Mastering Tableau 2023

Fourth Edition

Implement advanced business intelligence techniques, analytics, and machine learning models with Tableau

Marleen Meier

BIRMINGHAM—MUMBAI

Mastering Tableau 2023
Fourth Edition

Senior Publishing Product Manager: Gebin George

Acquisition Editor – Technical Reviews: Tejas Mhasvekar

Project Editor: Parvathy Nair

Content Development Editor: Elliot Dallow

Copy Editor: Safis Editing

Technical Editor: Karan Sonawane

Proofreader: Safis Editing

Indexer: Sejal Dsilva

Presentation Designer: Ganesh Bhadwalkar

Developer Relations Marketing Executive: Vignesh Raju

First published: November 2016

Second edition: February 2019

Third edition: May 2021

Fourth edition: August 2023

Production reference: 1230823

Published by Packt Publishing Ltd.
Grosvenor House
11 St Paul's Square
Birmingham
B3 1RB, UK.

ISBN 978-1-80323-376-5

www.packt.com

Forewords

For most of history, we have struggled with a lack of information, or data, to help make sense of our world. Even with the advent of computers and the internet, for a long time we relied on sampling and small datasets to make estimates of larger trends. But such estimates come with risks, above all a high level of uncertainty. Today, the tables have turned, and the exact opposite is true – we have too much information, too much data, and we are drowning in a sea of digital content. Large datasets mean no more need for estimations. A closer understanding of actual population trends is within reach, but it can become overwhelming when trying to identify meaningful patterns and insights buried within a surplus of data. Due to a confluence of technological advancements and societal shifts, particularly the global growth of the internet and smartphone usage, we have more data at our fingertips than we know what to do with. This surge in data is forecasted to accelerate as our world becomes ever more connected and the fusion of the online world with the offline world increases. Amid these changes, businesses find themselves compelled to make sense of all the data at hand, striving to learn how to use data as their differentiator, but the question we find ourselves repeatedly asking is *"How?"*

Proper business intelligence and analytics techniques are the answer. When done correctly, data can be whittled down gradually into valuable trends and insights. Tableau is a market leader in this realm of, what I like to call, data demystification. Notable for its intuitive interface and robust features, Tableau allows individuals and organizations alike to transform complex datasets into actionable intelligence. In *Mastering Tableau 2023*, author and renowned Tableau expert Marleen Meier takes you through everything you need to know when implementing the advanced offerings of Tableau.

I recently spent time with Marleen in her current home of Singapore, where, among other data topics, we discussed her work on the latest edition of *Mastering Tableau*. I was impressed by her enthusiasm for the tool and her dedication to keeping her publication updated with the latest features and capabilities. This is no small feat given how quickly the data landscape continues to change, with Tableau in turn adapting and expanding to meet market needs. This book does a commendable job of tackling the latest Tableau offering within the BI domain. From cover to cover, condensed into 16 chapters, you will master fundamental Tableau topics through visual explanations and hands-on, real-world examples. You will be guided through the use of fresh features in Tableau Server, Prep, and Desktop, as well as being challenged with advanced functionalities such as Python and R integrations geo-spatial analysis (a personal favorite of mine after time spent working on precisely this at Waze!), and time series analysis.

As a fellow data professional, lecturer, and leading voice in the field, analytics, especially visual analytics, lies close to my heart. It has been fascinating to experience firsthand the progression of low-code and no-code tools that democratize the use of data. It's incredible what you can do with Tableau today in just a few clicks or with a simple drag-and-drop motion, tasks that would have required extensive code and a team of developers in the past. I cannot think of a better way to master Tableau than through this book. As you will soon find, author Marleen Meier helps to simplify one's ability to harness the full potential of Tableau by detailing each concept with care, from basic dashboarding to advanced machine learning techniques. In the pages that follow, you will become more comfortable navigating Tableau as an advanced user. I hope you enjoy it as much as I have, and that you keep this valuable resource close by as you create and develop your own projects in Tableau moving forward.

Christina Stathopoulos

Founder, Dare to Data

I wonder what your journey to this book, and to Tableau, was? Have you been asked to do something with data? Build a dashboard? Design an infographic? Access a database at work? Monitor a business KPI? Uncover a connection between a multitude of datasets and their variables? Maybe you're a student who wants to know how to do all of the above and you're on a path to a qualification, or perhaps you're an individual looking for a new job or career?

Understanding more about data is the cornerstone of so many old and new career opportunities. And it's not just work: collecting and connecting people through data has always been important. Even our Stone Age ancestors were using tally sticks to record and share information long before abacuses, paper, and subsequently computers took over managing the flows from application A to application B that are so essential to business, sports, socializing, and, in effect, all of modern life.

Moving data (and the information it represents) is only half the problem. Sharing it in a way that benefits others is the other half. Deriving benefit often requires enrichment of the human context in which it is to be applied. When faced with constantly changing modern data infrastructures, finding context and delivering value pragmatically is, in my opinion, the largest part of why people turn to Tableau.

My own data journey started with AI and machine learning, followed by improving customer experiences across hundreds of websites. During those Dotcom years, I spent much time working with business problems, translating them into data problems, and then working out how to find different solutions for different businesses. This meant gaining familiarity with data, data structures and processes, and user interfaces and experiences, before then either acting on those findings directly or presenting them in a way that encouraged others to take action.

Using Tableau for the first time, it was apparent that it was designed to "help people see and understand data," which is the Tableau corporate mantra. It was more than just a visual endpoint to the flow of data (as understood by many who think Tableau is "just another dashboarding tool"). It was designed to encourage interactivity with data and enable people to find their own answers to new questions, not simply to be a static tabular visualisation to be observed. It utilized many principles of visual perception to encourage people to find their patterns, observe their own outliers, and look with their own eyes at their underlying data wherever it was stored, all without needing an introduction to coding or modern database administration.

Shortly after being introduced to Tableau, I met the author of this book, Marleen. Marleen was bridging the gap between people deep in data/data science and their business partners. A couple of the challenges were, "How can you get the business team closer to the data science team and, ultimately, the business data? How can you provide the context of the AI results and models in a manner that business partners can make sense of and apply?" It was clear that Marleen was up to the task of bridging this gap, and with Tableau, she had found a tool that would make it happen.

And now we have this book to read together and reference in the future. However you intend to use it, and whatever outcomes you wish to achieve, this book will allow you to get to grips with Tableau and, more importantly, the art of making any digital data more effective for us analog humans. In this book is advice regarding the linear tasks of data access and processing, moving toward the extremely non-linear process of problem solving and how to communicate data effectively with others.

Often, when faced with a new problem, it's unclear where to start. What is the first step I should be taking? Defining the problem first is always best, quickly followed by the question, "But what does the data say?" That first problem statement often changes as you learn more about the world as shown in the data you have available. The approaches in this book will serve you well regardless of the tool you are using, and in using Tableau, you'll appreciate the agility required to be effective in problem solving and communicating with data.

Using this book, I expect you'll gain a new appreciation of how to uncover your solutions, chipping away at your data tasks with newfound confidence and being ready to show your findings to your colleagues, friends, and family in a visual manner they will understand. Welcome to *Mastering Tableau*.

David Sigerson

Regional Field CTO, Tableau

Contributors

About the author

Marleen Meier is an accomplished analyst and author with a passion for statistics and data. Using traditional methodologies and more modern approaches such as machine learning and AI, Marleen is dedicated to driving meaningful insights.

Currently working as the APAC Data CoE Lead for ABN AMRO Clearing, Marleen is at the forefront of innovation and the implementation of data-driven strategies in a global financial environment.

With a strong focus on risk analytics, data visualization, data quality, and data control, Marleen constantly seeks to challenge the status quo and redefine best practices. She has lived and worked in various countries, including Germany, the Netherlands, the USA, and Singapore, allowing her to bring a diverse and global perspective to her work.

Marleen's dedication, expertise, and commitment to pushing the boundaries of data analysis make her a trusted authority in her field. Through her writing and speaking engagements, she aims to empower individuals and organizations to unlock the full potential of their data assets.

In Memory of Leo. We miss you greatly.

About the reviewers

Ruchi Arora is a technology and data executive with vast experience in transforming and scaling businesses. She has unique problem-solving capabilities and experience in AI/ML, analytics, and data product work that has consistently resulted in top-line growth, increased operational efficiency, and delighted customers.

Ruchi started her career as a software developer, but then shifted to AI data management and analytics. She has worked with different tech giants and Fortune 500 companies as a data leader. Ruchi is also a known speaker. She takes pride in solving complex business problems and helping industries through their digital transformation, RPA, and cloud journeys.

In addition, Ruchi is a diversity, equality, and inclusion advocate and an active member of many women in technology and data communities.

Ruchi is a volunteer for Women in Data, leading the Seattle chapter, and is also president of the Parents Association board at Bellevue Children's Academy.

Ruchi is a Harvard Business School graduate of the Leadership and General Management program and possesses a Master's in computer applications.

Jayen Thakker has 18 years of experience in the analytics field and is a seasoned professional in Tableau and Cognos Analytics. He has demonstrated his expertise by personally delivering nearly 100 training sessions on these platforms for clients and internal teams, further solidifying his position as a trusted leader in the industry. Jayen excels in acquiring new customers and driving upsells, while also serving as an enterprise solution architect, crafting effective analytics solutions for businesses. As a BI practice manager, he led a capable team of 80+ professionals, successfully delivering million-dollar projects in the field of BI and data warehousing. With a dedication to excellence, a passion for innovation, and a commitment to sharing knowledge, Jayen continues to make a significant impact in the analytics industry.

I would like to take this opportunity to thank my beloved family for supporting me while I was reviewing this book (and at other times as well). They are the ones who give me strength and patience for everything. Thank you, dear family.

One person who also believed in me for the book review is Muthukumar S M, who guided me to this opportunity and believed in me from the start. Thank you very much, Muthu.

Learn more on Discord

To join the Discord community for this book – where you can share feedback, ask questions to the author, and learn about new releases – follow the QR code below:

https://packt.link/tableau

Table of Contents

Chapter 10: Presenting with Tableau   371

Chapter 11: Designing Dashboards and Best Practices for Visualizations   401

Chapter 12: Leveraging Advanced Analytics 453

Preface

This edition of the bestselling Tableau guide will teach you how to leverage Tableau's newest features and offerings in various paradigms of the BI domain. Updated with fresh topics including the newest features in Tableau Server, Prep, and Desktop, as well as up-to-date examples and solutions to re-al-world challenges, this book will take you from mastering essential Tableau concepts to advanced functionalities. A new chapter on data governance has also been added.

Throughout this book, you will learn how to use various files and databases to connect to Tableau Desktop and Prep Builder to easily perform data preparation and handling, perform complex joins, spatial joins, unions, and data blending tasks using practical examples. You will also get to grips with executing data densification and explore other expert-level examples to help you with calculations, mapping, and visual design using Tableau Exchange.

Later chapters will teach you all about improving dashboard performance, connecting to Tableau Server, and understanding data visualization with hands-on examples. Finally, you will cover advanced use cases such as self-service analysis, time series analysis, and geo-spatial analysis, and connect Tableau to Python and R to implement programming functionalities within Tableau.

Finally, a brand-new chapter has been added that covers a very hot topic: data governance. You will explore an introduction to important features of Tableau Server that will get you prepared for compliance with GDPR and other data privacy and governance regulations.

By the end of this Tableau book, you will have mastered Tableau 2023 and you will be able to tackle common and advanced challenges in the data analytics space.

Who this book is for

This book is designed for business analysts, business intelligence professionals, and data analysts who want to master Tableau to solve a range of data science and business intelligence problems. Prior exposure to Tableau will help you get to grips with the features more quickly, but it is not a prerequisite.

What this book covers

Chapter 1, Reviewing the Basics, takes you through the basic and essential Tableau concepts needed to get you started.

Chapter 2, Getting Your Data Ready, is a theory-oriented chapter that will help you understand data preparation and henceforth work more easily with messy data.

Chapter 3, Using Tableau Prep Builder, discusses Tableau Prep Builder, the not-so-little Extract – Transform- Load (ETL) brother of Tableau Desktop.

Chapter 4, Learning about Joins, Blends, and Data Structures, answers the question of whether to use relationships, joins, or blends to combine data.

Chapter 5, Introducing Table Calculations, covers the special case of table calculations, which use the data order to assign values like ranks.

Chapter 6, Utilizing OData, Data Densification, Big Data, and Google BigQuery, teaches you how to leverage big data solutions and the concept of data densification.

Chapter 7, Practicing Level of Detail Calculations, helps you understand this advanced topic, which can change the aggregation of your data for certain calculations.

Chapter 8, Going Beyond the Basics, introduces you to advanced visualization concepts and Tableau Exchange, Extensions, Accelerators, and Connectors.

Chapter 9, Working with Maps, covers Tableau's internal, and some external, mapping capabilities using custom polygons, heatmaps, and layered maps.

Chapter 10, Presenting with Tableau, shows tips and tricks on how to use Tableau for presentation purposes.

Chapter 11, Designing Dashboards and Best Practices for Visualizations, takes you through different formatting techniques and design rules to maximize the aesthetics of your visualizations.

Chapter 12, Leveraging Advanced Analytics, will help you take your analytical skills to the next level with three advanced use cases to follow along with: self-service, time series, and geo-spatial analytics.

Chapter 13, Improving Performance, addresses various aspects of performance with the intent to empower you to create fast-loading dashboards for the best user experience.

Chapter 14, Exploring Tableau Server and Tableau Cloud, covers the different offerings and functionalities of Tableau Server, including Ask Data and Data Details.

Chapter 15, Integrating Programming Languages, shows you how to integrate R and Python with Tableau to enable (almost) unlimited analytics capabilities.

Chapter 16, Developing Data Governance Practices, introduces you to the vast and important topic of data governance and how to comply with regulations by using Tableau Server.

To get the most out of this book

Basic knowledge of Tableau will be an advantage and you will need a Tableau license after your 14-day free trial ends. You will also benefit from basic knowledge of R or Python if you wish to get the most out of *Chapter 15*, *Integrating Programming Languages*. You can, however, also follow along with the steps and learn as you go.

Other helpful installations will be mentioned in the book as needed, all in the realm of the average free-ware installation on Windows or Mac.

Download the example code files

The code bundle for the book is also hosted on GitHub at `https://github.com/PacktPublishing/Mastering-Tableau-2023-Fourth-Edition`. We also have other code bundles from our rich catalog of books and videos available at `https://github.com/PacktPublishing/`. Check them out!

Download the color images

We also provide a PDF file that has color images of the screenshots/diagrams used in this book. You can download it here: `https://packt.link/TybKH`.

Conventions used

There are a number of text conventions used throughout this book.

`CodeInText`: Indicates code words in text, database table names, folder names, filenames, file extensions, pathnames, dummy URLs, user input, and Twitter handles. For example: "When recording performance, Tableau initially creates a file in `My Tableau Repository\Logs`, named `performance_[timestamp].tab`."

A block of code is set as follows:

```
SCRIPT_REAL("x <- lm(.arg1 ~ .arg2 + .arg3 + .arg4) x$fitted", SUM(Profit),
COUNT(Quantity), SUM(Sales), AVG(Discount)
)
```

Bold: Indicates a new term, an important word, or words that you see on the screen, for example, in menus or dialog boxes, also appear in the text like this. For example: "Place **Profit_Expected** on the **Columns** shelf, next to **Profit**. Then click on either one and enable **Dual Axis**."

> Warnings or important notes appear like this.

Tips and tricks appear like this.

Get in touch

Feedback from our readers is always welcome.

General feedback: Email feedback@packtpub.com, and mention the book's title in the subject of your message. If you have questions about any aspect of this book, please email us at questions@packtpub.com.

Errata: Although we have taken every care to ensure the accuracy of our content, mistakes do happen. If you have found a mistake in this book we would be grateful if you would report this to us. Please visit, http://www.packtpub.com/submit-errata, selecting your book, click **Submit Errata**, and fill in the form.

Piracy: If you come across any illegal copies of our works in any form on the Internet, we would be grateful if you would provide us with the location address or website name. Please contact us at copyright@packtpub.com with a link to the material.

If you are interested in becoming an author: If there is a topic that you have expertise in and you are interested in either writing or contributing to a book, please visit http://authors.packtpub.com.

Share your thoughts

Now you've finished *Mastering Tableau 2023 - Fourth Edition*, we'd love to hear your thoughts! Scan the QR code below to go straight to the Amazon review page for this book and share your feedback or leave a review on the site that you purchased it from.

https://packt.link/r/1803233761

Your review is important to us and the tech community and will help us make sure we're delivering excellent quality content.

Download a free PDF copy of this book

Thanks for purchasing this book!

Do you like to read on the go but are unable to carry your print books everywhere?

Is your eBook purchase not compatible with the device of your choice?

Don't worry, now with every Packt book you get a DRM-free PDF version of that book at no cost.

Read anywhere, any place, on any device. Search, copy, and paste code from your favorite technical books directly into your application.

The perks don't stop there, you can get exclusive access to discounts, newsletters, and great free content in your inbox daily

Follow these simple steps to get the benefits:

1. Scan the QR code or visit the link below

https://packt.link/free-ebook/9781803233765

2. Submit your proof of purchase
3. That's it! We'll send your free PDF and other benefits to your email directly

1

Reviewing the Basics

Tableau is one of the leading tools used to solve **business intelligence (BI)** and analytics challenges. With this book, you will master Tableau's features and offerings in various paradigms of the BI domain. As an update to the successful *Mastering Tableau* series, this book covers the essential Tableau concepts, data preparation, and calculations with Tableau, all the way up to machine learning use cases.

This edition comes with new datasets, more examples of how to improve dashboard performance, and the most up-to-date know-how on data visualization, Tableau Server, and Tableau Prep Builder.

This new edition will also explore Tableau's connections with Python and R, Tableau extensions, joins, and unions, and last but not least, three new use cases of powerful self-service analytics, time-series analytics, and geo-spatial analytics in order to implement the learned content. By the end of this book, you'll have mastered the advanced offerings of Tableau and its latest updates, up to Tableau version 2023.

Those who are fairly new to Tableau should find this chapter helpful in getting up to speed quickly; however, since this book targets advanced topics, relatively little time is spent considering the basics. For a more thorough consideration of fundamental topics, consider *Learning Tableau,* written by Joshua Milligan and published by Packt Publishing.

In this chapter, we'll discuss the following topics:

- Creating worksheets and dashboards
- Connecting Tableau to your data
- Measure Names and Measure Values
- Three essential Tableau concepts
- Exporting data to other devices

Now, let's get started by exploring worksheet and dashboard creation in Tableau.

Creating worksheets and dashboards

At the heart of Tableau are **worksheets** and **dashboards**. Worksheets contain individual visualizations and dashboards contain one or more worksheets. Additionally, worksheets and dashboards may be combined into **stories** to communicate particular insights to the end user through a presentation environment. Lastly, all worksheets, dashboards, and stories are organized in **workbooks**, which can be accessed using Tableau Desktop, Server, Reader, or the Tableau mobile app.

At this point, I would like to introduce you to **Tableau Public** (`https://public.tableau.com/app/discover`). At times, you might need some inspiration, or you might want to replicate a dashboard created by another Tableau user. In this case, Tableau Public will be your place to go! It is a web-based collection of dashboards, as well as a creator's platform that allows you to design beautiful dashboards without a license or installation.

You can create your own profile—registration is free—and share all the dashboards you've created that you think the world shouldn't miss out on. The best part, however, is that you can download all of them, open them in your own version of Tableau, and start learning and replicating. Even without your own profile or registration, it is possible to download dashboards. In summary: Tableau Public is a free option but offers limited data source connectivity, data privacy, and feature availability. It does provide an excellent platform for sharing visualizations publicly though and brushing up on your Tableau skills without the need for a paid license.

In this section, we'll consider how to create worksheets and dashboards. Our intention here is to communicate the basics, but we'll also provide some insight that may prove helpful to more seasoned Tableau users.

Creating worksheets

Before creating a worksheet, we'll need to create a visualization to populate it with. At the most fundamental level, a visualization in Tableau is created by placing one or more **fields** on one or more **shelves**. As an example, note that the visualization created in the following diagram is generated by placing **Number of Records** on the **Text** shelf on the **Marks** card:

Figure 1.1: The Marks card

Having considered some basic theory, in the next subsection, you will get the chance to follow along in your own Tableau workbook. Let's go!

Creating a visualization

Now, let's explore the basics of creating a visualization using an exercise:

1. Navigate to `https://public.tableau.com/app/profile/marleen.meier` to locate and download the workbook associated with this chapter.

2. Open the file by double-clicking on the downloaded workbook.

3. In the workbook, find and select the tab labeled **Fundamentals of Visualizations**:

Figure 1.2: Navigating worksheet tabs

4. The dashboard is connected to two data sources; for this first exercise, we will use the **Summer-Olympics** data. Click on the data source **Summer-Olympics** in the top-left corner:

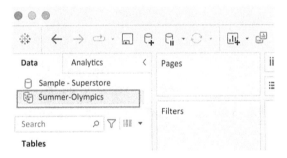

Figure 1.3: Data source

5. Locate **Sport** within the **Data** pane, which can be found on the left-hand side of the **Fundamentals of Visualizations** sheet:

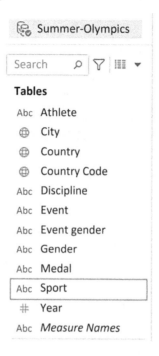

Figure 1.4: Dimensions on the Data pane

6. Drag **Sport** to **Color** on the **Marks** card and click **Add all members**:

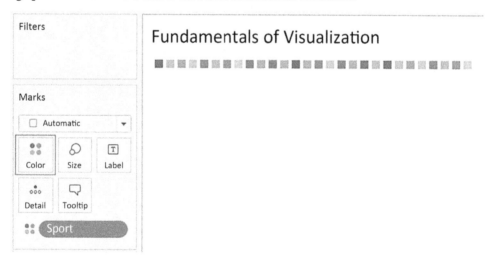

Figure 1.5: Dragging Color to the Marks card

7. Click on **Color** on the **Marks** card and then on **Edit Colors...** to adjust the colors of your visualization as desired. This will allow you to edit the colors used in your visualization, and **Transparency** and **Border** effects:

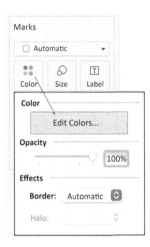

Figure 1.6: Edit Colors…

8. Now see what happens if you move **Sport** to the **Size**, **Label**, **Detail**, **Columns**, and **Rows** shelves. After placing **Sport** on each shelf, you can click on each shelf individually to access additional options.

9. Drop other fields on various shelves to continue exploring Tableau's behavior. One example could be, on an empty canvas, dragging **Year** to the **Columns** shelf, **Number of Records** to the **Rows** shelf, and **Medal** to **Color** on the **Marks** card. You will now see the number of medals per medal type over time:

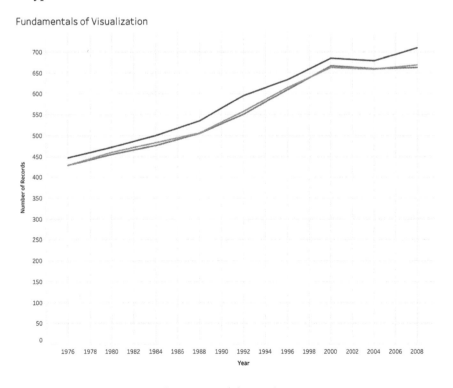

Figure 1.7: Medals over time

10. Did you come up with any interesting visualizations? Feel free to share them on Tableau Public. Add the tag **#MasteringTableau** if you want other readers of this book to find them—sharing is caring!

As you explore Tableau's behavior by dragging and dropping different fields onto different shelves, you'll notice that Tableau responds with default behaviors. These defaults, however, can be overridden, which we'll explore next.

Beyond the default behavior

In the preceding exercise, *Creating a visualization*, we can notice that the **Marks** card reads **Automatic**. This means that Tableau is providing the default view. The default view can easily be overridden by choosing a different selection from the drop-down menu:

Figure 1.8: The Marks card drop-down menu

By changing these settings on the **Marks** card, we can adjust the format in which your data will be displayed.

Another type of default behavior can be observed when dragging a field onto a shelf. For example, dragging and dropping a measure onto a shelf will typically result in the SUM( ) aggregation, which will sum up all the values to the highest level of aggregation. If no dimension is present, it will be the sum of all values. If a dimension is present on the **Marks** card, this same dimension will serve as the highest level of aggregation.

We will see an example of this behavior later in this section.

In Windows, you can override this default behavior by right-clicking and dragging a pill from the **Data** pane and dropping it onto a shelf. Tableau will respond with a dialog box with possible options:

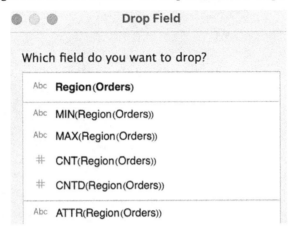

Figure 1.9: Changing the default aggregation

If you are working on macOS, you can right-click on the pill after you've dragged it to its location and then adjust the default behavior by changing the measure. This works on Windows as well. Another option is to right-click on the field while it is still in the **Data** pane on your left-hand side and select **Default Properties | Aggregation**.

Now, let's walk through an exercise where we'll override another default behavior on the **Marks** card:

1. In the workbook associated with this chapter, navigate to the **Overriding Defaults** worksheet.

2. Drag and drop **Year** from the data pane to the **Columns** shelf:

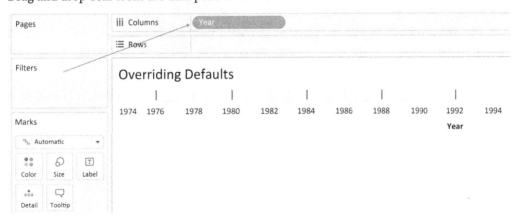

Figure 1.10: Year to Columns

3. Place **Number of Records** on the **Rows** shelf (which is automatically aggregated to **SUM(Number of Records)**) and **Sport** on the **Detail** shelf.

4. Click on the dropdown on the **Marks** card and select **Area**:

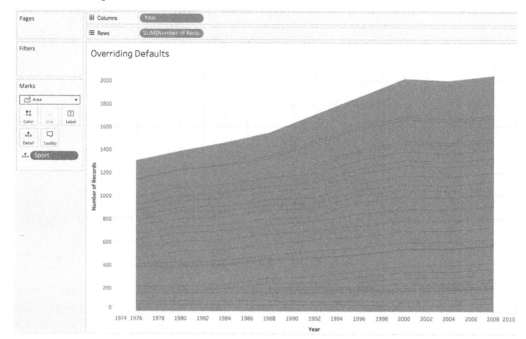

Figure 1.11: Area chart

In *Figure 1.11*, we can see the **Number of Records** over time (**Year**), where each line represents one type of **Sport**. We chose to visualize this in a stacked area chart.

Sorting and nested sorting

Now that you are familiar with the basics of dragging and dropping pills and are aware of Tableau's default behavior, the next thing most users want to do is to sort the data to draw first conclusions, regarding, for example, minimum and maximum values.

Navigate to the **Nested Sorting** tab and try to sort the countries by the amount of medals won, but separately for gold, silver, and bronze.

Did it work for you?

In Tableau, sorting and nested sorting can be done by simply clicking on the icon next to each column name:

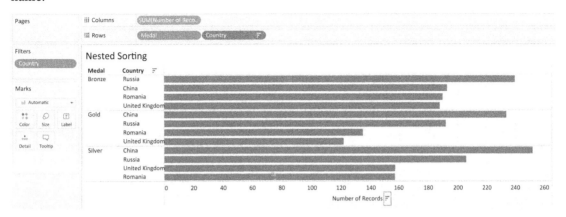

Figure 1.12: Sorting

To double-check the way of sorting, move your cursor onto the **Country** pile until the arrow appears in the right corner, click on the arrow next to a given field, in this case, **Country**, and select **Sort…**:

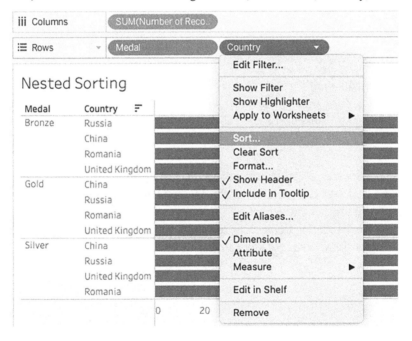

Figure 1.13: Sort settings

From the dropdown, select **Nested** and the desired **Field Name**, as well as the **Aggregation** type:

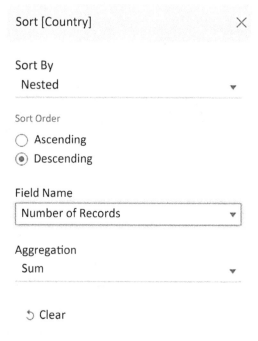

Sort [Country]   ✕

Sort By
Nested   ▾

Sort Order
○ Ascending
◉ Descending

Field Name
Number of Records   ▾

Aggregation
Sum   ▾

↺ Clear

Figure 1.14: Nested Sort

After having completed and understood **Sort** and **Nested Sort**, you will immediately be able to add value to your dashboards by presenting values in the most logical way. Now, we can move on to the next topic, the different default chart types Tableau comes with: **Show Me**.

Show Me

Show Me can help users new to Tableau to create the visualization they are looking for, such as bar charts, histograms, and area charts. It allows the Tableau author to create visualizations from input data at the click of a button. To understand how it works, let's refer to the following screenshot, which again makes use of the **Overriding Defaults** worksheet. This view can be accessed by clicking the **Show Me** button in the upper-right corner of any Tableau sheet:

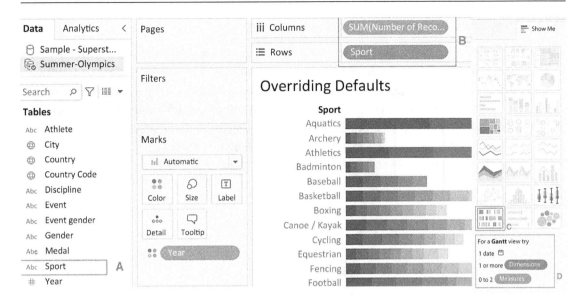

Figure 1.15: Show Me

Now let's look at the following aspects that are highlighted in the preceding screenshot:

- **A:** Selected fields in the **Data** pane
- **B:** Fields deployed in the view, that is, pills
- **C:** The recommended view, highlighted in the **Show Me** panel
- **D:** Help text that communicates the requirements for creating the recommended view or any selection choice over which the cursor is placed

Every icon in **Show Me** that isn't grayed out represents a visualization that can be created simply by clicking on it. For example, in the preceding screenshot, *Figure 1.15*, the Tableau author may choose to click on the area chart icon to create an area chart based on the selected and deployed fields.

Show Me options are highlighted based on two criteria: the selected fields in the **Data** pane and the fields deployed in the view.

Show Me may be effectively used for the following reasons:

- **Efficiency**: A proficient Tableau author already knows how to create the basic visualization types. **Show Me** automates these basic types and thus may be used for quicker production.

- **Inspiration**: Determining an effective way to visualize a dataset can be challenging. **Show Me** can help with this challenge by allowing the Tableau author to quickly consider various options.

- **Education**: An inexperienced Tableau author may access **Show Me** to better understand how various visualizations are created. By reading the help text displayed at the bottom of **Show Me** and changing the pill placement accordingly, much can be learned:

Figure 1.16: Show Me

These three reasons demonstrate the strong capabilities that **Show Me** provides for worksheet creation; however, be careful not to use it as a crutch. If you click on the various options without understanding how each visualization is created, you're not only shortchanging the educational process but you may also generate results that you don't understand and hence cannot explain to your stakeholders.

Once you are happy with the results and confident that the selected visualization puts enough emphasis on your data storytelling, your worksheet is ready for the next round of development. We've looked at some basic visualization creation and configuration techniques, so let's now look at how to group multiple worksheets into a dashboard.

Data storytelling is the art of using data to create a compelling story through visualizations such as graphs and charts. It combines the power of data analytics with storytelling techniques to convey complex information in an engaging and understandable way.

Creating dashboards

Although, as stated earlier in this section, a dashboard contains one or more worksheets, dashboards are much more than just static presentations. They're an essential part of Tableau's interactivity. In this section, we'll populate a dashboard with worksheets and then deploy actions for interactivity.

Let's begin by building a dashboard.

Building a dashboard

The following are the steps for building a dashboard:

1. In the workbook for this chapter, navigate to the **Building a Dashboard** tab.
2. In the **Dashboard** pane, located on the left side of the *Figure 1.17*, double-click on each of the following worksheets (in the order in which they are listed) to add them to the dashboard pane: **Count of Disciplines**, **Attendees**, **Medals**, and **Medal Shapes**:

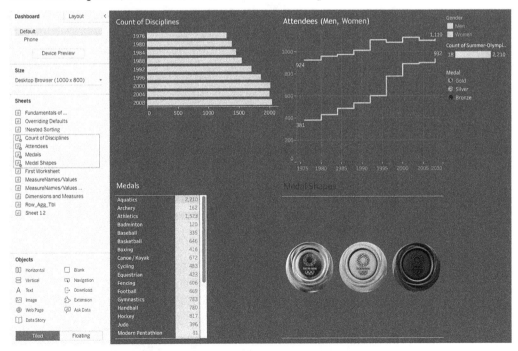

Figure 1.17: Creating a dashboard

3. In the bottom-right corner of the dashboard, click in the blank area (indicated by an arrow in *Figure 1.18*) to select a **container**. Containers are a selection of sheets that auto-adjust to fit next to/underneath each other on your dashboard:

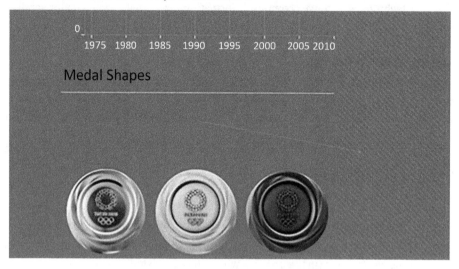

Figure 1.18: Deleting a container

4. After clicking in the blank area, you should see a blue border around the filter and the legends. This indicates that the vertical container is selected. Select the vertical container handle and delete it by clicking the **X**.

5. A selected container can also be dragged to a different location on the dashboard, replacing an existing sheet or sharing space. Note the gray shading in *Figure 1.19*, which communicates where the selection will be placed. Drag the **Attendees** worksheet by selecting and holding the handle and put it on top of the **Count of Disciplines** worksheet in order to swap the two:

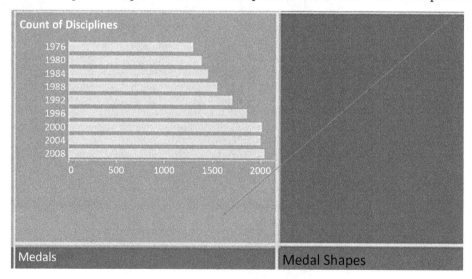

Figure 1.19: Moving worksheets

The gray shading provided by Tableau when dragging elements, such as worksheets and containers, onto a dashboard helpfully communicates where the elements will be placed. Take your time and observe carefully when placing an element on a dashboard or the results may be unexpected.

6. Note the **Floating** and **Tiled** buttons at the bottom left, next to your dashboard, as well as under the handle dropdown. If you select **Floating** instead of **Tiled**, your worksheets will not auto-adjust anymore and will be "floating" around the dashboard instead. This is a free form of worksheet arrangement on a dashboard, which is a powerful functionality, especially combined with transparent backgrounds. Note that floating can also be achieved by selecting it from the **More Options** dropdown on the right-hand side of every sheet in the dashboard:

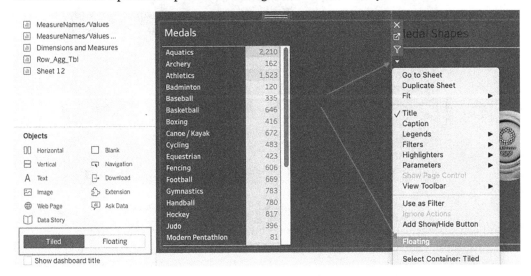

Figure 1.20: Tiled and Floating

7. Now, you can format the dashboard as desired. The following tips may prove helpful:

   • Adjust the sizes of the elements on the screen by hovering over the edges between each element and then clicking and dragging. Drag the edges of containers to adjust the size of each worksheet.

   • Make an element floating, as shown in *Figure 1.18*.

   • Create horizontal and vertical containers by dragging **Horizontal** and **Vertical** from the **Objects** pane onto the dashboard. Other objects, such as **Text**, **Image**, and **Blank**, can be added to containers too.

- Display the dashboard title by selecting **Dashboard** in the top pane, then **Show Title**. Double-click the title itself to adjust:

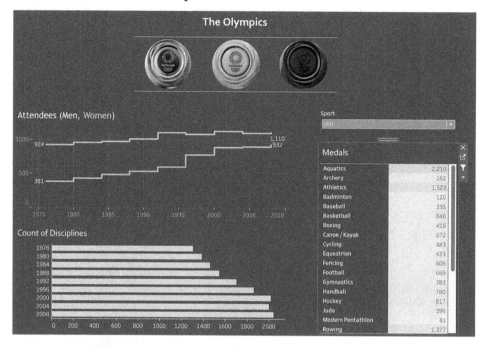

Figure 1.21: The Olympics dashboard

As you can see, you have just created your first dashboard. All worksheets are in place now. In the next part, we will add filter functionality to make the dashboard more interactive and meaningful.

Adding interactivity to a dashboard

One of the primary benefits of Tableau is the interactivity it provides for the end user. Dashboards aren't simply for viewing; they're meant for interaction. In this exercise, we'll add interactivity to the dashboard that was created in the previous exercise:

1. Select the **Medals** sheet on the dashboard and click on the drop-down arrow on the right-hand side, which will open a menu as shown in *Figure 1.22*. From there, select **Filters**, then **Sport**:

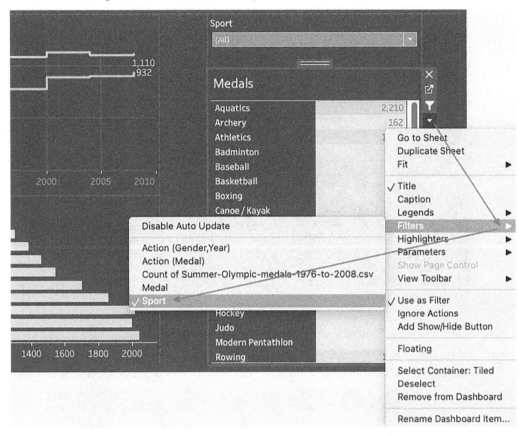

Figure 1.22: Adding a filter

2. Now select the newly created filter, **Sport**, click again on the drop-down options arrow, and select **Multiple Values (dropdown)**, as well as **Apply to Worksheets | All Using This Data Source**, as shown in *Figure 1.23*:

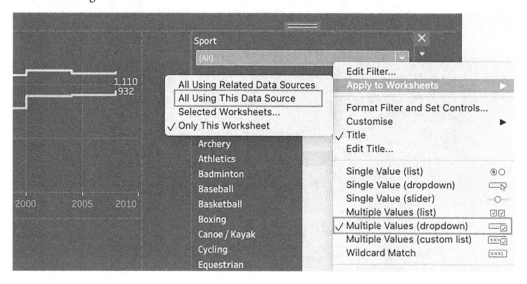

Figure 1.23: Filter settings

3. Lastly, place the filter above the **Medals** sheet by clicking and dragging it.

4. To use the images of the medals as a filter for the other worksheets on the dashboard pane, click the **Use as Filter** icon located at the top-right corner of the **Medals Shapes** worksheet:

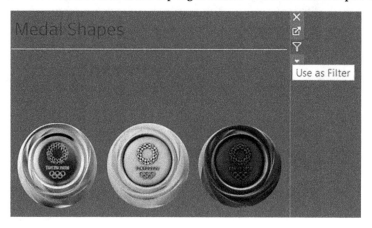

Figure 1.24: The Use as Filter option

5. Alternatively, navigate to **Dashboard | Actions....** In the dialog box, click **Add Action | Filter** and create a filter, as shown:

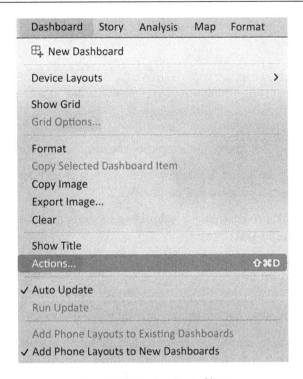

Figure 1.25: Navigating to filters

Edit Filter Action   ✕

Name

| Medal Shape | Insert ▼

Source Sheets

⊞ Building a Dashboard clean   ▼   Run action on

☐ Attendees   ○ Hover
☐ Count of Disciplines   ◉ Select
☑ Medal Shapes   ○ Menu
☐ Medals   ☐ Single-select only

Target Sheets

⊞ Building a Dashboard clean   ▼   Clearing the selection will

☑ Attendees   ○ Keep filtered values
☑ Count of Disciplines   ◉ Show all values
☑ Medal Shapes   ○ Exclude all values
☑ Medals

Figure 1.26: Adding a filter action

From here on in, you are good to go and use filters and action filters.

 In Tableau, filters are used to subset the underlying data based on certain conditions, while action filters allow users to interactively filter data by clicking on a visual element.

In *Chapter 13, Improving Performance*, this topic will be discussed in more detail.

Having completed the preceding dashboard exercise, you should now be able to click on various objects on the dashboard to observe the interactivity.

To learn some more advanced dashboard techniques, be sure to check out *Chapter 11, Designing Dashboards and Best Practices for Visualizations*.

To conclude, you have learned how to put existing worksheets, as tiled or floating objects, on a dashboard. You have changed the dashboard layout by dragging and dropping, as well as by using containers, filters, and action filters. Each of these core activities will be repeated multiple times throughout the book, so feel free to come back to this chapter and repeat the exercise steps whenever needed!

Next, you will learn how to connect your own data to Tableau and work with it.

Connecting Tableau to your data

At the time of writing, Tableau's data connection menu includes more than 90 different connection types. And that's somewhat of an understatement since some of those types contain multiple options. For example, **Other Files** includes more than 30 options. Of course, we won't cover the details for every connection type, but we will cover the basics. The official documentation on all connectors can be found here: https://help.tableau.com/current/pro/desktop/en-us/exampleconnections_overview.htm.

Upon opening a new instance of Tableau Desktop from within Tableau Desktop (**File** | **New**), you'll notice a **Connect to Data** link in the top-left corner of the workspace. Clicking on that link will enable you to connect to the data. Opening a new instance of Tableau from the application's location on your computer will bring up the blue **Connect** pane right away. Alternatively, you can click on the **New Data Source** icon on the toolbar.

Although in future chapters we'll connect to other data sources, here we'll limit the discussion to connecting to Microsoft Excel and text files.

Connecting to a file

Let's see how you can connect to a file, using Excel as an example:

1. In Tableau, navigate to **Data** | **New Data Source** | **Excel** to connect to the Sample - Superstore dataset that is installed with Tableau Desktop (it should be located on your hard drive under **My Tableau Repository** | **Data sources**).
2. Double-click on the **Orders** sheet.

3. Click on the **New Worksheet** tab, as shown in *Figure 1.27*:

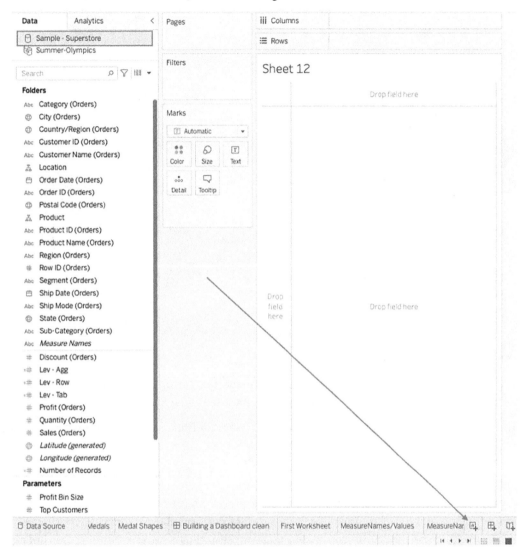

Figure 1.27: New worksheet

4. Rename the newly created tab to First Worksheet by right-clicking and selecting **Rename**.
5. Place **Discount** on the **Text** shelf in the **Marks** card.

6.   Double-click on **Profit** and **Sales**:

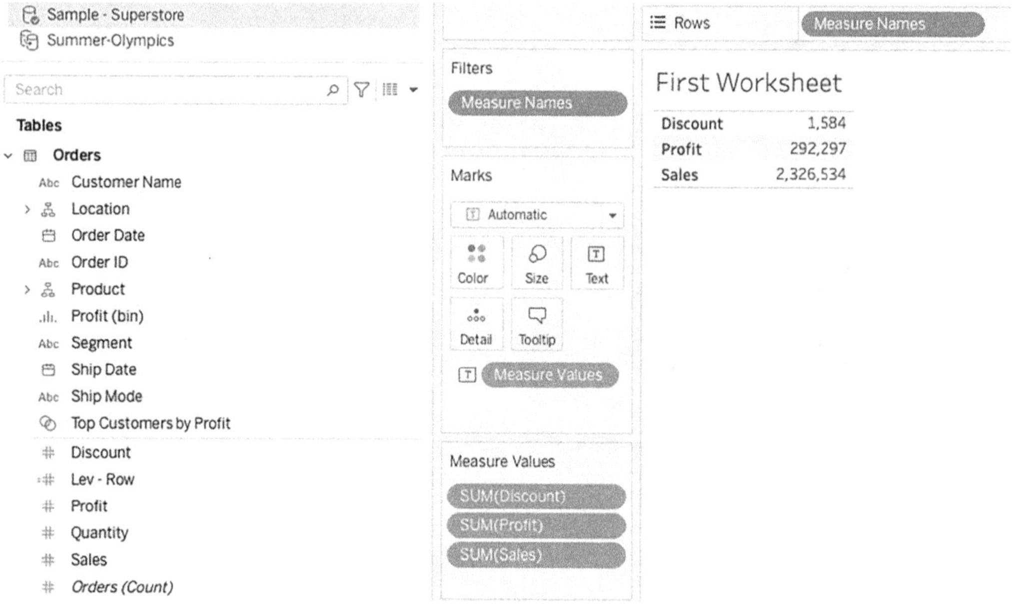

Figure 1.28: First worksheet

You've just created your first worksheet!

If you want to connect to a `.csv` file, you could use the **Text file** option. Later in this book, in *Chapter 12, Leveraging Advanced Analytics*, we will also connect to spatial files.

In this section, we learned how to connect to files. We'll continue with another important connection type in the next section: Tableau Server.

Connecting to Tableau Server

Connecting to Tableau Server is perhaps the single most important server connection type to consider, since it's frequently used to provide a better level of performance than may otherwise be possible. Additionally, connecting to Tableau Server enables the author to receive not only data but also information regarding how that data is to be interpreted—for example, whether a given field should be considered a measure or a dimension.

We'll discuss the difference between these terms in the *Dimensions and measures* section later in the chapter.

The following are the steps for connecting to Tableau Server:

1.   To complete this exercise, access to an instance of Tableau Server is necessary. If you don't have access to Tableau Server, consider installing a trial version on your local computer.

2.   In the workbook associated with this chapter, navigate to the **Connecting to Tableau Server** worksheet.

3.   Right-click on the `Superstore` data source and select **Publish to Server...**:

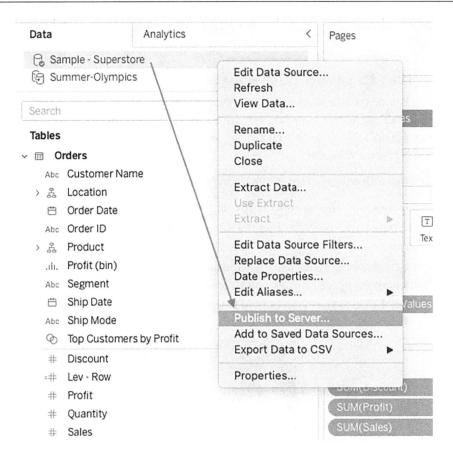

Figure 1.29: Publish to Server…

4. Log in to **Tableau Server** and follow the prompts to complete the publication of the data source.

5. Open a new instance of Tableau Desktop, select **Data | New Data Source | Tableau Server**, and then search for the Superstore dataset you just published and connect.

Having completed the preceding two exercises, let's discuss the most germane point, that is, **metadata**. Metadata is often defined as *data about data*. In the preceding case, the data source name, default aggregation, and default number formatting are all examples of consistency across multiple authors.

If you were to change a field name, for example, and then publish the data source to Tableau Server, the new field name would remain since Tableau remembers changes made to the metadata. This is important, for example, if your company has a policy regarding the use of decimal points when displaying currency; that policy will be easily adhered to if all Tableau authors start building workbooks by pointing to data sources where all formatting has been predefined.

Later on in this book, we will connect to other server types, like Google BigQuery, but the handling of all servers is pretty much the same and very straightforward. If you still have questions, you can always check out https://help.tableau.com/current/pro/desktop/en-us/exampleconnections_overview.htm.

Now, our last missing piece regarding connections is saved data sources. Please follow along with this as well.

Connecting to saved data sources

Connecting to a saved data source on a local machine is very similar to connecting to a data source published on Tableau Server. Metadata definitions associated with the local data source are preserved just as they are on Tableau Server. Of course, since the data source is local instead of remote, the publication process is different.

Let's explore the following steps to create a local data connection using an example:

1. In the workbook associated with this chapter, navigate to the **First Worksheet** tab.
2. In the **Data** pane, right-click on the Superstore data source and select **Add to Saved Data Sources**.
3. Using the resulting dialog box, save the data source as Superstore in **My Tableau Repository | Data sources**, which is located on your hard drive.
4. Click on the **Go to Start** icon located in the top-left part of your screen and observe the newly saved data source:

Figure 1.30: Saved Data Sources

You can save a local data source that points to a published data source on Tableau Server. First, connect to a published data source on Tableau Server. Then, right-click on the data source in your workspace and choose **Add to Saved Data Sources**. Now you can connect to Tableau Server directly from your start page!

Now that we've learned how to connect to files, Tableau Server, and saved data sources, we will continue our journey and dive into more details regarding **Measure Names** and **Measure Values**.

Measure Names and Measure Values

I've observed the following scenario frequently: a new Tableau author creates a worksheet and drags a measure to the **Text** shelf. They drag the second measure to various places on the view and get results that seem entirely unpredictable. The experience is very frustrating for the author since it's so easy to accomplish this in Microsoft Excel! The good news is that it's also easy to accomplish this in Tableau. It just requires a different approach.

Measure Names and **Measure Values** are generated fields in Tableau. They don't exist in the underlying data, but they're indispensable for creating many kinds of views. As may be guessed from its placement in the **Data** pane and its name, **Measure Names** is a dimension whose members are made up of the names of each measure in the underlying dataset. **Measure Values** contains the numbers or values of each measure in the dataset.

In this section, we'll watch what happens when these generated fields are used independently, then observe how they work elegantly together to create a view. Let's explore this with an exercise:

1. In the workbook associated with this chapter, navigate to the **MeasureNames/Values** and make sure that the Olympics data source is selected.

2. Drag **Measure Values** to the **Text** shelf and observe the results, all four values are printed on top of each other:

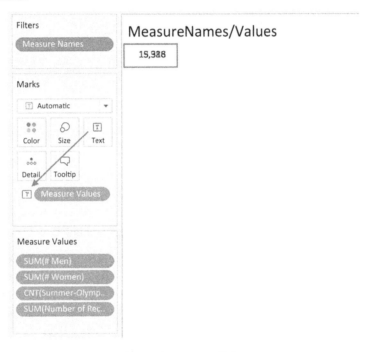

Figure 1.31: Measure Values

3. Clear the worksheet by clicking on the **Clear Sheet** icon on the toolbar:

Figure 1.32: Clear Sheet

4. Now, drag **Measure Names** to the **Rows** shelf and observe that the view merely displays **No Measure Values.**

5. Drag **Measure Values** to the **Text** shelf. Note the list of measures and associated values, each of the four values is printed in the respective row:

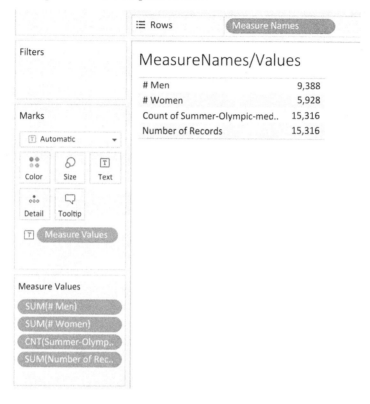

Figure 1.33: List of Measure Values

Perhaps the relationship between **Measure Names** and **Measure Values** is best explained by an analogy. Consider several pairs of socks and a partitioned sock drawer. *Step 2* is the equivalent of throwing the socks into a pile. The results are, well, disorganized. *Step 4* is the equivalent of an empty sock drawer with partitions. The partitions are all in place but where are the socks? *Step 5* is a partitioned drawer full of nicely organized socks. Measure Names is like the sock drawer. Measure Values is like the socks.

Independent of one another, they aren't of much use. Used together, they can be applied in many different ways.

Measure Names and Measure Values shortcuts

Tableau provides various shortcuts to quickly create the desired visualization. If you're new to the software, this shortcut behavior may not seem intuitive, but you'll gain an understanding of it. Let's use the following exercise to explore how you can use a shortcut to rapidly deploy Measure Names and Measure Values:

1. In the workbook associated with this chapter, navigate to the **MeasureNames/Values ShrtCts** worksheet.

2. Drag **# Women** onto **Text** in the **Marks** card.

3. Drag **# Men** directly on top of **# Women** in the view (**Show Me** appears):

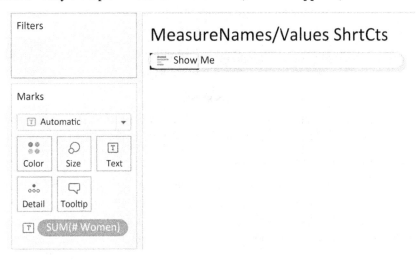

Figure 1.34: Show Me and Measures

4. Observe the results, including the appearance of the **Measure Values** shelf, the deployment of **Measure Names** on the **Rows** and **Filters** shelves, and **Measure Values** on the **Text** shelf:

Figure 1.35: Measure Values appearance

Several things happened in *step 2* of this exercise. After placing the # Men number on top of the # Women number in the view, Tableau did the following:

1. Deployed Measure Names on the **Filters** shelf:

   - Open the Measure Names filter by right-clicking and hit **Edit Filter...** Observe that only # Men and # Women are selected. This limits the view to display only those two measures.

2. Deployed Measure Names on the **Rows** shelf:

   - Measure Names is acting like a partitioned container, that is, like the sock drawer in the analogy. Because of the filter, the only rows that display are for # Men and # Women.

3. Displayed the **Measure Values** shelf:

   - The Measure Values shelf is somewhat redundant. Although it clearly shows the measures that are displayed in the view, it essentially acts as an easy way to access the filter. You can simply drag measures on and off of the Measure Values shelf to adjust the filter and thus display/hide additional Measure Values. You can also change the order within the Measure Values shelf to change the order of the measures in the view.

4. Deployed Measure Values on the **Text** shelf:

   - Measure Values is simply defining the numbers that will display for each row—in this case, the numbers associated with # Men and # Women.

If the visualization has an axis, the shortcut to deploy **Measure Names** and **Measure Values** requires the placement of a second measure on top of the axis of an initial measure. In *Figure 1.36*, **Year** is located on the **Columns** shelf and **Number of Records** on the Rows shelf. Note that the screenshot was taken while **# Women** was placed on top of the *y*-axis:

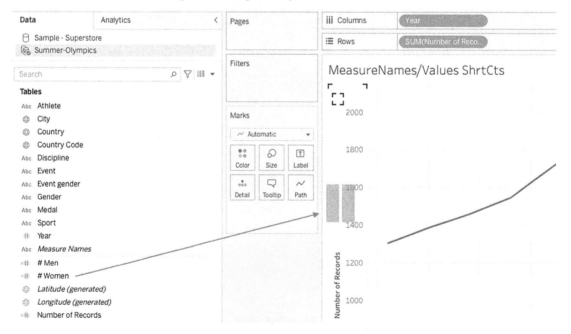

Figure 1.36: Axis shortcut

The resulting worksheet can be seen in *Figure 1.37*:

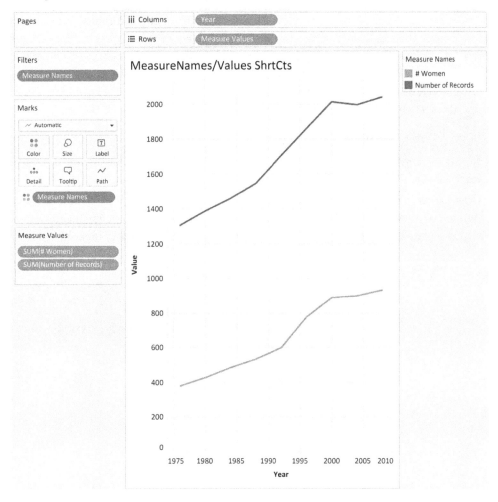

Figure 1.37: Two-line chart

The preceding section gave us a better understanding of **Measure Names** and **Measure Values**. You will come across those concepts more in your Tableau career, but now that you've successfully mastered the basics, let's move on to three other concepts that will be beneficial for your learning curve.

Three essential Tableau concepts

An important stop on the road to mastering Tableau involves three essential concepts. In this section, we'll discuss each of them:

- Dimensions and measures
- Row-level, aggregate-level, and table-level calculations
- Continuous and discrete

We'll start by defining **dimensions** and **measures**.

Dimensions and measures

Tableau categorizes every field from an underlying data source as either a **dimension** or a **measure**. A dimension is qualitative or, to use another word, categorical. A measure is quantitative or aggregable. A measure is usually a number but may be an aggregated, non-numeric field, such as MAX (Date). A dimension is usually a text, Boolean, or date field, but may also be a number, such as Number of Records. Dimensions provide meaning to numbers by slicing those numbers into separate parts/ categories. Measures without dimensions are mostly meaningless.

Let's look at an example to understand better:

1. In the workbook associated with this chapter, navigate to the Dimensions and Measures worksheet.

2. Drag Number of Records to the **Text** on the **Marks** Card. The result is mostly meaningless. The number of measures is **15,316**, but without the context supplied by slicing the measure across one or more dimensions, there is really no way to understand what it means:

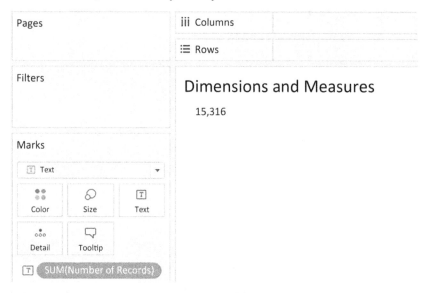

Figure 1.38: Worksheet without context

3. Place **Country** and **Year** on the **Columns** shelf and **Number of Records** on the **Rows** shelf:

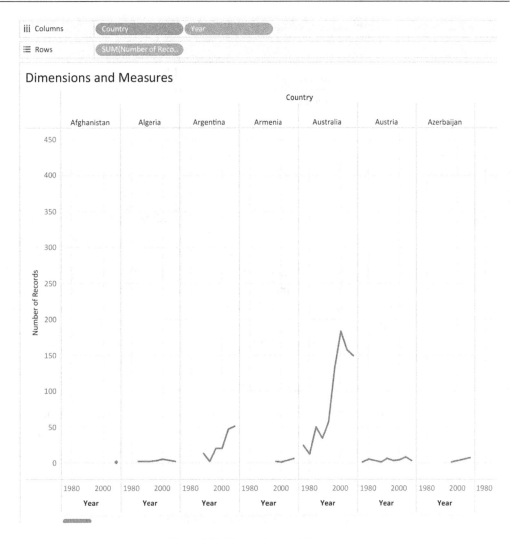

Figure 1.39: Dimensions and Measures

As shown in *Figure 1.39*, *step 3* brings meaning. Placing **Country** and **Year** on the **Columns** shelf provides context, which imparts meaning to the visualization.

Row-level, aggregate-level, and table-level calculations

There are three levels of calculations in Tableau: *row*, *aggregate*, and *table*. To understand how these three levels function, it's important to understand the Tableau processes. We'll do so with an example that considers the Number of Records and Quantity fields from the Superstore dataset.

Consider the following calculation types, calculated fields, and queries. A comparison to the commonly used language SQL will give us a better understanding of how to interpret Tableau calculations. Note that the SQL is slightly simplified for the sake of this example.

Let's take a deeper look at the three levels of calculations and consider the example in the following table:

Calculation type	Calculated field in Tableau	Query passed to data source

Row-level	`Number of Records/Quantity`	`SELECT Number of Records / Quantity)`
		
		`FROM Orders`

Aggregate-level	`[Number of Records])/ Sum(Quantity)`	`SELECT [Number of Records]),`
		
		`SUM(Quantity) FROM [Orders]`

Table level	`WINDOW_Sum([Number of Records])/ Quantity))`	`SELECT [Number of Records]),`
		
		`SUM(Quantity) FROM [Orders]`

For the row- and aggregate-level calculations, the computation is actually completed by the data source engine, as Tableau is an in-memory tool. Tableau merely displays the results. This, however, isn't the case for the table-level calculation. Although the query passed to the data source for the table-level calculation is identical to the query for the aggregate-level calculation, Tableau performs additional computations on the returned results. Let's explore this further with an exercise using the same calculated fields.

Let's look at the following steps and begin our exercise:

1. In the workbook associated with this chapter, navigate to the `Row_Agg_Tbl` worksheet.
2. Connect to the `Superstore` data source by clicking on `Sample - Superstore` in the **Data** section in the top-left corner.

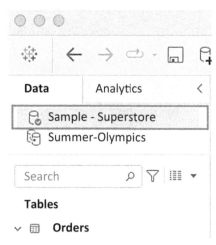

Figure 1.40: Connect to Superstore

3. Select **Analysis | Create Calculated Field** to create the following calculated fields. Note that each must be created separately; that is, it isn't possible in this context to create a single calculated field that contains all three calculations:

- Name the first calculation Lev – Row and enter the following code: [Number of Records]/[Quantity].
- Next, name the second calculation Lev – Agg and enter the following code: SUM ([Number of Records])/SUM (Quantity).
- Lastly, name the third calculation Lev – Tab and enter WINDOW_AVG ([Lev - Agg]).

4. In the **Data** pane, right-click on the three calculated fields you just created and select **Default Properties** | **Number format**.

5. In the resulting dialog box, select **Percentage** and click **OK**.

6. Place **Order Date** on the **Columns** shelf.

7. Place **Measure Names** on the **Rows** shelf and **Measure Values** on Text on the **Marks** card.

8. Exclude all values except for **Lev - Row**, **Lev - Agg**, and **Lev - Tab** by dragging them off the **Measure Values** shelf or removing them from the **Measure Names** filter:

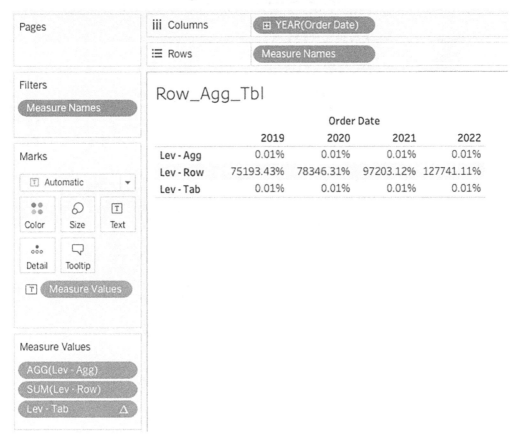

Figure 1.41: Level of calculations

- **Lev - Agg** is an aggregate-level calculation. The computation is completed by the data source engine. The sum of [Number of Records] is divided by the sum of [Quantity]. The results of the calculation are likely useful for the Tableau author.

- **Lev - Row** is a row-level calculation. The computation is completed by the data source engine. [Number of Records] is divided by [Quantity] for each row of the underlying data. The results are then summed across all rows. Of course, in this case, the row-level calculation doesn't provide useful results; however, since a new Tableau author may mistakenly create a row-level calculation when an aggregate-level calculation is what's really needed, the example is included here.

- **Lev - Tab** is a table calculation. Some of the computation is completed by the data source engine, that is, the aggregation. Tableau completes additional computation on the results returned from the data source engine based on the dimensions and level of detail in the data displayed in the sheet. Specifically, the results of **Lev - Agg** are summed and then divided by the number of members in the dimension. For the preceding example, this is:

$$\frac{26.29\% + 26.34\% + 26.30\% + 26.55\%}{4}$$

Once again, the results in this case aren't particularly helpful but do demonstrate knowledge that a budding Tableau author should possess.

Continuous and discrete

Continuous and discrete aren't concepts that are unique to Tableau. Indeed, both can be observed in many arenas. Consider the following example:

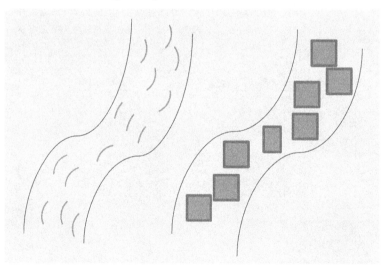

Figure 1.42: Continuous and discrete

The preceding diagram is of two rivers: *River-Left* and *River-Right*. Water is flowing in River-Left. River-Right is composed of ice cubes. Could you theoretically sort the ice cubes in River-Right? Yes! Is there any way to sort the water in River-Left? In other words, could you take buckets of water from the bottom of the river, cart those buckets upstream and pour the water back into River-Left, and thereby say "I have sorted the water in the river?" No.

The H_2O in River-Left is in a continuous form, that is, water. The H_2O in River-Right is in a discrete form, that is, ice.

Having considered continuous and discrete examples in nature, let's turn our attention back to Tableau. Continuous and discrete in Tableau can be more clearly understood with the following seven considerations:

1. Continuous is green. Discrete is blue:

    *   Select any field in the **Data** pane or place any field on a shelf and you'll note that it's either green or blue. Also, the icons associated with fields are either green or blue.

2. Continuous is always `numeric`. Discrete may be a `string`.

3. Continuous and discrete aren't synonymous with dimensions and measures:

    *   It's common for new Tableau authors to conflate continuous with measures and discrete with dimensions. They aren't synonymous. A measure may be either discrete or continuous.

    *   Also, a dimension, if it's a number, may be discrete or continuous. To prove this point, right-click on any numeric or date field in Tableau and note that you can convert it:

Figure 1.43: Converting between discrete and continuous

4. Discrete values can be sorted. Continuous values can't:

    •   Sortable/not sortable behavior is most easily observed with dates and a measure like
        Sum(Sales), as shown in the following example:

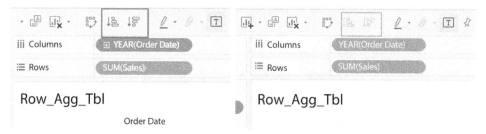

Figure 1.44: Left: continuous (not sortable). Right: discrete (sortable)

5. Continuous colors are gradients. Discrete colors are distinct:

    •   The following example shows **Sales** as continuous and then as discrete. Note the dif-
        ference in how colors are rendered. The left portion of the screenshot demonstrates
        the continuous results in gradients, and the right portion demonstrates the discrete
        results in distinctly colored categories:

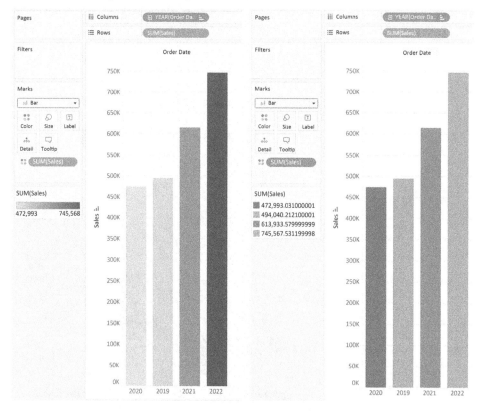

Figure 1.45: Sales as continuous (left) and discrete (right)

6. Continuous pills can be placed to the right of discrete pills, but not to the left because the discrete pills define the aggregation level:

  • The Tableau author is able to place **Region** to the right of **Year** when **Year** is discrete.

  • The Tableau author is unable to place **Region** to the right of **Year** when **Year** is continuous.

7. Continuous creates axes. Discrete creates headers:

  • Note in the right portion of the following screenshot that **Order Date** is continuous and the **Year of Order Date** axis is selected. Since **Year of Order Date** is an axis, the entire *x*-plane is selected. In the left portion, however, **Year(Order Date)** is discrete and **2014** is selected. Since 2014 is a header only, it's selected and not the entire *x*-plane:

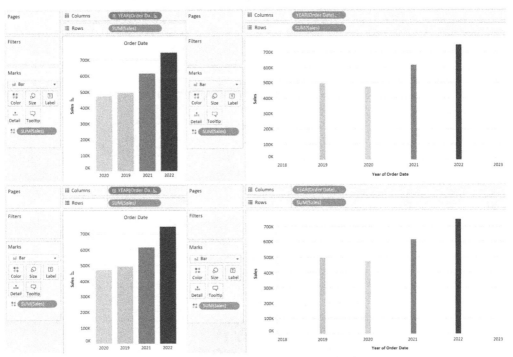

Figure 1.46: Continuous (Right) and discrete (left) dates

Congratulations, you just mastered three important concepts in Tableau: measures and dimensions, the level of calculations, and discrete and continuous values. With this knowledge alone, you will be able to create your first dashboards. I want to highly encourage you to do so; the learning curve when playing around with these tools will be very steep, and you will gain confidence quickly with practice! It will also help you to follow along in the upcoming chapters.

To conclude the basics, we will cover the export of dashboards to other devices next. Even if you don't feel ready to do so yet, it will round up the basic Tableau Desktop tour and will provide the raw diamond as a whole. We can then continue improving all bits and pieces in future chapters!

Exporting data to other devices

Once a dashboard looks as it's expected to, the developer has different choices for sharing the work. An upload to Tableau Server is the most likely option. The end user might not look at the results on just a laptop; they could use a tablet or cellphone, too.

Exporting data to a mobile phone

While developing a dashboard, Tableau Creator has the option to take a look at **Device Designer** or **Device Preview**. Whenever you are on a **Dashboard** tab, you can find it here:

Figure 1.47: Device Preview

Tableau comes with default phone settings. If needed, those defaults can be adjusted by clicking on **Phone** and then on the three dots. Once you're in the **Device Designer** mode, select a **Device type** option and you'll get choices of the most common models:

Figure 1.48: Device type set to Phone

Please be aware that you can only use the sheets that are in the default layout of your dashboard. If you want to add a default layout for a tablet, for example, go into **Device Designer** mode, select **Tablet**, and move the content in a way that the sheets you want to see on your tablet are within the device frame. Satisfied? Then add the new layout (highlighted in *Figure 1.50*) to the workbook. It will appear under the **Default** one in the top-left area:

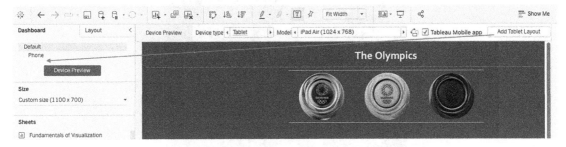

Figure 1.49: Add Tablet Layout

The user can now select the design needed whenever opening a workbook from Tableau Server.

Not only can your projects be viewed conveniently on a mobile device but you can also work on them on the go using Tableau Mobile! We'll cover this in the next section.

Tableau Mobile

In order to support flexible working, Tableau has created an app that can be downloaded from the App Store or from Google Play, called **Tableau Mobile**. Once installed on your phone and/or tablet, you will get the option to connect the app to Tableau Server or Tableau Online. Go ahead and publish the dashboard we created in this chapter, *The Olympics*, to either of those two instances. If you have questions regarding the publishing, please see *Chapter 14, Exploring Tableau Server and Tableau Cloud*, for further instructions.

At the bottom of your landing page, click **Explore** to see all the views you just published. Click on the **Building a Dashboard** view and see your previously created dashboard, **The Olympics**:

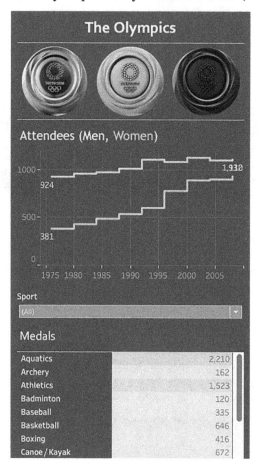

Figure 1.50: Mobile dashboard

And the best part is yet to come. The dashboard is fully interactive, so try the drop-down filter or the **Medals** filter. Also, try to click on a mark and select **Keep Only**. By clicking on the workbook icon at the top right, the first icon from the left, all the other sheets you created will be visible, making it possible to switch between sheets:

Figure 1.51: Sheet selection

Now, if you click the three dots at the top right, even more options will appear, such as **Revert**, **Alert**, **Subscribe**, and so on. To learn more about the different options that are also available on Tableau Server, see *Chapter 14, Exploring Tableau Server and Tableau Cloud*. For now, we can conclude that Tableau Mobile makes it easy to check your favorite dashboards wherever you are.

Summary

In this chapter, we covered the basics of Tableau. We began with some basic terminology, then we looked at the basics of creating worksheets and dashboards. We focused on default behavior and how to override that behavior, and we considered some best practices. Then, we reviewed the fundamental principles of Measure Names and Measure Values. After that, we explored three essential Tableau concepts: dimensions and measures; row-, aggregate-, and table-level calculations; and the concepts of continuous and discrete. Of particular importance is understanding that row- and aggregate-level calculations are computed by the data source engine, while table-level calculations are handled by Tableau. Finally, we saw how to adjust your dashboard for other devices, such as a cellphone or tablet and Tableau Mobile in action.

In the next chapter, we'll continue our Tableau exploration by looking at data. We'll consider how data is prepared using Tableau's data handling engine, Hyper, and explore some useful data preparation models and techniques.

Learn more on Discord

To join the Discord community for this book – where you can share feedback, ask questions to the author, and learn about new releases – follow the QR code below:

https://packt.link/tableau

2

Getting Your Data Ready

Have you ever asked yourself whether your data is clean enough to be analyzed? It's likely that everyone who works with data has, which is why this chapter is dedicated to getting your data ready for analysis, otherwise known as data cleaning.

The first part of this chapter is theory-oriented and does not include exercises. A careful reading of this information is encouraged since it provides a foundation for greater insight. The latter portion of the chapter provides various exercises specifically focused on data preparation.

Now let's dive into this fascinating topic with the goal of enriching our understanding and becoming ever-better data stewards.

In this chapter, we will discuss the following topics:

- Understanding Hyper
- Focusing on data preparation
- Surveying data
- Cleaning messy data

Since Tableau Desktop 10.5 has been on the market for some time, you may already have heard of Hyper. Regardless of whether you have or not, continue reading for a primer on this feature!

Understanding Hyper

In this section, we will explore Tableau's data-handling engine, and how it enables structured yet organic data mining processes in enterprises. Since the release of Tableau 10.5, we can make use of Hyper, a high-performing database, allowing us to query source data faster than ever before. Hyper is usually not well understood, even by advanced developers, because it's not an overt part of day-to-day activities; however, if you want to truly grasp how to prepare data for Tableau, this understanding is crucial.

Hyper originally started as a research project at the University of Munich in 2008. In 2016, it was acquired by Tableau and appointed as the dedicated data engine group of Tableau, maintaining its base and employees in Munich. Initially in Tableau 10.5, Hyper replaced the earlier data-handling engine only for extracts. It is still true that live connections are not touched by Hyper, but Tableau Prep Builder now runs on the Hyper engine too, with more use cases to follow. As stated on `tableau.com`, *"Hyper can slice and dice massive volumes of data in seconds, you will see up to 5X faster query speed and up to 3X faster extract creation speed."* And if you still can't get enough, there is always the option to use Hyper through API calls in your preferred programming language: `https://help.tableau.com/current/api/hyper_api/en-us/docs/hyper_api_reference.html`.

But what makes Hyper so fast? Let's have a look under the hood!

The Tableau data-handling engine

The vision shared by the founders of Hyper was to create a high-performing, next-generation database—one system, one state, no trade-offs, and no delays. And it worked—today, Hyper can serve general database purposes, data ingestion, and analytics at the same time.

Memory prices have decreased exponentially. The same goes for CPUs; transistor counts increased according to Moore's law, while other features stagnated. Memory is cheap but processing still needs to be improved.

Moore's Law is the observation made by Intel co-founder Gordon Moore that the number of transistors on a chip doubles every two years while the costs are halved. Information on Moore's Law can be found on Investopedia at `https://www.investopedia.com/terms/m/mooreslaw.asp`.

While experimenting with Hyper, the founders measured that handwritten C code is faster than any existing database engine, so they came up with the idea to transform Tableau queries into C code and optimize it simultaneously, all behind the scenes, so the Tableau user won't notice it. This translation and optimization come at a cost; traditional database engines can start executing code immediately. Tableau needs to first translate queries into code, optimize that code, then compile it into machine code, after which it can be executed. The big question is, is it still faster? As proven by many tests on Tableau Public and other workbooks, the answer is yes!

Furthermore, if there is a query estimated to be faster if executed without the compilation to machine code, Tableau has its own **virtual machine** (**VM**) on which the query will be executed right away. And next to this, Hyper can utilize 99% of available CPU computing power, whereas other parallel processes can only utilize 29% of available CPU compute. This is due to the unique and innovative technique of morsel-driven parallelization.

For those of you that want to know more about morsel-driven parallelization, a paper, which later on served as a baseline for the Hyper engine, can be found at `https://15721.courses.cs.cmu.edu/spring2016/papers/p743-leis.pdf`.

If you want to know more about the Hyper engine, I highly recommend the following video at `https://youtu.be/h2av4CX0k6s`.

Hyper parallelizes three steps of traditional data warehousing operations:

- Transactions and **Continuous Data Ingestion (Online Transaction Processing, or OLTP)**
- **Analytics (Online Analytical Processing, or OLAP)**
- **Beyond Relational (Online Beyond Relational Processing, or OBRP)**

Executing those steps simultaneously makes Hyper more efficient and more performant, as opposed to traditional systems where those three steps are separated and executed one after the other.

To sum up, Hyper is a highly specialized database engine that allows us as users to get the best out of our queries. If you recall, in *Chapter 1, Reviewing the Basics*, we already saw that every change on a sheet or dashboard, including drag and drop pills, filters, and calculated fields, among others, is translated into a query. Those queries are pretty much SQL lookalikes; however, in Tableau we call the querying engine VizQL.

VizQL, another hidden gem on your Tableau Desktop, is responsible for visualizing data in a chart format and is fully executed in memory. The advantage is that no additional space on the database side is required here. VizQL is generated when a user places a field on a shelf. VizQL is then translated into SQL, MDX, or **Tableau Query Language (TQL)** and passed to the backend data source with a driver.

Hyper takeaways

This overview of the Tableau data-handling engine demonstrates a flexible approach to interfacing with data. Knowledge of the data-handling engine can reduce data preparation and data modeling efforts, thus helping us streamline the overall data mining life cycle. Don't worry too much about data types and data that can be calculated based on the fields you have in your database. Tableau can do all the work for you in this respect. In the next section, we will discuss what you should consider from a data source perspective.

Focusing on data preparation

Tableau can be used effectively with various data preparation phases. Unfortunately, a single chapter is not sufficient to thoroughly explore how Tableau can be used in each phase. Indeed, such a thorough exploration may be worthy of an entire book! Our focus, therefore, will be directed to ward data preparation, since that phase has historically accounted for up to 60% of the data mining effort. Our goal will be to learn how Tableau can be used to streamline that effort.

Surveying data

Tableau can be a very effective tool for simply surveying data. Sometimes in the survey process, you may discover ways to clean the data or populate incomplete data based on existing fields. Sometimes, regretfully, there are simply not enough pieces of the puzzle to put together an entire dataset. In such cases, Tableau can be useful to communicate exactly what the gaps are, and this, in turn, may incentivize the organization to more fully populate the underlying data.

In this exercise, we will explore how to use Tableau to quickly discover the percentage of null values for each field in a dataset. Next, we'll explore how data might be extrapolated from existing fields to fill in the gaps.

Establishing null values

The following are the steps to survey the data:

1. If you haven't done so just yet, navigate to `https://public.tableau.com/profile/marleen.meier` to locate and download the workbook associated with this chapter.

2. Navigate to the worksheet entitled `Surveying & Exploring Data` and select `Happiness Report` data source.

3. Drag **Region** and **Country** to the **Rows** shelf. Observe that in some cases the **Region** field has **Null** values for some countries:

Figure 2.1: Null regions

4. Right-click and **Edit** the parameter entitled `Select Field`. Note that the **Data Type** is set to **Integer** and we can observe a list that contains an entry for each field name in the dataset:

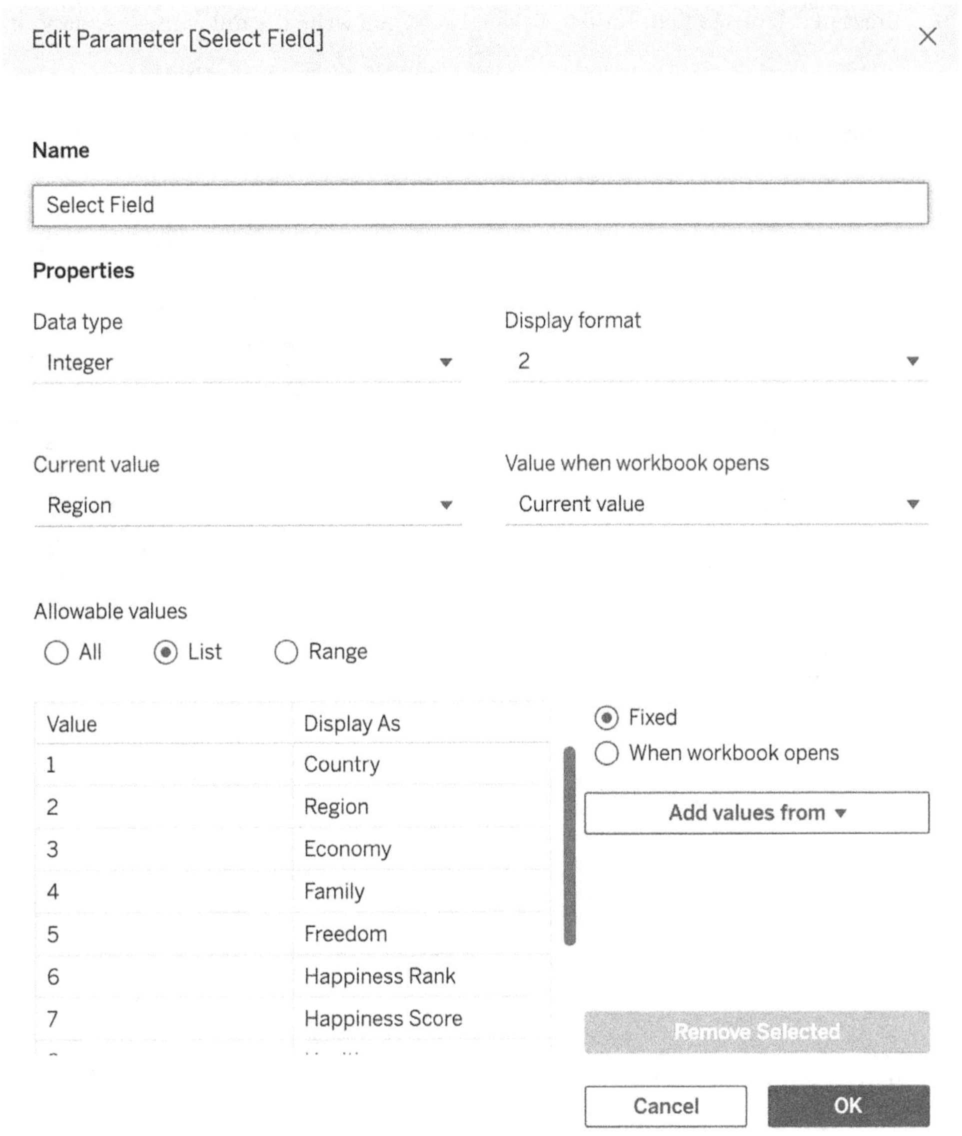

Edit Parameter [Select Field]   ×

Name

Select Field

Properties

Data type   Display format

Integer   ▼   2   ▼

Current value   Value when workbook opens

Region   ▼   Current value   ▼

Allowable values

○ All   ⦿ List   ○ Range

Value	Display As
1	Country
2	Region
3	Economy
4	Family
5	Freedom
6	Happiness Rank
7	Happiness Score

⦿ Fixed
○ When workbook opens

Add values from ▼

Remove Selected

Cancel   **OK**

Figure 2.2: Editing a parameter

5. In the **Data** pane, right-click on the parameter we just created and select **Show Parameter** Control.

6. Create a calculated field entitled % Populated and write the following calculation:

```
SUM([Number of Records]) / TOTAL(SUM([Number of Records]))
```

7. In the **Data** pane, right-click on % **Populated** and select **Default Properties | Number Format...**:

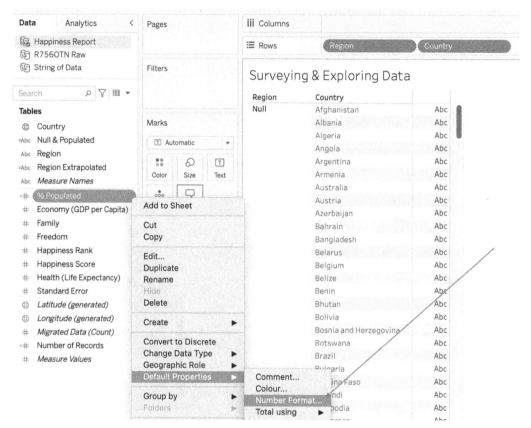

Figure 2.3: Adjusting default properties

8. In the resulting dialog box, choose **Percentage**.

9. Create a calculated field entitled Null & Populated and add the following code. Note that the complete case statement is fairly lengthy but also repetitive.

 In cases requiring a lengthy but repetitive calculation, consider using Excel to more quickly and accurately write the code. By using Excel's CONCATENATE function, you may be able to save time and avoid typos.

In the following code block, the code lines represent only a percentage of the total but should be sufficient to enable you to produce the whole block:

```
CASE [Select Field]
WHEN 1 THEN IF ISNULL ([Country]) THEN 'Null Values' ELSE
```

```
'Populated Values' END
WHEN 2 THEN IF ISNULL ([Region]) THEN 'Null Values' ELSE
'Populated Values' END
WHEN 3 THEN IF ISNULL ([Economy (GDP per Capita)]) THEN 'Null Values'
ELSE
'Populated Values' END
WHEN 4 THEN IF ISNULL ([Family]) THEN 'Null Values' ELSE
'Populated Values' END
WHEN 5 THEN IF ISNULL ([Freedom]) THEN 'Null Values' ELSE
'Populated Values' END
WHEN 6 THEN IF ISNULL ([Happiness Rank]) THEN 'Null Values' ELSE
'Populated Values' END
WHEN 7 THEN IF ISNULL ([Happiness Score]) THEN 'Null Values' ELSE
'Populated Values' END
WHEN 8 THEN IF ISNULL ([Health (Life Expectancy)]) THEN 'Null Values'
ELSE
'Populated Values' END
WHEN 9 THEN IF ISNULL ([Standard Error]) THEN 'Null Values' ELSE
'Populated Values' END
END
```

10. Remove **Region** and **Country** from the **Rows** shelf.

11. Place **Null & Populated** on the **Rows** and **Color** shelves and % **Populated** on the **Columns** and **Label** shelves:

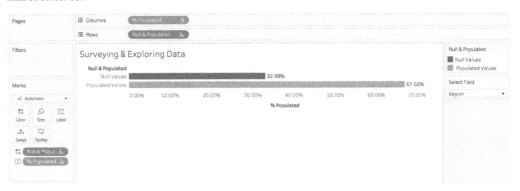

Figure 2.4: Populated values

12. Change the colors to red for **Null Values** and green for **Populated Values** if desired. You can do so by clicking on **Color** in the **Marks** card and **Edit Colors**.

13. Click on the arrow in the upper-right corner of the **Select Field** parameter on your sheet and select **Single Value List**.

14. Select various choices in the **Select Field** parameter and note that some fields have a high percentage of null values. For example, in the following diagram, **32.98%** of records do not have a value for **Region:**

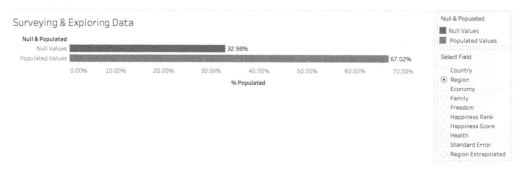

Figure 2.5: Comparing null and populated values

Building on this exercise, let's explore how we might clean and extrapolate data from existing data using the same dataset.

Extrapolating data

This exercise will expand on the previous exercise by cleaning existing data and populating some of the missing data from known information. We will assume that we know which country belongs to which region. We'll use that knowledge to fix errors in the Region field and also to fill in the gaps using Tableau:

1. Starting from where the previous exercise ended, create a calculated field entitled Region Extrapolated with the following code block:

```
CASE [Country]
WHEN 'Afghanistan' THEN 'Southern Asia'
WHEN 'Albania' THEN 'Central and Eastern Europe'
WHEN 'Algeria' THEN 'Middle East and Northern Africa'
WHEN 'Angola' THEN 'Sub-Saharan Africa'
WHEN 'Argentina' THEN 'Latin America and Caribbean'
WHEN 'Armenia' THEN 'Central and Eastern Europe'
WHEN 'Australia' THEN 'Australia and New Zealand'
WHEN 'Austria' THEN 'Western Europe'
//complete the case statement with the remaining fields in the data set
END
```

As an alternative to a **CASE** statement, you could use an **IF** statement like:

```
If [Country] = 'Afghanistan' then 'Southern Asia'
ELSEIF [Country] = 'Albania' then …
END
```

To speed up the tedious creation of a long calculated field, you could download the data to an Excel file and create the calculated field by concatenating the separate parts, as shown here:

	A	B	C	D
	SUM		fx =$B$2&" "&$C$2&A4&$C$2&" "&$D$2&" "&$C$2&B4&$C$2	
1				
2		WHEN		THEN
3				
4	Afghanistan	Southern Asia	=$B$2&" "&$C$2&A4&$C$2&" "&$D$2&" "&$C$2&B4&$C$2	
5	Albania	Central and Eastern Europe	WHEN 'Albania' THEN 'Central and Eastern Europe'	
6	Algeria	Middle East and Northern Af	WHEN 'Algeria' THEN 'Middle East and Northern Africa'	
7	Angola	Sub-Saharan Africa	WHEN 'Angola' THEN 'Sub-Saharan Africa'	
8	Argentina	Latin America and Caribbear	WHEN 'Argentina' THEN 'Latin America and Caribbean'	
9	Armenia	Central and Eastern Europe	WHEN 'Armenia' THEN 'Central and Eastern Europe'	
10	Australia	Australia and New Zealand	WHEN 'Australia' THEN 'Australia and New Zealand'	
11	Austria	Western Europe	WHEN 'Austria' THEN 'Western Europe'	
12	Azerbaijan	Central and Eastern Europe	WHEN 'Azerbaijan' THEN 'Central and Eastern Europe'	
13	Bahrain	Middle East and Northern Af	WHEN 'Bahrain' THEN 'Middle East and Northern Africa'	
14	Bangladesh	Southern Asia	WHEN 'Bangladesh' THEN 'Southern Asia'	
15	Belarus	Central and Eastern Europe	WHEN 'Belarus' THEN 'Central and Eastern Europe'	
16	Belgium	Western Europe	WHEN 'Belgium' THEN 'Western Europe'	
17	Belize	Latin America and Caribbear	WHEN 'Belize' THEN 'Latin America and Caribbean'	
18	Benin	Sub-Saharan Africa	WHEN 'Benin' THEN 'Sub-Saharan Africa'	
19	Bhutan	Southern Asia	WHEN 'Bhutan' THEN 'Southern Asia'	
20	Bolivia	Latin America and Caribbear	WHEN 'Bolivia' THEN 'Latin America and Caribbean'	

Figure 2.6: Compiling a calculation in Excel

You can then copy them from Excel into Tableau. However, for this exercise, I have created a backup field called Backup, which can be found in the Tableau workbook associated with this chapter, which contains the full calculation needed for the Region Extrapolated field. Use this at your convenience. The **Solutions** dashboard also contains all of the countries. You can therefore copy the Region Extrapolated field from that file too.

2. Add a **Region Extrapolated** option to the **Select Field** parameter:

Figure 2.7: Adding Region Extrapolated to the parameter

3. Add the following code to the `Null & Populated` calculated field:

```
WHEN 10 THEN IF ISNULL ([Region Extrapolated]) THEN 'Null Values' ELSE
'Populated Values' END
```

4. Note that the **Region Extrapolated** field is now fully populated:

Figure 2.8: Fully populated Region Extrapolated field

Now let's consider some of the specifics from the previous exercises.

Let's look at the following code block.

Note that the complete `CASE` statement is several lines long. The following is a representative portion:

```
CASE [% Populated]
WHEN 1 THEN IF ISNULL ([Country]) THEN 'Null Values' ELSE
'Populated Values' END
...
```

This case statement is a row-level calculation that considers each field in the dataset and determines which rows are populated and which are not. For example, in the representative line of the preceding code, every row of the `Country` field is evaluated for nulls. The reason for this is that a calculated field will add a new column to the existing data—only in Tableau, not in the data source itself—and every row will get a value. These values can be N/A or null values.

The following code is the equivalent of the quick table calculation `Percent of Total`:

```
SUM([Number of Records]) / TOTAL(SUM([Number of Records]))
```

In conjunction with the `Null & Populated` calculated field, it allows us to see what percentage of our fields are actually populated with values.

It's a good idea to get into the habit of writing table calculations from scratch, even if an equivalent quick table calculation is available. This will help you more clearly understand the table calculations.

The following CASE statement is an example of how you might use one or more fields to extrapolate what another field should be:

```
CASE [Country]
WHEN 'Afghanistan' THEN 'Southern Asia'
... END
```

For example, the Region field in the dataset had a large percentage of null values, and even the existing data had errors. Based on our knowledge of the business (that is, which country belongs to which region), we were able to use the Country field to achieve 100% population of the dataset with accurate information.

Nulls are a part of almost every extensive real dataset. Understanding how many nulls are present in each field can be vital to ensuring that you provide accurate business intelligence. It may be acceptable to tolerate some null values when the final results will not be substantially impacted, but too many nulls may invalidate results. However, as demonstrated here, in some cases, one or more fields can be used to extrapolate the values that should be entered into an underpopulated or erroneously populated field.

As demonstrated in this section, Tableau gives you the ability to effectively communicate to your data team which values are missing, which are erroneous, and how possible workarounds can be invaluable to the overall data mining effort. Next, we will look into data that is a bit messier and not in a nice column format. Don't worry, Tableau has us covered.

Cleaning messy data

The United States government provides helpful documentation for various bureaucratic processes. For example, the **Department of Health and Human Services (HSS)** provides lists of ICD-9 codes, otherwise known as International Statistical Classification of Diseases and Related Health Problems codes. Unfortunately, these codes are not always in easily accessible formats.

As an example, let's consider an actual HHS document known as R756OTN, which can be found at https://www.cms.gov/Regulations-and-Guidance/Guidance/Transmittals/downloads/R756OTN.pdf.

Cleaning the data

Navigate to the Cleaning the Data worksheet in the workbook accompanying this chapter and execute the following steps:

1. Within the **Data** pane, select the **R756OTN Raw** data source:

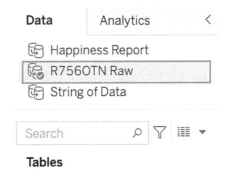

Figure 2.9: Selecting the raw file

2. Drag **Diagnosis** to the **Rows** shelf and choose **Add all members.** Click on the **AZ** sign to sort the **Diagnosis** column. Note the junk data that occurs in some rows:

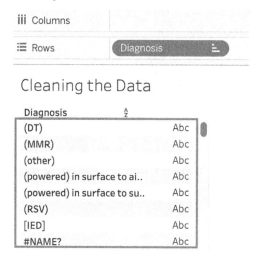

Figure 2.10: Adding Diagnosis to Rows

3. Create a calculated field named DX with the following code:

```
SPLIT([Diagnosis], " ", 1)
```

4. Create a calculated field named Null Hunting with the following code:

```
INT(MID([DX],2,1))
```

5. In the **Data** pane, drag Null Hunting from **Measures** to **Dimensions**.

6. Drag **Diagnosis, DX,** and **Null Hunting** to the **Rows** shelf. Observe that **Null** is returned when the second character in the **Diagnosis** field is not numeric:

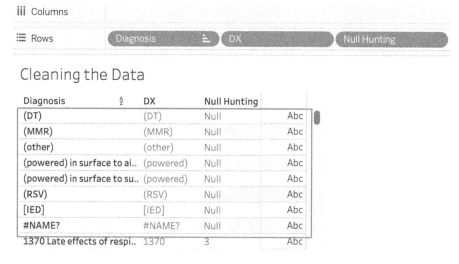

Figure 2.11: Ordering fields on Rows

7. Create a calculated field named `Exclude from ICD` codes containing the following code:

```
ISNULL([Null Hunting])
```

8. Clear the sheet of all fields, as demonstrated in *Chapter 1*, *Reviewing the Basics*, and set the **Marks** card to **Shape**.

9. Place **Exclude from ICD Codes** on the **Color**, and **Shape** shelves, and then place **DX** on the **Rows** shelf. Observe the rows labeled as **True**:

Figure 2.12: Excluding junk data

10. In order to exclude the junk data (that is, those rows where `Exclude from ICD Codes` equates to `True`), place `Exclude from ICD Codes` on the **Filter** shelf and deselect **True**.

11. Create a calculated field named `Diagnosis Text` containing the following code:

```
REPLACE([Diagnosis],[DX] + "","")
```

12. Place **Diagnosis Text** on the **Rows** shelf after **DX**. Also, remove **Exclude from ICD Codes** from the **Rows** shelf and the **Marks** card, and set the mark type to **Automatic**:

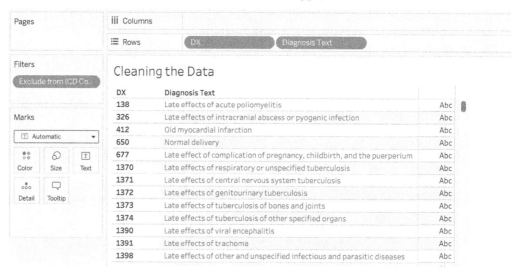

Figure 2.13: Observing the cleaned data

Now that we've completed the exercise, let's take a moment to consider the code we have used:

- The SPLIT function was introduced in Tableau 9.0:

  ```
  SPLIT([Diagnosis], " ", 1)
  ```

- As described in Tableau's help documentation about the function, the function does the following:

  Returns a substring from a string, as determined by the delimiter extracting the characters from the beginning or end of the string.

- This function can also be called directly in the **Data Source** tab when clicking on a column header and selecting **Split**. To extract characters from the end of the string, the token number (that is, the number at the end of the function) must be negative.

- Consider the following code, which we used to create the Null Hunting field:

  ```
  INT(MID([DX],2,1))
  ```

- The use of MID is quite straightforward and much the same as the corresponding function in Excel. The use of INT in this case, however, may be confusing. Casting an alpha character with an INT function will result in Tableau returning Null. This satisfactorily fulfills our purpose, since we simply need to discover those rows not starting with an integer by locating the nulls.

1. ISNULL is a Boolean function that simply returns TRUE in the case of Null:

  ```
  ISNULL([Null Hunting])
  ```

2. The `REPLACE` function was used while creating the `Diagnosis Text` field:

```
REPLACE([Diagnosis],[DX] + "","")
```

3. This calculated field uses the ICD-9 codes isolated in `DX` to remove those same codes from the `Diagnosis` field and thus provides a fairly clean description. Note the phrase *fairly clean*. The rows that were removed were initially associated with longer descriptions that thus included a carriage return. The resulting additional rows are what we removed in this exercise. Therefore, the longer descriptions are truncated in this solution using the `replace` calculation.

The final output for this exercise could be to export the data from Tableau as an additional source of data. This data could then be used by Tableau and other tools for future reporting needs. For example, the `DX` field could be useful in data blending.

Does Tableau offer a better approach that might solve the issue of truncated data associated with the preceding solution? Yes! Let's turn our attention to the next exercise, where we will consider regular expression functions.

Extracting data

Although, as shown in the previous exercise, *Cleaning the data*, the `SPLIT` function can be useful for cleaning clean data, regular expression functions are far more powerful, representing a broadening of the scope from Tableau's traditional focus on visualization and analytics to also include data cleaning capabilities.

Let's look at an example that requires us to deal with some pretty messy data in Tableau. Our objective will be to extract phone numbers.

The following are the steps:

1. If you have not already done so, please download the workbook from https://public.tableau.com/profile/marleen.meier and open it in Tableau.
2. Select the `Extracting the Data` tab.
3. In the **Data** pane, select the **String of Data** data source and drag the **String of Data** field to the **Rows** shelf. Observe the challenges associated with extracting the phone numbers:

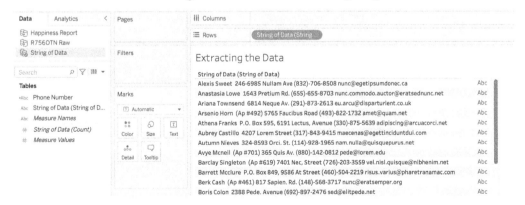

Figure 2.14: Extracting data from a messy data format

4. Access the underlying data by clicking the **View data** button and copying several rows:

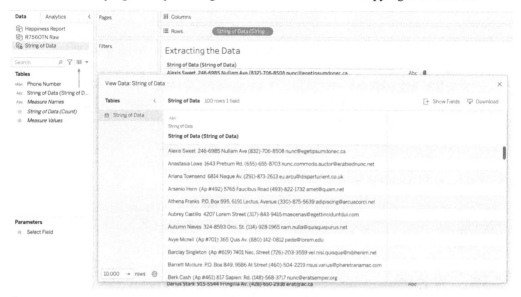

Figure 2.15: Accessing underlying data

5. Navigate to `http://regexpal.com/` and paste the data into the pane labeled **Test String**—that is, the second pane:

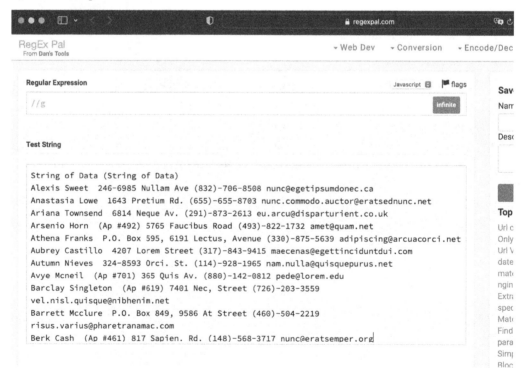

Figure 2.16: Regexpal

6. In the first pane (the one labeled **Regular Expression**), type the following:

```
\([0-9]{3}\)-[0-9]{3}-[0-9]{4}
```

7. Return to Tableau and create a calculated field called `Phone Number` with the following code block. Note the regular expression nested in the calculated field:

```
REGEXP_EXTRACT([String of Data (String of Data)],'(\([0-9]{3}\)-[0-9]{3}-
[0-9]{4})')
```

8. Place **Phone Number** on the **Rows** shelf, and observe the result:

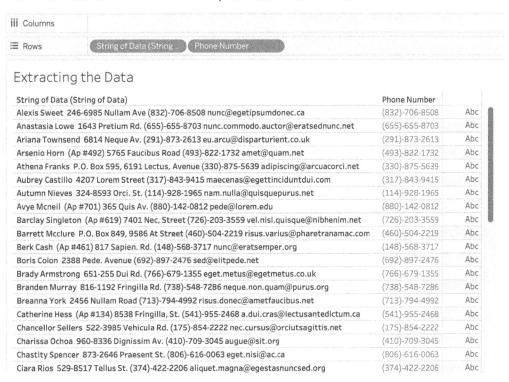

Figure 2.17: Extracting data final view

Now let's consider some of the specifics from the preceding exercise in more detail:

- Consider the following code block:

```
REGEXP_EXTRACT([String of Data],'()')
```

- The expression pattern is purposely excluded here as it will be covered in detail later. The '()' code acts as a placeholder for the expression pattern. The `REGEXP_EXTRACT` function used in this example is described in Tableau's help documentation as follows:

Returns a substring of the given string that matches the capturing group within the regular expression pattern.

- Note that as of the time of writing, the Tableau documentation does not communicate how to ensure that the pattern input section of the function is properly delimited. For this example, be sure to include '()' around the pattern input section to avoid a null output.

- Nesting within a calculated field that is itself nested within a VizQL query can affect performance (if there are too many levels of nesting/aggregation).

- There are numerous regular expression websites that allow you to enter your own code and help you out, so to speak, by providing immediate feedback based on sample data that you provide. http://regexpal.com/ is only one of those sites, so search as desired to find one that meets your needs!

- Now, consider the expression:

```
\([0-9]{3}\)-[0-9]{3}-[0-9]{4}
```

In this context, the \ indicates that the next character should not be treated as special but as literal. For our example, we are literally looking for an open parenthesis. [0-9] simply declares that we are looking for one or more digits. Alternatively, consider \d to achieve the same results. The {3} designates that we are looking for three consecutive digits.

As with the opening parenthesis at the beginning of the pattern, the \ character designates the closing parentheses as a literal. The - is a literal that specifically looks for a hyphen. The rest of the expression pattern should be decipherable based on the preceding information.

After reviewing this exercise, you may be curious about how to return just the email address. According to http://www.regular-expressions.info/email.html, the regular expression for email addresses adhering to the RFC 5322 standard is as follows:

```
(?:[a-z0-9!#$%&'*+/=?^_'{|}~-]+(?:\.[a-z0-9!#$%&'*+/=?^_'{|}~-
]+)*|"(?:[\x01-\x08\x0b\x0c\x0e-\x1f\x21\x23-\x5b\x5d-
\x7f]|\\[\x01-\x09\x0b\x0c\x0e-\x7f])*")@(?:(?:[a-z0-9](?:[a-z0-9-
]*[a-z0-9])?\.)+[a-z0-9](?:[a-z0-9-]*[a-
z0-9])?|\[(?:(?:25[0-5]|2[0-4][0-9]|[01]?[0-9][0-9]?)\.){3}(?:25[0-
5]|2[0-4][0-9]|[01]?[0-9][0-9]?|[a-z0-9-]*[a-z0-9]:(?:[\x01-
\x08\x0b\x0c\x0e-\x1f\x21-\x5a\x53-\x7f]|\\[\x01-\x09\x0b\x0c\x0e-
\x7f])+)\])
```

Emails do not always adhere to RFC 5322 standards, so additional work may be required to truly clean email address data.

Although I won't attempt a detailed explanation of this code, you can read all about it at http://www.regular-expressions.info/email.html, which is a great resource for learning more about regular expressions. Also, YouTube has several helpful regular expression tutorials.

The final output for this exercise should probably be used to enhance existing source data. **Data dumps** such as this example do not belong in data warehouses; however, even important and necessary data can be hidden in such dumps, and Tableau can be effectively used to extract it.

Summary

We began this chapter with a discussion of the Tableau data-handling engine. This illustrated the flexibility Tableau provides in working with data. The data-handling engine is important to understand in order to ensure that your data mining efforts are intelligently focused. Otherwise, your effort may be wasted on activities not relevant to Tableau.

Next, we focused on data preparation. We considered using Tableau to survey and also clean data. The data cleaning capabilities represented by the regular expression functions are particularly intriguing and are worth further investigation.

Having completed our first data-centric discussion, we'll continue with *Chapter 3, Using Tableau Prep Builder*, looking at one of the newer features Tableau has brought to the market. Tableau Prep Builder is a dedicated data pre-processing interface that is able to greatly reduce the amount of time you need for pre-processing. We'll take a look at cleaning, merging, filtering, joins, and the other functionality Tableau Prep Builder has to offer.

Learn more on Discord

To join the Discord community for this book – where you can share feedback, ask questions to the author, and learn about new releases – follow the QR code below:

`https://packt.link/tableau`

3

Using Tableau Prep Builder

Tableau Prep Builder was introduced with version 2018.1 of Tableau Desktop, but what can we use Tableau Prep Builder (henceforth referred to in this chapter as *Prep*) for? The core purpose of the tool is data preparation. The good news is, Prep is fully compatible with Tableau Desktop, and also with Tableau Server. That means you can execute jobs in Prep to clean your data with the click of a button. Additionally, Prep is as visual as its big brother, Tableau Desktop, meaning that you can see every step of data preparation in a fully visual format.

Therefore, let's dive into the **Graphical User Interface** (GUI) and be amazed by another high-end product, which will allow you to get initial data insights, enabling you to decide faster whether your dataset is worth analysis. Prep will pave the way for an even smoother Tableau Desktop experience.

In this chapter, the following topics will be discussed:

- Connecting to data
- The Prep GUI
- Data quality
- Additional options with Prep
- Exporting data

In order to get started, we need to load data. How to do so in Prep will be described in the following section.

Connecting to data

If you are familiar with Tableau Desktop, Prep will be an easy game for you. The handling and inter-faces are very similar, and connecting to data, if the connector is available in Prep, works the same whether it's a text file, a database, or an extract. At first sight, you might not even notice a difference between Prep and the Tableau Desktop GUIs, which provides the handy advantage that you can start prepping right away.

To get started, begin by opening Prep and click on + to open a file. The following screen will appear:

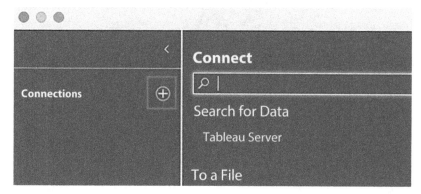

Figure 3.1: Connecting to data

From the preceding screenshot, we can see that you can choose the type of data you want to connect to in the search bar. Just as in Tableau, the repertoire of Prep includes multiple databases.

Now let's connect to a dataset with a practical exercise. For this exercise, we need the following dataset: https://www.kaggle.com/airbnb/boston. Please download calendar.csv, listings.csv, and reviews.csv. Alternatively, download them from the repository associated with this chapter on Tableau Public: https://github.com/PacktPublishing/Mastering-Tableau-2023-Fourth-Edition/ tree/main/Chapter03.

First, we are going to start with the calendar.csv file. Add it to the empty Prep canvas by making a connection with a text file, followed by the selection of your .csv file. You will now see the following screen:

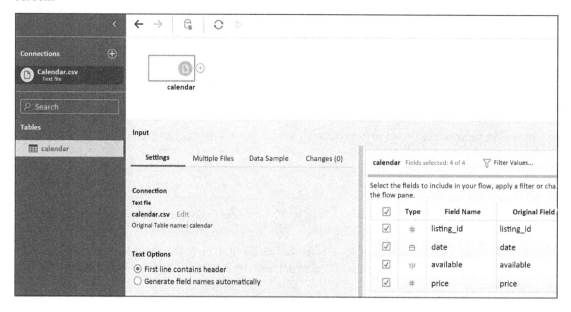

Figure 3.2: Input data

Congratulations—you've just made your first Prep connection. Here, you can manipulate and visualize your connected dataset as required!

In the following section, I will describe the GUI in more detail.

The Prep GUI

User experience is an important topic, not only when you build a dashboard but also when you use other aspects of Tableau. One of the biggest selling points of Tableau is and has always been the ease of using the GUI, and it is only one of the reasons Tableau is a much-loved tool by its customers.

The Prep GUI has two important canvases to look at. Right after you have connected data to Prep, the workspace will split into several parts:

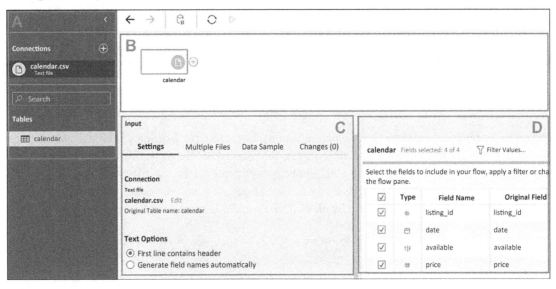

Figure 3.3: Prep workspace sections

Let's look at what we can see from the preceding screenshot:

A: The connection pane, showing you the input files available at the location selected.

B: The flow pane, which shows your current Prep flow. This always starts with an input step.

C: The input pane settings, which give you several options to configure your input.

D: The input pane samples, showing the fields you moved to the connection pane, including sample values.

In the input pane (**C**), you can use the wildcard union (multiple files) function to add multiple files from the same directory. Also, you can limit the sample set that Prep will print in order to increase performance. In the input pane samples (**D**), you can select and deselect the fields you want to import and change their data types. The data type options are, for example, strings, dates, or numbers.

The second GUI is the profile pane. Once you've selected the input data needed, click on the + in the flow pane and select **Add: Clean Step.** Now the profile pane will appear with the data grid:

In the preceding screenshot, the profile pane shows every column from the data source in two sections. The upper sections show aggregates. For example, column 2, **date**, shows the number of rows per date in a small histogram. The columns can all be sorted by clicking on the sort icon (a mini bar chart that appears when your mouse is hovering over a column) next to the column name and by selecting one item. Let's take, for example, **True**, in **available** (column 3). All related features will be highlighted:

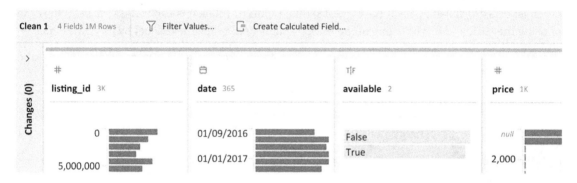

Figure 3.4: Cleaning data

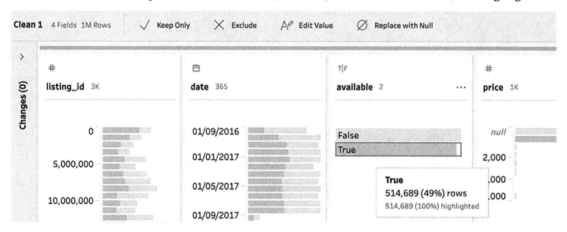

Figure 3.5: Visual filtering

This gives you the chance to get some insights into the data before we even start to clean it up. In the following screenshot, each row is shown as it is in the data source in the lower part of the profile pane:

10036037
10036192
10037387

listing...	date	available	price
4583526	16/02/2017	True	195
4583526	15/02/2017	True	195
4583526	14/02/2017	True	195
4583526	13/02/2017	True	195
4583526	12/02/2017	True	195
4583526	11/02/2017	True	195
4583526	10/02/2017	True	195

Figure 3.6: Data overview

So far we have seen that, after loading data in Prep, visual filters can be applied by clicking on a field or bar in one of the columns. The lower pane will always show the data source of the selection made at the row level. Next, we will continue by adding more data sources.

Getting to know Prep

Let's start with a practical example:

Next to the calendar.csv file, connect to the following files:

* listings.csv
* reviews.csv

Now, drag them onto the flow pane:

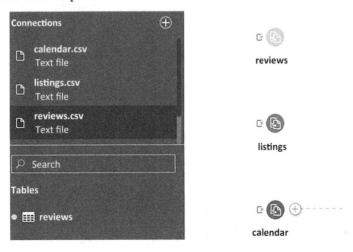

Figure 3.7: Multiple tables input

Can you answer the following questions?

- How many listings use the word "beach" in their description?
- What is the percentage of condominiums that are marked with "exact location"?
- On which day were the most reviews entered?

Without a tool like Prep, it is much more difficult to find the solution to these types of questions. Prep makes our data analytics journey much faster and easier and that is exactly the reason why I encourage you to spend the additional time and learn Prep as well as Tableau Desktop!

 Solutions can be found in the workbook associated with this chapter at the following link: `https://public.tableau.com/profile/marleen.meier`.

Here you see, as an example, I used the **sort** function on **date** in order to answer the third question: *On which day were the most reviews entered?*

reviews   Clean 3

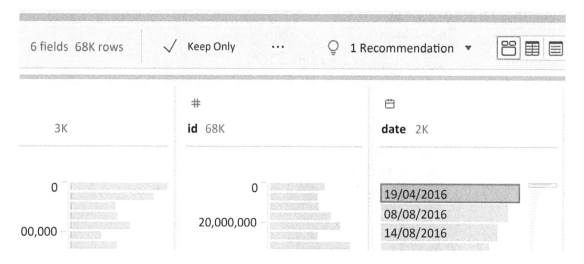

Figure 3.8: Sorting by date

As you can see, sorting this field ordered the dates by the number of entries, thus making it very simple to answer the question, *on which day were the most reviews entered?* After the first few clicks, it already starts to feel natural, doesn't it?

All the changes you made to the dataset can be traced back on the left side of the profile pane. But don't forget to add a proper name to each step: this will make it much easier for others, and yourself, to understand your process.

So, let's continue on to the data quality features of Prep.

Data quality

Prep comes with lots of different features. Sometimes, you might use many different tools to prepare your dataset in order to get it in the shape you desire. Other times, you might just run an aggregation (one feature) and be done. It really depends on the dataset itself and the expected output. The fact is, the closer your Prep output data is to what you need for your Tableau Desktop visualization, the more efficiently VizQL will run on Tableau Desktop. Fewer queries in Tableau Desktop means faster generation of dashboards.

To me, the best part about Prep is that it can handle a huge amount of data. Sometimes, I even use it for datasets I don't want to visualize in Tableau Desktop, just to get a quick overview of, for example, how many rows contain a specific word, how many columns are needed, what happens to the date range if I filter a particular value, and so on! Within a few minutes, I have insights that would have taken me much more time to get with database queries or Excel functions. I hope that by the end of this chapter, you will be able to cut your time spent data prepping in half (at least). We will divide the prepping features into five subcategories: cleaning, unions and joins, aggregating, pivoting, and scripting. Let's start with cleaning data!

Cleaning data

We have seen the following canvas before in the *The Prep GUI* section. To create the cleaning step, the user can simply click on + next to the input and select **Add: Clean Step**. During the cleaning step, multiple operations can be performed, such as filtering or creating a calculated field. Also note the recommendations Prep gives you:

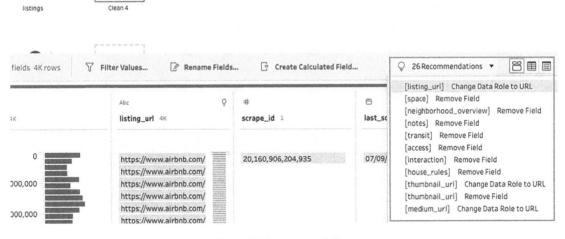

Figure 3.9: Recommendations

Prep analyzes the column content and proposes changes that might fit the data. The column **listing_url**, for example, is being recognized as a web page and therefore Prep recommends you change it to the data role URL. The second, third, and several more recommendations after **listing_url** are to remove certain columns. This is probably the case because the column does not contain any data or contains only a small amount of data. The list goes on.

This feature can be very useful, especially for unfamiliar datasets. My way of working would be to look at the recommendations, check whether they make sense, and execute the change—or not. Don't blindly trust these recommendations, but they can point out data flaws you might have missed otherwise.

Data is often messy, involving null values, typos from manual entries, different formatting, changes in another system, and so on. As a consequence, you will have to sort out the mess before you can get reliable results from an analysis or a dashboard. This section will show you how to clean data at the column level.

Once a value is selected within your clean step, you have the option to **Keep Only, Exclude, Edit Value,** or **Replace with Null:**

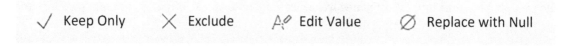

Figure 3.10: Quick access

None of these changes will change the data source itself. Prep is like an in-between step, or a filter between the original data source and your Tableau Desktop. Excluding a value, using the option you can see in Figure 3.10, will only remove it from Prep. However, if used later on as input for Tableau Desktop, there won't be an option to add that specific value back in. This option will remain in Prep only.

Another slightly hidden option is to click on the ellipses (...) next to the column headers (as shown in *Figure 3.11*) and select **Clean:**

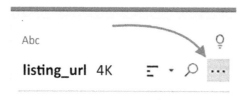

Figure 3.11: More options

This **Clean** functionality operates based on the data type of the column. In the preceding screenshot, the data type is a string (indicated by the **Abc** icon). For other data types, the option will be grayed out since **Clean** is only available for strings. The option allows you to make use of eight more cleaning features:

- Make Uppercase
- Make Lowercase
- Remove Letters

- Remove Numbers
- Remove Punctuation
- Trim Spaces
- Remove Extra Spaces
- Remove All Spaces

The data type can be changed just above each column header; you will find a symbol above the column name, which can be changed by clicking on it, just like in Tableau Desktop:

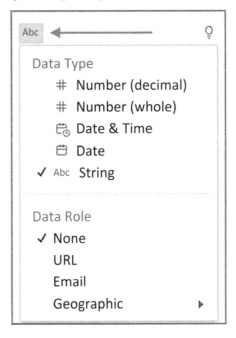

Figure 3.12: Changing Data Type

This comes in handy in case Prep misinterprets the data type of a column. A wrongly assigned data type can have an effect on the calculation you perform on it and how Tableau Desktop would visualize the column.

In the upcoming section, we will practice combining multiple datasets. You might want to combine, for example, order data with shipment data (using a join) or append 2020 sales data to your 2019 sales dataset (using a union). To find out how, read on!

Unions and joins

We will now join the three datasets, so that we may analyze and visualize them together. The nature of the three datasets (listings.csv, reviews.csv, and calendar.csv) requires a join but not a union. However, I will still walk you through the steps of a union in order for you to know when you need it!

Adding unions

A union in Tableau is the appending of data to an existing dataset. Imagine you have two Excel files. Both have the exact same header, but one contains data from 2019, and the other data from 2020. If you union the 2020 data to the 2019 data, you append the rows of the 2020 files to add them underneath the rows of the 2019 files. To perform a union, both datasets need to have almost the same layout/header. Why almost? You will see in the following exercise:

1. To begin this exercise, your Prep flow pane should look like this:

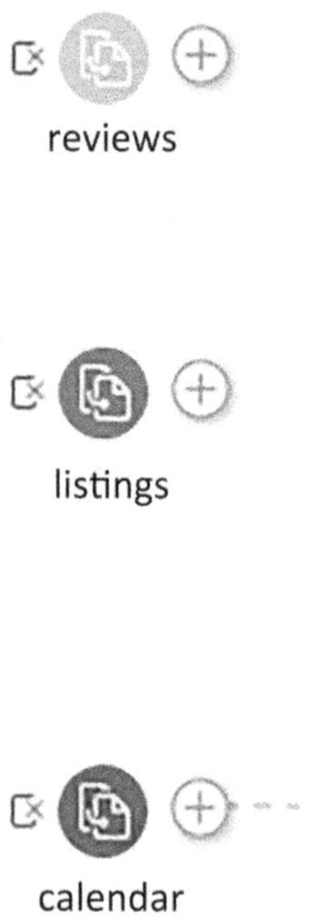

reviews

listings

calendar

Figure 3.13: Flow pane

2. Add a clean step by clicking + next to the **listings** dataset.

    You can change the color of each step according to your preferences by right-clicking on a step and selecting **Edit Color**.

3. Select the column **host_identity_verified** and filter on **True**:

Figure 3.14: Filtering on True

4. Now, create a calculated field, called `DatasetA_ID`, containing just a string, `'A'`:

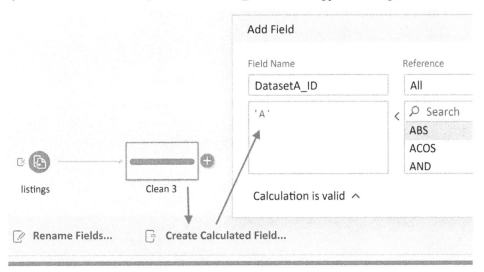

Figure 3.15: Creating a calculated field

5. Create a second cleaning step from the same listings data and filter this time on **True** in the host_identity_verified column:

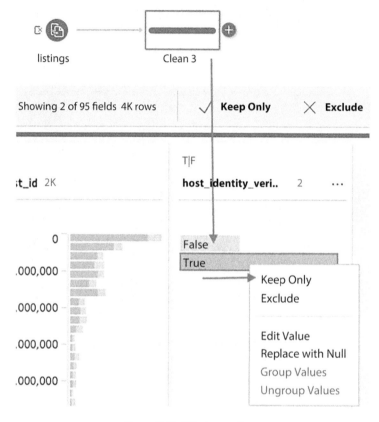

Figure 3.16: Filtering on True

6. Create a calculated field, DatasetB_ID, containing just a string, 'B', using the same process shown in *Figure 3.15*. Renaming the steps by right-clicking and hitting **Rename** helps to keep track of the applied changes. Your flow should look like the following:

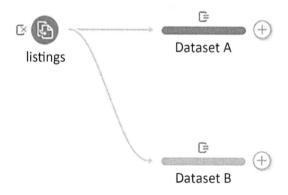

Figure 3.17: Visual flow

7. You have now created two datasets that can be combined using a union, without changing the original data. Union the two by either selecting **Union** after clicking on + next to **Dataset A** or by dragging one step over the other (**Dataset B** over **Dataset A** or vice versa):

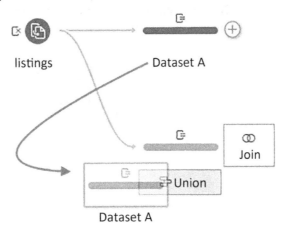

Figure 3.18: Union

8. Check whether all fields match by clicking on **Union 1** and looking at the input details at the bottom left of the screen:

Figure 3.19: Visual check

9. In the preceding screenshot, you can see that on the left, you have information about the union. From top to bottom: the **Inputs** and their respective colors (these are the same as in the flow pane), the **Resulting Fields**, showing 2 mismatching fields, and finally, the **Mismatched Fields** themselves: **DatasetA_ID** and **DatasetB_ID**. The colors next to each mismatched field show that our **DatasetB_ID** field does not exist in **DatasetA**, and the **DatasetA_ID** field does not exist in **DatasetB**.

10. In this case, we know that those columns can be appended even despite the different naming conventions. A better name for both fields would have been **Dataset_ID** (you can go a few steps back and try this out). Prep will not show any mismatches then. But for us here, we can go ahead and drag and drop one field on top of the other to merge them and thereby give Prep the permission to view them as one column:

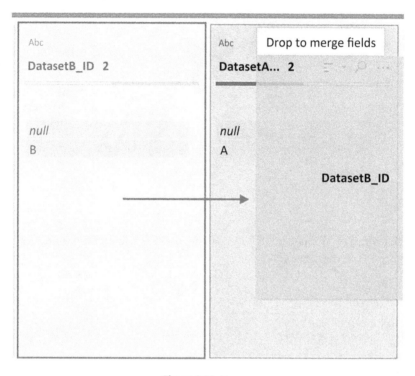

Figure 3.20: Merge

11. See how the **Resulting Fields** now show 0 mismatches, and how both dataset colors are now represented in the bar underneath the column header:

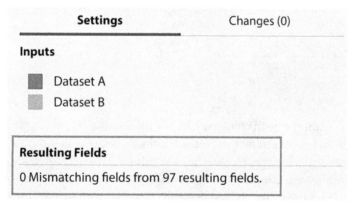

Figure 3.21: Color coding

12. Rename by selecting and right-clicking the union step from **Union 1** to **listings2**, and add a description by selecting and right-clicking the union step and hitting **Add Description** if you like—all the extra effort you make now will help you later with replication, documentation, and explanation.

Congratulations; your first union was a success. We first split the original listings dataset in to two and then combined them again into one. Stacking data with the same layout on top of each other, as we've done here, is a typical task for unions.

Wildcard unions

Instead of dragging one data input on top of another, as we did in the previous section, you can also tell Prep which files to union from a pre-defined directory. Oftentimes, departments have a shared location in which they store, for example, Excel files that are named something such as **Jan2023Revenue**, **Feb2023Revenue**, **Mar2023Revenue**, and so on. If you come across such a scenario, you can do the following:

1. Connect Prep to any one file that you want to use.

2. Click on the input data icon and select the **Tables** tab. You can now see that you can create a union given a certain condition:

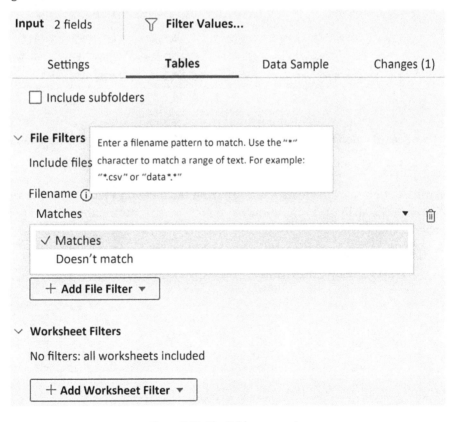

Figure 3.22: The Tables menu view

3.   I will select all matching filenames in that same directory that start with something (*) and end with **2023Revenue.xlsx**, and as you can see, Jan, Feb, and March will all be included, and you can even filter the input by using the **File** and **Worksheet** filter, and clicking **Apply** when you are done::

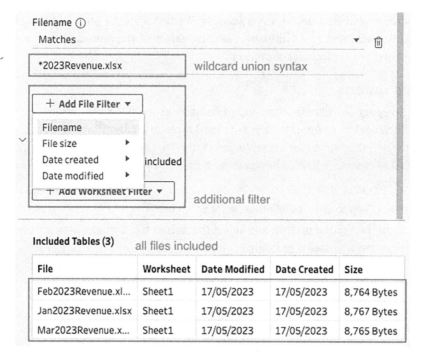

Figure 3.23: Filtering the unions

This is the wildcard union feature. It is really powerful! Try it out and see for yourself.

Adding joins

Now, we will continue to work in the same flow pane and focus on a join. As a quick refresher, a join appends data horizontally. As a rule of thumb, unions increase the number of rows and joins change the number of columns:

1.   Drag **listings2** onto **reviews** until the **Join** option appears.

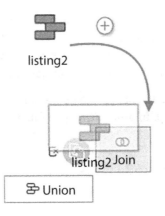

Figure 3.24: Join

2. Select **listing_id** from **reviews** and **id** from **listings2** for your join. Please note that you can change the join type by clicking on the Venn diagram under **Join Type**:

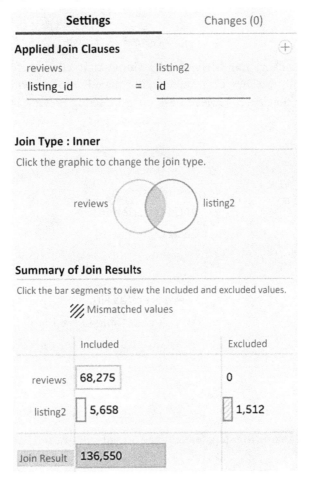

Figure 3.25: Visual check join

What the preceding overview tells us is that all 68,275 rows of the **reviews** dataset were matched to a row in the **listing2** dataset. However, we do have 756 mismatches from the **listing2** dataset. Our total **Join Result** is therefore 68,275 rows. But it is likely that not all listings have reviews and therefore we can safely assume that our join worked as expected.

3. Another check could be to change the join to a full outer join and dive deeper into the data later in Tableau Desktop. In order to get to a full outer join, simply click on the outer edge of the two circles:

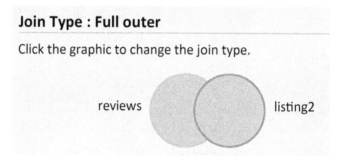

Join Type : Full outer

Click the graphic to change the join type.

reviews   listing2

Figure 3.26: Full join

4. If you want to check immediate results, simply right-click on, for example, the join symbol (represented by the Venn diagram icon, as shown in the following screenshot), and you'll be able to check the data in Tableau Desktop by selecting **Preview in Tableau Desktop**:

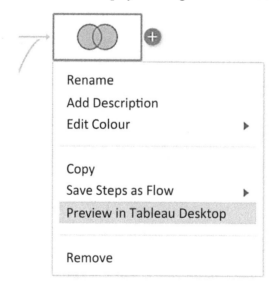

Rename

Add Description

Edit Colour ▶

Copy

Save Steps as Flow ▶

Preview in Tableau Desktop

Remove

Figure 3.27: Preview

5. We can also rename the step; let's change our join's name to lis&rev.

By now, we've seen how to clean data, and how to use unions and joins. The union part taught us how to append data vertically or underneath each other. The join part allowed us to combine data horizontally or next to each other. More specifically, we were able to combine the listings with their respective reviews. Instead of having two datasets, we have created one that allows us to look up a listing review, and in the same row, view all the data regarding the listing itself, like the type of listing, number of bedrooms, whether it has an ocean view, and so on.

Let's continue next with the aggregation step.

Aggregating

An aggregation is used when you want to change the granularity of your data. In our dataset, we have one row per review. However, we want to see if hosts that have been in the Airbnb business in Boston longer have more reviews compared to hosts that started more recently. In order to do so, we need to get an aggregated number of reviews per year that the host started offering listings. The **host_since** field will give us helpful information as well as the **reviewer_id** field. For the latter, we will count the distinct reviewers that left reviews. Let's do it!

Our current flow pane looks like this:

Figure 3.28: Flow pane

To aggregate the number of reviews, please take the following steps:

1. First, click on the + sign next to **lis&rev** and choose **Aggregate**:

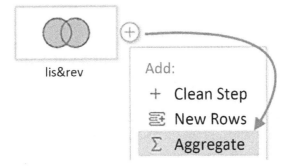

Figure 3.29: Aggregate

2. This will open a window entitled **Aggregate 1**. Our goal is to see how many people reviewed accommodation per year from when the host started offering listings; therefore, take the following actions.

    1. Using the search field in the **Additional Fields** pane, as can be seen on the left in *Figure 3.30*, add the **host_since** field to **Grouped Fields** by dragging and dropping.

    2. Add the **reviewer_id** to **Aggregated Fields**, also by dragging and dropping. Note that the default aggregation is **SUM**, as indicated by the arrow on the right:

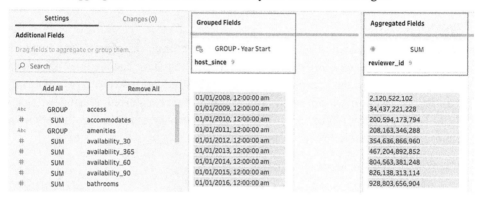

Figure 3.30: Aggregated fields

3. Change the **reviewer_id** aggregation by clicking on **SUM** under **Aggregated Fields**, and change it to **Count Distinct**:

Aggregated Fields

#	SUM
revi	✓ Sum ...
	Average
	Median
2,1	Count
34,	Count Distinct
200	Minimum

Figure 3.31: Count Distinct

4. This will change the default aggregation, **Sum** (where every review is counted), to **Count Distinct,** which counts the distinct reviewer ID aggregation. This will allow us to focus on how many different reviewers left reviews. This is just an arbitrary choice; feel free to try out the other aggregations and see how the data changes.

Let's have a look at the Tableau Desktop preview by right-clicking on the **Aggregate** step on our flow pane and selecting **Preview in Tableau Desktop**:

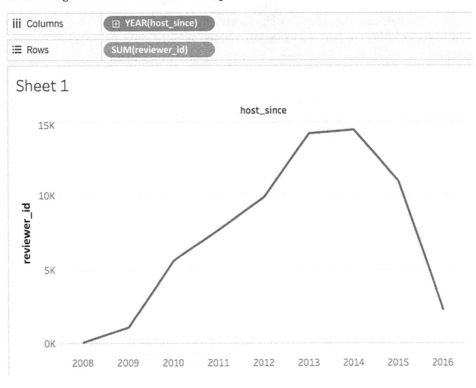

Figure 3.32: Host chart

In the preceding screenshot, we can see the distinct count of reviews per **host_since** date. Of course, in this specific example, Tableau Desktop could also count the reviews per **host_since** date if those were the only fields dragged onto the view without the help of Prep. But a benefit of aggregating prior to importing the data into Tableau Desktop is that you have less data to import; hence, it's possible to achieve better performance. If you want to continue analyzing the dataset in either Prep or Tableau Desktop, you can now ask further questions, such as the following:

- Which type of accommodation has the highest discount for staying a week rather than a day?
- Is there a correlation between the size of the accommodation and the monthly price?
- How many hosts (as a percentage) have more than one listing?

Good luck and happy dashboard building!

We'll finish this section here and look back at a graph consisting of only 9 datapoints, which we created by aggregating the almost 64,000 rows of **reviewer_id** data by the year that the host started offering the listing. The graph tells a story; 64,000 individual rows of data don't. That is why it is so important to always reduce your data, and aggregate it if possible. In the next section, we will talk about another important feature: pivoting.

Pivoting

Do you recognize a situation where you drag and drop your fields onto your Tableau Desktop row and column shelves but somehow the visualization doesn't do what you want? Chances are that you have to turn your data, or better, pivot it. If data that you expect to be in one column, spread over multiple rows, appears in multiple columns instead, it's a case for pivoting. The following example will showcase a need for pivoting.

For our pivot example, we will make use of another dataset. You can find it at `https://github.com/PacktPublishing/Mastering-Tableau-2023-Fourth-Edition/blob/main/Chapter03/Excel_Pivot.xlsx`. The dataset is very simple and looks like this:

	A	B	C	D
1	Day	Blue	Green	Yellow
2	1	3	4	3
3	2	4	7	4
4	3	3	5	2
5	4	2	6	3
6	5	3	5	2
7				

Figure 3.33: Excel input

It has three different colors that were observed on five different days, *x* amount of times. This data is a typical example of when pivoting is helpful to tidy up the data because multiple columns have the same purpose—**B**, **C**, and **D** are all observations. If you wanted to visualize this table, it could look like the following:

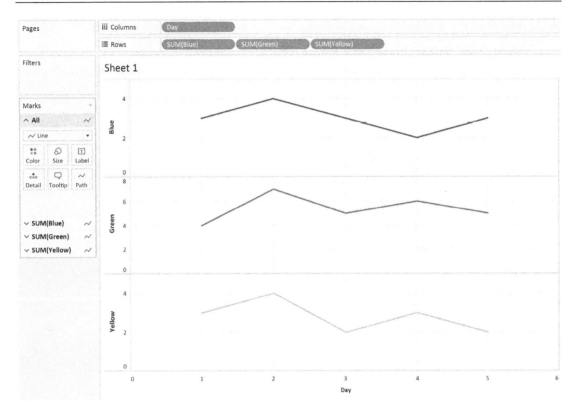

Figure 3.34: Pivot I

But you might be wondering, since the color scheme already indicates which color has been observed, wouldn't it be better to put all three lines in one graph? With separate lines per color, within one line chart? Let's accomplish this!

Begin by connecting the PivotDataSet to Prep, then follow these steps to pivot the data:

1. From Prep, connect to the Excel file we just created and add **PivotDataSet** to the flow pane, click on the + next to the input data step, and select **Pivot**. A new step called **Pivot 1** will appear:

PivotDataSet   Pivot 1

Figure 3.35: Adding a Pivot step

2. Click on the **Pivot 1** step in the flow pane, and *Figure 3.36* will appear at the bottom of your Prep window. Select all three colors from the **Fields** pane shown in **Step I**, and drag them onto the **Pivoted Fields** pane, as shown in **Step II**:

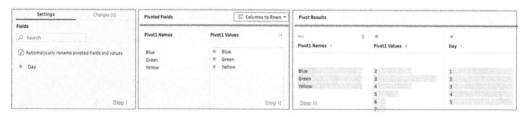

Figure 3.36: Pivot steps

3. Now, have a look at the **Pivot Results** pane, as shown in **Step III** of the preceding screenshot, and rename **Pivot1 Names** to **Colors** and **Pivot1 Values** to **Observations** by right-clicking and selecting **Rename**. Now click the + next to **Pivot 1**, and voilà, we now have a clean table, called **Clean 1**:

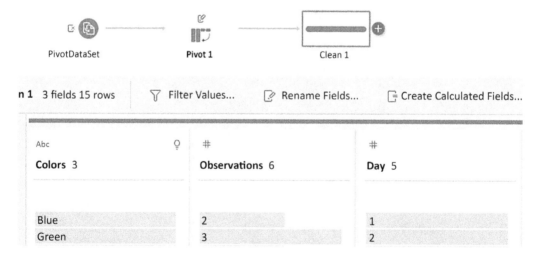

Figure 3.37: Pivot results

4. Remember our problem from the beginning? Our line chart can now be created in a different way, as shown in *Figure 3.38*. Note that **Colors** is a dimension now and the **Observations** are their own field, compared to before when they were located under the column header of each color:

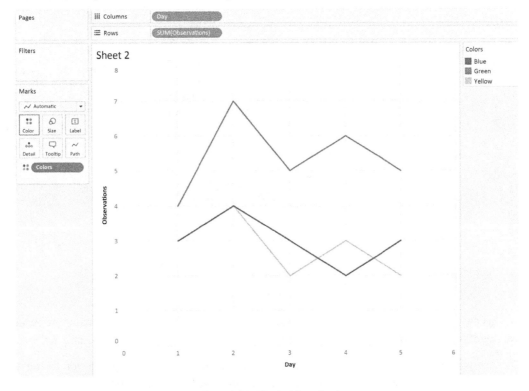

Figure 3.38: Pivoted line chart

 This is a simple use case for pivoting, but the technique here can be transferred to any other dataset. Prep has a built-in recommendation feature. Whenever you see a light bulb in the upper-right corner of a column, check it out and see if the recommendation applies to your needs.

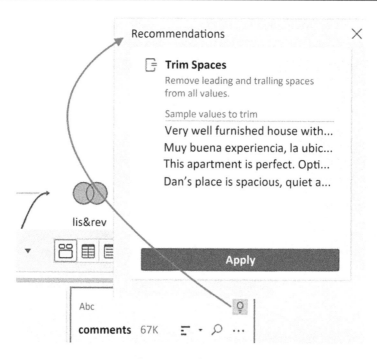

Figure 3.39: Trim spaces

In this case, Tableau recommends we remove all leading and trailing spaces, which is exactly what we need! As demonstrated here, it's always worth checking the recommendations.

Perfect; you are all set with the main Prep functionality. However, you might be wondering what you are supposed to do if you require any further preparation. No problem; Prep has you covered. Scripting is the newest addition to Prep and the most powerful of all; it is virtually limitless! Continue reading to explore Prep's scripting feature.

Scripting

The script functionality that we will discuss next is one of the features more recently added to Tableau. We will discuss it next because a programming language like Python or R gives you endless flexibility. If you ever reach the boundaries of Prep's offerings, you can fall back on scripting and write your own code to do exactly what you want.

In order to make use of it, you have to connect to Python (or R), outside of Tableau first. The following steps are based on the instructions from https://help.tableau.com/current/prep/en-us/prep_scripts_TabPy.htm for Python or https://help.tableau.com/current/prep/en-us/prep_scripts._R.htm for R.

For this exercise, we will be using the Boston Airbnb dataset, more specifically the `calendar` table. Download this dataset from `https://www.kaggle.com/airbnb/boston` and connect to the `calendar` table in Prep:

Figure 3.40: Calendar dataset

Now, let's take a step back and connect Python to Prep:

1. Download and install `Python` from `python.org` (or download and install R from `https://www.r-project.org/`).

2. Download and install `TabPy` by executing the following command in your terminal or on the command line:

   ```
   pip install tabpy
   ```

3. Alternatively, if using R, open R and execute:

   ```
   install.packages("Rserve", , "http://rforge.net")
   ```

4. Open `TabPy` on the command line/terminal by entering the following command:

   ```
   tabpy
   ```

   Or, in the R GUI, type:

   ```
   library(Rserve)
   Rserve()
   ```

5. Back in Prep, click on + on the right-hand side of the calendar table and add a **Clean Step**.

6. Add a calculated field called **PythonTest** (use **RTest** instead if you've chosen to experiment with R) with a string value, `"Test"`:

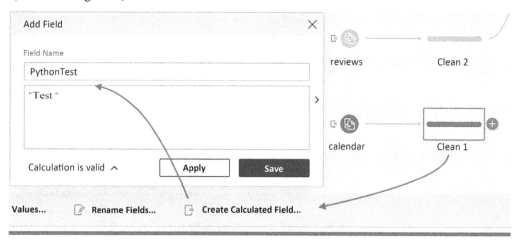

Figure 3.41: PythonTest

7. Now, click on + on the right-hand side of the **Clean 1** step and add **Script**.

8. By selecting the **Script** step, the **Settings** pane at the bottom (see *Figure 3.42*) will give you an option to connect to **Rserve** or **TabPy.** **Rserve** is the Tableau server for R and TabPy is the Tableau server for Python.

9. Choose your connection type by selecting **Rserve** or **Tableau Python (TabPy) Server.** Then open **Help | Settings and Performance | Manage Analytics Extension Connection.** In the upcoming window, connect Prep to TabPy by using **localhost** and **Port 9004** (if using R, connect to Rserve by selecting it under **Connection type** and using **localhost** and **Port 6311** in the same popup), and click **Sign In:**

    •   If using an SSL-encrypted Rserve server, **Port 4912** is the default port.

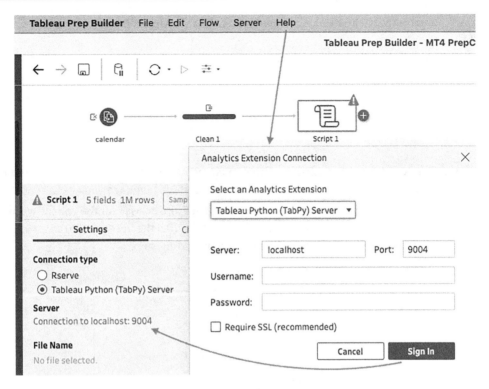

Figure 3.42: TabPy Server

10. Next, if experimenting with Python, create a .py file containing the following code and make sure the indentation is exactly the same:

```python
def ChangeString(df):
    df['PythonTest'] = 'Python'
    return df
```

Figure 3.43: The .py file

Alternatively, create a `.R` file containing the following code:

```
Get ChangeString<- add_column(
.data,
.before = 'Test'
.after = 'R') {
Return (data.frame ())
}
```

11. The script we just created is written to change an existing column in Prep and rename every row from Test to Python or R, depending on which language you've chosen.

12. We'll continue with the Python script. Back in Prep, browse for the `.py` file we just created and add the function name to the Prep interface. I called the file PrepTableau.py and the function name is ChangeString, as defined in the preceding step:

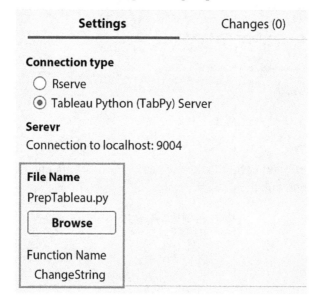

Figure 3.44: Adding a function

13. Observe that the **PythonTest** column has changed from **Test** to **Python**:

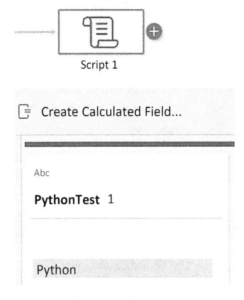

Figure 3.45: PythonTest

Our little experiment worked! And even though we used a very simplistic example, it shows that the scripting feature works, and you can just follow your creativity with what else you might be able to do by using scripting. Examples include everything from calculating an inverse normal distribution to machine learning with sentiment analysis or clustering.

You might have noticed that we did not import pandas in the script itself, but still used a pandas DataFrame. This is due to the fact that the pandas import comes with TabPy. You can see this in your command line/terminal after opening TabPy:

```
●  ○  ●                              marleenmeier — tabpy — 143×61
2023-05-17,14:33:56 [INFO] (base_handler.py:base_handler:115): Authentication is not a required feature for
2023-05-17,14:33:56 [INFO] (base_handler.py:base_handler:115): Authorization header not found
2023-05-17,14:33:56 [INFO] (base_handler.py:base_handler:115): function to evaluate=def _user_script(tabpy,
import pandas as pd
 def get_output_schema():
        return 'a17cef38-c7da-4014-a420-ab3ca676861b'
 def prep_string():
        return ['prep_string_type']
 def prep_bool():
        return ['prep_bool_type']
```

Figure 3.46: Importing pandas on the command line

If you want to use other libraries in your script, you can install them by using `pip install` on your command line/terminal. You only have to restart TabPy afterward and you will be able to use them too. Remember, always open TabPy on the terminal/command line first, or else Prep can't execute the script.

 At the time of writing, Prep does not support a script as input yet—you could, however, use a dummy `.csv` file as a workaround and add a script to the flow immediately after it.

Additional options with Prep

This section will discuss some smaller standalone, very powerful, and new Prep features. Some of you might have been using Prep since the very first release. With each release and each additional user and feedback given, Tableau was able to create a priority list of features that stakeholders—like you and I—really wished to see. The upcoming topics are some of the best examples. None of these features were present in the initial release but have made the product so much better, more valuable, and more complete. You are able now to save part of your flow and reuse it, write back your data to an external database, refresh parts of your dataset, and schedule flows with the Tableau Data Management add-on. Let's take a closer look and start with the "insert flow" function.

Insert Flow

An option in Prep is to add an existing flow to your own flow. For example, say someone already worked on the Boston Airbnb dataset and created a flow of the highlighted steps only:

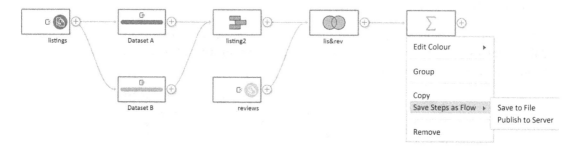

Figure 3.47: Save to File

You could save the steps you wish to insert into your flow by right-clicking and selecting **Save to File**, as shown in *Figure 3.47*. These steps could be inserted back into your flow by right-clicking on the canvas, selecting **Insert Flow**, and browsing your .tfl files for the previously downloaded file:

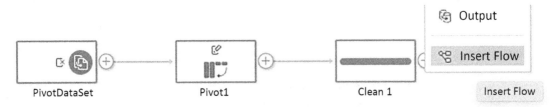

Figure 3.48: Insert Flow

This functionality is very convenient to share work and reuse already created steps. Next, we will look into another functionality that will allow you to refresh the data used in your Prep flow: incremental refresh.

Incremental refresh

Prep 2020.2 saw the introduction of the incremental refresh feature. After completing a flow and adding an output, you can decide whether you want a full or incremental refresh, and which field you want to use as an indicator. Imagine you have a dataset of infections per day of a particular disease. By the end of every day, you want to add the new data, which comes from a health ministry database, to your dataset. So, what are you going to do?

Typically, you would load the whole dataset, all of it, after the newest datapoints were added. But nothing changes about the datapoints older than that day; they will remain the same and you loaded them before already. Therefore, it is a waste of resources to reload the whole dataset. An incremental refresh will only load new datapoints and add them to the existing data, which has been built up over many days. You can imagine how much time and effort this will save. It is a much more sustainable way to keep your data up to date than a full refresh.

We are going to look at an example in the following workflow. It is important that an **Output** step is part of the flow:

Figure 3.49: Incremental refresh

To add the incremental refresh, take the following steps:

1. Click on the data input step and scroll down the **Settings** tab until you see the **Incremental Refresh** option. Then, check the **Enable incremental refresh** box:

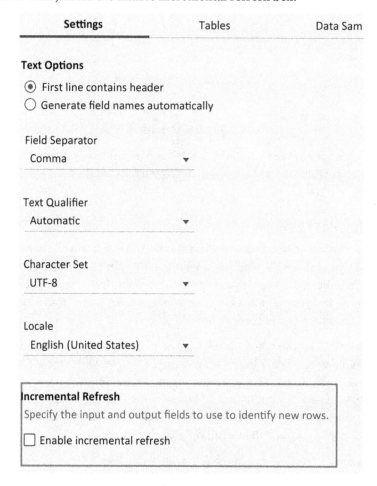

Figure 3.50: Set up Incremental Refresh

2. After you click on the **Enable incremental refresh** box, a dropdown will appear. This dropdown contains all fields that Prep finds useful as an indicator for a data refresh. Select, for example, the **date** field. It is the perfect field to use since as soon as a new date is added to the original data source, the refresh will start.

3. Prep will also ask you for the output field that will represent the **date** column in the output. In our case, it is still **date**:

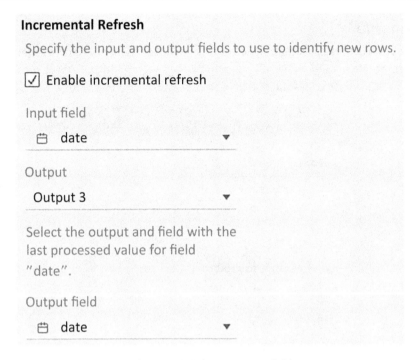

Incremental Refresh

Specify the input and output fields to use to identify new rows.

☑ Enable incremental refresh

Input field

🗓 date ▼

Output

Output 3 ▼

Select the output and field with the last processed value for field "date".

Output field

🗓 date ▼

Figure 3.51: Select an output field

4. After everything is set up, click on the **Output** step again and note how you can now select the type of refresh, full or incremental, you prefer for this flow by clicking on the drop-down menu on the **Run Flow** option:

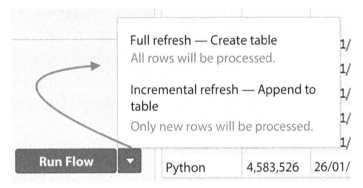

Figure 3.52: Refresh options

You just learned how to set up your data refresh—full as well as incremental. This will help you with the sustainable usage of compute resources and to always have your data up to date. Next, we will introduce another Tableau feature worth investigating—Bulk rename.

Bulk rename

This feature is a real time-saver! Simply select as many columns as you want to rename, right-click, and select **Rename Fields**. A new view will open that allows you to add a prefix or suffix to every selected column or you can replace specific text in each of them:

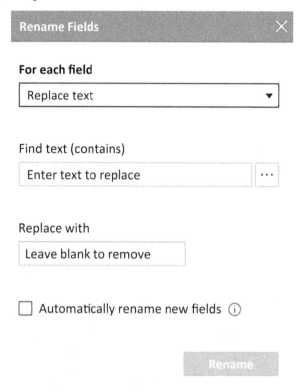

Figure 3.53: Bulk rename in action

You could then also leverage the **Find Text** function or automatically rename all new fields that might come in at a later stage, e.g., because IT added an additional column to your dataset.

Tableau Prep Conductor

With **Tableau Prep Conductor,** you can publish your Prep flows to Tableau Server, schedule them to run at a certain time, and always have refreshed data. The conductor is available in the Tableau Data Management add-on and doesn't ship with Tableau Desktop or Prep.

> For more information, please check https://www.tableau.com/products/add-ons/data-management.

Exporting data

Last, but not least, we may want to export our data. We have seen before that a right-click on a symbol in the flow pane offers the possibility to preview the data in Tableau Desktop:

1. If you want a flow to run according to a schedule or save it to a location, it's best to use **Add | Output**.

2. After you do this, the following screen will appear:

Figure 3.54: Save to file

3. The user now has the option to save the data to a file, and also to save it in Hyper file format as `.hyper`, as `.xlsx` (new in Tableau 2021.1), or as a `.csv` file.

4. Another option is to publish the newly generated data source directly to Tableau Server and make it available to other users. For this option, select **Publish as a data source** instead of **Save to File** from the dropdown.

5. A third option to save Prep output has been added to Tableau 2020.3: writing the resulting data to an external database. If you want to do so, select the **Database** table option from the drop-down. At the time of writing, seven databases are compatible with the write-back functionality, but more will be added based on user demand:

Figure 3.55: Save to external database

Since the Tableau release 2022.3, you can write back to CRM Analytics too. To do this, you need a Salesforce account and the according license. Therefore, we will not discuss this option further, but if you are a Salesforce Analytics user, check this out!

This section has shown us how to save our work and, even more so, the output of our Prep flows. To me, the ability to save output to an external database is the best new feature, because it is the easiest way to share my output in a structured and organized way with others. So not only I but also other users can work with the prepped data, saving additional work. The flow can then be reused not only by me but by anyone.

Summary

We started this chapter with an introduction to Prep. We looked at the GUI and how we can connect data to it. After that, we did some exercises regarding data preparation. This can be divided into five parts: data cleaning, unions and joins, aggregating, pivoting, and scripting. We also considered several additional options to improve the usefulness of your data, including inserting steps from other flows, and incremental refreshes. To round out this chapter on Prep, we looked at exporting data. Here, we saw that the new dataset can be saved as a file or data extract, written back to an external database, or pushed directly to Tableau Server.

Just like Tableau Desktop, Prep is very much self-explanatory and highly visual. Colors, symbols, and highlights make it easy to get used to this extract, transform, and load tool, which is invaluable for preparing your data before manipulating it on the main Tableau interface!

In the next chapter, we'll continue our exploration of data in Tableau. We'll explore how to prepare data for Tableau by looking at joins, blends, and data structures.

Learn more on Discord

To join the Discord community for this book – where you can share feedback, ask questions to the author, and learn about new releases – follow the QR code below:

`https://packt.link/tableau`

4

Learning about Joins, Blends, and Data Structures

Connecting Tableau to data often means more than connecting to a single table in a single data **source**. You may need to use Tableau to join multiple tables from a single data source. For this purpose, we can use joins, which combine a dataset row with another dataset's row if a given key value matches. You can also join tables from disparate data sources or union data with a similar metadata structure.

Sometimes, you may need to merge data that does not share a common row-level key, meaning if you were to match two datasets on a row level like in a join, you would duplicate data because the row data in one dataset is of much greater detail (for example, cities) than the other dataset (which might contain countries). In such cases, you will need to blend the data. This functionality allows you to, for example, show the count of cities per country without changing the city dataset to a country level.

Also, you may find instances when it is necessary to create multiple connections to a single data source in order to pivot the data in different ways. This is possible by manipulating the data structure, which can help you achieve data analysis from different angles using the same dataset. It may be required to discover answers to questions that are difficult or simply not possible with a single data structure.

In this chapter, we will discuss the following topics:

- Relationships
- Joins
- Unions
- Blends
- Understanding data structures

In version 2020.2, Tableau added functionality that will allow you to join or blend without specifying one of the two methods. It is called **relationships**. We will start this chapter off by explaining this new feature before we investigate the details of joins, blends, and more.

Relationships

Although this chapter will primarily focus on joins, blends, and the manipulation of data structures, let's begin with an introduction to **relationships**: a new functionality available since Tableau 2020.2, and one that the Tableau community has been waiting a long time for. It is the new default option in the data canvas; therefore, we will first investigate **relationships**, which belong to the **logical layer of the data model,** before diving deeper into the join and union functionalities that operate on the **physical layer.**

To read all about the physical and logical layers of Tableau's data model, visit the Tableau help pages: `https://help.tableau.com/current/online/en-us/datasource_datamodel.htm`.

For now, you can think of the logical layer as being able to count smarter. Imagine a customer table with unique customer names and an order table with hundreds of recorded orders. In a logical layer, a customer name with multiple orders (thus multiple rows of order and customer IDs in the order table) will be counted as one customer because the logical layer is smart and it recognizes the customer name, while the physical layer would count one customer for each order and hence it would count the same customer as multiple customers if they ordered multiple times. You could only solve this by counting distinct values (which is not required when using the logical layer).

In the following screenshot, you can see the data source canvas, with two datasets combined in a relationship on the left-hand side and the same datasets combined using a **join** on the right-hand side. Please note that relationships only show a line between the tables (**Orders, People,** and **Returns**) whereas joins indicate the type of join by two circles:

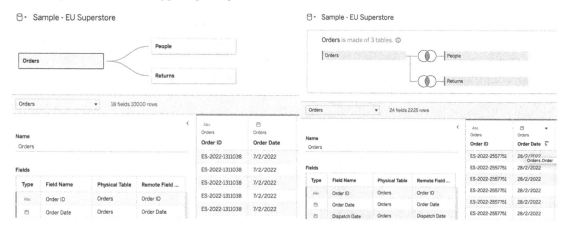

Figure 4.1: Relationships and joins on the data source canvas

A key difference is that the preview of the data, at the bottom, will show only data from the selected table in relationships, compared to all data when using joins. This makes sense because the granularity of data can change in relationships, depending on the fields you are using in your dashboard. Joins, however, have a fixed level of granularity, which is defined by the type of join and join clauses you choose.

Relationships are the default for Tableau Desktop 2020.2 and higher. However, if you still want to make use of the join functionality, you can drag a dataset into the data source canvas, click on the drop-down arrow, and select **Open...**:

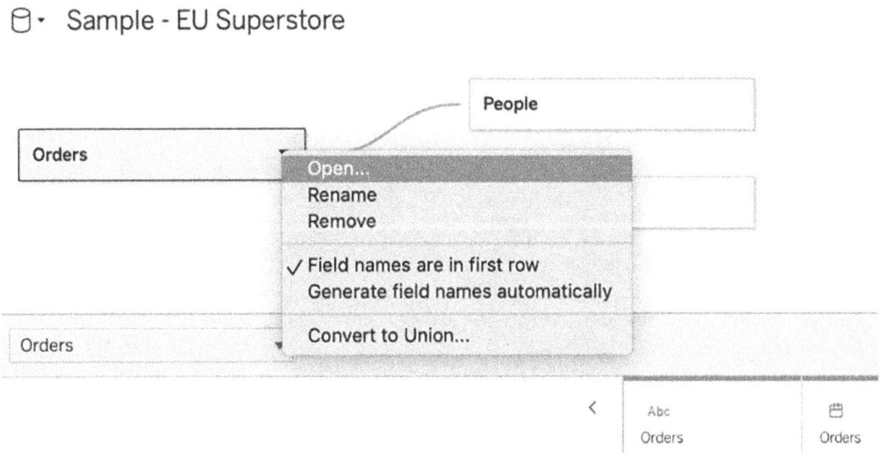

Figure 4.2: From relationship to join canvas

This will open the dataset as you used to see it in the data pane in Tableau in versions before 2020.2 and you will be able to use joins the old way, as we will describe in the *Joins* section.

The line between two datasets in a relationship (based on the logical layer) is called a **noodle** due to its al dente spaghetti looks – yum! Tableau detects a relationship as soon as you drag in the second data source to the data source canvas, but you can add more key columns or remove and adjust them if needed by clicking on the noodle itself:

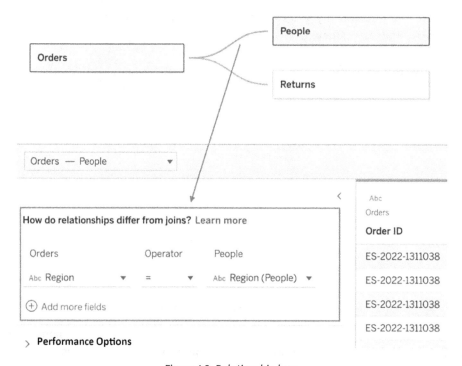

Figure 4.3: Relationship keys

If you open older dashboards in Tableau 2020.2 or later versions, you will see that the joined data will be shown as **Migrated**. This is intentional. Just click on the migrated data source and Tableau will switch from the logical to the physical layer, meaning you will see the join-based data source canvas instead of the relationship canvas.

Looking at the worksheet, you will notice differences as well. You will see that in the new relationships layout, the columns are divided by table name first and then split into **Dimensions** and **Measures** per data source, while in a join, the columns are divided into **Dimensions** and **Measures** and split by table name.

To conclude on relationships, the new data source layout makes it a lot easier to combine datasets and you do not have to decide upfront if you want to join or blend. People that are used to the old data source pane might have to get used to the new flexibility a bit, but for new Tableau users, it will be much easier to work with different datasets from the start. Nevertheless, we will still cover joins next, especially because the functionality is still part of Tableau in the physical layer.

Joins

This book assumes basic knowledge of joins, specifically inner, left-outer, right-outer, and full-outer joins. If you are not familiar with the basics of joins, consider taking W3Schools' SQL tutorial at `https://www.w3schools.com/sql/default.asp`. The basics are not difficult, so it won't take you long to get up to speed.

The following screenshot shows three related datasets:

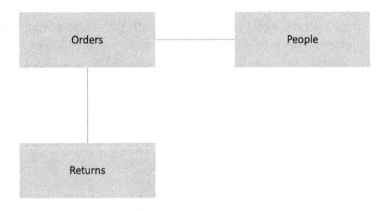

Figure 4.4: Related datasets

To better understand what Tableau does to your data when joining multiple tables, let us explore join queries.

Join queries

The following screenshot is a representation of the joined datasets in *Figure 4.4*:

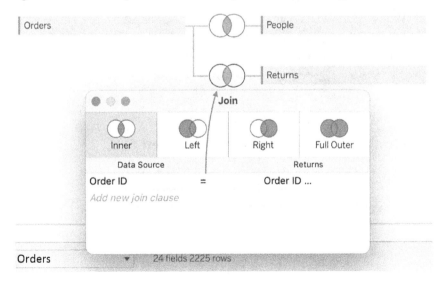

Figure 4.5: Join culling

The preceding screenshot represents an inner join between the **Orders** and **Returns** tables, connected through an inner join on the common key, **Order ID. Orders** and **People** are joined on the common key **Region.**

To better understand what has just been described, we will continue with a join culling exercise. We will look at the SQL queries generated by Tableau when building a simple view using these two tables, which will show us what Tableau does under the hood while we simply drag and drop.

Please follow these steps:

1. Locate and download the workbook associated with this chapter from `https://public.tableau.com/profile/marleen.meier/`.

2. Select the **Join Culling** worksheet and click on the **Sample - EU Superstore Join** data source.

3. From the menu, select **Help**, then **Settings and Performance**, and then **Start Performance Recording:**

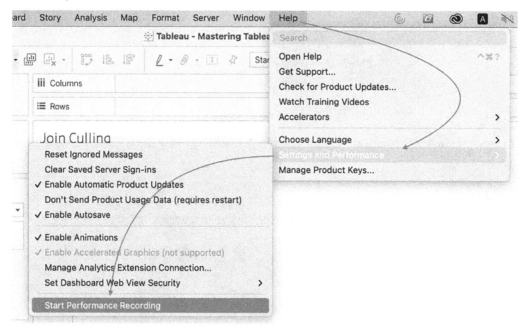

Figure 4.6: Start Performance Recording

4. Drag **People** to the **Rows** shelf and place **Sales** on the **Text** shelf:

Figure 4.7: Drag and drop

5. Stop the recording with **Help**, then **Settings and Performance**, and finally, **Stop Performance Recording**.

6. In the resulting **Performance Summary** dashboard, drag the time slider to `0.0000` and select both green bars: **Executing Query**. Now you see the two SQL queries generated by Tableau:

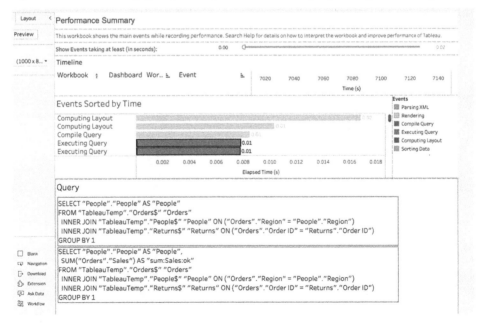

Figure 4.8: Performance recording

So far, we have connected Tableau to our dataset, then we created a very simple worksheet, showing us the number of sales for people. But, for Tableau to show the people's names and the sales amount, it needs to get data from two different tables: **Orders** and **People**. The performance recording in *Figure 4.8* shows how long each step of building the dashboard took and which query was sent to the database. Since we first dragged a dimension and then a measure into the worksheet, we see two queries. The second query combines both dragged piles; therefore, we will focus on the latter. Let's look at it in detail:

```
"SELECT ""People"".""People"" AS ""People"",
  SUM(""Orders"".""Sales"") AS ""sum:Sales:ok""
FROM ""TableauTemp"".""Orders$"" ""Orders""
  INNER JOIN ""TableauTemp"".""People$"" ""People"" ON (""Orders"".""Region"" =
""People"".""Region"")
  INNER JOIN ""TableauTemp"".""Returns$"" ""Returns"" ON (""Orders"".""Order
ID"" = ""Returns"".""Order ID"")
GROUP BY 1"
```

Note that an inner join was generated between the tables. This was a view behind the scenes of Tableau's **join feature**.

Now that the technical details have been discussed, let us look at joins in the dashboards themselves.

Join calculations

In Tableau, it is possible to join two files based on a calculation. You would use this functionality to resolve mismatches between two data sources. The calculated join can be accessed in the dropdown of each join.

See the following screenshot:

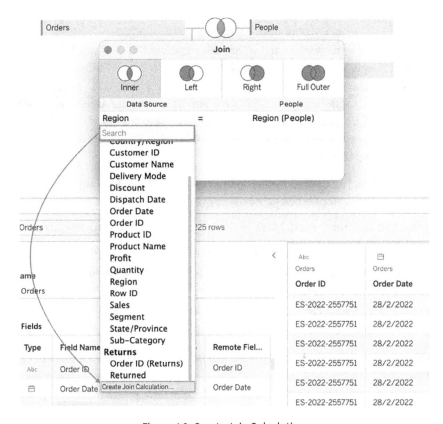

Figure 4.9: Create Join Calculation...

As an example, imagine a dataset that contains one column for **First Name**, and another column for **Last Name**. You want to join it to a second dataset that has one column called **Name**, containing the first and last name. One option to join those two datasets is to create a **Join Calculation** like the following in the first dataset:

```
[First Name] + ' ' + [Last Name]
```

Now, select the **Name** column in the second dataset and your keys should be matching!

If you want to know more about calculated joins, please check the Tableau help pages: https://help.tableau.com/current/pro/desktop/en-us/joining_tables.htm#use-calculations-to-resolve-mismatches-between-fields-in-a-join.

Spatial joins

In Tableau 2018.2, **spatial joins** were added. What this means is that you can join spatial fields from MapInfo tables and Shape, Esri, KML, TopoJSON, and GeoJSON files. You can also use CSV or Excel files and translate the data into spatial data by using the Tableau MAKEPOINT function (see *Chapter 12, Leveraging Advanced Analytics*). In practice, imagine two datasets, one about the location of basins, indicated by a spatial field, and a second dataset containing the locations of waterfowl sightings, also in a spatial column. Tableau allows you to join the two, which is very hard to do otherwise because most programs don't support spatial data.

To join on spatial columns, you have to select the **Intersects** field from the **Join** dropdown, only visible when working with spatial data.

For more information on joining spatial files in Tableau, read the following resources from Tableau:

- `https://help.tableau.com/current/pro/desktop/en-us/maps_spatial_join.htm`
- `https://www.tableau.com/about/blog/2018/8/perform-advanced-spatial-analysis-spatial-join-now-available-tableau-92166`
- `https://help.tableau.com/current/pro/desktop/en-us/maps_spatial_join.htm`
- `https://help.tableau.com/current/pro/desktop/en-us/examples_spatial_files.htm`

Alternatively to a horizontal join, you might need a vertical join, also called a **union**. A typical union use case is visualizing data that is stored in multiple files or tables over time. You might have a daily report, in which the column structure is the same but collected as a new file every day, stored in a monthly or yearly folder.

Combining those files gives so much more insight than looking at them one at a time! You will be able to analyze trends and daily or yearly changes or perform a year-to-date analysis. Thus, we will continue with an in-depth explanation of unions in Tableau next.

Unions

Sometimes you might want to analyze data with the same metadata structure that is stored in different files – for example, sales data from multiple years, different months, or countries. Instead of copying and pasting the data, you can union it. We already touched upon this topic in *Chapter 3, Using Tableau Prep Builder*, but a union is basically where Tableau will append new rows of data to existing columns with the same header. For the following exercise, we will use FIFA data (from the PlayStation game, not the World Cup). The data is from Kaggle (`https://www.kaggle.com/datasets/stefanoleone992/fifa-22-complete-player-dataset?resource=download`) and ships in multiple CSVs; each CSV contains data for one year and male/female are split too.

For our analysis, we want to combine all the files into one. Hence, we need to union, by taking the following steps:

1. Download the CSV files from GitHub (`https://github.com/PacktPublishing/Mastering-Tableau-2023-Fourth-Edition/tree/main/Chapter04`) or Kaggle (`https://www.kaggle.com/datasets/stefanoleone992/fifa-22-complete-player-dataset?resource=download`).

2.   In the dashboard belonging to this chapter, open the **Connect to data** pane, and click on **Text file:**

Figure 4.10: Text file

3.   Locate the downloaded FIFA data on your machine and connect to any one of the files.

4.   Create the union by dragging and dropping **a second file** from the left pane on top of the **initial file** until the word **Union** appears, a sign that when dropping the data now, the data will be used for a union:

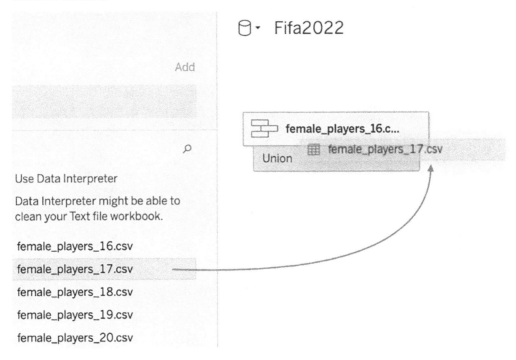

Figure 4.11: Union

5. Alternatively, click on the arrow of the primary dataset and select **Convert to Union...**:

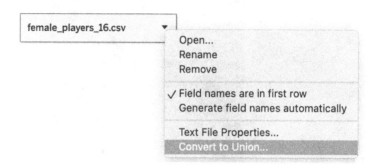

Figure 4.12: Convert to Union...

6. In the following popup (*Figure 4.13*), the user has the option to select all the data tables that should be part of the union individually by dragging and dropping or by using a **Wildcard** union, which includes all tables in a certain directory based on the naming convention—a * represents any character. players* will include any file that starts with players. Respectively, female* will include all files starting with female, and * will include all files:

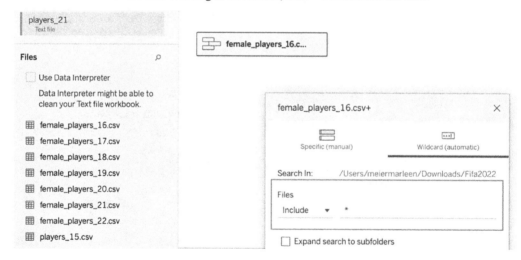

Figure 4.13: Edit Union...

Unions are used to combine data that is similar and can be appended underneath each other. They are most often used for multiple data files where each has a different date stamp, a different region, a different manager, and so forth. By using a union, you want to make the dataset more complete. We saw that Tableau allows unions by dragging and dropping, as well as right-clicking on the initial data source. We also talked about unions that combine one or more other datasets, using drag and drop or wildcards. *Figure 4.14* presents a typical union example:

Dataset A				Dataset B				Union		
Sales 2021				Sales 2022				Sales 2021&2022		
Year	Month	Sales		Year	Month	Sales		Year	Month	Sales
2021	12	639		2022	12	4323		2021	12	639
2021	11	3758		2022	11	5757		2021	11	3758
2021	10	6836		2022	10	4444		2021	10	6836
2021	9	1721		2022	9	625		2021	9	1721
2021	8	5942		2022	8	191		2021	8	5942
2021	7	9853		2022	7	6480		2021	7	9853
2021	6	7338		2022	6	4231		2021	6	7338
2021	5	6144		2022	5	2696		2021	5	6144
2021	4	7285		2022	4	4600		2021	4	7285
2021	3	7560		2022	3	6999		2021	3	7560
2021	2	561		2022	2	8123		2021	2	561
2021	1	7844		2022	1	9602		2021	1	7844
								2022	12	4323
								2022	11	5757
								2022	10	4444
								2022	9	625
								2022	8	191
								2022	7	6480
								2022	6	4231
								2022	5	2696
								2022	4	4600
								2022	3	6999
								2022	2	8123
								2022	1	9602

Figure 4.14: Union

Let us look at the aspects we need to remember:

- Unions append data in creating additional rows.
- A union should contain datasets that have many common columns.
- Unions should only be used for same-structured data stored across multiple data sources.
- Keep an eye on performance when using unions. With each additional dataset in the union, you will increase the complexity of Tableau's VizQL.

Since you just became a union expert, it's time to move on to the next feature Tableau offers: **blending**! Blending helps you to combine datasets that have a different level of granularity. Think *one-to-many* relationships between datasets. One dataset has a unique key per row; the other has multiple rows per key. To avoid duplicating rows in the first-mentioned dataset, Tableau deployed blending, long before relationships were part of the software package.

Blends

Relationships make data blending a little less needed and it can be seen as legacy functionality. But for the sake of completeness and for older Tableau versions (below 2020.2), let's consider a summary of data blending in the following sections. In a nutshell, data blending allows you to merge multiple disparate data sources into a single view. Understanding the following four points will give you a grasp of the main points regarding data blending:

- Data blending is typically used to merge data from multiple data sources. Although as of Tableau 10, joins are possible between multiple data sources, there are still cases when data blending is the only feasible option to merge data from two or more sources. In the following sections, we will see a practical example that demonstrates such a case.

- Data blending requires a shared dimension. A date dimension is often a viable candidate for blending multiple data sources.

- Data blending aggregates and then matches. On the other hand, joining matches and then aggregates.

- Data blending does not enable dimensions from a secondary data source. Attempting to use dimensions from a secondary data source will result in a * or null in the view. There is an exception to this rule, which we will discuss later, in the *Adding secondary dimensions* section.

Now that we have introduced relationships, joins, and unions, I would like to shift your focus a bit to data structures within your workbook. You might have set up the perfect join or union, started dragging and dropping fields onto your workbook canvas, used a filter, used a calculated field, and then received some unexpected results. Tableau is behaving, just not the way you like it. Why might that be?! The order of operation here is key. It is essential to know when which filter will be applied and how this affects your data. Therefore, next in line: the order of operations.

Exploring the order of operations

Isn't a data blend the same thing as a left join? This is a question that new Tableau authors often ask. The answer, of course, is no, but let us explore the differences. The following example is simple, even lighthearted, but does demonstrate profound consequences that can result from incorrect aggregation resulting from an erroneous join.

We will explore in which order aggregation happens in Tableau. This will help you understand how to use blends and joins more effectively.

For this example, we will use the following data:

Pants		Shirts	
Salesperson	**Pants Amount**	**Sales Associate**	**Shirts Amount**
Tanya	100	Tanya	50
Tanya	100	Tanya	50
Zhang	100	Zhang	50
Zhang	100	Zhang	50

Figure 4.15: Pants and shirts sales

In these tables, two people are listed: **Tanya** and **Zhang**. In one table, these people are members of the **Salesperson** dimension, and in the other, they are members of the **Sales Associate** dimension. Furthermore, **Tanya** and **Zhang** both sold $200 in pants and $100 in shirts. Let us explore new ways Tableau could connect to this data to better understand joining and data blending.

When you look at the spreadsheets associated with this exercise, you will notice additional columns. These columns will be used in a later exercise.

Please take the following steps:

1. In the workbook associated with this chapter, right-click on the Pants data source and look at the data by clicking **View data**. Do the same for the Shirts data source.

2. Open the Join data source by right-clicking on it and selecting **Edit Data Source**, and observe the join between the **Pants** and **Shirts** tables using **Salesperson/Sales Associate** as the common key:

 Join

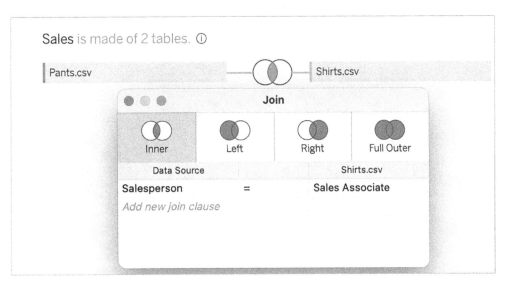

Figure 4.16: Join

3. On the **Pants** worksheet, select the **Pants** data source and place **Salesperson** on the **Rows** shelf and **Pants Amount** on the **Text** shelf:

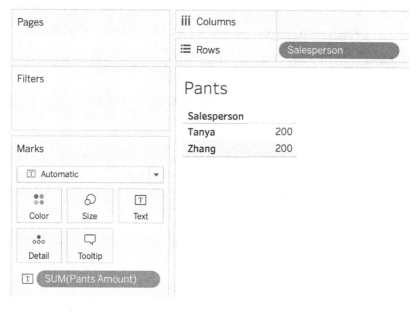

Figure 4.17: Setting up the worksheet

4. On the **Shirts** worksheet, select the **Shirts** data source and place **Sales Associate** on the **Rows** shelf and **Shirt Amount** on the **Text** shelf:

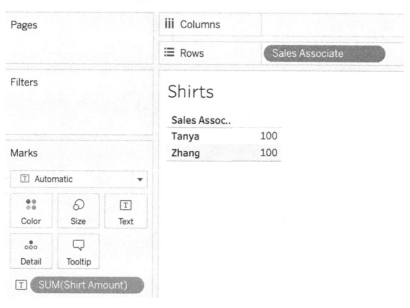

Figure 4.18: Shirts

5. On the **Join** worksheet, select the **Join** data source and place **Salesperson** on the **Rows** shelf. Next, double-click **Pants Amount** and **Shirt Amount** to place both on the view:

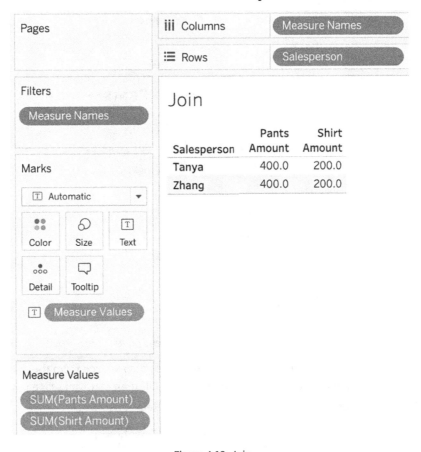

Figure 4.19: Join

6. On the **Blend – Pants Primary** worksheet, select the **Pants** data source and place **Salesperson** on the **Rows** shelf and **Pants Amount** on the **Text** shelf:

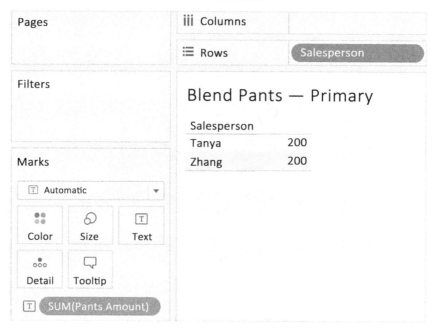

Figure 4.20: Blend pants

7. Stay on the same worksheet and select the Shirts data source from the data source pane on the left and double-click on **Shirt Amount**. Click **OK** if an error message pops up.

8. Select **Data** from the menu bar, then **Edit Blend Relationships...**:

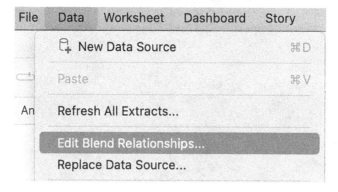

Figure 4.21: Edit Blend Relationships...

9. In the resulting dialog box, select Pants as the **Primary data source** and Shirts as the **Secondary data source**, then click on the **Custom** radio button, as shown in *Figure 4.22*, then click **Add....**

10. In the left column, select **Salesperson**, and in the right column, select **Sales Associate**. The left column represents data from the **Primary data source** and the right column represents all the data available in the **Secondary data source.**

11. Remove all other links, if any, and click **OK**. The results in the dialog box should match what is displayed in the following screenshot:

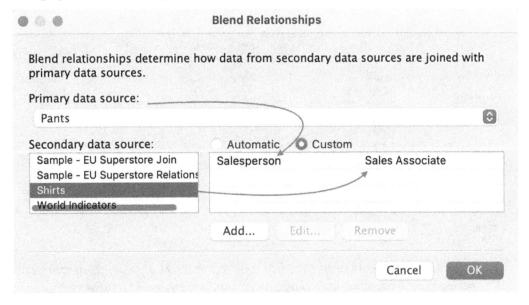

Figure 4.22: Blend Relationships

A little recap of what we have done so far: we are working with three data sources: **Pants, Shirts,** and **Join,** where **Join** consists of **Pants** and **Shirts**. We have also created a blend with **Pants** being the primary data source and we connected them by using **Salesperson** and **Sales Associate** as keys.

12. Do not get confused by the name **Blend Relationships**. This has nothing to do with the logical layer relationships. It is just the name of the pop-up window.

Going back to the exercise, continue with the following steps:

13. On the Blend – Shirts Primary worksheet, select the **Shirts** data source and place **Sales Associate** on the **Rows** shelf and **Shirt Amount** on the **Text** shelf:

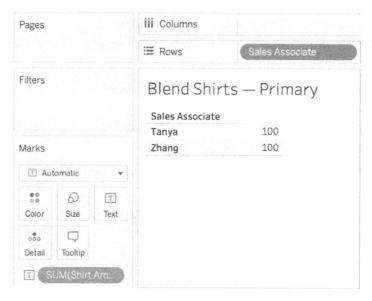

Figure 4.23: Blend Shirts – Primary

14. In the same workbook, select the Pants data source, make sure the chain icon next to **Salesperson** is connected/red, and double-click **Pants Amount** to add it to the view:

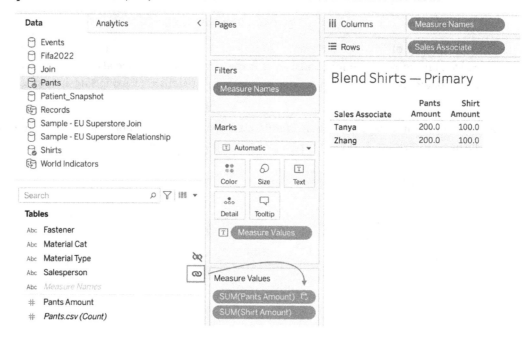

Figure 4.24: Finalizing the worksheet

15. Place all five worksheets on a dashboard. Format and arrange as desired. Now let us compare the results between the five worksheets in the following screenshot:

Pants

Salesperson	
Tanya	200
Zhang	200

Shirts

Sales Associate	
Tanya	100
Zhang	100

Join

Salesperson	Pants Amount	Shirt Amount
Tanya	400.0	200.0
Zhang	400.0	200.0

Blend Pants — Primary

Salesperson	
Tanya	200
Zhang	200

Blend Shirts — Primary

Sales Associate		Pants Amount	Shirt Amount
Tanya	200	200.0	100.0
Zhang	200	200.0	100.0

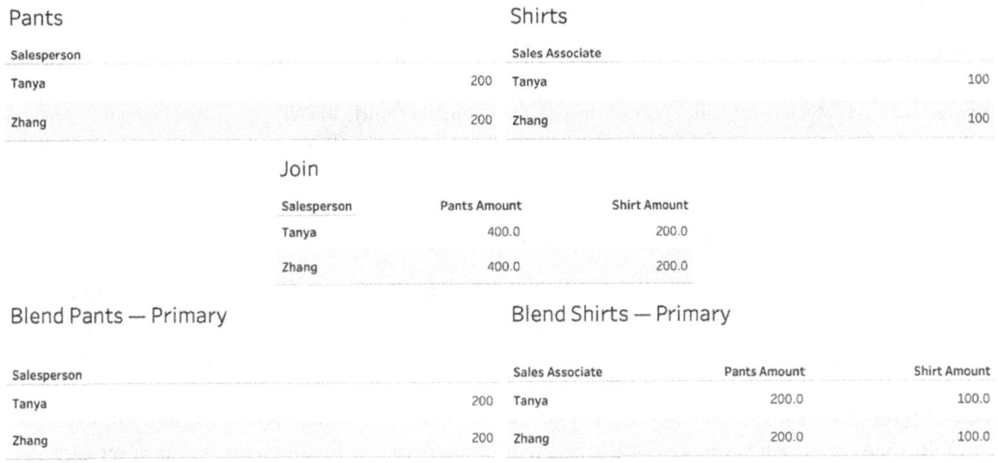

Figure 4.25: Comparison

In the preceding screenshot, the **Join** worksheet has double the expected results. Why? Because a join first matches the common key (in this case, **Salesperson/Sales Associate**) and then aggregates the results. The more matches found on a common key, the worse the problem will become. If multiple matches are found on a common key, the results will grow exponentially. Two matches will result in squared results, three will give cubed results, and so forth. This exponential effect is represented graphically in the following screenshot:

Salesperson	Sales Associate	JOIN	Pants Amount	Shirts Amount
Tanya	Tanya	Tanya	100	50
	=	Tanya	100	50
Tanya	Tanya	Tanya	100	50
		Tanya	100	50
Zhang	Zhang	Zhang	100	50
		Zhang	100	50
Zhang	Zhang	Zhang	100	50
		Zhang	100	50

Figure 4.26: Join

On the other hand, the blend functioned more efficiently, but before the blend could function properly, we had to edit the data relationship so that Tableau could connect the two data sources using the **Salesperson** and **Sales Associate** fields. If the two fields had been identically named (for example, **Salesperson**), Tableau would have automatically provided an option to blend between the data sources using those fields.

The results for the Blend Pants - Primary and Blend Shirts - Primary worksheets are correct. There is no exponential effect. Why? Because data blending first aggregates the results from both data sources, and then matches the results on a common dimension.

In this case, it is **Salesperson/Sales Associate**, as demonstrated in the following screenshot:

Salesperson	SUM(Pants Amount)	Sales Associate	SUM(Shirts Amount)	BLEND	Pants Amount	Shirts Amount
Tanya	200	Tanya	100	Tanya	200	100
Zhang	200	Zhang	100	Zhang	200	100

Figure 4.27: Blending results

What we saw in this exercise is that joins can change the data structure, so be careful when using them and be very aware of which columns are a suitable key. Also, do checks before and after joining your data, which can be as easy as counting rows and checking if this is the expected result.

Blending has advantages and disadvantages; adding dimensions, for example, is not that straightforward. But we will explore more details regarding secondary dimensions in the next section.

Adding secondary dimensions

Data blending, although particularly useful for connecting disparate data sources, has limitations. The most important limitation to be aware of is that data blending does not enable dimensions from a secondary data source. There is an exception to this limitation; that is, there is one way you can add a dimension from a secondary data source. Let us explore this further.

There are other fields besides **Salesperson/Sales Associate** and **Shirt Amount/Pants Amount** in the data sources. We will reference those fields in this exercise:

1. In the workbook associated with this chapter, select the Adding Secondary Dimensions worksheet.
2. Select the **Shirts** data source.

3. Add a relationship between the **Shirts** and **Pants** data sources for **Material Type**, taking the following steps:

    1. Select **Data** and then **Edit Relationships**.

    2. Ensure that **Shirts** is the primary data source and **Pants** is the secondary data source.

    3. Select the **Custom** radio button.

    4. Click **Add…**.

    5. Select **Material Type** in both the left and right columns:

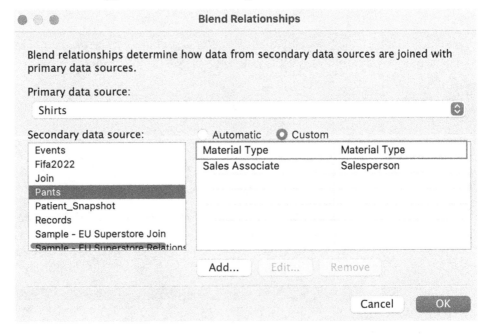

Figure 4.28: Custom blend relationships

    6. Click **OK** to return to the view.

4. Place **Material Type** on the **Rows** shelf.

5. Select the **Pants** data source and make sure that the chain-link icon next to **Material Type** in the **Data** pane is activated and that the chain-link icon next to **Salesperson** is deactivated. If the icon is a gray, broken chain link, it is not activated. If it is an orange, connected chain link, it is activated:

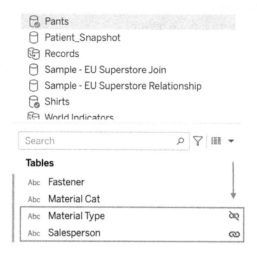

Figure 4.29: Shirts and Pants

6. Place **Material Cat** *before* **Material Type**, and **Fastener** *after* **Material Type** on the **Rows** shelf as follows:

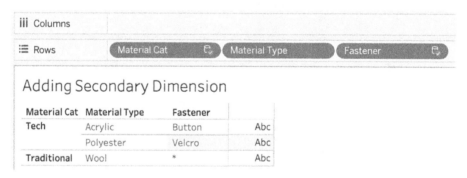

Figure 4.30: Secondary dimensions

Material Cat is a dimension from a secondary data source. Data blending does not enable dimensions from a secondary data source. Why does it work in this case? There are a few reasons:

*   There is a one-to-many relationship between **Material Cat** and **Material Type**; that is, each member of the **Material Type** dimension is matched with one and only one member of the **Material Cat** dimension.

- The view is blended on **Material Type**, not **Material Cat**. This is important because **Material Type** is at a lower level of granularity than **Material Cat**. Attempting to blend the view on **Material Cat** will not enable **Material Type** as a secondary dimension.

- Every member of the **Material Type** dimension within the primary data source also exists in the secondary data source.

Fastener is also a dimension from the secondary data source. In *Figure 4.35*, it displays * in one of the cells, thus demonstrating that **Fastener** is not working as a dimension should; that is, it is not slicing the data, as discussed in *Chapter 1, Reviewing the Basics*. The reason an asterisk is displayed is that there are multiple **Fastener** types associated with **Wool**. **Button** and **Velcro** display because **Acrylic** and **Polyester** each have only one **Fastener** type in the underlying data.

If you use blending, make sure that your main reason is to combine measures and that you do not need the dimensions on a detailed level. It is especially useful to know this before you create a dashboard, to prepare accordingly. Your data needs extra prepping (check *Chapter 3, Using Tableau Prep builder*) because neither a join nor a blend can bring you the expected data structure. Or you can make use of scaffolding, a technique that uses a helper data source—we will discuss this in the next section.

Introducing scaffolding

Scaffolding is a technique that introduces a second data source through blending to reshape and/or extend the initial data source. Scaffolding enables capabilities that extend Tableau to meet visualization and analytical needs that may otherwise be exceedingly difficult or altogether impossible. Joe Mako, who pioneered scaffolding in Tableau, tells a story in which he used the technique to recreate a dashboard using four worksheets. The original dashboard, which did not use scaffolding, required 80 worksheets painstakingly aligned pixel by pixel.

Among the many possibilities that scaffolding enables is extending Tableau's forecasting functionality. Tableau's native forecasting capabilities are sometimes criticized for lacking sophistication. Scaffolding can be used to address this criticism.

The following are the steps:

1. In the workbook associated with this chapter, select the Scaffolding worksheet and connect to the World Indicators data source.

2. Using Excel or a text editor, create a Records dataset. The following two-row table represents the Records dataset in its entirety:

	A	B
1	Record	
2	1	
3	2	
4		

Figure 4.31: Excel file

3. Connect Tableau to the dataset.

4. To be expedient, consider copying the dataset directly from Excel by using *Ctrl + C* and pasting it directly into Tableau with *Ctrl + V*.

5. Create a **Start Date** parameter in Tableau, with the settings seen in the following screenshot. Notice the highlighted sections in the screenshot by which you can set the desired display format:

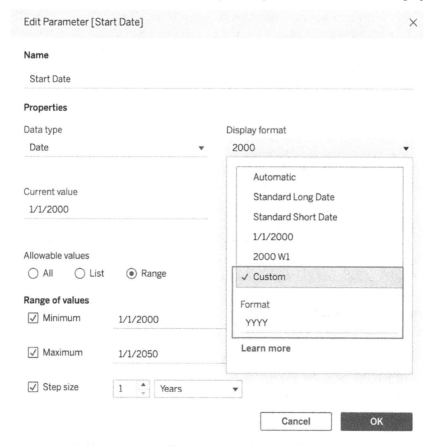

Figure 4.32: Display format

6. Create another parameter named **End Date** with identical settings.

7. In the **Data** pane, right-click on the **Start Date** and **End Date** parameters you just created and select **Show Parameter**:

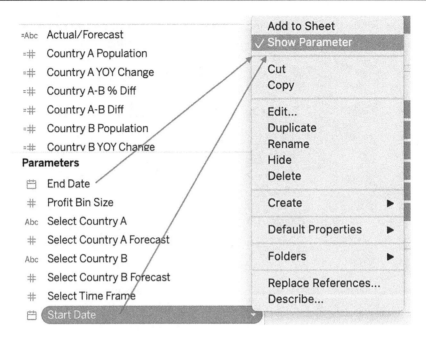

Figure 4.33: Show Parameter

8. Set the start and end dates as desired, for example, **2000 – 2027:**

Figure 4.34: Start and end dates

9. Select the **Records** data source and create a calculated field called **Date** with the following code:

```
IIF([Records]=1,[Start Date],[End Date])
```

10. Place the **Date** field on the **Rows** shelf.

11. Right-click on the **Date** field on the **Rows** shelf and select **Show Missing Values**. Note that all the dates between the start and end date settings now display:

Figure 4.35: Show Missing Values

12. Create a parameter named **Select Country A** with the settings shown in the following screenshot. Note that the list of countries was added with the **Add values from** button:

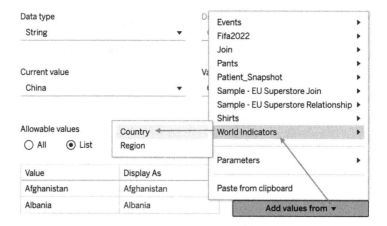

Figure 4.36: Add from field

13. Create another parameter named **Select Country B** with identical settings.

14. Create a parameter named **Select Country A Forecast** with the settings given in the following screenshot:

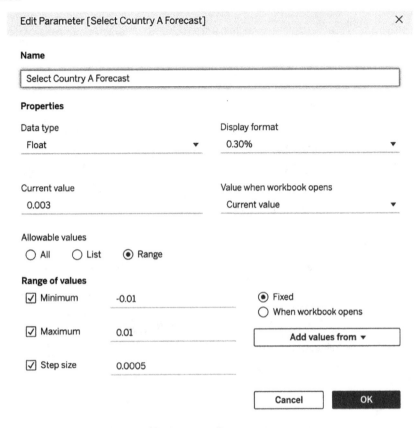

Figure 4.37: Edit parameter

15. Create another parameter named **Select Country B Forecast** with identical settings.

16. In the **Data** pane, right-click on the four parameters you just created (**Select Country A, Select Country B, Select Country A Forecast,** and **Select Country B Forecast**) and select **Show Parameter:**

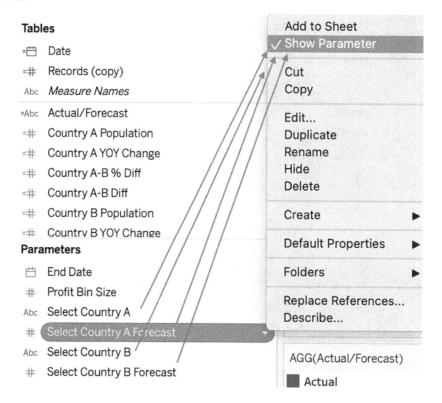

Figure 4.38: Show Parameter

17. Make sure that the **Date** field in the **World Indicators** data source has the orange chain-link icon deployed. This indicates it is used as a linking field:

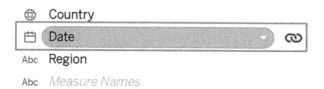

Figure 4.39: Link

18. Within the **World Indicators** dataset, create the following calculated fields:

Calculated field name	Calculated field code
Country A Population	`IIF([Country] = [Select Country A],[Population Total],NULL)`
Country B Population	`IIF([Country] = [Select Country B],[Population Total],NULL)`

19. Within the **Records** dataset, create the following calculated fields:

Calculated field name	Calculated field code
Actual/Forecast	`IIF(ISNULL(AVG([World Indicators].[Population Total])),"Forecast","Actual")`

Country A Population	`IF [Actual/Forecast] = "Actual" THEN SUM([World Indicators].[Country A Population]) ELSE PREVIOUS_VALUE(0)`
	`*[Select Country A Forecast] + PREVIOUS_VALUE(0)`
	`END`

Country A YOY Change	`([Country A Population] - LOOKUP([Country A Population], -1)) /` `ABS(LOOKUP([Country A Population], -1))`

Country B Population	`IF [Actual/Forecast] = "Actual" THEN SUM([World Indicators].[Country B Population]) ELSE PREVIOUS_VALUE(0)`
	`*[Select Country B Forecast] + PREVIOUS_VALUE(0)`
	`END`

Country B YOY Change	`([Country B Population] - LOOKUP([Country B Population], -1)) /` `ABS(LOOKUP([Country B Population], -1))`
Country A-B Diff	`[Country A Population] - [Country B Population]`
Country A-B % Diff	`[Country A-B Diff]/[Country A Population]`

20. Within the **Data** pane, right-click on **Country A YOY Change**, **Country B YOY Change**, and **Country A-B % Diff** and select **Default Properties | Number Format...** to change the default number format to **Percentage**:

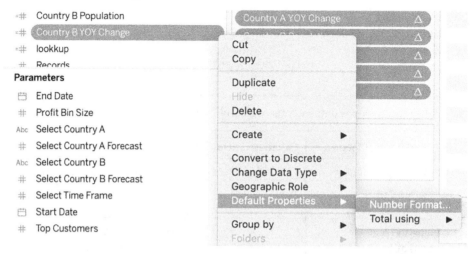

Figure 4.40: Default Properties

21. With the **Records** data source selected, place the **Actual/Forecast, Measure Values,** and **Measure Names** fields on the **Color, Text,** and **Columns** shelves, respectively:

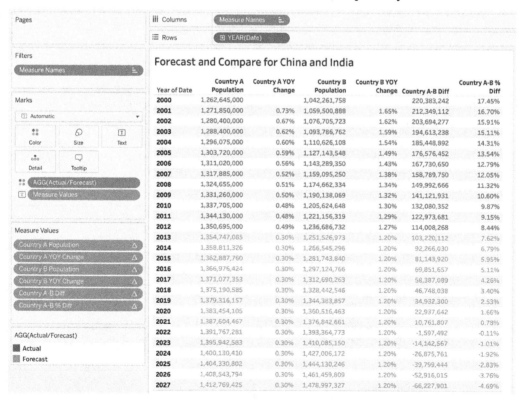

Figure 4.41: Forecast setup

22. Adjust the **Measure Values** shelf so that the fields that display are identical to the following screenshot. Also, ensure that **Compute Using** for each of these fields is set to **Table (down)**:

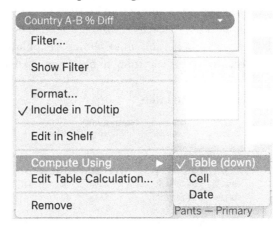

Figure 4.42: Compute Using

So, what have we achieved so far? We created a duplicated data structure that allows us to compare two countries in two separate columns, even though the data is in one column in the original dataset. This setup allows us to ask more advanced questions.

To demonstrate this, let us ask, *"When will India's population overtake China's?"* You can set the parameters as desired—I chose 0.45% and 1.20% as the average yearly growth rates, but feel free to choose any parameter you think works best for a country. In *Figure 4.48*, you see that with a growth rate of 0.45% and 1.20% for China and India, respectively, India will have more inhabitants than China by 2024. You can observe this by looking at the columns **Country A Population** and **Country B Population**. Everything in orange is a forecast, while everything in blue is actual data from our dataset:

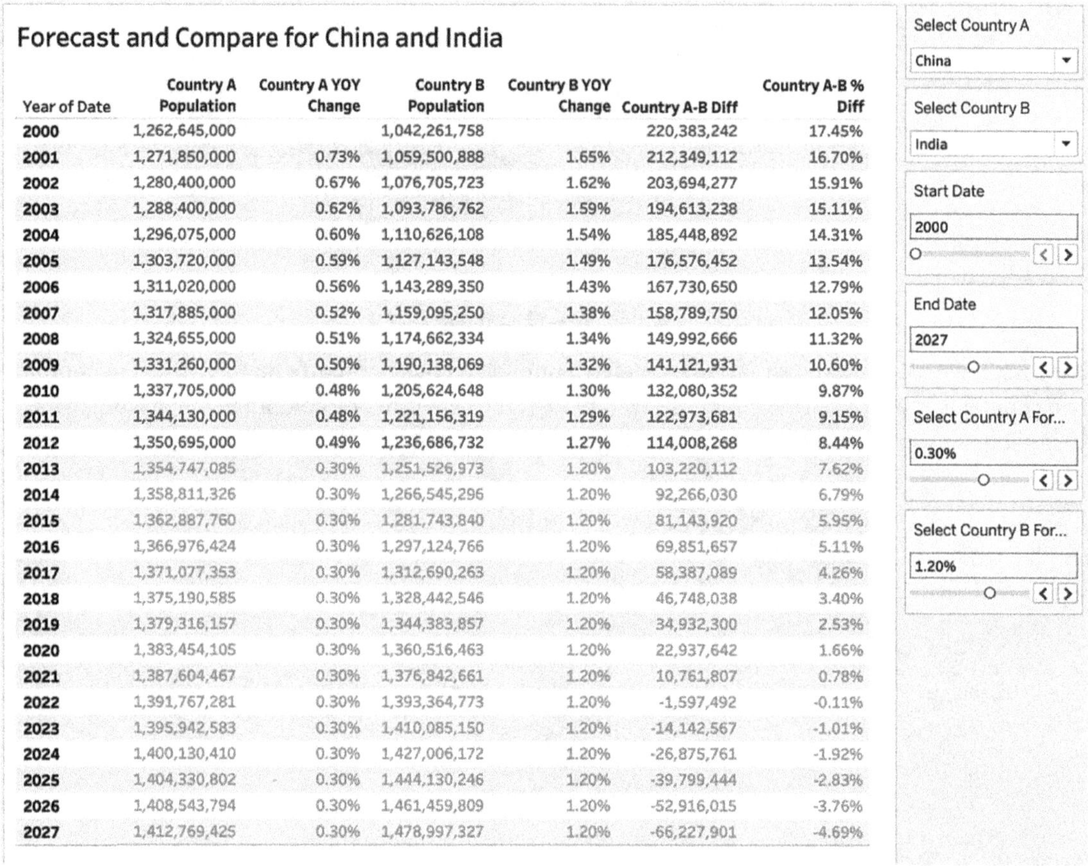

Forecast and Compare for China and India

Year of Date	Country A Population	Country A YOY Change	Country B Population	Country B YOY Change	Country A-B Diff	Country A-B % Diff
2000	1,262,645,000		1,042,261,758		220,383,242	17.45%
2001	1,271,850,000	0.73%	1,059,500,888	1.65%	212,349,112	16.70%
2002	1,280,400,000	0.67%	1,076,705,723	1.62%	203,694,277	15.91%
2003	1,288,400,000	0.62%	1,093,786,762	1.59%	194,613,238	15.11%
2004	1,296,075,000	0.60%	1,110,626,108	1.54%	185,448,892	14.31%
2005	1,303,720,000	0.59%	1,127,143,548	1.49%	176,576,452	13.54%
2006	1,311,020,000	0.56%	1,143,289,350	1.43%	167,730,650	12.79%
2007	1,317,885,000	0.52%	1,159,095,250	1.38%	158,789,750	12.05%
2008	1,324,655,000	0.51%	1,174,662,334	1.34%	149,992,666	11.32%
2009	1,331,260,000	0.50%	1,190,138,069	1.32%	141,121,931	10.60%
2010	1,337,705,000	0.48%	1,205,624,648	1.30%	132,080,352	9.87%
2011	1,344,130,000	0.48%	1,221,156,319	1.29%	122,973,681	9.15%
2012	1,350,695,000	0.49%	1,236,686,732	1.27%	114,008,268	8.44%
2013	1,354,747,085	0.30%	1,251,526,973	1.20%	103,220,112	7.62%
2014	1,358,811,326	0.30%	1,266,545,296	1.20%	92,266,030	6.79%
2015	1,362,887,760	0.30%	1,281,743,840	1.20%	81,143,920	5.95%
2016	1,366,976,424	0.30%	1,297,124,766	1.20%	69,851,657	5.11%
2017	1,371,077,353	0.30%	1,312,690,263	1.20%	58,387,089	4.26%
2018	1,375,190,585	0.30%	1,328,442,546	1.20%	46,748,038	3.40%
2019	1,379,316,157	0.30%	1,344,383,857	1.20%	34,932,300	2.53%
2020	1,383,454,105	0.30%	1,360,516,463	1.20%	22,937,642	1.66%
2021	1,387,604,467	0.30%	1,376,842,661	1.20%	10,761,807	0.78%
2022	1,391,767,281	0.30%	1,393,364,773	1.20%	-1,597,492	-0.11%
2023	1,395,942,583	0.30%	1,410,085,150	1.20%	-14,142,567	-1.01%
2024	1,400,130,410	0.30%	1,427,006,172	1.20%	-26,875,761	-1.92%
2025	1,404,330,802	0.30%	1,444,130,246	1.20%	-39,799,444	-2.83%
2026	1,408,543,794	0.30%	1,461,459,809	1.20%	-52,916,015	-3.76%
2027	1,412,769,425	0.30%	1,478,997,327	1.20%	-66,227,901	-4.69%

Select Country A: China

Select Country B: India

Start Date: 2000

End Date: 2027

Select Country A For...: 0.30%

Select Country B For...: 1.20%

Figure 4.43: Forecast dashboard

We are obviously already many years ahead; can you use this dashboard to figure out the actual average growth rate for China and India from 2012 to 2020 if I tell you that the population in 2020 was 1,439,323,776 in China and 1,380,004,385 in India? Share your results on Tableau Public with the tag **#MasteringTableau**!

One key to this exercise is data scaffolding. Data scaffolding produces data that does not exist in the data source. The **World Indicators** dataset only includes dates from 2000 to 2012 and obviously, the **Records** dataset does not contain any dates. By using the **Start Date** and **End Date** parameters coupled with the calculated **Date** field, we were able to produce any set of dates desired. We had to blend the data, rather than join or union, to keep the original data source intact and create all additional data outside of **World Indicators** itself.

The actual data scaffolding occurred upon selecting **Show Missing Values** from the **Date** field drop-down after it was placed on the **Rows** shelf. This allowed every year between **Start Date** and **End Date** to display, even when there were no matching years in the underlying data. *Chapter 6, Utilizing OData, Data Densification, Big Data, and Google BigQuery*, will explore something remarkably similar to data scaffolding, data densification, in more detail.

Let us look at a few of the calculated fields in more depth to better understand how forecasting works in this exercise:

Calculated field: `Actual/Forecast`:

```
IIF(ISNULL(AVG([World Indicators].[Population Total])),"Forecast","Actual")
```

The preceding code determines whether data exists in the **World Indicators** dataset. If the date is after 2012, no data exists and thus `Forecast` is returned.

Calculated field: `Country A Population`:

```
IF [Actual/Forecast] = "Actual" THEN SUM([World Indicators].[Country A
Population]) ELSE PREVIOUS_VALUE(0)
*[Select Country A Forecast] + PREVIOUS_VALUE(0) END
```

If forecasting is necessary to determine the value (that is, if the date is after 2012), the `ELSE` portion of this code is exercised. The `PREVIOUS_VALUE` function returns the value of the previous row and multiplies the results by the forecast and then adds the previous row.

Let's look at an example in the following table:

Previous Row Value (PRV)	1,000
Forecast (F)	0.01
PRV * F	10
Current Row Value	1,010

One important thing to note in the `Country A Population` calculated field is that the forecast is quite simple: multiply the previous population by a given forecast number and tally the results. Without changing the overall structure of the logic, this section of code could be modified with more sophisticated forecasting.

These exercises have shown that with a few other tricks and techniques, blending can be used to great effect in your data projects. Finally, we will talk about data structures in general such that you will better understand why Tableau is doing what it is doing and how you can achieve your visualization goals.

Understanding data structures

The right data structure is not easily definable. True, there are ground rules. For instance, tall data is generally better than wide data. A wide dataset with lots of columns can be difficult to work with, whereas the same data structured in a tall format with fewer columns but more rows is usually easier to work with.

But this is not always the case! Some business questions are more easily answered with wide data structures. And that is the crux of the matter. Business questions determine the right data structure. If one structure answers all questions, great! However, your questions may require multiple data structures. The **pivot** feature in Tableau helps you adjust data structures on the fly to answer different business questions.

Before beginning this exercise, make sure you understand the following points:

- Pivoting in Tableau is limited to Excel, text files, and Google Sheets; otherwise, you must use Custom SQL or Tableau Prep
- A pivot in Tableau is referred to as *unpivot* in database terminology

As a business analyst for a hospital, you are connecting Tableau to a daily snapshot of patient data. You have two questions:

- How many events occur on any given date? For example, how many patients check in on a given day?
- How much time expires between events? For example, what is the average stay for patients in the hospital for multiple days?

To answer these questions, take the following steps:

1. In the starter workbook associated with this chapter, select the `Time Frames` worksheet, and within the **Data** pane, select the **Patient_Snapshot** data source.
2. Click on the dropdown in the **Marks** card and select **Bar** as the chart type.
3. Right-click in the **Data** pane to create a parameter named **Select Time Frame** with the settings displayed in the following screenshot:

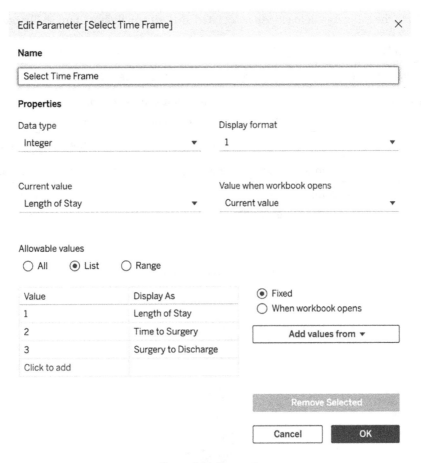

Figure 4.44: Parameter

4. Right-click on the parameter we just created and select **Show Parameter**.

5. Right-click in the **Data** pane to create a calculated field called **Selected Time Frame** with the following code:

```
CASE [Select Time Frame]
WHEN 1 THEN DATEDIFF('day',[Check-in Date],[Discharge Date])
WHEN 2 THEN DATEDIFF('day',[Surgery Date],[Discharge Date])
WHEN 3 THEN DATEDIFF('day',[Check-in Date],[Surgery Date])
END
```

6. Drag the following fields to the associated shelves and define them as directed:

Field name	Shelf directions
Patient Type	Drag to the **Filter** shelf and check **Inpatient**.
Check-in Date	Drag to the **Filter** shelf and select **Range of dates**. Also, right-click on the resulting filter and select **Show Filter**.
Check-in Date	Right-click and drag to the **Columns** shelf and select **MDY**.
Selected Time Frame	Right-click and drag to the **Rows** shelf and select **AVG**.
Selected Time Frame	Right-click and drag to the **Color** shelf and select **AVG**. Set colors as desired.

7. After these actions, your worksheet should look like the following:

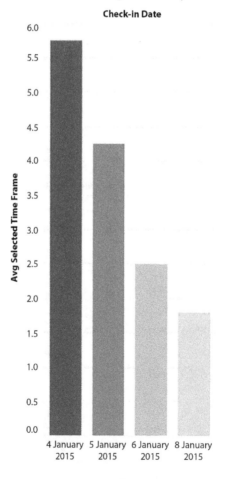

Figure 4.45: Initial dashboard

8. Right-click on the **Avg Selected Time Frame** axis and select **Edit Axis...**, as shown in the following figure. Then, delete the title:

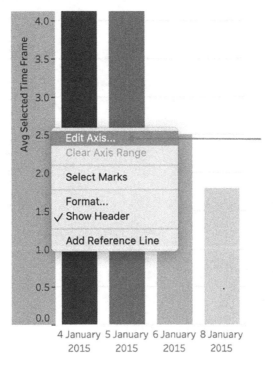

Figure 4.46: Edit Axis...

9. Select **Worksheet** | **Show Title**. Edit the title by inserting the parameter **Select Time Frame**, as shown in the following screenshot:

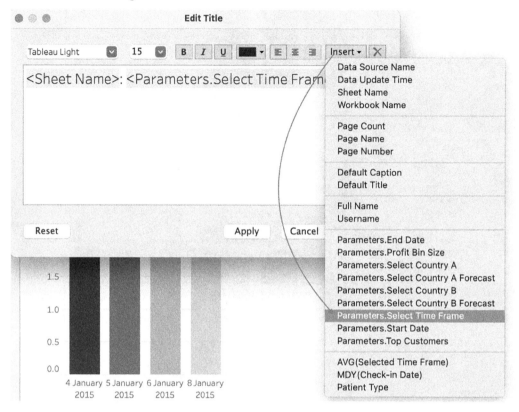

Figure 4.47: Add parameter

The data structure was ideal for the first part of this exercise. You were able to create the visualization quickly. The only section of moderate interest was setting up the **Selected Time Frame** calculated field with the associated parameter.

This allows the end user to choose which time frame they would like to view:

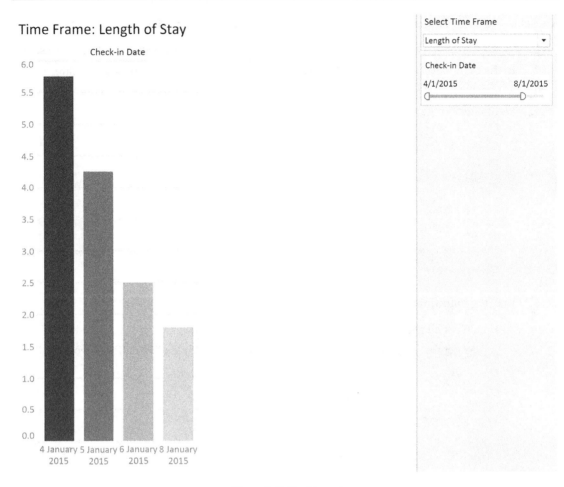

Figure 4.48: Dashboard

But what happens if you need to find out how many people were involved in a type of event per day?

This question is rather difficult to answer using the current data structure because we have one row per patient with multiple dates in that row. In *Figure 4.49*, you can see the difference: the right-hand side is our current data structure, and the left-hand side is the data structure that will make it easier to count events per day:

	A	B	C	D	E	F	G	H	I
1	Patient	Event	Date		Patient	Event A Date	Event B Date	Event C Date	
2	U	A	X		U	X	Y	Z	
3	U	B	Y		V	Y	X		
4	U	C	Z						
5	V	A	Y						
6	V	B	X						
7									
8									

Figure 4.49: Patient data structure

Therefore, in the second part of this exercise, we will try a different approach by pivoting the data:

1. In the starter workbook associated with this chapter, select the Events Per Date worksheet.
2. In the **Data** pane, right-click the **Patient_Snapshot** data source and choose **Duplicate**.
3. Rename the duplicate **Events**.
4. Right-click on the **Events** data source and choose **Edit Data Source...**:

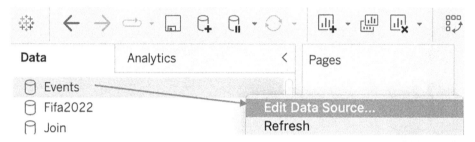

Figure 4.50: Edit Data Source...

5. Take the following steps:

    1. Select all five of the date fields with *Shift* or *Ctrl* + click.
    2. Select the drop-down option for any of the selected fields and choose **Pivot**:

Figure 4.51: Pivot

3. The pivot will turn rows and columns around and we will get a data structure just like in *Figure 4.49* on the left-hand side. Rename the pivoted fields **Event Type** and **Event Date**.

4. Select the Events Per Date worksheet and place the following fields on the associated shelves and define as directed:

Field name	Shelf directions
Event Date	Right-click and drag to the **Rows** shelf and select **MDY**
Event Type	Place after **Event Date** on the **Rows** shelf
Patient Type	Right-click and select **Show Filter**
Number of Records	Drag to the **Columns** shelf

5. From this, your worksheet should look like the following:

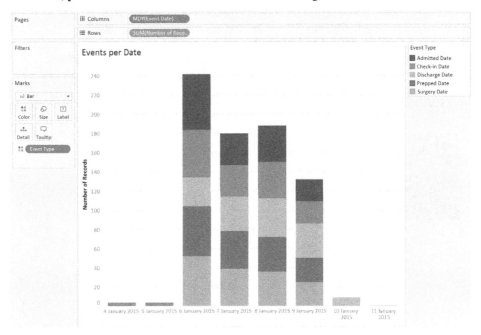

Figure 4.52: Events per Date

The original data structure was not well suited to this exercise; however, after duplicating the data source and pivoting, the task of counting events per day was quite simple since we were able to achieve this by using only three fields: **Event Date**, **Number of Records**, and **Event Type**. That is the main takeaway. If you find yourself struggling to create a visualization to answer a seemingly simple business question, consider pivoting.

Summary

We began this chapter with an introduction to relationships, followed by a discussion on joins, and discovered the queries Tableau uses to generate the respective data. Unions come in handy if identically formatted data, stored in multiple sheets or data sources, needs to be appended.

Then, we reviewed data blending to clearly understand how it differs from joining. We discovered that the primary limitation in data blending is that no dimensions are allowed from a secondary source; however, we also discovered that there are exceptions to this rule. We also discussed scaffolding, which can make data blending surprisingly fruitful.

Finally, we discussed data structures and learned how pivoting can make difficult or impossible visualizations easy. Having completed our second data-centric discussion, in the next chapter, we will discuss table calculations, partitioning, and addressing.

Learn more on Discord

To join the Discord community for this book – where you can share feedback, ask questions to the author, and learn about new releases – follow the QR code below:

```
https://packt.link/tableau
```

5

Introducing Table Calculations

The topic of table calculations in Tableau is so rich and deep that it alone could legitimately be the subject of an entire book. Exploring the various options that are available for each table calculation function and the various ways that table calculations can be applied is an interesting and rewarding endeavor. As you review the examples in this chapter, you will undoubtedly encounter techniques that you can apply in your day-to-day work; however, you may struggle to understand why some of these techniques work. This chapter was written to provide ways of thinking about table calculations that will prove useful in your journey toward mastering this fascinating topic. Along the way, some practical examples will be considered as well.

Of the dozens of blogs, forum posts, conference sessions, articles, and white papers reviewed for this chapter, Jonathan Drummy's blog post (`http://drawingwithnumbers.artisart.org/at-the-level-unlocking-the-mystery-part-1-ordinal-calcs/`), *At the Level – Unlocking the Mystery Part 1: Ordinal Calcs*, was the clearest and most insightful for understanding the various nuances of partitioning and addressing – the DNA of table calculations. In this chapter, we will discuss the following topics:

- Partition and direction of addressing
- Directional and non-directional addressing
- Exploring each unique table calculation function
- Application of functions

Let's go into more detail and start this chapter off with a general definition of table calculations and two resulting questions, which we will answer by the end of this chapter.

Partition and direction of addressing

As discussed in *Chapter 1*, *Reviewing the Basics*, calculated fields can be categorized as either row-level, aggregate-level, or table-level. For row- and aggregate-level calculations, the underlying data source engine does most (if not all) of the computational work and Tableau merely visualizes the results. For table calculations, Tableau also relies on the underlying data source engine and the available RAM on your machine to execute computational tasks; however, after that work is completed and a dataset is returned, Tableau performs additional processing before rendering the results.

Let us look at the definition of table calculations, as follows:

 A table calculation is a function performed on a cached dataset that has been generated as a result of a query from Tableau to the data source.

Let us consider a couple of points regarding the dataset in the cache mentioned in the preceding definition.

This cache is not simply the returned results of a query. Tableau may adjust the returned results. We will consider this in *Chapter 6, Utilizing OData, Data Densification, Big Data, and Google BigQuery*; Tableau may expand the cache through data densification but usually, it is user-driven. In table calculation terms, the cache is called a **partition**.

It is important to consider how the cache is structured. The dataset in the cache is the table used in your worksheet and, like all tables, is made up of rows and columns. This is particularly important for table calculations since a table calculation may be computed as it moves along the cache. The previous_value() table calculation will change whenever the cache structure changes because it will retrieve the value prior to the current one and this is very subjective. Is it prior in terms of date, value, or alphabetical order? It is up to you to tell Tableau how to structure the cache by using addressing and partitioning.

Most table calculations need to consider the cache structure. Such a table calculation is called **directional**. Alternatively, a table calculation may be computed based on the entire cache with no consideration for addressing and partitioning. The table calculation total(), for example, will calculate the total value, which does not change when the cache order changes. Another one is size(), the script_ and model functions. This type of table calculation is called **non-directional**.

 Note that in the Tableau documentation, the dataset in the cache is typically referred to as a partition. The structure of this chapter was designed with the intent of providing a simple schema for understanding table calculations.

The *Introducing functions* section explores each unique table calculation function. The *Application of functions* section explores how table calculations are applied to the view via partitioning and addressing dimensions.

Directional and non-directional addressing

We will begin this section by listing the different table calculation functions.

Tableau offers a wide range of table calculations, but if we narrow our consideration to unique groups of table calculation functions, we will discover that there are only 11:

Table Calculations
LOOKUP
PREVIOUS VALUE
RUNNING
WINDOW
FIRST
INDEX
LAST
RANK
SIZE
TOTAL
SCRIPT & MODEL

As mentioned in *Partition and direction of addressing*, table calculation functions operate on the cache and thus might change if the cache data changes, depending on the type of table calculation: directional or non-directional. In the following exercises, we will see directional and non-directional table calculation functions in action.

Let us have a closer look at directional and non-directional table calculations:

1. Navigate to https://public.tableau.com/profile/marleen.meier to locate and download the workbook associated with this chapter.
2. Navigate to the **Directional/Non-Directional** worksheet.
3. Create the calculated fields, as shown in the following table:

Name	Calculation	Notes
Lookup	LOOKUP(SUM([Sales]),-1)	Notice the -1 included in this calculation. This instructs Tableau to retrieve the value from the previous row.
Size	SIZE()	The SIZE function returns the number of rows in the partition. Therefore, as can be seen in the following screenshot, the size equals the total number of rows.
Window Sum	WINDOW_ SUM(SUM([Sales]))	The Window sum functions (WINDOW_SUM(expression, [start, end]) can operate either directionally or non-directionally. Since this example does not include the [start, end] option, it operates non-directionally.

Window Sum w/ Start&End	WINDOW_ SUM(SUM([Sales]),0,1)	This example of a window function is operating directionally, as can be seen by the inclusion of the [start, end] option.
Running Sum	RUNNING_ SUM(SUM([Sales]))	By their nature, RUNNING functions operate directionally since they consider previous rows in order to compute.

4. Place **Category** and **Ship Mode** on the **Rows** shelf.

5. Double-click on **Sales, Lookup, Size, Window Sum, Window Sum w/ Start&End**, and **Running Sum** to populate the view as shown in the following screenshot:

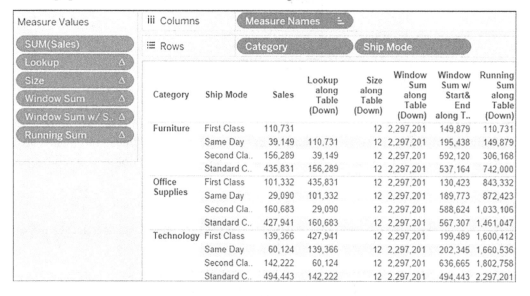

Figure 5.1: Table calculation

6. The table in *Figure 5.1* shows you that the Size function and the Window Sum function are the only two non-directional functions. All others present a number depending on the direction. For example, Lookup moves down and prints the value prior to the actual field. You can change the direction by clicking on the triangle of any table calculation field and selecting **Edit Table Calculation**.

This first exercise was an example of two table calculation categories: directional and non-directional. Now, we will move on to considering the table calculation functions individually. Regretfully, space does not allow us to explore all table calculations; however, to gain a working understanding, it should suffice to consider all but one of the unique groups of options. The four table calculations that begin with Script_, as well as the six Model_ functions, will be covered in *Chapter 15, Integrating Programming Languages*.

Although I added a real-world scenario at the end of each section in writing, the follow-along exercises focus on demonstrating table calculation functionality and considering how each interacts **directionally** or **non-directionally** with the dataset in the cache (also known as the **partition**).

Exploring each unique table calculation function

The following exercises will show us each table calculation individually; at the end of each section, you will find my thoughts on a real-world scenario.

Lookup and Total

The objectives of the following worksheet are to display those customers who made purchases in the last two days of 2013 and the associated absolute, as well as relative sales for the month of December.

In the following table, LOOKUP behaves directionally whereas TOTAL is non-directional. This behavior is easy to notice in the results. Follow these steps in order to do so:

1. In the workbook associated with this chapter, navigate to the **Lookup/Total** worksheet.

2. Drag **Customer Name** and **Order Date** onto the **Rows** shelf. Set **Order Date** to **Month/Day/Year** discrete by right-clicking and selecting **Day** as well as **Discrete**.

3. Place **Order Date** on the **Filters** shelf, choose to view only December 2013, and select **Month/Year** as the date format.

4. Create the following calculated fields:

Name	Calculation
Lookup Intervening Time	DATEDIFF('day',LOOKUP(Max([Order Date]),0), MAKEDATE(2013,12,31))
% Total Sales	SUM(Sales)/TOTAL(SUM([Sales]))

5. Right-click on % **Total Sales** and select **Default Properties | Number format** to set the number format to percentages with two decimal places.

6. Place **Lookup Intervening Time** on the **Filters** shelf and choose a range from 0 to 1.

7. Double-click on **Sales** and % **Total Sales** to place both fields on the view.

8.   Format as desired:

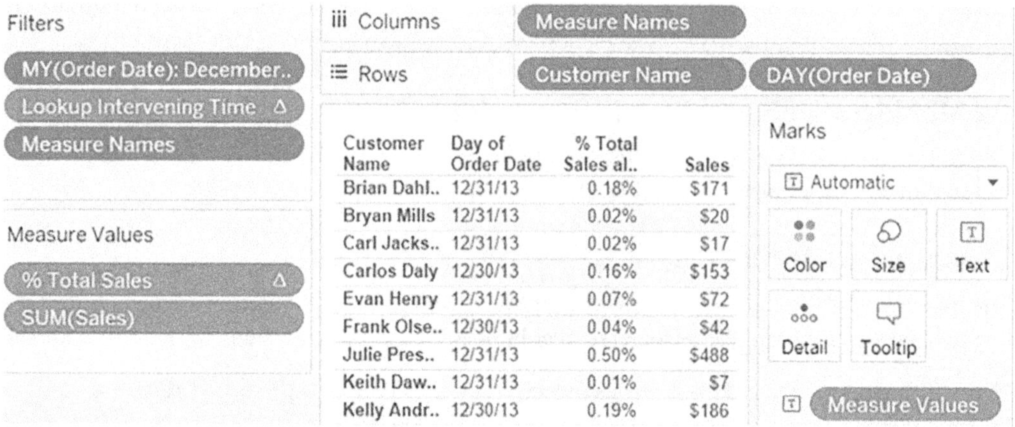

Figure 5.2: Total Sales

Let's consider how the preceding worksheet functions:

- The filter on **Order Date** ensures that the dataset returned to Tableau only includes data from the month of December 2013.

- The **% Total Sales** SUM(Sales)/TOTAL(SUM([Sales])) includes the TOTAL(SUM([Sales])) calculated field, which returns the total sales for the entire dataset. Dividing SUM([Sales]) by this total returns the percentage of the total.

- **Lookup Intervening Time:** DATEDIFF('day, LOOKUP(Max([Order Date]),0), MAKEDATE (2013,12,31)) will return an integer that reflects the difference between the date returned by the LOOKUP function and 12/31/2013. Note that the LOOKUP function has an offset of zero. This results in each row returning the date associated with that row. This differs from directional and non-directional table calculations, which include a LOOKUP function with an offset of -1, which causes each row in the view to return data associated with the previous row.

At first glance, you might think that you could simplify this workbook by removing **Lookup Intervening Time** from the **Filters** shelf and adjusting the filter on [Order Date] to display only the last two days of December. However, if you do this, **% Total Sales** will add up to 100% across all rows in the view, which would not satisfy the workbook's objectives. Think of **Lookup Intervening Time** as not filtering but hiding all but the last two days in December. This hiding ensures that the data necessary to calculate **% Total Sales** is in the dataset in cache/partition.

Real-world scenario: I use **Lookup** more often than **Total**. And both are invaluable when working with Tableau. We already saw that you use lookup for changes; you can think of a month-to-month comparison of profits, the number of employees today versus today last year, website click differences per day of the week, and so on.

For the table calculation total, you can use it every time you want to show the total number of something while still showing some level of aggregation in your dashboard. The percentage of **Total** in *Figure 5.2* is actually the perfect example.

Previous Value

The objectives of the following worksheet are to return the aggregate value of sales for each year and set next year's sales goal. Note that two options have been provided for determining next year's sales goal in order to demonstrate how PREVIOUS_VALUE differs from LOOKUP. Also, note that PREVIOUS_VALUE behaves directionally.

Let us have a look at the steps:

1. In the workbook associated with this chapter, navigate to the **Previous Value** worksheet.
2. Create the following calculated fields:

Name	Calculation
Next Year Goal Prv_Val	PREVIOUS_VALUE(SUM([Sales])) * 1.05
Next Year Goal Lkup	LOOKUP(SUM([Sales]),0) * 1.05

3. Place **Order Date** on the **Rows** shelf.
4. Double-click **Sales** and **Next Year Goal Prv_Val** to place each on the view.
5. Format as desired, or as seen in the following screenshot (by dragging the piles in **Measure Values**, the order will change accordingly in the view, as seen in the following screenshot):

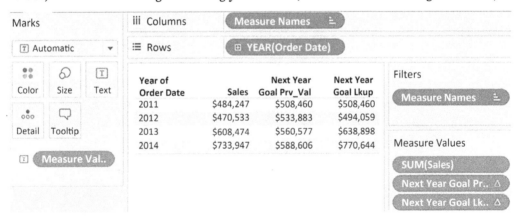

Figure 5.3: Next year

Let's consider how the preceding worksheet functions:

- **Next Year Goal Prv_Val**: PREVIOUS_VALUE(SUM([Sales])) *1.05 is applied in this worksheet, which retrieves the results from each previous row and adds 5%. In other words, the goal is a steady-state growth rate of 5% per year over all years.

- **Next Year Goal Lkup:** `LOOKUP(SUM([Sales]),0) * 1.05` is also applied to this worksheet; this calculation adds 5% to the current year's sales. In other words, the goal for next year is for sales that are 5% greater than this year. Previous years are not considered.

To better understand this exercise, consider the values associated with 2014 in the preceding screenshot. **Next Year Goal Prv_Val** is calculated via **2013 Next Year Goal Prv_Val**; that is, $560,577 * 1.05. On the other hand, **Next Year Goal Lkup** is calculated via the 2014 sales; that is, $733,947 * 1.05.

Real-world scenario: imagine you want to extrapolate a data point and keep extrapolating from that new value; for this, you use **Previous_Value**. One example is a bond that pays a frequent coupon. If your bond has a face value of 100 and it pays a 4% semi-annual coupon, you can calculate the final worth of the bond by using **Previous_Value**, just like we did with the **Next Year Goal Prv_Val** in the last exercise.

Running

The objective of the following worksheet is to display the running minimum profit, running average profit, and running maximum profit compared with **SUM(Profit)** for each month in the dataset.

The following example demonstrates how the `Running` functions behave directionally:

1. In the workbook associated with this chapter, navigate to the **Running** worksheet.
2. Create the following calculated fields:

Name	Calculation
Running Min	RUNNING_MIN(SUM([Profit]))
Running Max	RUNNING_MAX(SUM([Profit]))
Running Avg	RUNNING_AVG(SUM([Profit]))

3. Place **Order Date** on the **Columns** shelf and set it to **Month/Year** continuous. Place **Measure Values** on the **Rows** shelf.
4. Remove all instances of measures from the **Measure Values** shelf except for **Running Min, Running Max, Running Avg,** and **Profit**.
5. Move **SUM(Profit)** from the **Measure Values** shelf to the **Rows** shelf. Right-click on **SUM(Profit)** and select **Dual Axis**.
6. Format as desired.

Let's consider how the preceding worksheet functions:

- **Running Min**: `RUNNING_MIN(SUM([Profit]))` is visible in the preceding screenshot, which compares the current **SUM(Profit)** with the least **SUM(Profit)** recorded to that point in time. If the current **SUM(Profit)** is less than the least **SUM(Profit)** recorded to date, the current **SUM(Profit)** replaces the least **SUM(Profit)**.

- **Running Max**: `RUNNING_MAX(SUM([Profit]))` operates similarly to **Running Min**, except of course it looks for maximum values.

- **Running Avg**: `RUNNING_AVG(SUM([Profit]))` calculates the average **SUM(Profit)** based on every month to the current month.

Real-world scenario: again, there are plenty of examples for this table calculation. Think about year-to-date profits, population numbers based on childbirth (do not forget to subtract the deaths), the current number of open support tickets, and many more.

Window

The objective of the following worksheet is to display a directional instance of a `WINDOW` function and a non-directional instance.

Please follow these steps:

1. In the workbook associated with this chapter, navigate to the **Window** worksheet.

2. Create the following calculated fields:

Name	Calculation
Win Avg Directional	`WINDOW_AVG(SUM([Profit]),-2,0)`
Win Avg Non-Directional	`WINDOW_AVG(SUM([Profit]))`

3. Place **Order Date** on the **Columns** shelf and set it to **Month/Year** continuous. Place **Measure Values** on the **Rows** shelf.

4. Remove all instances of measures from the **Measure Values** shelf except **Win Avg Directional**, **Win Avg Non-Directional**, and **Profit**.

5. From the **Data** pane, drag another instance of **Profit** onto the **Rows** shelf. Right-click on the instance of **Profit** on the **Rows** shelf and select **Quick Table Calculation | Moving Average**. Right-click on the instance of **Profit** on the **Rows** shelf and select **Dual Axis**.

6. Right-click on the axis labeled **Moving Average of Profit** and select **Synchronize Axis**.

7.   Format as desired, or as seen in the following screenshot:

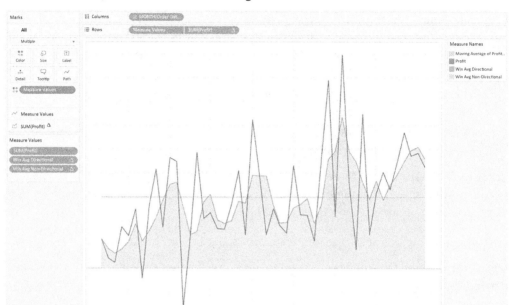

Figure 5.4: Window

Let's consider how the preceding worksheet functions:

- **Win Avg Directional:** Window_AVG(SUM([Profit]),-2,0) has a start point of -2 and an endpoint of 0, which signifies that Tableau will create a point based on the average of the SUM([Profit]) calculated on the current month and the previous two months. Changing the 0 to 2 would cause the average of each point to be calculated on the previous 2 months, the current month, and the next 2 months. Double-click on the instance of **Profit** on the **Rows** shelf to view the underlying code. (This is the instance of **Profit** that was changed into a table calculation by right-clicking and selecting **Quick Table Calculation | Moving Average**.) Note that the calculation is identical to the code created for **Win Avg Directional**. However, if you right-click on both pills and select **Edit Table Calculation**, you will notice that the resulting dialog boxes differ. The dialog box associated with **Profit** has more options, including the ability to change the previous and next values. Changing the previous and next values for **Win Avg Directional** requires adjusting the calculated field.

- **Win Avg Non-Directional:** WINDOW_AVG(SUM([Profit])) is associated with the horizontal line across the view. Note that it is not dependent on direction. Instead, it is a single value generated by the average of all aggregated **Profit** values in the dataset in the cache/partition and will therefore be the same no matter the order of the data points.

Real-world scenario: why would you want to use a window average? Because you want to smoothen the outliers, for example. A window average provides a steady representation of your data. Single highs or lows will be removed. If you analyze stock prices, you will notice that prices can differ throughout the year! By using the window averages or rather window standard deviations as an early warning indicator, you will be able to see price jumps more clearly and can, as an investor, act upon it. Steady growth or decline will, however, fall into the moving bands. This is not achievable by using fixed bands.

First and Last

The objective of the following worksheet is to display the first and last instance of the best-selling item in the Superstore dataset. Notice how the following example demonstrates that the FIRST and LAST functions behave directionally.

Take the following steps:

1. In the workbook associated with this chapter, navigate to the **First/Last** worksheet.
2. Create the following calculated fields:

Name	Calculation
First	FIRST()
Last	LAST()
First or Last	FIRST() = 0 OR LAST() = 0

3. Place **Product Name** on the **Filters** shelf, select the **Top** tab, and choose **Top 1** by **Sum** of **Sales**, as shown in the following screenshot:

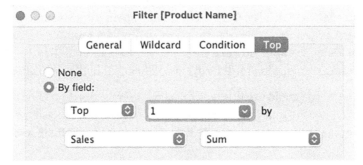

Figure 5.5: Top filter

4. Place **First or Last** on the **Filters** shelf and select **True** in the resulting dialog box.
5. Drag **Product Name**, **Order Date**, and **Row ID** onto the **Rows** shelf.
6. Set **Order Date** to **Month/Day/Year** discrete.
7. Double-click on **Sales**, **First**, and **Last** to place each on the view.
8. Right-click on **First**, **Last**, and **First or Last** and select **Compute Using | Table (down)**.

9. Format as desired:

Figure 5.6: First and Last

Let's consider how the preceding worksheet functions:

*   **First:** FIRST() starts at 0 and counts down to the last row of the dataset in the cache. In the preceding screenshot, note that the first instance of **Canon imageCLASS** occurs on 05/24/13. The fact that FIRST() ranges from 0 to -4 communicates that there are five instances of **Canon imageCLASS** in the dataset in the cache or within the window cache.

*   **Last:** LAST() starts at the last row of the dataset in the cache and counts down to 0. In the preceding screenshot, note that the last instance of **Canon imageCLASS** occurs on 11/18/14. The fact that LAST() ranges from **4** to **0** communicates that there are five instances of **Canon imageCLASS** in the dataset in the cache.

*   **First or Last:** FIRST() = 0 OR LAST() = 0, when placed on the **Filters** shelf and set to **True**, hides all instances of matching rows except the first and last.

*   The **Row ID** field is included in the view to make sure that the very first and last instances of **Canon imageCLASS** display. Otherwise, if there are multiple instances of **Canon imageCLASS** on the first or last date, the sales numbers will reflect multiple values. It's important to set **Compute Using** to **Table (down)** for each table calculation in the view. **Compute Using** is the same as **Addressing,** which will be discussed in detail in the *Application of functions* section.

Real-world scenario: you could use this type of calculation for the time between the last 5 orders per quarter, to see whether the time between orders is increasing or decreasing during the day. This can then help to improve marketing or schedule help desk hours more efficiently.

Index

The objective of the following worksheet is to list those states in the USA with over 50 postal codes represented in the underlying dataset.

Notice how the following example demonstrates that the INDEX function behaves directionally and can be seen as a count of rows:

1. In the workbook associated with this chapter, navigate to the **Index** worksheet.
2. Set the **Marks** card to **Circle**.
3. Place **State** on the **Rows** shelf and **Postal Code** on the **Detail** shelf.

4. Create a calculated field named **Index** with the code: INDEX( ). Drag **Index** onto the **Filters** shelf and select the **Range of values** filter. Choose to view only values that are 50 or greater by moving the slider to a minimum value of **50**.

5. Right-click on **Index** and select **Edit Table Calculation**. Select **Specific Dimensions** and check **Postal Code**:

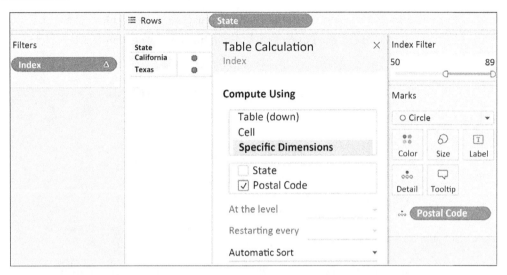

Figure 5.7: Index

6. Select **Analysis | Stack Marks | Off**, then review:

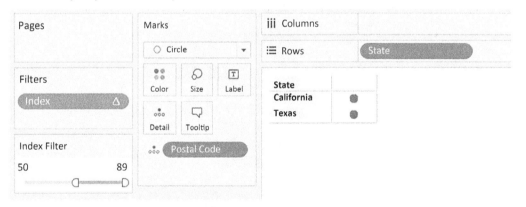

Figure 5.8: Final index

Let's consider how the preceding worksheet functions:

Index: INDEX( ) counts from 1 to n. As such, it behaves directionally. In this case, as a result of the partitioning and addressing settings, **Index** is counting postal codes. (Partitioning and addressing will be discussed in detail in the *Application of functions* section.) Setting the **Index** filter to display only values of 50 or more ensures that only those states with 50 or more postal codes are in the partition/ dataset in the cache display.

Real-world scenarios: most often, I use **Index** interchangeably with **First** and **Last**.

Rank

The objective of the following worksheet is to display the top three selling items in each region. This example will demonstrate how RANK interacts directionally with the dataset in the cache:

1. In the workbook associated with this chapter, navigate to the **Rank** worksheet.

2. Place **Product Name** on the **Filters** shelf, select the **Top** tab, and choose **Top 3** by **Sum** of **Sales**:

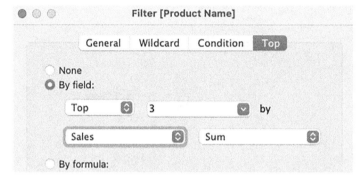

Figure 5.9: Filter

3. Place **Region** and **Product Name** on the **Rows** shelf and **Sales** on the **Columns** shelf.

4. Note that only two items display for each region:

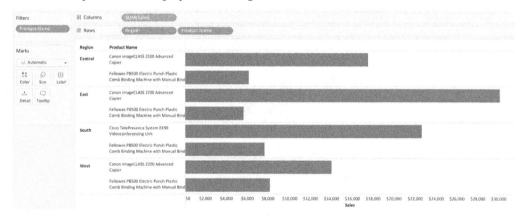

Figure 5.10: Reviewing the top two items

5. Create a calculated field named **Rank** with the code Rank(SUM(Sales)). Drag **Rank** between **Region** and **Product Name** onto the **Rows** shelf.

6. Note that before you can place **Rank** between the two pills on the **Rows** shelf, you have to cast it as discrete. One way to accomplish this is by placing **Rank** on the **Detail** shelf, right-clicking on the pill, and selecting **Discrete**.

7. Right-click on **Rank** and select **Compute Using | Product Name**.

8. Remove **Product Name** from the **Filters** shelf.

9. Press *Ctrl* (or press *Option* on Mac), and right-click and drag **Rank** from the **Rows** shelf onto the **Filters** shelf. Pressing the *Ctrl* key while dragging a pill from one shelf to another will create a copy of that pill. Failing to press the *Ctrl* key will, of course, simply result in moving the pill. In the resulting dialog box, select **1**, **2**, and **3**.

Format as desired:

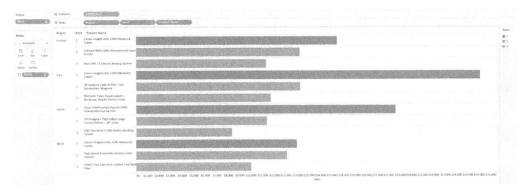

Figure 5.11: Rank

Let's consider how the preceding worksheet functions:

*   If you followed the step-by-step instructions for this exercise, you will have noticed that after placing **Region** and **Product Name** on the **Rows** shelf and filtering to show only the top three product names, the resulting visualization only showed two products in each region. This is because the filter on **Product Name** showed the top three products overall, but it so happened that two out of the three were always present in each region. But we actually wanted to show the top three per region rather than overall. To fix this issue, we employed the Rank table calculation function.

*   Let's understand how this works. Instead of writing the Rank(Sum(Sales)) function, the same code will be automatically generated by right-clicking on an instance of **Sales** on any shelf and selecting **Quick Table Calculation | Rank**. Note that **Rank** is counting the product names within each region. This demonstrates that the **Rank** table calculation operates directionally on the dataset in the cache/partition.

Real-world scenario: I use **Rank** when I want to filter a continuously changing view, divided into subsections – for example, the last three comments on each of my blog posts. Or when I want to show behavior over time, for example, the top 10 ranked products over the course of 2 years. This will result in a bump chart.

Size

The objective of the following worksheet is to display all states with five or fewer cities in the **Superstore** dataset. This example will demonstrate how SIZE utilizes the entire partition/dataset in the cache and is thus non-directional. We will also use the FIRST table calculation function, which is directional, in order to clean up the view.

Please follow along with the steps:

1. In the workbook associated with this chapter, navigate to the **Size** worksheet.
2. Set **Analysis | Stack Marks** to **Off**.
3. Create the following calculated fields:

Name	Calculation
Size	SIZE()
City Count	IF FIRST() = 0 THEN [Size] ELSE NULL END

4. Drag **State** onto the **Rows** shelf, **City** onto the **Detail** shelf, **City Count** onto the **Text/Label** shelf, and **Size** onto the **Detail** shelf.
5. Right-click on the **Size** filter and select **Compute Using | City**. Move **Size** from the **Marks** card to the **Filters** shelf.
6. In the resulting dialog box, select an **At most** value of **5**:

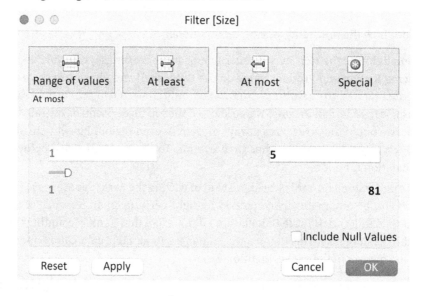

Figure 5.12: At most

7. On the **Marks** card, right-click on **City Count** and select **Edit Table Calculation**. Under **Nested Calculations**, select **City Count**.
8. Select **Compute Using | Specific Dimensions** and check **City**:

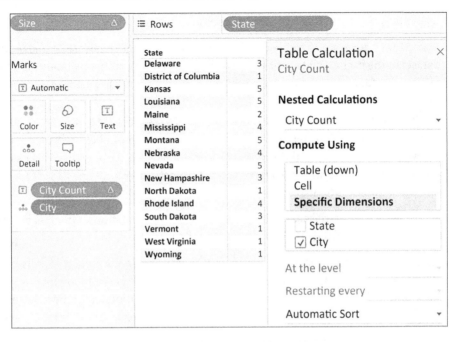

Figure 5.13: Specific Dimensions

9. Now use the dropdown under **Nested Calculations** again and select **Size**. Then, select **Compute Using | Specific Dimensions** and check **City**.

10. Observe the final view:

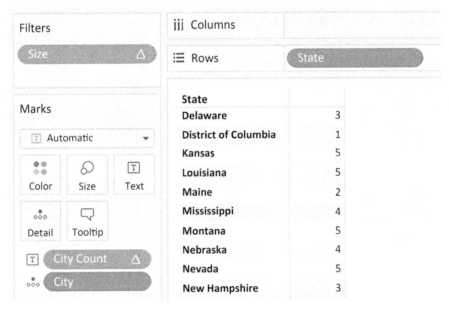

Figure 5.14: Final worksheet

Let's consider how the preceding worksheet functions:

- **Size:** `Size()` generates a single number, for example, 3 for Delaware, based on the partition/dataset in the cache. That number can change depending on the partitioning and addressing settings but does not change based on movement across the partition. As such, it behaves non-directionally.

- **City Count:** The `IF FIRST() = 0 THEN LOOKUP([Size],0) ELSE NULLEND` field is not strictly necessary. You could, instead, simply place **Size** on the **Text/Label** shelf. However, if you do so, you will note that the numbers in the view will look bold. This occurs because the numbers are actually repeated and then layered on top of each other. Utilizing `FIRST() = 0` causes only one set of numbers to display.

Note that the preceding exercise had an option for **Nested Calculations**, which is because the `Size` calculated field was referenced within the `City Count` calculated field.

Real-world scenario: **Size** is probably the least used. I honestly do not think I ever used it other than explaining and showcasing it. But what I saw others do with **Size** is the following; by turning on the grand total column view, **Size** can generate a non-default aggregation like standard deviation. Simply use this formula: `if size()=1 then sum({STDEV([Sales])}) else sum([Sales]) end`.

If you cannot get enough of table calculation, here are some more scenarios: `https://www.tableau.com/blog/top-10-tableau-table-calculations`.

Now that we have presented the different table calculations, we will see how they can be manipulated in the partitioning (scope) and addressing (direction) of calculations.

Application of functions

So far, we have covered the first of our two major questions: *What is the function?* Now we will proceed to the next question: *How is the function applied?*

Let's try to understand that question via the following three options, which are all applications of the `INDEX` function:

Category	Segment		
	Consumer	Corporate	Home Office
Furniture	1	2	3
Office Sup..	1	2	3
Technology	1	2	3

Category	Segment		
	Consumer	Corporate	Home Office
Furniture	1	1	1
Office Sup..	2	2	2
Technology	3	3	3

Category	Segment		
	Consumer	Corporate	Home Office
Furniture	1	2	3
Office Sup..	4	5	6
Technology	7	8	9

Figure 5.15: Applications

The INDEX function is used in each of these three screenshots; however, it is applied differently in each. The first and second screenshots both display 1, 2, and 3, but differ directionally. The third screenshot ranges from 1 to 9. So, how is INDEX being applied in each case?

Answering this question can be confusing because Tableau uses different terminology. Within Tableau itself, the way a table calculation is applied may be referred to as running along, moving along, compute using, or **partitioning (scoping)** and **addressing (direction)**. For our purposes, we will utilize the terms partitioning and addressing, which we will define here according to the Tableau documentation (https://help.tableau.com/current/pro/desktop/en-us/calculations_tablecalculations.htm):

> *The dimensions that define how to group the calculation, that is, define the scope of data it is performed on, are called partitioning fields. The table calculation is performed separately within each partition. The remaining dimensions, upon which the table calculation is performed, are called addressing fields, and determine the direction of the calculation.*

This basically means that the partition defines which fields are being used, for example, Segment. If you have three segments divided over three categories, you could look at each combination separately, all categories within one segment, or all segments within one category. The way you look at it is what Tableau calls addressing.

If a table calculation is utilized in the view, you can right-click on it and select **Edit Table Calculation**. Upon doing so, you will see a dialog box that will allow you to choose specific dimensions. If a dimension is checked, it is addressed. If it is unchecked, it is partitioned.

See an example in the following figure:

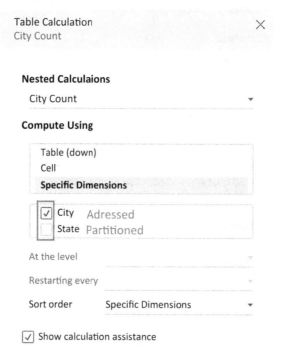

Figure 5.16: Addressing and partitioning

Tableau provides many out-of-the-box partitioning and addressing settings, including **Table (down)**, **Table (across)**, **Pane (down)**, and **Cell**. We will reference these options occasionally but will not give a detailed review. This leads us to our first partitioning and addressing guideline:

 Do not use the out-of-the-box partitioning and addressing settings provided by Tableau, including **Table (across)** and **Pane (down)**. Force yourself to click **Specific Dimensions** and manually define the partitioning and addressing so that you clearly understand how every table calculation is applied.

There are a couple of caveats to the preceding guideline:

- There is an exception, which is **Cell**. It is not possible to address individual cells in a view using partitioning and addressing. Instead, it is necessary to use **Compute Using** as **Cell** or, within the **Table Calculation** dialog box, to select **Cell**. Surprisingly, addressing a table calculation along each cell can be useful. An example is provided in the workbook associated with this chapter, on the worksheet **Percent of Total**. There it is used to show 100% for each cell divided into two categories.

- If you set partitioning and addressing for a given table calculation and then add dimensions to the view, usually, Tableau will not automatically adjust the partitioning and addressing settings; they are locked down. However, when using **Table (down)**, **Pane (across)**, and the like, Tableau will make automatic adjustments as dimensions are added to the view.

This leads us to our next guideline:

 Place all needed dimensions on the desired shelves *before* setting partitioning and addressing for table calculations.

Following these guidelines will help ensure that you are always clear about how your table calculations are being applied. It might take longer in the first place, but ultimately, you'll be more in control of table calculations and can develop faster.

Building a playground

Let us set up a simple playground environment to quickly and efficiently explore partitioning and addressing:

1. In the workbook associated with this chapter, navigate to the **Playground** worksheet.
2. Place **Category** on the **Rows** shelf and the **Index** calculation on the **Label** shelf.
3. The **Index** calculation is simply Index(). Click on the drop-down menu associated with **Index** and select **Edit Table Calculation**. In the resulting dialog box, click **Specific Dimensions**.

4.   Position the screen components optimally. See the following screenshot for one possible setup:

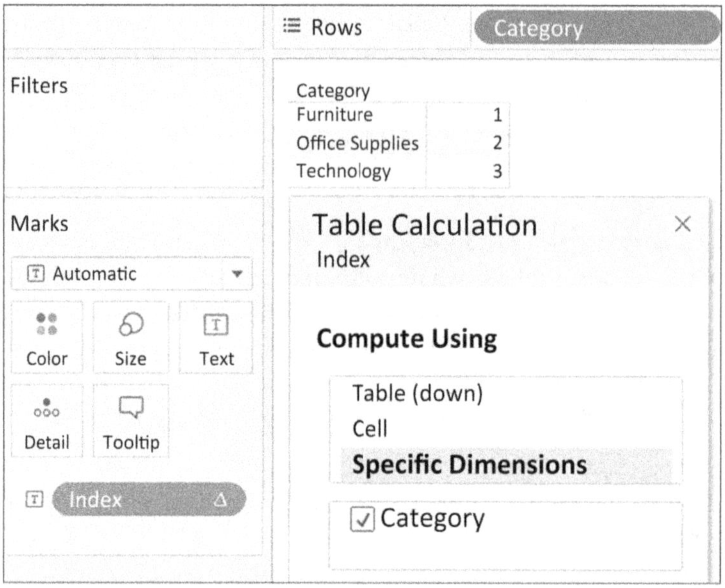

Figure 5.17: Building a playground

You can see in *Figure 5.17* that we created a worksheet displaying the three categories **Furniture**, **Office Supplies**, and **Technology**. By adding the **Index** field to the **Text** shelf, we have the minimum requirement to use a table calculation, which is one dimension and one table calculation. Now we can change the compute used in the table calculation and can spot what changes in the visualization. Later on, we will explore more complex examples; however, always start easy and increase the level of complexity slowly to fully understand what is happening.

In the following pages, we will utilize our playground extensively and modify it as necessary. However, for the sake of efficiency, we will need to keep the focus on the playground and the accompanying discussion narrow. The discussion will be confined to dimensions on the **Rows** and **Columns** shelves and the INDEX function on the **Text** shelf.

We could explore different functions on various shelves and the different options that they afford. For instance, placing a date field on the **Pages** shelf will cause a table calculation that uses the TOTAL function to display an option to compute the total across all pages. Regretfully, exploring every possible nuance is simply not possible in one chapter, but if you are interested in this topic, feel free to check out the Tableau help page for more content and examples: https://help.tableau.com/current/pro/desktop/en-us/functions_functions_tablecalculation.htm.

Partitioning and addressing with one dimension

Let us use our playground to start exploring partitioning and addressing with the simplest possible example:

Figure 5.18: Compute Using | Category

In this simple example, addressing **Category** causes each member of the **Category** dimension to be counted. This demonstrates that addressing a dimension determines the direction of the calculation. In our example, we have the **Table Calculation Index**, but **Index** depends on partitioning and addressing as we learned before. **Category** serves as a partition in the **Rows** shelf. We split the data into three: **Furniture, Office Supplies,** and **Technology.** Now we also say address **Category** for the **Table Calculation.** We did that by selecting **Category** from **Compute Using** (*Figure 5.18*). Now the **Table Calculation** will be applied to the categories and hence counts 1, 2, 3 categories.

If you were to select **Compute Using | Cell,** the partition into three categories would still remain in the view—you would still see **Furniture, Office Supplies,** and **Technology**—but the counting would happen per cell and not for the whole **Category** dimension. Hence, the **Index** will count 1, then move to the next cell and count 1, then the next cell and again count 1:

Figure 5.19: Compute Using | Cell

Now, let us consider partitioning and addressing with not one but two dimensions.

Partitioning and addressing with two dimensions

Two additional options are made available when partitioning and addressing two or more dimensions: **At the level** and **Restarting every**. You can compare this scenario to the task of counting all countries per continent. In this scenario, **At the level** will be countries since you are not counting streets or trees but countries. **Restarting** will be continents. After you are done counting countries for one continent, you start at 1 again for the next continent:

At the level	Deepest	▼
Restarting every	None	▼

Figure 5.20: Two dimensions

Both **At the level** and **Restarting every** allow the author to choose dimensions from a drop-down menu. **At the level** allows the author to choose what level to increment at, and as the name suggests, **Restarting every** allows the author to choose which dimensions to restart on. The examples here will provide context for your understanding.

Note that **At the level** has one additional choice: **Deepest**. In this case, setting **At the level** to **Deepest** is the same as selecting **Ship Mode**. This leads us to our next guideline:

 It is not necessary to choose the bottom dimension in the **At the level** drop-down menu. It is always identical to **Deepest**.

To recreate the iterations listed here, you will need to make some changes to the playground environment. In addition to **Category** on the **Rows** shelf and **Index** on the **Label** shelf, also place **Ship Mode** on the **Rows** shelf. We will not cover iterations that include one or more dimensions on the **Columns** shelf since the behavior of these possibilities is much the same.

As you consider and/or reproduce the following options, note that the **Addressing** order is important. For examples 3-5, **Category** is first on the addressing list. For options 6-8, **Ship Mode** is first on the list.

In the first example, configure the partitioning and addressing settings thus:

- **Partitioning: Category**
- **Addressing: Ship Mode**
- **At the level: -**
- **Restarting every: -**

This will produce the following visualization:

Category	Ship Mode	
Furniture	First Class	1
	Same Day	2
	Second Class	3
	Standard Class	4
Office Supplies	First Class	1
	Same Day	2
	Second Class	3
	Standard Class	4

Figure 5.21: Example 1

Here, we count the **Ship Mode** per **Category**.

In the second example, configure the partitioning and addressing settings thus:

- **Partitioning: Ship Mode**
- **Addressing: Category**
- **At the level: -**
- **Restarting every: -**

This will produce the following visualization:

Category	Ship Mode	
Furniture	First Class	1
	Same Day	1
	Second Class	1
	Standard Class	1
Office Supplies	First Class	2
	Same Day	2

Figure 5.22: Example 2

In this example, we count the **Category** per **Ship Mode**.

In the third example, configure the partitioning and addressing settings thus:

- **Partitioning: -**
- **Addressing: Category, Ship Mode**
- **At the level: Deepest**
- **Restarting every: None**

This will produce the following visualization:

Category	Ship Mode	
Furniture	First Class	1
	Same Day	2
	Second Class	3
	Standard Class	4
Office Supplies	First Class	5
	Same Day	6

Figure 5.23: Example 3

This time, we count the **Category** and **Ship Mode** combination.

In the fourth example, configure the partitioning and addressing settings thus:

- **Partitioning:** -
- **Addressing: Category, Ship Mode**
- **At the level: Deepest**
- **Restarting every: Category**

This will produce the following visualization:

Category	Ship Mode	
Furniture	First Class	1
	Same Day	2
	Second Class	3
	Standard Class	4
Office Supplies	First Class	1
	Same Day	2

Figure 5.24: Example 4

Here, we count the combination **Category** and **Ship Mode** and restart counting at every new **Category**.

In the fifth example, configure the partitioning and addressing settings thus:

- **Partitioning:** -
- **Addressing: Category, Ship Mode**
- **At the level: Category**
- **Restarting every: None**

This will produce the following visualization:

Category	Ship Mode	
Furniture	First Class	1
	Same Day	1
	Second Class	1
	Standard Class	1
Office Supplies	First Class	2
	Same Day	2

Figure 5.25: Example 5

We count the combination **Category** and **Ship Mode** that appears at the **Category** level. Since the **Category** level is higher in the hierarchy than **Ship Mode**, we end up counting only one value per **Category**.

In the sixth example, configure the partitioning and addressing settings thus:

* **Partitioning: -**
* **Addressing: Ship Mode, Category**
* **At the level: Deepest**
* **Restarting every: None**

This will produce the following visualization:

Category	Ship Mode	
Furniture	First Class	1
	Same Day	4
	Second Class	7
	Standard Class	10
Office Supplies	First Class	2
	Same Day	5
	Second Class	8
	Standard Class	11
Technology	First Class	3
	Same Day	6
	Second Class	9
	Standard Class	12

Figure 5.26: Example 6

We count the combination **Ship Mode** and **Category** at the **Ship Mode** level; hence, we count **First Class** and all the **Category** combinations with it before **Same Day** and its combinations with **Category**.

In the seventh example, configure the partitioning and addressing settings thus:

* **Partitioning: -**
* **Addressing: Ship Mode, Category**

- At the level: Deepest
- Restarting every: Ship Mode

This will produce the following visualization:

Category	Ship Mode	
Furniture	First Class	1
	Same Day	1
	Second Class	1
	Standard Class	1
Office Supplies	First Class	2
	Same Day	2

Figure 5.27: Example 7

We count the **Ship Mode** and **Category** combinations at the deepest level but we restart at every **Ship Mode**; therefore, we count **First Class** and **Furniture**, **First Class** and **Office Supplies**, then **First Class** and **Technology**. Then, we move on to **Same Day** and its combinations, restarting at 1 again.

In the eighth example, configure the partitioning and addressing settings thus:

- Partitioning: -
- Addressing: Ship Mode, Category
- At the level: Ship Mode
- Restarting every: None

This will produce the following visualization:

Category	Ship Mode	
Furniture	First Class	1
	Same Day	2
	Second Class	3
	Standard Class	4
Office Supplies	First Class	1
	Same Day	2

Figure 5.28: Example 8

We count the **Ship Mode** and **Category** combinations at the **Ship Mode** level.

Now, let's consider some of the possibilities presented here in more detail. Some of the options are identical. In fact, out of the nine options, only four are unique. Let's consider examples 1, 4, and 8, all of which have identical end results. Does this mean that each is truly identical? Options 1 and 4 are identical. Option 8, however, is slightly different. To understand this, note the description within the table calculation dialog box for option 8:

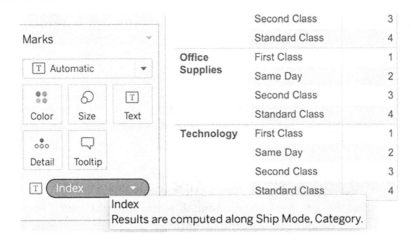

Figure 5.29: Index

The description in example 8 reads **Results are computed along Ship Mode, Category** (see *Figure 5.29*). The text in the description box for example 1 is identical to that for example 4: **Results are computed along Ship Mode for Category**, which can be translated as partitioning **Category** and addressing **Ship Mode**. This translation is identical to the actual partitioning/addressing setup accomplished in example 1. Therefore, examples 1 and 4 are identical. But does the slight difference to example 8 mean there are practical differences? No!

Example 6 may seem confusing at first. Why has the odd numbering sequence occurred? Because the order in which the dimensions are addressed differs from the order of dimensions on the **Rows** shelf. The addressing order is **Ship Mode, Category**. The order on the **Rows** shelf is **Category, Ship Mode**. Simply reversing the position of **Category** and **Ship Mode** on the **Rows** shelf and noting the change in the number sequence should help dispel any confusion:

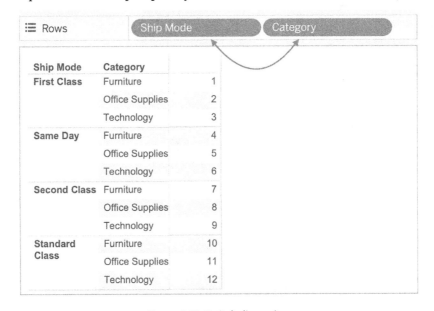

Figure 5.30: Switch dimensions

Is there any practical use for example 6? Yes. From time to time, it may be necessary to address dimensions in a different order than they are listed on a shelf. But this is not usually the case. This leads us to our next guideline:

 When addressing multiple dimensions for a table calculation, the order of addressing will usually reflect the order of dimensions on the **Rows** and/or **Columns** shelves.

Partitioning and addressing with three dimensions

Let us add another dimension to our playground and reorder things slightly. Place **Category** and **Region** on the Rows shelf and **Ship Mode** on the **Columns** shelf. **Index** should remain on **Text** in the **Marks** shelf. Also, add two filters. Filter **Region** to **East**, **South**, and **West**. Filter **Ship Mode** to **First Class**, **Second Class**, and **Standard Class**.

When partitioning and addressing three dimensions, the number of possible iterations jumps to 57; however, only 14 of these are unique. Here is a listing of those unique possibilities.

 Remember, addressing means selecting the dimensions in the table calculation settings while partitioning is the de-selection of dimensions, as described in *Figure 5.17*.

In the first example, configure the partitioning and addressing settings as:

- **Partitioning: Category, Region**
- **Addressing: Ship Mode**
- **At the level: -**
- **Restarting every: -**

This will produce the following visualization:

		Ship Mode		
Category	Region	First Class	Second Class	Standard Class
Furniture	East	1	2	3
	South	1	2	3
	West	1	2	3
Office Supplies	East	1	2	3
	South	1	2	3

Figure 5.31: Example 1

Here, we count the different **Ship Modes** per **Category** and **Region** combinations.

In the second example, configure the partitioning and addressing settings as:

- **Partitioning: Category, Ship Mode**
- **Addressing: Region**
- **At the level: -**
- **Restarting every: -**

This will produce the following visualization:

		Ship Mode		
Category	**Region**	**First Class**	**Second Class**	**Standard Class**
Furniture	East	1	1	1
	South	2	2	2
	West	3	3	3
Office Supplies	East	1	1	1
	South	2	2	2
	West	3	3	3

Figure 5.32: Example 2

Here we count the different **Regions** per **Category** and **Ship Mode** combinations.

In the third example, configure the partitioning and addressing settings as:

- **Partitioning: Region, Ship Mode**
- **Addressing: Category**
- **At the level: -**
- **Restarting every: -**

This will produce the following visualization:

		Ship Mode		
Category	**Region**	**First Class**	**Second Class**	**Standard Class**
Furniture	East	1	1	1
	South	1	1	1
	West	1	1	1
Office Supplies	East	2	2	2
	South	2	2	2
	West	2	2	2
Technology	East	3	3	3
	South	3	3	3
	West	3	3	3

Figure 5.33: Example 3

Here we count the different **Category** options per **Region** and **Ship Mode** combinations.

In the fourth example, configure the partitioning and addressing settings as:

- **Partitioning: Category**
- **Addressing: Region, Ship Mode**
- **At the level: Deepest**
- **Restarting every: None**

This will produce the following visualization:

Ship Mode

Category	Region	First Class	Second Class	Standard Class
Furniture	East	1	2	3
	South	4	5	6
	West	7	8	9
Office Supplies	East	1	2	3
	South	4	5	6
	West	7	8	9

Figure 5.34: Example 4

Here we count the different **Category** options per **Region** and **Ship Mode** combinations at the deepest level.

In the fifth example, configure the partitioning and addressing settings as:

- **Partitioning: Category**
- **Addressing: Ship Mode, Region**
- **At the level: Deepest**
- **Restarting every: None**

This will produce the following visualization:

Ship Mode

Category	Region	First Class	Second Class	Standard Class
Furniture	East	1	4	7
	South	2	5	8
	West	3	6	9
Office Supplies	East	1	4	7
	South	2	5	8
	West	3	6	9

Figure 5.35: Example 5

Here, we count the different **Category** options per **Ship Mode** and **Region** combinations at the deepest level.

In the sixth example, configure the partitioning and addressing settings as:

- **Partitioning: Region**
- **Addressing: Category, Ship Mode**
- **At the level: Deepest**
- **Restarting every: None**

This will produce the following visualization:

		Ship Mode		
Category	**Region**	**First Class**	**Second Class**	**Standard Class**
Furniture	East	1	2	3
	South	1	2	3
	West	1	2	3
Office Supplies	East	4	5	6
	South	4	5	6
	West	4	5	6
Technology	East	7	8	9
	South	7	8	9
	West	7	8	9

Figure 5.36: Example 6

Here, we count the different **Regions** per **Category** and **Ship Mode** combinations at the deepest level.

In the seventh example, configure the partitioning and addressing settings as:

- **Partitioning: Ship Mode**
- **Addressing: Category, Region**
- **At the level: Deepest**
- **Restarting every: None**

This will produce the following visualization:

Ship Mode

Category	Region	First Class	Second Class	Standard Class
Furniture	East	1	1	1
	South	2	2	2
	West	3	3	3
Office Supplies	East	4	4	4
	South	5	5	5
	West	6	6	6
Technology	East	7	7	7
	South	8	8	8
	West	9	9	9

Figure 5.37: Example 7

Here we count the different **Ship Modes** per **Category** and **Region** combinations at the deepest level.

In the eighth example, configure the partitioning and addressing settings as:

- **Partitioning: Ship Mode**
- **Addressing: Region, Category**
- **At the level: Deepest**
- **Restarting every: None**

This will produce the following visualization:

Ship Mode

Category	Region	First Class	Second Class	Standard Class
Furniture	East	1	1	1
	South	4	4	4
	West	7	7	7
Office Supplies	East	2	2	2
	South	5	5	5
	West	8	8	8
Technology	East	3	3	3
	South	6	6	6
	West	9	9	9

Figure 5.38: Example 8

Here we count the different **Ship Modes** per **Region** and **Category** combinations at the deepest level.

In the ninth example, configure the partitioning and addressing settings as:

- **Partitioning: -**
- **Addressing: Category, Ship Mode, Region**
- **At the level: Deepest**
- **Restarting every: None**

This will produce the following visualization:

		Ship Mode		
Category	**Region**	**First Class**	**Second Class**	**Standard Class**
Furniture	East	1	4	7
	South	2	5	8
	West	3	6	9
Office Supplies	East	10	13	16
	South	11	14	17
	West	12	15	18
Technology	East	19	22	25
	South	20	23	26
	West	21	24	27

Figure 5.39: Example 9

Here we count the **Category**, **Ship Mode**, and **Region** combinations at the deepest level.

In the tenth example, configure the partitioning and addressing settings as:

- **Partitioning: -**
- **Addressing: Ship Mode, Category, Region**
- **At the level: Deepest**
- **Restarting every: None**

This will produce the following visualization:

Ship Mode

Category	Region	First Class	Second Class	Standard Class
Furniture	East	1	10	19
	South	2	11	20
	West	3	12	21
Office Supplies	East	4	13	22
	South	5	14	23
	West	6	15	24
Technology	East	7	16	25
	South	8	17	26
	West	9	18	27

Figure 5.40: Example 10

Here we count the **Ship Mode, Category,** and **Region** combinations at the deepest level.

In the eleventh example, configure the partitioning and addressing settings as:

- **Partitioning: -**
- **Addressing: Ship Mode, Category, Region**
- **At the level: Category**
- **Restarting every: None**

This will produce the following visualization:

Ship Mode

Category	Region	First Class	Second Class	Standard Class
Furniture	East	1	4	7
	South	1	4	7
	West	1	4	7
Office Supplies	East	2	5	8
	South	2	5	8
	West	2	5	8
Technology	East	3	6	9
	South	3	6	9
	West	3	6	9

Figure 5.41: Example 11

Here we count the **Ship Mode, Category,** and **Region** combinations at the **Category** level.

In the twelfth example, configure the partitioning and addressing settings as:

- **Partitioning:** -
- **Addressing: Ship Mode, Region, Category**
- **At the level: Deepest**
- **Restarting every: None**

This will produce the following visualization:

		Ship Mode		
Category	**Region**	**First Class**	**Second Class**	**Standard Class**
Furniture	East	1	10	19
	South	4	13	22
	West	7	16	25
Office Supplies	East	2	11	20
	South	5	14	23
	West	8	17	26
Technology	East	3	12	21
	South	6	15	24
	West	9	18	27

Figure 5.42: Example 12

Here we count the **Ship Mode, Region,** and **Category** combinations at the deepest level.

In the thirteenth example, configure the partitioning and addressing settings as:

- **Partitioning:** -
- **Addressing: Ship Mode, Region, Category**
- **At the level: Deepest**
- **Restarting every: Ship Mode**

This will produce the following visualization:

Ship Mode

Category	Region	First Class	Second Class	Standard Class
Furniture	East	1	1	1
	South	4	4	4
	West	7	7	7
Office Supplies	East	2	2	2
	South	5	5	5
	West	8	8	8
Technology	East	3	3	3
	South	6	6	6
	West	9	9	9

Figure 5.43: Example 13

Here we count the **Ship Mode**, **Region**, and **Category** combinations at the deepest level.

In the fourteenth example, configure the partitioning and addressing settings as:

- **Partitioning:** -
- **Addressing: Region, Ship Mode, Category**
- **At the level: Deepest**
- **Restarting every: None**

This will produce the following visualization:

Ship Mode

Category	Region	First Class	Second Class	Standard Class
Furniture	East	1	4	7
	South	10	13	16
	West	19	22	25
Office Supplies	East	2	5	8
	South	11	14	17
	West	20	23	26
Technology	East	3	6	9
	South	12	15	18
	West	21	24	27

Figure 5.44: Example 14

We will not address the various instances of these possibilities. Instead, the reader is encouraged to recreate these 14 possibilities in Tableau to solidify their understanding of partitioning and addressing. Even better, consider recreating all 57 possible iterations and working to understand how Tableau produces each result. The process may be tedious, but the resulting understanding is invaluable, allowing the user to understand the things that Tableau is doing in the background when computing.

Guidelines: a reminder

Throughout this chapter, I laid out a series of partitioning and addressing guidelines. Here they are again as a quick reminder:

- Do not use the out-of-the-box partitioning and addressing settings provided by Tableau, including **Table** (across) and **Pane** (down). Force yourself to click **Specific Dimensions** and manually define the partitioning and addressing so that you clearly understand how every table calculation is applied.

- Place all needed dimensions on the desired shelves *before* setting partitioning and addressing for table calculations.

- It is not necessary to choose the bottom dimension in the **At the level** drop-down menu. It is always identical to **Deepest**.

- When addressing multiple dimensions for a table calculation, the order of addressing will usually reflect the order of dimensions on the **Rows** and/or **Columns** shelves.

Summary

In this chapter, we explored the inner workings of table calculations. We began by considering what the partition and direction of a table calculation are. In the thereafter following sections, we distinguished directional and non-directional addressing of table calculations, which eventually lead us to the **Edit Table Calculation** interface, and we identified it as the place to change partition and addressing (also called the scope and direction). As we explored, we surveyed each unique group of table calculation functions except for the Script_ and Model_ functions, which will be covered in more detail in *Chapter 15*, *Integrating Programming Languages*. We learned how to apply these functions to a view through partitioning and addressing, where partitioning can be seen as the scope and addressing as the direction of the calculation.

We have seen examples where we compared measures over different time periods, like weekly profit numbers, or comparing a part to the whole. We continued by considering standard deviation bands for stock price alerts, as well as the **Rank** function to produce a bump chart.

Using the knowledge of partitioning and addressing we gained in this chapter, in the next chapter, we will go on to explore data densification and big data.

Learn more on Discord

To join the Discord community for this book – where you can share feedback, ask questions to the author, and learn about new releases – follow the QR code below:

https://packt.link/tableau

6

Utilizing OData, Data Densification, Big Data, and Google BigQuery

Many questions that Tableau newbies have are not related to data preparation, joins, unions, data blending, or data structures, but rather, some of the following:

- How can I remove null dates from the view?
- Why does a table calculation display numbers that don't exist in the underlying data?
- How does Tableau work with big data?
- Will Tableau still perform well if I query millions of rows?

This chapter will answer all of the above. As always, the Tableau help pages provide an excellent resource too. Some useful links to explore these topics further are:

- Data densification: `https://help.tableau.com/current/pro/desktop/en-us/predictions_generated_marks.htm`
- Big data: `https://www.tableau.com/solutions/big-data`

In this chapter, we will discuss the following topics:

- Using the OData connector
- Data densification
- Domain completion
- Domain padding
- Big data
- Google BigQuery

We will start this chapter by introducing the OData connector. The city of Chicago makes data publicly available, just like other cities, countries, or public bodies. Check it out; you will be surprised how much data you can find online. In our case, we are extra lucky because the city of Chicago uses OData, which makes it even easier to analyze because Tableau has a direct connector to OData. Let's get started.

Using the OData connector

The exercises in this chapter can be followed by downloading the workbook associated with this chapter at `https://public.tableau.com/profile/marleen.meier`. The following steps explain how datasets from the web can be loaded directly into Tableau by using an OData endpoint – in this case, provided by the city of Chicago:

1. Navigate to `https://data.cityofchicago.org/Public-Safety/Crimes-2001-to-Present/` `ijzp-q8t2` and select the **More** icon (indicated by an ellipsis, **…**), followed by the **Access Data via OData** button:

Figure 6.1: Chicago Data Portal

2. Copy the **OData Endpoint** URL and open Tableau Desktop:

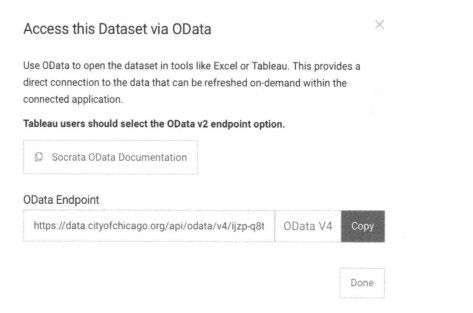

Figure 6.2: OData

3. In the **Data Source** pane, search for OData, and select the **OData** option:

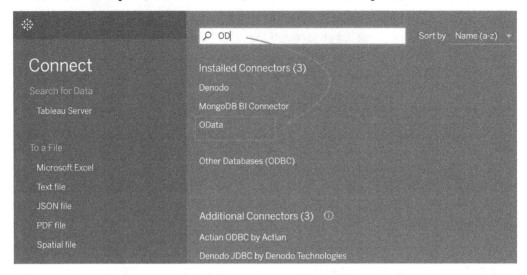

Figure 6.3: OData connector

4. In the **Server** field, copy in the **OData** endpoint from the Chicago Crime website. Authentication is not necessary, so select **Sign In** to get started:

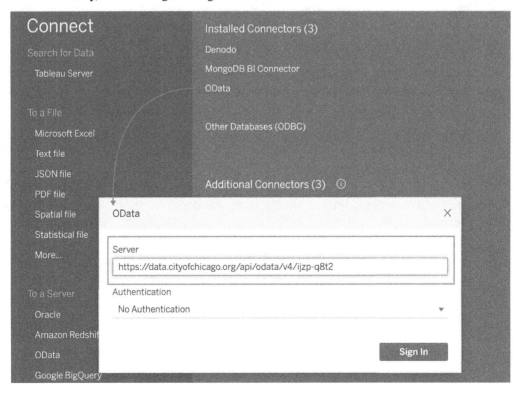

Figure 6.4: Server name

5. Start building your dashboard!

Now that we have the data connection all set up, we can continue with our first real exercise about data densification. Knowing about data densification will help you to troubleshoot if you see unexpected data output in your dashboard and will help you set up your visualization the right way to achieve your goals without having to troubleshoot at all.

Introducing data densification

Data densification is a largely undocumented aspect of Tableau that can be useful in many circumstances but can also be confusing when encountered unexpectedly. This section will provide information about data densification with the intent of dispelling confusion and providing the Tableau author with sufficient knowledge to use this feature to their advantage. Data densification, in its simplest form, is the addition of datapoints to a view that doesn't exist in the underlying dataset. This topic can be a bit confusing at first.

 If you would like to read more about it, please check the following article: `https://towardsdatascience.com/data-densification-in-tableau-93c0a6bfcc5f`

To begin understanding data densification, four terms should be defined: data densification, sparse data, domain completion, and domain padding. In addition to the definitions, each term will be discussed in detail by using examples to help improve understanding:

- **Data densification:** Displays datapoints for which there are no corresponding underlying data (by using, for example, domain completion or domain padding)
- **Sparse data:** A dataset that is missing multiple datapoints (think Swiss cheese)
- **Domain completion:** Making sparse data dense – domain completion is a data densification method that uses table calculations to fill the missing gaps, available in Tableau when two or more dimensions are in the view
- **Domain padding:** Adding datapoints to a sparse dataset – domain padding is a data densification method, available through the **Show Missing Values** feature in range piles (e.g., date and bin dimensions)

The definitions should be clear now; let's continue with hands-on exercises.

Domain completion

There are two types of data densification: domain completion and domain padding. **Domain completion** is the more complex of the two and can be deployed cleverly to solve sparse data issues, but may also appear unexpectedly and prove a challenge to address.

Grasping domain completion requires a good understanding of **dimensions** and **measures** – discrete and continuous –and **partitioning** and **addressing** within table calculations. If you need a refresher on those topics, please review *Chapter 1, Reviewing the Basics* (for **dimensions** and **measures**), and *Chapter 5, Introducing Table Calculations* (for **partitioning** and **addressing**) before you continue to the next exercise.

Now, let's consider how domain completion can be deployed, when it's helpful, and when it can be a problem.

Deploying domain completion

Domain completion can be activated in numerous and sometimes surprising and confusing ways. Adjusting the arrangement of pills on shelves, toggling dimensions between discrete and continuous, switching view types on the **Marks** card, adjusting partitioning, addressing, and other changes can impact domain completion activation. Although examples for every activation possibility will not be covered in this book, a review of typical domain completion scenarios should prove helpful.

Activating domain completion in a crosstab

The following steps will guide you through an example of domain completion.

Navigate to `https://public.tableau.com/profile/marleen.meier` to locate and download the workbook associated with this chapter or use the OData endpoint as described in the section *Using the OData connector*:

1. Navigate to the worksheet entitled `DC - Crosstab` in the starter workbook. Please note that this worksheet is not present in the solutions workbook. Due to the unique user OData connection, it is not possible to save this page with my credentials.
2. Ensure that **Analysis | Table Layout | Show Empty Rows** and **Show Empty Columns** are both *deselected*.
3. In the `Chicago Crime` dataset, create a calculated field named **Index** with the code `INDEX()`.
4. Add a **Location Description** filter to view only a few locations – for example, all the ones beginning with `AIRPORT`. Then place **Location Description** on the **Rows** shelf.

5. Place **Date** on the **Columns** shelf. Leave it at the **YEAR** aggregation and change it to a discrete value. Note that, as shown in the following screenshot, the view is sparsely populated:

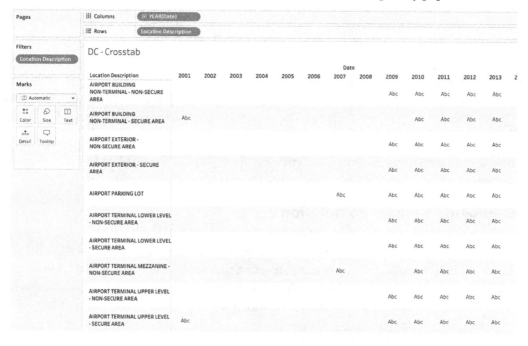

DC - Crosstab

Location Description	2001	2002	2003	2004	2005	2006	2007	2008	2009	2010	2011	2012	2013	2
AIRPORT BUILDING NON-TERMINAL - NON-SECURE AREA									Abc	Abc	Abc	Abc	Abc	
AIRPORT BUILDING NON-TERMINAL - SECURE AREA	Abc									Abc	Abc	Abc	Abc	
AIRPORT EXTERIOR - NON-SECURE AREA									Abc	Abc	Abc	Abc	Abc	
AIRPORT EXTERIOR - SECURE AREA									Abc	Abc	Abc	Abc	Abc	
AIRPORT PARKING LOT							Abc		Abc	Abc	Abc	Abc	Abc	
AIRPORT TERMINAL LOWER LEVEL - NON-SECURE AREA									Abc	Abc	Abc	Abc	Abc	
AIRPORT TERMINAL LOWER LEVEL - SECURE AREA									Abc	Abc	Abc	Abc	Abc	
AIRPORT TERMINAL MEZZANINE - NON-SECURE AREA							Abc			Abc	Abc	Abc	Abc	
AIRPORT TERMINAL UPPER LEVEL - NON-SECURE AREA									Abc	Abc	Abc	Abc	Abc	
AIRPORT TERMINAL UPPER LEVEL - SECURE AREA	Abc								Abc	Abc	Abc	Abc	Abc	

Figure 6.5: Crosstab

6. Place **Index** on the **Detail** shelf on the **Marks** card. Note that in the following screenshot, the view now reflects domain completion – that is, the view is fully populated:

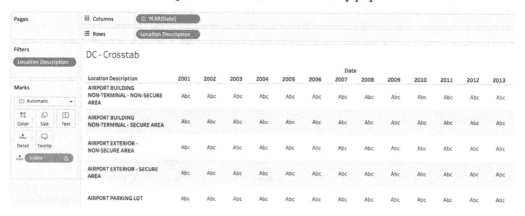

DC - Crosstab

Location Description	2001	2002	2003	2004	2005	2006	2007	2008	2009	2010	2011	2012	2013
AIRPORT BUILDING NON-TERMINAL - NON-SECURE AREA	Abc	Abc	Abc	Abc	Abc	Abc	Abc	Abc	Abc	Abc	Abc	Abc	Abc
AIRPORT BUILDING NON-TERMINAL - SECURE AREA	Abc	Abc	Abc	Abc	Abc	Abc	Abc	Abc	Abc	Abc	Abc	Abc	Abc
AIRPORT EXTERIOR - NON-SECURE AREA	Abc	Abc	Abc	Abc	Abc	Abc	Abc	Abc	Abc	Abc	Abc	Abc	Abc
AIRPORT EXTERIOR - SECURE AREA	Abc	Abc	Abc	Abc	Abc	Abc	Abc	Abc	Abc	Abc	Abc	Abc	Abc
AIRPORT PARKING LOT	Abc	Abc	Abc	Abc	Abc	Abc	Abc	Abc	Abc	Abc	Abc	Abc	Abc

Figure 6.6: Crosstab II

7. Right-click on **YEAR(Date)** and select **Continuous**. Note that data densification is deactivated:

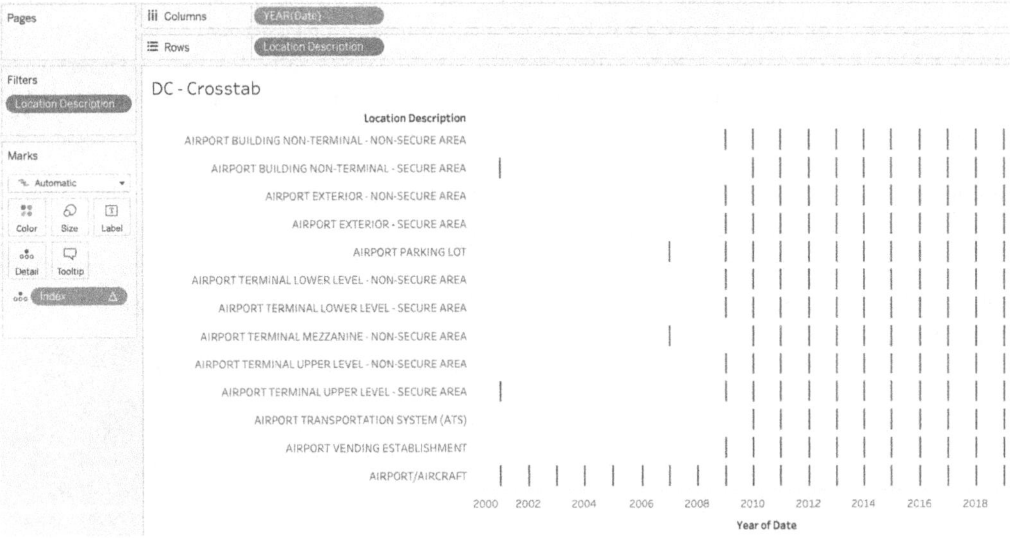

Figure 6.7: Crosstab III

8. Reset **YEAR(Date)** to **Discrete** and then right-click on **Index** and select **Edit Table Calculation**.

9. In the resulting dialog box, select **Specific Dimensions** and then observe the results for each of the following selections:

Select Specific Dimension	Data Densification Activated/Deactivated
Location Description	Activated
Year of Date	Activated
Location Description and Year of Date	Deactivated
No selection	Deactivated

The preceding exercise illustrates the following rule for deploying domain completion:

Given a crosstab with discrete dimensions on the **Rows** *and* **Columns** *shelves, utilizing a table calculation (in this case, the* **Index** *field) in which at least one dimension (but not all dimensions) is addressed activates domain completion.*

A key term in the preceding rule may have been confusing: addressed. Partitioning and addressing were covered in *Chapter 5, Introducing Table Calculations,* but will be defined again here to ensure understanding of this rule. Consider the following from the Tableau documentation (https://help.tableau.com/current/pro/desktop/en-us/calculations_tablecalculations.htm):

The dimensions that define how to group the calculation, that is, that define the scope of the data it is performed on, are called **partitioning fields**. The table calculation is performed separately within each partition. The remaining dimensions, upon which the table calculation is performed, are called **addressing fields**, and determine the direction of the calculation.

When editing a table calculation, you can choose to select/deselect specific dimensions. When a dimension is selected, that dimension is used to address the table calculation. When a dimension is not selected, the dimension is used to partition the table calculation. The following screenshot of a **Table Calculation** editing dialog box demonstrates addressing on **Location Description** and partitioning on **Year of Date**:

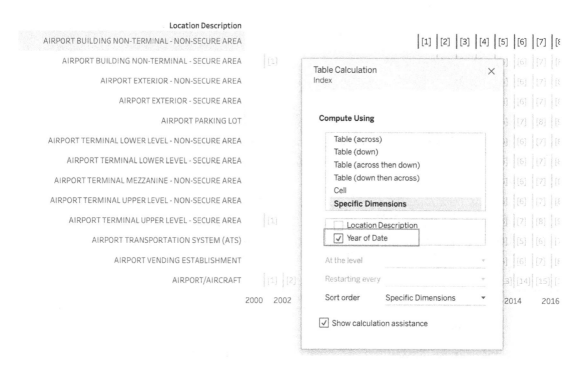

Figure 6.8: Table Calculation

We will now look at the remaining steps involved in activating domain completion in a crosstab:

1. Duplicate the worksheet from the previous exercise, `DC - Crosstab`. Name the new worksheet `DC - Crosstab II`.

2. Right-click on **Index** and select **Compute Using | Cell**. Note that the view is sparsely populated.

3. Select **Analysis | Table Layout | Show Empty Columns**. The view is now fully populated:

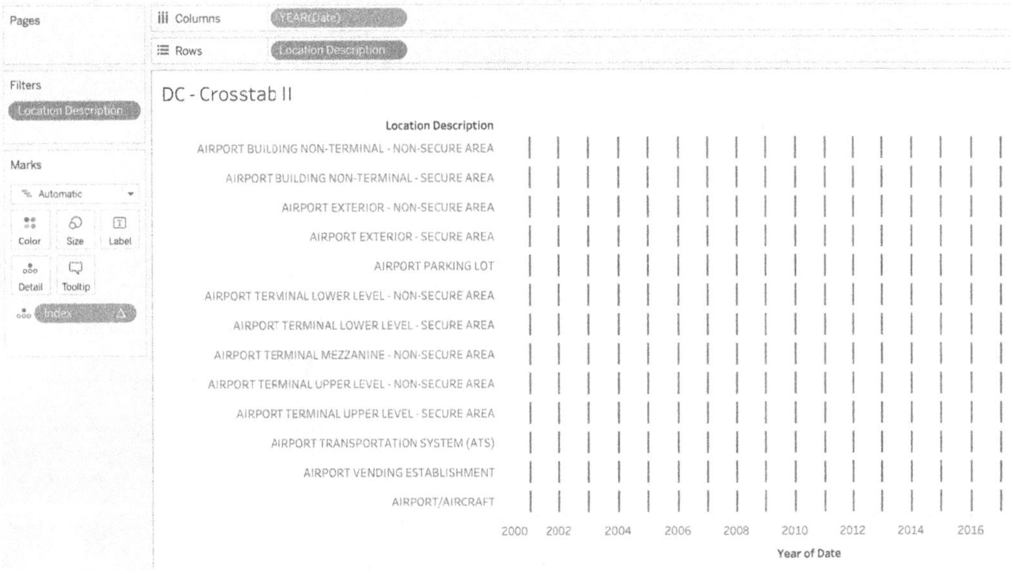

Figure 6.9: Crosstab

This exercise illustrates the following rules for deploying domain completion:

- Given a view with discrete dimensions (blue) on the **Rows** and **Columns** shelves, selecting **Compute Using | Cell** deactivates domain completion.
- Given a view with discrete dimensions (blue) on the **Rows** and **Columns** shelves, selecting **Analysis | Table Layout | Show Empty Rows/Columns** activates domain completion.

Setting **Compute Using** to **Cell** may raise a question: what about the other **Compute Using** options, such as **Table (across)** and **Table (down)**? These options are all variations of partitioning and addressing.

Activating domain completion through view types

We will now investigate activating domain completion through view types:

1. Duplicate the worksheet from the previous exercise, DC - Crosstab II. Name the new worksheet DC - View Types.
2. Remove **Index** from the **Marks** view card and deselect **Analysis | Table Layout | Show Empty Columns**. The view is now sparsely populated.

3. Change the **Marks** type from **Automatic** to **Line**. The view is now fully populated with more marks:

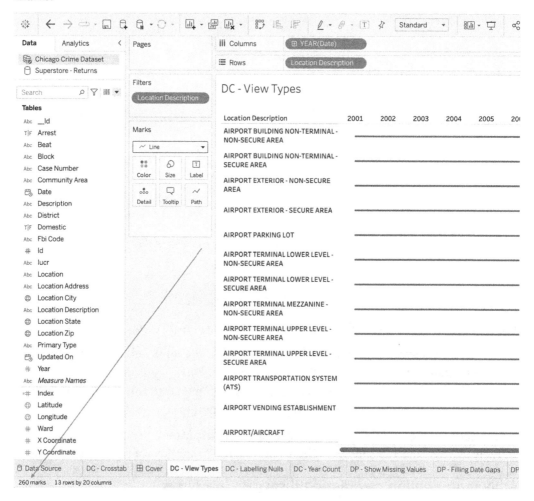

Figure 6.10: View types

4. Choose each view type option on the **Marks** card and observe which view types activate domain completion and which do not.

The preceding exercise illustrates the following rule for deploying data completion:

> Given a view with discrete dimensions on the **Rows** and **Columns** shelves, selecting the **Line, Area,** and **Polygon** view types from the **Marks** view card activates domain completion.

The usefulness of domain completion

Domain completion can be useful in many circumstances – for example, instead of filling in missing values manually, whenever you want to use a parameter, or when performing explanatory analysis. In fact, you may have gleaned some uses from the previous exercises even though they were designed merely for illustration purposes. The following exercise demonstrates using domain completion to display no data for cells without a value in a sparsely populated view.

Labeling nulls

Let us look at the following steps to begin the exercise:

1. Duplicate the worksheet from the previous exercise, `DC - View Types`. Name the new worksheet `DC - Labeling Nulls`.

2. Adjust the duplicated worksheet so that the view type is set to **Text**. Also, ensure that only **Location Description** and **Year** are deployed on the view. Be sure to leave **Location Description** on the **Filters** shelf so that a few locations are displayed.

3. Create a calculated field named **No Data** with the following code:

    ```
    IF ISNULL(COUNT([Case Number])) THEN 'No Data' ELSE 'Data' END
    ```

4. Place **Ward** and **No Data** on the **Text** shelf. Note that the text `No Data` does not display:

Figure 6.11: Labeling nulls

5. Place **Index** on the **Detail** shelf. Note that the text **No Data** does display. The domain completion portion of the exercise is now complete but consider making the visualization more appealing by utilizing a shape:

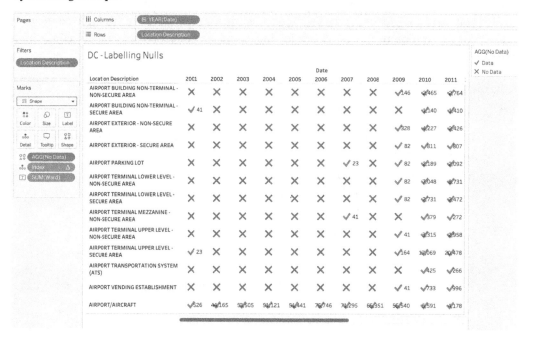

Figure 6.12: Labeling nulls, with additional formatting

I hope this exercise has given you a practical example of how domain completion works. Quite literally, you can think of domain completion as auto-filling the URL you start typing into your browser search bar. But what if you want to get rid of it altogether? We'll discuss this in the next section.

Removing unwanted domain completion

After being made aware of domain completion, a user will no longer be confused when unwanted marks are displayed in the view. But knowing how to remove those unwanted marks from the display can be a challenge. The following exercise shows a scenario of undesired domain completion and how to address the problem. The goal of the exercise is to display each year that a given crime has been reported with an accompanying filter to adjust the crimes that display based on the number of years that data is available:

1. In the workbook associated with this chapter, navigate to the DC – Year Count worksheet.
2. Select the Chicago Crime dataset in the **Data** pane.
3. Place **Description** on the **Filter** shelf and select **AGG PO HANDS NO/MIN INJURY**.

4. Place **Description** and **Date** on the **Rows** shelf, make **YEAR(Date)** discrete, and put **Ward** on the **Text** shelf. Format as desired. Note the missing value for **2001**, as shown in the following screenshot:

Figure 6.13: Year Count

This is not an instance of data densification since the dataset has a row for **2001**, despite the value for **Ward** being empty in that year. Therefore, **2001** has a null value.

5. To remove the fields containing null values, click on the drop-down menu associated with **SUM(Ward)** and select **Filter**. In the resulting dialog box, select **Special | Non-null values**:

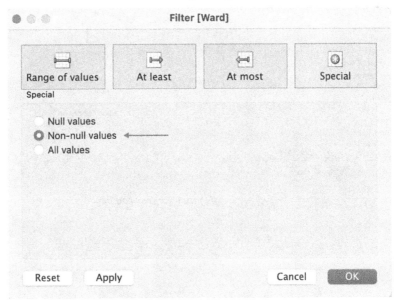

Figure 6.14: Filtering non-null values

6. Create a table calculation named Year Count with the following code:

    ```
    SIZE()
    ```

7. If you put the **Description** pill on the **Filters** shelf in *step 3*, please remove it for the following steps.

8. Place a discrete instance of **Year Count** on the **Columns** shelf. Note that the resulting number, **6411** (note, you may see a different number as the dataset is constantly updated), represents every column in the view:

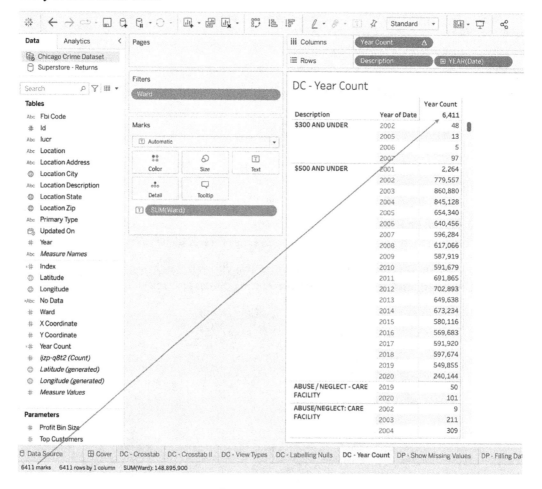

Figure 6.15: Year count

9. Right-click on **Year Count** and select **Compute Using | Date**. It appears as if the scenario discussed in *step 4* has returned. However, although the issue looks the same in the view, the underlying problem differs. **Year Count** is a table calculation and has caused domain completion. So, this time, we see one row for each year in the whole dataset, even though, for example, the combination of **$300 AND UNDER** and **2001** does not exist in the dataset. We see every year because of the table calculation **Year Count**:

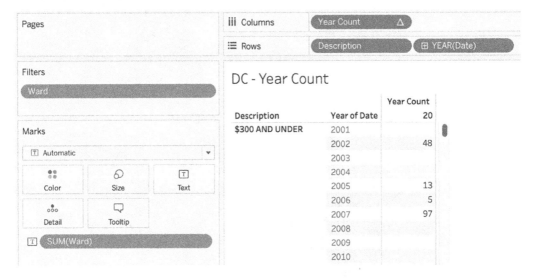

Figure 6.16: Year count domain completion

10. Right-click on **Year Count** and select **Edit Table Calculation.**

11. In the resulting dialog box, select **Specific Dimensions**. Make sure that **Description** and **Year of Date** are both checked and, by dragging and dropping, placed in the order shown in *Figure 6.17*. Leave **At the level** at **Deepest** and set **Restarting every** to **Description**. **Sort order** can remain as **Specific Dimensions,** and if you check the **Show calculation assistance** box, you will see yellow highlighters in the visualization, indicating the datapoints related to the selection:

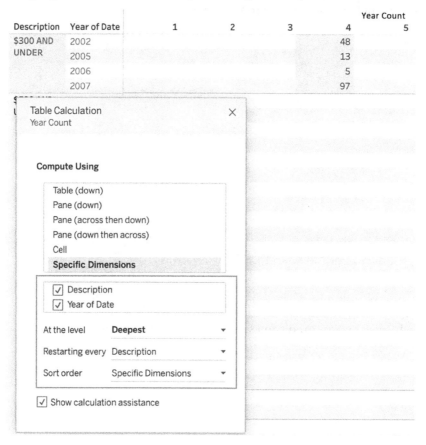

Description	Year of Date	1	2	3	Year Count 4	5
$300 AND UNDER	2002				48	
	2005				13	
	2006				5	
	2007				97	

Figure 6.17: Specific Dimensions

12. If you have more than one value for **Year Count**, complete the exercise by moving **Year Count** from the **Columns** shelf to the **Filters** shelf. Format as desired (this allows you to filter on dimensions with the same number of rows in the partition):

Figure 6.18: Completing the Year Count worksheet

The relevant section in the preceding rule for this exercise is "a table calculation in which at least one dimension is addressed (but not all dimensions) activates domain completion." The domain completion occurred when first deploying **Year Count**, which is a table calculation. Upon changing the addressing and partitioning of **Year Count** so that all dimensions were addressed (that is, no dimensions were partitioned), the issue was resolved.

Congratulations, you can cross domain completion off your "to learn" list. As mentioned in the introduction to this chapter, next in line is domain padding. You will want to know how to use domain padding because it helps you when working with dates and bins.

Domain padding

The second type of data densification is known as **domain padding**. We will now consider how domain padding is deployed and when it's useful.

Deploying domain padding

You may recall that one of the ways to deploy domain completion is **Analysis | Table Layout | Show Empty Rows/Columns**. The same is true of domain padding, as illustrated in the following exercise. This exercise demonstrates how to toggle domain padding on and off:

1. In the workbook associated with this chapter, select **Data | New Data Source** and connect to the `Sample Superstore` Excel workbook that ships with Tableau. It is located in **My Tableau Repository | Datasources+**.

2. In the resulting instance of the **Data Source** page, double-click on **Orders and Returns**. This will cause a relationship to be created on the field **Order ID**.

3. Name the data source `Superstore - Returns`.

4. Navigate to the worksheet entitled `DP - Show Missing Values` and select the **Superstore - Returns** data source that was just created.

5. Place **Ship Mode** and **State** on the **Rows** shelf. Next, place **Region** on the **Filters** shelf and select **West**. Lastly, put **SUM(Sales)** on the **Text** shelf. Note that, for example, **Wyoming** only appears for **Standard Class** shipping mode:

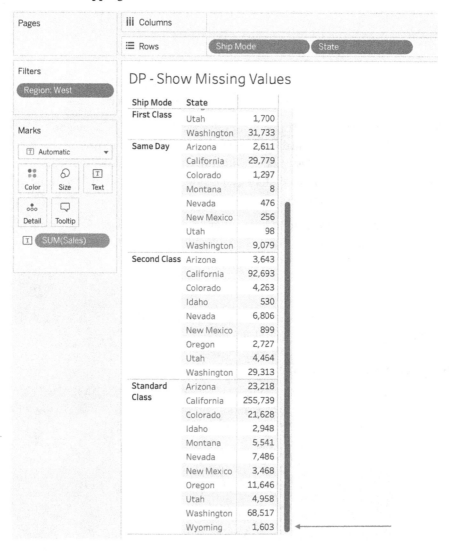

Figure 6.19: Show Missing Values

6. Select **Analysis | Table Layout | Show Empty Rows**:

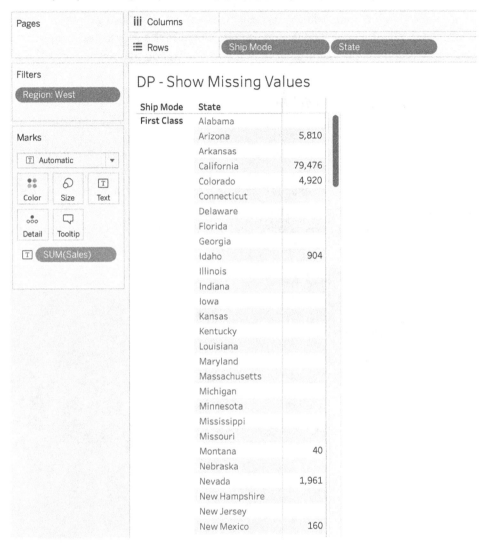

Figure 6.20: Show Missing Values II

And you can see domain padding in action. All states that have a value in some year or some region are showing now, even the ones that were filtered by **Region: West**. Now, the filter simply removes the **Sales** amount but does show all possible states.

It was necessary to point to a live data source, such as the instance of **Superstore** that ships with Tableau, because using an extract would not, in this case, activate domain padding, even if **Analysis | Table Layout | Show Empty Rows** was selected. The functionality gets lost as soon as you activate an extract.

The usefulness of domain padding

Domain padding is often useful when working with dates with gaps. Such gaps occur when some dates have associated values and some dates do not. As shown in the following example, returns do not occur every day in the Superstore dataset. Since a visualization that displays dates with gaps could be confusing, it might be helpful to fill in those gaps.

Using domain padding to fill in date gaps

We will now try to fill in the date gaps:

1. In the workbook associated with this chapter, navigate to the worksheet entitled DP - Filling Date Gaps.

2. Select the Superstore - Returns data source that was created in the previous exercise.

3. Place a discrete instance of **MDY(Order Date)** on the **Columns** shelf and place **Sales** on the **Rows** shelf. Note that every mark in the view is equally spaced, regardless of the length of time between dates:

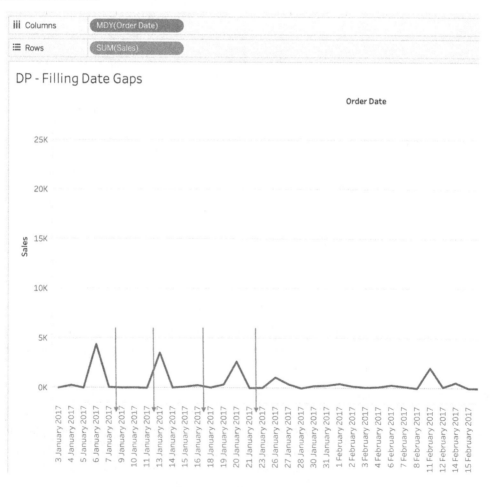

Figure 6.21: Filling Date Gaps

4. Right-click on **MDY(Order Date)** and select **Show Missing Values**.

5. Right-click on **SUM(Sales)** on the **Rows** shelf and select **Format**. In the resulting **Format** window, choose the **Pane** tab and select **Marks: Show at Default Value**:

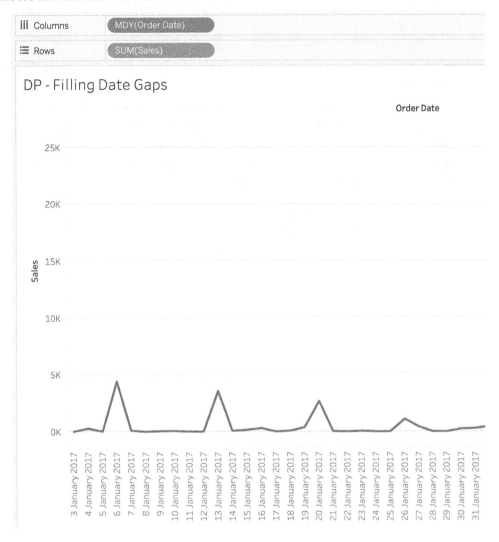

Figure 6.22: Filling Date Gaps II

Note that the distance between marks is now based on the length of time between dates. All dates with no value are displayed with **Sales** values of zero.

Problems of domain padding

Since domain padding can be toggled on or off through specific commands in Tableau (that is, **Show Missing Values** and **Show Empty Rows/Columns**), it's typically not a problem. There are a few scenarios, however, when domain padding may cause confusion, one of which is covered in the following example.

From a domain-padded visualization to a crosstab

Let's have a look at creating a crosstab from a domain-padded visualization:

1. In the workbook associated with this chapter, navigate to the worksheet entitled DP - From Viz to Crosstab.
2. Select the Superstore - Returns data source.
3. Right-click on **Discount** in the data pane and select **Create | Bins**. In the resulting dialog box, choose a bin size of **0.05**.
4. Place the newly created **Discount (bin)** dimension on the **Columns** shelf.
5. Right-click on **Discount (bin)** and ensure that **Show Missing Values** is selected.
6. Right-click and drag the **Discount** field from the **Data** pane to the **Rows** shelf. Select **CNT** as the measure. Note that some of the bins have no values. For example, as shown in the following screenshot, the **0.35** bin has no associated value:

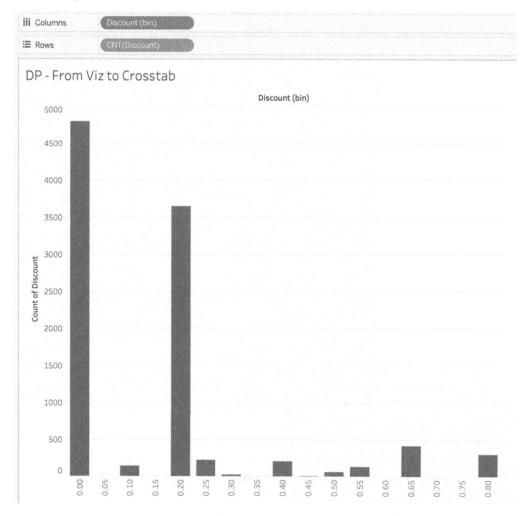

Figure 6.23: From Viz to Crosstab

7. Duplicate the sheet as a crosstab by right-clicking on the worksheet tab and selecting **Duplicate as Crosstab**. Note that **Show Missing Values** is still activated:

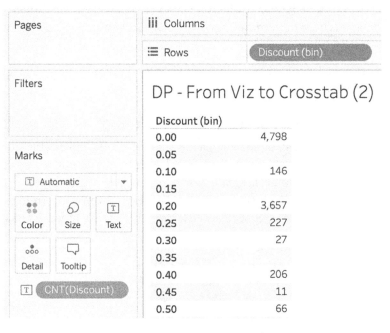

Figure 6.24: From Viz to Crosstab II

8. Complete the exercise by right-clicking on **Discount (bin)** and deselecting **Show Missing Values**:

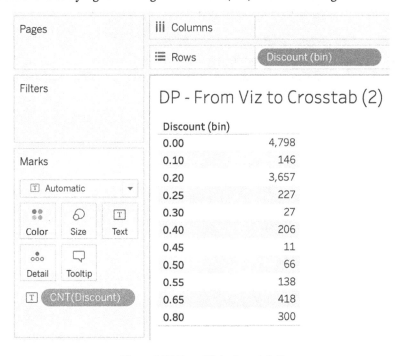

Figure 6.25: From Viz to Crosstab III

Utilizing **Show Missing Values** for bins or dates is often helpful in a visualization but may not be helpful in a crosstab view. This is especially true if there are many rows or columns without values. It would make it harder for a human to digest the amount of data and, since often associated with not being important, it is most of the time better to exclude missing values in crosstabs – simply to keep a better overview.

A special case of data densification will appear when working with predictive modeling. That's why we will discuss this next.

Data densification in predictive modeling

Besides trendlines and forecasts (accessible via the **Analytics** pane), Tableau Desktop currently supports three types of predictive modeling as built-in functions. More can be added by using, for example, a Python integration (see *Chapter 15, Integrating Programming Languages*). Linear regression, regularized linear regression, and Gaussian process regression are the ones you can currently choose from. Those can be called by using the Model_Quantile and Model_Percentile functions in a calculated field.

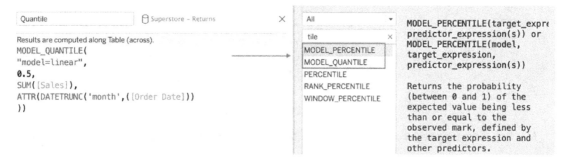

Figure 6.26: Built-in prediction functions

Given the DP - Show Missing Values Prediction worksheet in the **solutions** dashboard accompanying this chapter, you can see the Superstore Count(Orders) given each day in October 2020 and the respective daily 50% quantile.

For more information on built-in predictive analytics and `Model_Quantile`, please check `https://help.tableau.com/current/pro/desktop/en-us/predictions_overview.htm`.

Some days don't show data:

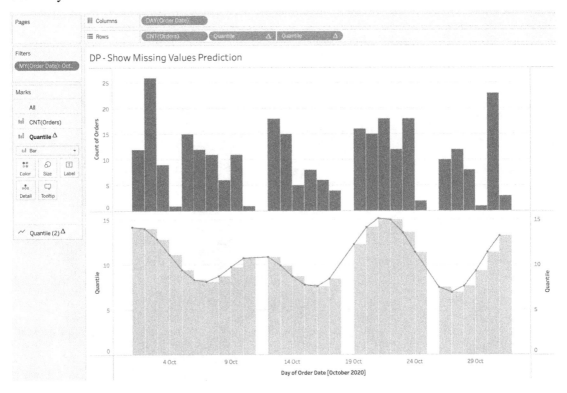

Figure 6.27: Missing values

But we can enable data densification to complete the view.

Turn on **Show Missing Values** by right-clicking on **DAY(Order Date)** on the **Columns** shelf.

Select **Analysis** | **Infer Properties from Missing Values** and see the completed prediction:

Figure 6.28: Data densification

I hope data densification has become a bit clearer now. It is a powerful feature and should be discussed more often. Spread the word! Data densification will enhance your visualizations (see *Figure 6.28*), interpolate datapoints for you, and can even be used in calculations – a non-existing number will suddenly be there – how cool! Our journey, however, will continue, and the topic we will discuss next is working with big data.

Tableau and big data

Perhaps the first challenge of big data is defining it adequately. It's a term so widely used as to be almost meaningless. For example, some may refer to data exceeding 1,048,576 rows as big data (which is the row limit in Microsoft 365, Excel 2019, Excel 2016, Excel 2013, Excel 2010, and Excel 2007), while others would only apply the term to datasets in the multiple-petabyte range. Definitions found on Wikipedia (https://en.wikipedia.org/wiki/Big_data) are so broad as to encompass both of these examples.

True, it is probably simplistic to consider data that merely exceeds Excel's row limitation as big data; nevertheless, from the perspective of an individual for whom Excel is the traditional data-processing application, the preceding definition fits.

Talking about big data goes hand in hand with parallel processing. For Tableau and working with big data, it is very important to know the partitions that your IT team has put in place for parallel processing. It could be, for example, the **YEAR**, **MONTH**, and **DAY** columns. If you use those columns that are also used as partitions in the database, your Tableau dashboard will perform so much better than trying to query on a random field in the dataset. So, first, put filters in place—preferably partitions. Then, build your dashboard on a subset of the data. Once you are all done, load the data you need and check the performance again. More information regarding performance is given in *Chapter 13, Improving Performance*.

Many organizations opt for a cloud-based solution, such as AWS, Azure, or GCP. Within **Google Cloud Platform (GCP)**, you will find BigQuery, which we will use for the next exercise.

Building a visualization with Google BigQuery

One big data solution is BigQuery from Google, next to many others from providers like Amazon, Alibaba, Azure, IBM, etc. For this section of the book, we have randomly chosen BigQuery, which you can test for free if you have a Gmail account. Other providers offer free tier accounts too. Since we are working with the cloud, you don't have to install anything, which makes Google Cloud a good platform for an exercise in this book.

To build a visualization with Google BigQuery, you will need to first set up access to BigQuery. The following exercise will point you in the right direction. Once you have set up access to BigQuery, you will be able to connect to the BigQuery sample datasets. In the remainder of the exercise, you will build a visualization while connected to BigQuery.

Assuming you have a good internet connection, the performance will likely exceed what you experience when working with a local copy of an extracted data source of a similar size.

Let's have a look at how we can use Google BigQuery in our Tableau dashboard:

1. Log in to your Google account, navigate to `https://cloud.google.com/bigquery/`, and follow the provided instructions to try **BigQuery** for free.
2. In the workbook associated with this chapter, navigate to the `BigQuery` worksheet.
3. Press *Ctrl + D* to connect to a data source. In the resulting window, select **Google BigQuery** and, when prompted, provide your Gmail login information.
4. On the **Data Source** page, choose any billing project you have set up when registering on GCP. In my case, it's called `BigDataProject`.
5. Then select the `publicdata` project, the `samples` dataset, and the `natality` table. This data is available to everyone and hence you should see it too.

6. The **natality** table provides birth demographics for the United States from 1969 to 2008:

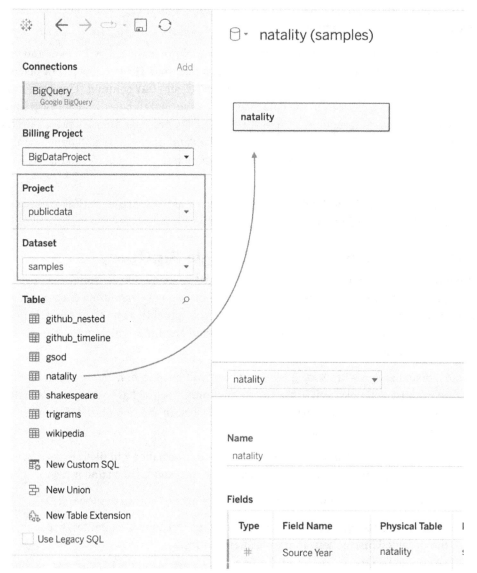

Figure 6.29: BigQuery

7. In the **Data** pane, double-click **natality(Count).**

8. From the **Data** pane, drag **Month** to the **Columns** shelf, and set it to **Discrete.**

9. Right-click on the *y* axis, **Count of natality,** and select **Edit Axis.** Deselect **Include Zero.**

10. Format as desired. This visualization displays the number of infants born in each month from 1969 to 2008:

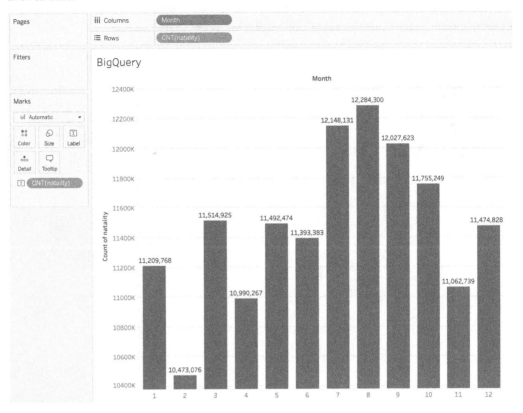

Figure 6.30: BigQuery visualization

Knowing the fields on which the big data engine is partitioned will help a lot when facing performance issues. If, for example, your data is partitioned by **Year**, always try to make use of this field in filters and calculations. *Chapter 13*, *Improving Performance*, contains more information on this topic.

As you can see, BigQuery allows us to visualize datasets containing millions of records quickly and easily.

Summary

We began this chapter with a discussion of data densification and discovered that there are two types of data densification: domain completion and domain padding. When reviewing these two types of data densification, we learned how each can be deployed, when each is useful, and when each can be problematic. Next, we explored big data with a walk-through of an example of how to use Tableau to connect to Google BigQuery.

In the next chapter, we will explore another functionality: level of detail calculations. Although table calculations remain an important part of everyday Tableau usage, we will discover how level of detail calculations can easily accomplish tasks that were previously only possible through complex table calculations.

Learn more on Discord

To join the Discord community for this book – where you can share feedback, ask questions to the author, and learn about new releases – follow the QR code below:

```
https://packt.link/tableau
```

7

Practicing Level of Detail Calculations

When we talk about **Level of Detail (LOD)** calculations in Tableau, we mean three expressions: FIXED, INCLUDE, and EXCLUDE. These three expressions open up a world of options by providing the ability to create calculations that target specific levels of granularity. In older versions of Tableau, data granularity for a worksheet was established by the dimensions in a view. If the view contained dimensions for, for example, **Region**, **State**, and **Postal Code**, but the author wanted to create a **City**-level calculation, the **City** dimension would need to be included on the view. Furthermore, there was no mechanism for excluding or ignoring a given **dimension** on a view. Admittedly, the desired results could normally be obtained through some complex and sometimes convoluted use of table calculations, data blends, and so on. Fortunately, LODs greatly simplify these use case scenarios and, in some cases, enable what was previously impossible.

In this chapter, we will discuss the following topics:

- Introducing LODs
- FIXED and EXCLUDE
- INCLUDE
- Building practical applications with LODs

The early sections of this chapter are more theory-based, but don't worry – you'll get to explore these concepts in a practical way in the *Building practical applications with LODs* section. Let's begin by introducing LODs and how they are used.

Introducing LODs

Tableau's default is to show measures in a view based on the dimensions also present in the view. If you have a dashboard with Sales data and dimensions like State and City, and you drag the State and Sales data onto the view, the Sales data will be divided by State, showing you Sales per State. If you want to divide the Sales data further into smaller chunks, you might add the City field, resulting in Sales data per City, per State. LODs can manipulate this default behavior.

After completing this chapter, you will be able to divide or partition measures by dimensions that are not in the view and show measures using fewer dimensions than are visible in the view.

To do this, we will build and use two **playgrounds**. Delivering reports as required by one's job duties may lead to a thorough knowledge of a limited set of capabilities; that is, a deep but narrow understanding. It can be difficult to set aside time (and justify that time) to explore the capabilities of Tableau that, on the surface, may seem to have no direct correlation to job duties. Playground environments can help overcome any difficulties and objections by providing efficient avenues of exploration. In this chapter, we'll build two playground environments specifically for LODs, to help make the task of deep and broad understanding easier by providing an efficient avenue for exploration and understanding. You can always come back to the workbook accompanying this chapter and test functionality related to LODs.

FIXED and EXCLUDE

The first playground we will build will be for the purpose of exploring two of the three LOD functions: FIXED and EXCLUDE. We will use a set of parameters and associated calculated fields to efficiently explore how these functions work.

Setting up the workbook

Much of the groundwork for this exercise has already been completed in the workbook associated with this chapter. The following steps will simply require you to open different calculations and parameters to see how they have been set up and why this works. Explanations are given along the way. If you do not have ready access to the workbook, you should be able to construct a similar one by referencing the following steps.

To complete the initial setup of a worksheet, take the following steps:

1. Navigate to https://public.tableau.com/profile/marleen.meier to locate and download the workbook associated with this chapter.

2. Open the workbook associated with this chapter and navigate to the Fixed and Exclude worksheet. The worksheet should look as follows:

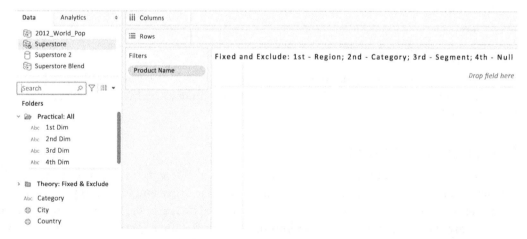

Figure 7.1: The worksheet

1. Select the Superstore data source and inspect the parameter named **1st Dim** by right-clicking and selecting **Edit**:

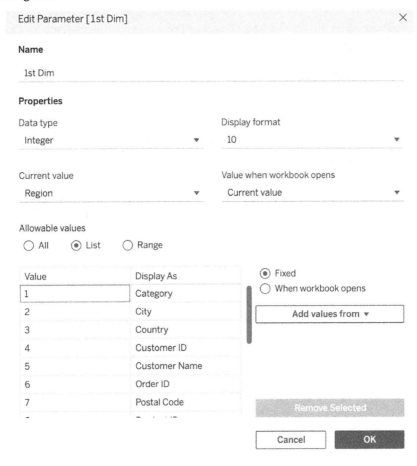

Figure 7.2: Parameter I

The parameters named **2nd Dim**, **3rd Dim**, and **4th Dim** are identical to **1st Dim**.

2. Note that except for **Order Date** and **Ship Date**, every dimension in the dataset is included in the list of values (see *Figure 7.2*). For the purposes of this exercise, **Category**, **Region**, **Segment**, **Ship Mode**, and **Sub-Category** are particularly important because these are dimensions with fewer members. Dimensions with many members are more difficult to use in this context.

3. Inspect the **Choose Fixed Dims, Choose Excluded Dims 1,** and **Choose Excluded Dims 2** parameters included in the workbook and note that we defined several integers under the **Value** column, each of which will later be visible as a string specified under the **Displays As** column in the parameter dropdown. The **Value** and **Display As** configurations for **Choose Fixed Dims** are as follows:

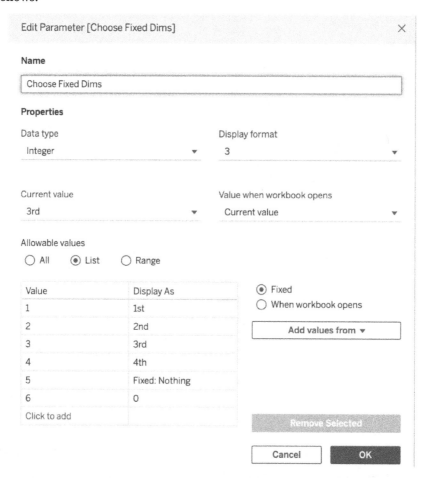

Figure 7.3: Parameter II

4. Inspect the calculated field named **1st Dim** (it is located under the **Practical: All** folder in the **Data** pane); this calculation makes use of the 1st Dim parameter and will cause a field to be displayed depending on the selection of the parameter. If the user selects **Category** in the **1st Dim** parameter, value 1 will be activated (according to the values specified in *Figure 7.2*). Value 1 then translates to the **Category** field in the calculated **1st Dim** field, as shown in the following screenshot:

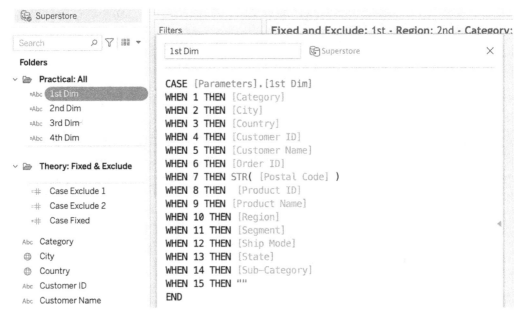

Figure 7.4: Calculated 1st Dim field

5. The calculated fields named **2nd Dim**, **3rd Dim**, and **4th Dim** are identical to **1st Dim** except that each references the parameter bearing its name; for example, the **2nd Dim** calculated field utilizes [Parameters].[2nd Dim].

These Case statements, in conjunction with the associated parameters, will allow you to choose which dimensions to view from a dropdown in the view as described in *step 5*.

6. Inspect the following calculated fields, which enable you to choose which LODs to employ and thus to compare and contrast differences and similarities:

Figure 7.5: Case Fixed

The **Case Fixed** calculation shows that if the user selects 1 in the **Choose Fixed Dims** parameter (which is being displayed as 1st), **1st Dim** will be fixed—no matter what the dashboard setup. That means that **SUM(Sales)** will be partitioned over **1st Dim**, no matter if it is part of the dashboard:

```
Case Exclude 1                          Superstore                          ×

CASE [Choose Excluded Dims 1]
WHEN 1 THEN SUM({EXCLUDE [1st Dim]: SUM([Sales])})
WHEN 2 THEN SUM({EXCLUDE [2nd Dim] : SUM([Sales])})
WHEN 3 THEN SUM({EXCLUDE [3rd Dim] : SUM([Sales])})
WHEN 4 THEN SUM({EXCLUDE [4th Dim]: SUM([Sales])})
WHEN 5 THEN 0
END
```

Figure 7.6: Case Exclude 1

The **Case Exclude 1** calculation shows that if the user selects 1 in the **Choose Excluded Dims 1** parameter (which will be displayed as 1st), **1st Dim** will be excluded from the calculation in the view.

That means that **SUM(Sales)** won't be partitioned over **1st Dim**, even if it is part of the view:

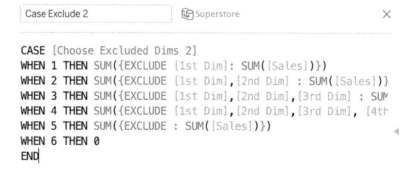

Figure 7.7: Case Exclude 2

The **Case Exclude 2** calculation shows that if the user selects 1 in the **Choose Excluded Dims 2** parameter (which will be displayed as **1st**), **1st Dim** will be excluded from the calculation in the view. That means that **SUM(Sales)** won't be partitioned over **1st Dim**, even if it is part of the view.

7. Now, right-click and open the context filter on **Product Name** for inspection. In the resulting dialog box, click the **Wildcard** tab and note the settings, as shown in the following screenshot. The filter has been set to show only product names that start with S (**Match value** is not case-sensitive.):

Figure 7.8: Wildcard filter

8. After clicking **OK**, right-click on the filter and click **Add to Context**. Note that context filters are denoted in gray:

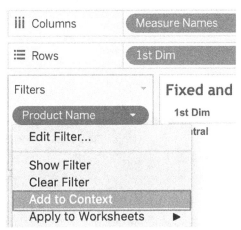

Figure 7.9: Gray context filter

9. Place the following dimensions on the **Rows** shelf: **1st Dim**, **2nd Dim**, **3rd Dim**, and **4th Dim**.

10. Drag **Measure Names** onto the **Filters** shelf and select **Sales**, **Case Fixed**, **Case Exclude 1**, and **Case Exclude 2**.

11. Add **Measure Values** to **Text** and **Measure Names** to **Columns**:

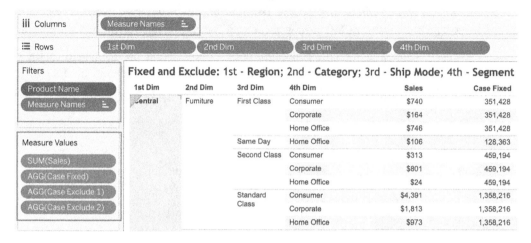

Fixed and Exclude: 1st - **Region**; 2nd - **Category**; 3rd - **Ship Mode**; 4th - **Segment**

1st Dim	2nd Dim	3rd Dim	4th Dim	Sales	Case Fixed
Central	Furniture	First Class	Consumer	$740	351,428
			Corporate	$164	351,428
			Home Office	$746	351,428
		Same Day	Home Office	$106	128,363
		Second Class	Consumer	$313	459,194
			Corporate	$801	459,194
			Home Office	$24	459,194
		Standard Class	Consumer	$4,391	1,358,216
			Corporate	$1,813	1,358,216
			Home Office	$973	1,358,216

Figure 7.10: Measure Values

12. Display every parameter by right-clicking each one and selecting **Show Parameter Control**. Order the parameter controls as follows:

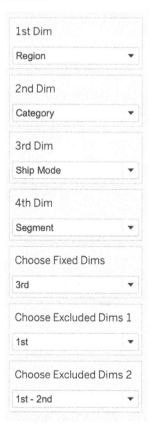

Figure 7.11: Final playground

By following the previous steps, we are now ready to build various tables to compare the different LODs because the parameters will allow us to select different dimensions and the calculated fields that incorporate the FIXED and EXCLUDE functions from Tableau. We will now continue using the playground and explain how LODs change calculated fields.

Understanding FIXED

Now that the playground environment is complete, let's build scenarios to better understand the FIXED and EXCLUDE functions. We'll begin with FIXED. The FIXED LOD considers only the dimensions to which it is directed. Thus, when fixed on a dimension, all other (if any) dimensions in the view are ignored. When the FIXED LOD is used without defining any dimension, the result will be a calculation ignoring all (if any) dimensions in the view.

Let's jump into the exercise and see this for ourselves:

1. Using the worksheet described previously, set the parameters as shown here:

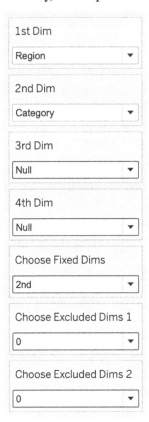

Figure 7.12: First example

What we achieve with the different parameters is that we show the **SUM(Sales)** per **Region** and each **Region** per **Category**, but we also fixed the **SUM(Sales)** calculation for the **Category** dimension in the **Case Fixed** column.

2. The **Case Fixed** column now displays the totals for each **Category** and ignores **Region** because we told the calculation to fix the **2nd Dim** (**Region**) and ignore the dimensions in the view itself. The effect of this is visible by comparing the **Sales** column and the **Case Fixed** column:

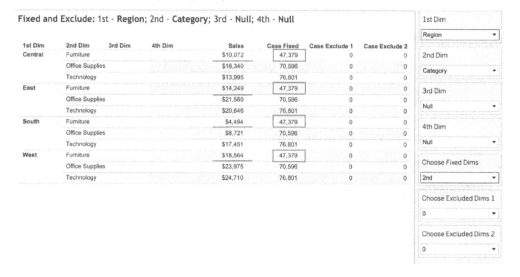

Figure 7.13: Case Fixed I

3. Check for yourself and do the math for **Furniture**:

$$10,072 + 14,249 + 4,494 + 18,564 = 47,379.$$

Even though the **Region** is visible in the view, the **SUM(Sales)** in the **Case Fixed** column ignores the **Region** and shows the results as if the **Category** dimension is the only dimension in the view. We manipulated the granularity of the data. In the **Case Fixed** column, **Region** is there for informative purposes only but does not affect the calculation of **SUM(Sales)**.

1. Now change the **Choose Fixed Dims** parameter to **1st** and note that **Case Fixed** now displays the totals for each **Region**:

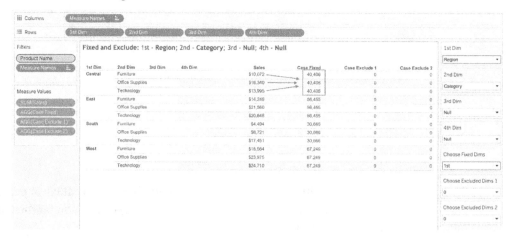

Figure 7.14: Case Fixed II

2. This time, we fix the calculation in the **Case Fixed** column to only take the **Region** into account but ignore the **Category**. Check for yourself and do the math for **Central**: 10,072 + 16,340 + 13,995 = 40,406.

Change the **Choose Fixed Dims** parameter to **Fixed: Nothing** and note that the amount reflects the total **SUM(Sales)**:

Fixed and Exclude: 1st - **Region**; 2nd - **Category**; 3rd - **Null**; 4th - **Null**

1st Dim	2nd Dim	3rd Dim	4th Dim	Sales	Case Fixed	Case Exclude 1	Case Exclude 2
Central	Furniture			$10,072	194,776	0	0
	Office Supplies			$16,340	194,776	0	0
	Technology			$13,995	194,776	0	0
East	Furniture			$14,249	194,776	0	0
	Office Supplies			$21,560	194,776	0	0
	Technology			$20,646	194,776	0	0
South	Furniture			$4,494	194,776	0	0
	Office Supplies			$8,721	194,776	0	0
	Technology			$17,451	194,776	0	0
West	Furniture			$18,564	194,776	0	0
	Office Supplies			$23,975	194,776	0	0
	Technology			$24,710	194,776	0	0

Figure 7.15: Fixed: Nothing

This time, we fixed the calculation to nothing, meaning that we ignore every dimension in the view. Check for yourself and do the math by summing the **Sales** values; the sum will be 194,776.

As is evident, the FIXED LOD considers only the dimensions to which it is directed. Thus, when fixed on **Category**, **Region** is ignored. And, as demonstrated, when fixed on **Region**, **Category** is ignored. Lastly, when **Choose Fixed Dims** is set to **Fixed: Nothing**, the entire dataset that is not restricted by the context filter on **Product Name** is displayed.

Next, let's look at a couple of new features introduced with Tableau 2021.1 that pertain to FIXED LODs.

Table-scoped expressions

A quick way to write a FIXED LOD expression when using a whole table as the scope is using code like the following:

```
{MAX([Order Date])}
```

If you use this calculation on the Superstore dataset, you will achieve the exact same as writing:

```
{FIXED: MAX([Order Date])}
```

No matter what you show in the view, this field will always retrieve the latest data from the whole table. Cool, right?

Quick LODs

Tableau 2021.1 allows us to create FIXED LODs faster. Simply drag the desired measure on top of a dimension and press *Ctrl* (or *Cmd* on macOS).

Now you will see the dimension highlighted in blue (see **Region** in *Figure 7.16*). Then drop the measure there and a new measure field (in this case, **Sales (Region)**) will be created.

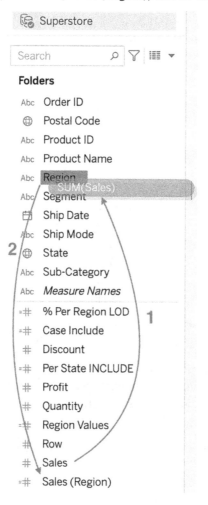

Figure 7.16: Quick LOD

Right-click on **Sales (Region)** and note that a FIXED LOD has been created:

```
{ FIXED [Region]: SUM([Sales]) }
```

Figure 7.17: Quick LOD II

If you're working with Tableau 2021.1 or higher, you can use this shortcut for FIXED LODs.

The playground we built was not only meant for FIXED but also for EXCLUDE. Let us have a look at EXCLUDE next.

Understanding EXCLUDE

Let's start understanding the EXCLUDE LOD. The EXCLUDE LOD will exclude any dimension to which it is directed. If your view contains **Region** and **Category** and you write an EXCLUDE LOD on **Category**, only **Region** will be considered in the calculations. The following example will make this clearer—our goal in this exercise is to calculate SUM(Sales) by using fewer dimensions than in the view. We want to exclude visible dimensions only from the calculation but still show the dimension values in the dashboard:

1. Set the parameters as shown in the following screenshot:

Figure 7.18: Fixed: Nothing

2. You can observe the following results:

Fixed and Exclude: 1st - **Region**; 2nd - **Category**; 3rd - **Segment**; 4th - **Null**

1st Dim	2nd Dim	3rd Dim	4th Dim	Sales	Case Fixed	Case Exclude 1	Case Exclude 2
Central	Furniture	Consumer		$5,444	0	26,738	0
		Corporate		$2,779	0	13,050	0
		Home Office		$1,849	0	7,592	0
	Office Supplies	Consumer		$9,085	0	31,861	0
		Corporate		$3,462	0	24,179	0
		Home Office		$3,793	0	14,556	0
	Technology	Consumer		$5,144	0	39,955	0
		Corporate		$3,848	0	23,766	0
		Home Office		$5,003	0	13,081	0
East	Furniture	Consumer		$6,941	0	26,738	0
		Corporate		$4,415	0	13,050	0
		Home Office		$2,893	0	7,592	0
	Office Supplies	Consumer		$11,361	0	31,861	0
		Corporate		$7,217	0	24,179	0
		Home Office		$2,982	0	14,556	0
	Technology	Consumer		$12,459	0	39,955	0
		Corporate		$8,011	0	23,766	0
		Home Office		$176	0	13,081	0
South	Furniture	Consumer		$2,052	0	26,738	0
		Corporate		$2,193	0	13,050	0
		Home Office		$249	0	7,592	0
	Office Supplies	Consumer		$3,393	0	31,861	0
		Corporate		$2,349	0	24,179	0
		Home Office		$2,978	0	14,556	0
	Technology	Consumer		$10,024	0	39,955	0
		Corporate		$6,046	0	23,766	0
		Home Office		$1,381	0	13,081	0
West	Furniture	Consumer		$12,301	0	26,738	0
		Corporate		$3,663	0	13,050	0
		Home Office		$2,600	0	7,592	0
	Office Supplies	Consumer		$8,022	0	31,861	0

Figure 7.19: Exclude I

Case Exclude 1 displays the total of each **Category** and **Segment** and ignores **Region**. For example, the total of the segment **Consumer** within the category **Furniture** is $26,738. That total is repeated for each **Region**. The relevant code that is generating these results is

```
SUM({EXCLUDE [Region] : SUM([Sales])})
```

3.   Make the following changes to the parameters:

Figure 7.20: Exclude II

Any LOD calculation can be used with multiple dimensions in a view. In this case, **Case Exclude 2** ignores two dimensions: **1st Dim** and **2nd Dim**, which are associated with **Region** and **Category**. The associated code for **Case Exclude 2** is therefore:

```
SUM({EXCLUDE [Region],[Category] : SUM([Sales])})
```

The associated code for **Case Fixed** is:

```
SUM({FIXED [Segment]: SUM([Sales])})
```

Case Exclude 2 and **Case Fixed** now have identical results. This is because excluding the first two dimensions is the same as fixing on the third dimension. Only the third dimension **Segment** is considered in both cases.

You can observe the results in the following screenshot:

Fixed and Exclude: 1st - **Region**; 2nd - **Category**; 3rd - **Segment**; 4th - **Null**

1st Dim	2nd Dim	3rd Dim	4th Dim	Sales	Case Fixed	Case Exclude 1	Case Exclude 2
Central	Furniture	Consumer		$5,444	98,554	26,738	98,554
		Corporate		$2,779	60,994	13,050	60,994
		Home Office		$1,849	35,228	7,592	35,228
	Office Supplies	Consumer		$9,085	98,554	31,861	98,554
		Corporate		$3,462	60,994	24,179	60,994
		Home Office		$3,793	35,228	14,556	35,228
	Technology	Consumer		$5,144	98,554	39,955	98,554
		Corporate		$3,848	60,994	23,766	60,994
		Home Office		$5,003	35,228	13,081	35,228
East	Furniture	Consumer		$6,941	98,554	26,738	98,554
		Corporate		$4,415	60,994	13,050	60,994
		Home Office		$2,893	35,228	7,592	35,228
	Office Supplies	Consumer		$11,361	98,554	31,861	98,554
		Corporate		$7,217	60,994	24,179	60,994
		Home Office		$2,982	35,228	14,556	35,228
	Technology	Consumer		$12,459	98,554	39,955	98,554
		Corporate		$8,011	60,994	23,766	60,994
		Home Office		$176	35,228	13,081	35,228
South	Furniture	Consumer		$2,052	98,554	26,738	98,554
		Corporate		$2,193	60,994	13,050	60,994
		Home Office		$249	35,228	7,592	35,228
	Office Supplies	Consumer		$3,393	98,554	31,861	98,554
		Corporate		$2,349	60,994	24,179	60,994
		Home Office		$2,978	35,228	14,556	35,228
	Technology	Consumer		$10,024	98,554	39,955	98,554
		Corporate		$6,046	60,994	23,766	60,994
		Home Office		$1,381	35,228	13,081	35,228
West	Furniture	Consumer		$12,301	98,554	26,738	98,554
		Corporate		$3,663	60,994	13,050	60,994
		Home Office		$2,600	35,228	7,592	35,228
	Office Supplies	Consumer		$8,022	98,554	31,861	98,554

Figure 7.21: Exclude II table

4.   Make the following changes to the parameters:

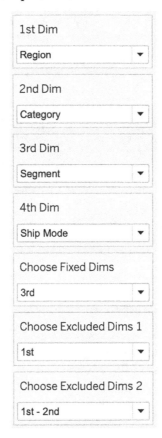

Figure 7.22: Change 4th dimension

5. You can observe the results as follows:

Fixed and Exclude: 1st - **Region**; 2nd - **Category**; 3rd - **Segment**; 4th - **Ship Mode**

1st Dim	2nd Dim	3rd Dim	4th Dim	Sales	Case Fixed	Case Exclude 1	Case Exclude 2
Central	Furniture	Consumer	First Class	$740	98,554	2,961	8,843
			Second Class	$313	98,554	6,493	24,765
			Standard Class	$4,391	98,554	17,147	62,011
		Corporate	First Class	$164	60,994	779	10,622
			Second Class	$801	60,994	3,139	8,818
			Standard Class	$1,813	60,994	8,934	38,997
		Home Office	First Class	$746	35,228	1,202	3,121
			Same Day	$106	35,228	517	2,616
			Second Class	$24	35,228	2,286	6,953
			Standard Class	$973	35,228	3,586	22,537
	Office Supplies	Consumer	First Class	$251	98,554	1,854	8,843
			Same Day	$160	98,554	2,165	2,935
			Second Class	$1,046	98,554	7,930	24,765
			Standard Class	$7,627	98,554	19,913	62,011
		Corporate	First Class	$1,819	60,994	4,977	10,622
			Same Day	$41	60,994	274	2,558
			Second Class	$427	60,994	3,225	8,818
			Standard Class	$1,176	60,994	15,703	38,997
		Home Office	First Class	$634	35,228	1,551	3,121
			Same Day	$172	35,228	1,419	2,616
			Second Class	$400	35,228	1,866	6,953
			Standard Class	$2,586	35,228	9,720	22,537
	Technology	Consumer	First Class	$260	98,554	4,028	8,843
			Same Day	$235	98,554	634	2,935
			Second Class	$1,062	98,554	10,342	24,765
			Standard Class	$3,587	98,554	24,951	62,011
		Corporate	First Class	$946	60,994	4,866	10,622
			Second Class	$783	60,994	2,454	8,818
			Standard Class	$2,119	60,994	14,360	38,997
		Home Office	First Class	$15	35,228	369	3,121
			Second Class	$1,637	35,228	2,802	6,953

Figure 7.23: Exclude III

6. Note that **Case Exclude 2** and **Case Fixed** no longer have identical results. This is because **Ship Mode** was introduced and **Case Exclude 2** considers **Ship Mode** whereas **Case Fixed** does not.

7. Experiment with other settings to further enhance your understanding of the FIXED and EXCLUDE LODs.

EXCLUDE will cause any dimension addressed in the LOD calculation to be removed from the calculation. Multiple dimensions can be part of an EXCLUDE LOD and common use cases include the direct comparison of values at a lower level of aggregation (fields that are in the view) to a higher aggregate (as if dimensions would be removed from the view). Let us assume you want to visualize the sales of categories in different regions as well as the total sales in each region. You might also want to calculate the difference from a single category in a region to the region overall. Isn't it so cool that LODs can solve this seemingly impossible scenario? I hope that the preceding exercise gave you a better feel for the EXCLUDE LOD.

As a quick interlude after those exercises on FIXED and EXCLUDE, let us take a closer look at Tableau's order of operations. As you now know, getting the same result for FIXED and EXCLUDE is not always the case – the order of operations will help us understand why.

Understanding Tableau's order of operations

The previous exercise led us to believe that the same results for FIXED and EXCLUDE can be achieved by fixing the dimensions that are not excluded and vice versa. However, the order in which Tableau executes a FIXED and an EXCLUDE LOD differs and can hence cause unexpected results. To avoid this, I will show you what to consider when using either FIXED or EXCLUDE LODs.

Let us have a look at the order of filtering:

1. Set the parameters as follows:

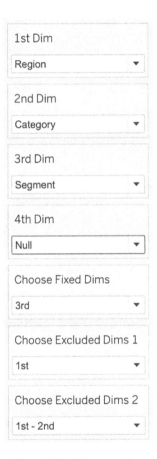

Figure 7.24: Set parameters

2. Observe the results:

Fixed and Exclude: 1st - Region; 2nd - Category; 3rd - Segment; 4th - Null

1st Dim	2nd Dim	3rd Dim	4th Dim	Sales	Case Fixed	Case Exclude 1	Case Exclude 2
Central	Furniture	Consumer		$5,444	98,554	26,738	98,554
		Corporate		$2,779	60,994	13,050	60,994
		Home Office		$1,849	35,228	7,592	35,228
	Office Supplies	Consumer		$9,085	98,554	31,861	98,554
		Corporate		$3,462	60,994	24,179	60,994
		Home Office		$3,793	35,228	14,556	35,228
	Technology	Consumer		$5,144	98,554	39,955	98,554
		Corporate		$3,848	60,994	23,766	60,994
		Home Office		$5,003	35,228	13,081	35,228
East	Furniture	Consumer		$6,941	98,554	26,738	98,554
		Corporate		$4,415	60,994	13,050	60,994
		Home Office		$2,893	35,228	7,592	35,228
	Office Supplies	Consumer		$11,361	98,554	31,861	98,554
		Corporate		$7,217	60,994	24,179	60,994
		Home Office		$2,982	35,228	14,556	35,228
	Technology	Consumer		$12,459	98,554	39,955	98,554
		Corporate		$8,011	60,994	23,766	60,994
		Home Office		$176	35,228	13,081	35,228
South	Furniture	Consumer		$2,052	98,554	26,738	98,554
		Corporate		$2,193	60,994	13,050	60,994
		Home Office		$249	35,228	7,592	35,228
	Office Supplies	Consumer		$3,393	98,554	31,861	98,554
		Corporate		$2,349	60,994	24,179	60,994
		Home Office		$2,978	35,228	14,556	35,228
	Technology	Consumer		$10,024	98,554	39,955	98,554
		Corporate		$6,046	60,994	23,766	60,994
		Home Office		$1,381	35,228	13,081	35,228
West	Furniture	Consumer		$12,301	98,554	26,738	98,554
		Corporate		$3,663	60,994	13,050	60,994
		Home Office		$2,600	35,228	7,592	35,228
	Office Supplies	Consumer		$8,022	98,554	31,861	98,554

Figure 7.25: Same results

Note that, as seen in the previous exercise, **Case Exclude 2** and **Case Fixed** are identical.

3. Right-click on the **Product Name** filter and select **Remove from Context**:

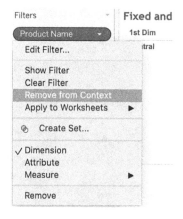

Figure 7.26: Remove from Context

4.   Observe the results in the following screenshot:

Fixed and Exclude: 1st - **Region**; 2nd - **Category**; 3rd - **Segment**; 4th - Null

1st Dim	2nd Dim	3rd Dim	4th Dim	Sales	Case Fixed	Case Exclude 1	Case Exclude 2
Central	Furniture	Consumer		$5,444	1,161,401	26,738	98,554
		Corporate		$2,779	706,146	13,050	60,994
		Home Office		$1,849	429,653	7,592	35,228
	Office Supplies	Consumer		$9,085	1,161,401	31,861	98,554
		Corporate		$3,462	706,146	24,179	60,994
		Home Office		$3,793	429,653	14,556	35,228
	Technology	Consumer		$5,144	1,161,401	39,955	98,554
		Corporate		$3,848	706,146	23,766	60,994
		Home Office		$5,003	429,653	13,081	35,228
East	Furniture	Consumer		$6,941	1,161,401	26,738	98,554
		Corporate		$4,415	706,146	13,050	60,994
		Home Office		$2,893	429,653	7,592	35,228
	Office Supplies	Consumer		$11,361	1,161,401	≠ 31,861	98,554
		Corporate		$7,217	706,146	24,179	60,994
		Home Office		$2,982	429,653	14,556	35,228
	Technology	Consumer		$12,459	1,161,401	39,955	98,554
		Corporate		$8,011	706,146	23,766	60,994
		Home Office		$176	429,653	13,081	35,228
South	Furniture	Consumer		$2,052	1,161,401	26,738	98,554
		Corporate		$2,193	706,146	13,050	60,994
		Home Office		$249	429,653	7,592	35,228
	Office Supplies	Consumer		$3,393	1,161,401	31,861	98,554
		Corporate		$2,349	706,146	24,179	60,994
		Home Office		$2,978	429,653	14,556	35,228
	Technology	Consumer		$10,024	1,161,401	39,955	98,554
		Corporate		$6,046	706,146	23,766	60,994
		Home Office		$1,381	429,653	13,081	35,228
West	Furniture	Consumer		$12,301	1,161,401	26,738	98,554
		Corporate		$3,663	706,146	13,050	60,994
		Home Office		$2,600	429,653	7,592	35,228
	Office Supplies	Consumer		$8,022	1,161,401	31,861	98,554

Figure 7.27: Without context filter

5.   **Case Exclude 2** and **Case Fixed** are no longer identical. **Case Fixed** is no longer impacted by the **Product Name** filter because the context was removed.

The behavior difference observed between EXCLUDE and FIXED in the preceding exercise reflects the underlying filter order of operations. As shown in *Figure 7.27*, **Context Filters** will impact FIXED, EXCLUDE, and INCLUDE calculations because the **Context Filter** is being applied first to the dataset, then the LOD. **Dimension Filters**, however, will only impact EXCLUDE and INCLUDE LODs because the FIXED LOD will be applied to the dataset first and then the dimension filter, followed by the EXCLUDE and INCLUDE LODs.

See the following diagram, a schematic representation of the order of operations in Tableau:

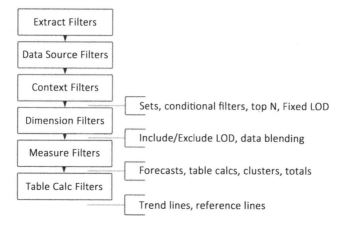

Figure 7.28: Order of operations

Figure 7.28 is sourced from Tableau's help pages, here: `https://help.tableau.com/current/pro/desktop/en-us/order_of_operations.htm`.

This page also contains more information on Tableau's order of operations.

We just saw that when using a context filter, `EXCLUDE` and `FIXED` LODs can result in the same numbers, whereas a dimension filter will cause the results to differ. This happens because Tableau executes the different requests after one another. As can be seen in the preceding diagram, the order of operations is:

1. Context filters
2. `FIXED` LOD
3. Dimension filters
4. `INCLUDE` and `EXCLUDE` LODs

This is important for you to know to choose the correct filter or LOD for your purpose.

Next, we will use a new playground, this time to show how `INCLUDE` LODs work.

INCLUDE

The second playground is mostly set up for you when using the accompanying workbook (`https://github.com/PacktPublishing/Mastering-Tableau-2023-Fourth-Edition/tree/main/Chapter07`). We will, however, add some calculated fields for the purpose of effective exploration. If you do not have ready access to the workbook, you should be able to construct a similar one by referencing the following information.

Setting up the workbook

In the following, we will set up a worksheet with which we can practice the `INCLUDE` LODs:

1. Open the workbook associated with this chapter and navigate to the `Exploring Include` worksheet.

2. The parameters and calculated fields named **1st Dim**, **2nd Dim**, **3rd Dim**, and **4th Dim** created in the previous exercises are also utilized for this worksheet.

3. Right-click on the **1st Dim** parameter and choose **Duplicate**.

4. Rename the duplicate `Choose Included Dims`.

5. Create a new calculated field named `Case Include` with the following code:

```
CASE [Choose Included Dims]
WHEN 1 THEN AVG({INCLUDE [Category]: SUM([Sales])})
WHEN 2 THEN AVG({INCLUDE [City]: SUM([Sales])})
WHEN 3 THEN AVG({INCLUDE [Country]: SUM([Sales])})
WHEN 4 THEN AVG({INCLUDE [Customer ID]: SUM([Sales])})
WHEN 5 THEN AVG({INCLUDE [Customer Name]: SUM([Sales])})
WHEN 6 THEN AVG({INCLUDE [Order ID]: SUM([Sales])})
WHEN 7 THEN AVG({INCLUDE [Postal Code]: SUM([Sales])})
WHEN 8 THEN AVG({INCLUDE [Product ID]: SUM([Sales])})
WHEN 9 THEN AVG({INCLUDE [Product Name]: SUM([Sales])})
WHEN 10 THEN AVG({INCLUDE [Region]: SUM([Sales])})
WHEN 11 THEN AVG({INCLUDE [Segment]: SUM([Sales])})
WHEN 12 THEN AVG({INCLUDE [Ship Mode]: SUM([Sales])})
WHEN 13 THEN AVG({INCLUDE [State]: SUM([Sales])})
WHEN 14 THEN AVG({INCLUDE [Sub-Category]: SUM([Sales])})
WHEN 15 THEN 0
END
```

6. Place **Case Include** on the **Detail** shelf.

7. Place the following measures and dimensions on their respective shelves:

Figure 7.29: Exploring INCLUDE

8. Display each of the following parameters by right-clicking each one and selecting **Show Parameter Control**:

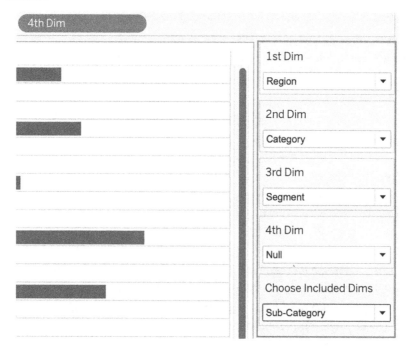

Figure 7.30: Parameters

After you have finished the initial setup, we can finally start to investigate the INCLUDE LOD.

Understanding INCLUDE

Now that the playground environment is complete, let's build a scenario to better understand INCLUDE. By now, you can probably imagine that if the FIXED and EXCLUDE LODs remove dimensions from a calculation, INCLUDE adds dimensions. Correct! It might happen that you want to include one or more dimensions in a calculation even though the view doesn't show them. The next example will make use of this functionality to show an average per sub-category without showing the sub-category. One would want to do this because the sub-category has so many additional values that the dashboard will be harder to read, and it will take longer to draw quick conclusions. Nevertheless, it is of interest to know the average per sub-category because the number of sub-categories might differ per **Region** and other dimensions, and thus including it will give insights into the real average sales.

Let's see it in action:

1. Set the parameters on the right-hand side as shown here:

Figure 7.31: Initial layout

2. Add two reference lines by clicking on **Analytics** and edit them using the following settings:

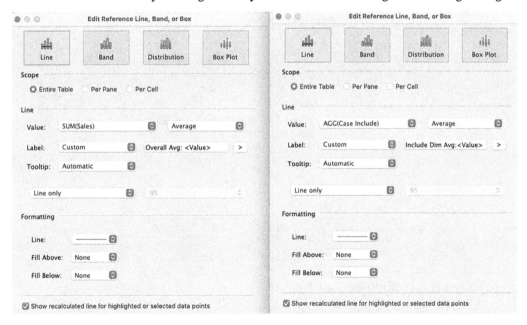

Figure 7.32: Reference line settings

3. Look at the following screenshot for the result. Note that both reference lines are equal:

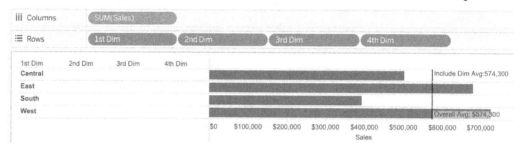

Figure 7.33: Sales per region and reference lines

4. If the reference lines are overlapping with each other, edit the formatting and set **Alignment** to **Top.** To access the formatting, click on the reference line in the view:

Figure 7.34: Format Reference Line

5. Now, set the parameters as shown here:

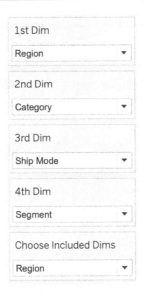

Figure 7.35: Format Reference Line

6.   In Tableau Desktop, you should now see the following. As before, both **Reference Lines** are equal:

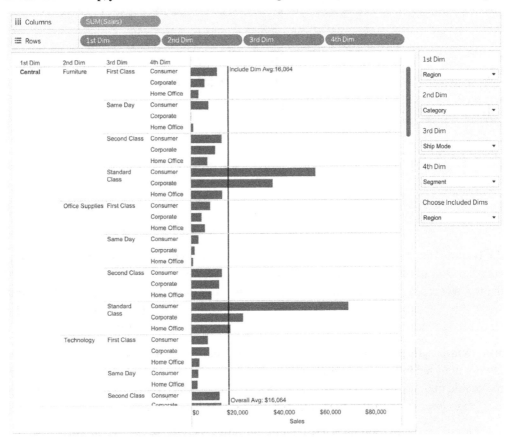

Figure 7.36: Reference Lines

7. Change the **Choose Included Dims** parameter to **Category, Ship Mode**, and **Segment**.

8. Note that the **Reference Lines** equal one another for each of these settings. This is because **Choose Included Dims** is only introducing dimensions already represented in the view.

9. Change the **Choose Included Dims** parameter to **Sub-Category** to see the additional reference line in its intended place:

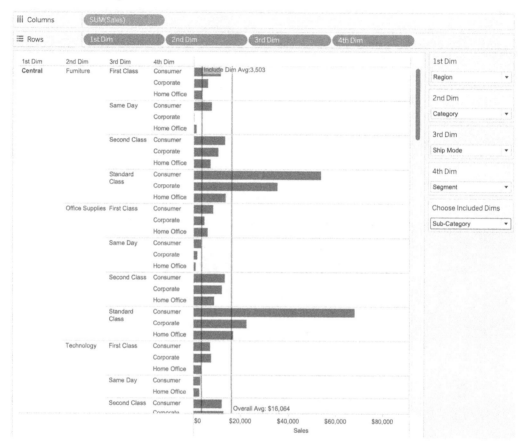

Figure 7.37: Showing an additional Reference Line

The **Include Dim Avg** reference line now includes **Sub-Category** in the average and therefore differs from the **Overall Avg** reference line. The average is smaller because the total **Sales** amount is being divided over more points than are visible in the view. Adding **Sub-Category** to the LOD leads to more rows, which leads to a smaller average per row. Furthermore, note that the **Sub-Category** dimension is not used in the view. LODs do not require a calculation to reside in the view.

To summarize, the INCLUDE LOD can manipulate a visualization in a way that partitions can be added that are not used in the view itself. Also, the naming convention for all three LODs will be your best mnemonic in understanding them: Fixed to fix the fields used, Include to add "missing" fields, and Exclude to remove unwanted fields from the calculations that are already present.

To get more hands-on training, we will continue with a few practical applications.

Building practical applications with LODs

The first portion of this chapter was designed to demonstrate how LODs work. The remainder will be dedicated to practical applications. Specifically, we will consider three typical challenges that previously were solved using other Tableau capabilities, such as table calculations and data blending.

This exercise will look at a problem that occurs when mixing a table calculation that calculates the percentage of the total with a dimension filter. We will consider the problem, a solution using a LOD calculation, and finish with a commentary section on the germane points of the solution.

Using the LOD FIXED calculation

Did you ever encounter a situation where you wanted to calculate the **Percent of Total** while only showing a subset of the **Total** dimension in your view? Well, you are not alone. But thanks to LODs, you will soon know how to solve this problem. The following steps will guide you through the exercise:

1. Open the workbook associated with this chapter and navigate to the worksheet entitled The Problem.

2. Select the 2012_World_Pop dataset.

3. Create a calculated field named Percent of Total with the following code:

   ```
   SUM([Population]) / TOTAL(SUM([Population]))
   ```

4. Right-click on **Percent of Total** and select **Default Properties | Number Format | Percentage**.

5. Place **Country** on the **Columns** shelf, **Measure Names** on the **Rows** shelf, and **Measure Values** on the **Text** shelf.

6. Remove **Number of Records** from the **Measure Values** shelf.

7. Right-click on **Percent of Total** and set it to **Compute Using | Country**.

8. Create a filter on **Country** such that only **Afghanistan** displays:

Figure 7.38: Population of Afghanistan

Afghanistan displays the percentage of the total as 100%. Obviously, this does not represent Afghanistan's percentage of the total population of the world. Let's investigate a possible solution—to solve the issue with a LOD, follow along with the exercise steps:

1. Duplicate the worksheet entitled The Problem and rename it Solution LOD.

2. Create a calculated field named `Percent of Total LOD` with the following code:

```
SUM([Population])/SUM({ FIXED : SUM([Population])})
```

3. Place **Percent of Total LOD** on the **Measure Values** shelf and note that the displayed percentage equals **0.43%**. If 0 displays, change the number formatting to percentage:

Figure 7.39: Percent of total

4. Remove the **Percent of Total** table calculation that was previously created from the **Measure Values** shelf:

	Country
	Afghanistan
Population	29,824,536
Percent of Total LOD	0.43%

Figure 7.40: Percent of total LOD

As you can see, problem solved! To better understand what is happening in the background, let's look at a query that Tableau generates for the worksheet entitled The Problem. Generated queries can be viewed by clicking **Help | Settings and Performance | Start Performance Recording**. (See *Chapter 11, Designing Dashboards and Best Practices for Visualizations*, for additional information regarding viewing Tableau's generated queries.)

The SQL statement is as follows:

```
SELECT
['2012_World_Pop$'].[Country] AS [Country],
SUM(['2012_World_Pop$'].[Population]) AS [SUM:Population:ok]
FROM
[dbo].['2012_World_Pop$'] ['2012_World_Pop$']
WHERE
(['2012_World_Pop$'].[Country] = 'Afghanistan')
GROUP BY
['2012_World_Pop$'].[Country]]
```

Note that the WHERE clause in the query is limiting the returned dataset to only those rows that have Afghanistan as **Country**. This WHERE clause was generated because of placing **Country** on the **Filters** shelf. By limiting the returned data, the processing requirements are shifted from Tableau to the underlying data source engine. In other words, the data source engine does the work of executing the query, and Tableau thus works with a smaller dataset. The reasoning behind this design is that data source engines are specifically engineered to efficiently query large datasets and typically have underlying hardware to support such activities. Furthermore, limiting the rows of data returned to Tableau can reduce inefficiencies due to latency.

Inefficiencies are further reduced because Tableau works from the cache whenever possible. Often, a user can perform various operations without generating a call to the underlying data source. However, in the preceding case, if a user were to select a different **Country** from the filter, Tableau would generate a new query to the data source. For example, if a user interacts with the filter and deselects Afghanistan and selects Albania, a new query with a corresponding WHERE clause is generated. Although the logic of Tableau's reliance on the data source engine is demonstrable, the problem proposed in the preceding example remains. What can a Tableau author do to calculate the percent of the whole regardless of filtering?

A solution is to create a table calculation that can also be used as a filter. The difference is that unlike in the worksheet The Problem, the query generated by Tableau to the data source returns the entire dataset. When a table calculation is used in a filter, the filtering does not take place until the underlying data is returned. In other words, Tableau performs the filtering. This preserves a percent of the total percentages regardless of which country population totals the user chooses to view. But a potential issue with table calculations is that the returned dataset may be quite large, which may cause performance challenges. Latency may be experienced due to the increased time required to return a large dataset, and Tableau may perform more slowly because of additional processing responsibilities to filter the dataset.

Our proposed solution, an LOD calculation, can address these challenges. Let's look at the SQL queries created by the Percent of Total LOD calculated field in the Solution LOD worksheet:

```
SELECT
[t0].[Country] AS [Country],
[t1].[ measure 0] AS
[TEMP(Calculation_418553293854285824)(2417030171)(0)],
[t0].[TEMP(Calculation_418553293854285824)(616435453)(0)] AS
[TEMP(Calculation_418553293854285824)(616435453)(0)]
FROM
( SELECT
['2012_World_Pop$'].[Country] AS [Country], SUM(['2012_World_Pop$'].
[Population])
AS [TEMP(Calculation_418553293854285824)(616435453)(0)]
FROM
[dbo].['2012_World_Pop$'] ['2012_World_Pop$']
WHERE
```

```
(['2012_World_Pop$'].[Country]= 'Afghanistan')
GROUP BY
['2012_World_Pop$'].[Country] ) [t0]
CROSS JOIN
( SELECT SUM(['2012_World_Pop$'].[Population]) AS [ measure 0] FROM
[dbo].['2012_World_Pop$'] ['2012_World_Pop$']
GROUP BY () ) [t1]
```

Note the term CROSS JOIN; the LOD calculation generates a query that instructs the underlying data source engine to return data in such a way as to allow Tableau to divide the population values of one or more countries by the world population total, thus returning the correct percentage of the total.

Using the LOD INCLUDE calculation

Next, we will practice the INCLUDE LOD calculation. In this exercise, we will create a worksheet that displays the following:

- Total sales per region
- The average of total sales across all regions
- The average of total sales across all states in each region

Using a LOD calculation to display these values is straightforward. Let's explore. Follow along with the exercise steps:

1. Select the Practical Include worksheet.
2. Select the Superstore dataset.
3. Create a calculated field named Per State INCLUDE with the following code:

   ```
   {INCLUDE [State]:SUM([Sales])}
   ```

4. Drag **Region** to the **Columns** shelf, **SUM(Sales)** to the **Rows** shelf, and **AVG(Per State INCLUDE)** to the **Details** shelf. Be sure to change **Per State INCLUDE** to an average aggregation.
5. Add two **Reference Lines** by right-clicking on the **Sales** axis and selecting **Add Reference Line**. Use the following settings:

Figure 7.41: Reference lines

6. Complete the worksheet by formatting it as desired:

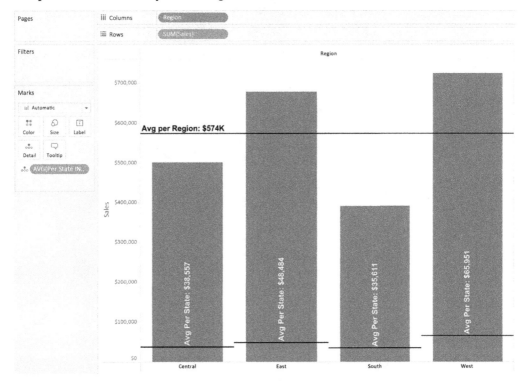

Figure 7.42: Average per Region and State

As you can see, thanks to the LOD, we can display a line chart per **Region**, as well as one for the whole dataset. This is possible because we included the **State** dimension in our **Per State INCLUDE** calculation. Using this calculated field to create a reference line allows Tableau to show not only the average per (visible) **Region** but also the average per **State** (invisible) per **Region**.

Using the LOD EXCLUDE calculation

In this exercise, we will create a worksheet using the Superstore dataset, which will calculate the percentage of sales generated by each city in a region.

Follow along with the exercise steps:

1. Select the Practical Exclude worksheet.
2. Select the Superstore dataset.
3. Create the following calculated fields:

Figure 7.43: Region Values and % Per Region LODs

4. Place **Region** and **City** on the **Rows** shelf.
5. Place **Measure Names** on the **Columns** shelf and **Measure Values** on the **Text** shelf.
6. Remove all instances of measures from the **Measure Values** shelf except **Sales**, **Region Values**, and **% Per Region LOD.**

7. In order for **% Per Region LOD** to display as a percentage, the number formatting must be adjusted. Simply right-click on the calculation in the **Data** pane and select **Default Properties | Number Format | Percentage**:

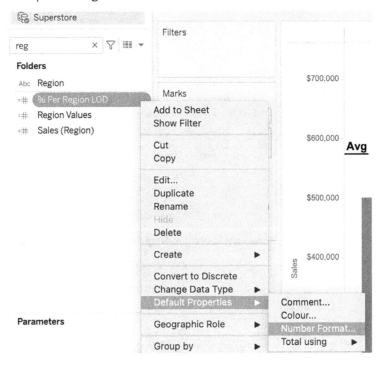

Figure 7.44: Change Number Format

8. Place an instance of **AGG(% Per Region LOD)** on the **Filter** shelf and adjust to display at least `0.1` (or 10%):

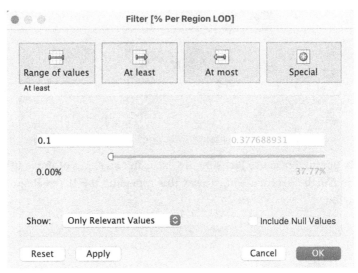

Figure 7.45: % filter

9. Observe the current view, with **Region** and **City** on the **Rows** shelf:

Region	City	Sales	Region Values	% Per Region LOD
Central	Houston	$64,505	501,240	12.87%
East	New York City	$256,368	678,781	37.77%
	Philadelphia	$109,077	678,781	16.07%
South	Jacksonville	$44,713	391,722	11.41%
West	Los Angeles	$175,851	725,458	24.24%
	San Francisco	$112,669	725,458	15.53%
	Seattle	$119,541	725,458	16.48%

Figure 7.46: Jacksonville still visible

10. Now, place **State** on the **Rows** shelf between **Region** and **City**. Note that **Jacksonville** disappears:

Region	State	City	Sales	Region Values	% Per Region LOD
Central	Texas	Houston	$64,505	501,240	12.87%
East	New York	New York City	$256,368	678,781	37.77%
	Pennsylvania	Philadelphia	$109,077	678,781	16.07%
West	California	Los Angeles	$175,851	725,458	24.24%
		San Francisco	$112,669	725,458	15.53%
	Washington	Seattle	$119,541	725,458	16.48%

Figure 7.47: Jacksonville disappears when Region is added to Rows

This is happening because **Jacksonville** exists in two states of the **South** region, in **Florida** as well as in **North Carolina**. You can see this replacing the % **Per Region LOD** filter with **City: Jacksonville:**

Figure 7.48: Jacksonville existing within two states

Our **Region Values** calculation excluded **City** and **State,** and so the % **Per Region LOD** will consider the **SUM(Sales)** for whatever is visible in the view, divided by the **Region Values**. With **Region** and **City** in the view only, the **SUM(Sales)** for Jacksonville is **44,713** (see *Figure 7.48*). That number divided by the **Region Values** of **391,722** (see *Figure 7.46*) is > 10%. But then we added **State** to the view, changing the **SUM(Sales)** to **39,133** for **Jacksonville** in **Florida** and **5,580** for **Jacksonville** in **North Carolina** (see *Figure 7.50*). Neither one of them, when divided by **391,722** for the **Region Values**, is above 10% and will therefore drop from the view due to our filter.

LODs are one of the more advanced topics when using Tableau, but they are very powerful and worth spending the time to understand. For more practical examples, I would recommend you check out the following website: `https://www.tableau.com/about/blog/LOD-expressions`. I remember that when I first started using Tableau, I did not think that I would ever want to show data based on dimensions that were not in my view or that I would want to exclude dimensions. But I needed to do that so many times, for example, when adding a calculation of the distance to the average of total rows to my dashboard or when a dimension had multiple max dates and you wanted to show the measure of each individual max date only. I have gone back to the documentation on LODs more often than you can imagine, and I can only encourage you to do the same; the more you read about LODs, the easier it will be to grasp the concept and use them naturally. The added flexibility LODs bring to your dashboard is incredible.

Summary

We began this chapter by exploring why LODs are so impactful and why their inclusion in Tableau was so lauded. Next, we built two playgrounds to explore how the three LODs—FIXED, EXCLUDE, and INCLUDE—work. Tableau's default is to base calculations on the dimensions visible in the view. For example, if you have states in your view, the sales amount will be presented by state. If you are adding cities, the sales amount will be adjusted by state, by city. But, if you want to manipulate this default logic, you can use LODs. They allow you to calculate measures based on any dimension, no matter whether that dimension is represented in the view or not. We also saw that FIXED LODs are higher in the order of operations in Tableau than EXCLUDE and INCLUDE LODs. This is important to remember so that you use the correct LOD and/or filter in your dashboard.

In the next chapter, we'll turn our attention to the visual side of Tableau and explore different chart types and less common but very useful visualizations.

Learn more on Discord

To join the Discord community for this book – where you can share feedback, ask questions to the author, and learn about new releases – follow the QR code below:

https://packt.link/tableau

8

Going Beyond the Basics

The assumption behind this chapter is that the you are familiar with basic chart types such as bar, line graph, treemap, pie, and area, and that you have used Tableau to build multiple charts. The intention of this chapter is to focus on how to improve visualization types you may already use on a regular basis, as well as introducing chart types with which you may be unfamiliar but that are, nonetheless, widely useful. I will then introduce you to Tableau Exchange, a platform that contains extensions, accelerators, and connectors, which offer some more exotic chart types.

Perhaps the most useful part of this chapter is not contained in the book at all but, rather, in the workbook associated with the chapter. Be sure to download that workbook (the link will be provided in the following section) to check out a wide range of visualization types.

This chapter will explore the following visualization types and topics:

- Improving popular visualizations
- Custom background images
- Tableau Exchange

    - Extensions
    - Accelerators
    - Connectors

Keep in mind that the content of your dashboard is the most important, but if you can have the same content with a nicer design, go for the nicer design. There is such a thing as **Beauty Bias** and **Design Driven Consumption.** You want to sell your product – make it look good! I hope the next sections will help you find your path and eventually make you a better dashboard designer.

Improving popular visualizations

Most popular visualizations are popular for good reason. Basic bar charts and line graphs are familiar, intuitive, and flexible and are thus widely used in data visualization. Other less basic visualizations such as bullet graphs and Pareto charts may not be something you use every day but are nonetheless useful additions to a data analyst's toolbox. And while these are all good, they could do more. In this section, we will explore ideas for how to tweak, extend, and even overhaul a few popular chart types.

Bullet graphs

The bullet graph was invented by Stephen Few and communicated publicly in 2006 through his book *Information Dashboard Design: The Effective Visual Communication of Data*. Stephen Few continues to be a strong voice in the data visualization space through his books and his blog, www.perceptualedge.com. Bullet graphs communicate efficiently and intuitively by packing a lot of information into a small space while remaining attractive and easy to read. Understandably, they have gained much popularity and are utilized for many purposes, as can be seen through a web search. The following two exercises communicate the basics of bullet graphs and how to improve on those basics. That is not to say that I have improved on the bullet graph in this chapter! The intent is merely to relay how this important visualization type can be more effectively used in Tableau. Let's get started.

Using bullet graphs

The following steps will teach you the basics of a bullet graph:

1. Navigate to https://public.tableau.com/profile/marleen.meier to locate and download the workbook associated with this chapter.

2. Navigate to the worksheet entitled Bullet Graph and select the CoffeeChain data source.

3. Place these fields on their respective shelves: **Profit** on **Columns**, **Market** on **Rows**, and **BudgetProfit** on **Detail** in the **Marks** card.

4. Right-click on the *x* axis and select **Add Reference Line**.

5. From the upper left-hand corner of the **Edit Reference Line, Band or Box** dialog box, select **Line**. Also, set **Scope** to **Per Cell**, **Value** to **SUM(Budget Profit)** as **Average**, and **Label** to **None**. Click **OK**:

Figure 8.1: Reference line

6. Let's add another reference line. This time, as an alternative method, click on the **Analytics** pane and drag **Reference Line** onto your worksheet. (You could obviously repeat the method in *Step 4* instead.)

7. Within the dialog box, select **Distribution** and set **Scope** to **Per Cell**. Set **Value** to **Percentages** with **90,95,100** and **Percent of** to **SUM(Budget Profit)**. Set **Label** to **None**. Click **OK**:

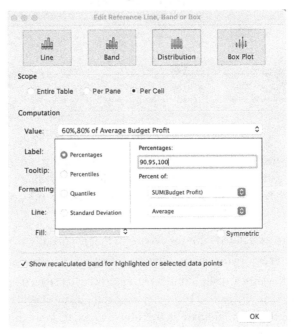

Figure 8.2: Percentiles

8. Create a calculated field called `Profit to Budget Profit Ratio` with the following code:

```
SUM([Profit])/SUM([Budget Profit])
```

9. Create another calculated field called `Quota Met?` with the following code:

```
SUM([Profit])>=SUM([Budget Profit])
```

10. Right-click on **Profit to Budget Profit Ratio** and select **Default Properties | Number Format | Percentage**.

11. Place **Profit to Budget Profit Ratio** on the **Label** shelf in the **Marks** card and **Quota Met?** on the **Color** shelf in the **Marks** card:

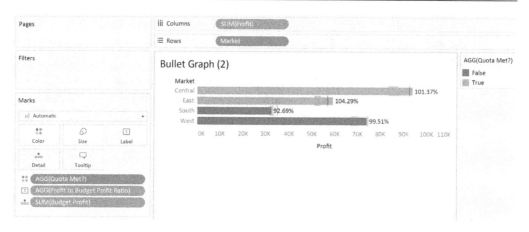

Figure 8.3: Preliminary bullet graph

As you survey our results thus far, you will notice that there are some important aspects to this visualization. For example, the reference lines and the colored bars clearly delineate when a quota was met and missed. Furthermore, the percentages communicate how close the actual profit was to the budgeted profit for each market. However, there are also some problems to address:

- The percentage associated with the **South** market is partially obscured.
- The background colors represented by the reference distribution are obscured.
- The colors of the bars are not intuitive. Orange is set to **True**, which signifies, in this case, the markets that made the quota. However, psychologically speaking, orange is a warning color used to communicate problems and, therefore, would be more intuitively associated with those markets that failed to make the quota. Furthermore, these colors are not easily distinguishable when presented in grayscale.
- The words **False** and **True** in the legend are not immediately intuitive.

In the upcoming steps, we will address those issues and show you possible solutions.

Bullet graphs — beyond the basics

To address the problems with the graph in the previous section, take the following steps:

1. Continuing from the previous exercise, access the **Data** pane on the left-hand portion of the screen, right-click on **Quota Met?**, and adjust the calculation as follows:

```
IF SUM([Profit])>=SUM([Budget Profit])
THEN 'Quota Met'
ELSE 'Quota Missed'
END
```

2. This calculation will create the string Quota Met if the profit is higher than the budgeted profit, or the string Quota Missed if the profit isn't higher than the budgeted profit. These two strings can be used as a legend and are more intuitive than the previous **True** and **False**.

3. Create a calculated field named `Greater of Profit or Budget Profit` with the following code:

```
IF SUM(Profit)>SUM([Budget Profit])
THEN SUM(Profit)
ELSE SUM([Budget Profit])
END
```

This calculation will show the profit amount if it is more than the budgeted amount, or the budgeted amount if the profit is smaller. This will help us to always show the bigger amount of the two.

4. Place **Greater of Profit or Budget Profit** on the **Columns** shelf after **Profit**. Also, right-click on the pill and select **Dual Axis**.

5. Right-click on the axis for **Greater of Profit or Budget Profit** and select **Synchronize Axis**.

6. Within the **Marks** card, select the pane labeled **All** and set the mark type to **Bar**.

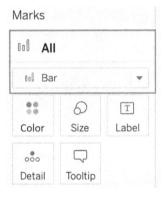

Figure 8.4: Marks card

7. Remove **Measure Names** from the **Color** shelf.

8. Within the **Marks** card, select the pane labeled **AGG(Greater of Profit or Budget Profit)**.

9. Click on the **Color** shelf and set **Opacity** to **0%**.

10. Within the **Marks** card, select the pane labeled **SUM(Profit)**.

11. Remove **AGG(Profit to Budget Profit Ratio)** from the **Marks** card and note that the percentage labels are no longer obscured.

12. Click on the **Color** shelf and select **Edit Colors**. Within the resulting dialog box, complete the following steps:

    1. Double-click on **Quota Met** and set the color to white.

    2. Double-click on **Quota Missed** and set the color to black.

13. After you have clicked **OK** for each dialog box and returned to the main screen, once again click on the **Color** shelf, and select black for **Border**.

14. Click on the **Size** shelf to narrow the width of the bars by dragging the slider to the left.

15. Right-click on the **Profit** axis and select **Edit Reference Line**. Then set **Value** to **90%,95%,100%** of **Average Budget Profit**:

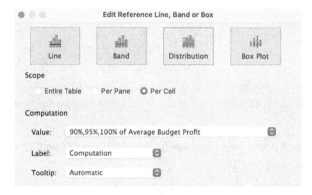

Figure 8.5: Reference line

16. In the same window, moving down to the **Formatting** section, set the **Fill** color to **Grey Light**. Click the **Fill Below** checkbox and the **Reverse** checkbox. Note that the background colors are now more easily distinguishable:

Figure 8.6: Background colors

17. Right-click on the axis labeled **Greater of Profit or Budget Profit** and deselect **Show Header**. You may wish to make some additional tweaks, but our result looks as follows:

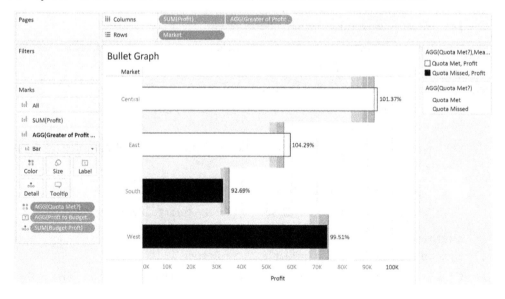

Figure 8.7: Improved bullet graph

Note that each of the aforementioned problems has now been addressed:

- The percentage numbers are no longer obscured.
- The background colors are easier to distinguish due to having narrowed the bars.
- The color of the bars is more intuitive. Furthermore, using black, white, and gray has circumvented any readability problems arising from color blindness or grayscale print.
- The words **False** and **True** in the legend have been replaced with the more descriptive terms **Quota Met** and **Quota Missed**.

By completing this section, you will have learned how tweaks can improve your visualization and the type of graph you choose. You can do this whenever the current choices you have made do not tell the full story yet. In addition to that, it is also a selling point. Your users like a nice design and clear dashboards. By improving your visualization with more advanced techniques, you will be able to improve your storytelling and marketing.

In the next section, we will continue to add complexity to known **visualizations**. This time we will create pie and donut charts and eventually combine the two.

Pies and donuts

Pie charts are normally frowned upon in data visualization circles. They simply have too many drawbacks. For instance, pie charts don't utilize space well on a rectangular screen. Treemaps fit much better. Also, the number of slices that are reasonable on a pie chart is fairly limited, perhaps six to eight at best. Once again, treemaps are superior because they can be sliced at a finer level of granularity while remaining useful. Lastly, when using pie charts, it can be difficult to discern which of two similarly sized slices is the largest. Treemaps are no better in this regard; however, if the viewer understands that treemap sorting is from the top left to the bottom right, that knowledge can be used to distinguish size differences. Of course, bar charts circumvent that particular problem entirely, since the eye can easily distinguish widths and heights but struggles with angles (pie charts) and volume (treemaps).

Despite these drawbacks, because of their popularity, pie charts will likely continue to be widely used in data visualization for years to come. People like them because they are different than the old, boring bar chart. Users are familiar with pie charts and they do not require any explanation and are a way to show proportions – just not the best way in my opinion. For the pessimistic Tableau author, the best course of action is to grin and bear it. But for one willing to explore and push frontier boundaries, good uses for pie charts can be discovered. The following exercise is one contribution to that exploration.

Pies and donuts on maps

Occasionally, there is a need (or perceived need) to construct pie charts atop a map. The process is not difficult (as you will see in the following exercise), but there are some shortcomings that cannot be easily overcome. We will discuss those shortcomings after the exercise.

The following are the steps:

1. Within the workbook associated with this chapter, navigate to the worksheet entitled `Pie Map` and select the `Superstore` data source.

2. In the **Data** pane, double-click on **State** to create a map of the United States.

3. Place **Sales** on the **Color** shelf. Click on the **Color** shelf and change the **Palette** to **Grey**:

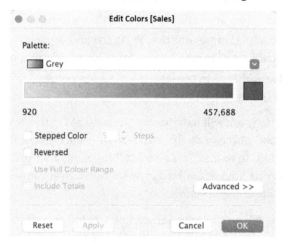

Figure 8.8: Edit Colors

4. Drag an additional copy of **Latitude (generated)** on the **Rows** shelf by holding *Ctrl* for Windows and *Command* for Mac and simultaneously dragging the pill to create two rows, each of which displays a map:

Figure 8.9: Latitude

5. In the **Marks** card, you will notice that there are now three panes: **All**, **Latitude (generated)**, and **Latitude (generated) (2)**. Click on **Latitude (generated) (2)** and set the mark type to **Pie**:

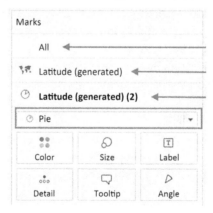

Figure 8.10: Marks card panes

6. Place **Category** on the **Color** shelf and **Sales** on the **Size** shelf.

7. To complete the visualization, right-click on the second instance of **Latitude (generated)** in the **Rows** shelf and select **Dual Axis**:

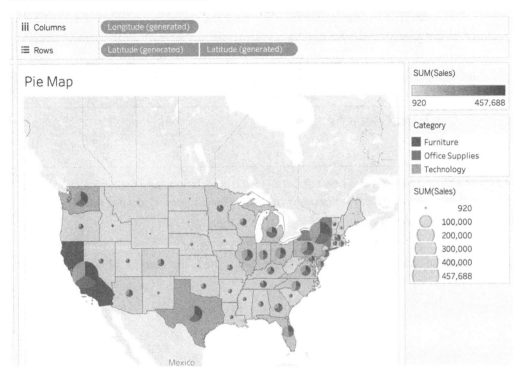

Figure 8.11: Pie map

Can you see issues in the visualization? Two should be immediately apparent:

- First, the smaller pies are difficult to see. Clicking on the drop-down menu for the **Size** legend and selecting **Edit Sizes** could partially address this problem, but pies in smaller states such as **Rhode Island** will continue to be problematic.
- Second, many states have the same light-gray background despite widely varying sales amounts.

The following approach will address these issues while also adding additional functionality.

Pies and donuts — beyond the basics

The following are the steps required to create a tile grid map with both a pie and donut chart on top of the map. By combining the different methods, we will be able to show more information at once without overloading the view:

1. Within the workbook associated with this chapter, navigate to the worksheet entitled `Altered Pie Map` and select the `Superstore` data source.

2. Create the following calculated fields:

Name	Code
Category State Sales	{FIXED State, Category: SUM(Sales)}
State Max	{FIXED State : MAX([Category State Sales])}
Top Selling Category per State	MAX(If [State Max] = [Category State Sales] then Category END)

3. We need those first two **Level of Detail (LOD)** calculations and the last calculation to show the sales per category, while also showing the best-selling category per state.

4. Within the **Marks** card, set the mark type to **Pie**.

5. Within the **Data** pane, select the **States** data source.

6. Click the chain link next to **State** in the **Data** pane to use **State** as a blended field:

Figure 8.12: Linking dimensions

7. Drag **Column** to the **Columns** shelf and **Row** to the **Rows** shelf.

8. From the **Superstore** data source, place **Category** on the **Color** shelf and **Sales** on the **Angle** shelf.

9. Place **State** on **Detail** in the **Marks** card.

10. Click on the **Size** shelf and adjust the size as desired.

11. At this point, you should see a rough map of the United States made up of pie charts. Next, we will further enhance the graphic by changing the pies into donuts:

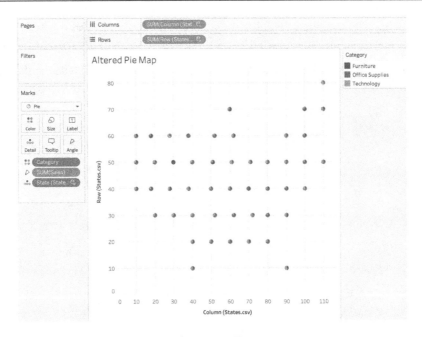

Figure 8.13: Map

12. Return to the **States** data source and place another instance of **Row** on the **Rows** shelf.

13. In the **Marks** card, select **Row (2)** and change the view type to **Circle**.

14. From the **Superstore** dataset, place **Top Selling Category per State** on the **Color** shelf:

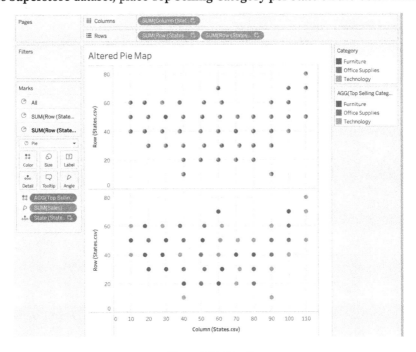

Figure 8.14: Map II

15. Place **Sales** on the **Label** shelf. Right-click on the instance of **Sales** you just placed on the **Label** shelf and select **Format**. Make the following adjustments in the **Format** window:

1. Set the **Numbers** formatting to **Currency (Custom)** with 0 decimal places and **Display Units** set to **Thousands (K)**:

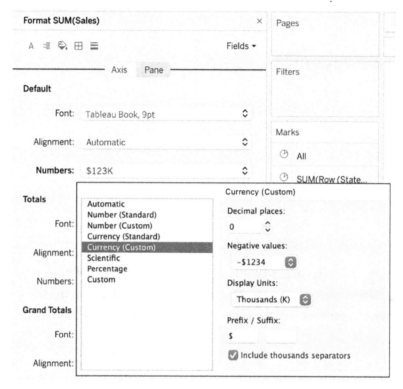

Figure 8.15: Formatting

2. Set **Alignment** to **Middle Centre**, as shown in the following screenshot, so that the numbers are centered over the circles:

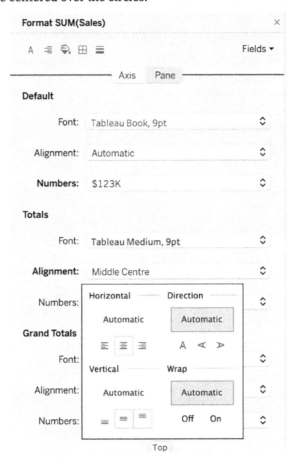

Figure 8.16: Alignment

3. In the **Rows** shelf, right-click on the second instance of **Row** and select **Dual Axis**.

4. Right-click on an instance of the **Row** axis and select **Synchronize Axis**.

5. Within the **Row (2)** instance on the **Marks** card, make sure that **Size** exceeds the **Size** of the **Row** instance in the **Marks** card to show the pie chart as an outer ring.

6. Within the **Row (2)** and **Row** instances of the **Marks** card, click on the **Color** shelf and select **Edit Colors**. Adjust the color settings as desired so that the color of the overlaying circle (the hole of the donut) can be distinguished from the underlying colors and yet continues to recognize which **Category** sold best. I selected the following:

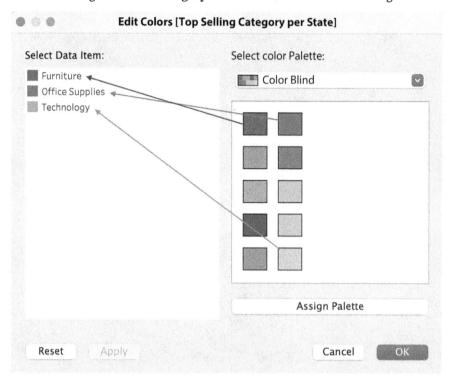

Figure 8.17: Color selection

7. Also, within the **Color** shelf, set **Border** to the desired color. I used white. I also used white as the color for **Label**.

8. Right-click on each axis and deselect **Show Header**. Select **Format | Lines** and set **Grid Lines** to **None**. Make other formatting changes as desired:

Altered Pie Map

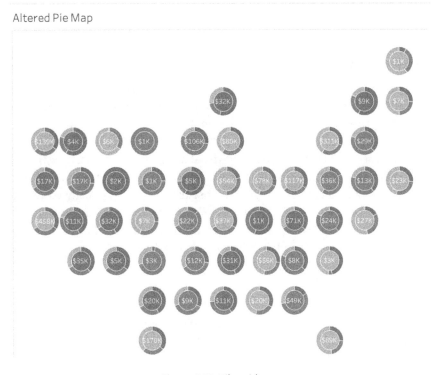

Figure 8.18: Tile grid map

At first glance, the visualization may look peculiar. It's called a **tile grid map** and although it's fairly new to the data visualization scene, it has begun to see usage at media outlets such as NPR. In the right setting, a tile grid map can be advantageous. Let's consider a couple of advantages the preceding exercise gives us.

First, the grid layout in combination with the **Log Sales** calculated field creates a map immediately evident as being the United States, while ensuring that the sizing of the various pie charts changes only moderately from greatest to least. Thus, each slice of each pie is reasonably visible; for example, the District of Columbia sales is as easily visible as California sales.

Second, the end user can clearly see the top-selling category for each state via the color of the inner circle (that is, the hole of the donut). This was accomplished with the LOD calculations. Thanks to the LOD, we were able to differentiate the best-selling category from the other two. Since all three categories live in the same column, you need to use an LOD calculation. You can refer to *Chapter 7, Practicing Level of Detail Calculations*, for more details on LOD calculations. The result is an information-dense visualization that uses pie charts in a practical, intuitive manner.

This section demonstrated some more creative approaches to show data from different angles in the same visualization. Next, we will continue to discuss another advanced visualization, Pareto charts.

Pareto charts

In the late 19th century, an Italian economist named Vilfredo Pareto observed that 80% of the land in Italy was owned by 20% of the people. As he looked around, he observed this mathematical phenomenon in many unexpected places. For example, he noted that 80% of the peas in his garden were produced from 20% of the peapods. As a result, the 80/20 rule has found its way into the popular vernacular. You can leverage this principle to create a clear visual hierarchy by emphasizing the most crucial elements or focal points. You can also use it as a tool for prioritization – what are your 20% most important tasks, datasets, and data quality issues? Work on those first. By giving priority you can focus your attention and ensure effective communication. But all of this requires another whole book. Let us focus first on how we can visualize an 80/20 phenomenon in Tableau. In the following exercise, we'll discuss how to build a basic Pareto chart and then how to expand that chart to make it even more useful.

Using Pareto charts

Of course, not every dataset is going to adhere to the 80/20 rule. Accordingly, the following exercise considers loan data from a community bank where 80% of the loan balance is not held by 20% of the bank's customers. Nonetheless, a Pareto chart can still be a very helpful analytical tool.

Take the following steps:

1. Within the workbook associated with this chapter, navigate to the worksheet entitled `Pareto - Basic` and select the `Bank data source`.

2. In the **Data** pane, change **Account #** to **Dimension**. Place **Account #** on the **Columns** shelf and **Current Loan Balance** on the **Rows** shelf.

3. Click on the **Fit** drop-down menu and choose **Entire View**.

4. Right-click on the **Account #** pill and select **Sort**. Set **Sort By** to **Field**, **Sort Order** to **Descending**, **Field Name** to **Current Loan Balance**, and **Aggregation** to **Sum**:

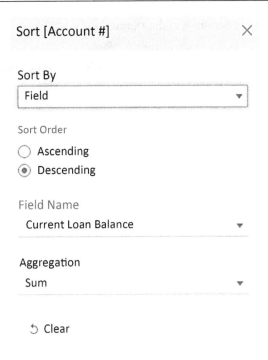

Figure 8.19: Sorting

5. Right-click on **SUM(Current Loan Balance)** Δ located on the **Rows** shelf and select **Add Table Calculation.** Choose the settings as shown in the following screenshot:

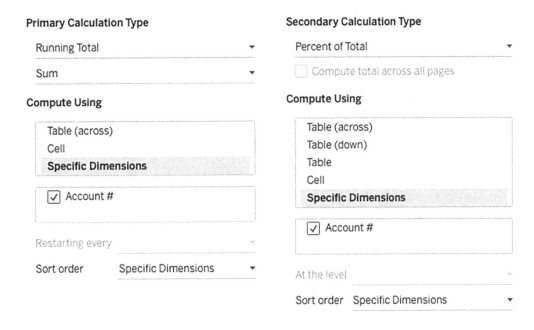

Figure 8.20: Table Calculation I

6. Drag an instance of **Account #** to the **Detail** shelf.

7. Click on the **Color** shelf and set **Border** to **None**.

8. Right-click on the instance of **Account #** that is on the **Columns** shelf and select **Measure |
    Count (Distinct)**. Note that a single vertical line displays:

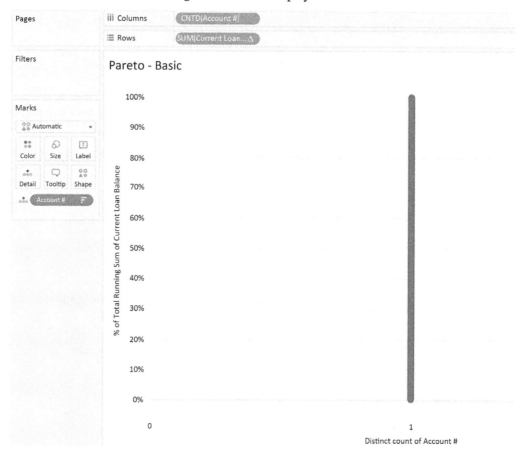

Figure 8.21: Pareto displaying a single vertical line

9. Once again, right-click on the instance of **CNTD(Account #)** on the **Columns** shelf and select **Add Table Calculation**. Configure the settings as shown in the following screenshot:

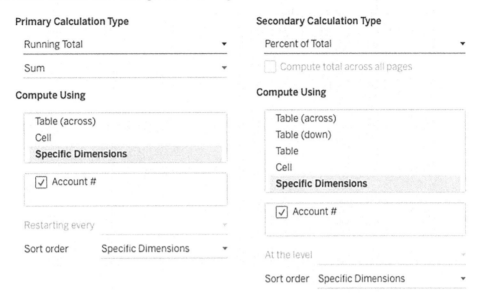

Figure 8.22: Table Calculation II

10. Click the **Analytics** tab in the upper left-hand corner of the screen and perform the following two steps:

    1. Drag **Constant Line** to **Table | SUM(Current Loan Balance)** Δ
    2. In the resulting dialog box, select **Constant** and set **Value** to **0.8**, as shown in the following screenshot:

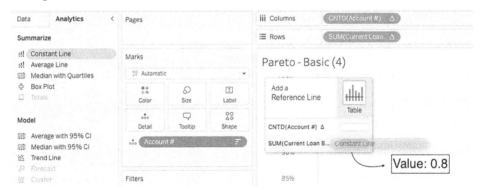

Figure 8.23: Constant Line

11. Repeat the previous step with the following differences:

    1. Drag **Constant Line** to **Table | CNTD(Account #)**
    2. In the resulting dialog box, select **Constant** and set **Value** to **0.2**

12. Drag **Current Loan Balance** to the **Rows** shelf. Place it to the right of the **SUM(Current Loan Balance)** Δ that is currently on the **Rows** shelf. Note that the axis is affected by a single loan with a much larger balance than the other loans:

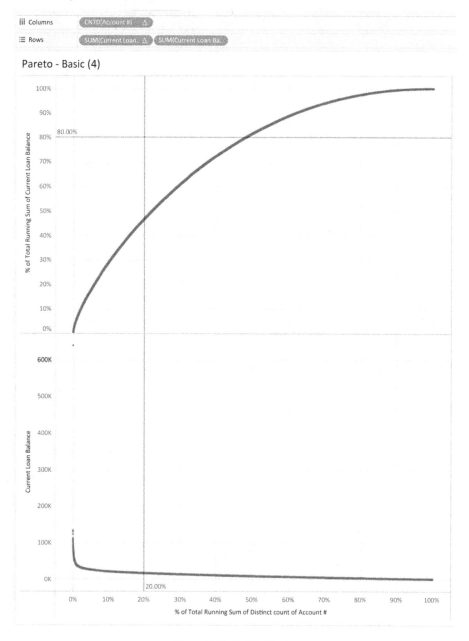

Figure 8.24: Pareto Basic

13. Right-click on the **Current Loan Balance** axis and select **Edit Axis**. In the resulting dialog box, set **Scale** to **Logarithmic** and close the window. This addresses the problem of the single large loan affecting the axis and thus obscuring the view of the other loans.

14. Within the **Marks** card, select the second instance of **SUM(Current Loan Balance)** Δ and set the mark type to **Bar:**

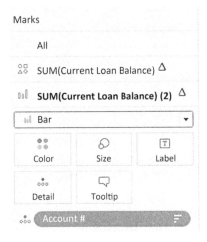

Figure 8.25: Select Bar

15. Right-click on **SUM(Current Loan Balance)** Δ on the **Rows** shelf and select **Dual Axis**.

16. Right-click on the **% of Total Running Sum of Current Loan Balance** axis and select **Move Marks Card to Front.** Change the colors, tooltips, and formatting as desired:

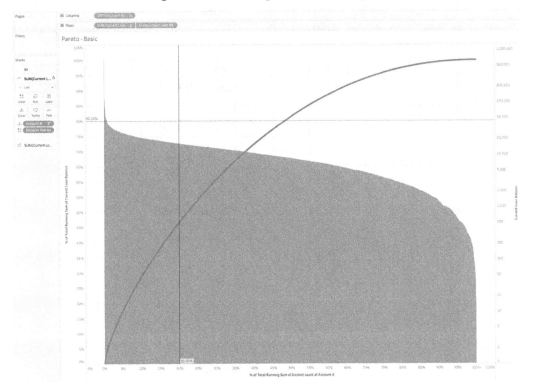

Figure 8.26: Pareto chart

There are positive aspects of this visualization to consider. First, the end user can quickly gain an initial understanding simply by observing both portions of the graph in conjunction with the values on the axes. The *y* axis on the left, for example, shows the percentage of each current loan in regard to the total amount of current loans, presented in a running sum such that we end up at 100%. The *y* axis on the right side shows the amount of those same loans. The *x* axis simply presents us with the unique account IDs or numbers. We can see that in this example, 20% of the accounts hold almost 60% of the loans and around 50% of the accounts hold 80% of the loans. Those are the two cross points of the red line and the two reference lines. Furthermore, the end user can hover the cursor over any part of the curve and see the resulting tooltip.

However, there are ways this visualization could be improved. For example, adding parameters to the two reference lines and rewording the axis labels to be less verbose would be quick ways to add additional value. Therefore, in the next exercise, we'll see if we can go a little beyond the current visualization.

Pareto charts — beyond the basics

In the previous exercise, we had to take a closer look in order to figure out what percentage of accounts account for how many loans. The following steps will show us how to create a parameter that will help us to spot the intersection:

1. Duplicate the sheet from the previous exercise and name the duplicate **Pareto - Improved**.
2. Remove both reference lines by selecting them and dragging them out of the worksheet.
3. Drag **SUM(Current Loan Balance) Δ** (the table calculation) from the **Rows** shelf to the **Data** pane. When prompted, name the field **Running % of Balance**.
4. Create and display a parameter with the following settings. This parameter will allow us to set any given value between 0 and 100%, and we will be able to see that area on the Pareto visualization in color:

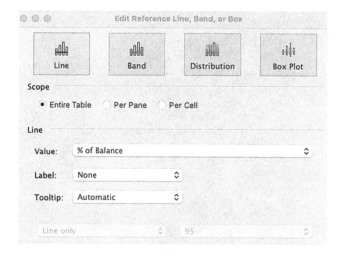

Figure 8.27: Editing the parameter

5. Right-click on the newly created parameter and select **Show Parameter**.

6. Create the following calculated fields:

Name	Code
Running % of Loans	`RUNNING_SUM(COUNTD([Account #]) / TOTAL(COUNTD([Account #])))`
Pareto Split	`IF [Running % of Balance] < [% of Balance] THEN "Makes up X% of Balance" ELSE "Makes up rest of Balance" END`
Pareto Split (label)	`IF LOOKUP([Pareto Split], -1) != LOOKUP([Pareto Split], 0) THEN MID(STR([Running % of Loans] * 100), 1, 5) + "% of loans make up " +MID(STR([% of Balance] * 100), 1, 5) +"% of balance" END`

7. The configuration that will result in the coloring of a selected area on the Pareto chart needs some extra attention; therefore, we created three calculations. With the help of those, we can change the color of parts of the visualization and add some explanatory text, as well as labels.

8. Select the **All** portion of the **Marks** card.

9. Drag **Pareto Split** to the **Detail** shelf. Click on the drop-down menu to the left of the **Pareto Split** pill on the **Marks** card and select **Color**:

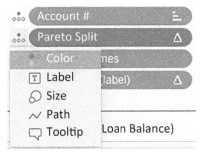

Figure 8.28: Pareto Split to Color

10. Select the **Running % of Balance Δ** portion of the **Marks** card. Set the mark type to **Line**.

11. Drag **Pareto Split (label)** to the **Label** shelf. Note that the expected label does not display:

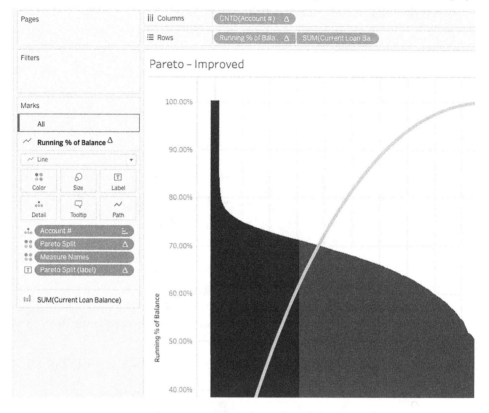

Figure 8.29: Pareto chart with no label

12. To address this, first click on the **Label** shelf and select **Allow labels to overlap other marks.**

13. Then, right-click **Pareto Split (label)** on the **Marks** card and select **Compute Using | Account #**. Now you will see the label:

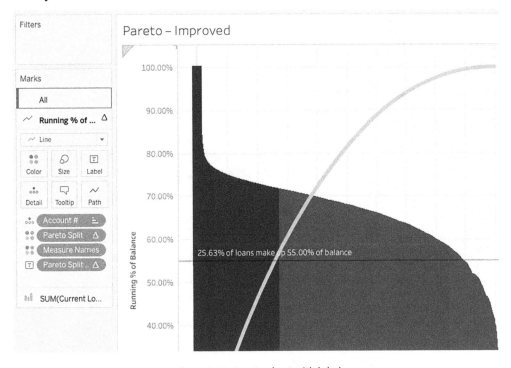

Figure 8.30: Pareto chart with label

14. Click the **Analytics** tab in the upper left-hand corner of the screen and perform the following two steps:

   1. Drag **Reference Line** to **Table | Δ Running % of Balance:**

Figure 8.31: Reference line

2. In the resulting dialog box, select **% of Balance** from the **Value** drop-down menu and set **Label** to **None**:

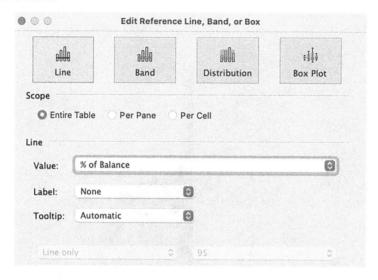

Figure 8.32: Reference line II

3. Change the colors, tooltips, and formatting as desired:

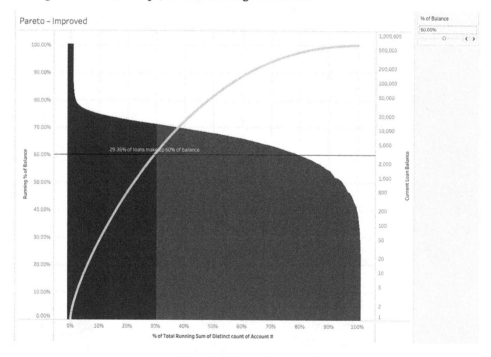

Figure 8.33: Pareto improved

As you will see in the screenshot, the end user now has a single parameter slider (in the top-right corner) that moves the horizontal reference line on the chart. As the end user moves the reference line, the text updates to display the loan and balance percentages. The colors also update as the end user adjusts the parameter to vertically communicate the percentage of loans under consideration. We were able to achieve this by creating the calculated fields `Pareto Split` and `Pareto Split (Label)`, which perform calculations on the data in the view in combination with the parameter.

The next section discusses a very powerful and still rarely used feature that will take your dashboards to the next level! Imagine a street view with houses in Tableau, whereby hovering over each house you will be able to see the rental/purchase price, the size, and maybe other characteristics. You can't imagine how to achieve this in Tableau? Well, continue reading! We will discuss diverse examples of maps, images, and even games like chess and darts in the next section.

Custom background images

Custom background images in Tableau open a world of potential. Imagine the ability to visualize any space. Possibilities encompass sports, health care, engineering, architecture, interior design, and much, much more. Despite this wealth of potential, background images in Tableau seem to me to be underutilized. Why? Part of the reason is because of the difficulty of generating datasets that can be used with background images.

Like the tile grid map discussed before, background images require a grid layout to pinpoint x and y coordinates. In the following section, we will address how to use Tableau to create a grid that can be superimposed on an image to instantly identify locations associated with x and y coordinates, and relatively quickly produce datasets that can be accessed by Tableau for visualization purposes.

Creating custom polygons

Geographic areas for which Tableau natively provides polygons include country, state/province, county, and postcode/zip code. This means, for example, that a filled map can easily be created for the countries of the world. Simply copy a list of countries and paste that list into Tableau. Next, set the view type in Tableau to **Filled Map** and place the country list on the **Detail** shelf. Tableau will automatically draw polygons for each of those countries.

Furthermore, special mapping needs may arise that require polygons to be drawn for areas that are not typically included on maps. For example, an organization may define sales regions that don't follow the usual map boundaries. Lastly, mapping needs may arise for custom images. A Tableau author may import an image of a basketball court or football pitch into Tableau and draw polygons to represent particular parts of the playing area. To create a filled map for each of these examples, for which Tableau does not natively provide polygons, custom polygons must be created.

Drawing a square around Null Island

In this section, we will start with the basics by drawing a simple square around the mythical Null Island, which is located at the intersection of the prime meridian and the equator.

We will progress to a more robust example that requires drawing polygons for every city in Texas. There is an option in Tableau that allows an author to **Show Data at Default Position** for unknown locations. Selecting this option will cause Tableau to set latitude and longitude coordinates of 0 (zero) for all unknown locations, thus creating a symbol on the world map 1,600 kilometers off the western coast of Africa. Tableau developers affectionately refer to this area as Null Island.

 Null Island even has its own YouTube video: `https://youtu.be/bjvIpI-1w84`.

In this exercise, we will draw a square around Null Island:

1. Recreate the following dataset in Excel:

	A	B	C
1	Point	Latitude	Longitude
2	0	-1	-1
3	1	-1	1
4	2	1	1
5	3	1	-1
6	4	-1	-1

2. Copy and paste the dataset into Tableau. By doing so, a new data source called `Clipboard_...` will appear:

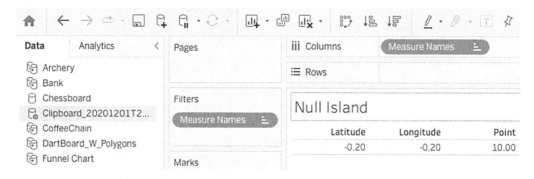

Figure 8.34: Null Island coordinates

3. Remove all fields from the worksheet.
4. Convert **Point** to a dimension. This can be accomplished by either right-clicking on **Point** and selecting **Convert to Dimension,** or by dragging it to the dimensions portion of the **Data** pane.
5. Double-click on **Latitude** and **Longitude**. It doesn't matter in which order; Tableau will automatically place **Longitude** on the **Columns** shelf and **Latitude** on the **Rows** shelf.

6. Select **Map | Background Maps | Streets**. You might have to zoom out a bit to see the land line:

Figure 8.35: Locating Null Island

7. Change the view type to **Line**, and drop **Point** on the **Path** shelf. You should see the following results:

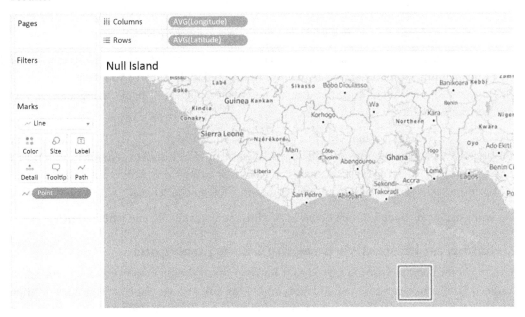

Figure 8.36: Locating Null Island II

8. Go back to your Excel file, switch the rows containing data for points 1 and 2, and copy the data again into Tableau.

9. Follow *Steps 2–7* and observe the resulting image:

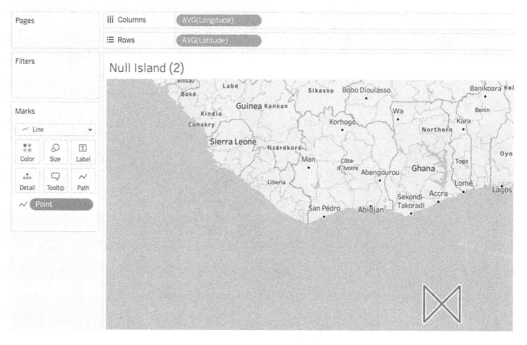

Figure 8.37: Incorrectly delineating Null Island

This interesting but incorrect image occurred because of incorrect point ordering. As a rule of thumb, when determining point order, select an order that would make sense if you were physically drawing the polygon. If you cannot draw the desired polygon on a sheet of paper using a given point order, neither can Tableau.

It is likely that you found completing this exercise in Tableau relatively easy. The challenge is in getting the data right, particularly the polygon points. A useful (and free) tool to generate polygon data can be found at http://powertoolsfortableau.com/tools/drawing-tool. This is one of many tools created by InterWorks that are helpful to address common Tableau challenges.

We will use it next to show which books in our library are available and which aren't.

Creating an interactive bookshelf using polygons

I am not very good at drawing myself, but I always loved the fancy polygon backgrounds I saw on Tableau Public, having shapes of all kinds, and being able to have Tableau interact with them, color them depending on a measure, or link an action to a specific area. Did you know, for example, that the continents can be reshaped to build the shape of a chicken? Well, Niccolo Cirone made a Tableau dashboard out of it, using polygons: https://www.theinformationlab.co.uk/2016/06/01/polygons-people-polygon-ize-image-tableau/.

Do you want to build fancy dashboards too but your drawing skills are mediocre, just like mine? Don't worry! This section will give you the tools to achieve it anyway. InterWorks has developed a tool similar to painting by numbers – the perfect application to build polygons without drawing too much yourself. You can find it here: `https://cbistudio.interworks.com`. All you need to do is find an image, upload it to the tool, and start drawing along the lines.

For this exercise, I searched for an image of a bookshelf on the internet. You can do the same and find an image for this exercise or download the image I used, which can be downloaded here: `https://github.com/PacktPublishing/Mastering-Tableau-2023-Fourth-Edition/Chapter08/bookshelf.png`:

1. Open the free drawing tool from InterWorks and select the **Images** option:

Figure 8.38: CBI Studio

2. Upload your image and select **Polygon** in the **I'M CREATING** section.

3. Now start at the edge of one book and click. An orange dot will appear. Now go to the next edge of the same book and click again. A line will be drawn along that edge of the book and the coordinates automatically appear in the list on the right-hand side:

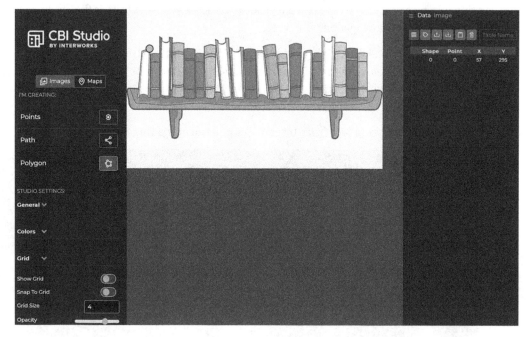

Figure 8.39: Drawing tool

4. The last dot of a book should be on top of the first dot (which is bigger than the rest). Hitting the first dot again will finalize the first polygon, which is indicated by a green color:

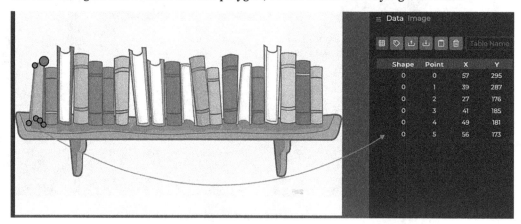

Figure 8.40: Finalizing the polygon

5. The next dot you set somewhere else will get a different shape ID and, hence, can be distin-
    guished as a different shape by Tableau later on. And remember, move along the outside of a
    book and avoid crossing lines.

6. When you are done outlining the books, download the data in .csv format and save the file
    to be used as a data source in Tableau. I did so, and in addition, I added **Name** and **Available**
    columns. You can see, furthermore, the unique shape ID, the point ID (the order in which
    you clicked on the screen), and x and y as a representation of the location within the image:

	A	B	C	D	E	F
1	shape id	point id	x	y	Name	Available
2	0	0	57	284	The brown book	No
3	0	1	83	284	The brown book	No
4	0	2	83	173	The brown book	No
5	0	3	60	173	The brown book	No
6	0	4	57	284	The brown book	Yes
7	1	0	117	173	The green book	Yes
8	1	1	117	309	The green book	Yes
9	1	2	145	309	The green book	Yes
10	1	3	145	176	The green book	Yes
11	1	4	117	173	The green book	Yes
12	2	0	175	176	The blue book	Yes
13	2	1	175	283	The blue book	Yes
14	2	2	196	283	The blue book	Yes
15	2	3	196	176	The blue book	Yes
16	2	4	175	176	The blue book	Yes
17	3	0	303	176	The purple book	No
18	3	1	303	292	The purple book	No
19	3	2	327	292	The purple book	No
20	3	3	327	173	The purple book	No
21	3	4	303	176	The purple book	No

Figure 8.41: Excel

7. Next, load the data in Tableau and place **X** on **Columns** and **Y** on **Rows**. Can you recognize the bookshelf yet? I only used four books for this exercise; therefore, not all show up:

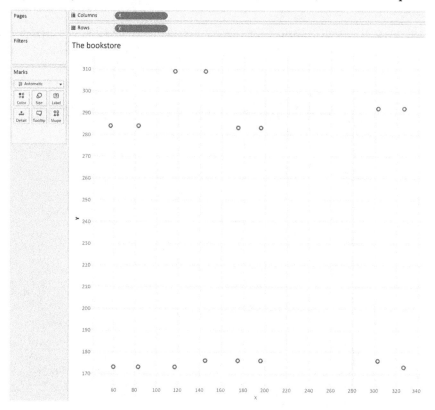

Figure 8.42: Bookstore

8. Before we can add the image to Tableau, we need the coordinates of the outermost points for the Tableau settings. Simply go back to the drawing tool and measure the edges. Note down the **X** and **Y** coordinates for the four edges. It might not be exactly the corners but the below values can be roughly translated to height = 400 and width = 648:

Figure 8.43: Drawing tool

9. Back in Tableau, click on **Map | Background Image** and select **The bookstore….** In the following popup, define a name and upload the image you used in the drawing tool. Also fill in the coordinates for the **X** and **Y** fields to represent the edges of the image:

Figure 8.44: Edit Background Image

10. Click on **Options** and select **Always Show Entire Image**. Then close this window:

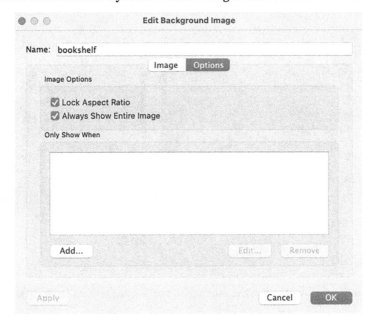

Figure 8.45: Edit Background Image options

11. Your image should appear on your worksheet now, with matching dots surrounding the books:

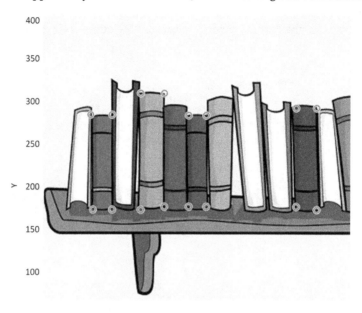

Figure 8.46: Bookshelf with dots

12. To create a surrounding line instead of dots, change the mark type to **Line** and place **Shape Id** on **Detail** and **Point Id** on **Path**:

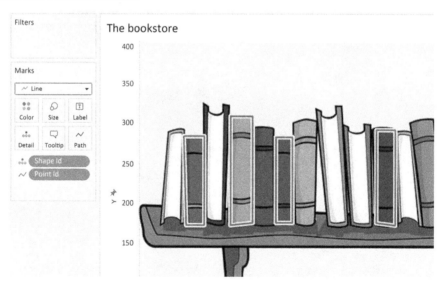

Figure 8.47: Bookshelf with lines

13. To create a polygon, change the mark type to **Polygon** and set **Opacity** in the **Color** shelf to 0%.

14. In addition, you can add a tooltip with the book name and availability after placing both fields on the **Detail** shelf:

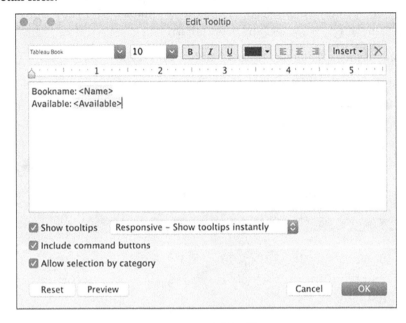

Figure 8.48: Edit tooltip

15. If you hover over the books, you can see the name as well as the availability:

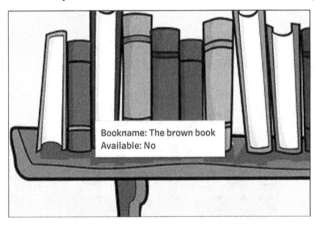

Figure 8.49: Using a tooltip

The best part about polygons is that they fill the whole area. In this example, no matter where you hover or click, the complete back of the book is covered because we drew an area rather than a point or a certain default shape. And this comes with endless options; imagine a big library where every book is a polygon, and you can connect live data to the polygon dataset with the up-to-date availability of any book. Aside from books, you can draw anything. What I have seen most in Tableau are floor plans, supermarket shelves, office layouts, shapes split into parts… polygons really allow you to get creative with your visualizations.

If you don't have an image at hand and you want to draw something very specific to your dashboard, you can use paid or free software like Adobe Illustrator Draw, Sketch, Sketsa SVG Editor, Boxy SVG, Gravit Designer, Vecteezy Editor, Vectr, Method Draw, Inkpad, iDesign, Affinity Designer, macSVG, Chartist.js, Plain Pattern, Inkscape, and many others.

Let us take our dashboard one step further before we move on:

1. Right-click on **Name** | **Aliases...**
2. Change the book as shown here and click **OK**:

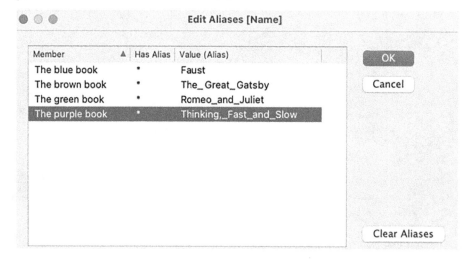

Figure 8.50: Picking another book

3. Remove the **X** and **Y** axis of The Bookstore worksheet.
4. Open a dashboard tab and call it **The Bookstore**:

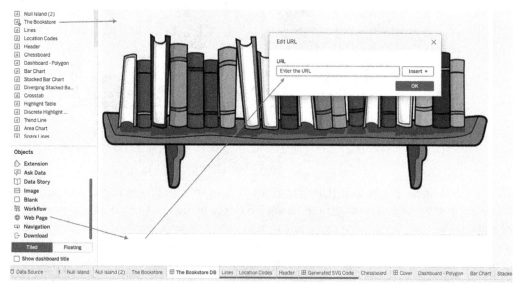

Figure 8.51: URL

5. Drag The Bookstore worksheet into the upper part of the dashboard and the **Web Page** object into the bottom half. Type into the URL popup: `https://en.wikipedia.org/wiki/`.

6. Select the **Web Page Object** and click on the arrow; choose **Add URL Action...**

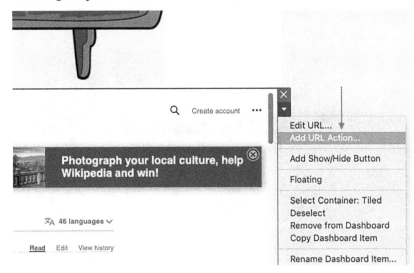

Figure 8.52: Add URL Action…

7. In the **Actions** window, add **Name** to the URL by selecting this field from the arrow dropdown:

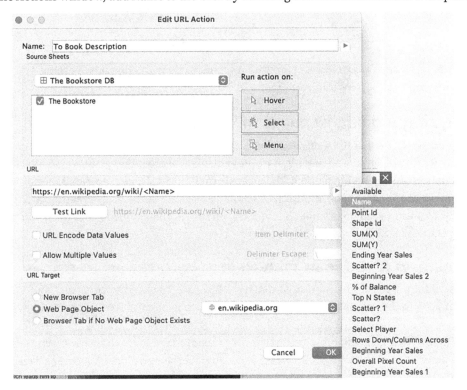

Figure 8.53: Description filter

8.   Click **OK** and select the different books to see the Wikipedia entry changing in your dashboard:

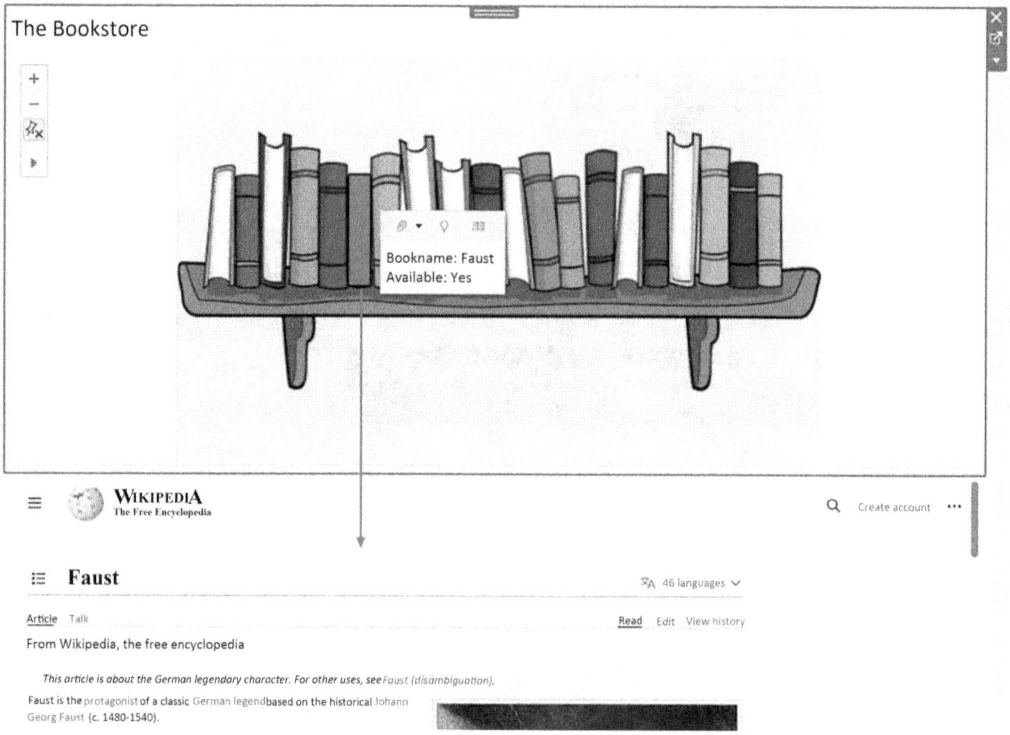

Figure 8.54: Wikipedia

I am sure you have a ton of ideas by now about what to do with polygons. Perhaps you would like to analyze a game of chess? We will do that next!

Analyzing a game of chess in Tableau

In this exercise, we will use Inkscape. But instead of drawing something in one of the tools, transforming it into polygons, and loading it in Tableau, we will create the code for an SVG file in Tableau, load it in Inkscape to see if it worked, then transform it into polygons, and load the converted version with x and y coordinates back into Tableau to analyze a game of chess. By creating an SVG file yourself, you will be able to recognize which X and Y coordinates Tableau needs, and thus, you will always be able to transform SVGs.

Creating an SVG file in Tableau

In this section, we will use Tableau to generate the XML required to construct an SVG file that can be opened with the vector graphic tool Inkscape, which is open source and is, thus, available free of charge. Visit inkscape.org to download the latest version. We will also need the Chessboard.png image, available on the Packt GitHub page: https://github.com/PacktPublishing/Mastering-Tableau-2023-Fourth-Edition/Chapter08/Chessboard.png. Please download that one as well.

Usually, polygons show their power even more when used in non-linear drawings. Our chessboard, however, is a good example in this case, because we will create the locations used by Tableau ourselves – creating a square is easier than a more complex shape because we can work with increments. Note that a grid with 10 rows and 10 columns is used in the following examples, which of course generates a grid of 100 cells. This will perform satisfactorily in Inkscape. However, if a large cell count is required, a professional graphics tool such as Adobe Illustrator may be required.

Creating a grid

The following exercise serves multiple purposes. The first purpose is to demonstrate how to use Tableau to create a grid. This chapter provides another opportunity to use data scaffolding, which was discussed in *Chapter 4, Learning about Joins, Blends, and Data Structures*. The difference is that in that chapter, dates were used for scaffolding purposes, whereas in the following section, bins are utilized. Additionally, this exercise requires many table calculations that will help reinforce the lessons learned in *Chapter 5, Introducing Table Calculations*. Lastly, this exercise makes use of data densification, which was discussed in *Chapter 6, Utilizing OData, Data Densification, Big Data, Google BigQuery*.

To get started, take the following steps:

1. Open a new Tableau workbook and name the first sheet **Header**.
2. Using Excel or a text editor, create a **Records** dataset. The following two-row table represents the **Records** dataset in its entirety:

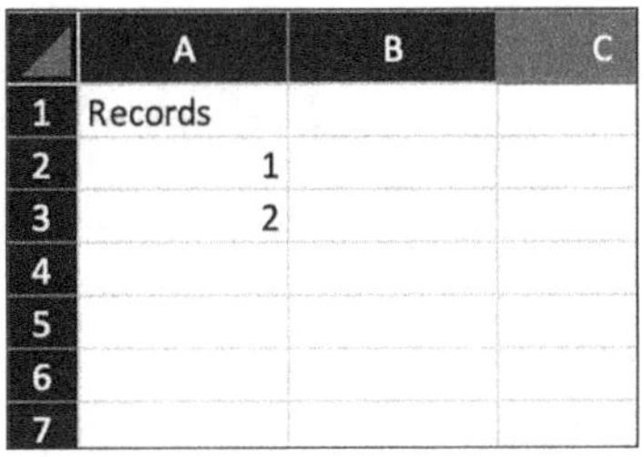

Figure 8.55: Excel

3. Connect Tableau to the **Records** dataset:

    •   For convenience, consider copying the dataset using *Ctrl + C* and pasting it directly into Tableau using *Ctrl + V*.

    •   Tableau will likely consider **Records** a measure. Drag **Records** to the **Dimensions** portion of the **Data** pane.

4. Create two parameters. Name one `Overall Pixel Count` and the other `Rows Down/Columns Across`. The settings for both are as follows:

    •   Data type: **Integer**

    •   Allowable values: **All**

5. Show both parameters. Set **Rows Down/Columns Across** to 10 and **Overall Pixel Count** to 1,000:

Rows Down/Columns Across

```
10
```

Overall Pixel Count

```
1,000
```

Figure 8.56: Showing the parameter

6. Create a calculated field named Concatenate Header with the following code:

```
'<?xml version="1.0" encoding="utf-8"?><svg version="1.1" id="Squares"
xmlns="http://www.w3.org/2000/svg"
xmlns:xlink="http://www.w3.org/1999/xlink" x="0px" y="0px" viewBox="0 0 '
+
STR( [Overall Pixel Count] ) + " " + STR([Overall Pixel Count])+ '"
style="enable-background:new 0 0 '+ STR([Overall Pixel Count]) + ' ' +
STR([Overall Pixel Count]) + ';" xml:space="preserve">
<style type="text/css"> .st0{fill:none;stroke:#000000;stroke-
miterlimit:10;}
</style>'
```

Note that entering line breaks in the **Calculated Field** dialog box may make the results difficult to extract from Tableau. In other words, remove all line breaks.

7. Now we have created a skeleton or template that will help us create multiple locations in order to draw a grid in Tableau.

8. Place the newly created calculated field on the **Text** shelf.

9. In the toolbar, choose to fit to **Entire View** to view the results; you can see that the parameters fill in **STR([Overall Pixel Count])** from **Concatenate Header**:

Figure 8.57: Concatenate Header

10. Create a new worksheet named **Location Codes.**

11. Create the following calculated fields:

Name	Code
Rows Down/Columns Across	`[Parameters].[Rows Down/Columns Across]`
Which Column?	`LAST()+1`
Which Row?	`INDEX()`
Grid Size	`[Overall Pixel Count]/LOOKUP([Which Column?],FIRST())`
X	`[Overall Pixel Count] - ([Grid Size] * ([Which Row?]))`
Y	`[Overall Pixel Count] - ([Grid Size] * ([Which Column?]-1))`
Count	`If [Records] = 1 THEN 1 ELSE [Rows Down/Columns Across] END`
Decicount	`If [Records] = 1 THEN 1 ELSE [Rows Down/Columns Across] END`
Location Codes	`Index()`
Concatenate Locations	`'<text transform="matrix(1 0 0 1 ' + STR([X])` `+ " " + STR([Y])` `+')">' + STR( [Location Codes] ) + '</text>'`

12. The created calculated fields will be used in the next steps to create a table of values, similar to the table of values that we generated in the drawing tool. Only now, we will do it ourselves and use SVG code instead of longitude and latitude values.

13. Right-click on **Count** and select **Create | Bins**. In the resulting dialog box, set **Size of bins** to 1:

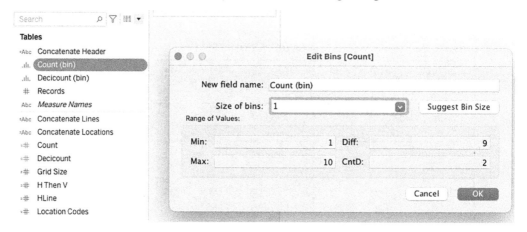

Figure 8.58: Count bin

14. Right-click on **Decicount** and select **Create | Bins**. In the resulting dialog box, set **Size of bins** to 1:

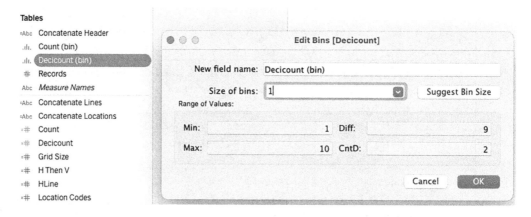

Figure 8.59: Count bin II

15. Place **Count (bin)**, **Decicount (bin)**, **Location Codes**, **X**, and **Y** on the **Rows** shelf. Be sure to place those fields in the order listed.

16. If your fields are green (meaning continuous), right-click on each field on the **Rows** shelf and set it to **Discrete**. Then:

    • Right-click on **Count (bin)** and **Decicount (bin)** and ensure that **Show Missing Values** is selected

    • Right-click on **Location Codes** and select **Compute Using | Table (Down)**

- Set the **Compute Using** value for **X** to **Count (bin)**
- Set the **Compute Using** value for **Y** to **Decicount (bin)**

Count (bin)	Decicount (..	Location Co..	X	Y		
1	1	1	900	100	Abc	
	2	2	900	200	Abc	
	3	3	900	300	Abc	
	4	4	900	400	Abc	
	5	5	900	500	Abc	
	6	6	900	600	Abc	
	7	7	900	700	Abc	
	8	8	900	800	Abc	
	9	9	900	900	Abc	
	10	10	900	1,000	Abc	
2	1	11	800	100	Abc	
	2	12	800	200	Abc	
	3	13	800	300	Abc	
	4	14	800	400	Abc	
	5	15	800	500	Abc	
	6	16	800	600	Abc	
	7	17	800	700	Abc	
	8	18	800	800	Abc	

Columns

Rows: Count (bin) · Decicount (bin) · Location Codes △ · X △ · Y △

Rows Down/Columns A... : 10

Overall Pixel Count : 1,000

Figure 8.60: Location Codes worksheet

17. Place **Concatenate Locations** on the **Text** shelf.

18. Right-click on the instance of **Concatenate Locations** you just placed on the **Text** shelf and select **Edit Table Calculations**.

19. At the top of the resulting dialog box, note that there are four options under **Nested Calculations: Grid Size, Which Column?, Which Row?,** and **Location Codes**. Set the **Compute Using** definition for each as follows:

   - **Nested Calculations: Grid Size > Compute Using: Table (down)**
   - **Nested Calculations: Which Column? > Compute Using: Specific Dimensions: Decicount (bin) > move this dimension to the top**
   - **Nested Calculations: Which Row? > Compute Using: Specific Dimensions: Count (bin) > move this dimension to the top**
   - **Nested Calculations: Location Codes > Compute Using: Table (down)**

20. In the toolbar, choose **Fit Width** to view the results; you can already see that multiple rows have been created. Those rows will later be used to draw a grid:

Count (bin)	Decicount (..	Location Co..	X	Y	
1	1	1	900	100	<text transform="matrix(1 0 0 1 900 10..
	2	2	900	200	<text transform="matrix(1 0 0 1 900 20..
	3	3	900	300	<text transform="matrix(1 0 0 1 900 30..
	4	4	900	400	<text transform="matrix(1 0 0 1 900 40..
	5	5	900	500	<text transform="matrix(1 0 0 1 900 50..
	6	6	900	600	<text transform="matrix(1 0 0 1 900 60..
	7	7	900	700	<text transform="matrix(1 0 0 1 900 70..
	8	8	900	800	<text transform="matrix(1 0 0 1 900 80..
	9	9	900	900	<text transform="matrix(1 0 0 1 900 90..
	10	10	900	1,000	<text transform="matrix(1 0 0 1 900 10..
2	1	11	800	100	<text transform="matrix(1 0 0 1 800 10..
	2	12	800	200	<text transform="matrix(1 0 0 1 800 20..
	3	13	800	300	<text transform="matrix(1 0 0 1 800 30..
	4	14	800	400	<text transform="matrix(1 0 0 1 800 40..
	5	15	800	500	<text transform="matrix(1 0 0 1 800 50..
	6	16	800	600	<text transform="matrix(1 0 0 1 800 60..
	7	17	800	700	<text transform="matrix(1 0 0 1 800 70..

Figure 8.61: Fit width

21. Now, create a new worksheet named **Lines**.
22. Create the following calculated fields:

Name	Compute Using Setting
H Then V	Index()
HLine	Last()
VLine	Index()-1
X1	IF [H Then V] = 1 THEN 0 ELSE [Overall Pixel Count] - ([Grid Size] * ([VLine])) END
Y1	IF [H Then V] = 2 THEN 0 ELSE [Overall Pixel Count] - ([Grid Size] * ([VLine])) END
X2	IF [H Then V] = 1 THEN [Overall Pixel Count] ELSE [Overall Pixel Count] - ([Grid Size] * ([VLine])) END
Y2	IF [H Then V] = 2 THEN [Overall Pixel Count] ELSE [Overall Pixel Count] - ([Grid Size] * ([VLine])) END

1. Next, place the following fields on the **Rows** shelf in the following order: **Count (bin)**, **Decicount (bin)**, **H Then V**, **HLine**, **VLine**, **Grid Size**, **Which Column?**, **X1**, **Y1**, **X2**, and **Y2**. Note that each should be cast as discrete.

2. Right-click on **Count(bin)** and **Decicount(bin)** and set each to **Show Missing Values**.

3. Right-click on each of the remaining fields on the **Rows** shelf and select **Edit Table Calculations**. Set the **Compute Using** definition of each field as shown in the following table:

Name	Nested Calculations	Compute Using Setting
H Then V	N/A	Count (bin)
HLine	N/A	Count (bin)
VLine	N/A	Decicount (bin)
Grid Size	Grid Size	Table (Down)
Grid Size	Which Column?	Decicount (bin)
X1, Y1, X2, Y2	H Then V	Count (bin)
X1, Y1, X2, Y2	Grid Size	Count (bin)
X1, Y1, X2, Y2	Which Column?	Count (bin)
X1, Y1, X2, Y2	VLine	Decicount (bin)

4. Note that some of the fields include nested table calculations. In such cases, the **Table Calculation** dialog box will include an extra option at the top entitled **Nested Calculations**:

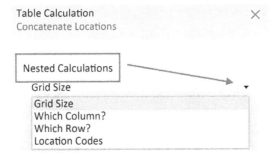

Figure 8.62: Nested calculation

5. **X1**, **X2**, **Y1**, and **Y2** need to be configured for four nested calculations. Start by opening the **X1** table calculation and then selecting **H Then V** from the **Nested Calculations** dropdown, and set **Compute Using** to **Count (bin)**. Then, in the same window, select **Grid Size** from the dropdown and enter the corresponding **Compute Using** setting. After all four dropdowns have been set, continue with **X2** and do the same.

6. Filter **H Then V** to display only **1** and **2**.

7. Create a calculated field called Concatenate Lines with the following code:

```
'<line class="st0" x1="' + STR([X1]) + '" y1="' + STR([Y1]) + '" x2="' +
STR( [X2] ) + '" y2="' + STR([Y2]) + '"/>'
```

8. This calculation will create a new string by including the fields **X1**, **X2**, **Y1**, and **Y2**. By doing so we multiply one row of code by as many rows as we want, each with a specific combination of **X1**, **X2**, **Y1**, and **Y2**.

9. Place **Concatenate Lines** on the **Text** shelf. Your worksheet should look as follows:

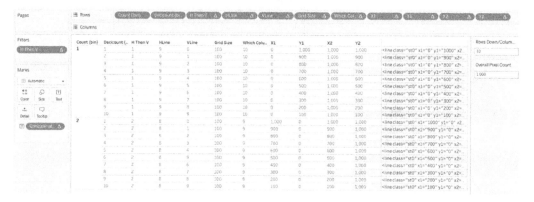

Figure 8.63: Concatenate Lines

10. Export the code from the three worksheets just created.

> Exporting the code from the three worksheets can be tricky since Tableau may try to input additional quotes for string values. I found the following approach works best:
>
> 1. Select **1** in the **Count (bin)** Rows
> 2. Press *Ctrl + A* (*Command + A* for Mac) to select all the contents of the worksheet.
> 3. Hover the cursor over the selected text in the view and pause until the tooltip command buttons appear.
> 4. Select the **View Data** icon at the right-hand side of the tooltip.
> 5. In the resulting **View Data** dialog box, select **Export All**.
> 6. Save the CSV file using the same name as each worksheet; for instance, the data exported from the Header worksheet will be named Header.csv.
> 7. Repeat the steps for the remaining worksheets **Header** and **Location Codes**.

11. Open an instance of your favorite text editor and save it as Grid and LocationCodes.svg.

12. Copy the data from the previously exported and saved Header.csv and paste it into Grid and LocationCodes.svg. Be sure not to include the header information; include only the XML code. For example, in the next screenshot, don't copy row 1, only copy row 2:

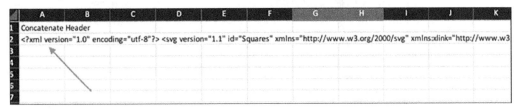

Figure 8.64: Excel

13. Using Excel, copy the required data from Location.csv and paste it into Grid and LocationCodes.svg. The required data only includes the column labeled Concatenate Locations. Do not include the other columns or the header. Include only the XML code. For example, in the following screenshot, we only copy column F:

A	B	C	D	E	F
Count (bin)	Decicount (t	Location Co	X	Y	
1	1	1	900	100	\<text transform="matrix(1 0 0 1 900 100)">1\</text>
	2	2	900	200	\<text transform="matrix(1 0 0 1 900 200)">2\</text>
	3	3	900	300	\<text transform="matrix(1 0 0 1 900 300)">3\</text>
	4	4	900	400	\<text transform="matrix(1 0 0 1 900 400)">4\</text>
	5	5	900	500	\<text transform="matrix(1 0 0 1 900 500)">5\</text>
	6	6	900	600	\<text transform="matrix(1 0 0 1 900 600)">6\</text>
	7	7	900	700	\<text transform="matrix(1 0 0 1 900 700)">7\</text>
	8	8	900	800	\<text transform="matrix(1 0 0 1 900 800)">8\</text>
	9	9	900	900	\<text transform="matrix(1 0 0 1 900 900)">9\</text>
	10	10	900	1,000	\<text transform="matrix(1 0 0 1 900 1000)">10\</text>
2	1	11	800	100	\<text transform="matrix(1 0 0 1 800 100)">11\</text>
	2	12	800	200	\<text transform="matrix(1 0 0 1 800 200)">12\</text>
	3	13	800	300	\<text transform="matrix(1 0 0 1 800 300)">13\</text>
	4	14	800	400	\<text transform="matrix(1 0 0 1 800 400)">14\</text>

Figure 8.65: Excel II

14. Using Excel, copy the required data from Lines.csv and paste it into Grid and LocationCodes.svg. Again, the required data only includes the column labeled Concatenate Lines. Do not include the other columns or the header, only the XML code.

15. Lastly, complete the SVG file by entering the \</svg> closing tag. The full code has been added for your convenience on the **Generated SVG Code** tab:

```
<text transform="matrix(1 0 0 1 200 300)">73</text>
<text transform="matrix(1 0 0 1 200 200)">72</text>
<text transform="matrix(1 0 0 1 200 100)">71</text>
<text transform="matrix(1 0 0 1 300 1000)">70</text>
<text transform="matrix(1 0 0 1 300 900)">69</text>
<text transform="matrix(1 0 0 1 300 800)">68</text>
<text transform="matrix(1 0 0 1 300 700)">67</text>
<text transform="matrix(1 0 0 1 300 600)">66</text>
<text transform="matrix(1 0 0 1 300 500)">65</text>
<text transform="matrix(1 0 0 1 300 400)">64</text>
<text transform="matrix(1 0 0 1 300 300)">63</text>
<text transform="matrix(1 0 0 1 300 200)">62</text>
<text transform="matrix(1 0 0 1 300 100)">61</text>
<text transform="matrix(1 0 0 1 400 1000)">60</text>
<text transform="matrix(1 0 0 1 400 900)">59</text>
```

| Null Island (2) | The Bookstore | Lines | Location Codes | Header | ⊞ **Generated SVG Code** | Chessboard |

Figure 8.66: Full code

16. Now, open the SVG file in Inkscape (`https://inkscape.org/`) and observe the grid:

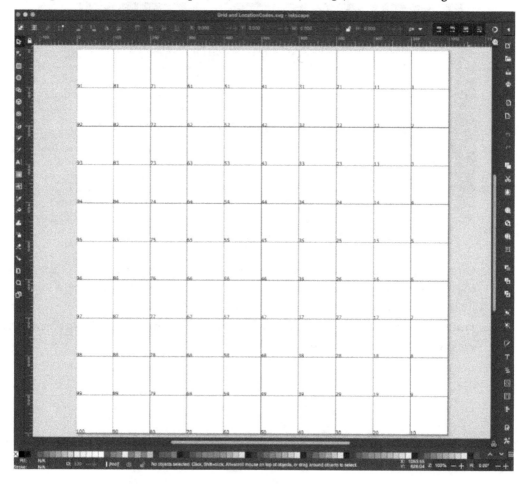

Figure 8.67: Inkscape II

If for some reason your code does not create a grid or you instead want to use the version that I created, you can find the SVG file together with all the other datasets on the following GitHub page: https://github.com/PacktPublishing/Mastering-Tableau-2023-Fourth-Edition/blob/main/Chapter08/GridandLocationCodes.svg.

We will cover an example of how to use the grid for a polygon data source in Tableau in the next exercise.

Using a grid to generate a dataset

Skilled chess players will complete a game in about 40 moves. In chess tournaments, data is routinely captured for each game, which provides opportunities for data visualization. In this exercise, we will use data from a chess game to visualize how often each square of a chessboard is occupied:

1. Within the workbook associated with this chapter, navigate to the worksheet entitled Chessboard.
2. Download the Chessboard.png pictures from this book's GitHub repository if you haven't done so yet.
3. Open the SVG file created in the previous exercise in Inkscape.

> If you did not complete the previous exercise, you can copy the XML code located on the dashboard, entitled **Generated SVG Code**, in the solution workbook associated with this chapter. Paste that code into a text editor and save it with an SVG extension, then open the file with Inkscape.

4. Within **Inkscape**, press *Ctrl + A* (*Command + A* for Mac) to select all. Group the selection using *Ctrl + G* (*Command + G* for Mac).
5. From the **Inkscape** menu, select **Layer | Layers and Objects**. The keyboard shortcut is *Shift + Ctrl + L* (*Shift + Command + L* for Mac).
6. Within the **Layers** palette that displays on the right-hand side of the screen, press the + icon to create a layer. Name the layer Chessboard. Then, create another layer named Grid:

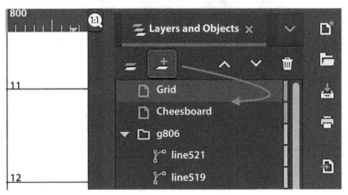

Figure 8.68: Layers

7. Click on any line or number in the view. Right-click on that same line or number and select **Move to layer**. Choose the **Grid** layer.

8. Select **File** | **Import** and choose the Chessboard.png image.

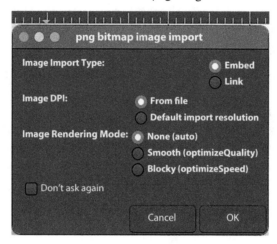

Figure 8.69: Image import

9. Make sure that the image is placed on the **Chessboard** layer so that the location code numbers are not obscured. Position the chessboard image such that location code **81** is centered over the top left-hand square of the chessboard. Since the chessboard is only composed of 64 squares, it will not encompass all 100 squares that the grid provides:

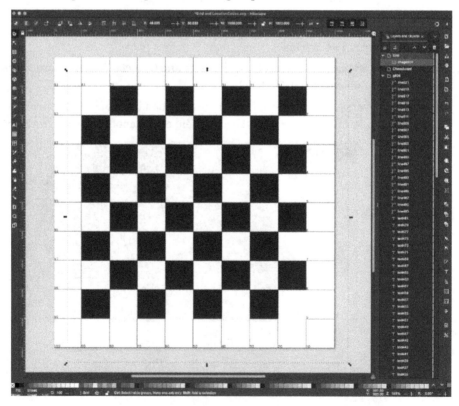

Figure 8.70: Chessboard

At this point, you can generate a dataset based on how often each location is occupied. For example, you might note that for one game, position 81 was occupied for 40 moves, in which case the player may simply have never moved that rook. However, in another game the position may be occupied for only 10 moves, perhaps indicating the player performed a castle early in the game. The point of layering the chess game and the square file was to identify which square belongs to which field on a chess board.

Visualizing a chess game

In this exercise, we will take a look at a dataset generated from a chess game and discover how to visualize the results based on the work done in the previous exercises. The following are the steps:

1. Within the workbook associated with this chapter, navigate to the worksheet entitled Chessboard and select the Chessboard data source.

    In order to follow the next step, you will need to download the assets associated with this chapter. To do so, simply follow the link to the GitHub repository for this book: https://github.com/PacktPublishing/Mastering-Tableau-2023-Fourth-Edition/tree/main/Chapter08.

2. Right-click on the Chessboard data source and select **Edit Data Source** in order to examine the dataset.

3. In the dialog box asking **Where is the data file?**, steer to the Chessboard.xlsx file provided with the assets associated with this chapter.

4. The table named **Board Grid** contains each location code and the **X** and **Y** coordinates associated with each location code. This dataset was taken from the **Location Codes** worksheet created earlier in this chapter. The table named **Squares Occupied** contains the fields **Location Code** and **Moves Occupied**. **Board Grid** and **Squares Occupied** are connected using a left join on **Location Code**:

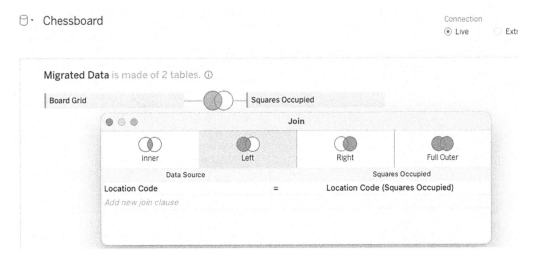

Figure 8.71: Join

5. On the Chessboard worksheet, select **Map | Background Images | Chessboard**.

6. In the resulting dialog box, click **Add Image** to add a background image.

7. Fill out the **Edit Background Image** dialog box as shown:

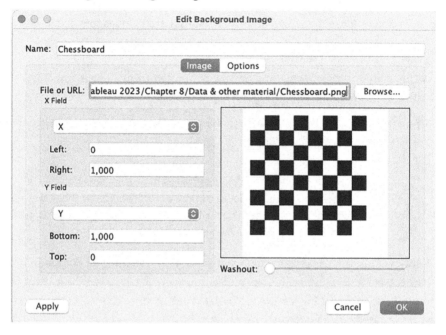

Figure 8.72: Chessboard background image

8. Place the fields **X**, **Y** (both as **Dimension**), and **Location Code** on the **Columns**, **Rows**, and **Detail** shelves respectively, and the **Moves Occupied** field on **Color** while selecting the **Marks** type **Density**:

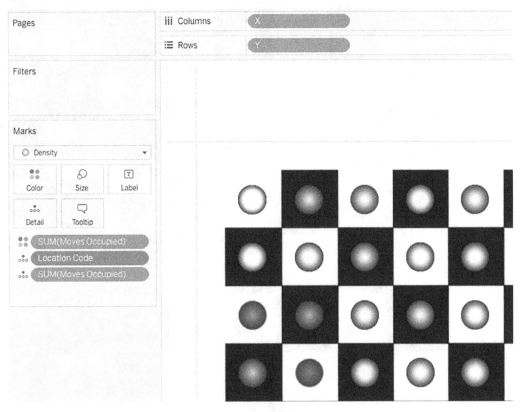

Figure 8.73: Chessboard background image II

9. Right-click on the **X** and **Y** axes and set both to **Fixed**, with a **Fixed start** value of **0** and a **Fixed end** value of **875**.

10. Edit the **Y** axis and set it to **Reversed**. Do not reverse the **X** axis.

 This last step was performed because the data has been structured to mirror the **X** and **Y** coordinate setup that is the default in most graphic tools. In these tools, the upper left-hand corner is where **X** and **Y** both equal **0**.

11. Adjust **Color**, **Size**, **Shape**, and so on as desired:

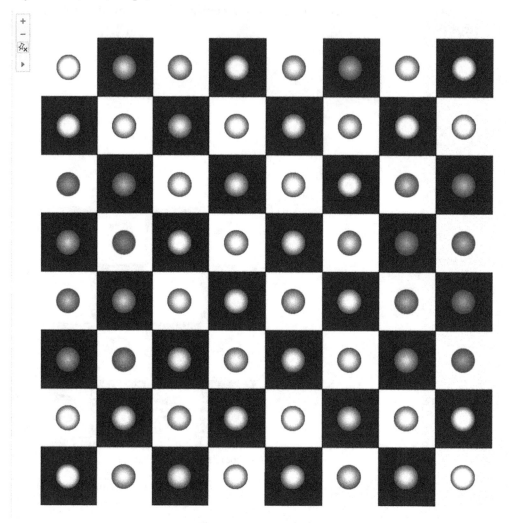

Figure 8.74: Chessboard

In the screenshot, the brighter the circle, the more frequently this space was occupied for a move. The darker the circle, the less frequently it was occupied. By hovering over a field, the amount of occupation will show as well.

To recap, we started off by creating an SVG file. We did so by creating three different code types, Header, Location Codes, and Lines, according to the standards of an SVG file. We then copied those three code pieces into a text editor program and saved them as an SVG file. Then we downloaded the Inkscape application and opened the SVG file to check and see the result of our work, a 10-by-10 square field.

We added an image of a chessboard to Inkscape and aligned the two. Now we can see which square number will be associated with which chessboard field. Just like in the bookshelf example, it is necessary to identify the shape ID, that is, the chessboard field ID. Based on the chessboard field IDs, we were able to generate a second dataset containing the number of moves for which a field was occupied. By joining the Board Grid dataset with the Occupied Moves dataset, we got ourselves a use case. We added a background image of a chessboard to Tableau and on top of it, we drew squares and colored and also sized them, depending on the number of moves those fields were occupied for during the chess games. The numbers are very specific to each game, of course, but by collecting the data for multiple games, we are able to visually analyze chess strategies and maybe even tell who the better player was. If you like chess, feel free to try it out and compare the different visual results per game, or see whether you usually end up with the same pattern and whether this is also true for your opponent.

Talking about games, in the next exercise, we will visualize a dartboard. This exercise will be shorter than the chess one. Follow along with the steps and learn more about polygons.

Creating polygons on a background image

Utilizing shapes on specific points of a visualization was sufficient for the previous exercise, but sometimes it may be advantageous to use polygons to outline shapes. In this section, we will utilize polygons on a background image, and unlike with the books, we will fill out the areas such that the background image is not needed (as much) anymore.

The following are the required steps:

1. Within the workbook associated with this chapter, navigate to the worksheet entitled Dashboard - Polygon and select the Dartboard_W_Polygon data source.

 If you did not already do so when completing the previous exercise, download the images provided on GitHub. Unzip the contents to a directory of your choosing.

2. Select **Map | Background Images | Dartboard - Polygon**. In the **Background Images** dialog box, select **Add Image**. Fill out the dialog box as shown:

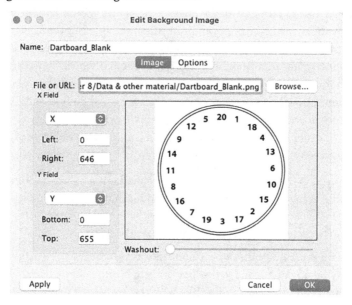

Figure 8.75: Dartboard background image

3. Create a parameter with the following configuration:

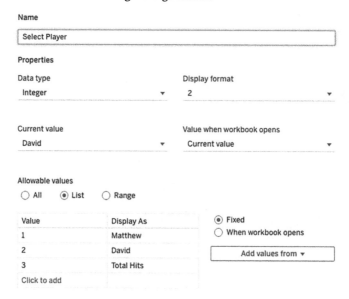

Figure 8.76: Parameter

4. This parameter will be used to either switch between player 1: **Matthew** and player 2: **David** or show the dart hits of both.

5. Display the parameter created in the previous step by right-clicking on it at the bottom of the **Data** pane and selecting **Show Parameter Control.**

6. Create a calculated field called `Total Hits` with the following code:

```
[David]+[Matthew]
```

7. Then, create a calculated field called `Case` with the following code:

```
CASE [Select Player]
WHEN 1 THEN SUM([Matthew])
WHEN 2 THEN SUM([David])
WHEN 3 THEN SUM([Total Hits])
END
```

8. Set the **Marks** card to **Polygon.**

9. Survey the **Data** pane to ensure that **Point** and **Shape** are both dimensions (blue color). The other fields are measures:

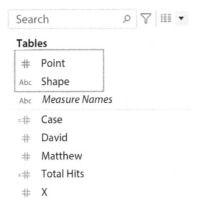

Figure 8.77: Dimensions and measures

10. Place the fields **X, Y, Point, Shape,** and **Case** on their respective shelves:

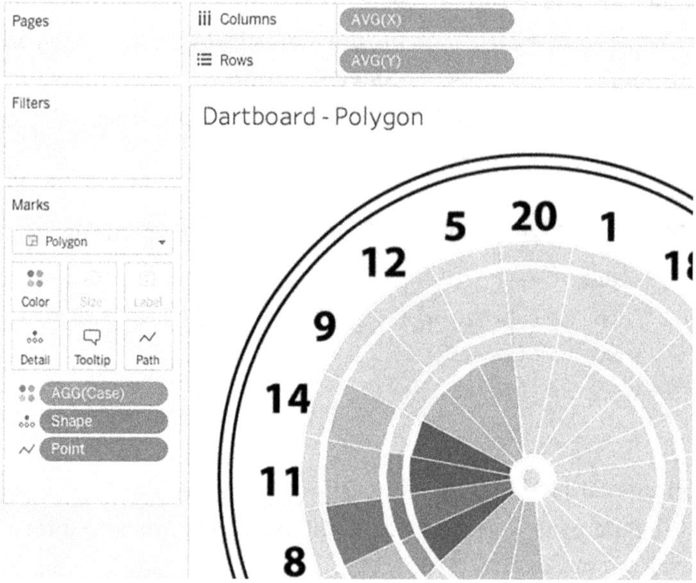

Figure 8.78: Dartboard polygon

11. Right-click on each axis and set the **Range** from **0** to **650.**

12. Click on the **Color** shelf and select **Edit Colors.** Adjust the color as desired. One possibility is represented in the following screenshot:

Figure 8.79: Custom Diverging

Your final worksheet should look like the following:

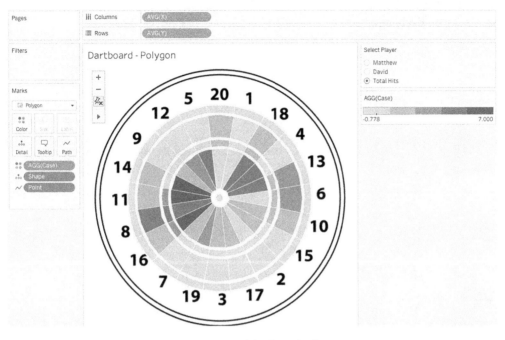

Figure 8.80: Final dartboard polygon

The final dashboard shows a dartboard with different colors. The gray color means that this area has not been hit during the game, whereas the redder the color of a field is, the more often it has been hit. By using the parameter, you can compare Matthew's score with David's, or you can show the total hits, like in the preceding screenshot.

You may have noticed that the curved sections of the polygons in this exercise aren't quite perfect. Look, for example, at the triple ring and double ring areas surrounding the bullseye; you can see that the area is not 100% even. That's simply the nature of working with points on a Cartesian grid in Tableau. This means that Tableau is based on a grid structure, so every curve we draw will still be many small lines connecting dots on a grid layout. The more dots you have and the shorter the lines between the dots, the more likely you will draw curves evenly. But if you followed along with the bookshelf exercise, you can see that a lot of effort has to go into such a background image. Nevertheless, I believe that polygons are absolutely worth it. Here we used fun exercises that might not add value to your day-to-day job, but think about a picture-perfect landing page that you designed in a different program. By using polygons, you can make the design elements clickable and interactive.

The next topic is a little bit different from the rest of this chapter. Have you heard about Tableau Exchange yet? Tableau Exchange is a newer edition to the Tableau universe that combines three products: extensions, accelerators, and connectors. Interested? Continue with the next section!

Tableau Exchange

To access Tableau Exchange, go to this website: `https://exchange.tableau.com`.

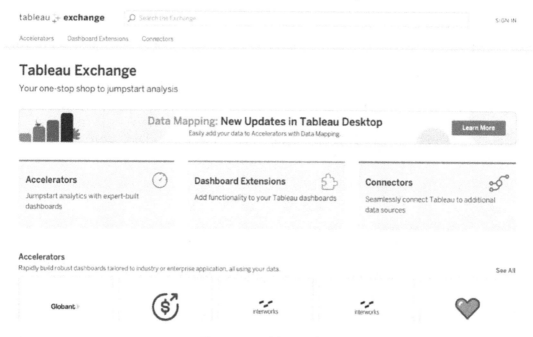

Figure 8.81: Tableau Exchange

Accelerators and extensions can also be accessed from within Tableau Server and/or Tableau Desktop. Let us dive right into Tableau Exchange and see what it has to offer!

Tableau extensions

Extensions are the oldest product and are accessible from the **Object** pane on your Tableau dashboard. Basically, extensions allow you to use third-party tools directly in Tableau. Some selected extensions are available at `https://extensiongallery.tableau.com`, and the list is always growing.

Please be aware that Tableau does not provide support or guarantees/security measures for extensions. Those APIs are built by external parties and should be treated as such. Check with your IT security team first if you want to use them at work.

Let's have a look at one example from Infotopics – a Sankey chart extension.

Using an extension

In the associated workbook, create a new sheet called Show me More and select the Coffee Chain dataset. Now reproduce the following worksheet layout by adding **Type** to **Columns**, **Product Type** to **Rows**, and **Profit** to the **Text** shelf:

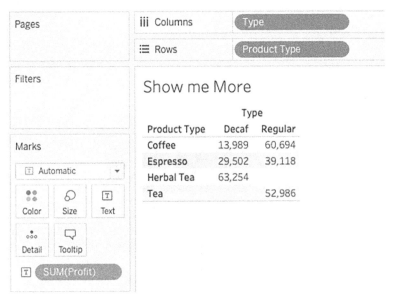

Figure 8.82: Show me More

We want to utilize a Sankey chart for this worksheet, which is a kind of flow chart that shows, based on the size of flow-lines, how much of a given measure and a given dimension flows into a second given dimension. In this case, we want to know how much **Profit** from **Regular** type products comes from **Coffee**, **Espresso**, **Herbal Tea**, or **Tea**, and how much **Profit** can be associated with the **Decaf** types.

Let's say you know how to build a Sankey chart using calculated fields, but it is time-consuming. Instead, there is an **extension** to do so. The following are the steps required to use the extension and ultimately save us time when building a Sankey chart:

1. In the associated workbook, open a **Dashboard** tab and call it Show me More DB.

2. Drag the **Show me More DB** sheet onto the dashboard. Now also drag the **Extension** object onto the dashboard:

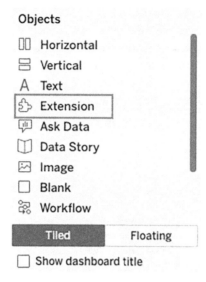

Figure 8.83: Extension

3. From Tableau 2021.1, you will see the following pop-up window:

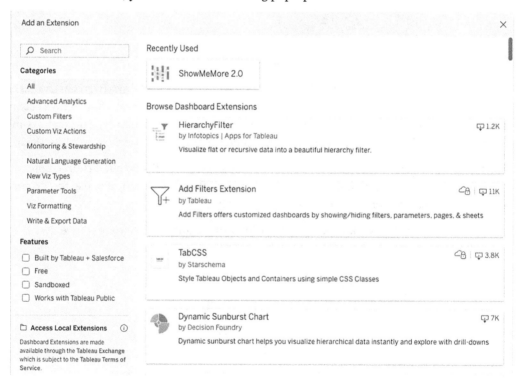

Figure 8.84: Extension Gallery

4. In the **Extension Gallery** search for the **Show Me More 2.0** extension. Click on it and select **Add to Dashboard** on the next screen:

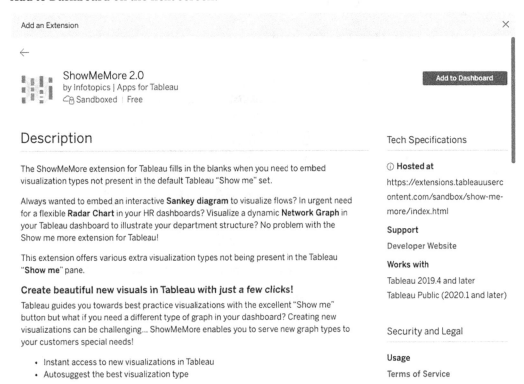

Figure 8.85: Show Me More 2

5. Then, select **Get started** and choose the **Sankey Diagram** visualization:

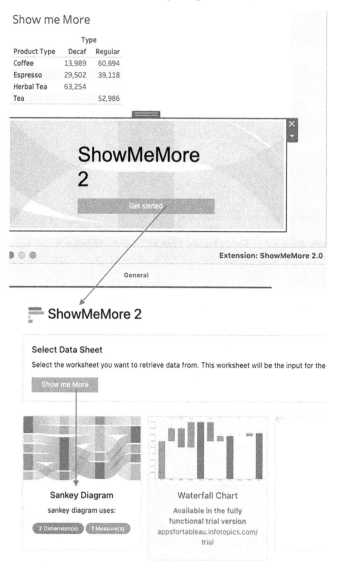

Figure 8.86: Show Me More II

6. After selecting the Sankey diagram, configure the variables as follows. There are many more options, as partly shown in *Figure 8.87*; feel free to test them out:

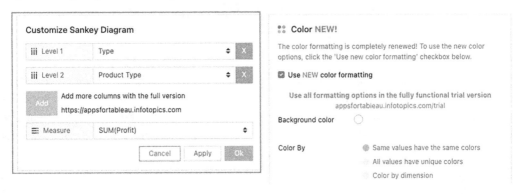

Figure 8.87: Sankey diagram settings

7. Hit the **Ok** button, and voilà, you have your Sankey diagram:

Show me More

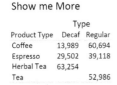

Product Type	Type	
	Decaf	Regular
Coffee	13,989	60,694
Espresso	29,502	39,118
Herbal Tea	63,254	
Tea		52,986

Figure 8.88: Sankey diagram

Besides this Sankey chart, I would highly recommend you have a look at the extensions library. There are many extensions for multiple different use cases; some are free, some have to be paid for, but you can also build your own. It is worth taking a look! The next section will be dedicated to a special extension, which is the most advertised new feature in Tableau 2021.1, **Einstein Discovery**.

Accelerators

This feature works on a more basic level: how to design, structure, and put together a dashboard. Accelerators are pre-defined dashboards from different sectors and with different focus points. Currently, there are over 100 available in multiple languages, catering to different departments, industries, and enterprise applications. Instead of starting from scratch, you can use an **Accelerator** dashboard by clicking on the links on your Tableau Desktop landing page, or Tableau Server:

Figure 8.89: Tableau landing page

In *Figure 8.89*, the two dashboards on the left always show on the Tableau Desktop landing page, and you are familiar with those already: the Superstore and the World Indicators datasets. Next to them you can see an icon of two people with a headset. That is the third accelerator dashboard that I loaded. But looking at the top right, in the red frame, you can see a hyperlink called **More Accelerators**; click on it.

Imagine that you want to use financial trading data and an accelerator dashboard to kick-start your project. Search for *trading*:

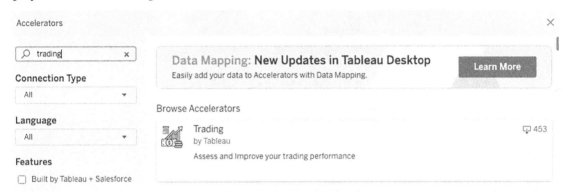

Figure 8.90: Search accelerator

By clicking on the **Trading by Tableau** dashboard, a new Tableau workbook will open – with a fully built trading dashboard and, even better, data mapping capabilities, which means that you can replace the current data with different data without breaking the dashboard layout and pre-build functionality. The description in each of the accelerator dashboards contains the *data mapping possible* or *impossible* information.

When your new dashboard is open, you will see the following popup:

Figure 8.91: Data mapper

Click on **Get Started** and connect your desired dataset to the accelerator dashboard.

 You can use this dataset as a test: `https://www.kaggle.com/datasets/georgezakharov/ historical-data-on-the-trading-of-cryptocurrencies.`

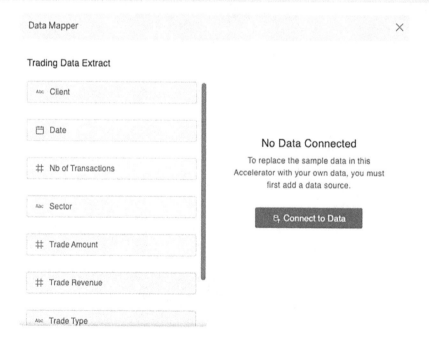

Figure 8.92: Data mapper II

Once loaded, you can start mapping the fields one by one:

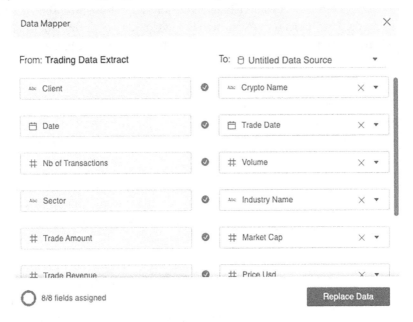

Figure 8.93: Mapping data

It is important to know that you do not have to map all fields; however, if visualizations in the workbook make use of an unmapped column, those instances will appear null.

After the mapping is done, your dashboard is ready to use! Sample-check that everything looks as desired and your job is done!

Great, isn't it? Such a time-saver; I really enjoy this new feature in Tableau.

Connectors

The last section that Tableau Exchange has to offer is **connectors**. Here you can find connectors to databases that are not listed in the **Connect** pane of your Tableau Desktop.

To sum up, Tableau Exchange is a platform where you can find various tools to enhance your data analysis and quickly derive meaningful insights. It offers Tableau accelerators, which are pre-built dashboards created by experts, extensions that offer functionality that is not native to Tableau, and connectors, which allow you to connect to databases that are not listed in the default pane. A true, free marketplace to jump-start your Tableau successes.

Einstein Discovery

We discussed Tableau exchange in the previous section; however, one other similarly beyond-basics feature deserves some attention too. But before we continue, a bit of backstory. In August 2019 Tableau was acquired by Salesforce. Probably most of you know Salesforce and even work with it, but for all other readers, Salesforce is a cloud-native **Customer Relationship Management** (CRM) tool. Next to that, the company also developed an analytics portion, which allows Salesforce users to analyze data from a CRM system and other data sources.

Connecting Salesforce to Tableau was possible long before the acquisition, but what's new in Tableau 2021.1 is that the analytics piece of Salesforce is available for integration into Tableau, as an extension and in calculated fields. The Tableau community is very excited about this feature because of the built-in machine learning capability and real-time prediction power. This piece of software is called Einstein Discovery.

 In order to make use of Einstein Discovery, you need a Salesforce license and, more specifically, the analytics license for Salesforce. The licensing details can be found here: `https://www.salesforce.com/editions-pricing/crm-analytics/`.

Now, to give you an idea of what Einstein Discovery can do for you, I will walk you through an imaginary use case. On a supply chain data dashboard, you discover that the shipment time can be improved, but you don't know which factors cause the delays. In this instance, you might decide to use Einstein Discovery for its analysis capabilities.

First, you drag the **Extensions** object onto the dashboard, just like we did with the **Show me More** extension. You then select the **Einstein Discovery** item, at which point a browser window will open to ask you to log in to Salesforce. After you have done so, you can select which model you want to use on your Tableau dashboard. The model (for example, a machine learning model) has to be prepared in Salesforce beforehand. Then, Einstein Discovery will be a part of your dashboard, and your worksheet will show the output from the model running in the background on Salesforce. In our example, the model will more easily be able to find the relevant variables used on your dashboard that are best suited to predict the time of delivery, and it will recommend actions you can take to improve the shipment time.

 A video of the described use case and another use case can be viewed at `https://youtu.be/dMWuy6mVE_o`.

Alternatively, you can call a Salesforce model directly in a calculated field. How this works is described here: `https://help.tableau.com/current/pro/desktop/en-us/einstein_discovery_predictions.htm`.

If you want to try out these new features, there is a way to test out the new Einstein capabilities if you do not have a Salesforce license yet. It is a longer process to set up but for those of you who do want to try, please check out this video for assistance: `https://youtu.be/ZReSwXK0reo`.

Those are the cornerstones of the bespoke new Einstein features in Tableau 2021.1. Going into detail on the functionality of the Salesforce platform is unfortunately out of the scope of this book, but if you have Salesforce in place, I would most certainly recommend that you set up the connection and test out running some models. Even if you do not use Salesforce, the licensing might change over time, so hopefully we can all run those models soon. For the time being, don't worry, as we will discuss machine learning model integration in *Chapter 15, Integrating Programming Languages*.

Summary

We began this chapter by considering how to tweak popular visualization types. Specifically, we fine-tuned a bullet graph, considered a very different approach to using pie charts in mapping, and ended by tweaking a Pareto chart. Next, we turned our attention to custom background images, where we considered how to build a grid using XML to generate an SVG file, to expedite generated data for use with background images. Then, we completed the chapter by building polygons on a background image and had a quick excursion into the world of Tableau Exchange. We discussed accelerators, extensions, and connectors but also Einstein Discovery, which is a separate product sold by Salesforce.

There are too many options to cover them all in this book but since you are an expert in replicating by now, I added more sheets with other visualizations to the solutions workbook for you to play with. You will find sheets with bar charts, stacked bar charts, diverging stacked bar charts, crosstabs, highlight tables, discrete highlight tables, trend lines, area charts, sparklines, combo charts, dual axis, histograms, box and whisker plots, scatterplots, filled maps, symbol maps, treemaps, tree bar charts, Gantt charts, KPI charts, funnel charts, jittered distribution, calendars, bump charts, slopegraphs, waterfall, target, and bar-in-bar charts. Always make sure to use the chart that is most suitable for your data and will add value to the story you try to tell. If you still need a little bit of help with deciding on the appropriate visualization technique, I advise you to look at the following dashboard published on Tableau Public: `https://public.tableau.com/en-us/gallery/visual-vocabulary`. This dashboard was made to show you which visualization type to use, depending on the data you have.

In the next chapter, we will turn our attention to mapping, where we will consider how to extend Tableau's native mapping capabilities without ever leaving the interface, as well as how to extend Tableau's mapping capabilities with other technology.

Learn more on Discord

To join the Discord community for this book – where you can share feedback, ask questions to the author, and learn about new releases – follow the QR code below:

`https://packt.link/tableau`

Working with Maps

When I conduct Tableau classes and workshops for people who are using Tableau for the first time, I find that demonstrating **mapping** is always a big hit, sometimes resulting in murmurs of appreciation and surprise. People have told me on multiple occasions that Tableau's mapping capability was the key feature that caused them to take notice of and consider Tableau's offerings more seriously. Tableau's out-of-the-box mapping capabilities are powerful and flexible. You may be surprised at how much you can accomplish without ever leaving the user interface. But these out-of-the-box capabilities are just the tip of the iceberg. With proper guidance (which I will attempt to provide in this chapter), you can expand beyond the native mapping functionality and explore techniques that will greatly enhance your workbooks' functionality and aesthetics.

In this chapter, we will discuss the following topics:

- Extending Tableau's mapping capabilities without leaving Tableau
- Creating custom polygons
- Heatmaps
- Dual axes and map layering
- Extending Tableau mapping with other technology
- Swapping maps
- Custom geocoding

The default mapping capability of Tableau is a big selling point. Take any city, region, country, or other geographical location, place it on a Tableau worksheet, and you get a nice map; add a measure like **Sales** to the **Color** shelf and your map colors change according to sales figures. In the following section, we will go a step further and enhance this capability with the less obvious features Tableau has to offer, like measuring distances on a map and plotting additional data (for example, weather data) in the background.

Extending Tableau's mapping capabilities without leaving Tableau

In our everyday lives, a map can be helpful for better understanding the world around us. For instance, maps are often used on websites, television, or in printed media to present demographic information. In such instances, the mapping requirement is **static** since the immediate goal does not require movement. Some businesses only have static mapping requirements—for example, a retail chain might create a visualization that includes a map to better understand sales performance in a given region. In such cases, movement between locations is not a direct need.

Often, however, a map is needed to navigate from point A to point B. This kind of mapping requirement is more complicated, because it encompasses static needs (what restaurant is nearby?), but must also deliver additional information, such as routes and distances (how can I get to that restaurant?). These **dynamic** mapping needs assume that movement is *required* to fulfill a demand. Many businesses need to understand routes and mileage, that is, how to get from point A to point B and the distances involved. These dynamic mapping requirements can vary greatly but most of these needs share at least two things in common: routes and distances.

In the following exercise, we will consider flight routes and associated distances in Australia. Specifically, we will cover how to extract longitude and latitude numbers from Tableau and use that information in conjunction with trigonometry to calculate the mileage between various points. Along the way, we will utilize data blending, table calculations, mapping, and **Level of Detail (LOD)** calculations for a robust exercise that touches on many advanced features.

Please take the following steps:

1. Navigate to `https://public.tableau.com/profile/marleen.meier` to locate and download the workbook associated with this chapter.
2. Open the workbook and navigate to the `Map` worksheet.
3. Select **Transit Data** in the **Data** pane and double-click on **City**, then change **City** from **Detail** to **Label** in the **Marks** card.
4. In the following screenshot, note that the cities **Mackay** and **Brisbane** are the only cities that display. This issue depends on your country setting, but the following is an example of an issue that may be encountered. If you see it, click on **14 unknown**, in the bottom-right corner:

Figure 9.1: Australia

Caveat: if you are in the **United States**, Melbourne in Florida will display. If you are in another country, you may get different results.

5. Select **Edit Locations...**:

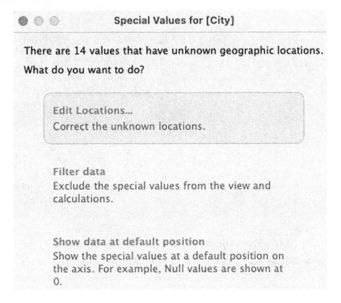

Figure 9.2: Edit Locations…

6. Change **Country/Region** to **Fixed | Australia**:

Figure 9.3: Select Australia

Australia is now displayed on the map:

Figure 9.4: Australia

7. Navigate to the `Miles` worksheet and place the **Trip ID** and **City** fields on the **Rows** shelf, and **Latitude (generated)** and **Longitude (generated)** on the **Text** shelf, as seen in the following screenshot:

Figure 9.5: Distances

Your screen should look like the preceding screenshot. Note that the crosstab is pretty cluttered. Ideally, **Latitude** and **Longitude** should be displayed in separate columns. Unfortunately, we can't do this with the generated latitude and longitude because, although they are listed under the **Measures** portion of the **Data** pane, Tableau doesn't treat them as measures. In order to complete the exercise, we will need to be able to access the latitude and longitude coordinates from a separate data source.

8. To do this, begin by clicking on the Map worksheet tab.

9. Right-click on the visualization and select **View Data**. Copy all the data in the **Summary** tab of the resulting dialog box, by selecting every cell and clicking **Copy**.

10. Close the dialog box and press *Ctrl + V* (*Command + V* for Mac) to create a new dataset in Tableau. Rename the resulting dataset (now called Clipboard_[timestamp]) to Lat Long. Also, name the worksheet Lat Long.

11. In the Lat Long worksheet, rename Latitude (generated) and Longitude (generated) to Lat and Long.

12. Return to the Miles worksheet and, within the Transit Data data source, create two calculated fields: one called LAT, containing the code AVG([Lat Long].[Lat]), and one called LONG, containing the code AVG([Lat Long].[Long]).

13. Remove **Latitude (generated)** and **Longitude (generated)** from **Text** on the **Marks** card.

14. Place **Measure Names** on the **Columns** shelf and the **Filter** shelf and select **Lat** and **Long**. Also, place **Measure Values** on the **Text** shelf. Now, we have the ability to treat latitude and longitude as true measures.

15. Create two more calculated fields: one called Lookup Lat, containing the code Lookup(Lat,-1), and one called Lookup Long, containing the code Lookup(Long, -1). Place the two newly created calculated fields on the **Measure Values** shelf.

16. Create a calculated field named Great Circle Distance Formula with the following code:

```
3959 * ACOS (
SIN(RADIANS([Lat])) * SIN(RADIANS([Lookup Lat]))+ COS(RADIANS([Lat]))
* COS(RADIANS([Lookup Lat])) * COS(RADIANS([Lookup Long]) -
RADIANS([Long]))
)
```

For kilometers, change 3959 to 6378. This number represents the radius of the Earth and it needs to be updated from miles to kilometers.

17. Place the newly created calculated field **Great Circle Distance Formula** on the **Measure Values** shelf.

18. Change the calculation for **Great Circle Distance Formula** so that it computes using **City** by clicking on the field itself and selecting **Compute Using: City**.

19. Adjust the following calculations accordingly:

Name	Code
Lookup Lat	IFNULL(LOOKUP(Lat,-1), LOOKUP(Lat,1))
Lookup Long	IFNULL(LOOKUP(Long,-1), LOOKUP(Long,1))

20. Select the Map worksheet and set the **Marks** type to **Line**.

21. Place **Trip ID** on the **Detail** shelf.

22. Drag **City** to the bottom of the **Marks** card view.

23. Place the **Great Circle Distance Formula** field on the **Tooltip** shelf. Double-check that it is still set to **Compute Using: City**:

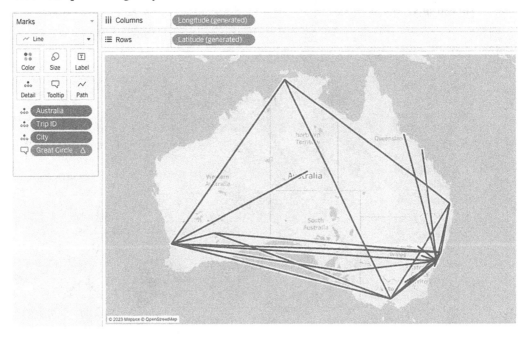

Figure 9.6: Australia distances

24. Create two more calculated fields, one called `Source City`, containing the following code:

```
{ FIXED [Trip ID]:MIN(IF [Dest/Orig]='Source' THEN City END)}
```

The second calculated field should be called `Destination City` and contain the following code:

```
{ FIXED [Trip ID]:MIN(IF [Dest/Orig]='Destination' THEN City END)}
```

25. Use the newly created calculated fields to format as desired. In particular, notice that in the following screenshot, **Source City** is on the **Color** shelf and **Destination City** is used on the **Tooltip** shelf:

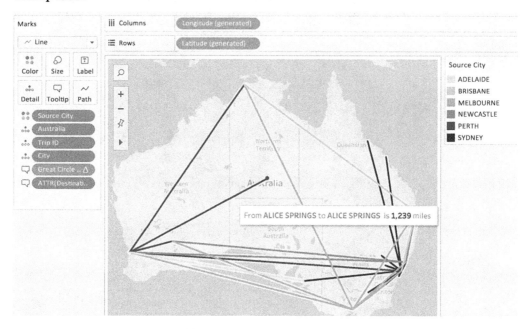

Figure 9.7: Flights

To sum up what we have done here, initially, we added a dataset to Tableau. We then needed to copy the latitudes and longitudes per city out of the workbook in order to create a second data source, which we then used as a blend to look up latitude and longitude values. With the help of LOD calculations, we could identify the source and destination cities, and lastly, we were able to measure the distance between cities by using the so-called great circle formula. Each color in the visualization represents a starting city; for example, all green lines measure distances from Perth to other cities. By hovering over a line, the source and destination city, as well as the distance measured in miles (or kilometers), will show.

If you wanted to analyze shipment routes or any other distances between two points, you now know exactly how to visualize this kind of data in Tableau.

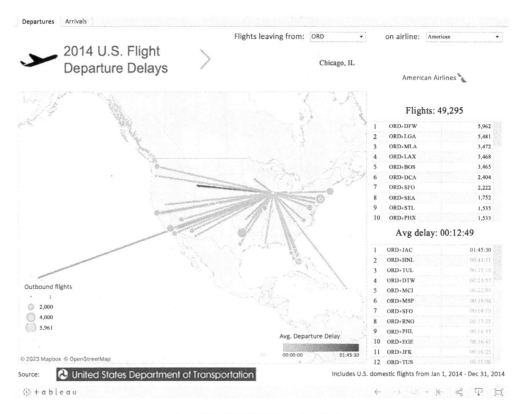

Figure 9.8: U.S. Flight Departure Delays

In *Figure 9.8*, you can see another, similar visualization, which is definitely worth checking out (try to replicate it!): https://www.tableau.com/solutions/workbook/big-data-more-common-now-ever.

In the next section, we will discuss how to leverage a combination of maps and polygons to further extend our Tableau toolbox.

Creating custom polygons

Geographic areas for which Tableau natively provides polygons include worldwide airport codes, cities, countries, regions, territories, states, provinces, and some postcodes and second-level administrative districts (county-equivalents): U.S. area codes, **Core-Based Statistical Areas (CBSAs)**, **Metropolitan Statistical Areas (MSAs)**, congressional districts, and ZIP codes. This means, for example, that a filled map can easily be created for the countries of the world. Simply copy a list of the world's countries (*Ctrl + C*) and paste that list into Tableau by pressing *Ctrl + V* while your mouse is located on an empty worksheet in Tableau Desktop. A new data source will be added to the top right under **Data**. Next, set the **View** type in Tableau to **Filled Map** and place the country list on the **Detail** shelf. Tableau will automatically draw polygons for each of those data points:

None
Airport
Area Code (US)
CBSA/MSA (US)
City
Congressional District (US)
✓ Country/Region
County
NUTS Europe
State/Province
ZIP Code/Postcode

Create from   ▶

Figure 9.9: Native polygons

There are some geographic types for which Tableau will not automatically provide polygons. These include telephone area codes. For these geographic types, Tableau will draw a symbol map but not a filled map, like so:

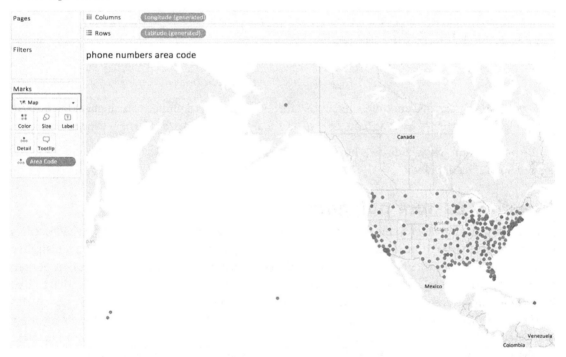

Figure 9.10: Filled map failed

Even though the filled map **Marks** type is chosen, Tableau is not able to fill the map because the outlines of those areas are unknown to Tableau. Furthermore, special mapping needs may arise that require polygons to be drawn for areas that are not typically included on maps. For example, an organization may define sales regions that don't follow the usual map boundaries. Or, a Tableau author may import an image of a basketball court or football pitch into Tableau and draw polygons to represent particular parts of the playing area. An alternative, which we discussed in more detail in *Chapter 8, Going Beyond the Basics*, could be mapping bookshelves in a store.

But other than drawing polygons yourself, there are also file types that support drawing polygons. One of those file types is .shp. In the next exercise, we will make use of such a file and create polygons for Texas.

Polygons for Texas

By processing an example of the aforementioned .shp file type, Tableau can create polygons. Let's try this out and show the population of Texas as polygons on a map of Texas:

1. Open the **Texas Department of Transportation** page: https://gis-txdot.opendata. arcgis.com/datasets/txdot-city-boundaries/explore?location=30.990445%2C-100.168292%2C6.68.

2. Use the **Download** dropdown and download **Shapefile**:

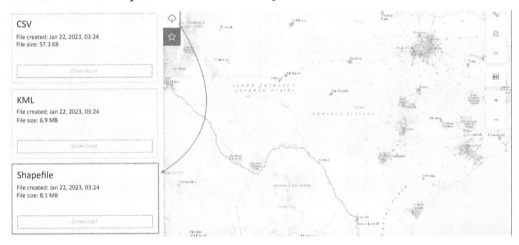

Figure 9.11: Texas data

In your download directory, you should find multiple files:

∨ ▣ TxDOT_City_Boundaries	--	Folder	Today at 8:39 PM
🗋 Cities.prj	145 bytes	Document	Today at 8:39 PM
🗋 Cities.cpg	5 bytes	Document	Today at 8:39 PM
🗋 Cities.dbf	177 KB	Document	Today at 8:39 PM
🗋 Cities.shx	10 KB	Document	Today at 8:39 PM
🗋 Cities.shp	17.5 MB	Document	Today at 8:39 PM

Figure 9.12: Texas city boundaries

If you were to open a `.shp` file in a text editor, you would see the following:

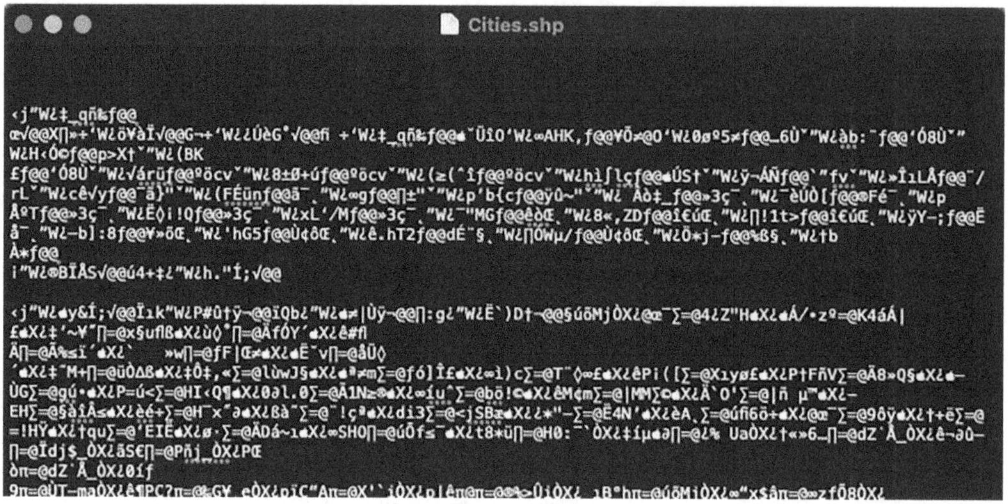

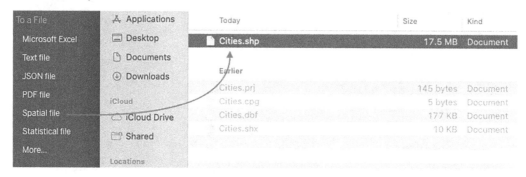

Figure 9.13: .shp in a text editor

3. Luckily, Tableau has native capabilities to read `.shp` files. In the workbook associated with this chapter, navigate to the `City Limits` worksheet and select **Data** | **New Data Source** | **Text File**.

4. Navigate to your downloads directory or the path where you saved the Texas shapefiles and select the `.shp` file:

Figure 9.14: Loading a spatial file

5. In the next screenshot, you can see how Tableau was able to read the `.shp` file and how it created an additional field called **Geometry** that indicates that we are looking at polygons and multipolygons in this file:

Figure 9.15: Geometry

6. Open a new worksheet and drag **Geometry** onto the empty canvas:

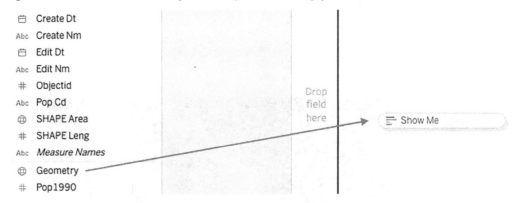

Figure 9.16: Adding geometry

7. And look at that! Tableau created polygons around areas in Texas right away:

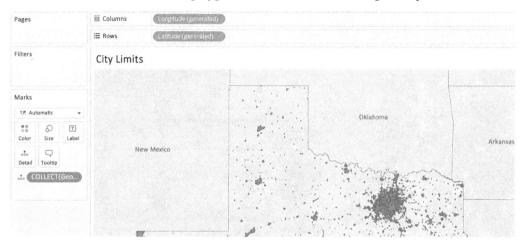

Figure 9.17: Texas polygons

8. Feel free to adjust the formatting via **Map | Background Maps | Dark**.

9. Put the **City Nm** field on **Detail** and **Pop2010** on **Color** in the **Marks** card. (The color used in *Figure 9.17* is **Temperature Diverging**.)

10. Your worksheet should look as follows:

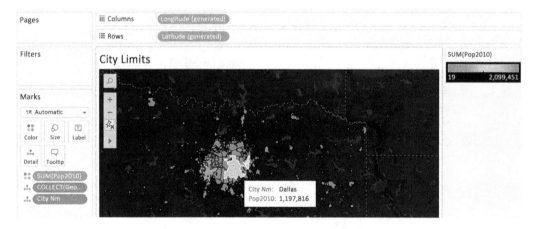

Figure 9.18: Texas city boundaries

You can see that we have a nice dark map now with polygons on top. The polygons define the area per city name (using the field **City Nm**) as published by the government of Texas. By placing the measure of the population in 2010 (using the field **Pop2010**) on the **Color** shelf, we can also see that the areas with red polygons had the highest number of inhabitants in 2010 and dark green the least.

You might not like the polygons or maybe you are wondering if a spatial file like a .shp will only allow you to use polygons. Luckily, the answer is we can change the map, no matter whether it's a spatial file or not. I really like heatmaps to display geographical density, so let's use them in the next section.

Heatmaps

I want to share a feature with you that was part of an earlier Tableau release and has proven to be very useful when working with geographical data. It is the **Marks** type **Density** with which you can create heatmaps. This new feature is not limited to maps; you can also use it for any other type of chart. However, it is most efficient for dense data where patterns cannot be spotted easily.

The following steps will illustrate an example of creating a **heatmap**:

1. Open the Citylimits tab in the workbook related to this chapter. If you did not complete the previous exercise, please open the Citylimits tab from the solutions workbook of this chapter.
2. Duplicate the worksheet, and call it City Limits (2).
3. Set the **Marks** card type to **Density**:

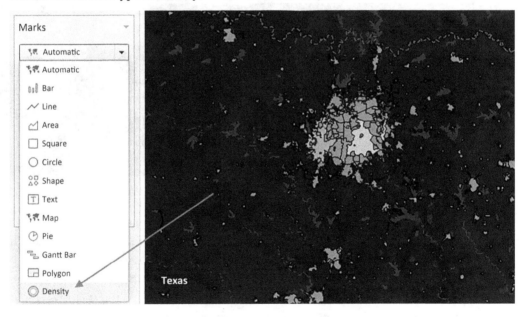

Figure 9.19: Texas city density

4. Click on **Color** in the **Marks** card and select any color you like. I chose **Density Gold Dark**.

5. Decrease **Size** in the **Marks** card by dragging the slider to the left. Drag until you like the size of the circles on your map:

Figure 9.20: Heatmap

Heatmaps can show you a spatial concentration and are perfect for very dense datasets. In the preceding figure, you can see that we lost the surroundings of the city, the polygon structure; however, we can still see the densely populated areas and now every city has the same size, making it easier to compare smaller with bigger geographic locations. And we were able to prove that a spatial file does not need to be used with polygons.

In the Tableau 2020.4 release, another feature was added: map layers. What they are and what they are used for will be described in the next section.

Dual axes and layering maps

You might recall that on many different occasions throughout the previous chapters, we used dual axes. A dual axis visualization can also be achieved with maps, and, even better, since the Tableau 2020.4 release, maps can be layered. We simply add another layer with the same structure (which, in this case, is a map), and per layer, we can display different data.

We will look at two exercises, the first one being about the use of dual axes and the second one including include map layers.

Using dual axes

Let's get started:

1. First, we need a dataset. I simply created one in Excel myself; feel free to create your own, copy what you see in the following screenshot, or download the file from this book's GitHub repository (https://github.com/PacktPublishing/Mastering-Tableau-2023-Fourth-Edition/blob/main/Chapter09/Freight.xlsx). Name the file freight:

	B	C	D	E	F	G	H	I	J
1	Transportation	Goods	Ordered	Delivered	Origin	Origin Country	Destination	Destination Country	Weight
2	Plane	Furniture	1/1/21	22/1/21	Lisbon	Portugal	London	United Kingdom	75
3	Train	Furniture	1/1/21	17/1/21	London	United Kingdom	Paris	France	54
4	Ship	Furniture	1/1/21	24/1/21	Venice	Italy	Palma	Italy	59
5	Ship	Furniture	1/1/21	7/1/21	Rotterdam	Netherlands	Hamburg	Germany	86
6	Plane	Office	1/1/21	4/1/21	Rotterdam	Netherlands	Rome	Italy	71
7	Plane	Office	1/1/21	12/1/21	Rome	Italy	Kiev	Ukraine	52
8	Transporter	Office	1/1/21	14/1/21	Rome	Italy	Vienna	Austria	91
9	Plane	Office	2/1/21	17/1/21	Amsterdam	Netherlands	Warsaw	Poland	56
10	Plane	Office	2/1/21	4/1/21	London	United Kingdom	Reykjavík	Iceland	99
11	Transporter	Books	2/1/21	15/1/21	Hamburg	Germany	Berlin	Germany	51
12	Plane	Books	2/1/21	23/1/21	Athens	Greece	Tallinn	Estonia	85
13	Train	Books	2/1/21	27/1/21	Paris	France	Madrid	Spain	82
14	Train	Books	2/1/21	24/1/21	Warsaw	Poland	Budapest	Hungary	82
15	Ship	Books	2/1/21	15/1/21	Helsinki	Finland	Glasgow	United Kingdom	62
16	Ship	Clothes	3/1/21	9/1/21	Glasgow	United Kingdom	Reykjavík	Iceland	93
17	Plane	Clothes	4/1/21	12/1/21	Reykjavík	Iceland	Istanbul	Turkey	54
18	Plane	Clothes	5/1/21	26/1/21	Istanbul	Turkey	Naples	Italy	75
19	Plane	Clothes	6/1/21	2/2/21	Palermo	Italy	Tunis	Tunisia	97

Figure 9.21: Excel

2. Connect the new dataset to Tableau and open a new worksheet called Dual-axis map.

3. Double-click on **Origin Country** and the following map will appear:

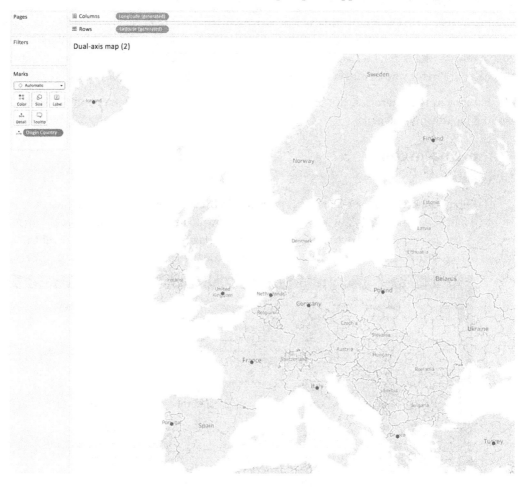

Figure 9.22: Dual-axis map

4. Change the **Marks** card type to a filled map and drag **Goods** onto the **Color** shelf:

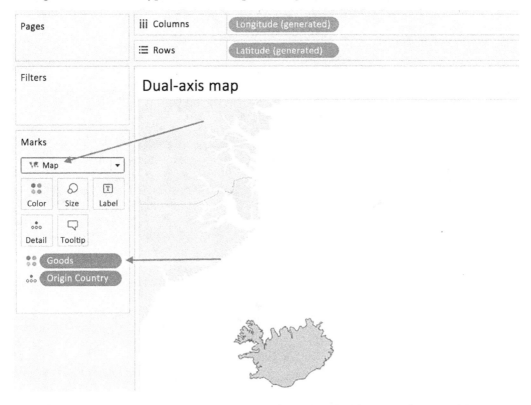

Figure 9.23: Dual-axis map II

5. Click on **Longitude** in the **Columns** shelf, press *Ctrl* (or *Command* on Mac), and simultaneously move the field to its right. You should have copied a second copy of the **Longitude** field to the **Columns** shelf:

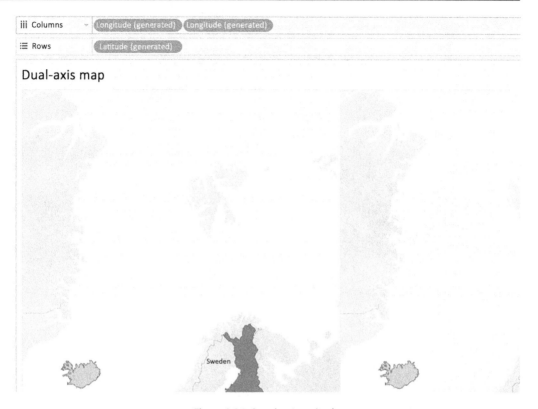

Figure 9.24: Copying Longitude

6. You can also see that the **Marks** card maintains two layers now, plus an additional **All** layer, just like dual axes on a bar chart would:

Figure 9.25: Marks card

7. On the bottom layer, replace **Goods** with **Origin** on the **Color** shelf and see how the second map now shows colored dots representing cities:

Figure 9.26: Dual-axis map

8. Click on the right **Longitude** field in the **Columns** shelf and select **Dual Axis**.

You created your first layered map! Each country's color represents the types of goods it ships. The dots indicate the cities for train, ship, plane, or truck transport:

Figure 9.27: Dual-axis map

After completing the first basic exercise, we will move on to a more complex one, using the newer map layering functionality.

Adding map layers

We want to visualize the transport routes with a line from the start to the destination city. We also want to show the time to delivery as well as the weight of the shipment. We will continue using the `freight` dataset from before; we just need to do some adjustments:

1. The `freight` dataset does not have longitudes or latitudes, which are crucial for some of Tableau's spatial calculated fields, like `MAKEPOINT`, which we will need later on. Open Google Maps and type in a city from the dataset, for example, `Lisbon`. In the URL, you will be able to find the longitude and latitude:

Figure 9.28: Google Maps

2. Copy them and add them to a separate Excel sheet, as shown in the following screenshot, and call it `latlong`:

	A	B	C
1	City	Lat	Long
2	Lisbon	38.7436057	-9.2302432
3	London	51.507351	-0.127758
4	Venice	45.440845	12.315515
5	Rotterdam	51.924419	4.477733
6	Rome	41.902782	12.496365
7	Amsterdam	52.3547925	4.7638775
8	Hamburg	53.5586526	9.6476426
9	Athens	37.9908997	23.7033199
10	Paris	48.8589507	2.2770201
11	Warsaw	52.2330653	20.9211112
12	Helsinki	60.11021	24.7385058
13	Glasgow	55.8555734	-4.3725409

Figure 9.29: Excel

3. We needed to use a new Excel sheet because we have to create a spatial field for destinations as well as the origin. Since some cities are an origin as well as a destination, we will create two inner joins; both times, the initial freight Excel sheet will connect to the recently created latlong Excel sheet (if you downloaded the data from GitHub, the latlong table is the second tab in the Freight.xlsx):

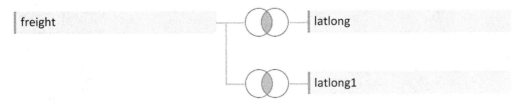

Figure 9.30: Join

4. The only difference will be that the first join is made on **Origin** and **City** and the second on **Destination** and **City**. Rename the **latlong** data sources by double-clicking on the name, to avoid confusion:

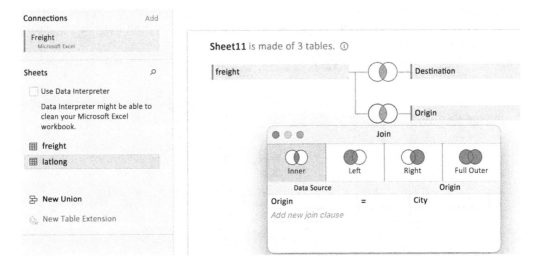

Figure 9.31: Join II

5. Open a new workbook and name it 4-layer map. Create a calculated field called Line, with the following code:

```
MAKELINE(MAKEPOINT([Lat (Origin)], [Long (Origin)]), MAKEPOINT([Lat
(Destination)], [Long (Destination)]))
```

6. The Tableau description shows that to make a point based on a spatial location, Tableau needs the longitude and latitude, or coordinates.

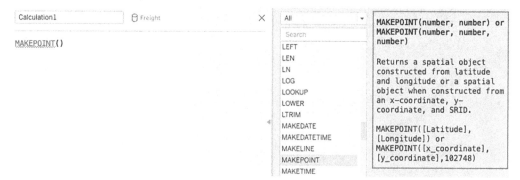

Figure 9.32: MAKEPOINT

7. Create another calculated field called Days to delivery, with the following code:

```
[Delivered]-[Ordered]
```

8. Double-click on **City** from the **Origin** file and a map will appear, but you will encounter **12 unknown**. Click on the error and then **Edit Locations…**:

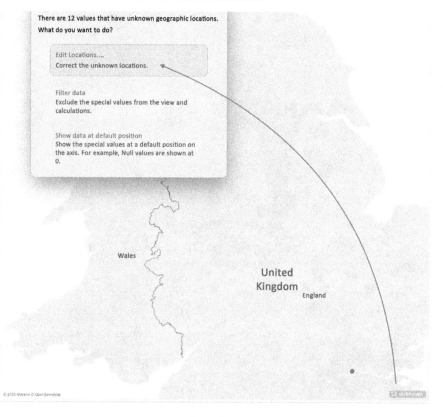

Figure 9.33: Unknown cities

9. You will see that Tableau uses **United Kingdom** (it might be different for you) as a default country to find every city, but Tableau is unsuccessful because we have cities all over Europe in our dataset. Instead of a **Fixed** location, use the **From field** option and select **Origin Country**. Now this field will be used as a country per city in our dataset:

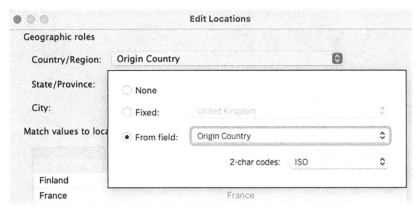

Figure 9.34: Origin Country

10. Tableau automatically adds **Origin Country** to the view on the **Detail** shelf and displays the cities correctly now. You can also achieve the previous step by placing **Origin Country** on the **Detail** shelf directly:

Figure 9.35: Origin cities

11. Since one of our goals is to draw lines between the **Origin** and **Destination** cities, it only makes sense to also add **Destination**, correct? Double-click on **Destination** to add it to the visualization.

12. We now have all **Origin** and **Destination** cities in our view, but we won't be able to distinguish between them because they are all on the same layer. Therefore, drag the just-added **Destination** field from the **Detail** shelf to the upper-left corner of your view, until the **Add a Marks Layer** sign appears:

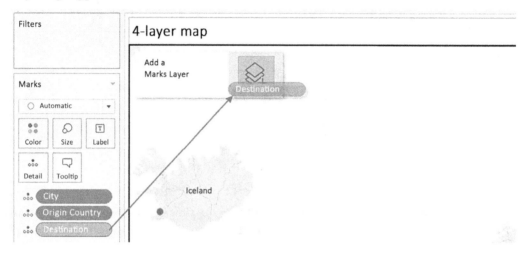

Figure 9.36: Freight II

13. You will now see that the **Marks** card shows two layers:

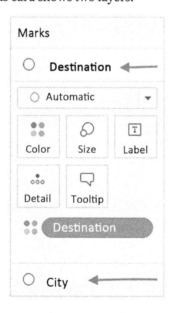

Figure 9.37: Marks

14. Rename the Destination layer to Destination Country by double-clicking on the name.

15. Add another layer by dragging **Line** onto **Add a Marks Layer** and add **Days to Delivery** to **Color**. Name this layer Line and select the **Automatic** type from the **Marks** card dropdown:

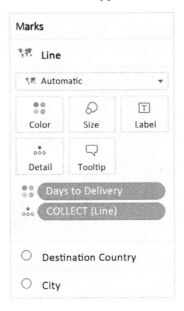

Figure 9.38: Marks layer

16. Add another layer by dragging **City** onto **Add a Marks Layer** and call it City (2). Add **Destination Country** to **Detail**. Select the **Automatic** type from the **Marks** card dropdown:

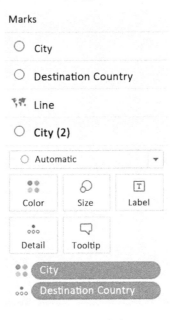

Figure 9.39: Marks layer

17. Lastly, go back to the **Destination Country** layer, change **Destination Country** to **Detail**, and put **Weight** on **Color**. Select **Map** from the **Marks** card dropdown:

Figure 9.40: Marks layer

18. Sort by dragging and dropping the layers in the following order: **Line**, **City**, **City (2)**, and **Destination Country**. Your worksheet should now look as follows:

Figure 9.41: Map

19. In order to make the visualization a bit easier to interpret, put **Origin** on the **Filters** shelf and select only a few origins of your choosing.

20. And to distinguish the **Origin** from the **Destination**, open the **City** and **City (2)** map layers and change **City** and **City (Destination)** respectively from **Detail** to **Shape**. Select one shape for the **Origin** and another for the **Destination**, for example, filled circles for **Origin** and crosses for **Destination**. You can also color the shapes by clicking on the **Color** shelf:

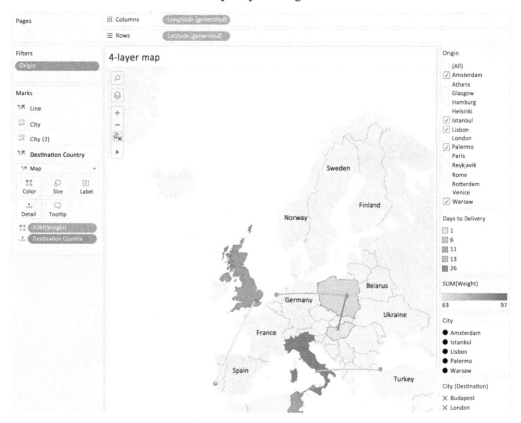

Figure 9.42: Final layered map

Now, let's look at what we have created. We can see that goods are being transported from every circle to a cross city. Both cities are connected by a yellow-to-red range colored line. More yellow-toned means that the delivery was fast, and more red-toned means that the delivery took longer. The destination country is colored in a turquoise-to-dark-blue color range. The darker the color, the more weight has been transported there. We can easily spot that Italy received the heaviest transport, coming from Istanbul and being delivered within 6 days. The slowest delivery was from Budapest to Warsaw, which took 26 days.

I hope that this exercise showed you the benefits of layered maps. Each layer allows you to use **Color**, **Shape**, **Size**, **Label**, and other **Marks** in its unique way, opening new paths for your analysis. In the next section, we will go even further and use external technology for maps in Tableau.

Extending Tableau mapping with other technology

Next, we will consider how to extend Tableau's mapping capabilities with other tools. Tableau's developers were careful to create a mapping interface that is readily extensible. Some areas of this extensibility, such as connecting to a **Web Map Service (WMS)** server, are available directly from the interface; we'll explore that next.

Using custom maps with a WMS

The easiest way to bring a custom map into Tableau is directly from Desktop. We need a properly formatted URL that points to a WMS server. Tableau Desktop can connect to any WMS server that supports the WMS 1.0.0, 1.1.0, or 1.1.1 standards.

 A good place to find a list of such URLs is http://directory.spatineo.com, which provides information on a ton of different mapping services.

The following exercise was inspired by Jeffrey A. Shaffer's article *Building weather radar in Tableau in under 1 minute*, which can be accessed here: https://www.dataplusscience.com/TableauWeatherRadar. html. However, we will include a different map and our source is the *NASA Earth Observation* data (https://neo.gsfc.nasa.gov/). In this exercise, we will see that by plotting additional data—in the form of background images—underneath your dataset, you will be able to make better decisions for your business. For example, if your sales figures are dependent on good (or bad) weather or your production is at risk of close-by wildfires, you will be able to see this all in one Tableau dashboard:

1. Open the workbook associated with this chapter and navigate to the WMS Server worksheet via the Desktop.
2. Select the Superstore data source.
3. Place **State/Province** on the **Detail** shelf.
4. Copy the http://neo.gsfc.nasa.gov/wms/wms URL, then in Tableau, navigate to **Map | Background Maps | Add WMS Map**. Paste the URL and click **OK**:

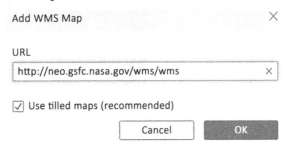

Figure 9.43: Add WMS Map

5. In the **Marks** card, set the **View** type to **Map**.

6. Click on the **Color** shelf to turn on **Border**, set the color to white, and set **Opacity** to 0%:

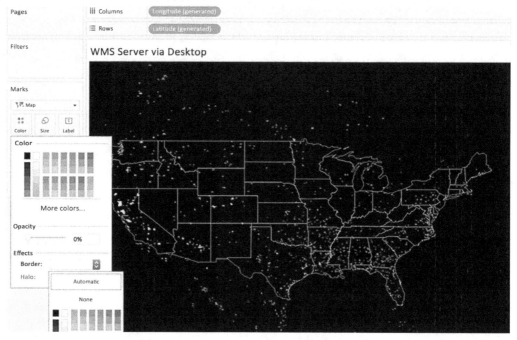

Figure 9.44: Active fires map

7. You can now see the active fires from the last month. But, by clicking on **Map | Background Layers**, more options will appear. Take a look at the left-hand side of your screen and select any other info domain you are interested in; how about **Average Land Surface Temperature**?

Figure 9.45: Land Surface Temperature map

8. Or **Cloud Fraction** (don't forget to first deselect a map before you select a new one):

Figure 9.46: Cloud Fraction map

This feature will give you endless ways to analyze data related to geographic locations. Let's say you own an online store. You could check if the sale of specific products is higher in specific areas, for example, umbrellas in rainy areas and sun protection in hotter regions. You can then continue to analyze if the market is already satisfied or if it makes sense to invest in marketing for those regions. Or maybe you want to move stock to regions where more sales are expected due to a weather change. Feel free to share your findings on Tableau Public and make sure to use the tag **#MasteringTableau**.

> Before we proceed, here's a note on tiling and zooming. Since high-resolution maps may be many gigabytes, it's impractical to require you to download an entire map in order to zoom in on one small area. Tiles solve this problem by enabling multiple zoom levels. A zoom level of 0 results in a single tile (often a 256 x 256-pixel PNG image) that displays the entire map. As the zoom levels increase, the number of map tiles increases exponentially. Also, a proportionally smaller section of the map displays; that is, as the zoom level increases, the area of the entire map that displays decreases and the total number of tiles required to fill the display remains constant. This helps control the amount of data downloaded at any given time.

Next, we'll explore Mapbox.

Exploring Mapbox

Mapbox provides custom maps and integrates natively with Tableau. To learn how to build your own custom maps, you can check out its website here: `https://www.mapbox.com/`. Starting with Tableau 2019.3, multiple Mapbox styles are even available by default:

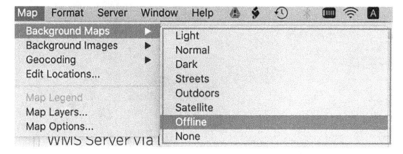

Figure 9.47: Background Maps

Next to that, Mapbox itself provides an extended mapping service with an accompanying web application that enables users to customize maps. This customizability encompasses fonts, colors, background images, and more. Mapbox provides basic services free of charge but, of course, more maps and greater bandwidth needs will require an upgrade with an accompanying fee.

This exercise will show you how to connect to **Mapbox**:

1. Navigate to `https://www.mapbox.com` and create an account.
2. After completing the signup and logging in to **Mapbox,** click on the **Studio** link:

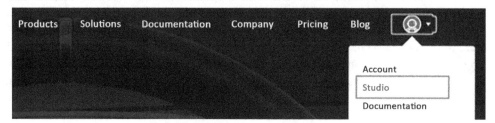

Figure 9.48: Mapbox

3. Click **New Style** and start creating a map. I chose **Monochrome | Dark | Customize Monochrome.**
4. The Mapbox editor should open. Adjust the map based on your needs:

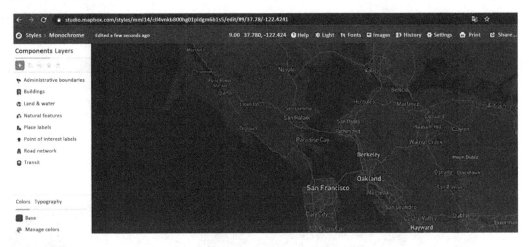

Figure 9.49: Mapbox integration

5. Click **Share** (in the top-right corner) once you are done. Select **Third party** | **Tableau** and copy the URL:

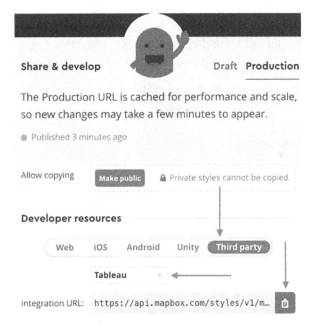

Figure 9.50: Mapbox integration

6. In the workbook associated with this chapter, navigate to the Mapbox Classic worksheet and select **Map** | **Background Maps** | **Add Mapbox Map**.

7. Add a **Style Name** (I used MasteringTableau) and copy the URL. Click **OK**.

8. Select the Superstore data source, double-click on **State**, and select the **MasteringTableau** map style via the **Map | Background Maps | MasteringTableau** path:

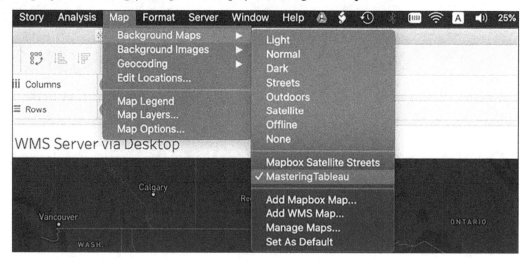

Figure 9.51: Background Maps

As you can see, Tableau makes use of the map we previously created in Mapbox. Great! So, this means you can customize your map just the way you like it.

A manual on how to create custom maps and everything else you need to know about Mapbox can be found here: https://docs.mapbox.com/studio-manual/guides/.

Swapping maps

We will now create a dashboard that allows the end user to choose between the various maps we just discussed. The technique used for this exercise is known as **sheet swapping**. However, a deeper dive into this technique is presented in *Chapter 11, Designing Dashboard and Best Practices for Visualizations*.

Let's look at the necessary steps:

1. Navigate to the MapSwap sheet in the workbook associated with this chapter. Double-click on **State**. Set the **Marks** card view to **Map**, click on **Color**, set **Opacity** to **0%**, and lastly, set **Border** to **Automatic**:

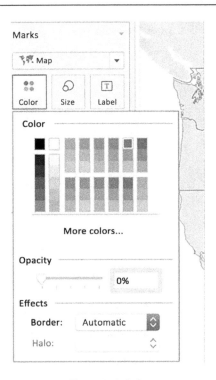

Figure 9.52: Color

2. Duplicate the **MapSwap** sheet twice:

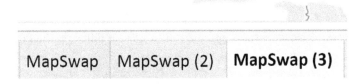

Figure 9.53: Duplicate MapSwap sheet

3. Select the **MapSwap** sheet and navigate to **Map | Background Maps | Normal**.
4. Select the **MapSwap (2)** sheet and navigate to **Map | Background Maps | Dark**.
5. Select the **MapSwap (3)** sheet and navigate to **Map | Background Maps | Satellite**.

6. Create a parameter called **Show Sheet** like so:

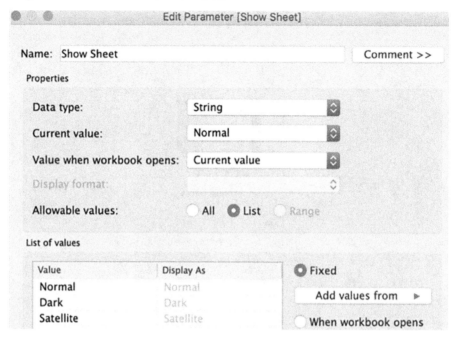

Figure 9.54: Parameter

7. Right-click on the parameter in the **Data** pane and select **Show Parameter Control.**

8. Create a calculated field called Show Sheet Filter like the following:

   [Show Sheet]

9. Select the MapSwap worksheet and place **Show Sheet Filter** on the **Filters** shelf. Select **Select from list** and **Normal:**

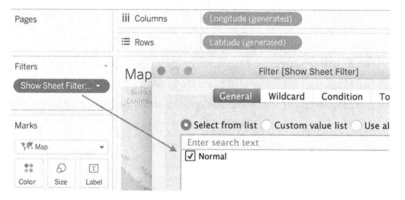

Figure 9.55: Sheet filter

10. Select the MapSwap (2) worksheet and place **Show Sheet Filter** on the **Filters** shelf. This time, select **Custom value list** and type Dark:

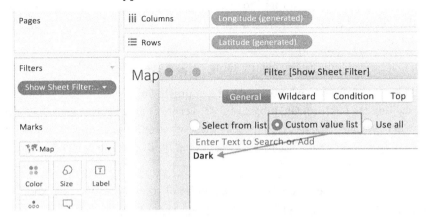

Figure 9.56: Custom value list

11. Repeat the previous step on the MapSwap (3) sheet and type Satellite instead of Dark.

12. Create a dashboard and call it db_MapSwap. Place a vertical container on the dashboard.

13. Place all three **MapSwap** sheets in the vertical container and hide their titles.

14. Select a different map style and see how your map changes:

Figure 9.57: Swap map

You might have seen a feature like dark/light or day/night backgrounds on your own computer or maybe on websites like YouTube or IDEs like PyCharm. With the **MapSwap** function, you can now offer the same comfort to your users on your Tableau dashboards.

Custom geocoding

Before we close this chapter, I wanted to share a quick tip that I saw on LinkedIn some weeks ago. The post describing the following exercise came from Klaus Schulte, a German professor and 2018 *Iron Viz* Champion.

He shared that he had built a grid map by using custom geocoding. Let's try to replicate it!

Download hex map data somewhere or create it yourself. For this exercise, you can use the hex map data from my Tableau Public or GitHub: https://github.com/PacktPublishing/Mastering-Tableau-2023-Fourth-Edition/blob/main/Chapter09/hexmap.xlsx. If you want to create it yourself, please review the polygon exercise in *Chapter 8, Going Beyond the Basics*. You can create the file the same way we created the book polygons:

1. Place the hexmap file in the Mapsources folder of your Tableau repository.
2. Connect Tableau Desktop to the default Superstore data.
3. Double-click on **State/Province:**

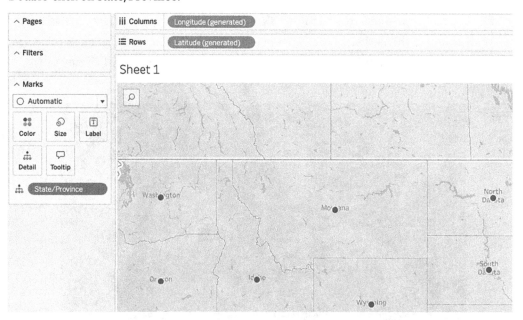

Figure 9.58: Normal map

4. Click on **State/Province** in the **Data** pane and select **Geographic Role | Hexmap.xlsx.**
5. Click on **Map | Background Layers** and set the **Washout (%)** to 100%.

6. The result will look like this:

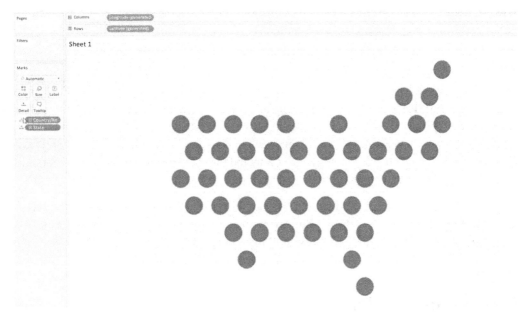

Figure 9.59: XX(will be Figure 9.59)

So why this effort? Because a grid map distributes the states evenly, if you did this without it, you wouldn't be able to distinguish between states in close proximity and would miss some far away:

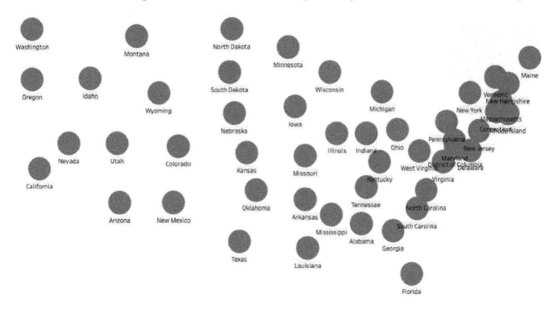

Figure 9.60: If no grid map

Thank you Klaus for this great tip! By the way, a hex map is not only applicable to the U.S.. Try it with Europe, Africa, South America, or the **Asia-Pacific (APAC)** region as well! Whenever you work with variances in size, a grid map comes in handy.

Summary

In this chapter, we explored how to extend Tableau's mapping capabilities without leaving the interface by capturing Tableau-generated latitude and longitude data and how to look this up on Google. We created polygons and a heatmap for Texas based on a `.shp` file as well as a dashboard with a dual map axis and another dashboard with 4 map layers. Next, we explored various ways to extend Tableau's mapping using other technology. We connected to a WMS server and then explored the Mapbox offering, followed by an excursion to the world of polygons.

In the next chapter, we will explore using Tableau for presentations. Specifically, we will look at how to get the best images out of Tableau, how to effectively and efficiently use Tableau with PowerPoint, and how to use Tableau directly for presentations without relying on third-party tools.

Learn more on Discord

To join the Discord community for this book – where you can share feedback, ask questions to the author, and learn about new releases – follow the QR code below:

`https://packt.link/tableau`

10

Presenting with Tableau

All Tableau authors are essentially storytellers. Analyzing data is more than just puzzle-solving; it is a search for a story that will make a difference. Topics can range from Airbnb to the Zika virus, and may be pleasantly diverting or life-changing, but they all serve a common need: to tell a story. This chapter is dedicated to helping you stock your toolkit of knowledge with ideas and methods for using Tableau to make presentations that engage, delight, and make a difference.

This chapter will explore the following presentation-centric topics:

- Getting the best images out of Tableau
- From Tableau to PowerPoint
- Embedding Tableau into PowerPoint
- Animating Tableau
- Story points and dashboards for presentations
- Presentation resources

Getting the best images out of Tableau

In this section, we will review options for exporting an image from Tableau into other applications and discuss the pros and cons of each method. We'll begin by surveying various screenshot applications and then we will consider methods that are available directly in Tableau.

Perhaps the easiest way to capture an image in Tableau is to use a screen capture tool. The following are some screen capture tools that won't impact your pocketbook:

- **Grab** is a screen capture utility natively available on macOS. Grab is located in the **Utilities** folder under **Applications**. You can also access it via the following shortcuts: *Shift + Command + 3* for a screenshot, *Shift + Command + 4* for a partial screenshot, and *Shift + Command + 5* for a timer screenshot.
- **Snipping Tool** is installed by default with Windows, a very simple tool with few bells and whistles, easy to use and effective.

- **Greenshot** is an open-source screen capture tool with many features. Visit http://getgreenshot.org/ to download the application and learn more.

- **Microsoft Office OneNote** includes a screen capture feature. If you have OneNote installed, simply press *Windows + S* to activate the screen capture or else press *Windows + N* and then the *S* key for activation.

 General rule of thumb: Capture a screenshot bigger than is needed because capturing more pixels will increase the quality. You can then decrease the size and make it fit for purpose, keeping more pixels on a smaller surface. (For very small objects, increase the scale of your computer display temporarily to get more pixels per square centimeter.)

Now that we have covered the tools for image capturing, let us have a look into the native capabilities that ship with Tableau.

Tableau's native export capabilities

One of the shortcomings of screen capture tools is that they are limited to **raster images**. Raster images are often sufficient for documentation or a PowerPoint presentation but are subject to pixelation if enlarged. Vector images, on the other hand, do not pixelate when enlarged and may therefore provide sharper image quality. Natively, Tableau includes both raster and vector export options. These options are discussed in the following list.

Tableau can export images in three formats, accessible via **Worksheet** | **Export** | **Image:**

- **SVG** is the only vector image offered in Tableau at the time of writing. Use this format to avoid pixelation if enlarged. If your image has lots of fine details and textures, SVGs are at a disadvantage because they are based on points and paths rather than single pixels.

- **JPEG** is a raster image format that is good for high-resolution images such as photographs, but does not work very well for low-color images, such as those typically deployed in Tableau. Export an image from Tableau in JPEG format and then zoom in close. Note that the white space (especially white space surrounding text) includes stray pixels of various colors. These are known as **artifacts** or **noise**. Although these pixels are not visible unless zoomed in, the overall impact on an exported image is that it can look blurry. Thus, there is rarely, if ever, a reason to export to JPEG from Tableau.

- Like JPEG images, **PNG** images are raster. The advantage of the PNG format is that it works well with both high-color images such as photographs and low-color images like those typically used in Tableau. Export an image from Tableau in PNG format and zoom in to observe that, although pixelation occurs, the white space comprises only white. Unlike JPEG images, no artifacts or noise appear. PNG should be considered the format of choice when using a raster image.

- **BMP** is a raster image format that looks quite nice but is uncompressed and can thus result in large image files. Today, the BMP format is considered antiquated and should typically be avoided.

I suggest you try all four of them. Luckily, Tableau also provides us with a native feature to export to a PDF as a vector image, as well as exporting to PowerPoint directly. In the next section, we will take a look at the PowerPoint export feature and some variations to it.

From Tableau to PowerPoint

PowerPoint is ubiquitous. Some may argue that other presentation tools such as Prezi are superior, but for many organizations (probably the vast majority) PowerPoint remains the software of choice.

 Prezi is a tool that can be accessed via the web. Typically, you won't see classical slides but an interactive, moving presentation. Templates are available online and they offer free as well as paid tiers. You can check it out here: `www.prezi.com`.

As such, it's important to integrate Tableau and PowerPoint efficiently and effectively. It is possible to export your dashboard directly into PowerPoint. You will find the option under **File | Export As PowerPoint...**:

File	Data	Worksheet	Dashboard	Story	Analysis
New					⌘ N
Open...					⌘ O
Close					⌘ W
Save					⌘ S
Save As...					⇧ ⌘ S
Revert to Saved					⌥ ⌘ E
Export As Version...					
Export Packaged Workbook...					
Export As PowerPoint...					

Figure 10.1: Export As PowerPoint...

After making this selection, you will be asked whether you want to export the current view or a selection of sheets from the workbook:

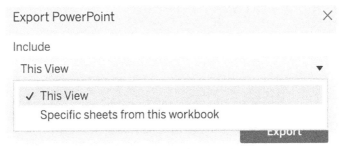

Figure 10.2: Export PowerPoint

Try both options to see how the native Tableau export functionality appears in PowerPoint. If you want to put in a little extra effort, there are options to create a PowerPoint implementation of Tableau via a different route. These alternatives might present added value for you. The following exercises explore the various techniques for doing so and the added value they offer.

Creating a template

For this first PowerPoint-centric exercise, you will create a template that will be utilized in future exercises. It will include common PowerPoint elements such as a header and a footer. The size of the template will be 1200 x 900, which adheres to the 4:3 aspect ratio typically used for PowerPoint presentations. Of course, if your company is using another aspect ratio, you can always adjust! Let's look at the following steps:

1. Navigate to `https://public.tableau.com/profile/marleen.meier` to locate and download the workbook associated with this chapter.

2. Create a new worksheet and select the `Superstore` dataset.

3. Name the worksheet `Header`.

4. Place **Sales** on the **Color** shelf in the **Marks** card.

5. Click on **Color** in the **Marks** card, click **Edit Colors...**, and then select the gray color palette and set **Opacity** to `50%`:

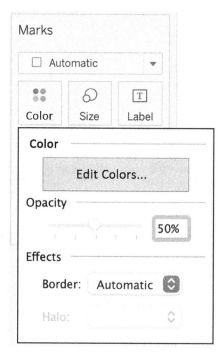

Figure 10.3: Opacity

6. Duplicate the `Header` worksheet and name the duplicate `Footer1`.

7. Click on **Color** in the **Marks** card, click **Edit Colors...**, and then select the blue color palette:

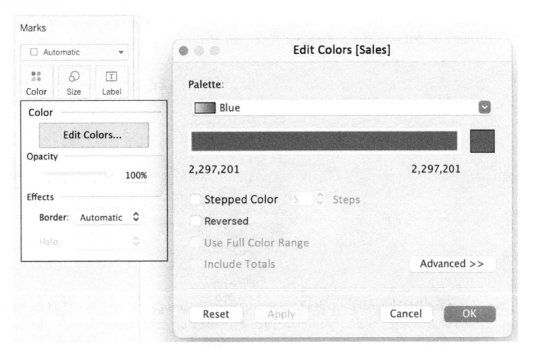

Figure 10.4: Color palette

8. Duplicate the Footer1 worksheet and name the duplicate Footer2.

9. Click on **Color** in the **Marks** card, click **Edit Colors...**, and then select the gray color palette and set **Opacity** to 50%.

10. Create a new dashboard called Template.

11. Within the **Dashboard** pane, set the **Size** to **Custom size (1200 x 700)**:

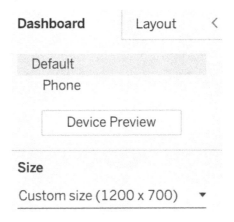

Figure 10.5: Custom size for the dashboard

12. Display the dashboard title via **Dashboard | Show Title**.

13. Double-click on the **title**. In the resulting dialog box, left-justify the text if needed.

14. In the **Dashboard** pane, make sure that **Tiled** is selected. This way, you make sure that the single worksheets stay in place and don't overlap with one another:

Figure 10.6: Tiled

15. From the **Dashboard** pane, drag **Blank** from the **Objects** panel and place it on the left-hand side of the dashboard. Be careful to place it so that it stretches from the top to the bottom of the dashboard, as shown in the following screenshot:

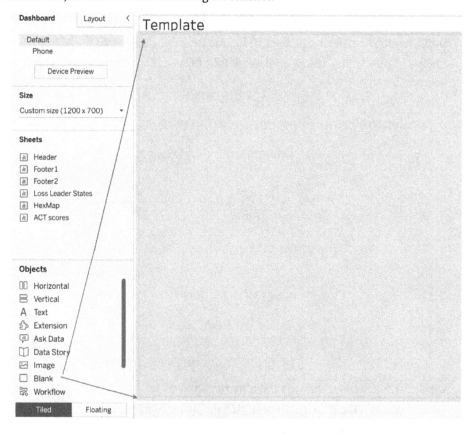

Figure 10.7: Adding a blank space

16. Repeat the previous step for the right-hand side, the middle, and the bottom of the dashboard. When creating the bottom margin, be sure to position the object so that it stretches from the far right to the far left of the dashboard. Your final layout should contain four containers and a left-aligned title at the top, like so:

Figure 10.8: Layout

17. Size the blank objects to create appropriate margins. This can be accomplished by dragging the inner edge of each **Blank** object (that is, the edges facing the center) as far to the right or left or bottom as possible:

Figure 10.9: Increasing size

18. Change the bottom margin one more time by approximately doubling the height by selecting the container and dragging the bottom line downward, as indicated by the arrows in *Figure 10.9*.

19. In the **Objects** portion of the **Dashboard** pane, click **Floating**.

20. Drag the **Header**, **Footer1**, and **Footer2** assets onto the dashboard. It does not matter where you place them; we will align the worksheets shortly. If a **Sales** legend appears, delete it.

21. Right-click on the title of each asset and select **Hide title**.

22. In the **Layout** pane, enter the following values for each worksheet:

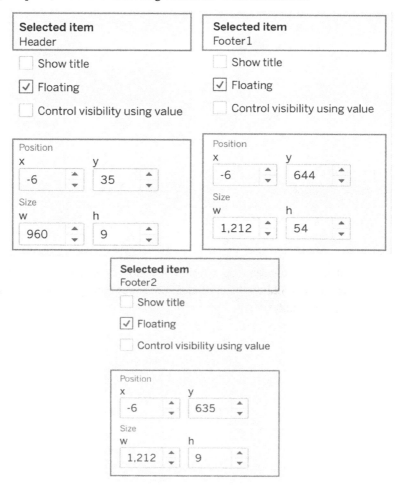

Figure 10.10: Changing position

23. Set each worksheet to **Entire View** by clicking in the toolbar on the **Fit** drop-down menu next to the word **Standard** and selecting **Entire View:**

Figure 10.11: Changing view

24. The results should be a line for the header just under the title stretching across 80% of the dashboard and two bars at the bottom stretching across the entire dashboard:

Figure 10.12: Layout

25. Click on the container located underneath the **Template** title.

26. If you have not already done so, download the assets associated with this chapter. A link is provided in the workbook.

27. Select **Floating** below the **Objects** pane:

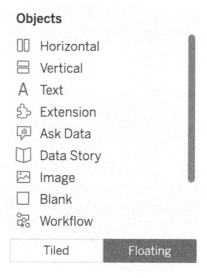

Figure 10.13: Floating

28. Drag an **Image** object from the **Objects** portion of the **Dashboard** pane onto the dashboard. When prompted, select the `tableau-logo.png` image supplied with this chapter:

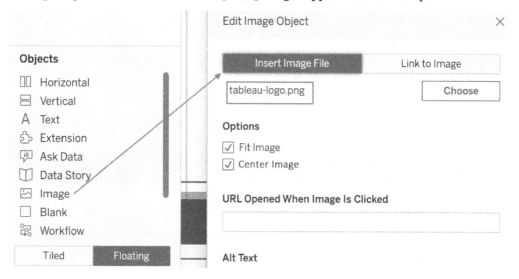

Figure 10.14: Adding an image

29. Select the option **Fit Image** and **Center Image** and then click **OK**.

30. Position the image via the **Layout** pane as follows:

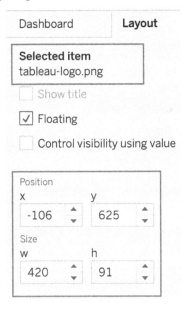

Figure 10.15: Position logo

Your PowerPoint template is now ready to use:

Figure 10.16: Template

For every screenshot you will take now, you will always have the same design surrounding it. By doing so, your presentations will look more appealing, and your audience will soon recognize your work by its design. A template such as this can also help you follow company design guidelines. As an extra tip, make sure that you use matching colors for headers, footers, and your graphs!

Next, we will go through some examples to see the template in use.

Creating a dashboard for print

This exercise will utilize the template created previously and incorporate a dashboard, which will then be suitable for printing and/or presenting. Basic instructions are provided, but specifics are left to individual preference:

1. Right-click on the tab entitled `Template` created in the previous exercise, *Creating a template*, and select **Duplicate**.

2. Rename the duplicate dashboard `Superstore Loss Leaders`.

3. Populate the **Superstore Loss Leaders** dashboard with the worksheets `HexMap` and `Loss Leaders States`. (These are two worksheets I put together based on the `Superstore` dataset, showing the **Profit Ratio** on a hex map as well as a list with the **Bottom 20 Profit States** to identify where more work needs to be done.) Arrange as desired. An example layout is given as follows:

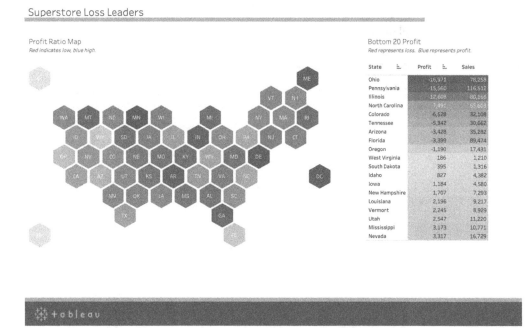

Figure 10.17: Dashboard and template

The dashboard on top of the template looks great, doesn't it? It immediately looks more interesting and presentation worthy. But are you asking, why did we choose to work with that specific layout? Well, let me elaborate: if you want to show a Tableau dashboard in a printed version or you have to export the dashboard into PowerPoint, it is important to remember that all interactivity will be lost.

One of the highlights and biggest selling points of Tableau—interactivity—doesn't work on a 2D print. But obviously, you don't want to recreate graphs that already exist in some form on your Tableau Server, and you don't have to. Just make sure that your audience understands the visualization without being able to click on a field or hover over to show more info:

- **Tip 1:** The dashboard in *Figure 10.17* has been adjusted to the colors of the template to make it appear as if the two belong together.

- **Tip 2:** A **hexagon map (hex map)** has been used instead of the default map that comes with Tableau. The reason is that smaller states on the east coast disappear when printed in the actual ratio and Alaska and Hawaii are so far away that they usually don't fit on the map either. A hex map gives the same space to each state and hence, even if printed, the user can see what's going on in Alaska as well as in Rhode Island.

- **Tip 3:** The colors indicate that the profit ratio is especially bad in Ohio and Colorado, but your audience might want to know more. That's when the table comes into play. The profit ratio is profit divided by sales and the table shows both numbers so that the audience can get a better picture of the current situation and you can avoid them asking.

- **Tip 4:** In order to avoid a printed scroll-down bar, I selected the bottom 20 states only. If the topic is loss leaders, it is not very likely that you will need to show all the states that do well.

I hope this example gave you some ideas on how to prepare your dashboard for printing! If printing happens more frequently, I advise you to add it as a page to your interactive dashboard on Tableau Server such that you always have it ready to go if asked for. If you are interested in replicating the hex map, check *Chapter 8*, *Going Beyond the Basics*, or go ahead and check out the following article: `https://www.tableau.com/about/blog/2017/1/viz-whiz-hex-tile-maps-64713`.

Next, we will look at another example, this time an automation for a weekly PowerPoint presentation.

Semi-automating a PowerPoint presentation

The previous exercises (*Creating a template* and *Creating a dashboard for print*) demonstrated two methods for generating a template for a PowerPoint presentation and gave you some tips on how to adjust your dashboard for printing and/or PowerPoint presentations. Usually, however, your Tableau dashboard isn't static, and the data will change by the next time you need it. You can, of course, export a new PowerPoint file with the updated data, but you might have other slides as well that you don't want to lose. The following steps will help you with a semi-automated way of updating your PowerPoint presentation:

1. Open the dashboard created previously entitled `Superstore Loss Leaders`.

2. Click on **Dashboard | Export Image...**:

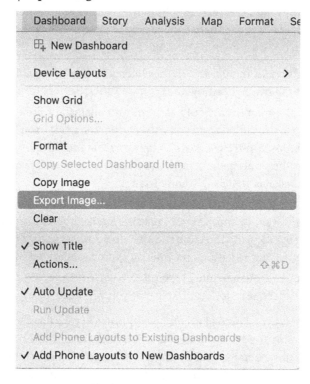

Figure 10.18: Export Image...

3. Click **OK** and, in the resulting dialog box, choose to save the image as `SuperstoreLossLeaders.png`.

4. Open the PowerPoint presentation. Open a slide.

5. Select the **Insert** ribbon and choose **Pictures | Picture from File...**:

Figure 10.19: Inserting a picture into PowerPoint

6. Navigate to the PNG image you just exported.

7. In the **Insert** dialog box, choose the drop-down selector next to **Insert** and select **Insert and Link** for Windows, or select **Options | Link to File | Insert** for Mac. Note that this step is important because it will allow pictures to be swapped out easily, as will be demonstrated:

Figure 10.20: Link to File

8. Save the PowerPoint presentation as `AutoUpdate.pptx`.
9. Close PowerPoint. In Tableau, modify the dashboard; for example, remove a state from the table.
10. Overwrite the previously exported `SuperstoreLossLeaders.png` image via **Dashboard | Export Image**....
11. Open `AutoUpdate.pptx` and note that the new image of the dashboard displays.

Something I come across frequently when I teach in Tableau classes is people who are responsible for providing PowerPoint presentations on a weekly or monthly basis. These presentations include charts and graphs that are updated, but the overall layout remains unchanged. The technique covered in the preceding exercise can make that process much quicker. Although Tableau Desktop only allows the author to update one image at a time, Tableau Server can be configured to export multiple images simultaneously, thereby making the process even more efficient. Exporting images from Tableau Server is discussed in *Chapter 14, Exploring Tableau Server and Tableau Cloud*.

Wouldn't it be even nicer if we could present our web browser, Tableau Server, directly on a slide, including all the interactivity? The next section will cover this while sharing some thoughts on doing so.

Embedding Tableau into PowerPoint

It is possible to embed Tableau directly into a PowerPoint presentation or, to be more accurate, it's possible to embed a web browser through which an instance of Tableau Server may be accessed. There are various methods for accomplishing this, including the Web Viewer app, a third-party add-in called LiveWeb, and VBA code.

The Web Viewer app is available at `https://appsource.microsoft.com/en-us/product/office/WA104295828?tab=Overview`. Although it works well for Tableau Public, the default Tableau Server settings disallow access via Web Viewer. Your Tableau Server Admin will be able to help change the settings though. LiveWeb (available at `http://skp.mvps.org/liveweb.htm`) works well but requires an additional installation. You must download the installation from the URL provided and start PowerPoint. You will then be able to add another add-in to your PowerPoint ribbon, which, in return, allows you to add a Tableau Server URL that will be displayed directly in Tableau. Detailed instructions can be found on the website too.

Embedding Tableau into Google Slides

Google Slides is another widely used presentation tool and, due to its web-based nature, a convenient one. Just like in PowerPoint, you can insert images, audio, and video but unfortunately no web page or a Tableau dashboard.

At the time of writing, I could not find a workaround either. However, if you don't want to switch between applications, Google Slides can be embedded into Tableau, so the other way around. This limits the tools at least to one!

Let's give it a try:

 You do need a Google account to do this.

1. Open Google Slides, `https://docs.google.com/presentation`, and click on **Blank** to open a new presentation.

    Type something like:

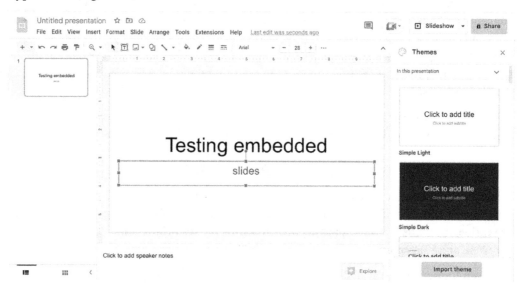

Figure 10.21: Google Slides

2. Fill a second page:

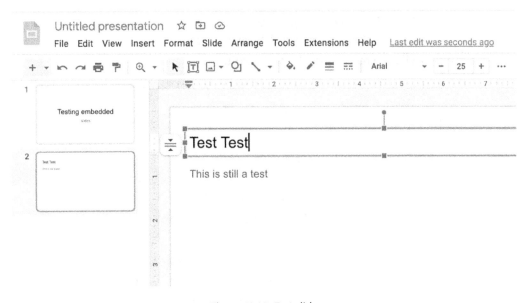

Figure 10.22: Test slides

3.   Click on **File | Share | Publish to web.**

4.   Change the dropdown **Auto-advance slides** to **every minute**. Then click on **Publish:**

Publish to the web   ✕

This document is not published to the web.

Make your content visible to anyone by publishing it to the web. You can link to or embed your document. Learn more

Link	Embed

Auto-advance slides:

every minute ▾

☐ Start slideshow as soon as the player loads

☐ Restart the slideshow after the last slide

Publish

▸ Published content & settings

Figure 10.23: Publish to the web

5. Copy the URL that now appears.

6. Open a new dashboard page in your Tableau workbook.

7. Drag the **Web Page** object onto the dashboard:

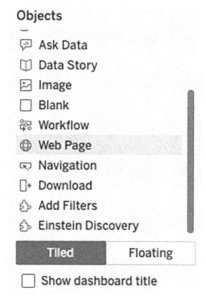

Figure 10.24: Web Page

8. Paste the URL that you previously copied from Google Slides and remove the highlighted part, &delayms=60000:

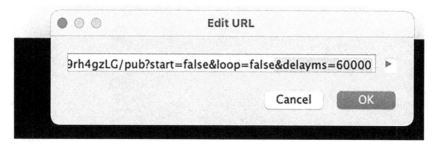

Figure 10.25: URL

9. Now you should be able to see your presentation in Tableau! The control for the slides can be found at the bottom left:

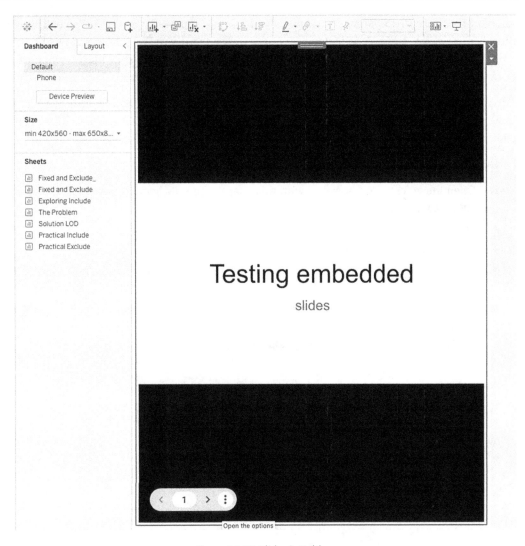

Figure 10.26: Slides in Tableau

In this section, you have learned how you can embed Google Slides into a Tableau dashboard and hence use one tool instead of switching between two. Next, we will discuss ways to bring animation to Tableau that can support your data storytelling.

Animating Tableau

Including animation in a presentation can be very effective for engaging an audience. Hans Rosling accomplishes this admirably with his popular YouTube video *200 Countries, 200 Years, 4 Minutes* (`https://youtu.be/jbkSRLYSojo`). In this video, Rosling uses data visualization to track wealth and life expectancy over time. His combination of data visualization with insightful commentary and a passion for his message makes Rosling's video a must-see for anyone interested in making appealing presentations using data.

Animations are easy to implement and are available via Tableau Reader as well as Tableau Server (since the 2020.1 release). At the time of writing, I have only encountered one drawback; worksheets with animations that are uploaded to Tableau Server will provide a single-speed level, whereas Tableau Desktop will show three. Regardless, that should not stop you from using this functionality.

The following exercise tracks ACT testing scores from 1991 to 2015. Complete the exercise to learn how to create an animation in Tableau and discover whether standardized testing results in the United States have improved over time.

Perform the following steps:

1. Open the workbook associated with this chapter and navigate to the worksheet entitled ACT 1991–2015.
2. Select the ACT data source.
3. Rename the sheet ACT scores.
4. Place **Year** on the **Columns** shelf, **Score Value** on the **Rows** shelf, and **Score Type** on **Color** in the **Marks** card.
5. Right-click on the **Score Value** axis and select **Edit Axis....** In the resulting dialog box, deselect **Include zero**.
6. Place **Year** on the **Pages** shelf. Your view should look like the following:

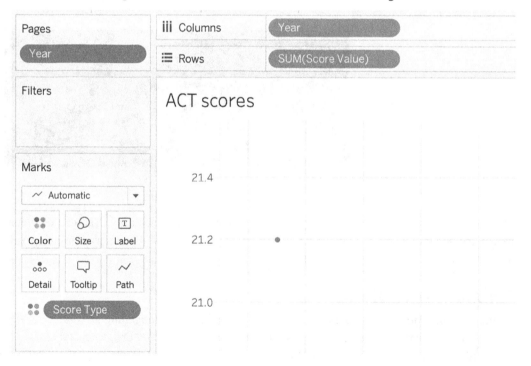

Figure 10.27: ACT scores – 1991

7. In the **Current Page** panel that appears on the worksheet, check **Show history**. Click on the arrow to open the dropdown and align all parameters as shown in the following screenshot:

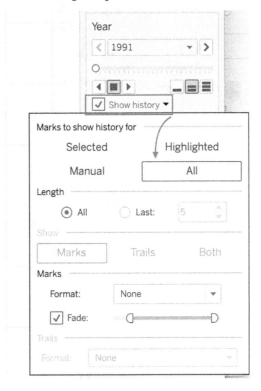

Figure 10.28: Aligning parameters

8. In the **Marks** card, click on the drop-down menu to change the view type from **Automatic** to **Circle**.

9. Click on the **Show history** drop-down menu again and note that both the **Show** options and the **Trails** options are now available. Under **Show**, select **Both**.

10. Click on the **Format** drop-down menu under **Trails** and then select the dashed line option:

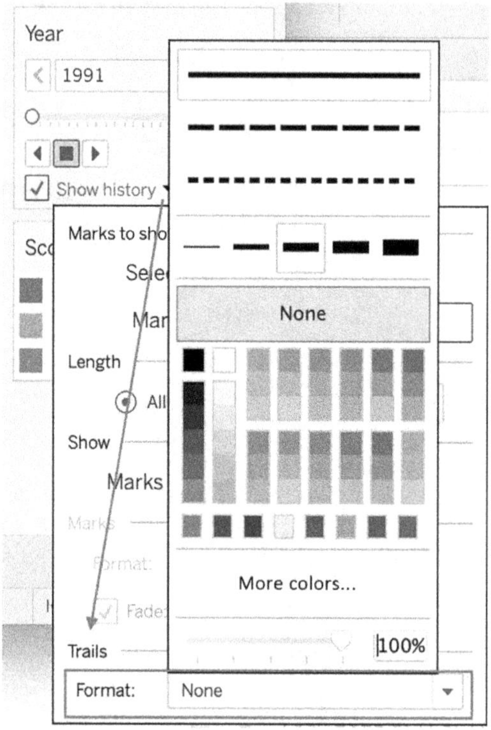

Figure 10.29: Dashed line

11. To briefly extend the theme of creating dashed lines in Tableau, to discover how to create multiple lines with varying dash types, check out `https://boraberan.wordpress.com/2015/11/22/quick-tip-creating-your-own-dashed-line-styles-in-tableau/`, where Bora Beran has pioneered a method using calculated fields to insert null values to achieve differing line effects.

> Dashed and doted lines have been available for basic line charts since Tableau 2023.2

12. Now, click on the play button and see how Tableau walks through each year, one at a time:

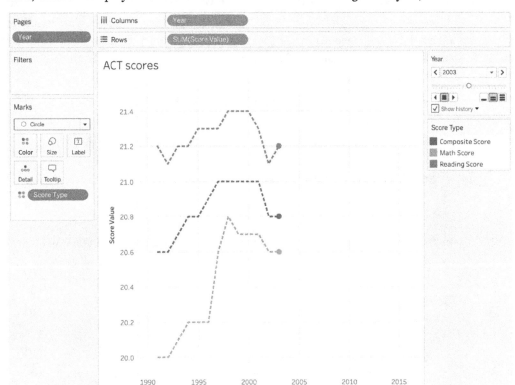

Figure 10.30: Animation

Even though this functionality is not a good use case for thorough analytics, it does help when visualizing change over time, for example, while giving a presentation or for any other kind of storytelling. I most recently used it to show how product clusters changed over time, with the conclusion that clusters should not remain static. I then continued to search for early identification of such change in clusters in order to adjust pricing and marketing accordingly.

To conclude, animations are possible in Tableau using a functionality called **Pages**. I hope you will find many use cases for this feature. Next, we will use the animation features in a different way, by showing you how to export multiple images with it.

Using an animation to export many images

There are at least two reasons why it may be necessary to export many images from a timeline. First, it may be analytically advantageous to see separate images for each time snapshot; for example, a separate image for each day in a month. Second, it may be necessary to create an animation outside of Tableau, perhaps in PowerPoint.

The next two exercises *Using an animation to export many images* and *Using an animation in Tableau to create an animation in PowerPoint* cover both scenarios:

 Note that the following steps assume that the previous exercise was completed.

1. Open the workbook associated with this chapter and navigate to the worksheet entitled ACT scores:

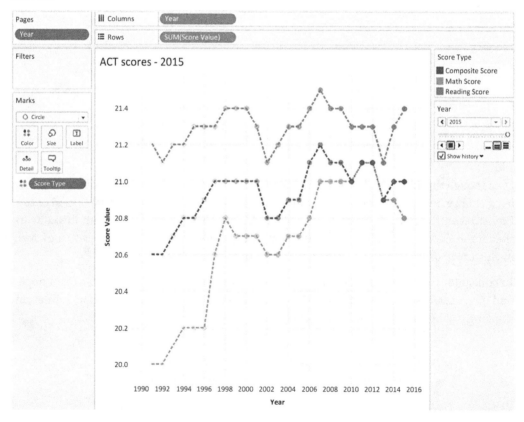

Figure 10.31: ACT scores final

2. Select **File** | **Page Setup....** At the bottom of the resulting dialog box, under **Pages Shelf**, select **Show all pages**:

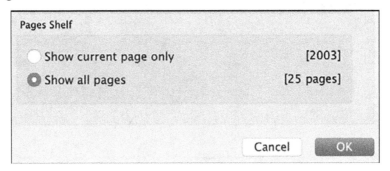

Figure 10.32: Show all pages

3. Select **File** | **Print to PDF**. Mac users should select **File** | **Print.**

4. In the resulting dialog box, set **Range** to **Active Sheet**. Also, set the orientation to **Landscape**.

5. Click **OK** and save the PDF as `Animation.pdf` to a location of your choice.

6. Navigate to `https://www.pdftoppt.com/`. Upload `Animation.pdf` and convert it into a Power-Point. An email will be sent a few minutes after conversion.

7. Download the file via the link provided in the email and open it in PowerPoint.

8. Within PowerPoint, select **File** | **Save As**. Within the **Save As** type drop-down menu, select ***.png**:

Figure 10.33: Animation.png

9. When prompted, choose to export **All Slides**:

Figure 10.34: All Slides

10. Save the PowerPoint presentation. Note that when PowerPoint finishes saving, a dialog box will display stating that each slide in the presentation has been saved as a separate file.

11. Open and inspect the saved PNG files as desired:

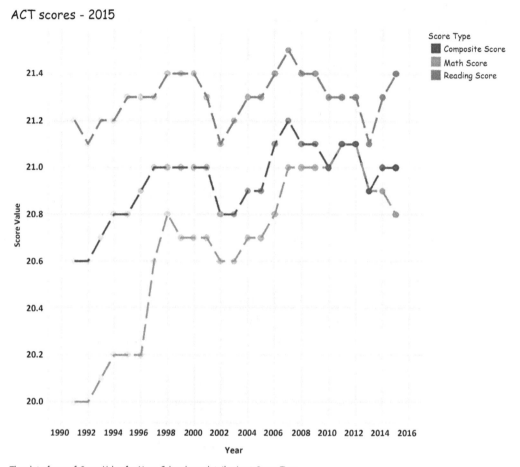

The plot of sum of Score Value for Year. Color shows details about Score Type.

Figure 10.35: Last slide as .png

By following all the preceding steps, you should have been able to save multiple images at once. This is hopefully a time-saver for you, and even though it might not happen too often, it will benefit you to know about this option.

Using an animation in Tableau to create an animation in PowerPoint

This exercise will show you how to create an animation from the mass of images we saved in the preceding exercise. Hence, we will use the files created previously to animate in PowerPoint:

1. Access the PowerPoint presentation downloaded from `https://www.pdftoppt.com/` in the previous exercise.

2. In the **View** ribbon, select **Slide Sorter** under the **Presentation Views** group.

3. Select **all slides** in the PowerPoint presentation except for the last one.

4. On the **Transition** ribbon under the **Timing** group, set to advance the slide after 0.1 seconds:

Figure 10.36: Advancing the slide

5. Press *F5* to see the animation.

Isn't this cool? You can see a similar simulation to what you would see in Tableau using Pages! To further improve the animation in PowerPoint, consider the following additional steps:

- Upload the initial PDF to `https://pdfresizer.com/crop` and crop the size as desired.

- If the animation is too slow in PowerPoint, it is likely that all the text and drawing elements are maintained. For example, the background grid is made up of individual lines. Rendering all text and drawing elements is resource-intensive. Consider creating a separate PowerPoint presentation using the PNG images created in the *Using an animation to export many images* exercise. This will lead to a quicker, smoother-running animation.

I hope that this section has given you some ideas on how you can improve and impress with PowerPoint. Using these newly acquired techniques, you might not even need Prezi after all. However, this chapter wouldn't be complete without mentioning story points, a feature that will bring you a long way if you don't want to use PowerPoint at all.

Story points and dashboards for presentations

Story points are Tableau's answer to PowerPoint. As such, both share fundamental similarities. A PowerPoint presentation provides a linear approach to communication. So do story points in Tableau. A PowerPoint presentation provides slides, each of which is a blank canvas that provides a user with infinite possibilities to communicate ideas. A story in Tableau provides story points for the same purpose.

Although there are fundamental similarities, it is important to understand that Tableau story points and PowerPoint presentations often do not fulfill the same role. Each has advantages over the other, and so a list of pros and cons should be considered.

We can view the pros and cons of PowerPoint and Tableau story points in the following table:

PowerPoint		Tableau story points	
Pros	**Cons**	**Pros**	**Cons**
Can be quick and easy to create	Difficult to automate based on changes to underlying data	Automatically updates as underlying data changes	Can be more difficult to create
Easily fits different resolutions	Difficult to create a presentation that allows for a departure from linear thought	Easily allows nonlinear exploration in the middle of a presentation	Requires forethought regarding resolution size

So how do you decide between using PowerPoint and Tableau when making presentations? Perhaps the following list will help:

When to use PowerPoint	When to use Tableau story points
A presentation where the audience has little opportunity for immediate feedback	A presentation where immediate feedback is likely and exploratory questions may be asked
A one-time presentation comprising clearly delineated points	A reusable presentation with updates mostly based on changes to underlying data
A presentation where the monitor resolution size may not be known in advance	A presentation where the monitor resolution size is known or assumed

The basics of creating and using story points are straightforward, and also, at the time of writing, there is not much beyond the basics. Since the focus of this book is on more advanced Tableau ideas and concepts, those basics will not be considered here. If you need to quickly understand story point basics, I recommend reading through the following pages: `https://help.tableau.com/current/pro/desktop/en-us/stories.htm`.

I like story points and I like to use them especially when my audience has its own version of Tableau open in front of them and can follow along with their own actions. It is a great way to give people a deeper understanding because it allows you to show more complexity than a static screenshot. If you are looking to improve your presentation skills in general, continue reading the next section.

Presentation resources

Using story points effectively in Tableau is perhaps more of an artistic consideration than a technical one. Although this book attempts to consistently consider best practices for data visualization and to encourage attractive and user-friendly worksheets and dashboards, a discussion of effective presentation techniques is beyond its scope.

If you would like to improve your ability to create effective presentations, consider the following resources:

- **Tableau story points:** Learning by example is invaluable. Fine examples of story points can be found on Tableau. To learn from one of the most engaging, navigate to `https://help.tableau.com/current/pro/desktop/en-us/story_example.htm`.

- **TEDx talks:** TEDx talks are great for learning and can even be listened to while commuting or being away from your desk in general. One video I would recommend is The 3 Magic Ingredients of Amazing Presentations by Phil Waknell `https://www.youtube.com/watch?v=yoD8RMq2OkU`.

- **Blogs:** One of the more interesting posts discussing Tableau story points in combination with good presentation methodology can be found here: `https://www.artofvisualization.com/blog/10-secrets-perfect-tableau-story`.

Even though these presentation skills are beyond the scope of this chapter, I do hope that the preceding resources have given you food for thought.

Summary

We began this chapter by exploring various screen capture tools as well as Tableau's native export capabilities. Next, we turned our consideration to PowerPoint, where we explored various methods for creating PowerPoint presentations from Tableau workbooks, and even explored how to embed a live instance of Tableau into PowerPoint. Next, we considered Tableau animation. Lastly, we explored how to use story points and dashboards for presentations. In *Chapter 11, Designing Dashboards and Best Practices for Visualizations*, we will turn our attention to dashboarding, where we will push beyond the normal boundaries of the typical dashboard, but not lose focus of the practical applications.

Learn more on Discord

To join the Discord community for this book – where you can share feedback, ask questions to the author, and learn about new releases – follow the QR code below:

`https://packt.link/tableau`

11

Designing Dashboards and Best Practices for Visualizations

Now, we will delve into the essential principles and best practices of data visualization, focusing specifically on dashboard design. By exploring how to present data in a visually compelling and informative manner, you will gain the knowledge and learn techniques that will help to create impactful dashboards to effectively communicate insights, drive decision-making, and engage your audience. This chapter was influenced by some giants in data visualization: *The Functional Art* by Alberto Cairo, *Information Dashboard Design* by Stephen Few, *The Big Book of Dashboards* by Steve Wexley, Jeffrey Shaffer, and Andy Cotgraeve, *Universal Principles of Design* by William Lidwell, Kritina Holden, and Jill Butler, *Data Story* by Nancy Duarte, and *The Visual Display of Quantitative Information* by Edward Tufte.

In this chapter, we will cover the following topics:

- Visualization design theory
- Formatting rules
- Color rules
- Visualization type rules
- Keeping visualizations simple
- Dashboard design
- Dashboard best practices
- Something extra

Now that we have defined the topics of this chapter, let's dive into design theory, which will provide you with rules that can be applied to every single dashboard you will build.

Visualization design theory

Your visualization thought process should always begin with the basics of design from the lowest level. In other words, we will start talking about the worksheets displayed on dashboards and ensure that those worksheets are well designed.

Therefore, our discussion will begin with a consideration of visualization design principles, such as the following collection, which is inspired by the *7 principles of design*: https://www.turing.com/kb/what-are-the-7-principles-of-design-detailed-breakdown:

- **Emphasize** what is most important
- **Amplify** important data points
- **Align and balance** elements with appropriate use of color, size, and texture
- Use **contrast** to highlight elements or groups
- **Limit** the use of colors or fonts to three to increase brand identity and keep control
- Use human-user friendly **proportions**, like the golden cut
- Keep the user's eye **moving** in a Z line
- Use **lines** for benchmarks or thresholds
- Use **white space** to organize and structure

Thus, in the next section, *Formatting rules*, we will consider various rules, while keeping in mind that once you're comfortable with the basics, rules can be broken to serve a purpose.

Formatting rules

The following formatting rules encompass **fonts**, **lines**, and **bands**. Fonts are, of course, an obvious formatting consideration. Lines and bands, however, may not be something you typically work with—but in Tableau, lines and bands should certainly be considered. This illustrates that data visualization is closely related to graphic design, where lines and bands play a much bigger role than they do in, for example, Excel, and that formatting considers much more than just the textual layout.

Keep the font choice simple

Typically, using one or two fonts on a dashboard is advisable. More fonts can create a confusing environment and interfere with readability.

Fonts chosen for titles should be thick and solid, while body fonts should be easy to read. In Tableau, choosing appropriate fonts is simple: select **Format** | **Font** to display the **Format Font** window to see and choose the fonts you like.

The Tableau fonts always work, like Tableau Bold, Tableau Book, Tableau Medium, Tableau Light, and so on. And for a special occasion, I like to use Corbel or play around with new fonts.

Use lines in order of visibility

We tend to order line visibility in the following order: trend line, chart line, reference line, drop line, and grid line. For example, trend-line visibility should be greater than reference-line visibility. Visibility is usually enhanced by increasing the line thickness but may be enhanced via color saturation or by choosing a dotted or dashed line over a solid line. Let's look at each of the line types, in order of decreasing visibility:

- **Trend lines:** The trend line, if present, is usually the most visible line on the graph. Trend lines are displayed via the **Analytics** pane and can be adjusted via **Format | Lines:**

  - **Use case:** A time series with many data points and lots of fluctuation over time. Use a trend line to show an overall direction (increase/decrease over time) and thus make it easier for your users to process the information.

- **Chart lines:** The chart line (for example, the line used on a time series chart) should not be so heavy as to obscure twists and turns in the data. Although a chart line may be displayed as dotted or dashed by utilizing the **Pages** shelf, this is usually not advisable because it may obscure visibility. The thickness of a chart line can be adjusted by clicking on the **Size** shelf in the **Marks remove bold** area:

  - **Use case:** This is the actual line of a line chart.

- **Reference lines:** Usually less prevalent than trend lines and can be formatted via **Format | Reference lines:**

  - **Use case:** A straight line to show, e.g., a threshold that is static for at least one dimension within the view of your dashboard.

- **Drop lines:** Not frequently used. To deploy drop lines, right-click in a blank portion of your **view** and select **Drop lines | Show drop lines**. Next, click a point in the view to display a drop line. To format drop lines, select **Format | Drop Lines**. Drop lines are relevant only if at least one axis is utilized in the visualization:

  - **Use case:** To mark the line from a point on your chart to the axis. It can help you to identify the specific value associated with that data point.

- **Zero lines:** These are sometimes referred to as baselines, and only display if zero or negative values are included in the view, or positive numerical values are relatively close to zero. Format zero lines via **Format | Lines:**

  - **Use case:** If you aren't happy with the default zero line, you can format it. It can help distinguish where positive values start and negative ones end (and vice versa).

- **Grid lines:** These should be the most muted lines on the view and may be dispensed with altogether. Format grid lines via **Format | Lines:**

  - **Use case:** Grid lines help the eye to identify values of data points that are otherwise far away from the axis. Use them to help users to better understand values in your visualization.

Use bands in groups of three to five

Visualizations composed of a tall table of text or horizontal bars should segment dimension members into groups of three to five.

Please follow along with the steps to experience an efficient use of bands in Tableau:

1. Navigate to `https://public.tableau.com/profile/marleen.meier` to locate and download the workbook associated with this chapter.

2. Navigate to the `Banding` worksheet.

3. Select the `Superstore` data source and place **Product Name** on the **Rows** shelf.

4. Double-click on **Discount, Profit, Quantity**, and **Sales**. Note that after completing this step, Tableau defaults to banding every other row. This default formatting is fine for a short table but is quite busy for a tall table, and it may lead to performance issues with large datasets.

5. Navigate to **Format | Shading** and set **Band Size** under **Row Banding** so that three to five lines of text are encompassed by each band. Be sure to set an appropriate color for both **Pane** and **Header**:

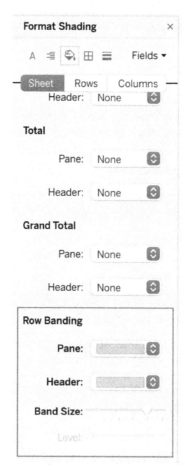

Figure 11.1: Format Shading

The *Band in Groups of Three to Five* rule is influenced by Dona W. Wong, who, in her book *The Wall Street Journal Guide to Information Graphics*, recommends separating long tables or bar charts with thin lines to separate the bars into groups of three to five to help readers read across.

Color rules

It seems slightly ironic to discuss color rules in a book that will be printed in black and white (to download the color images, look here: `https://packt.link/TybKH`. Of course, that may not be true if you are reading this book on an electronic device). Nevertheless, even in a monochromatic setting, a discussion of color is relevant. For example, the exclusive use of black text communicates something different compared to using variations of gray. The following list of color rules should be helpful to ensure that you use colors effectively in a variety of settings.

Keep colors simple and limited

Stick to the basic hues and provide only a few (perhaps three to five) hue variations. In his book *The Functional Art: An Introduction to Information Graphics and Visualization*, Alberto Cairo provides insight as to why this is important:

> *The limited capacity of our visual working memory helps explain why it's not advisable to use more than four or five colors or pictograms to identify different phenomena on maps and charts.*

Respect the psychological implications of colors

There is a color vocabulary in every region of the world so pervasive that it's second nature. Red is often used for love or danger; in some Asian countries, it can also mean fortune and is common for wedding dresses. Green can mean luck, whereas in Mexico, green represents independence. Green traffic signals tell us to go, and red to stop. Similarly, colors on dashboards are often used with a purpose. Reds and oranges are usually associated with negative performance, while blues and greens are associated with positive performance. Using colors counterintuitively can cause confusion, so be aware of color usage and your audience and their interpretation.

Be colorblind-friendly

A quick Google search told me that *"There are an estimated 300 million people in the world with color vision deficiency. 1 in 12 men and 1 in 200 women are color blind."* Therefore, it is quite likely that you will have a colorblind or color-vision-deficient person in your audience at some point in your career. Colorblindness is usually manifested as an inability to distinguish between red and green, or blue and yellow. Red/green and blue/yellow are on opposite sides of the color wheel.

Consequently, the challenges these color combinations present for colorblind individuals can be easily recreated with image editing software such as Photoshop. If you are not colorblind, convert an image with these color combinations into grayscale and observe. The challenge presented to the 8.0% of men and 0.5% of women who are colorblind becomes immediately obvious! Or, use the following website to upload an image of your dashboard and experience how your user might see the colors used: `https://www.color-blindness.com/coblis-color-blindness-simulator/`.

Use pure colors sparingly

The resulting colors from the following exercise should be a very vibrant red, green, and blue. Depending on the monitor, you may even find it difficult to stare directly at the colors. These are known as **pure colors** and should be used sparingly, perhaps only to highlight particularly important items or alerts in, for example, breached thresholds.

Please follow these steps:

1. Open the workbook associated with this chapter and navigate to the Pure Colors worksheet.
2. Select the Superstore data source and place **Category** on both the **Rows** shelf and the **Color** shelf.
3. Set **Fit** to **Entire View**.
4. Click on the **Color** shelf and choose **Edit Colors…**.
5. In the **Edit Colors** dialog box, select one after the other member—that is, **Furniture**, **Office Supplies**, and **Technology**, and select blue, green, and red, respectively:

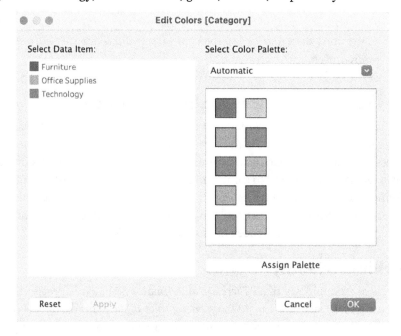

Figure 11.2: Colors

See for yourself how you experience looking at those pure colors and select three other, less vibrant, colors to compare. Too vibrant colors can be very heavy on your eye and make it hard to focus. Colors that are too similar, however, are hard to distinguish between. Finding a good balance is key.

Choose color variations over symbol variation

Deciphering different symbols takes more mental energy for the end user than distinguishing colors. Therefore, color variation should be used over symbol variation.

See the following scatter plot for an example of symbol variation:

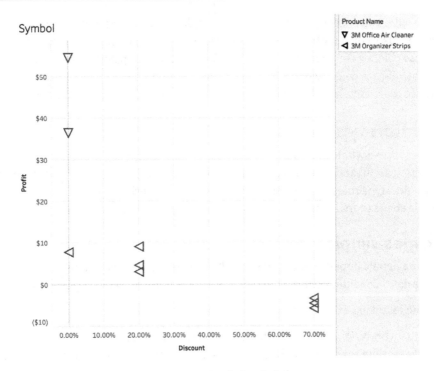

Figure 11.3: Symbol variation

See the same with color variation:

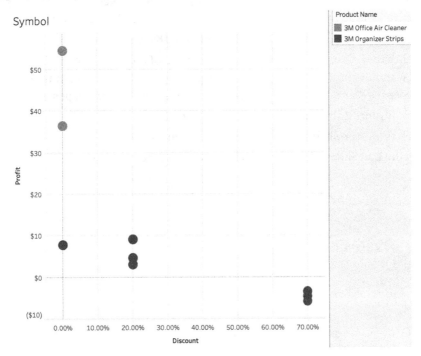

Figure 11.4: Color variation

To sum up the color rules, keep your color palette simple and be aware of your regional and cultural color meanings. Also, consider that people in your audience might have a color deficiency; tools can help you choose colors wisely, and Tableau also offers a colorblind palette. Use pure colors sparingly since too many vibrant colors will make it hard for the audience to focus on the important items. Lastly, don't use too many shapes in one view; instead, use color to distinguish between categories.

Visualization type rules

This section deserves a whole separate book and is interlinked with many other disciplines like story-telling, communication, and persuasion; as such, we won't take the time here to delve into a lengthy list of visualization-type rules but, rather, highlight a few frequently discussed ones. We will consider keeping simple shapes versus complex ones and the effective use of pie charts.

Keep shapes simple

Too many shape details impede comprehension. This is because shape details draw the user's focus away from the data. Consider the following exercise using two different shopping cart images.

Let's look at the following exercise steps:

1. Open the workbook associated with this chapter and navigate to the `Simple Shopping Cart` worksheet. Note that the visualization is a scatter plot that shows the top-10-selling subcategories in terms of total sales and profits.

2. Navigate to the `Shapes` directory located in the `My Tableau` repository. On my computer, the path is `C:\Users\Marleen Meier\Documents\My Tableau Repository\Shapes`. Locate the respective Tableau repository on your machine and open the `Shapes` directory

3. Within the `Shapes` directory, create a folder named `My Shapes`.

4. Reference the link included in the comment section of the worksheet to download assets associated with this chapter. In the downloaded material, find the images entitled `Shopping_Cart` and `Shopping_Cart_3D`, and then copy those images into the `My Shapes` directory.

5. In Tableau, access the `Simple Shopping Cart` worksheet.

6. Click on the **Shape** shelf and then select **More Shapes**.

7. Within the **Edit Shape** dialog box, click the **Reload Shapes** button:

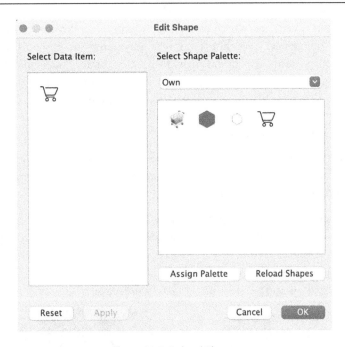

Figure 11.5: Reload Shapes

8. Select the **My Shapes** palette and set the shape to Shopping_Cart.

9. After closing the dialog box, click on the **Size** shelf and adjust as desired. Also, adjust other aspects of the visualization as desired.

10. Navigate to the 3D Shopping Cart worksheet and then repeat *steps 6–9* above. Instead of using Shopping_Cart, use Shopping_Cart_3D. See the following screenshot for a comparison of the simple and 3D shopping carts:

Figure 11.6: 2D versus 3D

Compare the two visualizations. Which version of the shopping cart is more attractive? It's likely that the cart with the 3D look was your choice. So, why not choose the more attractive image? Making visualizations attractive is only a secondary concern. The primary goal is to display the data as clearly and efficiently as possible. A simple shape is grasped more quickly and intuitively than a complex shape. Besides, the cuteness of the 3D image will quickly wear off.

Use pie charts sparingly

Edward Tufte makes an acrid comment against the use of pie charts in his book *The Visual Display of Quantitative Information,* saying that a table is always better than a pie chart because we humans fail to interpret the visual dimension of pie charts.

The present sentiment in data visualization circles is largely sympathetic to Tufte's criticism. There may, however, be some exceptions—that is, some circumstances where a pie chart is optimal. Consider the following visualization:

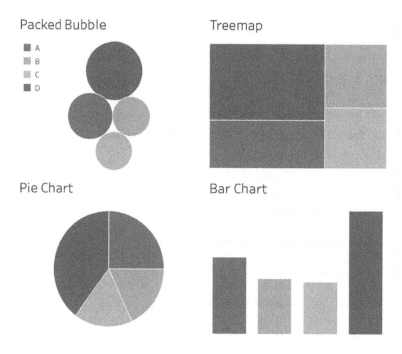

Figure 11.7: Comparing visualizations

Which of the four visualizations best demonstrates that A accounts for 25% of the whole? Clearly, it's the pie chart! Therefore, perhaps it is fairer to refer to pie charts as limited and to use them sparingly, as opposed to considering them inherently undesirable.

Often, building visualizations is a balancing act. It's not uncommon to encounter contradictory directions from books, blogs, consultants, and even within organizations. One person may insist on utilizing every pixel of space while another advocates for simplicity and white space. One counsels a guided approach, while another recommends building wide-open dashboards that allow end users to discover their own path.

Avant-garde types may crave esoteric visualizations, while those of a more conservative bent prefer to stay with convention. Let's explore a few of the more common competing requests and then suggest compromises.

Make the dashboard simple and robust

Occam's razor suggests that the simplest possible solution to any problem is probably the right one. Yet, sometimes, even the simplest solution is rather complex. This is OK! Complexity in Tableau dashboarding need not be shunned. But a clear understanding of some basic guidelines can help the author intelligently determine how to compromise between demands for simplicity and demands for robustness:

- *More frequent data updates necessitate simpler design*: Some Tableau dashboards may be near real-time. Third-party technology may be utilized to force a browser that displays a dashboard via Tableau Server to refresh every few minutes, to ensure the latest data is displayed. In such cases, the design should be quite simple. The end user must be able to see immediately all pertinent data and should not use that dashboard for extensive analysis. Conversely, a dashboard that is refreshed monthly can support high complexity and thus may be used for deep exploration.

- *Greater end user expertise supports greater dashboard complexity*: Know thy users. If they want easy, at-a-glance visualizations, keep the dashboards simple. If they like deep dives, design accordingly.

- *Smaller audiences require more precise design*: If only a few people monitor a given dashboard, it may require a highly customized approach. In such cases, specifications may be detailed, which are complex and difficult to execute and maintain. This is because the small user base has expectations that may not be natively easy to produce in Tableau.

- *Screen resolution and visualization complexity are proportional*: Users with low-resolution devices will need to interact simply with a dashboard. Thus, the design of such a dashboard will likely be correspondingly uncomplicated. Conversely, high-resolution devices support greater complexity.

- *Greater distance from the screen requires larger dashboard elements*: If the dashboard is designed for conference room viewing, the elements on the dashboard may need to be large to meet the viewing needs of those far from the screen. Thus, the dashboard will likely be relatively simple. Conversely, a dashboard to be viewed primarily on end users' desktops can be more complex.

Although these points are all about simple versus complex, do not equate simple with easy. A simple and elegantly designed dashboard can be more difficult to create than a complex dashboard.

As Steve Jobs said, simplicity can be harder than complexity; however, simplicity can move mountains.

Present dense information well

Normally, a line graph should have a max of four or five lines. However, there are times when you may wish to display many lines. A compromise can be achieved by presenting many lines and empowering the end user to highlight as desired. The following line graph displays the percentage of internet usage by country from 2000 to 2012. The user can select a country, which will then change color, and compare it to the rest.

We can see this example in the following screenshot:

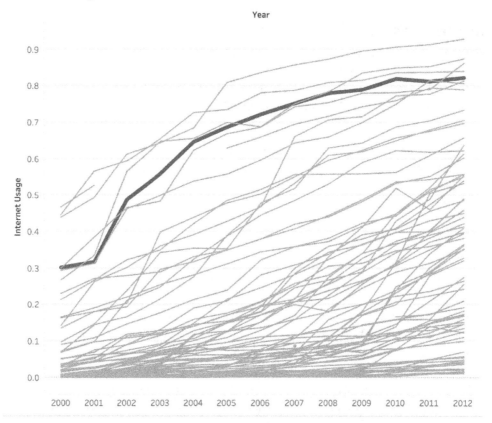

Figure 11.8: A many-line chart

When using line charts versus many-line charts, it should not be important how a line performs compared to a specific other line but, rather, how one line behaves in a lake of other lines.

Tell a story

In her book *Data Story*, Nancy Duarte explains in great detail the various techniques one could use to tell a story with data, and many overlap with visualization design theory, which was discussed earlier. We will now zoom in on a few new, storytelling-specific aspects:

Explore data points to drill deeper into lower levels of aggregation. Visualization in Tooltip (see the *Maximizing documentation on a dashboard* section of this chapter) is a great way to do this as well as Actions (see the *Dashboard best practices* section of this chapter).

Relate your data; for example, if a distance, size, time, or speed is hard to grasp, convert it into something known. Or, *"If the Sun were as big as a football and the Moon as big as… then the distance between the two would be from here to x."* Or, as a very specific example, instead of showing the amount of sugar in mg, present it as a count of sugar cubes or relate it to the recommended daily intake.

Use rhetoric to lead the reader through your viewpoint of the story, by incorporating emotive words, rhetorical questions, and interjections.

If your data is somewhat related to humans – and it often is – humanize it. Talk to people and learn about problems; you can then add qualitative information to your dashboard. Watch out to not make assumptions.

You will realize that telling a story isn't as easy as one might think:

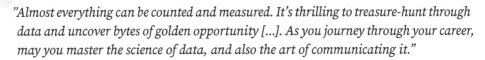

> *"Almost everything can be counted and measured. It's thrilling to treasure-hunt through data and uncover bytes of golden opportunity [...]. As you journey through your career, may you master the science of data, and also the art of communicating it."*
>
> *Nancy Duarte – Data Story*

You can choose to tell the story by using directive dashboard design (i.e., a dashboard that guides the viewer), or you could decide to build a dashboard that allows the discovery of numerous stories. Your choice will differ, depending on the given dataset and audience. If you choose to create a platform for story discovery, be sure to take the *New York Times* approach suggested by Grimwade in Alberto Cairo's book *The Functional Art: An Introduction to Information Graphics and Visualization*: *"Provide hints, pointers, and good documentation to lead your end user to successfully interact with the story you wish to tell or to successfully discover their own story."*

Maximize documentation on a dashboard

In the *Telling a story* section, we considered the suggestion of providing hints, pointers, and good documentation, but there's an issue. These things take up space. Dashboard space is precious. Often, Tableau authors are asked to squeeze more and more stuff onto a dashboard and, hence, look for ways to conserve space. Here are some suggestions to maximize documentation on a dashboard while minimally impacting screen real estate:

- **Craft titles for clear communication**: Titles are expected. Not just a title for a dashboard and worksheets on the dashboard, but also titles for legends, filters, and other objects. These titles can be used for effective and efficient documentation. For instance, a filter should not just read **Market**. Instead, it should say something such as **Select a Market**. Notice the imperative statement. The user is being told to do something, and this is a helpful hint. Adding a couple of words to a title will usually not impact dashboard space.

- **Use subtitles to relay instructions**: A subtitle will take up some extra space, but it does not have to be much. A small, italicized font immediately underneath a title is an obvious place a user will look for guidance. Consider an example: **red represents loss**. This short sentence could be used as a subtitle that may eliminate the need for a legend and, thus, actually save space.

- **Use intuitive icons**: Consider a use case of navigating from one dashboard to another. Of course, you could associate an action with some hyperlinked text that states it navigates to another dashboard. But this seems unnecessary when an action can be associated with a small, innocuous arrow, such as what is natively used in PowerPoint, to communicate the same thing.

- **Store more extensive documentation in a tooltip associated with a help icon:** A small question mark in the upper-right corner of an application is common. Currently, I'm composing this chapter in Word, which has such a question mark. In a Tableau dashboard, the lightbulb icon is often used for the same purpose. This clearly communicates where to go if additional help is required. As shown in the following exercise, it's easy to create.

Follow these steps to create an informative tooltip to help users:

1. Open the workbook associated with this chapter and navigate to the Help worksheet.
2. Hover over the light bulb on the worksheet and note the text that appears:

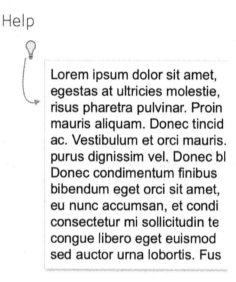

Figure 11.9: Lorem ipsum

 Note that the *Lorem ipsum...* text shown in the preceding screenshot is commonly used by web designers, who borrowed it from typesetters, who have used this Latin text as a placeholder for centuries. Visit www.loremipsum.io to learn more.

The text in this worksheet was deployed via **Worksheet | Tooltip**. This worksheet could be thoughtfully placed on a dashboard (for example, in the upper-right corner) to give very detailed documentation that minimally impacts space.

Visualization types

Another important set of rules is which visualization to use for what data type! To just pick out a few examples:

- Use a spine chart for deviation data
- Use a scatter plot or heatmap for correlation
- Use a line chart or seismogram for time series

- Use a bar, lollipop, or bump chart for ranking
- Use a histogram or box plot for distributions
- Use a treemap, grid plot, or waterfall for part of a whole data
- Use bars, radar, or bullet graphs to reflect magnitudes
- Use flow, dot-density, or heatmaps for spatial data
- Use Sankey charts, waterfall, or network graphs for flows

This list is by far not exhaustive; if you want to get additional information on this topic, I highly recommend checking out the *Visual Vocabulary* that Andy Kriebel created, which was inspired by the *Financial Times* (`https://ft-interactive.github.io/visual-vocabulary/`), available on Tableau Public: `https://public.tableau.com/profile/andy.kriebel#!/vizhome/VisualVocabulary/VisualVocabulary`. Each category contains multiple suitable visualization types; you can click on a given category to see details:

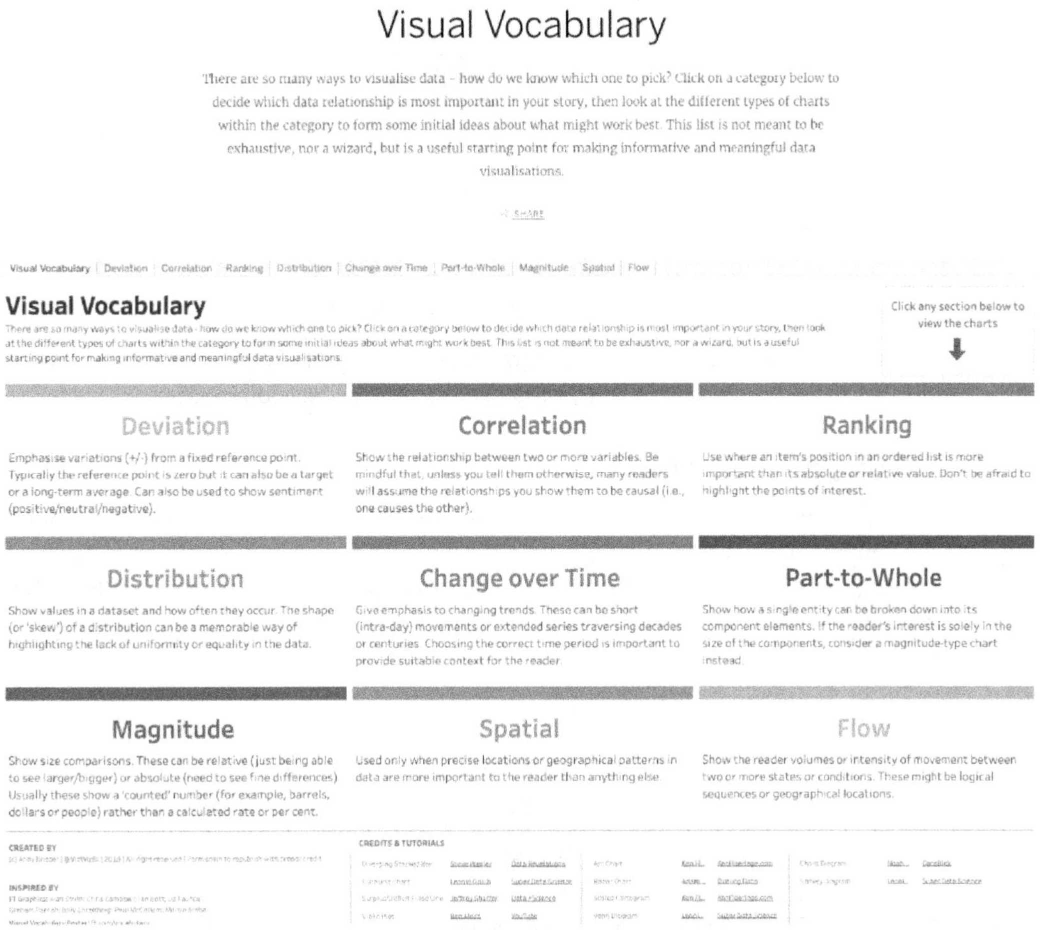

Figure 11.10: Visual Vocabulary

Here is, for example, the detail page for the category **Distribution**:

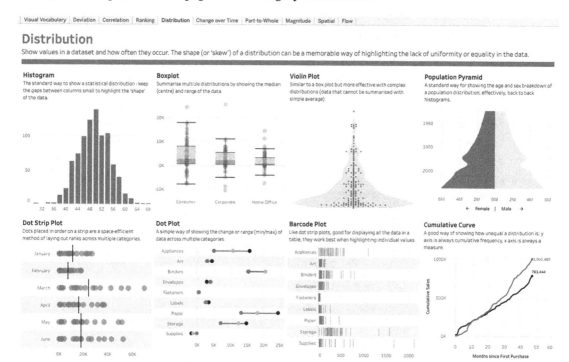

Figure 11.11: Visual Vocabulary – Distribution

Picking a well-matching visualization type for your graph is the very start of creating a good dashboard. Make it your priority to spend some time on this topic; it is a crucial decision in most projects.

Keep visualizations simple

Some people tire of seeing the same chart types over and over. This leads to requests such as, can we spice up the dashboard a bit? Normally, such sentiments should be resisted. As stated at the beginning of this chapter, introducing variety for its own sake is counterproductive. Nevertheless, there are times when a less common visualization type may be a better choice than a more popular type. When are those times?

Use less common chart types in the following scenarios:

*   The chart is used to catch the end user's attention.
*   The chart type presents the data more effectively.

Sometimes, a less common chart type can be effectively used to catch the end user's attention for some goal, such as humor, making a salient point, or making the visualization more memorable. One such example can be found on the Tableau 404 error page. Navigate to `http://www.tableau.com/asdf` and observe Bigfoot in a packed bubble chart. Note that this page changes from time to time, so you may see Elvis, aliens, or some other visualization.

An example of the second point is using a treemap over a pie chart. Both are non-Cartesian chart types (visualizations with no fields on the **Rows** or **Columns** shelves) used to show parts of a whole. Pie charts are the more common of the two, but treemaps usually present the data better. There are at least three reasons for this:

- A treemap can represent more data points.
- The rectangular nature of a treemap fits monitor space more efficiently.
- Pie slice sizes are more difficult to distinguish than sizes of treemap segments.

Sometimes, using a less common visualization type may elicit complaints: *I like pie charts. Give me a pie chart!* In such cases, a compromise may be possible. Later in this chapter, we will consider sheet swapping. As you will learn, sheet swapping can allow the end user to determine which visualization type to view. In the end, if a compromise is not possible and the person responsible for your paycheck desires a less-than-ideal chart type... well, I recommend you do as they ask!

Dashboard design

Now that we have completed our discussion of visualization theory, let's turn our attention to dashboard design. We'll begin by asking the question, what is a dashboard? This is rather difficult to answer; however, its usage in everyday conversation in many organizations would suggest that people have a definite idea as to what a dashboard is. Furthermore, search engine results provide no shortage of definitions. But those definitions can differ significantly and even be contradictory.

Why is it so difficult to define a dashboard? In part, it is because data visualization as a whole, and dashboarding specifically, is an emerging field that combines many other disciplines. These disciplines include statistical analysis, graphic and web design, computer science, and even journalism. An emerging field with so many components is a moving target and, as such, is difficult to define.

For our purposes, we will begin with Stephen Few's definition as it first appeared in an issue of *Intelligent Enterprise* in 2004. He states that a dashboard is a visual display of vital statistics we need to reach, and all these details are present on a sole screen so that this information can be observed in one place. Then, we'll extend and adapt that definition for Tableau dashboards.

Although this definition is good, Tableau takes a broader approach. For instance, a Tableau dashboard may be contained on a single screen but can be designed (and quite effectively so) to require scrolling. More importantly, Tableau dashboards are typically interactive, which opens up a world of exploration, analysis, and design options. Therefore, let's attempt a Tableau-centric dashboard definition:

A Tableau dashboard is a display that contains one or more data visualizations designed to enable a user to quickly view metrics. This display may provide interactive elements, such as filtering, highlighting, and drill-down capabilities that enable further exploration and analysis.

Dashboard layout

The layout of a dashboard is important for the same reason that the layout of a magazine foldout or a web page is important. Placing the right information in the right place helps the viewer quickly and efficiently gather information and draw conclusions.

In order to appreciate this fact, consider the last time you had to hunt through a poorly constructed web page to find important information. Your time could have been better used actually applying that important information!

The Golden Ratio layout

You have probably heard of the Fibonacci sequence or the Golden Ratio. Since it may have been a few years since you attended a math class, a brief reminder may prove helpful.

The Fibonacci sequence is a series of numbers where every number is the sum of the previous two numbers—for example, 1, 1, 2, 3, 5, 8, 13, 21.

A Golden Rectangle is achieved when the ratio of the longest side to the shortest side of a rectangle is approximately 1.618. This ratio is known as the Golden Ratio. Mathematically, the Golden Ratio is represented as follows:

$$\varphi = \frac{1 + \sqrt{5}}{2} \approx 1.61803398874989$$

You can see the connection between the Fibonacci sequence and the Golden Ratio when dividing each number of the Fibonacci sequence by the previous number; for example, take the following sequence:

0, 1, 1, 2, 3, 5, 8, 13, 21, 34

This leads to the following:

$$\frac{1}{1} = 1, \quad \frac{2}{1} = 2, \quad \frac{3}{2} = 1.5, \quad \frac{5}{3} = 1.67, \quad \frac{8}{5} = 1.6,$$

$$\frac{13}{8} = 1.625, \quad \frac{21}{13} = 1.615, \quad \frac{34}{21} = 1.619$$

Now, let's consider a dashboard layout using the Golden Ratio. The layout shown here is constructed of rectangles so that each is 1.618 times longer or taller than the next. The spiral (known as the Golden Spiral) is displayed to demonstrate the order of the rectangles:

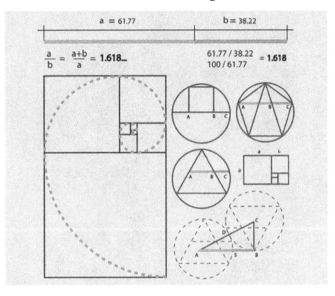

Figure 11.12: Golden Ratio (https://www.pixpa.com/blog/golden-ratio)

The Fibonacci sequence/Golden Rectangle/Golden Ratio appears endlessly in nature and throughout history. Many seashells and flowers adhere closely to the Fibonacci sequence. The Great Pyramid of Giza appears to have been constructed with the Golden Ratio in mind. Phidias likely used the Golden Ratio to design his statues for the Athenian Parthenon. Indeed, the Parthenon itself was designed with Golden Rectangle proportions. Even if more recent studies have shown that the ratio can't be replicated to decimals, nature and art are still very close to the mathematics behind it.

So, does the Golden Ratio, as pictured in the preceding diagram, represent the ideal dashboard layout? Perhaps it's more pertinent to say that this image represents one acceptable dashboard layout. The ideal is not so much found in the abstract as it's found in the application. Dashboard layouts may sometimes approximate the Golden Ratio but, as we will see, other dashboard layouts may be better for different scenarios.

The dashboard pictured here (which is also available in the Tableau workbook that accompanies this chapter) utilizes the Golden Rectangle:

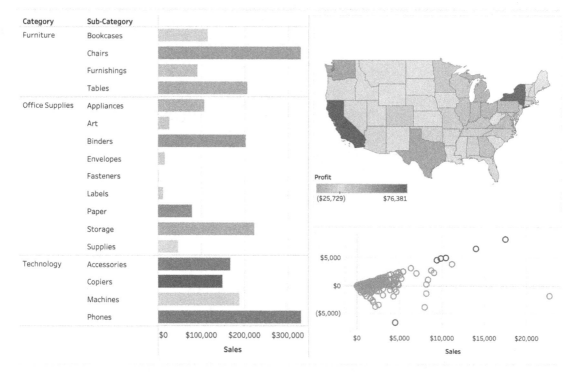

Figure 11.13: Golden Rectangle

Notice that this example does not attempt to follow the Golden Ratio through to smaller and smaller rectangles. There are practical limits.

The Golden Rectangle layout is particularly good for guiding the viewer from coarser to finer granularity. In this example, the left portion of the dashboard displays the coarsest granularity, 17 subcategories. The map is next. Finally, the scatter plot displays the finest granularity. Creating actions that follow this path would make a natural interaction for the end user. For example, an end user might first click on **Tables** and then click on the state of **Pennsylvania** to observe outliers in the scatter plot.

The quad layout

The quad layout divides a dashboard into four more or less equal quadrants. It's easy to implement. On a blank dashboard, simply double-click on four worksheets in the **Dashboard** pane. The result is a quad layout, though some small adjustments may need to be made to account for legends, filters, and parameters. To observe a quad layout, refer to the diagram in *Figure 11.7*.

The small multiple layout

A small multiple layout displays many views on a single dashboard. Like the quad layout, a small multiple layout can be implemented simply by double-clicking on each desired worksheet in the **Dashboard** pane.

Small multiples are useful when viewing information that utilizes the same visualization type repeatedly. Also, a consistent theme is helpful; for example, the following screenshot demonstrates a theme of profit performance per state in the USA. Attempting to create a small multiple layout with multiple visualization types and multiple themes will likely be messy and difficult to interact with:

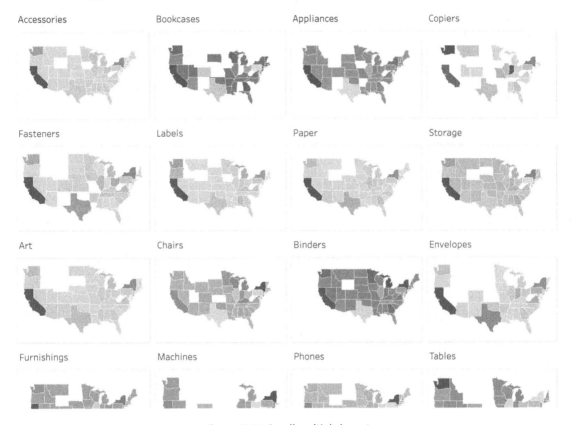

Figure 11.14: Small multiple layouts

Some layouts are essentially variations of a theme. For instance, a layout that displays three views where one view on the dashboard covers double the real estate of each of the other views may essentially be a variation of the quad layout. Other layouts defy easy categorization and are unique to a given dashboard. Regardless, this will hopefully provide some food for thought as you design dashboards in the future.

We already mentioned the next section when we discussed compromises – sheet swapping, which is a great feature for compromises. If your stakeholder asks you to build something you know might not be as good or doesn't follow a visualization best practice, you can always add a sheet swap, making your stakeholders happy and delivering an alternative to other users. We will walk through a sheet-swapping exercise in the next section.

Utilize sheet swapping

Sheet selection, often referred to as sheet swapping, allows the Tableau author to hide and display visualizations, as well as to move worksheets on and off the dashboard.

These techniques have been used in creative ways with some very impressive results. For example, Tableau Zen Master Joshua Milligan has built various games, including tic-tac-toe and blackjack, using sheet selection. For our purposes, we will stick to using sheet selection to assist with creating dashboards that adhere to the design principles we've discussed.

In the *Use pie charts sparingly* section, we discussed pie charts and treemaps, and we noted that a treemap is a better visualization. However, people are often more comfortable with pie charts. As a compromise, in the first exercise, we will review an example that allows the end user to choose whether to see a pie chart or a treemap.

Please follow these steps:

1. Open the workbook associated with this chapter and navigate to the `Population Pie` worksheet.

2. Select the `World Indicators` data source and note the calculated field, called `Blank`. The code is composed of single quotes with a space in between.

3. Place **Blank** on the **Columns** shelf.

4. In the view, select all pie slices via *Ctrl + A* or by dragging a marquee around the entire pie. Non-Cartesian visualization types (for example, visualizations with no fields on the **Rows or Columns** shelves) require this step for sheet swapping to work. Otherwise, when placing the worksheet in a vertical container on a dashboard, the worksheet will not properly stretch to fill the width of the container.

5. Right-click on any pie slice and choose **Annotate | Mark**.

6. In the resulting dialog box, delete all the text except `<Country>`:

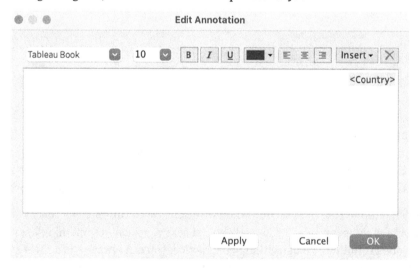

Figure 11.15: Annotation

7. Position and format the annotations as desired. Note that additional adjustments may be required once the pie chart has been deployed on a dashboard.

8. Create a parameter named Select Chart Type with the following settings:

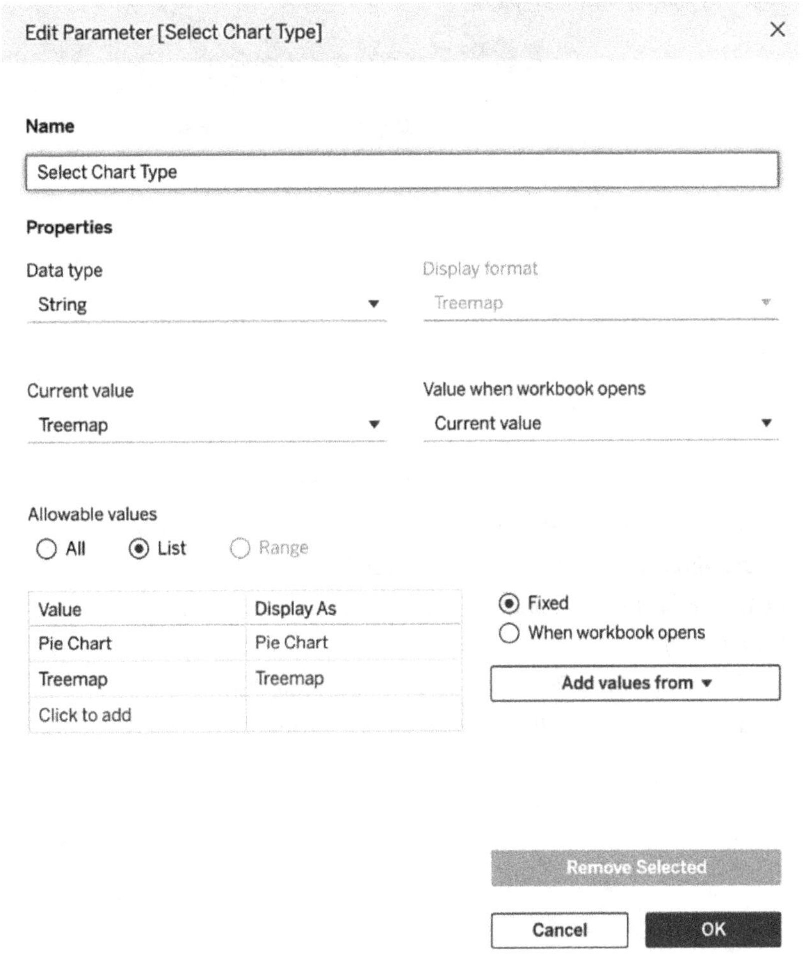

Figure 11.16: Parameter

9. Create a calculated field entitled Sheet Swap containing the following code:

```
[Select Chart Type]
```

10. Place **Sheet Swap** on the **Filters** shelf and select **Pie Chart** in the resulting dialog box.

11. Display the parameter by right-clicking on **Select Chart Type** and choosing **Show Parameter Control**.

12. Navigate to the Population Tree worksheet.

13. Place **Blank** on the **Columns** shelf.

14. Place **Sheet Swap** on the **Filters** shelf and select **Treemap** in the resulting dialog box.

15. If **Treemap** does not display as a choice, make sure that the **Select Chart Type** parameter is toggled to **Treemap** and click **OK**:

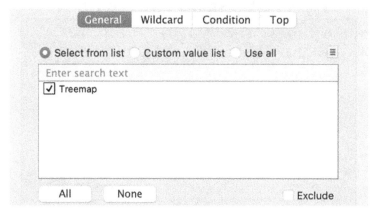

Figure 11.17: Filter

16. Create a new dashboard entitled `Latin American Population`.

17. In the **Dashboard** pane, double-click on **Vertical** to place a vertical container on the dashboard.

18. In the **Dashboard** pane, double-click on **Population Tree** and **Population Pie** in order to add them to the view.

19. Right-click on the titles **Population Tree** and **Population Pie**, then select **Hide Title** for both.

20. Place **Population Map** and **Population Change** on our dashboard, then position them as desired:

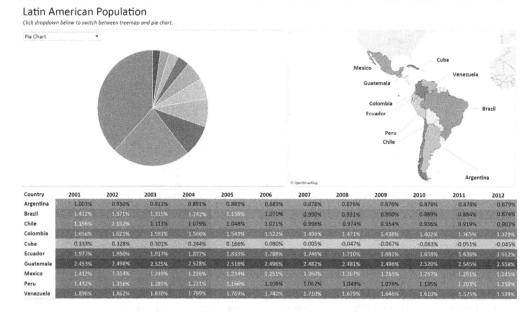

Figure 11.18: Dashboard

21. Shift-drag the **Select Chart Type** parameter over our **Treemap** to float the control; position it as desired.

22. Delete all legends and quick filters. Format, document, and position all dashboard elements as desired. The user can now determine whether to view a **Treemap** or a **Pie Chart**.

The following is an example of the dashboard with a treemap:

Latin American Population
Click dropdown below to switch between treemap and pie chart.

Country	2001	2002	2003	2004	2005	2006	2007	2008	2009	2010	2011	2012
Argentina	1.003%	0.950%	0.911%	0.891%	0.885%	0.883%	0.878%	0.876%	0.876%	0.876%	0.878%	0.879%
Brazil	1.412%	1.371%	1.315%	1.242%	1.159%	1.070%	0.990%	0.931%	0.900%	0.889%	0.884%	0.874%
Chile	1.196%	1.152%	1.113%	1.079%	1.048%	1.021%	0.996%	0.974%	0.954%	0.936%	0.919%	0.903%
Colombia	1.656%	1.621%	1.591%	1.566%	1.543%	1.522%	1.499%	1.471%	1.438%	1.402%	1.365%	1.329%
Cuba	0.333%	0.328%	0.301%	0.244%	0.166%	0.080%	0.005%	-0.047%	-0.067%	-0.063%	-0.051%	-0.045%
Ecuador	1.977%	1.950%	1.917%	1.877%	1.833%	1.788%	1.746%	1.710%	1.681%	1.658%	1.636%	1.612%
Guatemala	2.453%	2.498%	2.525%	2.528%	2.516%	2.496%	2.482%	2.481%	2.496%	2.520%	2.545%	2.558%
Mexico	1.412%	1.314%	1.249%	1.226%	1.234%	1.251%	1.260%	1.267%	1.265%	1.257%	1.251%	1.245%
Peru	1.492%	1.358%	1.285%	1.221%	1.166%	1.109%	1.062%	1.049%	1.078%	1.135%	1.203%	1.259%
Venezuela	1.896%	1.862%	1.830%	1.799%	1.769%	1.740%	1.710%	1.679%	1.646%	1.610%	1.575%	1.539%

Figure 11.19: Dashboard with treemap

The following is with a pie chart:

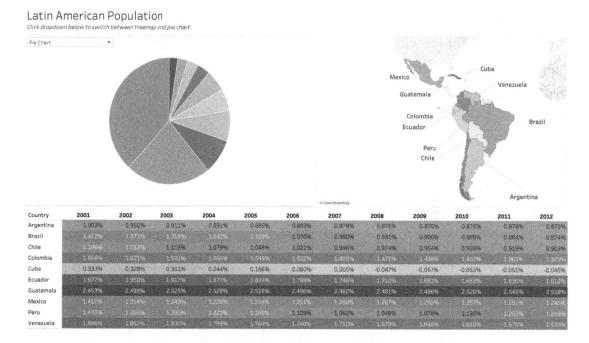

Latin American Population
Click dropdown below to switch between treemap and pie chart.

Country	2001	2002	2003	2004	2005	2006	2007	2008	2009	2010	2011	2012
Argentina	1.003%	0.950%	0.911%	0.891%	0.885%	0.883%	0.878%	0.876%	0.876%	0.876%	0.878%	0.879%
Brazil	1.412%	1.371%	1.316%	1.242%	1.159%	1.070%	0.990%	0.931%	0.900%	0.889%	0.884%	0.874%
Chile	1.196%	1.152%	1.113%	1.079%	1.048%	1.021%	0.996%	0.974%	0.954%	0.936%	0.919%	0.903%
Colombia	1.656%	1.621%	1.591%	1.566%	1.543%	1.522%	1.499%	1.471%	1.438%	1.402%	1.365%	1.329%
Cuba	0.333%	0.328%	0.301%	0.244%	0.166%	0.080%	0.005%	-0.047%	-0.067%	-0.063%	-0.051%	-0.045%
Ecuador	1.977%	1.950%	1.917%	1.877%	1.833%	1.788%	1.746%	1.710%	1.681%	1.658%	1.636%	1.612%
Guatemala	2.453%	2.498%	2.525%	2.528%	2.516%	2.496%	2.482%	2.481%	2.496%	2.520%	2.545%	2.558%
Mexico	1.412%	1.314%	1.249%	1.226%	1.234%	1.251%	1.260%	1.267%	1.265%	1.257%	1.251%	1.245%
Peru	1.432%	1.356%	1.285%	1.221%	1.166%	1.109%	1.062%	1.049%	1.078%	1.135%	1.203%	1.259%
Venezuela	1.896%	1.862%	1.830%	1.799%	1.769%	1.740%	1.710%	1.679%	1.646%	1.610%	1.575%	1.539%

Figure 11.20: Pie chart

You can use the sheet swap feature in case some of your users prefer one visualization over the other. Next, we will create a filter menu that can be hidden on the dashboard. In the *Maximizing documentation on a dashboard* section, the point was made that dashboard space is precious. Therefore, in the second exercise, *Creating a collapsible menu*, we will review an example that will use sheet selection to allow the end user to show or hide filters and, thus, make more efficient use of screen real estate.

Create a collapsible menu

Please follow these steps to learn how to add a collapsible filter menu to your dashboards:

1. Duplicate the dashboard we created in the preceding exercise and rename it Collapsible Menu. If you did not complete the preceding exercise, use the dashboard included in the solution workbook provided with this chapter.

2. Select any of the worksheets on the dashboard and click on the arrow; choose the filters **Country** and **Years Only** to be displayed.

Figure 11.21: Filters

3. The two filters will be placed in a container on the right-hand side of the dashboard. Double-click on the two horizontal lines in the top middle of one filter to select the container instead. The surrounding lines will appear blue. Select **Add Show/Hide Button**:

Figure 11.22: Add Show/Hide Button

4. Note that an **X** is visible next to the filters. In **Presentation Mode**, this button can now be used to minimize the filter:

Figure 11.23: Countries

In this section, we learned that by using containers and a filter, Tableau can automatically resize the selected worksheet within the container. This feature can be used to make it seem as if a worksheet can be swapped. However, Tableau basically just minimizes one and maximizes the other, even though this is not visible to the user's eye. Brilliant, isn't it?

After completing this exercise, you may think, OK, the filters do not technically display on the dashboard, but they are still visible at the side. While this is true in Tableau Desktop, if you can upload the workbook to an instance of Tableau Server, you will note that when clicking on the menu icon, the filters appear and disappear and do not display at the side.

The collapsible menu is a very nice add-on and contributes to the simplicity of your dashboard. If you read the last, third edition of this book, you might remember that it was a tedious process – and more of a workaround than a feature to get a collapsible menu to function. Now, with **Add Show/Hide Button**, it is a piece of cake. Users can focus on the data and use the filter only if needed.

Dashboard best practices

Visualization best practices are not limited to visual features; actions, filters, and organizing data can be just as important. A few of those features that Tableau has to offer shall be mentioned in this section. Each of them will help you to either improve the user experience or keep track of what you have built—since, sometimes, you can get lost when working with many different worksheets.

We will start by discussing six different types of **Actions**, followed by the **Download** and **Navigation Object**, then the **Used In feature**, and lastly, the **Item Hierarchy.** All contribute to a better dashboard-building experience. Let's start!

Actions

Implicitly, we have discussed this a few times before, but let's have an explicit look at what we can achieve with regard to visualization and dashboard design by using **Actions**. Actions come into play if you want your user to be redirected by clicking or hovering on data in a visualization. This can be helpful if you have a lot of data to show and don't want to put it all on the same dashboard. Neither should you, because it is distracting, and if it is hierarchical data, actions are the perfect way to implement a drill-down technique.

The following sections will explain all the different actions you can use in Tableau to add interactivity, supporting a clean and effective dashboard design.

Filter actions

In this example, we will use a filter action to show data initially hidden. By doing so, we will make sure to present smaller chunks of data at a time, and the user can drill down to any point of interest. Follow these steps:

1. Please open the worksheet Quantity by State:

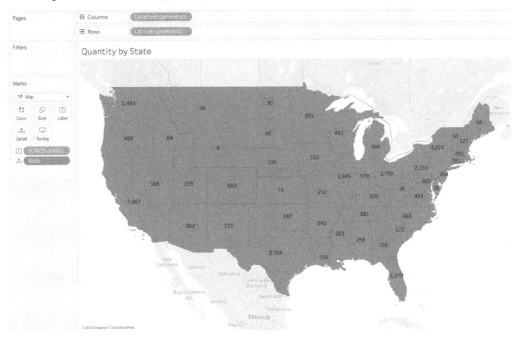

Figure 11.24: Map

You can see in the preceding screenshot that each state represents the quantity of a given product sold. But wouldn't it be nice to see more details by clicking on a given state? In order to do so, we must set up actions.

2. First, we need a second worksheet we want to use in our action. Please open the worksheet Profit by State by Category:

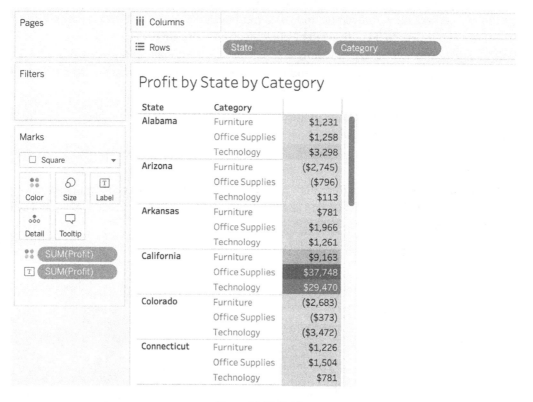

Figure 11.25: Table

You can see in the preceding screenshot that every state, every category, and the corresponding profit are shown.

3. Now, go back to the worksheet Quantity by State to enable an action that will prompt the user to go to the Profit by State by Category worksheet, and then filter it on the state they clicked on.

4. On the Quantity by State worksheet, select **Worksheet** | **Actions**; the following window will appear. Click on the **Add Action** button and select **Filter...**:

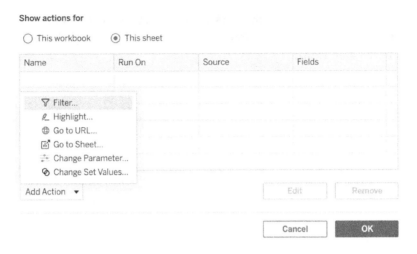

Figure 11.26: Filter action

5. In the next window, add a filter action called **Map to table (quantity to profit)** and copy the settings, as shown in the screenshot. Then, click **OK:**

Figure 11.27: Filter Action parameter

6.   If you now click on a state on the worksheet Quantity by State (Source Sheet), Tableau will look for that same **State** on the target sheet and filter accordingly. The following is an example after clicking on **Texas**:

Figure 11.28: Filtered table

The filter action discussed in this section can be used to declutter your dashboard. Following design principles often means less is more, and if you have lots of data points to share, a drill-down or filter action can help you achieve this goal. Present high-level data first, then present a more detailed data layer behind a filter action. You can also add a sentence for your users below the title, like *Click on a state to see more details.*

Highlight actions

Other options are, for example, a highlight action. This is more useful for worksheets on the same page because it will simply highlight applicable fields. You can show all data on the same dashboard, but the highlight action makes it easier for your users to find related data points. Follow these steps:

1. Please open the dashboard Qty & Profit, which combines the two worksheets we used previously:

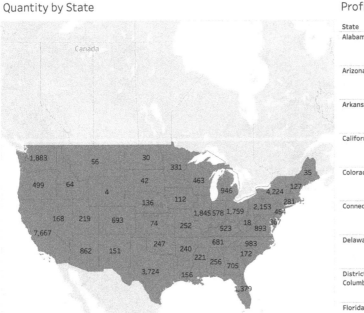

Figure 11.29: Dashboard

2. Click on **Dashboard | Actions**, and this time, copy the following **Highlight Action** parameters:

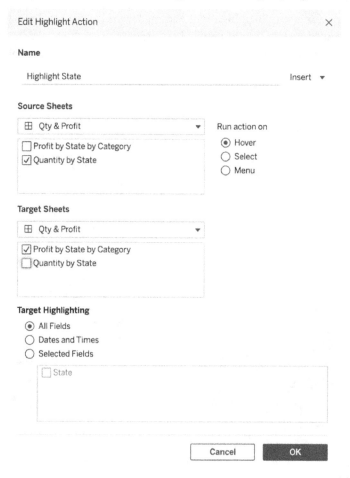

Figure 11.30: Highlight Action

3. The preceding parameters mean that, on the Qty & Profit dashboard, our source worksheet will be Quantity by State, and by hovering over it, the corresponding data on the target sheet will be highlighted. In this case, the only common data is **State**, so the highlighter will only take **State** into account. The result looks like this:

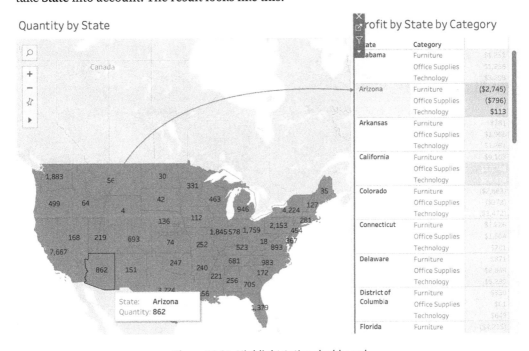

Figure 11.31: Highlight Action dashboard

By hovering over Arizona on the map, the same state will be highlighted in the right-hand table. As you can see, implementing a highlight filter can help your users find related data points faster. In contrast to the navigation action, this filter should be used for worksheets on the same page and as visual help to find a value.

URL actions

The next action is the URL action. This one allows you to open a URL when clicking on a data point in the dashboard. Follow these steps:

1. Go to the Quantity by State worksheet and open **Worksheet | Actions**.
2. Delete every action that is visible.

3. Now, select **Add Action** and select **Go to URL....** Copy all the parameters, as shown below, and click on the arrow next to the Wikipedia URL. Fields from your data source will appear, which enables you to add a field to the URL that will automatically return a value based on the dashboard. Select **State:**

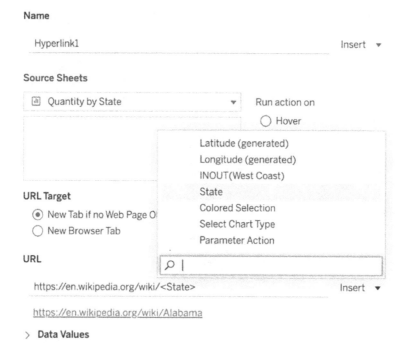

Figure 11.32: URL action

4. Click on a state on your map on the **Quantity by State** worksheet, and see how Wikipedia will open the respective web page.

URL actions are very useful when you want to show your users additional information available on websites. You can also use latitude and longitude values to open Google Maps or link the URL action to internal company websites with regulations, or maybe a ticketing system.

Navigation actions

The next action used to be commonly used in combination with a button to give the user a more interactive experience. Instead of clicking on tabs to go from one to another page, you will add buttons with an action to go to a specific sheet:

1. Go to the Qty & Profit dashboard and create a calculated field called String with the code "Go back to [...]". This will serve as our button shortly.
2. Open a new worksheet and call it Button.
3. Place the calculated field **String** by dragging and dropping **Details** as well as **Label** onto it.
4. Select **Shape** from the **Marks** card dropdown and select any shape (and color) of your choice.
5. Hide the title and disable **Tooltip.**

6. Click on **Label** and select **Bottom-Center Alignment**. The result will look as follows:

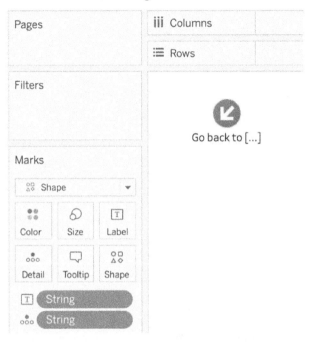

Figure 11.33: Button

7. Go back to the Qty & Profit dashboard, select **Floating**, and drag the Button worksheet onto the dashboard—for example, into the bottom-left corner:

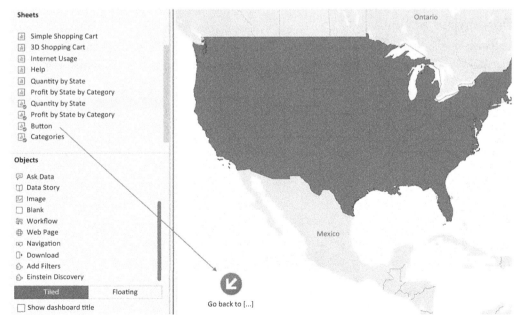

Figure 11.34: Button on the dashboard

8. Click on **Dashboard | Actions** and copy the following parameter:

Edit Go to Sheet Action   ×

Name

| Go To Sheet Action |

Source Sheets

⊞ Qty & Profit   ▼   Run action on

☑ Button   ○ Hover
☐ Categories   ⦿ Select
☐ Profit by State by Category   ○ Menu
☐ Quantity by State   ☐ Single-select only

Target Sheets

⊞ Latin American Population   ▼

                                        Cancel   OK

Figure 11.35: Go To Sheet Action

9. Click **OK** and click on the `Button` worksheet on the `Qty & Profit` dashboard.

It will now take you back to the `Latin American Population` dashboard! Nowadays, this action is less used since the release of a specific navigation object, but it is useful to know about it for the sake of completeness.

Parameter actions

The next one in line is **Parameter Actions**. This one is used to change a parameter by clicking on a data point in the dashboard rather than using the parameter control. Follow these steps:

1. Place the `Categories` worksheet on the `Qty & Profit` dashboard—for example, in the top-right corner:

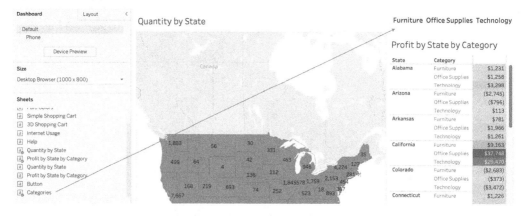

Figure 11.36: Parameter Actions

2. Click on **Dashboard** | **Actions** and copy the following parameters:

Name

Parameter Action   Insert ▾

Source Sheets

⊞ Qty & Profit   ▾   Run action on

☐ Button   ◉ Hover
☑ Categories   ○ Select
☑ Profit by State by Category   ○ Menu
☐ Quantity by State

Target Parameter   Clearing the selection will

Abc Parameter Action   ▾   ◉ Keep current value
     ○ Set value to

Source Field   Aggregation

Abc Category (...   ▾   None   ▾

Figure 11.37: Parameter Action setup

3. Create a calculated field called `Cat Param` with the following code:

```
If [Parameter Action] = [Category]
Then [Category]
Else ""
END
```

4. Place **Cat Param** on the **Filter** shelf on the worksheet `Profit by State by Category`, select the empty value, and enable **Exclude**, as shown here, before selecting **OK**:

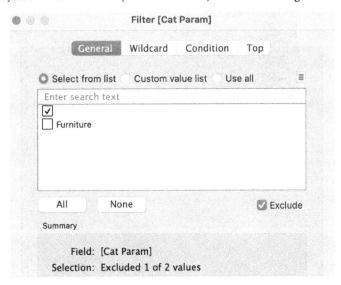

Figure 11.38: Category filter

5. If you now hover over any **Category** at the top, the following table will adjust accordingly:

Quantity by State

Furniture	Office Supplies	Technology

Category: Tec

Profit by State by Category

State	Category	
Alabama	Technology	$3,298
Arizona	Technology	$113
Arkansas	Technology	$1,261
California	Technology	$29,470
Colorado	Technology	($3,472)
Connecticut	Technology	$781
Delaware	Technology	$6,239
District of Columbia	Technology	$649
Florida	Technology	$531
Georgia	Technology	$4,400
Idaho	Technology	$92
Illinois	Technology	$4,823
Indiana	Technology	$11,001
Iowa	Technology	$318
Kansas	Technology	$175
Kentucky	Technology	$4,157

Figure 11.39: Category-filtered dashboard

Set actions

The last action that we will discuss is the set action. A set splits your data in two, **In** or **Out**. If you were to create a set called animals based on the following list: [cat, tree, dog, leopard, house, car], you would mark cat, dog, and leopard as **In** and tree, house, and car as **Out**. You can then use the set as a new field for your dashboard. Follow these steps:

1. Go to the `Qty & Profit` dashboard and select the western states `California`, `Oregon`, and `Washington`. Note that the pop-up window shows two rings in the top-right part. Using this icon is one way to create a set; go ahead and click on it:

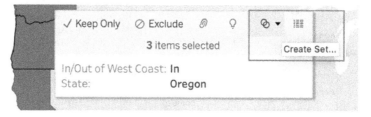

Figure 11.40: Set action

2. The following window will open; click **OK**:

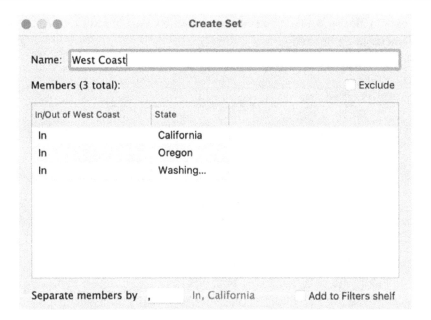

Figure 11.41: Set

In the data pane, a new field has been created—a set called West Coast.

3. See how it works by changing the Profit by State by Category worksheet as follows, removing **State** from **Rows**, and adding **West Coast** instead (you can remove **Cat Param** from the filter shelf or leave it; both will work):

Profit by State by Category

In/Out of W..	Category	
In	Furniture	$14,869
	Office Supplies	$49,109
	Technology	$44,616
Out	Furniture	$3,582
	Office Supplies	$73,382
	Technology	$100,839

Figure 11.42: Setting field states

The profit in the **Out** band takes into account all states except for California, Oregon, and Washington, whereas the **In** band shows numbers relative to those three aforementioned states.

4. Go back to the `Qty & Profit` dashboard and select **Dashboard | Actions** to copy the following parameter into a **Set Action**:

Name

| Set Action | Insert ▼ |

Source Sheets

| ⊞ Qty & Profit ▼ |

☐ Button
☐ Categories
☐ Profit by State by Category
☑ Quantity by State

Run action on

○ Hover
◉ Select
○ Menu
☐ Single-select only

Target Set

| West Coast ▼ |

Running the action will

◉ Assign values to set

Clearing the selection will

◉ Keep set values

Figure 11.43: Set Action parameter

5. If you now click on any one or multiple states, all selected states will be the **In** group of your set. Therefore, the profit numbers will show the profit of your selection against the rest, like so:

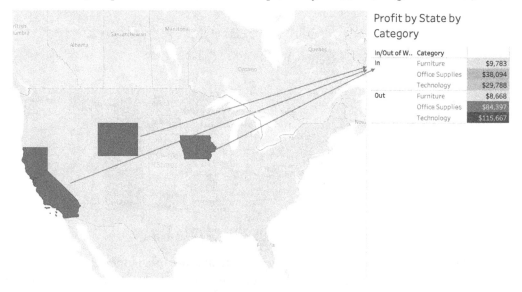

Figure 11.44: Set action dashboard

6. You can also rename the **In** and **Out** values by clicking and selecting **Edit Alias...**:

Figure 11.45: Edit Alias...

Those were the six Tableau actions; with the **Filter** and **Highlight** actions, you can make it easier for your users to find more detailed information by drilling down. The **Go to Sheet** and **Go to URL** actions can be seen as interactive buttons that will redirect your user to additional information, either on the web or on another sheet. And lastly, the **Change Parameter** and **Change Set** actions can be used to adjust a predefined value or multiple values, which will allow your users to interact with and analyze the data from different angles.

Download

Next to actions, another item that's part of the user experience is a built-in download button. Adding such a button to your dashboard will allow your users to share an image or a screenshot, if they like, with others, use it for documentation, or use it for presentation purposes. Adding a button is super easy; just follow these steps:

1. Open the dashboard `Golden Rectangle`, select **Floating** in the bottom-left corner, and drag **Download** to the top-right corner:

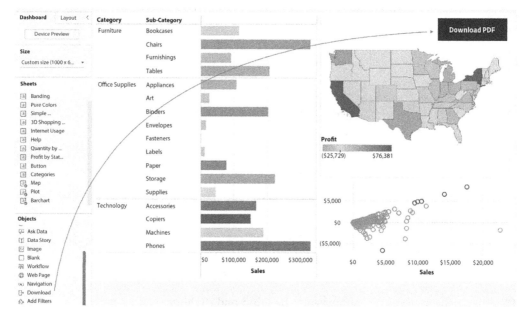

Figure 11.46: Download button

2. In **Presentation Mode**, click (*Alt* + click for non-presentation mode) on the newly added button; a **Print to PDF** popup will appear:

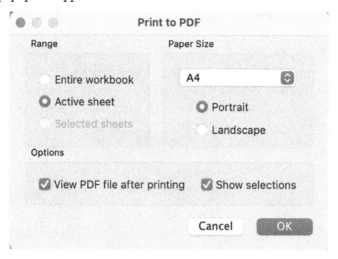

Figure 11.47: Print to PDF

3. Click **OK**, after which you can open the dashboard as a PDF from your desktop.

That's it! In only one simple step, you can make many users that like to have a printout very happy.

A Tableau workbook as well as Tableau dashboards can become very overwhelming, depending on how many worksheets are used to create them. Luckily, Tableau helps us with organizational features like **Item hierarchy** and **Used In**.

Item hierarchy

As we briefly mentioned in the *Creating a collapsible menu* section, if you open the Latin American Population dashboard, you will notice **Item hierarchy** at the bottom left of the **Layout** pane. By clicking on the arrow next to the word **Tiled,** you will be able to see all the different parts of the dashboards and the worksheets used in each container. You can also spot containers in containers and the structure of your layout:

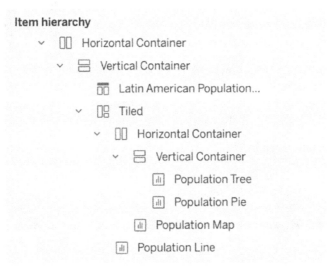

Figure 11.48: Item hierarchy extended

Try to keep a logical order within your item hierarchy. This will make it easier for you to make changes to your dashboard later on. Which logic you choose is up to you; one I use often is high-level to more detailed, most important to least important, or from spacious worksheets to smaller ones. A nice article on keeping your dashboard clean can be found here: https://www.thedataschool.co.uk/joe-beaven/layout-containers-how-to-get-your-item-hierarchy-under-control.

Used In

The **Used In** feature shows you on which dashboards a certain worksheet is used. Just right-click on a worksheet and select **Used In**:

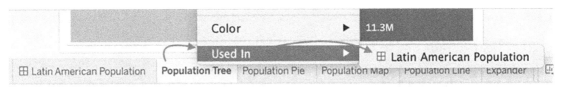

Figure 11.49: Used In

This feature is especially useful if you want to make changes to a worksheet. Before execution, you can check which dashboards will be affected, and the risk of breaking an existing dashboard will decrease tremendously.

Something extra

When I first started using Tableau I was, and still am, a really big fan of Makeover Monday (https://www.makeovermonday.co.uk). Makeover Monday is an initiative hosted by Eva Murray and Andy Kriebel. Every Monday, the Tableau community (you) is given a dataset accompanied by a visualization and asked to improve it. Those can come from newspapers or websites for example. The participants will then analyze the dataset, build a dashboard, and publish that version on Twitter using the hashtag **#makeovermonday**. If you compare the work from the community with the original work, you will surely learn to see which dashboards work best and which designs you prefer, and thus you can slowly develop your own style, especially when participating.

The learnings from the first years of Makeover Monday were summarized in a book with the same title. In 2022, Makeover Monday took a break but is back now in a slightly different format and led by Andy alone. Check it out; it is worth it. Below are some examples and my explanation of why it works; you will recognize the rules we have discussed in this chapter (which I will put in brackets):

The first example was published in *The Guardian* and shows a decrease in exported goods in the UK in January 2020.

Link to the data: https://data.world/makeovermonday/2021w13.

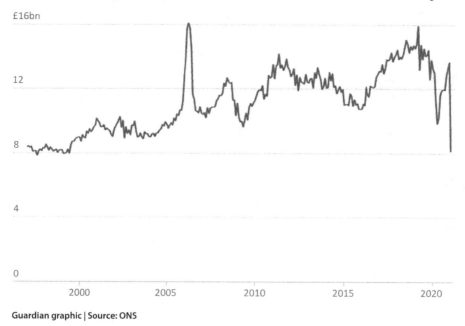

Figure 11.50: UK exports

What works?

Using a line chart (rule: keeping visualizations simple) for time series data is a good idea. I also like that the line is red (rule: psychological implications of colors) because the visualization is showing something negative, a steep drop in exports. The Y-axis indicates the monetary value of those changes, giving me as the user an idea of the absolute loss.

Now let's see what the Makeover Monday folks came up with:

Kimberly Furdell created the chart shown in *Figure 11.51* and without reading much further, ask yourself, what are the differences compared to the original visualization, and which one do you prefer and why?

Link to the visualization: `https://public.tableau.com/app/profile/kimberly.furdell/viz/UKexportstoEU_16172321299550/Dashboard1`.

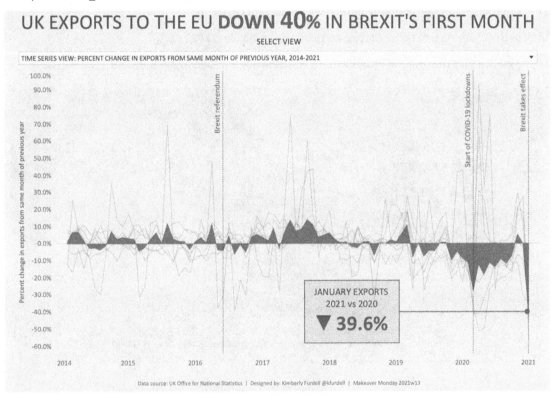

Figure 11.51: Brexit exports

Why it works better

The story from the article published in *The Guardian* revolved around the 40% drop in exports in January 2021 compared to January 2020. That the number was related to the previous year was not clear in the original visualization, and Kimberly has enough information in her visualization that you do not need to read the full article to understand (rule: maximizing documentation on a dashboard). To support the storyline further, Kimberly did an excellent job in changing the graph.

This visualization works better because the *Y*-axis shows a percentage. Now, you can clearly see that the drop in January 2021 is more severe than the drop in 2020, which looked similar to the original graph because of the nature of absolute values. Increasing the time series data by more years stresses that the developments are outside the past years' range. The gray lines on her dashboard represent the various export categories, and as such, it is a great idea to have an area chart for the total values, and line charts, in a less prominent color, for the details (rule: presenting dense information, using pure colors sparingly). The reference lines indicating events during this period of time make the story complete (rule: telling a story). Lastly, users wondering which category contributed the most to the drastic export decline can select a second view, a horizontal bar chart, from the drop-down menu (design: sheet swapping).

Next, we will look at another Makeover Monday challenge and two examples of how to do it better.

This time, we are concerned about the caffeine content in various coffees from different known chains. The article and data were initially published on `www.which.co.uk`.

Link to the challenge: `https://data.world/makeovermonday/2023w9`.

Here you can find the original visualization, which is not that bad in my opinion:

	Single-shot espresso	Cappuccino	Filter/brewed Coffee
Caffè Nero	45mg (30ml)	110–115mg (355ml)	n/a
Costa (Signature blend)	100mg (30ml)	325mg (362ml)	n/a
Greggs	75mg (28ml)	197mg (341ml)	225mg (341ml)
Pret	180mg (30ml)	180mg (350ml)	271mg (350ml)
Starbucks	33mg (25ml)	66mg (350ml)	102mg (350ml)

HIGH STREET COFFEE CAFFEINE CONTENT COMPARED

Caffeine content in mg (drink size in ml)

Figure 11.52: Coffee

What works?

The coffee cup images are good; without checking the table or reading the header, you will know that this visualization is about coffee. It will catch your attention. There is a limited use of colors but the background is not my favorite; the blue is catchy but unrelated to the topic and a bit heavy on the eye. The table, however, works; is it easy to compare the different drinks per brand and the same drinks across different brands (rule: keep it simple and robust).

Showing the caffeine as well as the ml amount is almost too much information and could be better normalized. But let's see what the Tableau community came up with.

This first example, *Figure 11.53*, was published by Will Sutton. He created a story, where each page is a step toward the improved version. What a great idea!

Link to the visualization: `https://public.tableau.com/app/profile/wjsutton/viz/HighStreetCaffeine/ImprovingabarchartMakeoverMonday2023Week9`.

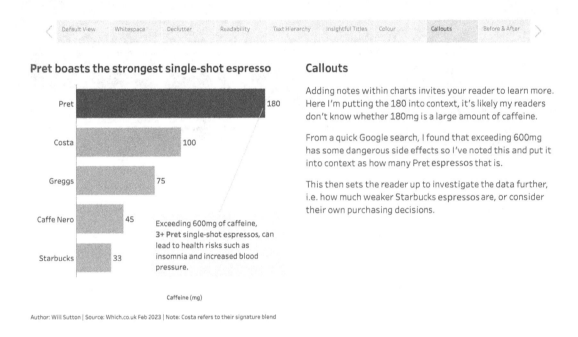

Figure 11.53: Callouts

Why it works better

Part of why it works better can be seen next to the horizontal bar chart; the numbers were put into context (rule: telling a story). Other than that, Will changed the table to a very simple bar chart; he focuses on one drink only and marks the highest possible health risk by imposing espresso in a dark red (rules: making a dashboard simple and robust, simple colors). He walks the user through a story, whereas the original table leaves a lot of room for context and answers to unknown questions.

But I will show you a redo with all the coffee chains and all the drinks too; this next one is by Gabriela Comanescu.

Link to the visualization: `https://public.tableau.com/app/profile/gabriela.comanescu/viz/HowmuchcaffeineisinyourcoffeeMakeoverMonday/Coffee`.

Figure 11.54: Caffeine

Why it works better

Gabriela picked up the theme of the original post, using coffee as an image to catch the user's attention. She, however, used a true-to-life image of coffee beans as background for her visualization, rather than an illustration. Her color choice is very simple; the font is kept in an off-white color, which could almost be the milk on top of the coffee (rule: simple colors). But what I like the most is that she normalized the data. For all beverages, she is showing the caffeine in mg per 100 ml. This makes every drink comparable, and hence, it makes sense to plot them each as a circular bar chart. Within seconds, the user can spot the highest caffeine content per drink and is able to compare them with each other too. Using a circular bar is genius, because it looks to me like stirring the coffee (rule: making a dashboard simple and robust, presenting dense information, and psychological implications of colors).

That was my take on Makeover Monday, and I hope, by now, you are a fan too. If you ever tweet your version of any given dataset, please tag **#MasteringTableau** so that readers of this book and I can check out your work.

Last but not least, another page that I highly recommend is Visual Capitalist (`https://www.visualcapitalist.com`). Its dashboards are so perfectly designed that you should really try and learn from them.

Summary

We began this chapter by considering visualization design theory. We looked at formatting rules, color rules, and rules about which visualization types to use and which we need to avoid. We also explored how to compromise when contradictory design goals are expressed by end users. Then, we discussed dashboard design principles. We covered three popular layouts: the Golden Rectangle, quad, and small multiple.

Afterward, we looked at how to use sheet selection techniques as an ally in good design. Specifically, we explored how to allow the end user to choose which visualization type to view, and how to hide and display filters so as to make the best use of screen real estate. Next, we discussed actions and download buttons for a better user experience, as well as item hierarchies and the **Used In** feature, which is very handy for organizing your dashboard. This, in turn, will help to improve the layout design. Finally, to combine everything we learned, we analyzed three Makeover Monday dashboards and explained why those work based on the rules discussed prior.

In the next chapter, we will focus on use cases. Going from a dataset to a product will be the theme, and we will practice doing this with, inter alia, geospatial data. The knowledge you gained from the previous chapters will be very useful!

Learn more on Discord

To join the Discord community for this book – where you can share feedback, ask questions to the author, and learn about new releases – follow the QR code below:

```
https://packt.link/tableau
```

12

Leveraging Advanced Analytics

This chapter focuses on advanced self-service analytics. Self-service analytics can be seen as a form of business intelligence, where people in a business are encouraged to execute queries on datasets themselves, instead of placing requests for queries in a backlog with their IT team. Then, query analysis can be done, which should lead to more insights and data-driven decision-making. But how do you start creating useful self-service dashboards if it's your first time doing so? How do you go from a dataset to a product? Have you ever asked yourself how other people start working on a dashboard, how they clean data, and how they come up with a dashboard design? If so, this is the right chapter for you! I want to share three use cases with you, written as a train of thought in order to give you an idea about how I work. Please note that this is just my personal experience; there are many different ways to reach your goal.

We will cover the following topics:

- Visualizing world indices correlations
- Geo-spatial analytics with Chicago traffic violations
- Extending geo-spatial analytics with distance measures

Now that we have had this introduction, we are good to go and can start with the first use case.

Visualizing world indices correlations

Imagine you are working on the world indices dataset and your line manager gives you the following task:

Create a dashboard for me in which I can easily spot all correlated world indices and their distribution. I need it by tomorrow morning.

Now, take a few minutes before you continue reading and think about how you would tackle this task. The dataset contains 67 columns with various indices, like birth registrations or emission values, exports and imports, and forest areas, divided into 188 rows, where each row represents one country.

Write down your planned steps, open the workbook related to this chapter from `https://public.tableau.com/profile/marleen.meier`, and follow your steps; time it in order to get a better feel for time estimates when working with Tableau. This way, you can make sure that you can deliver on time and manage expectations if you are ever asked how long it will take to build a certain dashboard.

Plotting a scattergraph

And now, I will illustrate one way I could imagine solving this task:

1. First, I open the `world-indices` file in Tableau Prep Builder in order to get more details on the dataset itself; this will help me to describe the data but also to spot obvious data flaws like null values, duplicate entries, and so on:

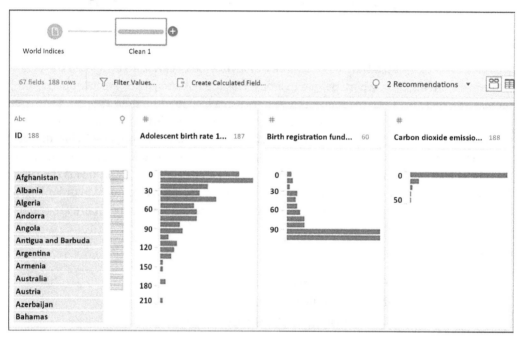

Figure 12.1: Tableau Prep Builder

With this dataset, I actually didn't spot any obvious data quality issues in Prep Builder, nor a need to further prepare the data. It's 1 row per country—which you can see in the evenly distributed bars in the **ID** column—and 65 columns for the different indices per country. Since no data preparation is needed, I decide to continue directly with Tableau Desktop. I close Tableau Prep Builder and open Tableau Desktop.

2. My next thought is, how can I visualize all correlations at once, yet not have it be too much information? I have 65 different columns, which makes for 4,225 possible combinations. No, I decide that displaying everything won't work. The task is very generic; therefore, I decide to go for a two-parameter approach, which will enable my end user to select each of the index combinations themselves. I start sketching what the dashboard might look like and come up with the following:

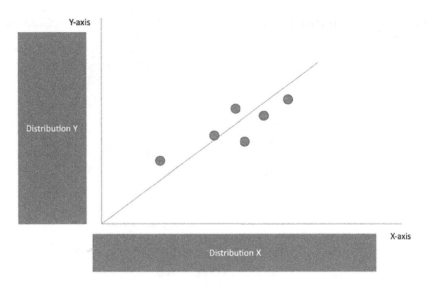

Figure 12.2: Sketch

3.   In order to execute my plan, I first create two parameters, which I name **X-Axis** and **Y-Axis**, which will be used to define the respective axes x and y.

4.   I define both parameters as **String** and paste all field names from the clipboard into both of the parameters. To do this, I open the input file in Excel, transpose the header row to a column, and press *Ctrl + C*. The data can now be pasted into the parameter via the **Paste from Clipboard** option. This saves time and is less error-prone:

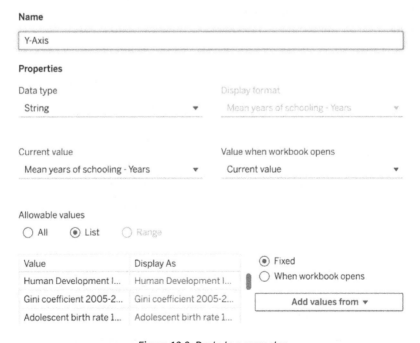

Figure 12.3: Paste to parameter

5. I also want the parameters to be visible on the dashboard, so I select **Show Parameter**:

Figure 12.4: Show Parameter

6. If you were to test the parameter now, nothing would happen. We need a calculated field that defines that if a selection from the parameter has been made, Tableau will select the appropriate field. I create the following calculated field to achieve this (this field has been made part of the `Starter` and `Solution` workbooks to make your life easier):

Figure 12.5: Calculated field

7. Now we will do the same thing for the **Y-Axis** parameter.

    In order to create the calculated field for **Y-Axis** quicker, copy and paste the **X-Axis** calculated field into Excel and find and replace `[Parameters].[X-Axis]` with `[Parameters].[Y-Axis]`.

8. Drag the **X-Axis** calculated field to **Columns** and **Y-Axis** to **Rows**. Also, put the **ID** field on the **Detail** shelf.

9. In order to see the correlation analytics from Tableau, drag **Trend Line** onto the sheet:

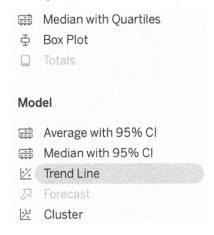

Figure 12.6: Trend Line

10. The sheet with the trend line looks as follows. When hovering over the trend line, you will see the equation of the line, the **R-Squared** value, and the value for **P-value**:

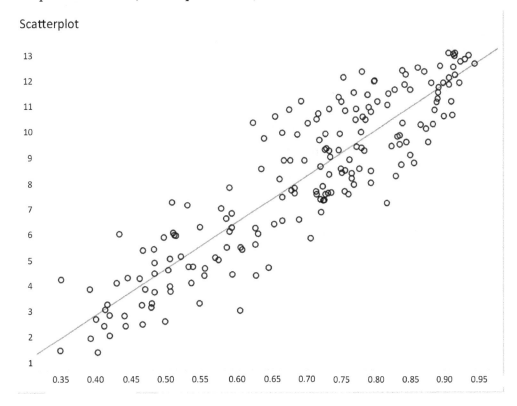

Figure 12.7: Trend line values

The **Y-Axis** equation means that, for each point on the x-axis, the y-axis value will increase by 17.9717, starting at point 0 on the x-axis and point -4.33685 on the y-axis. Thus, overall the y-term increases faster than the (also increasing) x-term. The **R-Squared** value explains how much variance is explained by the trend line (80.81%), and lastly, **P-value** explains the significance of the model. A **P-value** value smaller than 0.05 is considered significant and means there is a 5% chance that the data is following the trend line randomly. The trend line in the preceding figure has a **P-value** of less than 0.01%. We can safely assume, therefore, that there is a real relationship between the two variables.

11. To see more coefficients, right-click on the line and select **Describe Trend Line...**:

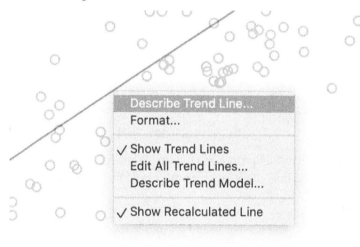

Figure 12.8: Describe Trend Line...

The following window will appear:

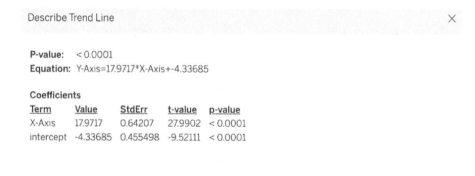

Figure 12.9: Trend line information

12. Alternatively, you can select the **Describe Trend Model...** option and you will see this:

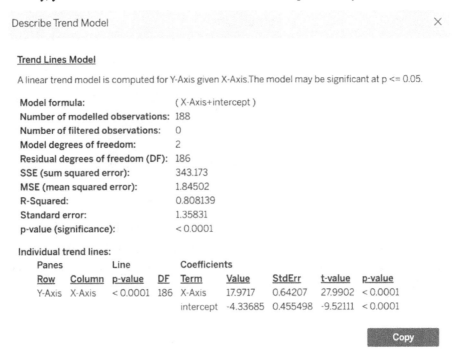

Figure 12.10: Trend model information

If you want to learn more about interpreting trend lines, you can read the following article: https://onlinehelp.tableau.com/current/pro/desktop/en-us/trendlines_add.htm.

13. I get a bit distracted by the grid lines, so I decide to remove them by right-clicking on the screen and selecting **Format...**:

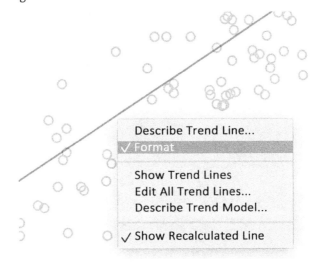

Figure 12.11: Formatting

14. I select the fifth option in the **Format** window, the lines, and set the **Grid Lines** value to **None**:

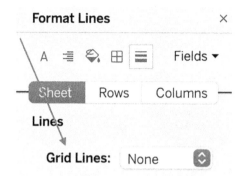

Figure 12.12: Removing grid lines

15. I also change **Marks** from **Automatic** to **Circle** and change the color to black.

16. Now, I think it would be helpful to show on the scatterplot which country each point represents, so I change the **ID** field from **Detail** to **Label** in the **Marks** card; however, this looks a bit too chaotic:

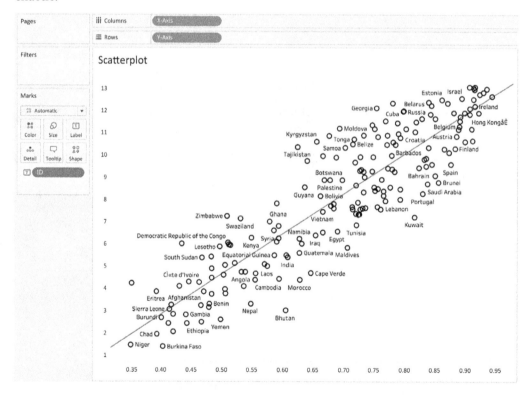

Figure 12.13: ID to text

17. I click on the undo arrow and add a highlighter function by right-clicking on **ID** and selecting **Show Highlighter**. Now, the end user will be able to search for a country and that point will be highlighted in the scatterplot:

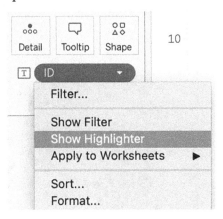

Figure 12.14: Show Highlighter

18. I also want the country name to be shown clearly in red when hovering over any points, and I achieve this by changing the **ID** color in **Edit Tooltip** to red and increasing the size:

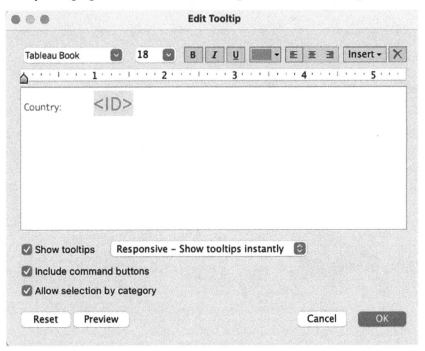

Figure 12.15: Tooltip

The result looks as follows:

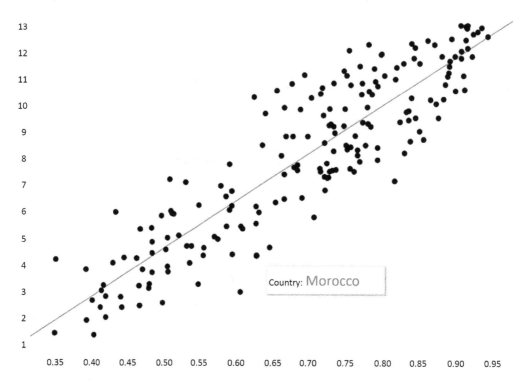

Figure 12.16: Hovering over a point

19. I have already added the trend line, and I now want to show the **Pearson R**, also called **R-Squared**, value in the view such that the user knows if two indices are correlated; however, it is not possible to set the **Describe Trend Line** or **Describe Trend Model** option to always be shown. Hence, I will calculate the value myself in a new field; I use the CORR() function to do this:

Pearson R	🗊 Self Sevice Analytics – World Indices

```
ROUND(CORR( [X-Axis],[Y-Axis]),3)
```

Figure 12.17: Pearson R

20. But I want to show some text that indicates if two variables are correlated or not instead of the value itself because I want to make my dashboard clear. Therefore, I create another calculated field called `Correlation yes or no` with the following code:

```
IF [Pearson R] > 0.7 then 'The two variables <' + [Parameters].[X-Axis]+
'> and <'+ [Parameters].[Y-Axis]+ '> have a very strong positive
correlation of: ' + STR([Pearson R])
ELSEIF [Pearson R] < 0.7 and [Pearson R] > 0.4 then 'The two variables
<'  + [Parameters].[X-Axis] + '> and <'+ [Parameters].[Y-Axis]+ '> have a
strong positive correlation of: '  + STR([Pearson R])
ELSEIF [Pearson R] < 0.4 and [Pearson R] > 0.2 then 'The two variables
<'  + [Parameters].[X-Axis] + '> and <'+ [Parameters].[Y-Axis]+ '> have a
moderate positive correlation of: ' + STR([Pearson R])
ELSEIF [Pearson R] <0.2 and [Pearson R] > -0.2 then 'The two variables <'
+ [Parameters].[X-Axis] + '> and <'+ [Parameters].[Y-Axis]+ '> have no or
a weak correlation of:' + STR([Pearson R])
ELSEIF [Pearson R] < -0.2 and [Pearson R] >-0.4 then 'The two variables
<'  + [Parameters].[X-Axis] + '> and <'+ [Parameters].[Y-Axis]+ '> have a
moderate negative correlation of: '+ STR([Pearson R])
ELSEIF [Pearson R] < -0.4 and [Pearson R] > -0.7 then 'The two variables
<'  + [Parameters].[X-Axis] + '> and <'+ [Parameters].[Y-Axis]+ '> have a
strong negative correlation of: ' + STR([Pearson R])
ELSEIF [Pearson R] < -0.7 THEN 'The two variables <'  + [Parameters].
[X-Axis] + '> and <'+ [Parameters].[Y-Axis]+ '> have a very strong
negative correlation of: ' + STR([Pearson R])
END
```

21. This being done, I create a new sheet and place **Correlation yes or no** on the **Text** shelf. The sheet looks very simple, as you can see:

The two variables <Human Development Index HDI-2014> and <Mean years of schooling -Years> have a very strong positive correlation of: 0.899

Figure 12.18: Correlation on text

22. I right-click on the title and choose **Hide Title**.

Finally, almost everything is ready to build the dashboard from the sketch at the beginning of this section. Only the distributions for each of the two axes are still missing.

Adding axis distributions

We have made a start, but now I want to add the distribution plots for the *x*- and *y*-axes next to the scatterplot. I take the following steps:

1. I start with the *x*-axis, open another worksheet, and drag **X-Axis** to **Rows**. Next, I click on the just-added **green pill X-Axis** and select **Measure | Count**. Now right-click on **X-Axis** in the data pane and select **Create | Bins....** In the pop-up, hit **OK**. Lastly, I drag the new dimension **X-Axis (bin)** to **Columns**.

2. After I close the **Edit Axis [X-Axis]** window, I right-click on **X-Axis** and deselect **Show Header** to not show the header anymore.

3. I continue with **Y-Axis** on another new worksheet and drag **Y-Axis** to **Columns**. Next, I change the **Y-Axis** on **Columns** by clicking on it and selecting **Measure | Count**. Now, right-click on **Y-Axis** in the data pane and select **Create | Bins....** In the pop-up, I hit **OK**.

Figure 12.19: Bins

4. Lastly, I drag the new dimension **Y-Axis (bin)** to **Rows**.

5. I change the color to gray in the **Marks** card and select **Entire View** at the top of the page.

6. The *y*-axis distribution should be aligned with the scatterplot; therefore, I click on **Y-Axis (bin) | Sort | Descending**. Next, I right-click on **Y-Axis** and deselect **Show Header** to not show the header anymore.

7. In order to put everything together, I open a dashboard page and call it `Distribution`, then I put the `Scatterplot` worksheet at the bottom of the page and the `Correlation` worksheet at the top of the dashboard canvas.

8. I add the distribution worksheets to the related sides of the scatterplot (`Y-Axis` to the *y*-axis and `X-Axis` to the *x*-axis).

9. I also add a blank in the lower left-hand corner to align the distribution with the scatterplot edges:

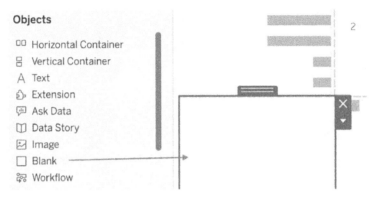

Figure 12.20: Adding a blank

The final layout looks like this:

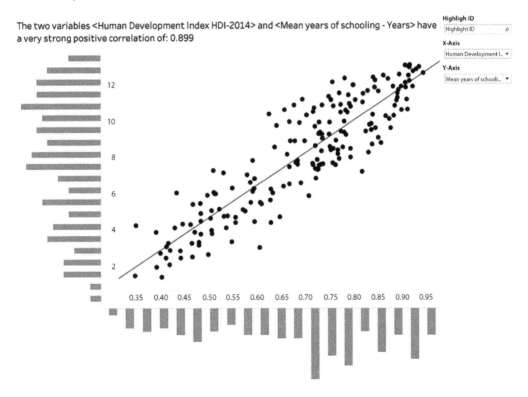

Figure 12.21: Final layout

10. I want to give the distribution more meaning and add an action that will highlight the country in both distribution plots. I do this so the user can see where a country is located in the range of all countries within one index because it can be hard to see in the scatterplot sometimes. The scatterplot, on the other hand, can be used to get more insights into the relationship between the two indices. For the **Highlight** action, I need to set the parameters as follows:

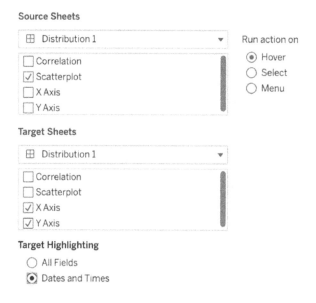

Figure 12.22: Highlight

11. And in order for the highlighter to work on the **X-Axis** and **Y-Axis** sheets, please add **ID** to the **Detail** shelf in both worksheets.

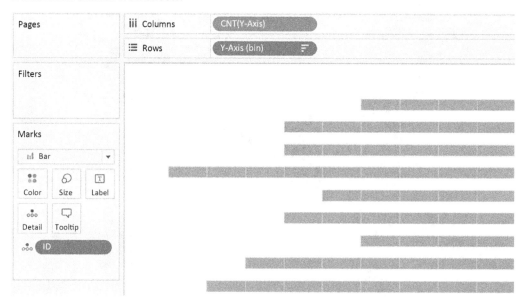

Figure 12.23: Adding ID

Now, look at the following screenshot:

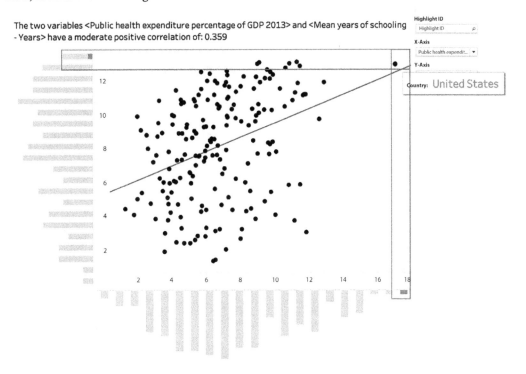

Figure 12.24: Correlation

I selected Public health expenditure percentage of GDP 2013 on the **X-Axis** and Mean years of schooling – Years on the **Y-Axis**. I had to resize the **X-Axis bin** in the **Data** pane by right-clicking | **Edit** | **Suggest Bin Size** | **OK**. I can see that the overall correlation between these two measures is positively moderate at a correlation coefficient of 0.359. But by hovering over the dots, you can now investigate which countries have what effect on this correlation. For countries close to the trend line, the correlation coefficient is closer to the true factor. For example, the United States in the top-right corner has a value of 16.8 for the *x*-axis (health expenditure) and 12.76 for the *y*-axis (years of schooling). If you multiply 12.76 by 0.359 (correlation coefficient), you get 4.581, which is almost exactly the difference between 12.76 and 16.8. Now, if you search for Sierra Leone (bottom-right), you get *x* and *y* values of 11.4 and 2.9. Here, the multiplication with the correlation coefficient won't explain the relationship as well. This can be easily seen in the scatterplot because Sierra Leone is far away from the trend line. I really like this dashboard because it simplifies relationships between variables and can help novices as well as senior users understand data.

Adding a correlation matrix

After clicking through the dashboard and testing the functionality, I realize that it's hard to remember which combinations I have already tried, and also, I wish I could filter for highly correlated combinations. To address this, I want to add one more dashboard to this workbook: a correlation matrix with all combinations, color-coded, and with an option to filter:

1. First, I go back to my **Data Source** tab and add the same dataset again, but with a new name: `World Indices Correlation Matrix`. I even add it twice because I need every index correlated against every other index:

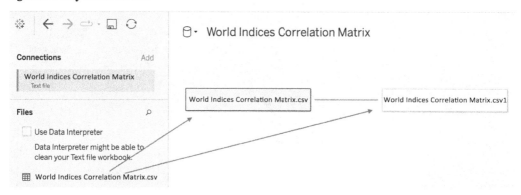

Figure 12.25: World Indices Correlation Matrix

2. The key used is **ID**:

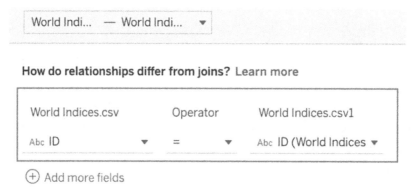

Figure 12.26: ID as a key

3. Then, I need to pivot both tables because instead of having one column per index, I need one column with all index names and a second column with all values in order to create a table with each of them. I select all fields except **ID** and use **Pivot**:

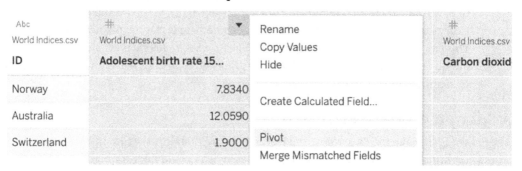

Figure 12.27: Pivoting

4. This results in three columns. I rename **Pivot Field Values** to **Value Index A** and **Pivot Field Names** to **Index A**:

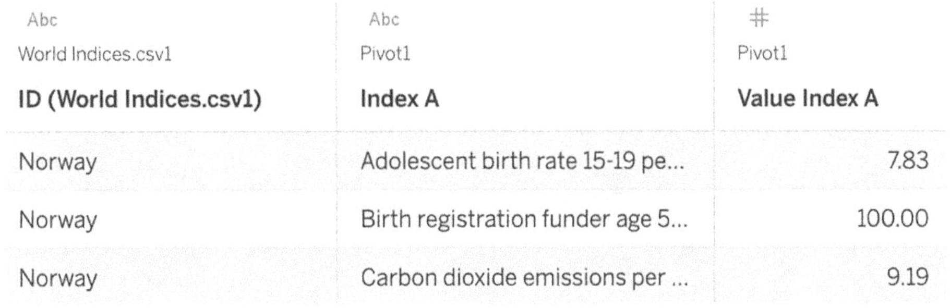

Abc	Abc	#
World Indices.csv1	Pivot1	Pivot1
ID (World Indices.csv1)	**Index A**	**Value Index A**
Norway	Adolescent birth rate 15-19 pe...	7.83
Norway	Birth registration funder age 5...	100.00
Norway	Carbon dioxide emissions per ...	9.19

Figure 12.28: Renaming columns

5. Now I do this again with the second table and rename the columns **Index B** and **Value Index B**.

6. I open a new worksheet and place **Index B** on **Columns**, and **Index A** on **Rows**. I create a calculated field named **Pearson R** with the code `CORR([Value Index B], [Value Index A])` and place it on **Filters**, **Color**, and **Text**. After right-clicking on **Pearson R** in the **Filters** shelf, I select **Show Filter**:

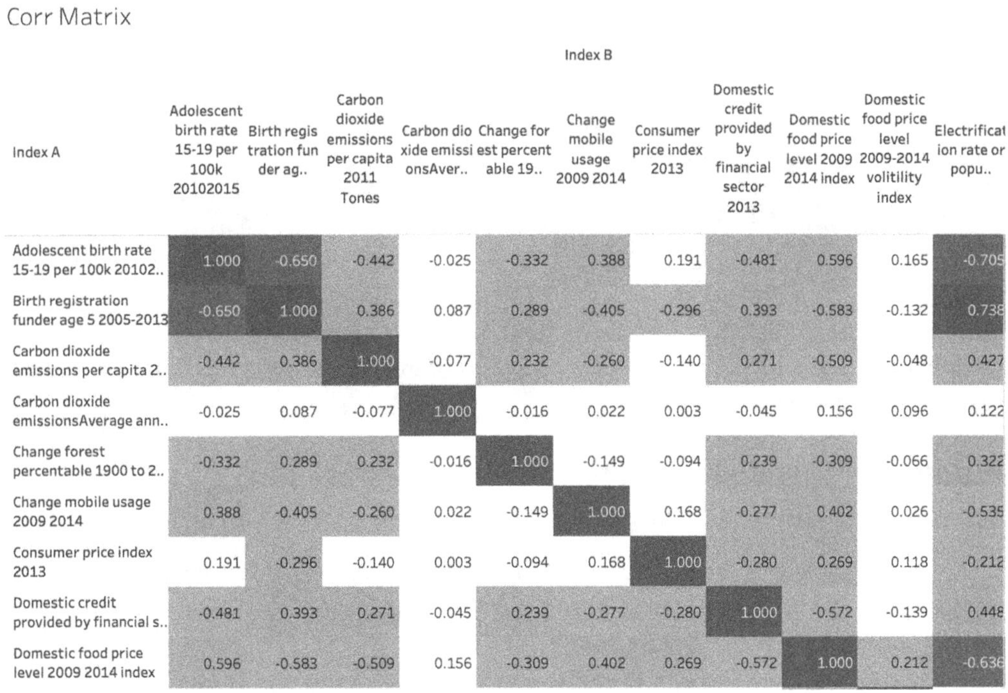

Corr Matrix

					Index B						
Index A	Adolescent birth rate 15-19 per 100k 20102015	Birth regis tration fun der ag..	Carbon dioxide emissions per capita 2011 Tones	Carbon dio xide emissi onsAver..	Change for est percent able 19..	Change mobile usage 2009 2014	Consumer price index 2013	Domestic credit provided by financial sector 2013	Domestic food price level 2009 2014 index	Domestic food price level 2009-2014 volitility index	Electrificat ion rate or popu..
Adolescent birth rate 15-19 per 100k 20102..	1.000	-0.650	-0.442	-0.025	-0.332	0.388	0.191	-0.481	0.596	0.165	-0.705
Birth registration funder age 5 2005-2013	-0.650	1.000	0.386	0.087	0.289	-0.405	-0.296	0.393	-0.583	-0.132	0.738
Carbon dioxide emissions per capita 2..	-0.442	0.386	1.000	-0.077	0.232	-0.260	-0.140	0.271	-0.509	-0.048	0.427
Carbon dioxide emissionsAverage ann..	-0.025	0.087	-0.077	1.000	-0.016	0.022	0.003	-0.045	0.156	0.096	0.122
Change forest percentable 1900 to 2..	-0.332	0.289	0.232	-0.016	1.000	-0.149	-0.094	0.239	-0.309	-0.066	0.322
Change mobile usage 2009 2014	0.388	-0.405	-0.260	0.022	-0.149	1.000	0.168	-0.277	0.402	0.026	-0.535
Consumer price index 2013	0.191	-0.296	-0.140	0.003	-0.094	0.168	1.000	-0.280	0.269	0.118	-0.212
Domestic credit provided by financial s..	-0.481	0.393	0.271	-0.045	0.239	-0.277	-0.280	1.000	-0.572	-0.139	0.448
Domestic food price level 2009 2014 index	0.596	-0.583	-0.509	0.156	-0.309	0.402	0.269	-0.572	1.000	0.212	-0.636

Figure 12.29: Correlation matrix

The colors can be adjusted as you like; I chose a 5-stepped color scheme from red to black, indicating that red fields are negatively correlated and black ones positively correlated.

7. I open a new dashboard tab and place the worksheet on it. Try adjusting the filter such that you only see the highly correlated range 0.89–0.99, just to have a smaller dataset to work with for now:

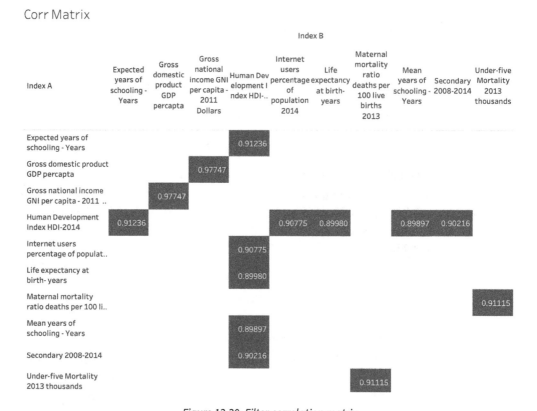

Figure 12.30: Filter correlation matrix

This section helped us create a heatmap of all possible combinations, and we color-coded the correlation value and added a filter to focus on points of interest. In the preceding screenshot, you can see the highly correlated indices.

Finalizing the dashboard

To avoid any confusion, I want to explain the **Pearson R** filter for the user and finalize the dashboard:

1. I start by adding the text field Pearson R ranges explained to the dashboard. Given more time, I could make it a drop-down parameter just like the **X-Axis** and **Y-Axis** fields:

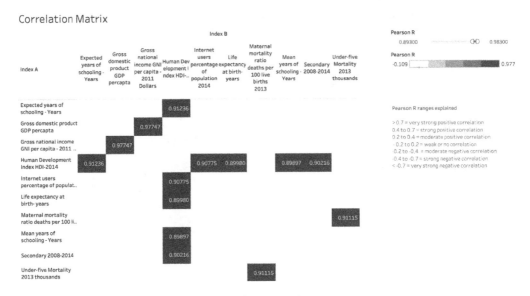

Figure 12.31: Adding text about Pearson R

2. To finalize everything, three actions are needed. First, two **Parameter** actions are needed to enable clicking on the correlation matrix to change the values for the **X-Axis** and **Y-Axis** parameters, the first of which should be customized as follows:

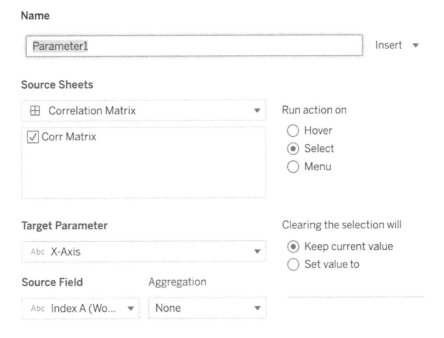

Figure 12.32: Parameter action 1

The action in the preceding screenshot will change the **X-Axis** parameter to the value from **Index A**.

3. Now, I edit the second **Parameter** action as follows:

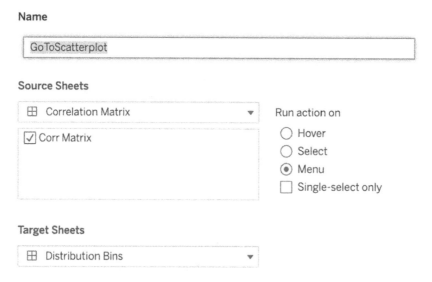

Name

| Parameter2 | Insert ▼ |

Source Sheets

⊞ Correlation Matrix ▼

☑ Corr Matrix

Run action on
- ○ Hover
- ◉ Select
- ○ Menu

Target Parameter

Abc Y-Axis ▼

Clearing the selection will
- ◉ Keep current value
- ○ Set value to

Source Field   **Aggregation**

Abc Index B (W... ▼   None ▼

Figure 12.33: Parameter action 2

The action in the preceding figure will change the **Y-Axis** parameter to the value from **Index B**.

4. Lastly, I add a **Sheet Navigation** action called **GoToScatterplot**, which allows the user to change the dashboard after selecting an index combination:

Name

| GoToScatterplot |

Source Sheets

⊞ Correlation Matrix ▼

☑ Corr Matrix

Run action on
- ○ Hover
- ○ Select
- ◉ Menu
- ☐ Single-select only

Target Sheets

⊞ Distribution Bins ▼

Figure 12.34: Sheet Navigation action

The preceding action will show a menu to go to the trend line dashboard.

5. The user can now select a value and click on it. In the background, the parameters **X-Axis** and **Y-Axis** will be adjusted to the two indices that relate to that same field. For example, for **Mean years of schooling** and **Human Development Index**, a hyperlink appears:

Figure 12.35: Menu

6. The user will be redirected to the dashboard with a trend line that is now prefiltered and shows the same two indices: **Mean years of schooling** and **Human Development Index**:

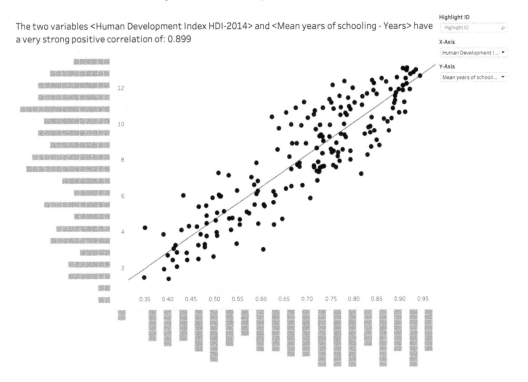

Figure 12.36: Filtered visualization

From this, we can see that the two selected indices are positively correlated by 89.9%. We can also see the distribution per index on the *x*- and *y*-axes.

This was a lengthy exercise, but I wanted to present you with my full thought process and look at dashboard creation. With more time, I would definitely add some more insights, for instance:

- Add an explanation for each index
- Add a more thorough explanation for the correlation
- Add the p-value or other coefficients to the analysis and change the text accordingly

And don't forget to get feedback and check with your stakeholders if you are on the right track. Some people use sketches, then work on a draft, and then ask for feedback again, until the product is finalized. I tend to ask my stakeholders questions to better understand what they need and let them walk me through the process they want to replace or change with the Tableau dashboard. Then, I present a full version or intermediate version, depending on the complexity and timelines. You should avoid spending hours or days on something that is not what the stakeholder wants.

But now, let us have a look at a second, shorter use case that incorporates geo-spatial data.

Geo-spatial analytics with Chicago traffic violations

It's Wednesday morning; your manager comes into your office wanting to check the red-light violations in the last year in Chicago. They ask if you can build a dashboard for that purpose. In particular, you're asked to highlight where the most violations happen and whether there is an overall trend in Chicago traffic light violations over the last few years. You are given two datasets, one with the camera locations and one with the violations, and are told that the dashboard is needed within the next hour. What do you do?

Before you continue reading, think about how you would approach this problem. Take five minutes, think about the steps you would take, and sketch a dashboard design.

The following is an overview of how I would do it:

1. Open the datasets in Tableau Prep Builder.
2. Join the two datasets.
3. Clean the data if needed.
4. Open the output in Tableau.
5. Use a map to visualize the locations of cameras, if possible.
6. Add the number of violations per camera.
7. Establish whether there is a monthly trend.

What follows is a rough sketch of how I would design the dashboard:

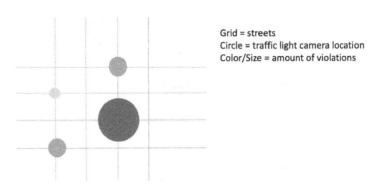

Grid = streets
Circle = traffic light camera location
Color/Size = amount of violations

Figure 12.37: Sketch

Up next is a step-by-step description of what I would do. The corresponding Tableau dashboard can be downloaded from Tableau Public, the Tableau Prep Builder file is available on GitHub (`https://github.com/PacktPublishing/Mastering-Tableau-2023-Fourth-Edition/tree/main/Chapter12`), and the dataset itself is publicly available here: `https://data.cityofchicago.org/Transportation/Red-Light-Camera-Violations/spqx-js37`.

Preparing the data

After loading both files into Tableau Prep Builder, I see that a join on **LONGITUDE** and **LATITUDE** doesn't get me anywhere because almost all records are mismatches:

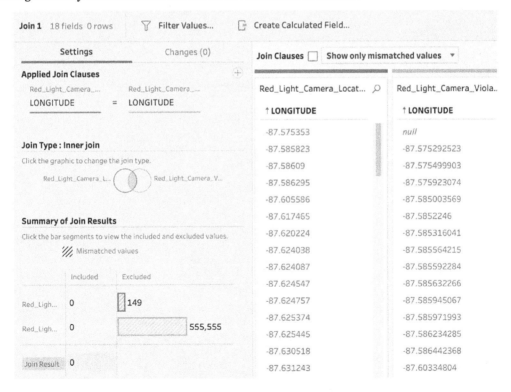

Figure 12.38: Join I

I try a different approach: a join on the intersections. This results, again, in **0** joined rows, but this time I see why. In one dataset, the **INTERSECTION** values are separated by dashes (-), and in the other dataset, it's **AND**; also, one uses capital letters, and the other one doesn't:

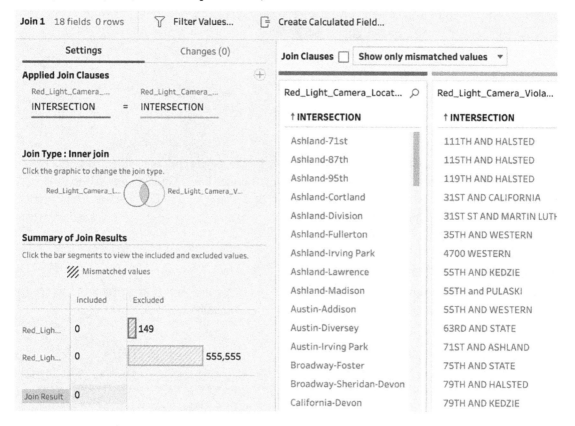

Figure 12.39: Join II

I could add a cleaning step to make all the letters uppercase and split the intersections into two parts. I can execute **Custom Split...** on - as well as on **AND**:

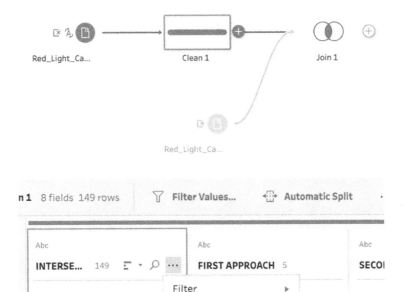

Figure 12.40: Data prepping

Then, I notice that the intersection order is different; for example, Ashland-71st and 71ST AND ASHLAND. I might consider restructuring the datasets and creating a loop that would put the two streets in alphabetical order in the two splits, but I don't have time for this now.

Another solution is to first join split 1 and split 1 as well as split 2 and split 2. In a second join, I could join split 1 and split 2 as well as split 2 and split 1. Afterward, I could union the two joins and create an output file (or directly load the Prep Builder dataset into Tableau Desktop). With this approach, I would still not include all the data, but I would have 380,000 rows out of 444,000. This could be enough to get a rough idea of patterns. If I have any time left, I can continue mapping the remaining mismatches.

However, I instead decide to drop the locations dataset altogether and just use the violations dataset because I realize that I would only miss locations in which no violation has happened yet. The locations of violations are sufficient for now. If you were, however, to determine if a traffic light control stopped working, you have to use both datasets.

Building a map of intersections

I continue by opening the violations dataset in Tableau:

1. Longitude and latitude values are not automatically recognized, so I have to change both to **Number (decimal)** by clicking on the data type icon:

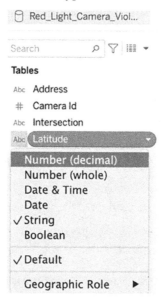

Figure 12.41: Change data type

2. Then, I change the **Longitude** and **Latitude** fields to **Measure** by clicking on the drop-down arrow on the field as shown in the preceding figure and selecting **Convert to Measure**.

3. Now I can click on the data type icon again and change the two fields to **Latitude** and **Longitude**:

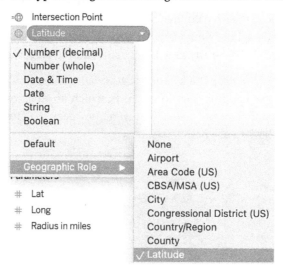

Figure 12.42: Changing the geographic role

4. By dragging **Longitude** to **Columns**, **Latitude** to **Rows,** and **Intersection** to the **Text** shelf, I visualize the red-light locations—at least the ones that have ever had a violation:

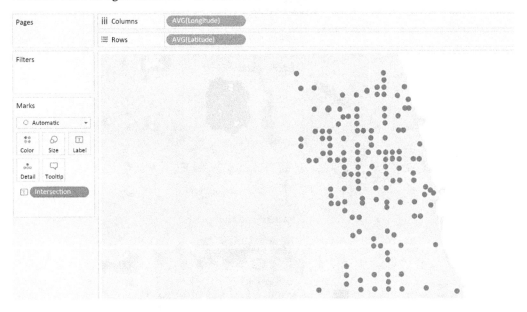

Figure 12.43: Intersections in Chicago

5. The name of the worksheet will be Intersection, and since I am looking at violations, I change the color in the **Marks** card to red. Lastly, I don't need to see the intersection name, so I change **Intersection** from **Text** to **Detail**.

6. Next, I like the map better when it shows a few more details, so I use **Background Layers...** to select some more options:

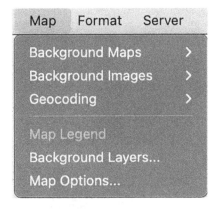

Figure 12.44: Background Layers...

Select all the layers you want to see on the map:

Figure 12.45: Map of Chicago

Another nice functionality of Tableau is that you can add **Data Layer** to your view. You can see the option in the bottom-left corner of the preceding screenshot.

7. I use the **Population** layer by **Census Tract,** as I hope it will give me some details on whether more or fewer violations happen in densely populated areas:

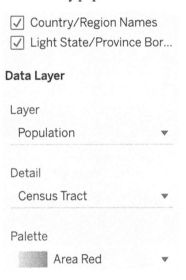

Data Layer

Layer

Population ▼

Detail

Census Tract ▼

Palette

Area Red ▼

Figure 12.46: Data layers

In the following screenshot, you can see how it looks—note that the darker the red, the denser the area is populated:

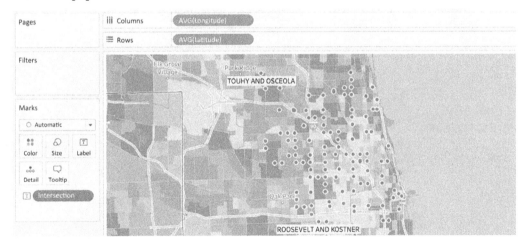

Figure 12.47: Intersection visualization

8. I add **MONTH(Violation Date)** to **Pages**; that way, my boss can play with the months and see where and when the number of violations changes:

Figure 12.48: Pages

9. Of course, I need to add the **Violations** field to make **Pages** work properly. I decide to use the **Density** feature of Tableau, using red as the color:

Figure 12.49: Density visualization

Adding a corresponding heatmap worksheet

After clicking on the **Pages** play button, I notice a pattern for some months. I want to take a closer look, so I open a new worksheet:

1. I call the new worksheet **Heatmap** and place **MONTH(Violation Date)** on **Columns** and **YEAR(Violation Date)** on **Rows**. Then, I drag **Violations** to the **Color** shelf and select red-gold to get the following:

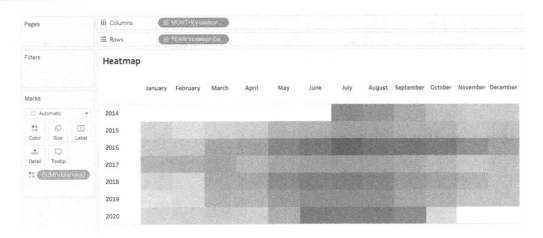

Figure 12.50: Heatmap

There are definitely more red-light violations in the summertime, and 2016 and 2020 show the most violations.

2. Last but not least, I add a new worksheet called Trend?. I drag **MONTH(Violation Date)** and drop it on the **Columns** shelf. The **Violations** field should be placed on **Rows**. I make sure that both measures are **Continuous (green)**. From the **Analytics** pane, I drag the linear **Trend Line** onto the worksheet. Next, I drag **Forecast** into the view:

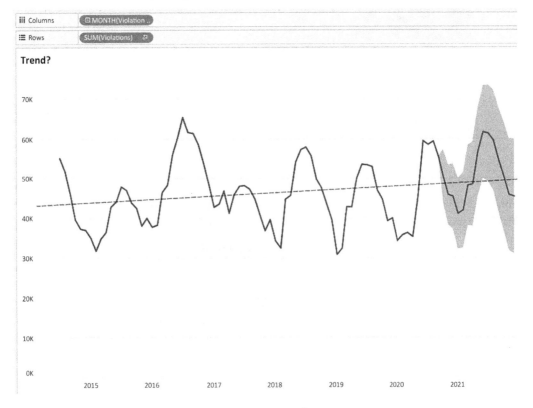

Figure 12.51: Line chart

In the preceding figure, you can see that the overall trend of red-light violations increases slightly over the years. The forecast shows us that the seasonality of there being more red-light violations in the summertime will probably continue in 2021.

Feel free to check by the end of 2021 how good Tableau's forecast model was! The City of Chicago datasets are continuously refreshed.

Finalizing the dashboard

The hour is almost over and I am just placing the three worksheets onto a dashboard, calling it **Red-Light Violations**, and formatting it a bit; it looks as follows:

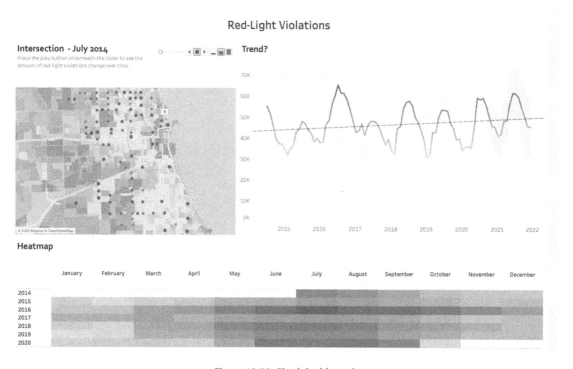

Figure 12.52: Final dashboard

You can find the final dashboard in the Tableau workbook associated with this chapter on Tableau Public, here: https://public.tableau.com/profile/marleen.meier/.

Can the dashboard be improved? Yes, it always can. But after this first iteration, my boss can let me know if anything needs to be adjusted and I can do so. I am sure that I could spend many more hours improving it, but most of the time, dashboarding is more about prompt delivery. And a full production model is a different story compared to an ad hoc question or a one-off exercise, especially if you work in an agile manner, split your work into deliverables, get feedback, and continue working on it.

Extending geo-spatial analytics with distance measures

Our last use case is also geo-spatial analysis on the same Chicago traffic dataset, but this time, we will add another component. We will look to rent a new place but with the requirement that there are no more than n intersections in a radius of x and Navy Pier should be at most y miles away. The variables n, x, and y should be interactive in order for us to make changes and have a very flexible dashboard experience. The questions to ask about this task are:

- How can we add any given location in Chicago to our dataset? It is currently only showing intersections and violations.
- How can we make the n, x, and y variables?
- How can we add a radius indicator to any given point on the map?
- How can we measure the distance between two variable points?

All those questions will be answered in the following steps:

1. Go back to the workbook related to this chapter.
2. Right-click on the worksheet called **Intersection** and click on **Duplicate**.
3. Rename the new worksheet Rental.
4. Remove **MONTH(Violation Date)** from **Pages** and **SUM(Violations)** from the **Color** shelf and the red text (sub-heading) from the title to make the worksheet look like this:

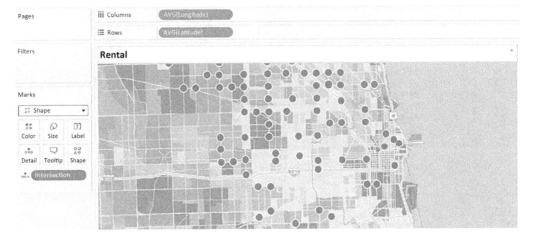

Figure 12.53: Intersections

5. Change the **Marks** type to **Map.**

6. Click on **Map** | **Map Layer** and change **Data Layer** to **No Data Layer**:

Data Layer

Layer

No Data Layer   ▼

Make Default

Figure 12.54: Map layer

7. Place **Violation Date** on the **Filters** shelf and select the year **2020**.

8. Drag **Violations** onto the **Color** shelf and select the **Red** color palette:

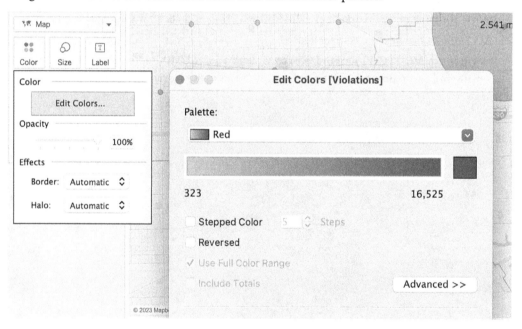

Figure 12.55: Edit colors

We now have a map of Chicago in front of us, on which each point represents an intersection at which violations have happened in 2020. The darker the dot, the more violations there are that were registered at that intersection.

Adding measure points to the map

Next, we have to add functionality that will allow us to set a mark on the map and start measuring from there. This can be achieved by creating longitude and latitude parameters and using them in a calculated field:

1. Create the following parameters, Lat and Long:

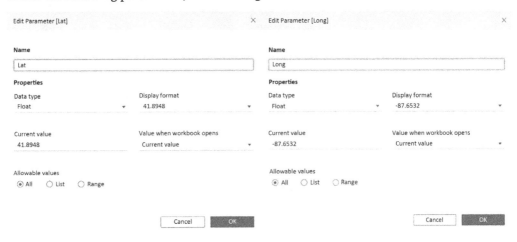

Figure 12.56: Parameters

2. Right-click each of the parameters and select **Show Parameter**.

3. Create a calculated field called Address manual:

```
MAKEPOINT([Lat], [Long])
```

4. Drag **Address manual** onto the map, on top of the **Add a Marks Layer** pop-up:

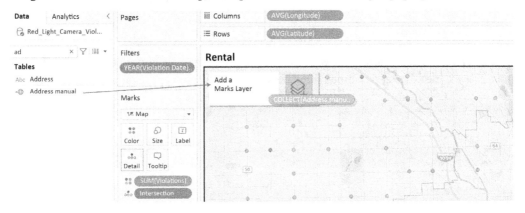

Figure 12.57: Add a layer

5. Change the **Marks** type of the new layer to **Map**.

6. After these steps, we have a map with intersections, color-coded numbers of violations, and a point that we can change by using the Lat and Long parameters. The user can use, for example, Google Maps to find the latitude and longitude; simply select a point on Google Maps that represents a rental home location:

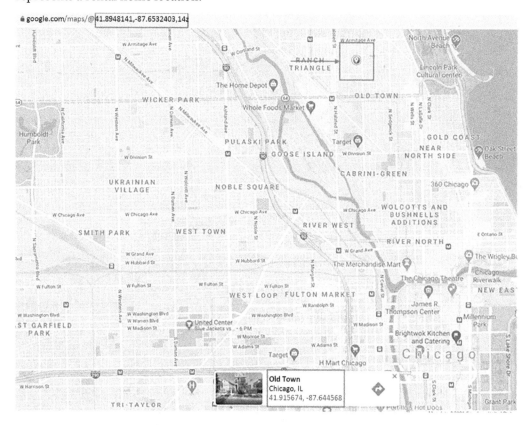

Figure 12.58: Google Maps

7. The latitude and longitude will show in the URL and at the bottom of the page. Type them into the Lat and Long parameters and the same points will appear on our Tableau map:

Figure 12.59: Latitude and longitude

Adding the distance line

In the next steps, we will add a radius and a distance line starting at Navy Pier:

1. Create another parameter called Radius in miles and set the current value to 1.1.
2. Right-click on the Radius in miles parameter and select **Show Parameter**.
3. Create a calculated field called Buffer, which will be used as our radius around the **Address manual** point:

```
BUFFER([Address manual],[Radius in miles], 'miles')
```

4. Drag the **Buffer** field onto the map just like we did with the **Address manual** field, on top of the **Add a Marks Layer** pop-up.
5. Change the **Marks** type of this new layer to **Map**.

6.   Click on **Color**, change the opacity to **50%**, and choose a gray color:

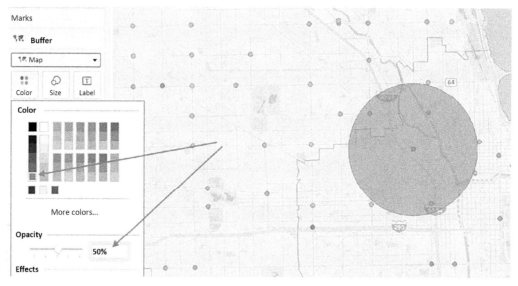

Figure 12.60: Map with radius

The **Navy Pier** coordinates are shown in the URL in the following figure (41.8859088,-87.6064094):

Figure 12.61: Navy Pier

7.   Create a calculated field as follows:

```
MAKEPOINT(41.892133, -87.604045)
```

8.   Drag the **Navy Pier** field onto the map on top of the **Add a Marks Layer** pop-up.

9.   Change the **Marks** type to **Map**.

10. In order to connect **Navy Pier** to our **Address manual** point and measure the distance, create another calculated field called `Line`:

```
MAKELINE([Address manual], [Navy Pier])
```

11. To measure the distance between the two, create a `Distance` field with the following code:

```
DISTANCE([Address manual], [Navy Pier], 'miles')
```

12. Place the **Line** field onto the map on top of the **Add a Marks Layer** pop-up.

13. Change the **Marks** type in the new layer to **Map**.

14. Place **Distance** on the **Label** shelf, change the measure to **Average**, and click on **Label** to add the text `miles`:

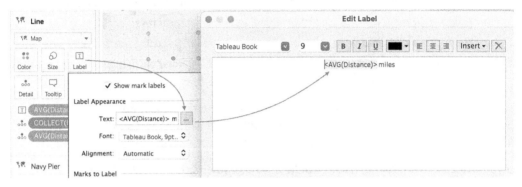

Figure 12.62: Edit label

Our dashboard now looks as follows:

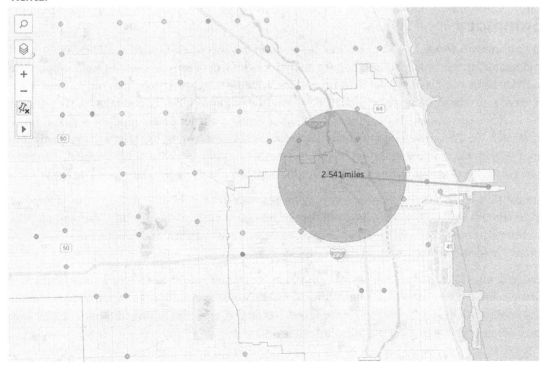

Figure 12.63: Final dashboard

And this makes it complete. The radius clearly shows how many intersections are within a certain distance; you can see the number of intersection violations by hovering over the points. The line from Navy Pier to our current location **Address manual** tells us how far away those two points are from each other.

To answer our questions from the beginning:

- *How can we add any given location in Chicago to our dataset? It is currently only showing intersections and violations.* By using the `Makepoint()` function in a calculated field.
- *How can we make the n, x, and y variables?* By using parameters.
- *How can we add a radius to any given point on the map?* By using the `Buffer()` function.
- *How can we measure the distance between two variable points?* By using the `Distance()` function; by adding the `MakeLine()` function, a line will be drawn.

This use case can be recreated for the number of supermarkets in an area, schools, public transport points, and so on. Be creative and feel free to upload your dashboards to Tableau Public, and don't forget to add the **#MasteringTableau** tag!

If you work a lot with spatial data, I would also recommend that you check out these links:

- `https://www.tableau.com/about/blog/2019/6/geospatial-analysis-made-easy-two-new-spatial-functions-makepoint-and-makeline`
- `https://www.tableau.com/about/blog/2020/3/seeing-and-understanding-proximity-made-easy-buffer-calculations`

Summary

In this chapter, we explored the fascinating world of advanced self-service analytics. We began by understanding the concept of self-service analytics as a form of business intelligence, empowering individuals to directly query datasets and unlock valuable insights. Throughout our journey, we uncovered three captivating use cases that showcased the power of self-service analytics. We unraveled the intricate correlations between world indices, gaining a deeper understanding of global market dynamics. We then delved into the realm of Chicago traffic violations, using geo-spatial analytics to uncover patterns and potential areas for improvement. Lastly, we extended our geo-spatial analysis, utilizing distance measures to determine the optimal radius for housing locations based on key variables.

Amidst these diverse scenarios, one key lesson resonated throughout: a well-structured approach is paramount when embarking on a self-service analytics project. By carefully planning our work, familiarizing ourselves with the data, employing descriptive statistics, and adapting our plans based on intermediate results, we paved the way for success.

And remember, a dashboard is never really finished: you can always change things; your audience might change; and stakeholder wishes might differ. Deliver a working visualization with basic functionality and continue to develop after you get feedback. Depending on your backlog or other circumstances, the minimum viable product might be just what you need.

As we conclude this chapter, I urge you to reflect on the insights gained and consider how these principles can be applied to your own self-service analytics endeavors. Remember, while my experiences have served as a guide, there are various paths that can lead you to your goals. Embrace the power of self-service analytics, empower yourself with data, and unlock a world of possibilities in your quest for informed decision-making. While doing this, give your IT team a rest and let them focus on the heavier implementations that are out of scope for you.

The next chapter will be all about improving performance. With more and more data, performance is key and could mean the difference between success and failure.

Learn more on Discord

To join the Discord community for this book – where you can share feedback, ask questions to the author, and learn about new releases – follow the QR code below:

`https://packt.link/tableau`

13

Improving Performance

Once people are familiar with Tableau's functionality, they soon run into another type of issue: performance. You might all have experienced staring at the screen while reading *Loading Data* or *Executing Query*. But don't worry, we've got you! If designed accordingly, Tableau dashboards can perform very well, even with large amounts of data.

This chapter will address various aspects of performance with the intent of empowering you with techniques to create workbooks that load quickly and respond snappily to end user interaction.

In this chapter, we will discuss the following topics:

- Understanding the performance-recording dashboard
- Hardware and on-the-fly techniques
- Connecting to data sources
- Working with extracts
- Using filters wisely
- Efficient calculations
- Other ways to improve performance

As you can see, there are many topics we have to cover with regard to performance improvement. Therefore, let's not lose any time and dive right in. Our first topic will be performance recording, which is the first thing you should look at when experiencing a drop in performance because it helps you identify the source of all the slowness.

Understanding the performance-recording dashboard

Tableau includes a performance-recording feature as part of the installation package and it ships as a dashboard named `PerformanceRecording.twb`. The dashboard gives the Tableau author an easy way to understand and troubleshoot performance problems. The following exercises and associated discussion points will review various aspects of the performance-recording dashboard, including how to generate it, how to use it to improve performance, and how it's constructed.

Perform the following steps:

1. Navigate to `https://public.tableau.com/profile/marleen.meier` to locate and download the workbook associated with this chapter.

2. Navigate to the `Types of Events` worksheet.

3. Select **Help | Settings and Performance | Start Performance Recording**.

4. Press *F5* on Windows or *Command + R* on macOS to refresh the view.

5. Select **Help | Settings and Performance | Stop Performance Recording**. A new dashboard will open:

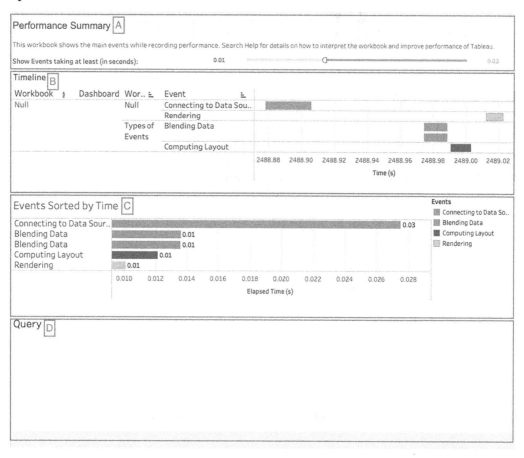

Figure 13.1: Performance summary

There are four main parts to be looked at:

A) **Performance Summary** shows the amount of time the dashboard needed to execute all the steps that happened between *step 3* (start performance recording) and *step 5* (stop performance recording). The slider can be used to filter.

B) **Timeline** shows which step happened when and how long it took.

C) The steps are also color-coded and can be found in the **Events** bar chart as well.

D) **Query** will only show details when clicking on any event in (B) or (C).

Let's continue with the next steps:

1. Drag the **Events** timeline slider in (**A**) to the far left to show all events.
2. Within **Events Sorted by Time** (**C**), click on any green bar entitled **Executing Query**. Note that the **Query** section is now populated by the VizQL belonging to the highlighted bar:

Figure 13.2: Events

3. To see the query in its entirety, navigate to the **Query** worksheet and set the fit to **Entire View** (by **Query**, Tableau is referring to a VizQL query). Note that an especially long query may not be recorded in its entirety. In order to see every line of such a query, reference the log files located in **My Tableau Repository**.

The preceding steps were intended to provide you with an initial look at what the performance-recording dashboard can be used for. I usually use it to check whether a particular query took significantly longer than others. I then look at the query on the **Query** tab and check which part is affected by reading the fields used, try to change it, and then run the performance dashboard again to see how things change. Now, let's look at some more details.

If you access the **Events** worksheet from the performance-recording dashboard, you will see the different events. We will now discuss those events and their impact on performance in more detail:

Event type	Performance considerations
Connecting to Data Source	Poor performance when connecting to the data source could indicate network latency or database issues, or even outdated drivers.
Generating Extract	Aggregating data and hiding unused columns before you extract can increase performance because it will decrease the total column and row count, respectively.
Compile Query	Compile Query performance problems could indicate database issues.
Executing Query	If a query takes too long, you can improve performance by filtering data you don't need or hiding fields you don't use. Refer to the *Using filters wisely* section in this chapter for more information.
Sorting Data	Performance issues related to sorting issues may indicate too many marks in the view. This sorting issue can also be caused by table calculations that depend on sorting data in the view.
Geocoding	Geocoding performance issues may indicate too many marks in the view, internet latency issues, poor hardware, or a poor graphics card.
Blending Data	Blending Data performance may be improved by reducing the amount of underlying data or by filtering.
Computing Table Calculations	Since table calculations are typically performed locally, complex calculations may tax the end user's computer.
Computing Totals	The Computing Totals performance may be improved by reducing the amount of underlying data or by filtering.
Computing Layout	Computing Layout performance issues may be indicative of a dashboard with too many worksheets or elements such as images.

After this overview, which you can always come back to, we will dive a little deeper and research what happens when performance recording is activated. Note that the following assumes that the author is working on Tableau Desktop and not Tableau Server. In *Chapter 14, Exploring Tableau Server and Tableau Cloud*, we will cover performance recording on Tableau Server.

When recording performance, Tableau initially creates a file in `My Tableau Repository\Logs`, named `performance_[timestamp].tab`. Additionally, there is a file named `PerformanceRecording_new.twb` located in the Tableau program directory, for example, `C:\Program Files\Tableau\Tableau.[version]\Performance`. That file is automatically opened once the recording stops, thereby allowing the author to peruse the results.

We just learned how we can record performance metrics and use the dashboard that ships with Tableau Desktop and Tableau Server (if enabled by admin) on said topic. In the next sections, we will guide you step by step through the different options that you can consider to improve the overall performance.

Hardware and on-the-fly techniques

Even though Tableau Desktop does not need a lot in terms of hardware, it still happens that company desktops or laptops are underpowered, especially if you are a so-called business user who does not require programming tools or lots of processing power in your day-to-day work.

Therefore, in this section, we will discuss the technical requirements. As per `www.tableau.com`, the latest technical requirements are:

Windows	Microsoft Windows 8/8.1, Windows 10 (x64), Windows 11
	2 GB memory
	1.5 GB minimum free disk space
	CPUs must support SSE4.2 and POPCNT instruction sets
Mac	macOS Catalina 10.15, macOS Big Sur 11.4+, macOS Monterey 12.6+ (for Tableau 2022.3+), and macOS Ventura (for Tableau 2022.3+)
	Intel processors or Apple Silicon processors (using Rosetta)
	1.5 GB minimum free disk space

Now that we have our basics straight, let us take a look at a feature that can slow down your performance unwillingly and how to solve it. Our first on-the-fly technique is called auto updates.

Auto updates can be accessed either via the icon located on the toolbar, via **Worksheet** | **Auto Updates**, or by using the shortcut key *F10* on Windows or *Option + Command + 0* on Mac. Auto updates give the author the option of pausing/resuming auto updates for the worksheet and/or for filters and can come in very handy if you want to make multiple changes to your layout but want to avoid Tableau loading after every change because every load means a new query is sent to your underlying data source and has to be processed, which will cost processing power. You can simply pause the update, make your changes, and then run the update once.

The following exercise demonstrates how this works:

1. Open the workbook associated with this chapter and navigate to the `Auto Updates` worksheet.
2. In the **Data** pane, select the `Superstore` dataset.
3. Place **State** on the **Rows** shelf.

4. Deselect **Auto Update Worksheet** via the toolbar:

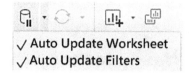

Figure 13.3: Auto Update Worksheet

5. Place **City** on the **Rows** shelf to the right of **State**. Note that the view does not update.
6. Enable **Auto Update Worksheet** via the toolbar. The view now updates.
7. Right-click on **State** on the **Rows** shelf and select **Show Filter**.
8. Right-click on **City** on the **Rows** shelf and select **Show Filter**.
9. On the **City** filter, click the drop-down menu and select **Multiple Values (list)** and **Only Relevant Values**:

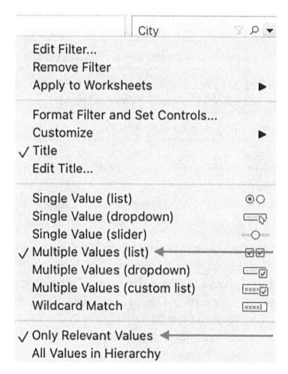

Figure 13.4: Only Relevant Values

10. Deselect **Auto Update Filters** as shown in *Figure 13.3*.
11. In the **State** filter, select only **Alabama**. Note that the **City** filter does not update.
12. Enable **Auto Update Filters** via the toolbar. The **City** filter now updates.

Auto updates can be very helpful. The author may pause auto updates, make multiple changes, and then resume auto updates, thereby saving time and increasing performance indirectly.

As a side note, cascading filters such as **Only Relevant Values** or **All Values in Context** may not populate when using the pause button or auto updates as they are reliant on a query being passed first.

The Run Update feature

The **Run Update** icon to the right of the pause/resume auto updates option is meant to refresh once, while the user can keep the disabled **Auto Update** feature in place. The following brief example should help clarify this option:

1. Duplicate the **previous** worksheet called Auto Updates and name the duplicate Run Updates.
2. Pause all updates by clicking on the **Pause Auto Updates** icon.
3. Select several states at random in the **State** filter.
4. Click on the **Run Update** icon as shown in *Figure 13.5* and select either **Update Filters** or **Update Worksheet**. The shortcut key for running an update is *F9* on Windows. The shortcut on macOS is *Shift + Command + 0*:

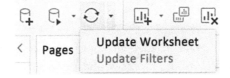

Figure 13.5: Running an update

5. Select several more states at random in the **State** filter. Note that auto updating is still paused.

To repeat, **Run Update** allows the Tableau author to intermittently refresh the view while keeping auto updates paused. The two update features that we just discussed will make your life as a dashboard developer easier by being able to make multiple changes before loading and hence waiting for the refreshed data, but if you want to tackle performance issues at their core, you need some more tools to hand. The following section will introduce extracts, a really good feature for speeding up calculations and rendering in general.

Small extracts

Although extracts will be discussed in more detail in the *Working with extracts* section, it seems fitting to mention extracts in the context of performance considerations while authoring. Even under optimal conditions, working with large data sources can be slow. If constant access to the entire dataset while authoring is not necessary, consider creating a small, local extract. Author as much of the workbook as possible and then, when all the underlying data is truly needed, point to the original data source.

The following steps show a brief example of this technique in action:

1. In the workbook associated with this chapter, navigate to the Small Local Extract worksheet.
2. Select **Data** | **New Data Source** to choose a desired data source. This exercise assumes Superstore.xls, which installs with Tableau, but you can take any dataset you like.

3. Drag any field to the **Text** shelf. In my example, I used `Number of Records`, which is a calculated field containing solely the number 1.

4. Right-click on the data source (for me: `Superstore`) and select **Extract Data...**:

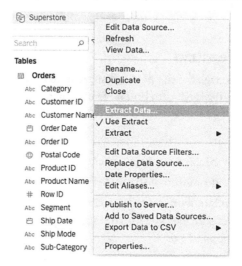

Figure 13.6: Extracting data

5. At the bottom of the **Extract Data...** dialog box, select **Top**, your data source, and choose **1000**. In the following figure, **Orders** has been chosen, which is one of the two parts of the superstore join:

Figure 13.7: Top rows

6. Click the **Extract** button and note that number of records now displays 1000 rows.

7. In the **Data** pane, right-click on **Superstore** and deselect **Use Extract**. Note that **Number of Records** has reverted to its original value.

 By creating a small, local extract, the Tableau author alleviates two performance inhibitors: network latency and dataset size.

This section gave you the knowledge of how to reduce your dataset temporarily and the option to get back to the original size, both without leaving the Tableau interface. This is a great way to speed up your dashboard-building process and avoid long waits. In the next section, we will talk about how to connect to data sources to achieve the best possible performance.

Connecting to data sources

One of the beauties of Tableau is the ease with which you can connect to many different data sources in various ways. As mentioned earlier in this book, there are many connectors defined in Tableau for interfacing with a variety of data sources. Furthermore, this flexibility extends beyond simply connecting to single tables or files.

 Although Tableau makes it easy to connect to various data sources, it should be stressed that Tableau is not an **Extract, Transform, and Load** (**ETL**) tool. If complex joins and complex data blending are required to generate useful results, it may be advisable to perform ETL work outside of Tableau, for example, in Tableau Prep Builder (see *Chapter 3, Using Tableau Prep Builder*, for more information on this service). ETL work will ideally lead to better data modeling and thus easier authoring and quicker performance in Tableau.

The four ways in which Tableau connects to data are as follows:

*   Tableau may connect to a single table. This is ideal as it allows the most functionality and easiest troubleshooting while enabling Tableau to send the simplest queries and thus perform optimally. However, it is not always possible to connect to a single table and, although ideal, it is not reasonable to have such a strict limitation. The relationship between data sources and reporting tools is constantly changing. A reporting tool that is inflexible in the way it can connect to data will likely not be successful, no matter how elegant and beautiful the end results.

*   The second option is relationships, a newer, more flexible way to combine two or more datasets. The level of detail will be defined per worksheet rather than in the **Data Source** tab, which makes this feature very powerful.

*   The third way in which Tableau may connect to data is via joining. One table may not supply all the necessary data, but by joining two or more tables, all the needed data may be accessible. As the joins become more and more complex, performance may be impacted, and troubleshooting may become difficult. Fortunately, Tableau can assume referential integrity and thus work quite efficiently with even complex joins. More information can be found here: https://help.tableau.com/current/pro/desktop/en-us/joins_xbd_perf.htm.

- Finally, Tableau may utilize data blending. Data blending often performs admirably, provided no more than one of the blended data sources is large and dimensions that are used for blending have relatively few members.

Relationships should be chosen over joining and joining should be chosen instead of blending whenever possible. When blending multiple, large data sources, performance can be seriously impacted. The problem is further compounded when blending on high-cardinality dimensions. Also, data blending limits some functionality, such as the ability to use dimensions, row-level calculations, or LOD expressions, from a secondary data source.

However, there are exceptions, two of which are discussed here:

- First, data blending is advantageous (and usually necessary) when there is no common key shared between two tables.
- Secondly, in some instances, cross-joining will not work, and a data blend is required. For example, use data blending when you work with two datasets that have different granularities and relationships are not possible or when a cross-database join is not possible (for example, to cubes or extract-only connections), or when you have big datasets for which a blend will improve performance.

 More info can be found here: https://help.tableau.com/current/pro/desktop/ en-us/multiple_connections.htm.

For these reasons, consider as a guideline that data blending should normally be avoided if a joining option exists.

Chapter 4, Learning about Joins, Blends, and Data Structures, provides detailed information about joining and blending. For the purposes of this chapter, joining and blending discussions will be limited to performance considerations.

Working efficiently with large data sources

This section will cover some basics of database tuning and ways to work efficiently with large data sources. Since the topic is more focused on data sources than on Tableau, no exercises are included.

If you are connecting to large data sources and are experiencing performance problems, a conversation with a **database administrator** (DBA) may be beneficial.

Clear communication coupled with a small amount of database work could dramatically improve performance. The conversation should include database-tuning points, such as explicitly defining primary and foreign keys, defining columns as *not null*, and indexing. Each point will be discussed here.

Defining primary and foreign keys

Primary and foreign keys are essential for joining tables. A primary key is composed of one or more columns in a table. The primary key should be unique for every row. Joining on a non-unique, row-level key may lead to erroneous results, as explored in *Chapter 4, Learning about Joins, Blends, and Data Structures*. Explicitly defining primary keys in the database helps to ensure that each key value is unique:

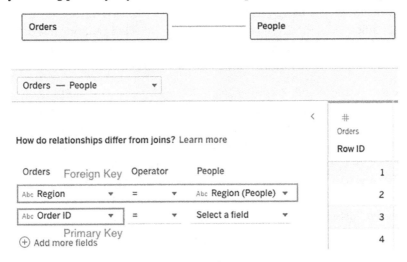

Figure 13.8: Database keys

A foreign key is composed of one or more columns in a table that uniquely identify rows in another table. This unique identification occurs as a result of the foreign key in one table referencing the primary key in another table. Explicitly defining foreign keys in the database enables Tableau to bypass many integrity checks, thereby improving performance.

Defining columns as NOT NULL

Tableau has published multiple white papers on performance improvement tips and tricks (https://help.tableau.com/current/pro/desktop/en-us/performance_tips.htm) that state that programmers and Tableau Desktop do not like NULL data. Define each column in your tables with an explicit NOT NULL if possible.

In practice, database admins debate when it is and isn't appropriate to define columns as NOT NULL; however, two things are clear:

- A primary or foreign key should be defined as NOT NULL. This is self-evident since primary and foreign keys must be unique by definition.
- Also, any column that is to be indexed should be defined as NOT NULL since, otherwise, an index may be unusable.

Indexing is discussed more fully in the next section.

Indexing

Let's consider the following two questions regarding indexing:

- What is an index?
- What should be indexed?

The first of our two questions may be easily answered by a DBA but is likely uncharted waters for the average Tableau author. So, to clarify, an index is a copy of selected columns in a database table that has been optimized for efficient searching. Since these copied columns include pointers to the original columns, they can be accessed to quickly find given rows and return the required data.

A small example may prove helpful. According to the Boeing Company, the 787 Dreamliner has about 2.3 million parts. Imagine a table that lists all these parts in the **Part_Name** column. Your task is to search this column for every part starting with the "fuse" string. On a non-indexed column, this would require the examination of every row of data in the database. Such a search could be quite slow. Fortunately, indexes can be used to reduce the number of rows searched, thus making the process much faster. One type of structured data used for indexing is B-tree. A B-tree data structure is sorted. Thus, when accessing an index using a B-tree data structure to search for all parts starting with *fuse*, not every row has to be considered. Instead, the database can skip straight to *fs* and quickly return the desired rows.

Now let's move on to the second question on indexing. What should be indexed? This question can be answered succinctly: ideally, all columns used for joining or filtering should be indexed in the data source.

Although there are some basic performance considerations for creating more efficient joins in Tableau (for example, avoid an outer join when a left join will suffice), join performance is largely determined outside of Tableau. Therefore, it is typically more important to index columns used in joins than those used for filtering.

To continue with our discussion of manipulating data sources, the next section will cover how Tableau can be used to create summarized datasets through extracting.

Working with extracts

This section will discuss what a Tableau data extract is as well as how to efficiently construct an extract. A colleague of mine recently consulted with a relatively small mobile phone service provider. Even though the company was small, the volume could be in excess of 1,000,000 calls per day. Management at the company insisted on the ability to interface with detailed visualizations of individual calls in Tableau workbooks. The performance of the workbooks was, understandably, a problem. Was such low-level detail necessary? Might less detail and snappier workbooks have led to better business decisions?

In order to balance business needs with practical performance requirements, businesses often need to ascertain what level of detail is genuinely helpful for reporting. Often, detailed granularity is not necessary. When such is the case, a summary table may provide sufficient business insight while enabling quick performance. In the case of the mobile phone service provider, a daily snapshot of call volumes may have sufficed. Even an hourly snapshot would have greatly reduced the table size and improved Tableau's performance.

To address this common business need, an extract is a proprietary compressed data source created by Tableau Desktop. Since its release, the file extension for an extract has changed from .tde to the .hyper format. Thus, the new format makes use of the Hyper engine, which was discussed in *Chapter 1, Reviewing the Basics*. An extract can be stored locally and accessed by Tableau to render visualizations.

Consider the following points that make an extract file an excellent choice for improved performance:

- Extracts can be quickly generated at an aggregate level.
- Extracts are a columnar store, which records as sequences of columns.
- Relational databases typically store data using a **Row Store** methodology.

In the following example, note that **Row Store** is excellent for returning individual rows, whereas **Column Store** is much better for returning aggregated data.

Here is an example table:

	Table		
	Instrument	Store	Price
Row 1	Selmer Trumpet	North	$3,500
Row 2	Conn French Horn	East	$4,500
Row 3	Getzen Trombone	South	$2,500
Row 4	Miraphone Tuba	West	$9,000

Here is a **Row Store** table in a database:

Row 1	Selmer Trumpet
	North
	$3,500
Row 2	Conn French Horn
	East
	$4,500
Row 3	Getzen Trombone
	South
	$2,500
Row 4	Miraphone Tuba
	West
	$9,000

Here is a **Column Store** table in a database:

Instrument	Selmer Trumpet
	Conn French Horn
	Getzen Trombone
	Miraphone Tuba
Store	North
	East
	South
	West
Price	$3,500
	$4,500
	$2,500
	$9,000

I hope you could see that in a **Column Store** table, each n row of a certain attribute makes up for the first row. For example, the first row of Instrument, the first row of Store, and the first row of Price all relate to one entry, whereas in a **Row Store** table, all rows that belong to the same entry are in consecutive order.

To sum up what we have learned so far in this section, extracts use compression techniques to reduce file size while maintaining performance and utilize RAM and hard drive space for optimal performance. Neither of those two things happens when using a live connection to a database—therefore, extracts can improve the performance of your dashboard whenever the database can't.

Constructing an extract

This section will discuss extracts from a performance aspect. Other aspects of extracts, such as scheduling and incremental refreshes, will not be considered here, but you can find more information here: https://help.tableau.com/current/pro/desktop/en-us/extracting_refresh.htm.

As we discussed in the *Small extracts* section earlier, an extract is created via **Data | [Data Source] | Extract Data**. From the resulting dialog box, we can take the following actions:

- **Filter the extract as needed**: Sometimes, an extract that precisely reflects a data source is warranted, but often filtering various fields will still populate the extract with the required data while shrinking the size and improving performance. To add a filter, simply click **Add...** to access a dialog box identical to the **Filter** dialog box used within a worksheet.

- **Aggregate to the level of granularity represented in the view**: Aggregation not only reduces the file size but can also be helpful from a security standpoint. Without aggregation, an extract is constructed using row-level data. Therefore, the Tableau author should note that if the extract is built without choosing to aggregate, any sensitive row-level data is accessible:

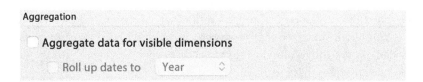

Figure 13.9: Aggregation

- **Reduce the number of rows**: As shown in the *Small extracts* section, reducing the number of rows can allow the author to create a small, local extract for quick workbook building, after which the original data source can be accessed for complete analysis:

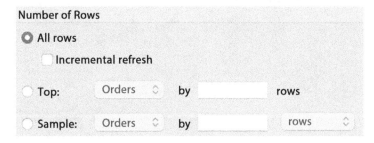

Figure 13.10: Reducing rows

- **Hide all unused fields**: This option excludes all columns that are not used in the workbook from the extract. This can significantly reduce the extract size and increase performance:

Figure 13.11: Hiding fields

By taking these four measures, your performance should improve immediately. Feel free to test it yourself by using the performance-recording tool and creating different extracts of the same data source. Using aggregation and performance-recording actions will be discussed next.

Aggregation

The following exercise will use two aggregates from a single data source, one at the **State** level and the other at the **City** level. These aggregated data sources will be used to create two worksheets. Each of these worksheets will be placed on a dashboard along with a third worksheet with row-level information. Finally, filter actions will be created to tie the three worksheets together. The purpose of the exercise is to demonstrate how small extracts might be used in conjunction with a larger dataset to create a more performant dashboard:

1. Open the workbook associated with this chapter and navigate to the State Agg worksheet.
2. In the **Data** pane, select the State Agg data source.
3. Create a filled map using state by placing **State** on the **Detail** shelf and selecting **Filled Map** from the **Marks** card.
4. Right-click on the State Agg data source and select **Extract Data**.

5. Note that Tableau displays an error stating that it cannot find the referenced file. You can either point to the instance of `Superstore` that ships with Tableau or you can use the instance provided via the GitHub link: `https://github.com/PacktPublishing/Mastering-Tableau-2023-Fourth-Edition/tree/main`.

6. After connecting to the data source, Tableau will display the **Extract Data** dialog box. Within the dialog box, select **Aggregate data for visible dimensions** and **All rows**. Click the **Hide All Unused Fields** button and then click on **Extract**:

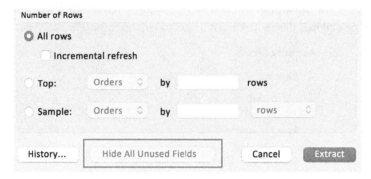

Figure 13.12: Extracting data

Note that the resulting extract only contains **State**. Also note that the data has been aggregated so that no underlying data is available.

7. Navigate to the `City Agg` worksheet.

8. In the **Data** pane, select the `City Agg` data source. Note that this data source has already been extracted and so only contains **State**, **City**, and **Sales**. Also note that the data has been aggregated so that no underlying data is available.

9. Place **City** on the **Rows** shelf, **Sales** on the **Text** shelf, and **State** on the **Detail** shelf. Don't forget to include **State** even though it does not display on the view. It must be used so that the dashboard created at the end of the exercise works correctly.

10. Navigate to the `Row Detail` worksheet and select the `Superstore` dataset.

11. Create a crosstab view that displays **Customer Name**, **Order ID**, **Row ID**, **Profit**, and **Sales**. One quick way to create this view is to double-click on each field.

12. Navigate to the `Agg Dash` dashboard and place each of the three worksheets on the dashboard.

13. Create a blend relationship between **City** and **State** from the **Superstore** and **City Agg** data source:

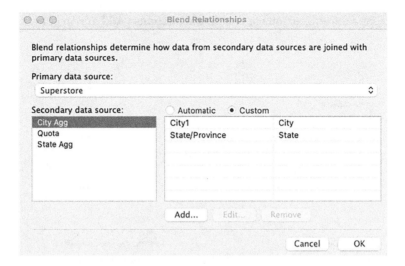

Figure 13.13: Blend

14. Create the following action via **Dashboard** | **Actions** | **Add Action** | **Filter**:

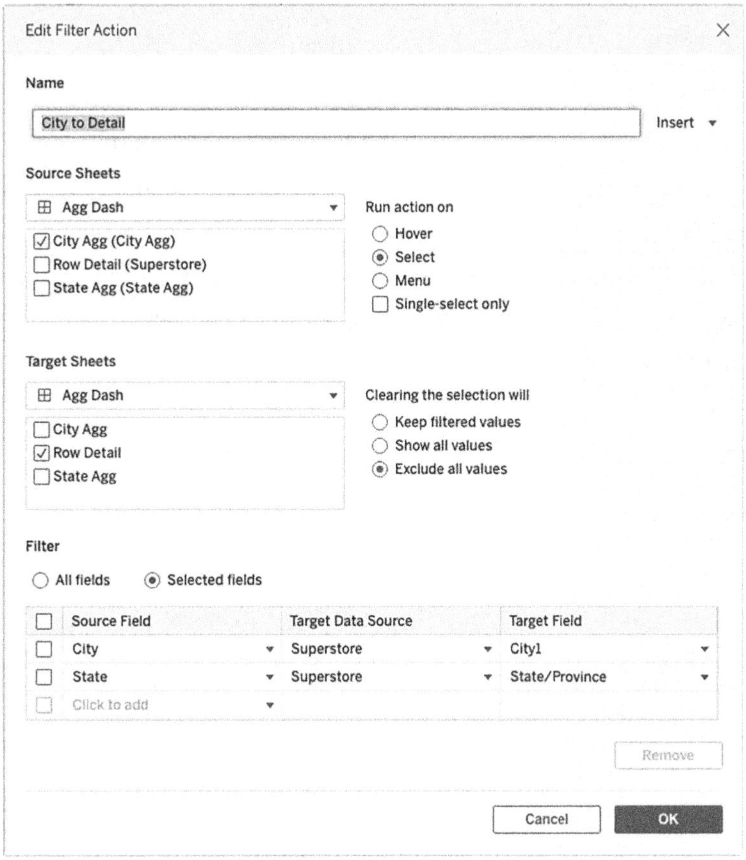

Figure 13.14: Adding City to Detail action

15. Create the following action via **Dashboard | Actions | Add Action | Filter**:

Name

| State to City | Insert ▾ |

Source Sheets

⊞ Agg Dash ▾

☐ City Agg (SS – City Agg)
☐ Row Detail (Superstore)
☑ State Agg (SS – State Agg)

Run action on

○ Hover
◉ Select
○ Menu
☐ Single-select only

Target Sheets

⊞ Agg Dash ▾

☑ City Agg
☐ Row Detail
☐ State Agg

Clearing the selection will

○ Keep filtered values
○ Show all values
◉ Exclude all values

Filter

◉ All fields   ○ Selected fields

Figure 13.15: Adding State to City action

16. After creating these two actions, in the dashboard, click on the **State** field.
17. Then, click on the **City** field.
18. Click on a blank portion of the City Agg worksheet to exclude all values on **Row Detail**.
19. Click on a blank portion of the State Agg worksheet to exclude all values on **City Agg**.
20. Format the dashboard as desired:

Figure 13.16: Action on dashboard

Having completed this exercise, note that the resulting dashboard is performant for the following reasons:

- When the user first opens the dashboard, only **State Agg** displays. This is performant for two reasons. First, displaying a single worksheet as opposed to every worksheet when opening the dashboard causes fewer initial queries and less rendering. Second, accessing a small extract is quicker than accessing a larger data source.

- Since the City Agg worksheet is also accessing a small extract, when the user clicks on a state, the **City Agg** worksheet will appear quickly.

- When the user clicks on **City**, a call is made to the data source that only includes the information for that city. A relatively small amount of data is pulled, and performance should be good for even larger datasets.

Another aspect of good performance practice, apart from using aggregate extracts, should be considered for this exercise. The dashboard contains no quick filters. Often, using quick filters on a dashboard is unnecessary. If the worksheets on the dashboard can be used to filter, those worksheets can essentially do double duty. That is to say, worksheets can provide valuable analysis while simultaneously acting as filters for other worksheets on the dashboard. This represents a performance improvement over using quick filters since adding quick filters would cause additional queries to be sent to the underlying data source.

In the preceding dashboard, each worksheet references a different data source. Therefore, you may ask, how are the action filters able to function across the different data sources? The answer can be found in the filter action dialog box. As shown in *Figure 13.14* and *Figure 13.15*, **All** fields are considered **Target Filters**. Tableau simply matches any fields of the same name across each data source. Extracts can be optimized for even better performance results. We'll cover this in the next section.

Optimizing extracts

Optimization accelerates performance by materializing calculated fields when possible. This means that Tableau generates values for calculated fields in the extract so that those values can be looked up instead of calculated. If you were to use table calculations, Tableau would have to calculate the values each time you change the view.

 Note that not all calculated fields are materialized. Fields that are not materialized include table calculations, changeable or unstable functions, such as NOW() and TODAY(), and calculated fields using parameters.

When an extract is first created, it is automatically optimized. In other words, calculated fields are automatically materialized when possible. However, over the course of time, calculated fields may be altered that will cause the extract to drop materialized fields. At such times, open **Data | [Data Source] | Extract** and click on **Compute Calculations Now** in order to regenerate the materialized fields:

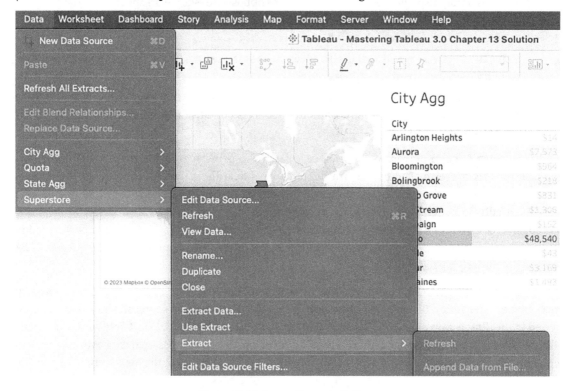

Figure 13.17: Computing calculations

If an extract is set to refresh on Tableau Server, the extract is automatically optimized for each refresh.

Finally, if you make use of parameters in your dashboard, check whether you can eliminate those and use calculations instead to improve performance. Also, split calculations if they can't be materialized as a whole. Put the part that can be materialized in one calculated field and the non-materialized part in another. If parts of the calculation can be calculated within the extract creation, you will gain performance.

The advantage of using extracts has now been discussed in great detail, so let's move on and see how we can make the most out of filters.

Using filters wisely

Filters generally improve performance in Tableau. For example, when using a dimension filter to view only the West region, a query is passed to the underlying data source, resulting in information being returned for just that region. By reducing the amount of data returned, performance improves. This is because less data means reduced network bandwidth load, reduced database processing requirements, and reduced processing requirements for the local computer.

Filters can also negatively impact Tableau's performance. For example, using **only relevant values** causes additional queries to be sent to the underlying data source, thereby slowing down the response time. Also, creating quick filters from high-cardinality dimensions can impair performance.

Tableau's filters are executed in a specific order, so keep this in mind when using them. The following flowchart, along with a link to an hour-long presentation, may help you grasp the concept fully: `https://help.tableau.com/current/pro/desktop/en-us/order_of_operations.htm`:

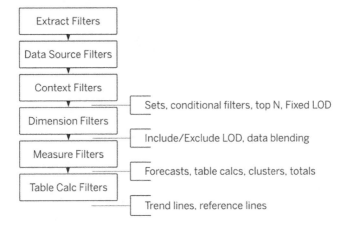

Figure 13.18: Filtering the order of operations

The rest of this section follows, step by step, the order of operations. By the end of it, you will know which filters to use in which situation so as to achieve the best performance for your dashboards.

Extract filters

Extract filters remove data from the extracted data source. Simply put, the data isn't there. Thus, performance is enhanced by reducing the overall amount of data. Performance may also be improved since extracted data uses Tableau's proprietary columnar dataset.

Furthermore, extracts are always flattened, which will have performance advantages over connecting to datasets using joins. To create an extract filter, begin by selecting **Data** | **[Data Source]** | **Extract Data**. In the resulting dialog box, choose to add a filter.

Data source filters

Data source filters are applied throughout the workbook. For example, if you create a data source filter that removes all members of the **Country** dimension except the USA, the **Country** dimension will only include the USA for all worksheets in the workbook.

Data source filters improve performance in the same way as dimension and measure filters; that is, data source filters cause Tableau to generate a query to the underlying data source, which will limit the data that is returned. Less returned data generally results in quicker processing and rendering. A further advantage that data source filters offer is ease of authoring. For example, if the Tableau author knows in advance that an entire workbook is going to be USA-centric, creating a data source filter saves you the trouble of applying a dimension filter to every worksheet in the workbook using that data source.

Also note that data source filters occur quite early in the process flow. All calculations (including calculations using fixed LOD expressions that are rendered before dimension and measure filters are triggered) respect data source filters.

To create a data source filter, click the **Data Source** tab located in the bottom-left corner of **Tableau Desktop**. Then, click on the **Add** link located in the top-right corner of the page:

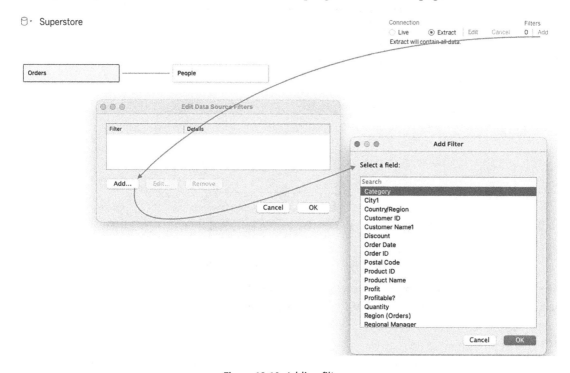

Figure 13.19: Adding filters

Context filters

A context filter is created simply by right-clicking on a field in the **Filter** shelf and selecting **Add to Context:**

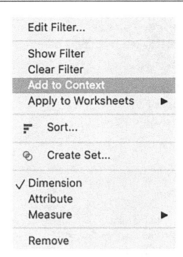

Figure 13.20: Context filters

Dimension and measure filters are independent. Each filter queries the data source independently and returns results. A context filter, on the other hand, will force dimension and measure filters to depend on it. This behavior can be helpful (and necessary) for getting the right answer in some circumstances. For instance, if a Tableau author accesses the **Superstore** dataset and uses a filter on **Product Names** to return the top-10 selling product names in a single category, it will be necessary for **Category** to be defined as a context filter. Otherwise, the **Product Names** filter will return the top 10 overall. Because of this, context filters improve performance.

Dimension and measure filters

Dimension and measure filters can improve performance. Since either a dimension filter or a measure filter will cause Tableau to generate a query to the underlying data source, which will limit the data that is returned, performance is improved. Simply put, the smaller the returned dataset, the better the performance.

However, dimension and measure filters can degrade performance. Since Tableau not only generates queries to the underlying data source in order to display visualizations but also generates queries to display filters, more displayed filters will slow performance. Furthermore, displayed filters on high-cardinality dimensions can inhibit performance. (A dimension with many members is referred to as having high cardinality.) Consider the example of a filter that displays every customer in a dataset. Performance for such a filter might be slow because every customer in the underlying dataset must be located and returned, and then Tableau has to render and display each of these customers in the filter.

When using two or more dimension or measure filters on a view, a relevant filter may be used to limit the choices that display. For example, if a view includes a filter for city and postal code, the latter might be set to show **Only Relevant Values:**

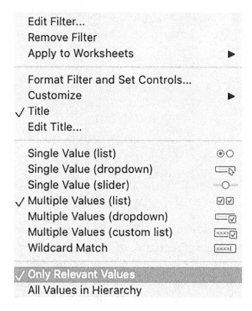

Figure 13.21: Only Relevant Values

This is advantageous to the end user in that it adjusts the number of postal codes that display to reflect only those pertinent to the cities selected in the first filter. However, using relative filters will cause additional queries to be sent to the data source and thus may degrade performance.

Table calculation filters

Using table calculations as filters does not have the same corresponding performance enhancements as dimension or measure filters. As discussed above, dimension and measure filters reduce the returned dataset, while table calculation filters do not. In the Tableau process flow, table calculations are not rendered until after the data is returned from the data source. This means that table calculations cannot be used to generate queries to limit returned data. Or, to put it another way, table calculation filters cause all data related to a given dimension or measure to be returned, after which Tableau executes the filter on the returned dataset.

To demonstrate this, perform the following steps:

1. Open the workbook associated with this chapter and navigate to the Late Filter worksheet.
2. In the **Data** pane, select the Superstore data source.
3. Create a calculated field named Cust Name Tbl Calc with the following code:

   ```
   LOOKUP( MAX( [Customer Name] ),0 )
   ```

4. Place **Customer Name** on the **Rows** shelf.
5. Place **Cust Name Tbl Calc** on the **Filters** shelf and constrain to show only **Aaron Bergman.**

6. Place **Sales** on the **Text** shelf.

7. Right-click on **Sales** and select **Quick Table Calculation | Rank**.

In this exercise, the entire list of customers is returned to Tableau, after which Tableau deploys the filter. Essentially, using **Cust Name Tbl Calc** as a filter merely hides the underlying data. This is useful because the rank returned for **Aaron Bergman** is correct. Merely filtering on **Customer Name** would return a rank of **1** for **Aaron Bergman**. Unfortunately, the correct results come with a performance hit. Running the performance recorder on this exercise will show that the table calculation negatively impacts performance.

Fortunately, with the advent of LOD calculations, using table calculations as filters is often not necessary. LODs are calculated fields that include or exclude data independent of the current view. For more information, please refer to *Chapter 5, Introducing Table Calculations*.

Using actions instead of filters

Another way to improve performance might be to use actions instead of filters. You can develop a dashboard that shows a high-level overview first and goes into detail only once the user selects something. The mechanics are similar to the ones we showed in the *Aggregation* section; however, aggregation happens per worksheet and not on the data source itself. By selecting a mark in the high-level overview, an action will be triggered. The user can dive deeper into details, but the level of detail will only be increased step by step. Hence, less data has to be loaded at once.

A very nice presentation regarding this topic can be found at `https://youtu.be/veLlZ1btoms`. Or if you are interested in learning more about the Hot-Warm-Cold method, feel free to read this article: `https://gemshare.org/2019/08/16/hot-warm-cold-data-architecture-best-practices/`.

The next topic we will be discussing involves calculations. How can we write a calculation in the most efficient and performant way?

Efficient calculations

Calculations may be constructed differently and yet accomplish the same thing. Look, for instance, at the following example, which shows that an `IF` statement can be replaced by simpler code:

Scenario I	Scenario II

Create a calculated field with the following code:
 	
`IF SUM (Profit) > 0 THEN 'Profitable'`
`ELSE 'Unprofitable' END`
 	
Place the calculated field on the **Color** shelf.
	Create a calculated field with the following code:
	
	`SUM (Profit) > 0`
	
	Place the calculated field on the **Color** shelf.
	
	Right-click on **True** and **False** in the resulting legend and rename **Profitable** and **Unprofitable**.

Since either of these scenarios will return the desired results, which should be used? The deciding factor is performance. This section will explore what to do and what to avoid when creating calculated fields in order to maximize performance.

Prioritizing code values

Calculations that use Boolean values or numbers are more performant than those that use dates. Calculations that use dates, in turn, are more performant than those using strings. This is not only true of Tableau, but also in computer science as a whole.

Based on this information, **Scenario II** listed in the preceding table is more performant than **Scenario I**. **Scenario I** causes Tableau to create a query that requires the data source engine to handle strings for reporting profitability, whereas **Scenario II** sends only 1s and 0s to determine profitability. The third step for **Scenario II** (that is, aliasing **True** and **False** to **Profitable** and **Unprofitable**) is merely a labeling change that happens after the aggregate dataset is returned from the data source, which is quick and easy for Tableau.

Level-of-detail calculations or table calculations

In some instances, a **level-of-detail (LOD)** calculation might be faster than a table calculation and vice versa. If you are not sure, try both to see which one performs better. You can, of course, run a performance recording too. Also, if they're not really needed, use neither. Refer to the following diagram, which explains when to choose which:

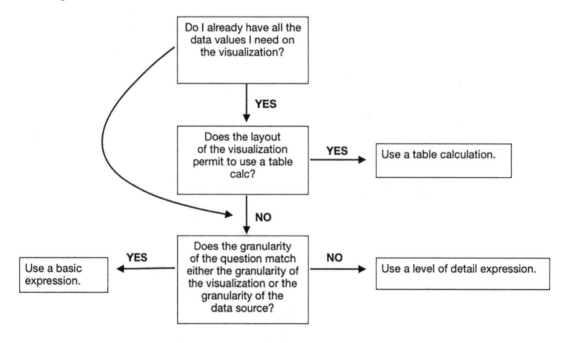

Figure 13.22: Choosing a calculation type

This diagram, along with more advice about selecting a calculation type, can be accessed at https:// www.tableau.com/about/blog/2016/4/guide-choosing-right-calculation-your-question-53667.

Other ways to improve performance

To conclude this chapter, let's consider a few other possibilities for improving performance.

Avoid overcrowding a dashboard

Often, end users want to see everything at once on a dashboard. Although this may be perceived as beneficial, it often is not. Consider the inclusion of a large crosstab on a dashboard. Does scrolling through pages of details add to the analytical value of the dashboard? Perhaps the answer is "no." Furthermore, an excess of information on a dashboard may obscure important insights. Diplomatically arguing for leaner dashboards may lead to better decision making as well as better performance.

Fixing dashboard sizing

Dashboards can be set to an exact size or to **Range** or **Automatic**. Exact size results in quicker performance because once Tableau Server has rendered a view for one end user, that render stays in the cache and can be reused for the next end user that accesses that dashboard. **Automatic** and **Range**, on the other hand, cause Tableau Server to attempt to determine the resolution size used by each end user and render the dashboard accordingly. This means that Tableau Server does not use the instance of the dashboard stored in the cache for the next end user. This, in turn, impacts performance.

Use Tableau Prep Builder

This has been mentioned before but is very relevant, therefore I will repeat: **If complex joins and complex data blending are required to generate useful results, it may be advisable to perform ETL work outside of Tableau**, for example, in Tableau Prep Builder (see *Chapter 3, Using Tableau Prep Builder*, for more information on this service). ETL work will ideally lead to better data modeling, aggregated data, or data that contains additional columns already that you would otherwise have to create in Tableau Desktop, and thus using Prep Builder leads to easier authoring and quicker performance in Tableau.

Setting expectations

If an end user is expecting near-instantaneous performance, then, of course, anything less is disappointing. Explaining in advance that a complicated, detail-oriented dashboard may not be performant can help in at least two ways. First, upon explaining the likely performance problems, a compromise may be reached that results in the creation of a less complicated dashboard that still delivers valuable information. Second, if it is absolutely necessary for the dashboard to be complicated and detail-oriented, at least the end user has been warned that patience may be needed when interfacing it.

Workbook Optimizer

Finally, for the lazy ones among us – or one might say – efficient ones, Tableau released a fantastic feature not that long ago: the Workbook Optimizer. It checks your workbook based on a set of rules and will respond with three types of categories: take action, needs review, and passed. Thus, it completes performance checks using the well-known RAG (red-amber-green) or traffic light system for you.

At the time of writing, rules include: calculation length, calculation using multiple data sources, dashboard size not fixed, filter uses conditional logic, filter uses "only relevant values," live data connections, multiple connections in a data source, nested calculations, non-materialized calculations, number of data sources, number of filters, number of layout containers, number of LOD calculations, number of views in a dashboard, number of workbook sheets, unused data sources, unused fields, uses data blending, uses date calculations, and uses grouping. I am sure, however, there are more rules to come and it will become increasingly easy to have a high-performing dashboard. You can access the Workbook Optimizer feature by selecting **Server | Run Optimizer**:

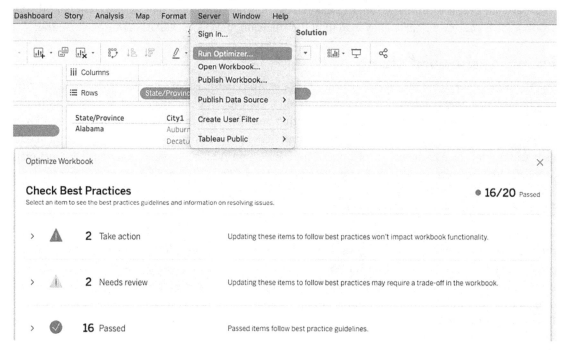

Figure 13.23: Run Optimizer

You will then be able to drill down per category and see where your dashboard needs improvement. For most of the rules, some human intervention is required but for some, a click of a button is sufficient, like in *Figure 13.24*. Observe the icons below the rule – the wrench indicates that Tableau can fix this for you.

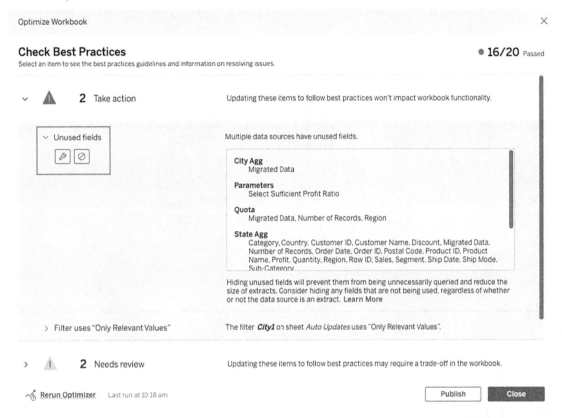

Figure 13.24: Unused fields

For each rule, Tableau also provides a **Learn More** hyperlink that will redirect you to one of the Tableau help pages with further explanation.

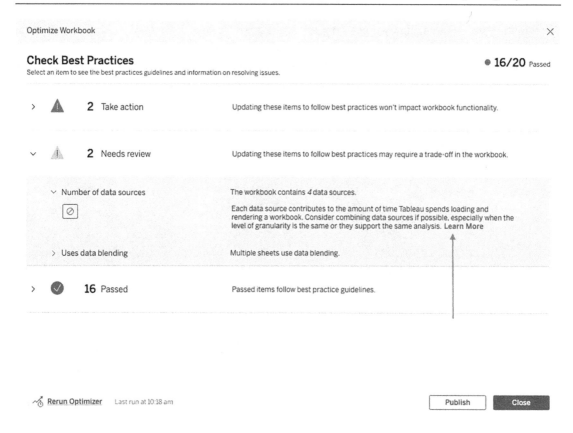

Figure 13.25: Number of data sources

Isn't this feature amazing?! From now on, always make sure to use the **Run Optimizer** button!

Summary

We began this chapter with a discussion of the performance-recording dashboard. This was important because many of the subsequent exercises utilized the performance-recording dashboard to examine underlying queries. Next, we discussed hardware and on-the-fly techniques, where the intent was to communicate hardware considerations for good Tableau performance and, in the absence of optimal hardware, techniques for squeezing the best possible performance out of any computer.

Then we covered working with data sources, including joining, blending, and efficiently working with data sources. This was followed by a discussion on generating and using extracts as efficiently as possible. By focusing on data sources for these three sections, we learned best practices and what to avoid when working with either remote datasets or extracts. The next sections explored performance implications for various types of filters and calculations. Lastly, we looked at additional performance considerations, where we explored a few more thoughts regarding dashboard performance as well as setting expectations.

In the next chapter, we will turn our attention to Tableau Server. Tableau Server is a dense topic worthy of its own book; therefore, our exploration will be truncated to only focus on Tableau Server from the Tableau Desktop author's perspective.

Learn more on Discord

To join the Discord community for this book – where you can share feedback, ask questions to the author, and learn about new releases – follow the QR code below:

`https://packt.link/tableau`

14

Exploring Tableau Server and Tableau Cloud

Tableau Server and Tableau Cloud are online solutions for sharing, distributing, and collaborating on content created in Tableau Desktop and/or Tableau Public. Its benefits include providing an environment where end users can securely view, explore, and refresh both real-time and scheduled data visualizations. The main difference between Tableau Server and Tableau Cloud is that Tableau Server needs to be maintained by you, while Tableau Cloud is fully hosted in the cloud by Tableau and backed up by Amazon Web Services infrastructure. For ease of reading, we will further refer to both as Tableau Server.

The scope of this chapter is limited to the Tableau Desktop author's interaction with Tableau Server. Topics such as installation and upgrades, authentication and access, security configuration, and command-line utilities are not related to the Tableau Desktop author's interaction with Tableau Server and are thus not included in this chapter. However, the help documentation is quite good. Also consider watching some videos from Tableau Software about Tableau Server (for example, `https://www.youtube.com/c/tableausoftware/search?query=Tableau%20Server`). If you have questions related to any of the topics listed here or regarding any other Tableau Server topics, be sure to visit the online help site at `https://www.tableau.com/support/help`.

This chapter will explore the following topics:

- Publishing a data source to Tableau Server
- Web authoring
- Maintaining workbooks on Tableau Server
- More Tableau Server settings and features

Tableau Server is a fantastic way to take your company's Tableau adoption to the next level. The most important question on your mind is probably, how can you bring your Tableau dashboards from Desktop to Server? That is exactly what we are going to show you in the first section.

Publishing a data source to Tableau Server

So, you purchased Tableau Desktop, became a pro dashboard developer, and now you want to share your work with your colleagues. Do they all need a Tableau Desktop license and installation to see your visualizations? Luckily, the answer is: NO! The best way to share Tableau dashboards is on Tableau Server. This way, your colleagues only need a Tableau Server viewing license, which is much cheaper than the developer license, and they can fully interact with the dashboard you built and uploaded to Server. A detailed description of the different roles in Tableau Server license models can be found here: `https://help.tableau.com/current/server/en-us/license_manage.htm`.

This chapter assumes the reader has access to Tableau Server with sufficient privileges to publish data sources and edit in the web authoring environment. If you do not have access to Tableau Server but would like to work through the exercises in this chapter, consider downloading the trial version, which, as of the time of writing, provides full functionality for two weeks.

But how do you upload your dashboard from Desktop to Server? Let us look at the following steps to see how we can publish a data source to Tableau Server:

1. Navigate to `https://public.tableau.com/profile/marleen.meier` to locate and download the workbook associated with this chapter.

2. Navigate to the `Publish` worksheet.

3. Make sure the data source is `My Superstore`.

4. If you have not already done so, log in to your instance of **Tableau Server** by clicking on **Server | Sign In...**:

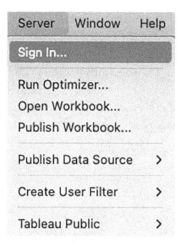

Figure 14.1: Server—Sign In…

5. In the **Data** pane, select the `My Superstore` data source.

6. Select **Server** | **Publish Data Source** | **My Superstore**:

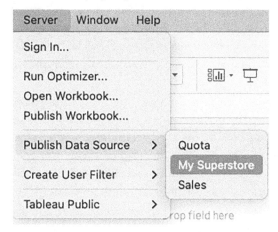

Figure 14.2: Server—Publish Data Source

7. In the resulting dialog box, input your desired settings.

If you have different projects on your Tableau Server, you can choose which project to publish the data source to. You can also change the name if you like or add a description, which comes in handy, especially if you have lots of different data sources and you want to allow your users to look for the one they need. By adding tags, you will add a metadata layer that will allow your Tableau Server users to search for a given data source based on tags. You can also change the permissions. Your setup might be that different users are in different groups, so here you can select which group is allowed which permissions. And lastly, you can immediately upload the workbook with the data source such that both are available on Tableau Server.

Tableau file types

We will continue our discussion of Tableau Server by considering the various Tableau file types. This may seem a surprising place to continue but as you read, you will discover that a clear understanding of file types provides the Tableau Desktop author with foundational knowledge for efficiently and effectively interacting with Tableau Server.

The file types discussed previously that are relevant for understanding how to interact with Tableau Server are considered in some depth. The file types that are not relevant for understanding Tableau Server are considered only briefly. Some file types (for example, those associated with license activation) are not considered.

Tableau data source

Let us now look at the various data sources available in Tableau. Look at the following Tableau data file:

- **File format type:** XML.
- **What it contains:** Metadata.

- **Why it's useful:** The .tds file is important because it allows the Tableau author to define default formatting and aggregation, calculated fields, data types, field types, and more. Furthermore, the .tds file can be published to Tableau Server and thus accessed by other authors in the environment. This effectively makes a .tds file a playbook, which ensures consistency across the organization. This important feature will be explored more fully in the *Tableau Server architecture* section.

- **How it's generated:** A .tds file can be generated by right-clicking on a data source in the **Data** pane and selecting **Add to Saved Data Sources...**, followed by selecting **Tableau Data Source** in the resulting dialog box. A .tds file can also be generated when publishing to Tableau Server via **Server | Publish Data Source | [data source]**. The *Publishing a data source to Tableau Server* section demonstrates how to publish a .tds file and also a .tdsx file.

- **How to access it:** The .tds file type is usually accessed in one of two places. First, it can be stored in **My Tableau Repository | Datasources**. When stored in this directory, a .tds file will display in the left portion of the **Start** page under the **Saved Data Sources** section. The second place a .tds file is often stored is on Tableau Server. Navigating to **Data | New Data Source** and choosing **Tableau Server** allows the Tableau author to point to the .tds and .tdsx files that have been published to Tableau Server.

Tableau packaged data source

Look at the following Tableau data file details:

- **File format type:** Compressed.
- **What it contains:** Metadata and a data extract.
- **Why it is useful:** The .tdsx file is useful because it can be accessed for both metadata and data. Tableau authors can access a .tdsx file located on Tableau Server as a data source, thus eliminating the need for a workbook to connect directly to an external data source. A published .tdsx file can be placed on a schedule so that it is regularly updated from the underlying data source.

- **How it is generated:** A .tdsx file can be generated by right-clicking on a data source in the **Data** pane and selecting **Add to Saved Data Sources...**, followed by selecting **Tableau Packaged Data Source** in the resulting dialog box. Like the .tds file, the .tdsx file can also be generated when publishing to Tableau Server via **Server | Publish Data Source | [data source]**. See the next exercise section for more details.

- **How to access it:** A .tdsx file is accessed in the same way a .tds file is. First, it can be stored in **My Tableau Repository | Datasources**. When stored in this directory, a .tdsx file will display in the left portion of the **Start Page** under the **Saved Data Sources** section. The second place a .tdsx file is often stored is on Tableau Server. Selecting **Data | New Data Source** and choosing **Tableau Server** allows the Tableau author to point to the .tds and .tdsx files that have been published to a given instance of Tableau Server.

Tableau workbook

Next to data sources, we have Tableau workbooks. Take a look at the following Tableau data file details:

- **File format type:** XML.

- **What it contains:** Metadata and schema. The schema defines the visualizations in the workbook. Note that schema, in this context, refers to the XML that defines the visual components of the workbook, including the visualizations displayed on worksheets as well as the layout of dashboards and stories.

- **Why it is useful:** The .twb file type is the file type most often used by the Tableau author. It is necessary for creating visualizations that point to a live dataset. Thus, real-time solutions will utilize this file type.

- **How it is generated:** A .twb file is created via **File | Save As**, then by selecting the .twb file type in the resulting dialog box.

- **How to access it:** A .twb file can be opened via Tableau Desktop or accessed via a browser that points to an instance of Tableau Server. Since a .twb file is XML, it can be opened, viewed, and updated via a text editor.

Tableau packaged workbook

Look at the following Tableau data file details:

- **File format type:** Compressed.

- **What it contains:** Metadata, schema, and optionally, one or more data extracts.

- **Why it's useful:** The .twbx file type is required for use with Tableau Reader. It can also be effectively used with Tableau Server when accessing data sources to which Tableau Server does not directly connect, such as flat files and Microsoft Excel and Access files. Drawbacks to the .twbx file will be discussed next.

- **How it's generated:** A .twbx file is created via **File | Save As**, then by selecting the .twbx file type in the resulting dialog box.

- **How to access it:** A .twbx file can be opened via Tableau Desktop or accessed via a browser that points to an instance of Tableau Server. Since a .twbx file is a compressed file, it can also be unzipped via a compression utility, such as WinZip or 7-Zip.

Other file types

The remaining file types you should be familiar with are not particularly relevant to Tableau Server and will thus only be briefly discussed here. There might be some issues with the compatibility of Tableau Desktop extracts and Tableau Server versions. A full list of compatibility scenarios can be found at https://help.tableau.com/current/desktopdeploy/en-us/desktop_deploy_compatibility.htm.

Let's take a look at the following other file types:

- **Tableau Data Extract:** The .hyper file can be generated via the following: if a .twb file is opened in Tableau Desktop, a .hyper file can be created by right-clicking on a data source in the **Data** pane and selecting **Extract Data**. After selecting the desired options, Tableau will provide a dialog box for the author to save the file in a given location. The extract file can be used to create a local snapshot of a data source for a quicker authoring experience. That same local snapshot is also portable and can thus be used offline.

- **Tableau Bookmark:** The .tbm file can be generated via **Window | Bookmark | Create Bookmark.** It can be useful for duplicating worksheets across multiple workbooks and also for sharing formatting across multiple workbooks.

- **Tableau Map Source:** In *Chapter 9, Working with Maps,* we discussed the use of Mapbox and WMS; if you would save these dashboards, you could do so in .tms format.

- **Tableau Preferences Source:** The .tps file can be used to create custom color palettes. This can be helpful when an organization wishes to use its color scheme within Tableau workbooks. The .tps file that Tableau utilizes is called Preferences.tps and is located in the My Tableau Repository. Since it's an XML format, it can be altered via a text editor. Matt Francis has posted a helpful blog at https://wannabedatarockstar.blogspot.com/ that clearly communicates how to adjust this file. You can also reference the Tableau help page.

Now that we've discussed the different file types, let's talk about web authoring.

Web authoring

After you have published a dashboard to Tableau Server, how do you go about editing it? Well, Tableau offers two options. In the first option, both you and everyone else who has access and the rights to download the dashboard can download it, edit it in Tableau Desktop, and overwrite the latest version on Tableau Server with a new upload. The other option is to edit the dashboard live on Server. This feature is called **web authoring**. Web authoring is a Tableau Server feature that provides an interface for authoring that is similar to Tableau Desktop. Originally, the web authoring interface was limited, but more features are introduced with each version. Thus, the capability gap between the Tableau Server web authoring environment and Tableau Desktop has shrunk. The web authoring environment provides robust capabilities for creating and applying table calculations and provides capabilities for creating dashboards.

As of the time of writing, some features are still missing altogether in the Tableau Server web authoring environment, but the following link will give you an overview of what is out there, comparing Tableau Desktop and Tableau Server web authoring functionality: https://help.tableau.com/current/pro/desktop/en-us/server_desktop_web_edit_differences.htm.

Next, two very brief exercises will demonstrate how to access the authoring environment within Tableau Server. Keep in mind that the Tableau Server admin needs to grant the respective rights to users to do so.

Editing an existing workbook with web authoring

Let's perform the following steps to edit an existing workbook on Tableau Server:

1. Log in to an instance of Tableau Server.
2. Select the My Superstore data source that we uploaded in the *Publishing a data source to Tableau Server* section.

3. Select **New, Workbook** to create a workbook based on the published data source:

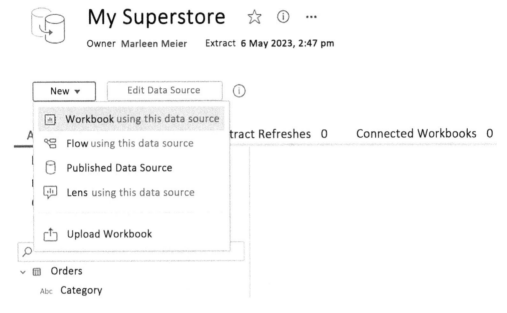

Figure 14.3: Published data source

4. Drag **Category** on to **Columns** and **Profit** on to **Rows**.

5. Now click on **File | Publish As...** and in the popup, choose a name for the workbook (I called mine Test), and hit **Publish**:

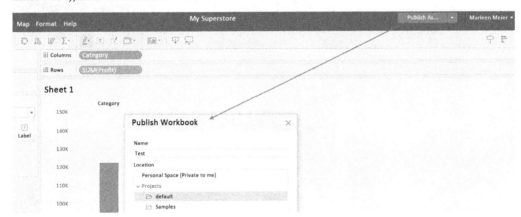

Figure 14.4: Publish Workbook

6.   If you go back now to the default folder of Tableau Server, you will see an additional workbook called **Test**, next to the **My Superstore** published data source:

Figure 14.5: Workbook view

7.   If you want to continue editing the Test workbook, simply open it on Tableau Server and select the **Edit** button:

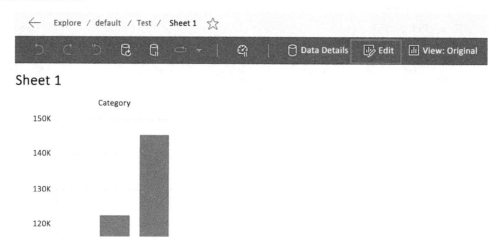

Figure 14.6: Web authoring

This is as easy as it gets.

So far, we have published a dataset, built a workbook from that dataset on Tableau Server, and perhaps you even edited the workbook. If not yet, no worries, we will do so in the next exercise.

Understanding the Tableau Server web authoring environment

Let's perform the following steps to understand the Tableau Server web authoring environment:

1. Access the workbook associated with this chapter and note the Sales & Quota worksheet:

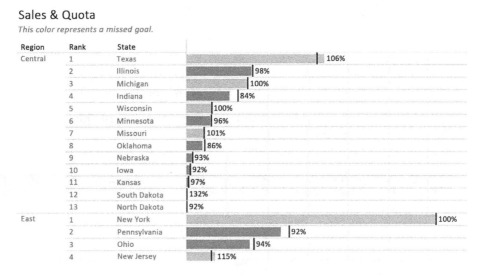

Figure 14.7: Web authoring II

2. Publish the worksheet to an instance of Tableau Server by clicking on **Server | Publish Workbook**. In the window that appears, rename the workbook to Sales & Quota and make sure that only the **Sales & Quota** worksheet will be uploaded:

Figure 14.8: Publish Workbook

3. The following popup will appear:

Figure 14.9: Publish Workbook II

4. Open the worksheet on Tableau Server by clicking on the **Sales & Quota** published view, and click on **Edit** to access web authoring:

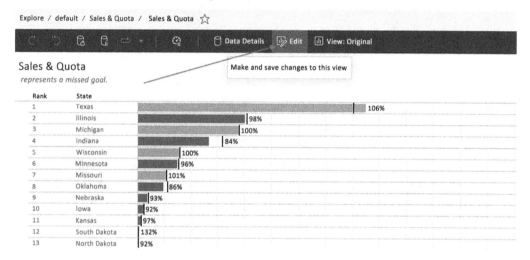

Figure 14.10: Accessing web authoring

5. From here, you should see an interface similar to the one you are used to from Tableau Desktop. This is what web authoring is all about—you have most of the Tableau Desktop functionality online and you don't even need to open Tableau Desktop as long as your workbook has been published to Tableau Server. Let's try it!

6. The first thing you might notice is that even though we didn't publish the Cover or Publish sheet, it is visible in the web authoring view. You can right-click on either one to make this worksheet accessible for Tableau Server users that don't have access to web authoring by selecting **Publish**:

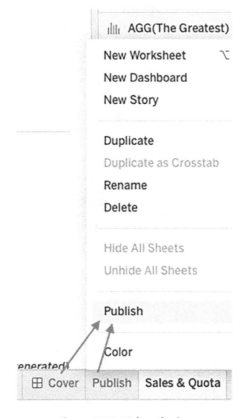

Figure 14.11: Web authoring

7. Next, on the Sales & Quota tab, press the *Ctrl* (Windows) or *Command* (macOS) button on your keyboard and, while doing so, drag the **Quota Met?** field to the **Rows** shelf:

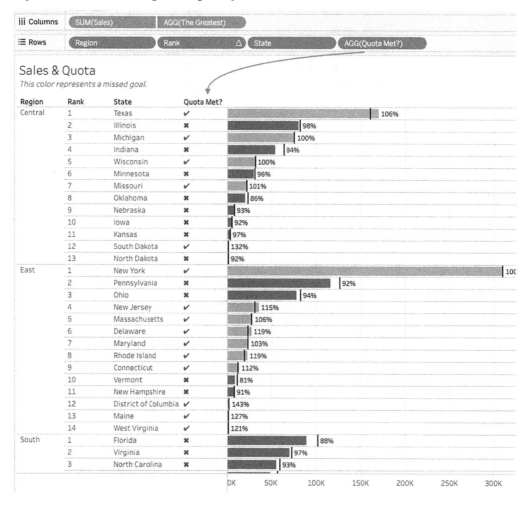

Figure 14.12: Web authoring II

8. You will see that crosses and checkmarks appear in the view. This shows us that we can not only use a color to indicate whether we met a quota but also a mark in the view with this simple calculated field: IF SUM([Sales]) >= [Quota] THEN "✓" ELSE "✗" END. Feel free to try out the other operations you are used to handling with ease in Tableau Desktop, including the following:

- Creating a calculated field
- Adding a filter
- Adjusting the tooltip
- Creating a new worksheet
- Creating a dashboard

After you are done with editing, try clicking on the cross in the upper-right corner. You will see that your changes aren't visible in the dashboard. Click **Edit** again to go back to web authoring mode and tada! **Quota Met?** is still visible on the **Rows** shelf. Depending on your Server settings, Tableau does auto-save but you have to use the **Publish** button to make changes visible on Server for your viewers.

Maintaining workbooks on Tableau Server

We have talked about the dashboard editing options and auto-save, but we have not yet discussed how we can keep track of changes and make sure that we don't lose important information in the process of producing new information. This section will provide help on how to maintain workbooks on Tableau Server, starting with revision history.

Revision history

You, as a Tableau dashboard developer or even a Tableau Server admin, want to make sure that your users are always looking at the right data. But then this happens: you edit a dashboard and after your edit, the dashboard displays faulty information. A user calls you and wants the old dashboard back immediately. What do you do? Use revision history!

Tableau Server ships with a revision history that ensures that the past 25 versions of each workbook and data source are retrievable. This setting can be enabled or disabled by the Tableau Server admin. In Tableau Desktop, if you attempt to upload a workbook or data source with the same name as a previously uploaded file, Tableau Desktop will display a warning such as **Workbook name is already in use**:

Figure 14.13: Overwriting data source

Publishing will overwrite the existing data source. If you proceed with the upload, revision control will be activated, and the previous version of the file will remain accessible as a revision. To access the revision history for individual workbooks and data sources in Tableau Server, simply select any data source or workbook you uploaded and click on the three dots at the bottom right. In the popup, select **Revision History...**:

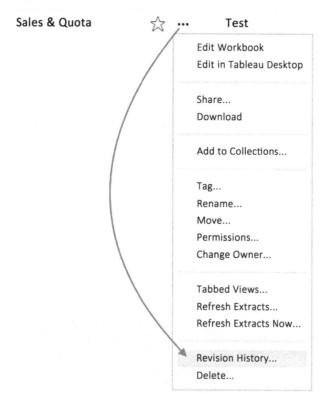

Figure 14.14: Revision History...

This will open a dialog box where you can choose which previous version to restore:

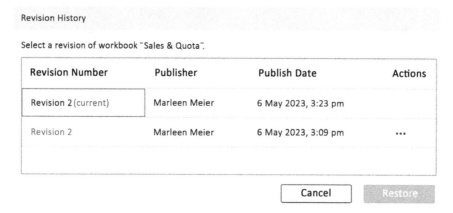

Figure 14.15: Revision History II

Revision histories are so helpful! I hope you will not have to use them often but it's always good to have options. The next question many organizations have is, how can I make sure that users only see what they are supposed to see and not just everything that has been published to Tableau Server? One solution is user filters. We will discuss this topic next!

User filters

Students often ask me something along the lines of the following question: I have sales managers over various territories. It's important that the sales managers see only their metrics; that is, not the metrics of the other sales managers. In order to accomplish this, do I have to create separate workbooks for each sales manager?

Fortunately, the answer is no. Tableau provides user filters that allow the Tableau author to make sure that each of those sales managers sees only the information for which they have clearance. To demonstrate this, take the following steps:

1. This exercise needs more than one user on Tableau Server. Therefore, go ahead and create at least one additional user on Tableau Server by clicking on **Users** | **Add Users**. I used a second email address that I own to do so:

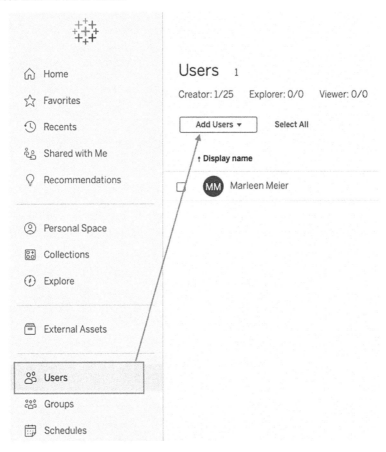

Figure 14.16: Add Users

2. As an optional step, you can change an account's display name. To change the display name of an account, log in to `https://www.tableau.com/`, click on **User | Edit Account**, and make the desired changes to the first and last name entries.

3. As a second optional step, instead of assigning single users to a filter, you can also assign groups of users. To do so, you can create different groups, as follows:

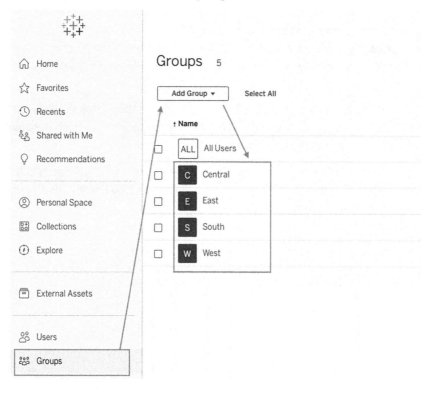

Figure 14.17: Add Group

4. You can then split the users on your Tableau Server instance into **Central**, **East**, **South**, and **West** regions by selecting a user and then **Group Membership...** under **Actions**:

Figure 14.18: Add Group II

5. Now, access the workbook associated with this chapter and navigate to the View Level User Filter worksheet. Note that the view is a field map of the USA with **State** on the **Detail** shelf, **Region** on the **Color** shelf, and **Sales** on the **Label** shelf.

6. Log in to an instance of Tableau Server via **Server | Sign In from Tableau Desktop**.

7. Select **Server | Create User Filter | Region...** (only accessible from Tableau Desktop):

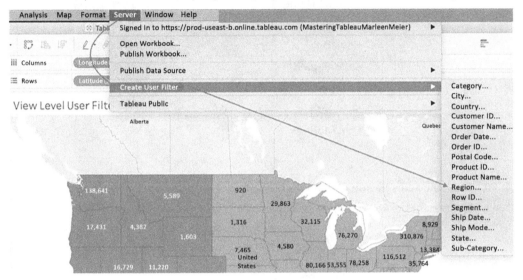

Figure 14.19: Create User Filter

8. In the resulting **User Filter** dialog box, you can now assign either a single user or a group to a region. Name the user filter Sales Region and click on **OK**:

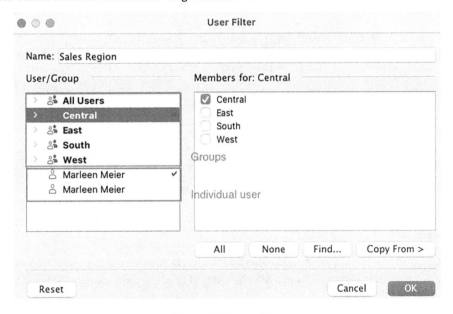

Figure 14.20: User Filter

9.   Note that **Sales Region** is now actually added to the **Sets** portion of the **Data** pane:

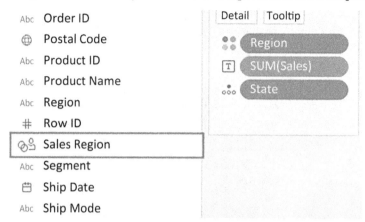

Figure 14.21: Set added

10.   Place the **Sales Region** on the **Filters** shelf.

11.   In the right portion of the status bar, click on the dropdown to access the user filter:

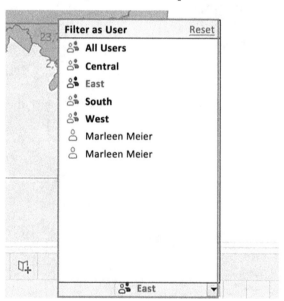

Figure 14.22: Switching between filters

12.   Choose a different group or user and note that the results displayed change depending on the settings from *Figure 14.20*.

Once the workbook is published to Tableau Server, users who access the workbook will only see the information the filter allows. This can also be applied to saved data sources at the data source level.

One important thing to note is, as opposed to simply adding a dimension filter to the **Filters** shelf, you might want to consider adding the **Sales Region** to the **Data Source** filter. This is important because any user with web authoring permission can simply remove a filter from the **Filters** shelf. In the case of this exercise, the user would then be able to see metrics for every region. Data source filters, however, cannot be removed via the web authoring environment and are thus more secure. Furthermore, a data source filter is workbook-wide, which further secures the data. However, if you don't have web authoring enabled, the **Filters** shelf serves its purpose.

> For more details on filters and Tableau's order of operation, please check *Chapter 13, Improving Performance*.

More Tableau Server settings and features

Once a dashboard has been published, users can set alerts, certify data sources, subscribe, add comments to a dashboard, and more, depending on their permissions. This section will address the different functionalities in two different places: on a worksheet and on a view. Next to those, Tableau Server has many more functionalities, especially settings for site admins, which are—unfortunately—out of the scope of this book.

Features on the worksheet level

By *features on the worksheet level*, I mean the settings that are available to you after selecting a project and a certain worksheet like so:

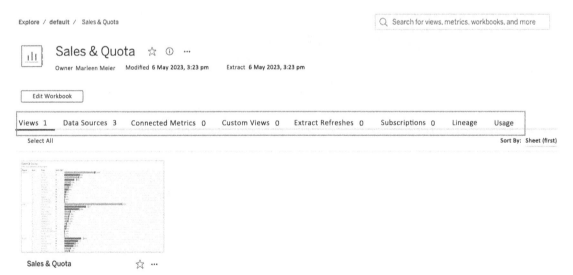

Figure 14.23: Tableau Server

On this level, we see eight different tabs, which we will discuss over the next few pages.

Views: Views show a thumbnail of all the worksheets or dashboards that have been published within one workbook. When uploading a workbook to Tableau Server, you can select all the views that should show here:

Sheet Name	Title
☐ Cover	⊞
☑ Sales & Quota	Sales & Quota This color …
☐ Sales & Quota Web Authored	Sales & Quota Web Authored …
☐ View Level User Filter	View Level User Filter

Only Dashboards		None	All

☑ Show selections
☐ Include external files

⟋⟋ **Workbook Optimizer**   Publish

Figure 14.24: Publish Workbook

By clicking on the three dots next to a View, more options will show, as can be seen in the following screenshot:

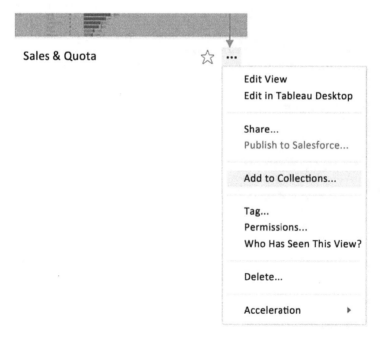

Sales & Quota   ☆ •••

Edit View
Edit in Tableau Desktop

Share…
Publish to Salesforce…

Add to Collections…

Tag…
Permissions…
Who Has Seen This View?

Delete…

Acceleration   ▶

Figure 14.25: Options

The different options are self-explanatory: you can edit the view (also referred to as web authoring, which we've discussed earlier in the chapter), and you can share the view with other users, where Tableau will send an email with an image and a hyperlink to the user you shared the view with. You can also add tags that will help other users find the view, you can check which user or group has permission to open the view and who has seen this view, and lastly, you can delete it. Which of those options will display is a matter of the configuration in Tableau Server, so your admin can enable or disable the different features to show or else they might be grayed out.

Data Sources: The next tab is **Data Sources**. It will give you an overview of the data sources used to create this workbook:

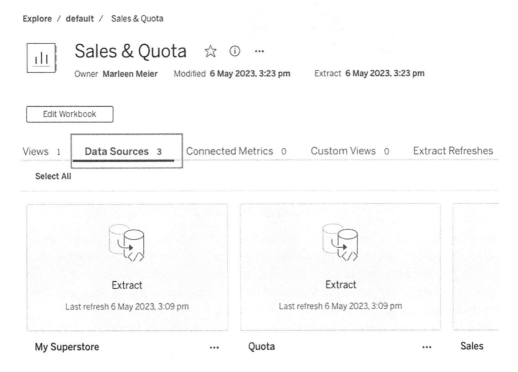

Figure 14.26: Data Sources

You will be able to see which type of data sources were used; for example, with an extract of live connections, by clicking on the three dots by each source, you will again be able to see more settings, depending on the settings of your Tableau Server:

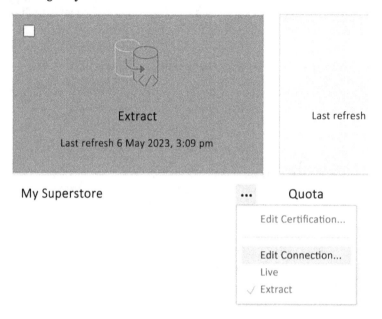

Figure 14.27: Data Sources II

Connected Metrics: Next in line are the connected metrics. This is a relatively new feature. To see metrics, you first have to set them up in a view. We will get to this in the second part of this section, but basically, it allows you to select pieces of different dashboards and views and combine those data points as metrics to monitor your data. Metrics make use of a specific data mark in your view. Therefore, you might need to adjust your view to show the one mark you want to use.

For example, if you have a dashboard with daily profits over the past year but your metrics should show only the last profit data point, you will have to create a new view in order to use the explicit last profit in a metric, even though the data is already part of the initial view. However, a big advantage is that you don't need to connect to different data sources, as the connections that are already set up in the different workbooks will be leveraged.

More details regarding metrics can be found here: `https://www.tableau.com/about/blog/2020/5/introducing-metrics-headlines-your-data`.

Extract Refreshes: When using extracts as the data source, you can define a refresh schedule while uploading the workbook to Tableau Server or even after you published the workbook. The different schedules can be set by your server admin. If you set the extract refresh to run at 7 AM every day, for example, Tableau Server will access the data source, perhaps a SQL database, at 7 AM, and load the data, and you will in return see the latest data in your Tableau dashboard. Using extracts tends to perform better than a live connection, depending on the amount of data and the type of data source, but be aware that the data in the dashboard will always be as old as your latest extract.

Subscriptions: Subscriptions can be set on a view level; we will get to this in the next section. But on a workbook level, you will be able to see all subscriptions that are active for a certain workbook.

Lineage: Lineage is another rather new feature on Tableau Server. It is only available through the Data Management add-on, at additional cost, and will show you the dependencies of a data source.

For more information on lineage, please check `https://help.tableau.com/current/server/en-us/dm_lineage.htm`.

Usage: The **Usage** tab gives you insights into how many people viewed your dashboard and how many other users added your dashboard as a favorite.

 The usage data can be accessed from the Tableau database too and hence can be used for further analytics.

Lastly, please note the three dots on a workbook page, which contain more options as well as options we have seen before:

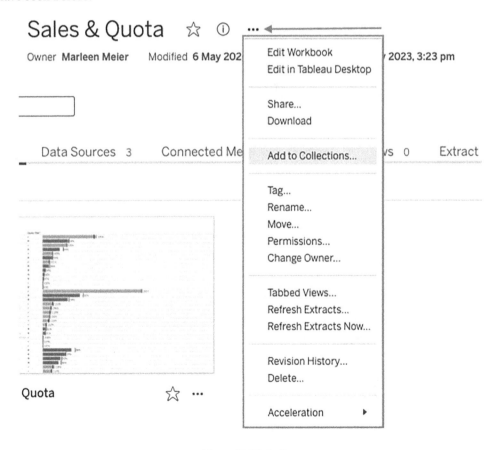

Figure 14.28: Options

Again, which ones you will be able to use depends on the permissions the Tableau Server admins gave you.

The available options look a little bit different when the selection is based on a published data source, like the My Superstore data source that we published to Tableau Server at the beginning of this chapter:

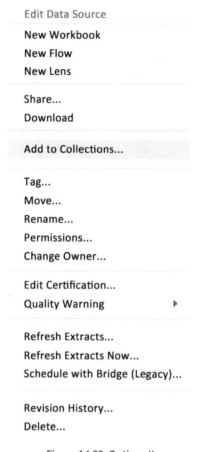

Figure 14.29: Options II

Most of the items are self-explanatory, but I want to point out **Quality Warning**, which is available at an additional cost within the Data Management add-on. This feature will allow you to alert every user of the data or any workbook based on the data to be extra careful when using it.

Depending on the settings, Tableau Server will show warnings of various types, such as **Deprecated**, **Stale data**, **Under maintenance**, and **Sensitive data**, which are selectable from a dropdown.

You can also decide whether you want to show the type on the data source only or also on the related workbooks. The following is an example of on the data source only:

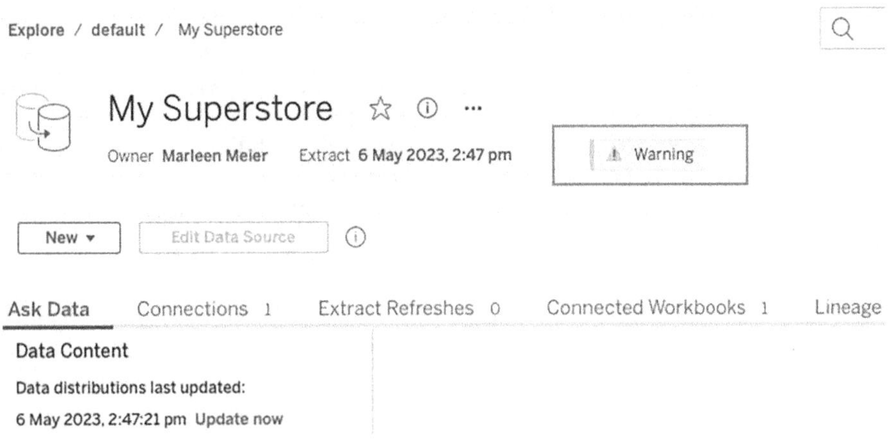

Figure 14.30: Data quality warning

And here is an example of how the warning looks on the workbook level:

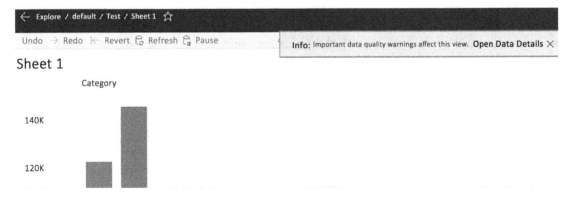

Figure 14.31: Data quality warning II

And even when opening the view:

Figure 14.32: Data quality warning III

This is a very powerful feature and shows how Tableau matures more and more with each release. Data quality is the focal point for many data strategies and the base of all analytics. Tableau Server is adapted to it and provides you with features that will grow along with your data strategy and quality measures.

Ask Data: The last item before we continue with the view level is **Ask Data**, which is only available for Tableau Server. To access **Ask Data**, select a published data source and click on the first tab. Now the fun part starts, where Tableau Server will help you build visualizations based on **Natural Language Processing (NLP)**:

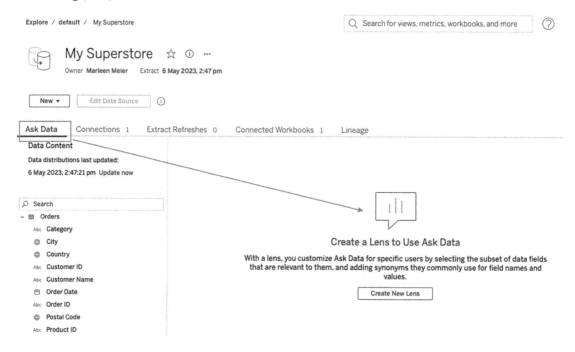

Figure 14.33: Ask Data

On the left-hand side, you see all available fields, and in the middle, you can create a so-called **lens**. A lens can be user- or group-specific and serves the purpose of making it easier for users to ask the right questions and hence retrieve the right information using NLP on a data source. It is thus a more structured and governed approach of NLP. You will even see more tips popping up:

Optimize for Ask Data

Customize this lens to give your users the best Ask Data experience.

- **Hide unnecessary fields**
  Click the pencil icon at the top of the Fields panel.

- **Add synonyms for field names and values**
  Hover over individual fields and click the pencil icon.

- **Customize the Recommended Visualizations list**
  To link to a visualization, while viewing it, click the pin icon in the toolbar.

Figure 14.34: Ask Data II

But back to creating a lens. First, select the fields you want to make available to your users:

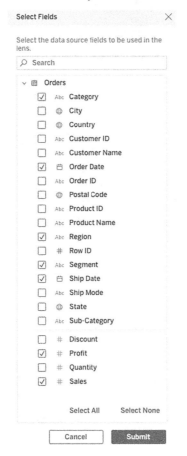

Figure 14.35: Select Fields

Submit your setting and see how the **Data** pane on the right has changed – it is much more limited now:

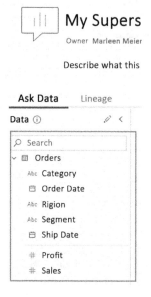

Figure 14.36: Data

And now, your users can start asking for information like:

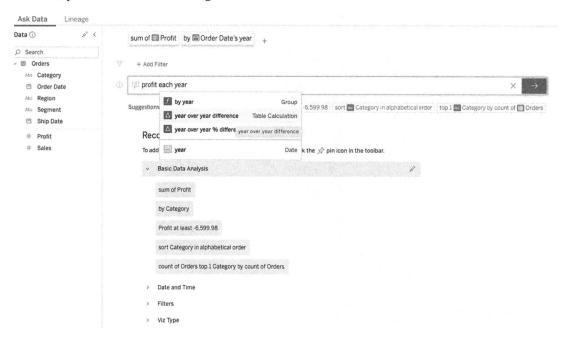

Figure 14.37 Ask Data III

You can see that I typed profit each year and Tableau proposed four different options to choose from. I select the third one and hit the arrow button. See what happens now:

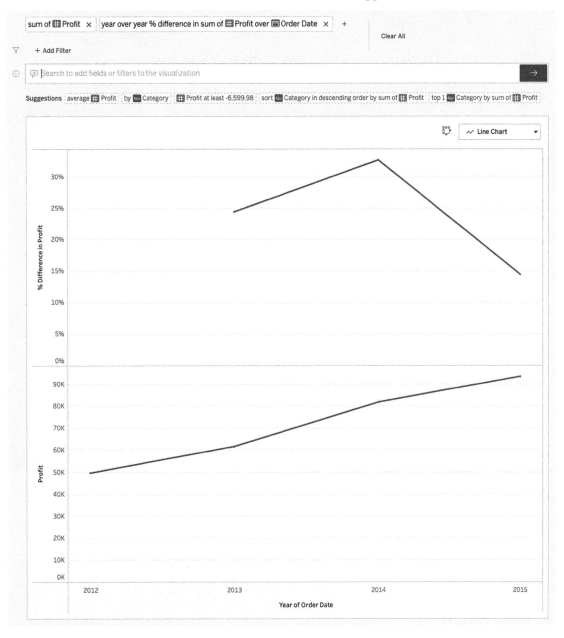

Figure 14.38: Ask Data graph

Tableau Server created a view. You can also add synonyms for each entry in your dataset and try out one of the many suggestions that Tableau has for you.

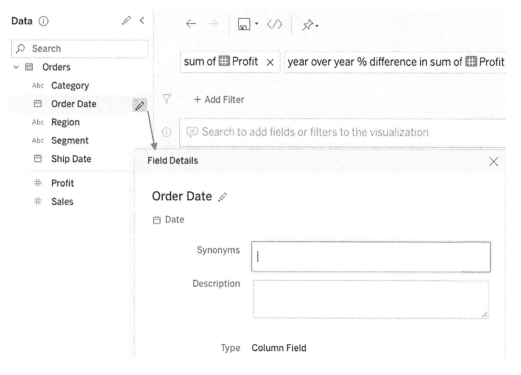

Figure 14.39: Field Details

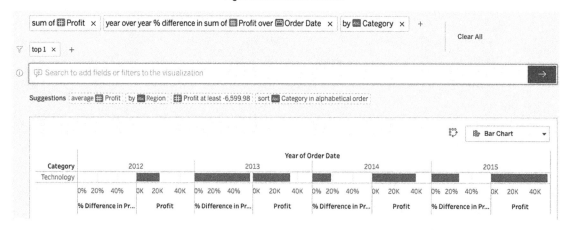

Figure 14.40: Ask Data plot

How cool is **Ask Data**? In my opinion, this feature is especially powerful because, even though Tableau is very intuitive, many people are not as data-savvy as you are. Providing a high-quality dataset and publishing it to Tableau Server will allow even more people to become data-driven and perform a quick analysis themselves. This will help you to focus on more complex dashboards, while ad hoc questions can be answered using this feature.

Tableau ships with more self-service insight features; check *Chapter 13, Improving Performance*, for more details.

Features on the view level

We have covered all settings on the workbook level, so now we will take a closer look at a lower level, the view. The view looks something like this, and the settings in the red frame are of interest for this section:

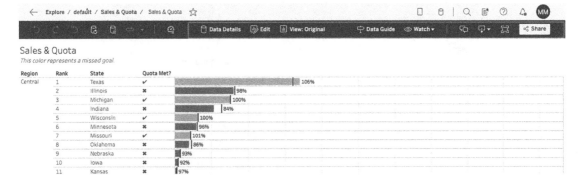

Figure 14.41: View-level features

Data Details: The **Data Details** tab will show more details regarding the data source used in the view. This feature is available at an additional cost within the Data Management add-on. The popup that will appear on the right side has three different sections: **Views of this sheet, Data Sources,** and **Fields in Use:**

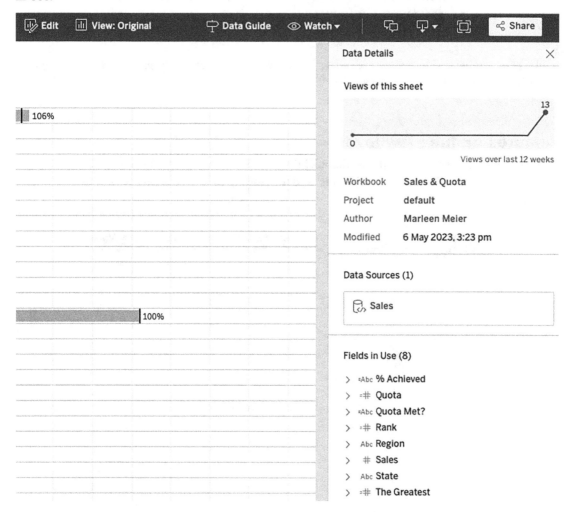

Figure 14.42: Data details

In the last section, you will have the option to open each field individually. If it is a calculated field, the calculation will show, while if it is a field from the original data source, the data type and description will be visible (if a description has been added):

Figure 14.43: Data details II

Edit: You know this one already. **Edit** allows you to enter the web authoring environment on Tableau Server.

View: The **View** tab allows you to add a view other than the default and save it. The next time you open the dashboard, you can select the view you created by clicking on this tab and the saved settings will be applied all at once. Your view may contain, for example, a specific filter selection, a different parameter selection than the default view, and maybe a set that is most important to you. Instead of having to change filters, parameters, and sets every time you open the view, you can use the **View** tab:

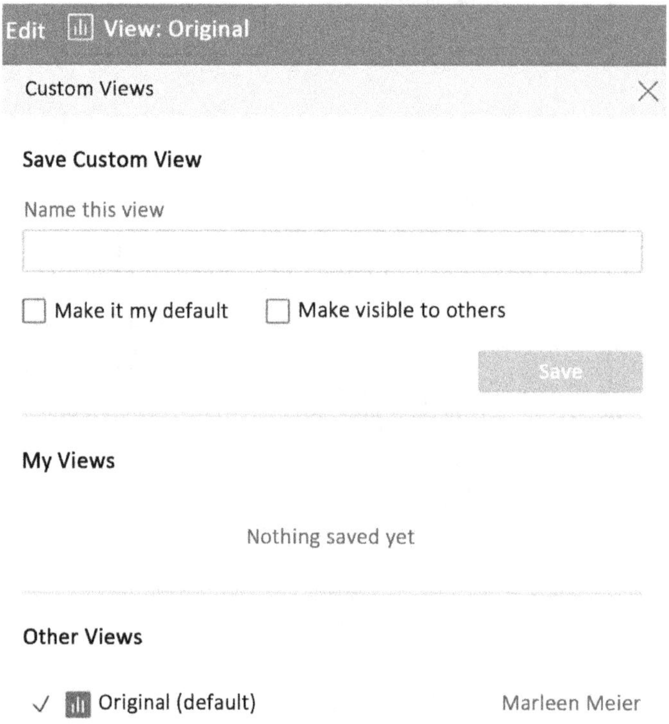

Edit   📊 **View: Original**

Custom Views   ✕

Save Custom View

Name this view

[   ]

☐ Make it my default   ☐ Make visible to others

                                                        Save

My Views

Nothing saved yet

Other Views

✓ 📊 Original (default)   Marleen Meier

Figure 14.44: Custom views

Data Guide is a summary of the data in the dashboard. Self-explanatory, isn't it?!

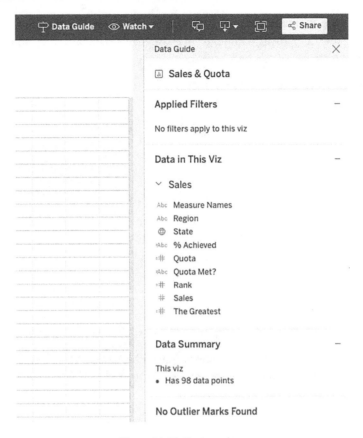

Figure 14.45: Custom views

Watch contains **Subscriptions, Metrics,** and **Alerts:**

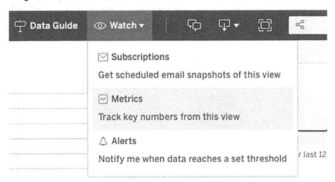

Figure 14.46: Custom views

Alerts: As of the time of writing, an alert can be set on a continuous numerical axis only. However, there are ideas being discussed on the Tableau forum that will increase the flexibility of setting alerts.

In the Tableau Ideas forum, users can write down what ideas they have for future releases and the community can vote for them. Ideas with high votes are likely to be picked up soon. You can find the forum here: https://community.tableau.com/community/ideas.

Click on the **Alerts** button and text on the right side will show:

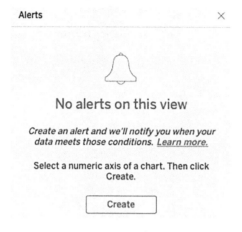

Figure 14.47: Alerts

After selecting a numeric axis (like **Sales**), a new popup will appear in which a condition and a threshold can be entered. Also, the frequency of the threshold check can be specified:

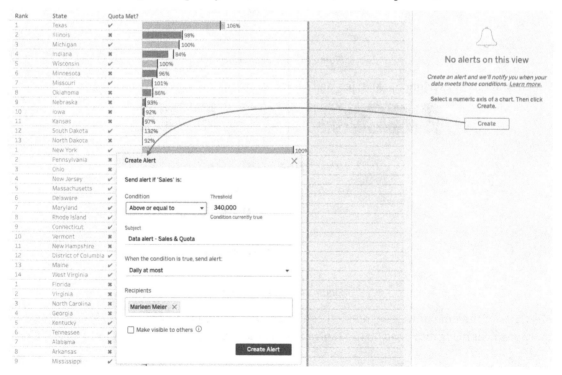

Figure 14.48: Alerts II

If an alert is set, all users and groups specified in that alert will receive an email once the threshold has been breached. The email will contain a static image and a link to the interactive version on Tableau Server.

Metrics: As mentioned before, this is a relatively new feature. In order to create a metric, select a mark in any view and click on the **Metrics** tab. The following screen opens on the right side of the view:

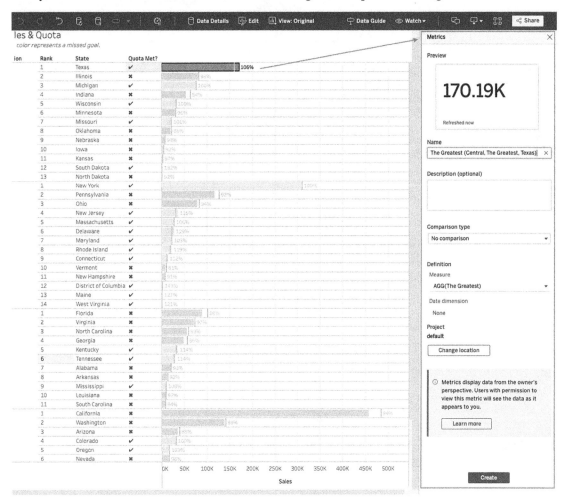

Figure 14.49: Metrics

The **Metrics** feature is very well integrated with Tableau Mobile and hence can be used to show key performance indicators to anyone, wherever they are. After clicking **Create**, the metric view can be accessed from the project it has been saved to.

Subscribe: Subscriptions are meant to be used for frequent-email updates. They work in a similar way to alerts; people or groups can be subscribed and will receive an email with an overview of the relevant dashboard at a set time. The scheduling can be predefined by the administrator: for example, every morning at 7 AM.

Share: By clicking on **Share**, a popup opens that allows you to share the URL to the view with anyone that is known to Tableau Server. That person will receive an email with the link. Make sure that that user has access to the project or else they will fail to open the view:

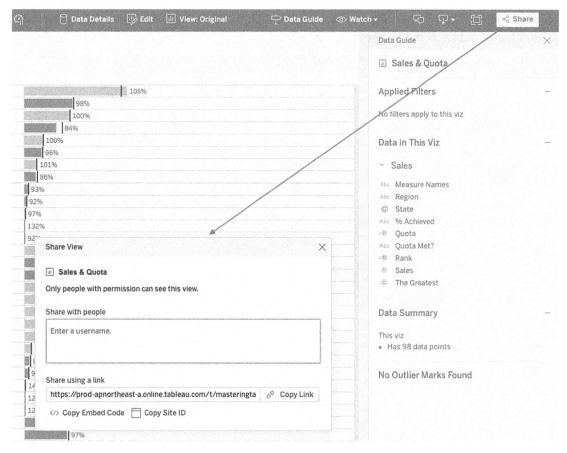

Figure 14.50: Share view

Download: Tableau Server also offers a download functionality. Depending on the configuration done by your admin, you can select between different formats for downloading purposes:

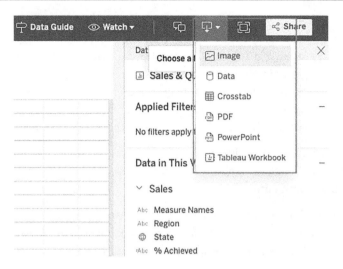

Figure 14.51: Download

Comments: Last but not least, you can comment on views—original or edited, both are possible. To do so, click on the **Comments** button in the upper-right corner:

Figure 14.52: Comments

You can mention a colleague in the comment with @colleaguesname, and they will receive an email with your comment in it. It is also possible to add screenshots to your comment.

Summary

We began this chapter by looking at Tableau Server settings, we learned that revision history features can provide a safety net against inadvertently overwriting files. We explored a section on the Tableau Server web authoring environment, which compared that environment with Tableau Desktop. This section's main purpose was to establish a knowledge base for determining which personnel should have Tableau Desktop licenses and for whom the web authoring capabilities of Tableau Server should suffice.

Then we discussed user filters. User filters enable the Tableau author to ensure that users are only able to access data for which they have clearance. And finally, we looked at some handy features, such as alerts, subscriptions, commenting, and others.

In the next chapter, we will branch out from the Tableau world and will consider how to integrate it with R and Python. Knowledge of programming integration will help the Tableau author accomplish analytics tasks beyond Tableau's capabilities, while still using Tableau to visualize the results.

Learn more on Discord

To join the Discord community for this book – where you can share feedback, ask questions to the author, and learn about new releases – follow the QR code below:

`https://packt.link/tableau`

15

Integrating Programming Languages

After 14 chapters full of Tableau functionality and exercises, what are we still missing? Correct, the one feature that opens a whole new universe of opportunities: programming integration! If you need a function that isn't covered natively by Tableau's calculated fields and you know how to code it, you can fall back on programming integrations. To be precise, two languages are supported: R and Python.

Imagine the following scenario: you deal with a financial dataset and want to add an options pricing formula to your Tableau dashboard. You look up the formula and see that you have all the required variables, like strike price, stock price, and volatility, but you also need a probability density function, which you can't find in Tableau. In this case, you can fall back to the programming integration and run the calculation in R or Python and send back the output—great, isn't it? Now imagine a second scenario: you're working on a sentiment analysis project. You could calculate the sentiment in Python outside of Tableau and then use the output as input for your model, but wouldn't it be great if you could have it all in Tableau? Well, you can by using the programming tool integration.

In this chapter, we will cover the following topics:

- Integrating programming languages
- R installation and integration
- Implementing R functionality
- Python installation and integration
- Implementing Python functionality

Integrating programming languages

How does integration empower Tableau? It happens through calculated fields. Tableau dynamically interfaces with Rserve or TabPy to pass values and receive results. And Tableau Prep Builder also has R and Python integration as we saw in *Chapter 3, Using Tableau Prep Builder*! So, let's not waste any time and jump right in.

Basic Tableau-to-R and Tableau-to-Python integration is quite simple: the view shows data based on a calculated field, with the help of which Tableau pushes data to Rserve or TabPy respectively and then retrieves the results via a table calculation:

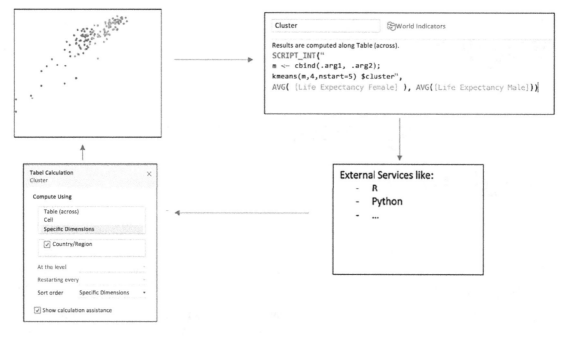

Figure 15.1: Tableau external services

Naturally, whether you are viewing a workbook on Tableau Desktop or via Tableau Server, if you wish to run R and Python calculations, then Rserve or TabPy must be accessible.

For a proper understanding of the integration, let's also look at the Tableau/R workflow as an example. The terms used in the following diagram, which you may be unfamiliar with, will be explained throughout this chapter:

Tableau/R Workflow

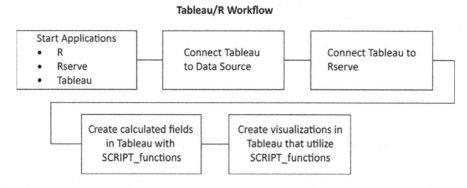

Figure 15.2: Tableau/R workflow

The preceding screenshot can be used likewise for Python. Let's begin with R since it was the first available integration.

R installation and integration

To adequately understand how Tableau and R work together, it's important to grasp the big picture. To facilitate that understanding, we'll cover high-level concepts and information in this section before delving into calculated fields and R scripting details.

Installing R is typically not difficult, but it does involve more than simply double-clicking on an executable. To successfully connect Tableau with R, you will need to make sure that permissions are correctly set and that various components—some required and some that are just nice to have—are correctly implemented. We will cover the basics, review a couple of the typical challenges faced during installation, and provide troubleshooting guidance.

Perform the following steps to install R:

1. Download R by visiting http://www.r-project.org/, click on the **download** R hyperlink, and choose a CRAN mirror. Note that R works best in a Linux or Unix environment; however, to learn R and begin working with Tableau/R functionality to complete the exercises in this chapter, installing the Windows version is adequate.

2. Install R by double-clicking on the downloaded executable.

3. Open R.

Various issues may arise when installing R. For example, you may experience problems due to insufficient permissions for the R working directory. This issue may first become evident when attempting to install R packages. To rectify the problem, determine the working directory in R with the getwd() function. Next, either change the working directory via setwd() or, at the operating system level—whichever you feel more comfortable with—set the appropriate read and execute permissions for the working directory.

Issues can also arise due to security system and port configuration problems. By default, Tableau will connect to Rserve via port 6311. Alternatively, within Tableau, you can specify a different port when connecting to R.

 The documentation at http://www.r-project.org/ provides detailed information regarding overcoming a variety of installation challenges.

Although not required, RStudio Desktop provides a better user interface than the default R GUI that installs with R. RStudio includes a console that features intelligent code completion (that is, IntelliSense), a workspace browser that provides easy access to files, packages, and help, a data viewer, and much more all within a single, unified environment:

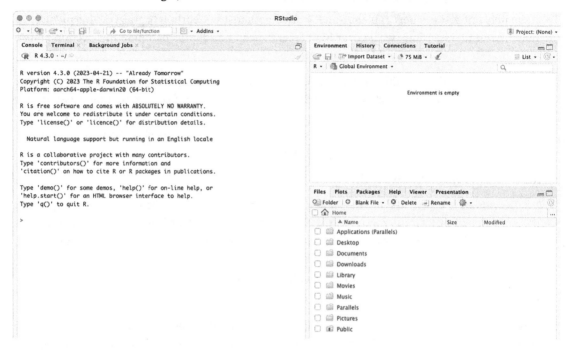

Figure 15.3: RStudio

The open-source edition of RStudio is sufficient for many uses. You can download the application via `https://posit.co/download/rstudio-desktop/`. Just choose for yourself which one you like better out of the Desktop and R GUI versions.

Open R:

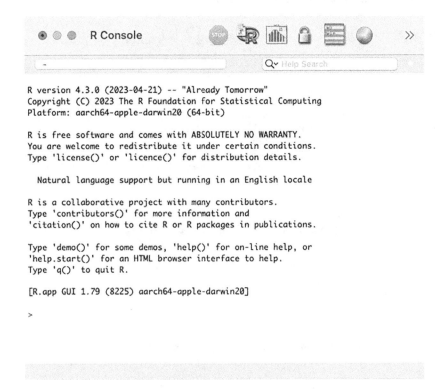

Figure 15.4: R GUI

To establish a connection with Tableau, you will need to start Rserve. Technically, Rserve is a separate package; however, by default, it is installed with R:

- To make sure that the Rserve package is installed, within R, enter the following command:

```
rownames(installed.packages())
```

- Several packages should be listed, including RServe. If for some reason the Rserve package did not install with your instance of R, you can do so via:

```
install.packages("Rserve")
```

- To start Rserve, enter `library(Rserve); Rserve()`.

The semicolon (;) represents a new line of code in R:

Figure 15.5: Rserve initialization

Now that you have successfully installed R and started Rserve, you are ready to connect Tableau to R. Within Tableau, select **Help | Settings and Performance | Manage Analytics Extension Connection...**:

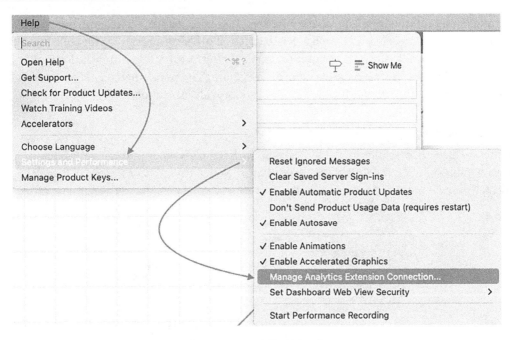

Figure 15.6: Analytics Extension

The **Manage Analytics Extensions Connection** screen will open; select **RServe**. The default settings in the following screenshot will work for most local installations:

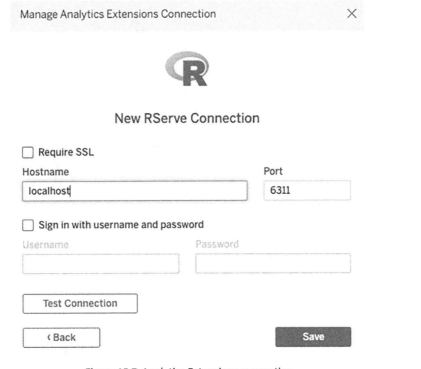

Figure 15.7: Analytics Extensions connection

While integrating Tableau with R doesn't require any interaction with an R interface, you will probably want to try out your R code in a GUI, such as R GUI or RStudio, before embedding the code into Tableau. This will allow you to take advantage of useful accompanying features relevant to the R language, such as help, examples, and sample datasets tailored to R. Note that the calculated field editor in Tableau simply acts as a pass-through for R code and does not provide any support.

Implementing R functionality

Now that we have successfully connected Tableau with R, let's write some code in Tableau to invoke R. Within Tableau, open the **Calculated Field Editor.** Notice the class of functions beginning with SCRIPT_, as shown in the following screenshot:

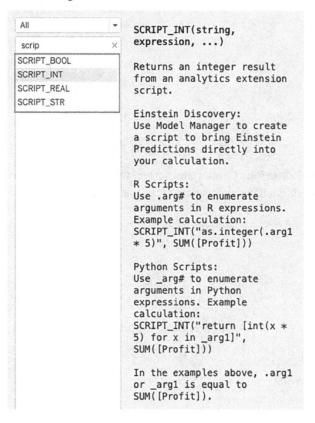

Figure 15.8: SCRIPT_ functions

The SCRIPT_ functions are used by Tableau to invoke R. The function names communicate the data type of the returned results; SCRIPT_REAL returns float values, SCRIPT_BOOL returns true or false values, and so forth.

The syntax of a `SCRIPT_` function is represented in the following diagram:

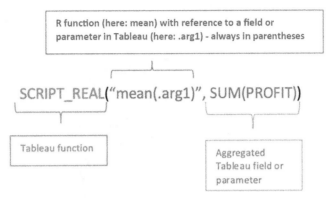

Figure 15.9: R script syntax

The preceding example code calculates the average profit, but we will get to more examples in the next sections. Let's start by reproducing Tableau functionality using the R integration and hence prove that R is working properly.

Reproducing native Tableau functionality in R

For our first exercise, we will use the AVG, MEDIAN, and STDEV functions in Tableau and compare the results with the mean, median, and sd R functions. This will allow you to practice the SCRIPT_ functions, begin to understand R syntax, and compare the results generated by Tableau with those generated by R.

Perform the following steps:

1. Navigate to `https://public.tableau.com/profile/marleen.meier/` to locate and download the workbook associated with this chapter.
2. Navigate to the `median | mean | sd` worksheet.
3. Select the `Superstore` data source.
4. Create the following Tableau-centric calculations:

    *   Tab Avg: `WINDOW_AVG(SUM(Sales))`
    *   Tab Median: `WINDOW_MEDIAN(SUM(Sales))`
    *   Tab Stdev: `WINDOW_STDEV(SUM(Sales))`

5. Place the **Region** dimension on the **Rows** shelf and **Sales** on the **Text** shelf.

6. Double-click on **Tab Avg**, **Tab Median**, and **Tab Stdev**. They will now appear on the **Measures Values** shelf:

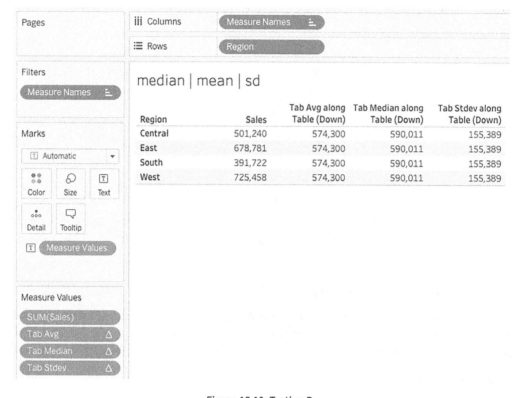

Figure 15.10: Testing R

7. Make sure R is installed, connected, and running as per the instructions in the *R installation and integration* section.

8. If you haven't installed the Rserve package yet, type install.packages("Rserve") into your R interface to install the Rserve package.

9. Next, type library(Rserve); Rserve() into the R interface. You may see the following error:

    ```
    Fatal error: you must specify '--save', '--no-save' or '--vanilla'
    ```

    In this case, type Rserve(args = "--no-save"). R requires you to make a choice of saving, not saving, or a combination (vanilla) after your session ends (not saving is my preferred option but the other two will work too).

10. Connect R to Tableau as demonstrated in the *R installation and integration* section. After you have done so, return to Tableau and click the **Test Connection** button to see if it works:

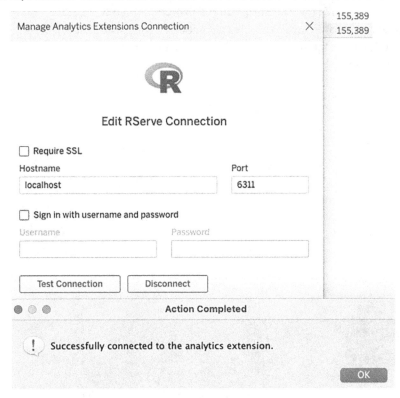

Figure 15.11: Testing R connection

11. Click **OK** to close the windows.

12. Create the following R-centric calculations in Tableau. Note that R functions (such as mean) are case-sensitive:

- R - mean: `SCRIPT_INT("mean(.arg1)", SUM(Sales))`
- R - median: `SCRIPT_REAL ("median(.arg1)", SUM(Sales))`
- R - sd: `SCRIPT_INT("sd(.arg1)", SUM(Sales))`

13. Place each of the R-calculated fields on the **Measure Values** shelf and arrange them so that the same types of calculations are next to each other but alternating Tableau and R-centric; for example, **Tab Avg** then **R – mean** then **Tab Median** then **R – median** and so on. Since `SCRIPT_` functions are categorized as table calculations (more on that later), be sure that each instance of the R-calculated fields as well as the Tableau-calculated fields use **Compute Using** set to **Table (Down)**:

Figure 15.12: Tableau versus R output

14. Observe that the Tableau and R functions show identical results.

Note that `INT` has been replaced with `REAL` in the median calculations, demonstrating that, as the names suggest, `SCRIPT_REAL` uses float values and `SCRIPT_INT` uses integers. In the case of the median, the `SCRIPT_INT` function results in a rounding difference – try it out and see for yourself!

This was our very first exercise with R integration—easy, right? The purpose of this exercise was mainly to show you that the R calculation works and therefore we compared three of the same calculations, each one calculated by Tableau as well as R. Or in other words, replicating Tableau functionality to prove that the R integration works as expected. The next exercise will be something that we can't do with Tableau's built-in functionality (as of the time of writing). We are going to calculate a regression analysis with more than two variables.

Using R for regression calculations

Succinctly stated, regression analysis is a technique for estimating variable relationships. There are several types of regression analyses, the most popular of which is linear regression. As demonstrated in the following screenshot, linear regression estimates a line that best fits the data and is a built-in function in Tableau.

You only need two measures on **Rows** and **Columns** as well as a dimension to partition the points in your view. Then, you go to **Analysis** and drag the **Trend Line** onto your screen and select **Linear**:

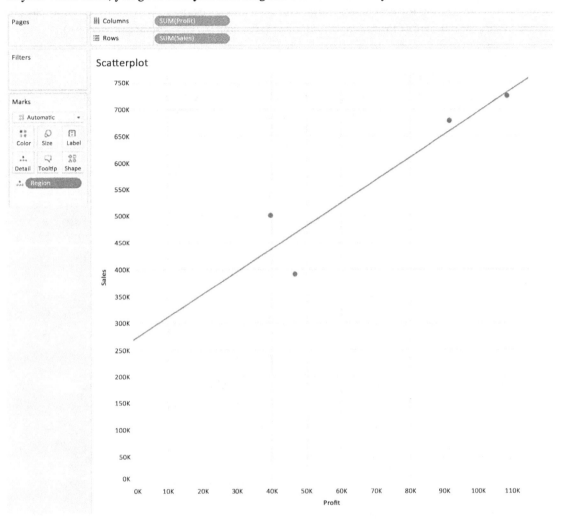

Figure 15.13: Scatterplot

Notice that this screenshot is from Tableau. You can access it by clicking on the **Scatterplot** worksheet in the workbook associated with this chapter. It's a simple scatterplot with trend lines turned on. Trend lines, in Tableau, default to linear but also include logarithmic, exponential, and polynomial options, which are all examples of regression analysis. By accessing **Worksheet** | **Export** | **Data** in a visualization utilizing a trend line, you can generate an **Access** database with predictions and residuals for marks on the view. But this is a tedious process and does not give a robust, dynamic solution for implementing more vigorous uses of linear regression. Using R provides much more flexibility.

Linear regression may use single or multiple variables. Single-variable equations are great for learning, but multiple-variable equations are typically necessary for real-world applications. The following exercise includes multiple-variable equations. Our goal for this exercise is to determine how closely a linear regression model of **Profit** fits COUNT(Quantity), SUM(Sales), and AVG(Discount):

1. Navigate to the Regression worksheet.
2. Select the Superstore data source.
3. Build the basic layout by placing **Profit** on the **Columns** shelf and **State** on the **Rows** shelf and filtering to **Top 10** by **Sum** of **Profit** by placing **State** on the **Filters** shelf as well:

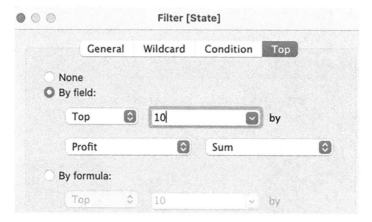

Figure 15.14: Filter top 10

4. Create a calculated field entitled Profit_Expected utilizing the following code:

```
SCRIPT_REAL("
x <- lm(.arg1 ~ .arg2 + .arg3 + .arg4)
x$fitted",
SUM(Profit), COUNT(Quantity), SUM(Sales), AVG(Discount)
)
```

The details of this function will be explained shortly.

5. Create a calculated field entitled % Diff that calculates the percent difference between SUM(Profit) and Profit_Expected:

```
SUM(Profit)/Profit_Expected - 1
```

6. Create a calculated field entitled Profit_Expected (residuals) to return the difference between SUM(Profit) and Profit_Expected in terms of dollars:

```
SCRIPT_REAL("
x <- lm(.arg1 ~ .arg2 + .arg3 + .arg4)
x$residuals",
SUM(Profit),COUNT(Quantity), SUM(Sales), AVG(Discount))
```

7. Place **Profit_Expected** on the **Columns** shelf, next to **Profit**. Then, click on either one and enable **Dual Axis**.

8. Right-click on one axis and select **Synchronize Axis**.

9. In the **SUM(Profit)** section on the **Marks** card, move **% Diff** onto the **Color** shelf. Select the **Red-Black Diverging** palette as well as **2 Steps** in **Stepped Color**. This way, all positive values will be black and all negative ones red. Make sure that **Bar** is selected as the view type.

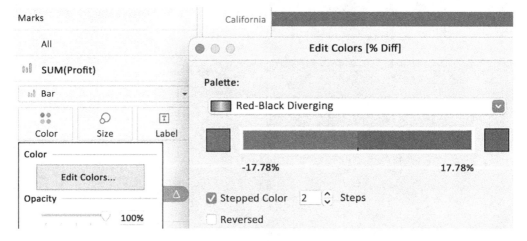

Figure 15.15: Color coding

10. From the menu, select **Analysis | Stack Marks | Off**.

11. In the **Profit_Expected** section on the **Marks** card, move **Profit_Expected (residuals)**, **% Diff**, and **Profit_Expected** to the **Label** shelf. Make sure that **Gantt Bar** is selected as the view type.

12. Double-check that all table calculations (indicated by the triangle sign: **Profit_Expected (residuals)**, **% Diff**, and **Profit_Expected**) are using **State** for the computation:

Figure 15.16: Compute using

13. Click on **Label** and the three dots in the **Text** section and edit the label to your liking:

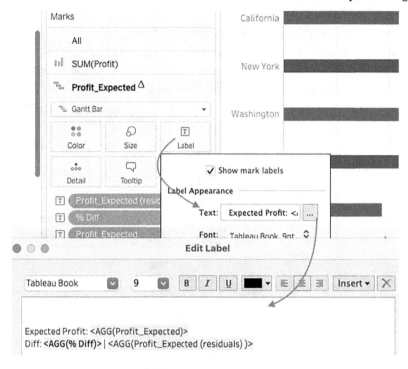

Figure 15.17: Expected profits

Adjust the size of the **Bar** and **Gantt Bar** as desired and observe the results:

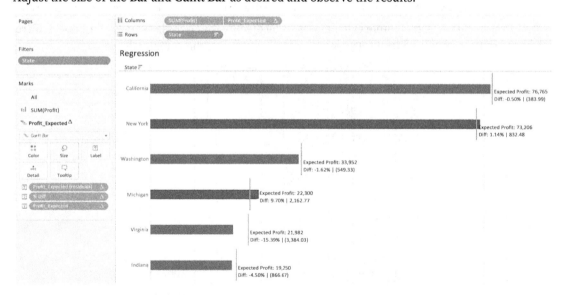

Figure 15.18: Regression

The visualization in *Figure 15.18* shows a comparison of the actual profit, the expected profit, and the difference between the two. This calculation is especially helpful in retail markets but also in financial planning for any company.

Now that we've completed the exercise, let's take a moment to consider some of the code we used in this exercise:

`SCRIPT_REAL`	This Tableau function calls the R engine and returns a float value.

`"x <- lm(.arg1 ~`
`.arg2 +.arg3+.arg4);`
`x$residuals"`
	This is an R expression that houses a variable, a function, and an argument, and then returns predicted values.

`x <-`	This is the variable to be populated by the subsequent R function.
`lm(.arg1 ~ .arg2 + .arg3` `+.arg4)`	This R function is used to fit linear models. It can be used to return regression based on variables provided by the argument. The information in the parentheses is called an argument and is used to fit the model. Specifically, the response is to the left of the tilde (~), and the model is to the right. Thus, this is a multi-variable linear regression where `.arg1 = SUM(Profit)`, `.arg2 = COUNT(Quantity)`, `.arg3 = SUM(Sales)`, and `.arg4 = AVG(Discount)`. In English, the argument could be read as `SUM(Profit)`, and is modeled as the combined terms of `COUNT(Quantity)`, `SUM(Sales)`, and `AVG(Discount)`.
`x$fitted`	The `lm` function returns many values as part of its model object, including coefficients, residuals, rank, and fitted values. `x$fitted` is referencing the fitted values generated as a result of passing data to the model.

`", SUM(Profit),`
`COUNT(Quantity),`
`SUM(Sales) ,`
`AVG(Discount))`
	These are the parameters used to populate the `.arg#` variables. Note that the double-quote (`"`) designates the end of the code passed to R, and the comma (`,`) designates the second half of the Tableau function, that is, the expression.

After having successfully implemented the regression, we will now investigate a different statistical method that is often used to differentiate between subsets within a dataset, called clustering.

Clustering in Tableau using R

Clustering is used to select smaller subsets of data with members sharing similar characteristics from a larger dataset. As an example, consider a marketing scenario. You have a large customer base to which you plan to send advertising material; however, cost prohibits you from sending material to every customer. Clustering the dataset will return groupings of customers with similar characteristics. You can then survey the results and choose a target group.

Major methods for clustering include hierarchical and k-means. Hierarchical clustering is more thorough and thus more time-consuming. It generates a series of models that range from 1, which includes all data points, to n, where each data point is an individual model. k-means clustering is a quicker method in which the user or another function defines the number of clusters. For example, a user may choose to create four clusters from a dataset of a thousand members.

Clustering capabilities are included with Tableau. You can find this functionality under the **Analytics** tab. The clustering implementation in Tableau is based on four pillars:

- Solid methodology
- Repeatable results
- A quick processing time
- Ease of use

Be sure to check out more details here (`https://help.tableau.com/current/pro/desktop/en-us/clustering.htm`) and the tab **Clustering (Tableau native)** in the accompanying solutions workbook.

There are numerous ways the Tableau development team could have approached clustering. R, for instance, provides many different clustering packages that use different approaches. A Tableau author may have good reason to choose one of these different approaches. For example, clustering results are always identical when using the native Tableau clustering capabilities. But they do not have to be. By using R for clustering, the underlying data and the view may remain unchanged, yet clustering could differ with each refresh because the function will stop at the best result (local minimum) before it has seen the whole dataset. The trade-off between using a so-called local minimum versus a global minimum for performance has been proven to be worth it. But depending on the order of numbers, the local minimum can differ each time you run the function. This could be advantageous to you if looking for edge cases where marks may switch between clusters. The following example explores such a case.

Our goal in this exercise is to create four clusters out of the countries of the world based on birth rate and infant mortality rate:

1. Navigate to the `Cluster (R)` worksheet.
2. Select the `World Indicators` data source (this dataset ships with Tableau and can be found under **Saved Data Sources**).
3. Build the initial view by placing **Infant Mortality Rate** on the **Columns** shelf, **Birth Rate** on the **Rows** shelf, and **Country/Region** on the **Details** shelf.

   Right-click on each axis and select **Logarithmic** and deselect **Include Zero**. This will spread the data points more uniformly and will help make the visualization more aesthetically pleasing and easier to read:

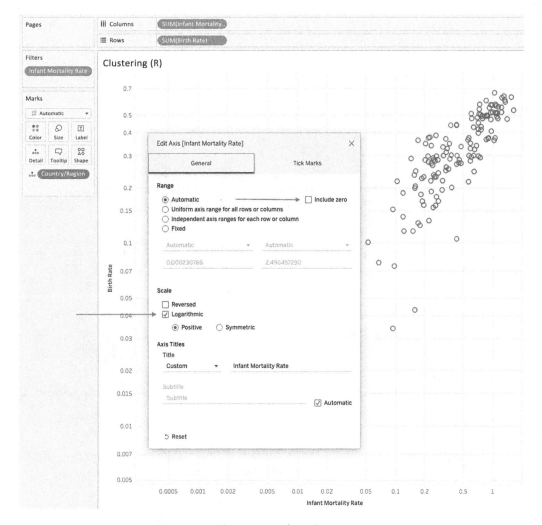

Figure 15.19: Clustering

4. Create a calculated field named Cluster with the following code:

```
SCRIPT_INT("
m <- cbind(.arg1, .arg2);
kmeans(m,4,nstart=5)$cluster",
AVG( [Life Expectancy Female] ), AVG([Life Expectancy Male]))
```

The details of this code will be explained at the end of this exercise.

Drag the **Cluster** field you just created to the **Detail** and the **Color** shelves. Note that the Rserve engine throws an error:

An error occurred while communicating with the Analytics Extension data s... ✕

Error Code: 6116DD27

> An error occurred while communicating with the Analytics Extension.
> An error occurred while communicating with the Analytics Extension. Error in
> do_one(nmeth): NA/NaN/Inf in foreign function call 9arg 1)

Go to Support   **Copy Error Message**

Figure 15.20: Error handling

This is because nulls exist in the underlying dataset. For example, the data does not include the **Infant Mortality Rate** for *Puerto Rico*.

 If you encounter this error with other measures, the same solution applies.

To rectify the error, drag an instance of **Infant Mortality Rate** onto the **Filters** shelf. Within the **Filter** dialog box, select the values as shown to remove all values below 0.01:

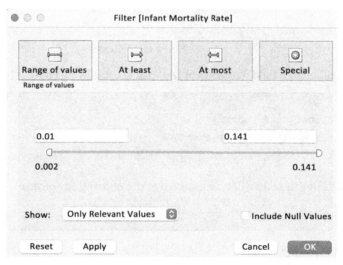

Figure 15.21: Filter

5. Make sure that you set **Cluster** to **Discrete** and **Compute Using | Country/Region** to avoid another error: *error in k-means (m, 4, nstart = 5): more cluster centers than distinct data points.*

6. The resulting view should look like the following screenshot:

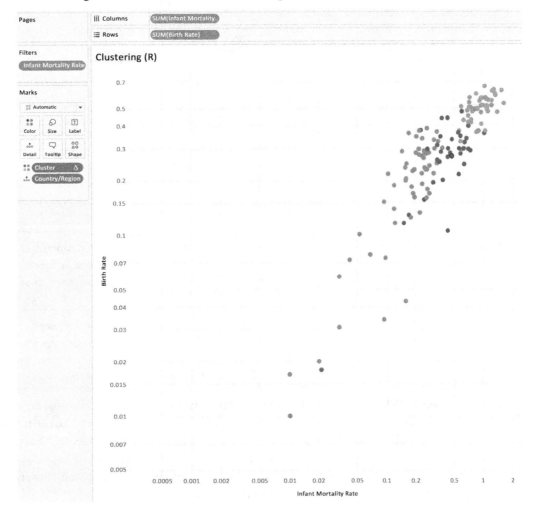

Figure 15.22: Clustering

7. Press *F5* and observe that the clustering changes with each refresh.

Now that we've completed the exercise, let's take a moment to consider some of the code we saw:

`SCRIPT_REAL`	This Tableau functions calls the R engine and returns a float value.
`"m <- cbind(.arg1, .arg2);` `kmeans(m,4,nstart=1)$cluster"`	This is the R expression that houses a variable, a function, and an argument, and then returns clusters.
`m <-`	This is the variable to be populated by the subsequent R function.
`cbind`	This R function combines the following `.arg#` variables into columns.
`(.arg1, .arg2)`	The variables within the parentheses are referred to as an argument. Each variable contains vector information. Specifically, `.arg1 = AVG( [Infant Mortality Rate] )` and `.arg2 = AVG([Birth Rate])`.
`kmeans(m,4,nstart=1)$cluster"`	`kmeans` declares the method of clustering. `m` contains the vector created by the `cbind` argument. The `4` integer declares the number of clusters. `nstart` declares the number of random sets.
`", AVG( [Infant Mortality Rate]` `), AVG([Birth Rate]))`	These are the parameters used to populate the `.arg#` variables. Note that the double-quote (") designates the end of the code passed to R, and the comma (,) designates the second half of the Tableau function, that is, the expression.

What did we achieve? Well, we were able to categorize the countries in our dataset into four subgroups, based on life expectancy. We show the results of the clustering on a scatterplot with the two measures, infant mortality, and birth rate. This way, we can indirectly analyze four measures at the same time, which in this case are **Infant Mortality Rate**, **Birth Rate**, **Country/Region**, and **Life Expectancy**. The R clustering is based on a _k_-means approach, which differs from the Tableau default clustering and can be adjusted to any approach that it is possible to execute in R.

Next, we are going to check out the world of quantiles.

Introducing quantiles

Quantiles are often considered synonymous with quartiles. They are not. Quantiles are the sets that make up an evenly divided population of values. A quartile is a type of quantile—as is a quintile, a tercile, and a decile, for example. To understand how quantiles evenly divide a population of values, imagine multiplying a population by 1/4, 2/4, 3/4, and 4/4, and you get 4 quartiles. To get quintiles, you multiply the population by 1/5, 2/5, 3/5, 4/5, 5/5, and so forth.

Tableau allows you to view quantiles by right-clicking on an axis and choosing **Add Reference Line |
Distribution | Computation | Quantiles**:

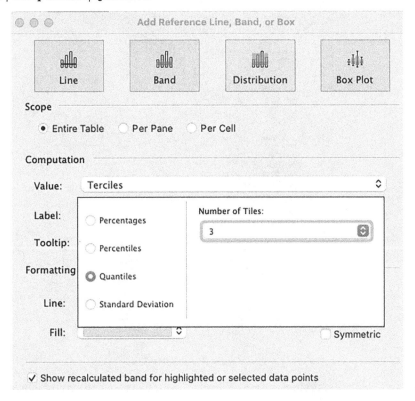

Figure 15.23: Terciles

But you can also change the number of tiles to 4, 5, or any other number to create quartiles, quintiles,
and so on. The functionality of quantiles thus accessed, however, is quite limited. Primarily, this is
because reference lines do not generate measures that can be placed on shelves. This limits the visualization options. Generating quantiles via R greatly expands those options.

Our goal for this exercise is to create *n* quantiles through R to view the customer distribution by sales.
We will further expand the exercise by creating parameters that restrict the number of members in the
total dataset to a given percentile range. Finally, we will fine-tune the visualization by adding jittering.

Let's have a look at the following steps:

1. Navigate to the Quantiles worksheet.
2. Select the Superstore data source.
3. Change the view type to **Shape** on the **Marks** card.

4.   Drag **Sales** to the **Rows** shelf, **Customer Name** to the **Details** shelf, and **Region** to the **Color** shelf:

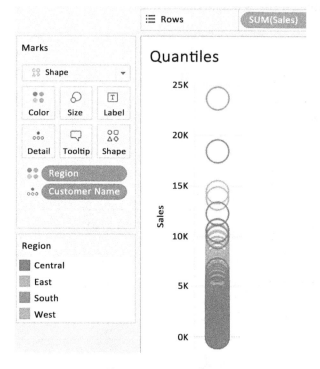

Figure 15.24: Quantiles

5.   Create and display a parameter entitled `Number of quantiles` with the following settings:

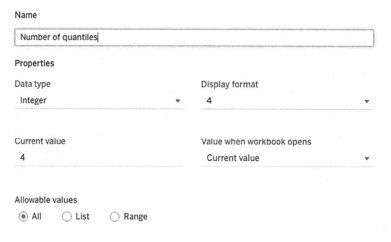

Figure 15.25: Quantile parameter

6.   Right-click on the created parameter and select **Show Parameter**.

7.   Create a calculated field entitled `Quantiles` with the following code:

```
SCRIPT_REAL("
x <- .arg1;
```

```
    y <- .arg2[1];
    m <- c(1:y)/y;
    n <- length(x);
    z <- c(1:n); for (i in c(1:n)) z[i] <- 0;
    for (j in c(1:y)) for (i in c(1:n)) z[i] <- if (x[i] <= quantile(x,m)[j]
    && z[i] == 0 ) j else z[i];
    z;"
    , SUM(Sales), [Number of quantiles])
```

The details of this code will be explained at the end of this exercise.

8. Right-click on the newly created calculated field `Quantiles` and select **Convert to Discrete**.

9. Create and display two parameters, **Select Percentile Bottom Range** and **Select Percentile Top Range**. Use the following settings for both:

Figure 15.26: Percentile parameter

10. Right-click on both newly created parameters and select **Show Parameter**.

11. Create a calculated field entitled `Percentile` with the following code:

```
    RANK_PERCENTILE(SUM([Sales])) < [Select Percentile Top Range]
    AND
    RANK_PERCENTILE(SUM([Sales])) > [Select Percentile Bottom Range]
```

12. Drag **Quantiles** to the **Columns** shelf and set **Compute Using** to **Customer Name**.

13. Drag **Percentile** to the **Filters** shelf, click **OK**, then set **Compute Using** to **Customer Name**. Open the filter again and select the value **True**.

So, let's recapture what we have done so far. We plotted the sales values per region, then we added an R script that creates quantiles out of the sales dot cloud. We also created a parameter that lets us select how many quantiles we want to see in the view since we learned that quantiles don't always have to be quartiles but could also be terciles or quintiles, or more.

Next up we will see this view in action, and we will add jittering.

14. You may wish to add these additional steps to further enhance the visualization. To utilize jittering, create an index calculated field, Index(), and place that field on the **Columns** shelf. Set **Compute Using** to **Customer Name**. Be sure to deselect **Show Header** so **Index** does not display in the view.

15. Right-click on each axis and select **Logarithmic** and deselect **Include Zero**. You should see the following on your screen:

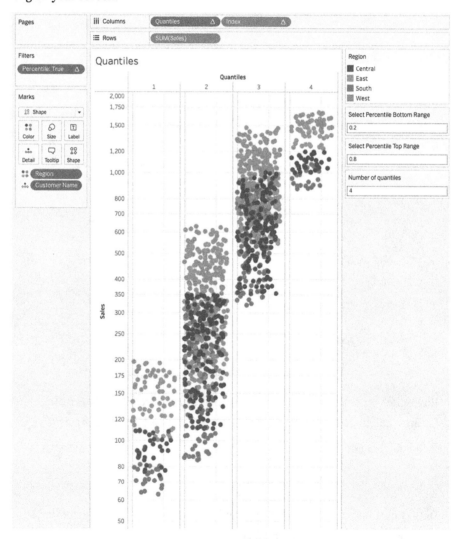

Figure 15.27: Quantiles dashboard

In the preceding figure, you can see that we decided to show four quantiles (utilizing the **Number of quantiles** parameter), which as such are called quartiles. By adding the Index() function to columns, we were able to divide the quantiles into each of the four components. One conclusion from this dashboard could be that, in each of the four quantiles, the West region has the highest sales figures, and the South region has the lowest. However, the Central and South regions come remarkably close to each other in the third quantile. Based on this information, we could do some further analysis on what is going on in those regions specifically and why the Central region's sales decreased in that quantile compared to the other regions.

Now that we've completed the exercise, let's take a moment to consider some of the code we looked at in this exercise:

`SCRIPT_REAL`	This Tableau function calls the R engine and returns a float value.
`x <- .arg1;`	x is the variable on which we'll create quantiles. The variable, in this case, is [Sales].
`y <- .arg2[1];`	This variable sets the quantile count. [1] forces a single number to be set and not a vector.
`m <- c(1:y)/y;`	m distributes probabilities evenly from 1:y.
`n <- length(x);`	This sets the size of the loops. The loops are discussed below.
`z <- c(1:n); for (i in c(1:n)) z[i] = 0;`	z sets the initial response vector by setting everything to 0.
`for (j in c(1:y)) for (i in c(1:n)) z[i] = if (x[i] <= quantile(x,m)[j] && z[i] == 0 ) j else z[i];`	For each quantile, we go through the z vector, and for each entry, we test whether the value of x is less than the upper limit of that quantile. If x has previously been set, we leave it. Otherwise, z[i] = that quantile (j).

In this exercise, you saw that by using R, a Tableau default functionality such as clustering can be extended and will give your dashboard users more freedom to answer new questions that come up while using the dashboard because it will be possible for them to change, for example, parameters and see the visualization changing. Now that we've learned about a few possible R use cases, it is time to discuss something worth your attention, the performance challenges that come along with using programming integrations with Tableau.

Performance challenges

R scripts are table calculations. Like all table calculations, this means that you can only utilize fields that are on your view. Also, it's important that you set partitioning and addressing correctly; otherwise, you may receive unexpected results.

In the *Introducing quantiles* section, you may have noticed that the greater the number of quantiles set with the **Number of quantiles** parameter, the longer it takes the results to display. This is because R runs the loops in the **Quantile** calculated field one iteration for each quantile. For example, if the **Number of quantiles** parameter is set to 1, the loop is instigated only once. If it is set to 2, it runs twice, and so forth. The rule of thumb is that R code is executed once for every partition. The more partitions, the slower the performance. Therefore, when using R code, reduce the number of partitions whenever possible.

This was the R part of this chapter. I hope you enjoyed it and that it has given you the inspiration to produce your own ideas to extend the functionality we have shared so far. We will now continue with the other very well-known programming language: Python. Luckily for us, Tableau also has an integration layer with Python.

Python installation and integration

Python is an interpreted programming language and is very well known for its readability. The first release was in 1991, so quite some time ago (longer than most people would guess), and it was developed by Guido van Rossum. TabPy is an external service that will allow you to connect Python and Tableau—similar to Rserve. By using TabPy, you will be able to parse fields from your Tableau dashboard to Python, execute a calculation, and send back the result as a newly calculated field to Tableau. Or you can also call functions that you implemented in Python, again in a calculated field. A more extensive article on TabPy can be found here: `https://tableaumagic.com/tableau-and-python-an-introduction`.

Installing Python is typically not difficult, but it does involve more than simply double-clicking on an executable. To successfully connect Tableau with Python, you might have to install some libraries and execute comments on the command line. The following paragraphs will guide you through this process.

The easiest way to install Python is by performing the following steps:

1. Download, for example, Anaconda with the Python 3.10 version: `https://www.anaconda.com`. Any other Python interpreter will work too.

    To integrate Python and Tableau, some additional steps are needed:

2. Open, for example, Jupyter Notebook within Anaconda and write:

    ```
    !pip install tabpy
    ```

    Alternatively, execute the following command on the command line or Terminal (for Mac) in your Python directory:

    ```
    pip install tabpy
    ```

3. Navigate to the directory where TabPy has been installed via the command line or Terminal (for Mac) and type tabpy into the command line or Terminal interface:

```
● ● ●                        🖫 site-packages — tabpy — 121×24
[(base) marleenmeier@marleens-Mini ~ % cd anaconda3/lib/python3.10/site-packages ◄─────────────────
[(base) marleenmeier@marleens-Mini site-packages % tabpy ◄──────────────────────
2023-05-13,12:55:59 [INFO] (app.py:app:299): Parsing config file /Users/marleenmeier/anaconda3/lib/python3.10/site-packag
es/tabpy/tabpy_server/app/../common/default.conf
2023-05-13,12:55:59 [INFO] (app.py:app:497): Loading state from state file /Users/marleenmeier/anaconda3/lib/python3.10/s
ite-packages/tabpy/tabpy_server/state.ini
2023-05-13,12:55:59 [INFO] (app.py:app:391): Password file is not specified: Authentication is not enabled
2023-05-13,12:55:59 [INFO] (app.py:app:406): Call context logging is disabled
2023-05-13,12:55:59 [INFO] (app.py:app:180): Initializing TabPy...
2023-05-13,12:55:59 [INFO] (callbacks.py:callbacks:43): Initializing TabPy Server...
2023-05-13,12:55:59 [INFO] (app.py:app:184): Done initializing TabPy.
2023-05-13,12:55:59 [INFO] (app.py:app:122): Setting max request size to 104857600 bytes
2023-05-13,12:55:59 [INFO] (callbacks.py:callbacks:64): Initializing models...
2023-05-13,12:55:59 [INFO] (app.py:app:150): Web service listening on port 9004
```

Figure 15.28: Starting TabPy

4. You are now connected to the tabpy server, which must remain open while running Tableau and Python combined.

5. If you encounter any other issues with TabPy, for example, version incompatibilities, a quick Google search will go a long way.

6. Open Tableau, select **Help** | **Settings and Performance** | **Manage Analytics Extension Connection**, select localhost for **Server**, and enter 9004 for **Port**:

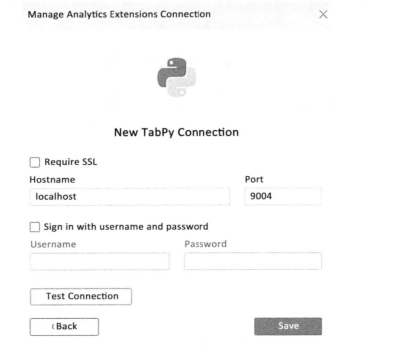

Figure 15.29: Analytics Extension connection

7. As you can see in the previous screenshot, it is possible to set up usernames, passwords, and SSL if you have any security concerns or for a bigger enterprise-wide rollout.

8. Click on **Test Connection** and you should see the following popup:

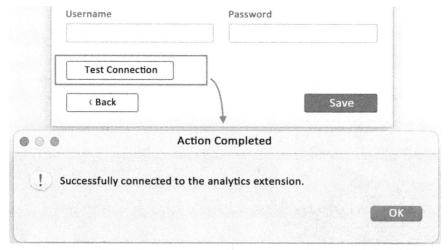

Figure 15.30: Testing the analytics extension

The full documentation on how to get TabPy up and running can be found at https://github.com/ tableau/TabPy. If you don't want to or cannot install TabPy on your machine, Tableau also offers a Docker container that will install the latest version of TabPy. You can find more information here: https://hub.docker.com/r/emhemh/tabpy/.

Implementing Python functionality

Just like R, TabPy makes use of the SCRIPT_ functions in Tableau. In the next sections, we will practice working with TabPy and will look at multiple use cases. Tableau calculations using TabPy look very similar to R's. For TabPy, it is important to add a return statement to the calculated field and notice that arguments are noted with an underscore instead of a dot:

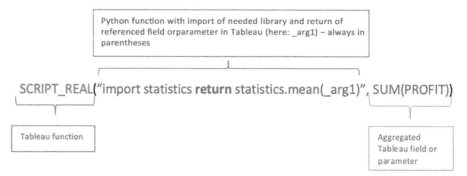

Figure 15.31: Python TabPy syntax

This will be manifested in the next exercises; we will first investigate random number generators.

Random and random normal

Many calculations are easily accessible via the calculated fields, others via the table calculations—and then there are some hidden functions. Hidden because those are not (yet) fully supported or tested; therefore, use them with care. If you tried to find the function Random, for example, you would not be able to. But you can still use the Random() function, as can be seen here:

Figure 15.32: Random

Another option is using TabPy to get the Random function. We will look at random as well as random normal with the variables mu and sigma. This will let us draw random numbers from a distribution, a method often used in statistics and quantitative modeling, among other areas, to simulate, reproduce, or calculate probabilities; mu and sigma are the mean and standard deviation defining the distribution.

Generating random numbers

Perform the following steps to create a dot cloud of random variables with a specific underlying distribution, defined by the mean and standard deviation:

1. Create an Excel sheet with one Index column and rows with the numbers 1-1,000. This is needed to have an initial dataset with the number of rows we want to use for the random number generator.

2. Save the file and connect Tableau to this Excel sheet. You should see one imported measure called **Index** (just like the header in your Excel file).

3. Connect Tableau to Python as described in *Python installation and integration*.

4. Create a calculated field called Random, which should look as follows:

```
SCRIPT_REAL("
from numpy import random as rd
return rd.random(_arg1[0]).tolist()",
SIZE()
)
```

5. Drag **Index** to **Rows** and **Random** to **Columns**.

6.   Disable **Aggregate Measures** on the **Analysis** tab.

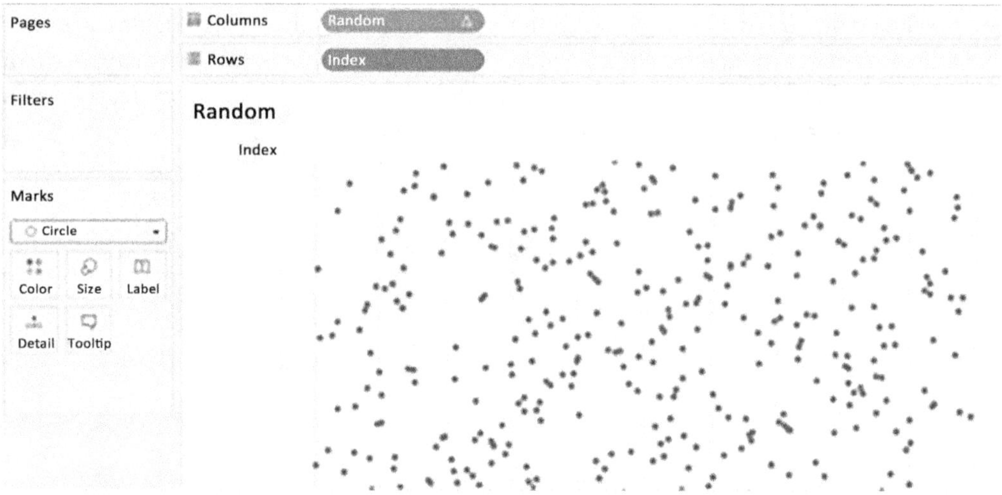

Figure 15.33: Random visualized

In the preceding screenshot, you can see the 1,000 random data points. Let's consider some of the code used in this exercise that allowed us to generate this visualization:

SCRIPT_REAL	This Tableau function calls the Python engine and returns a float value.
"from numpy import random as rd	In this part of the code, we need the Python library numpy, and from that library, we need the module random, which we will load with the shorter name rd.
return	This command is simply needed to return a value.
rd.random(_arg1[0]).tolist()"	In this step, we call the module rd that we imported before. From the rd module, we retrieve the random function. The _arg1[0] is needed to activate the function given a certain value. And lastly, we put all the retrieved values in a list of values by adding .tolist().
SIZE()	This is the value that will be replacing _arg1 and _arg1 is required by the random function. We use SIZE() to fulfill the requirement because it will return the number of rows in the partition and is sufficient to get a random number back from the function.

We got exactly 1,000 numbers because our initial Excel sheet had 1,000 rows. By using calculated fields, you can add columns to a data frame but no rows. Therefore, we need a data source that will provide us with the data schema. In the next section, we will learn how to specify a random number drawn from a normal distribution.

Random normal

Now, let's reproduce a random variable with a normal distribution. This technique is often used in statistical modeling to calculate probabilities. The random normal values can be used instead of or in addition to observations you already collected. Once we know how to use a normal distribution, you can extend this knowledge and create other distributions in Tableau as well:

1. Reuse the workbook from the previous exercise.

2. Create a `Random Normal` calculated field:

```
SCRIPT_REAL("
from numpy import random as rd
mu, sigma = 0, 1
return (rd.normal(mu, sigma, _arg1[0])).tolist()
",
SIZE()
)
```

3. Place **Random Normal** on **Columns** and **Index** on **Rows**.

4. Disable **Aggregate Measures** on the **Analysis** tab.

5. Select a **Marks** type of **Circle**. You can now see a plot with the 1,000 data points normally distributed:

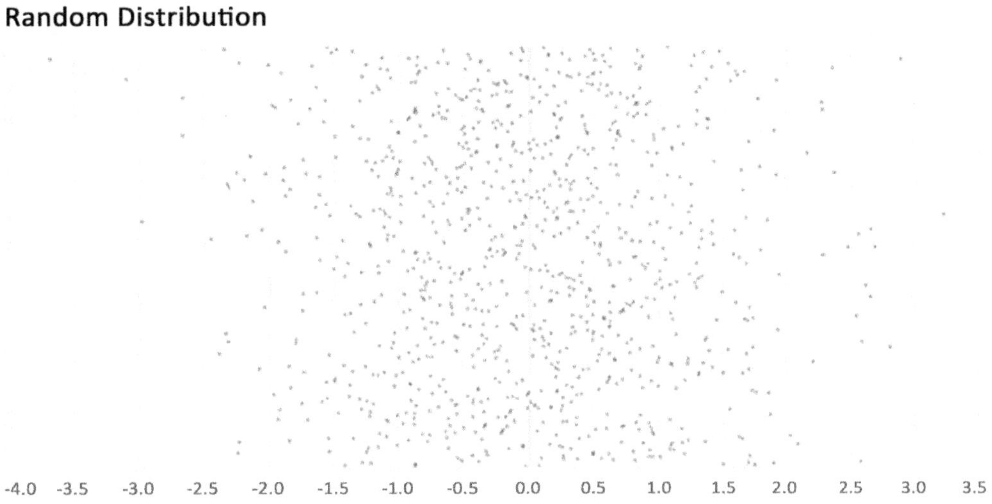

Random Distribution

Figure 15.34: Normal distribution visualized

To give your users more flexibility, you can also add parameters to your view that interact with the Python integration. For example, create the following two parameters:

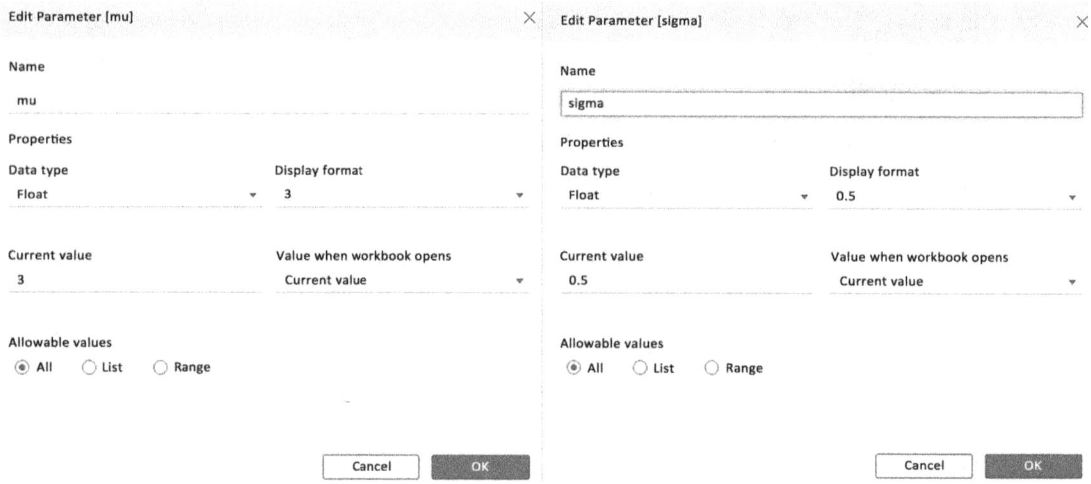

Figure 15.35: The sigma and mu parameters

Then, create a calculated field called `Random Normal Param` like:

```
SCRIPT_REAL("
from numpy import random as rd
mu, sigma = _arg2, _arg3
return (rd.normal(mu, sigma, _arg1[0])).tolist()
",
SIZE(), [mu], [sigma]
)
```

Add the parameter control to your view so your users can decide which variables they want to pass to Python:

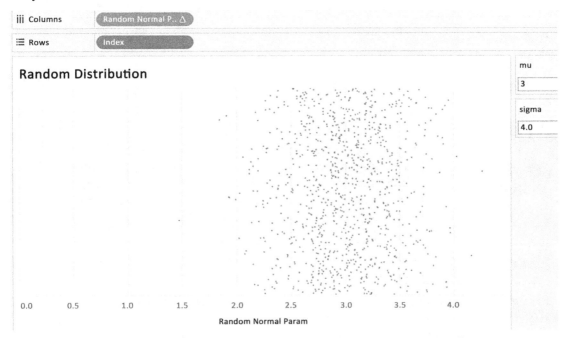

Figure 15.36: Final normal distribution worksheet

Compared to our prior visualization with the normal distribution, you can see in the preceding screenshot that by changing the mu parameter to 10, we change the mean to 10 and thus can move the whole dot cloud in any direction. With the random number being available in Tableau, you can, for example, visualize a Monte Carlo simulation, which is used in many real-life applications because it can model possible probability outcomes and thus helps interested parties understand the impact of risk and uncertainty.

 More information on how to calculate a Monte Carlo simulation in Tableau can be found here – https://jacksontwo.com/exploring-python-tableau – and more general Monte Carlo content can be found here: https://www.ibm.com/topics/monte-carlo-simulation.

Before moving on, let's again consider some of the key lines of code that were used in this exercise:

`SCRIPT_REAL`	This Tableau function calls the Python engine and returns a float value.
`"from numpy import random as rd`	In this part of the code, we need the Python library numpy, and from that library, we need the module `random`, which we will load with the shorter name `rd`.
`mu, sigma = _arg2,_ arg3`	This part defines that we will refer to `mu` and `sigma` with `_arg2` and `_arg3`.
`return`	This command is simply needed to return a value.
`rd.normal(mu, sigma, _arg1[0])).tolist()`	In this step, we call the module `rd` that we imported before. From the `rd` module, we retrieve the `random` function. The `_arg1[0]` is needed to activate the function given a certain value. Optional values are `mu` and `sigma`. This time, we will use those two as well. And lastly, we put all the retrieved values in a list of values by adding `.tolist()`.
`SIZE(), [mu], [sigma]`	This is the value that will be replacing `_arg1`, `_arg2`, and `_arg3`. Just like before, we use `SIZE()` to activate the function. The optional values `mu` and `sigma` will be pointing to the parameter we created before.

After finishing the first two exercises with TabPy, we learned how we can use a random number in Tableau. Next, we changed the random number to a random number drawn from a normal distribution and added parameters to the dashboard such that the user can change `mu` and `sigma` of the normal distribution. Of course, you can change the function in TabPy to other distributions as well.

The next topic is more advanced. We will use TabPy to execute a sentiment analysis on newspaper headlines from 2003 to 2021.

Calculating sentiment analysis

Alongside machine learning and artificial intelligence, another term is being used increasingly: **Natural Language Processing** (NLP). This is the process of machines understanding words and their meaning. Sentiment analysis falls into this category; the technique has different flavors but one of them is to measure polarity, that is, whether the speaker has a positive or negative opinion. Use cases are, for example, datasets of reviews, tweets, comments, plots, lyrics, and so on. Let's have a look!

This exercise is based on the idea of Brit Cava, who used the Makeover Monday data from the top 100 songs' lyrics to try out the Tableau-Python integration. You can find the blog post here: https://www.tableau.com/about/blog/2016/12/using-python-sentiment-analysis-tableau-63606. Let's reproduce it with this Australian Broadcasting Corporation dataset containing one million news headlines: https://www.kaggle.com/datasets/therohk/million-headlines.

1. Navigate to the `Sentiment Analysis` tab in the workbook associated with the chapter.
2. Connect to the `Headlines` data source.
3. Connect Tableau to Python.
4. Create a `Sentiment Score` calculated field. The formatting, for example, indented text, is important:

```
SCRIPT_REAL("
from nltk.sentiment import SentimentIntensityAnalyzer
text = _arg1
scores = []
sid = SentimentIntensityAnalyzer()
for word in text:
    ss = sid.polarity_scores(word)
scores.append(ss['compound'])
return scores "
,ATTR([headline_text]))
```

5. Create a Color Coding calculated field:

    ```
    IIF ([Sentiment Scores] >= 0, 'Positivity', 'Negativity')
    ```

6. Place **publish_date** on the **Rows** shelf, as well as **MONTH(publish_date)**.

7. Put **Sentiment Score** on **Columns**.

8. Add **Color Coding** to the **Color** shelf. And **headline_text** to **Details**. Lastly, drag an average line from the **Analytics** pane on the view (**Per Cell**):

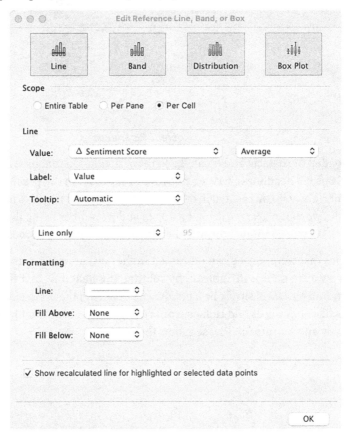

Figure 15.37: Sentiment Score

Limit the data as needed, considering the performance of your PC. I am showing 2019-2021 and only Jan, Feb, Nov, and Dec to compare the differences between the beginning and end of the years:

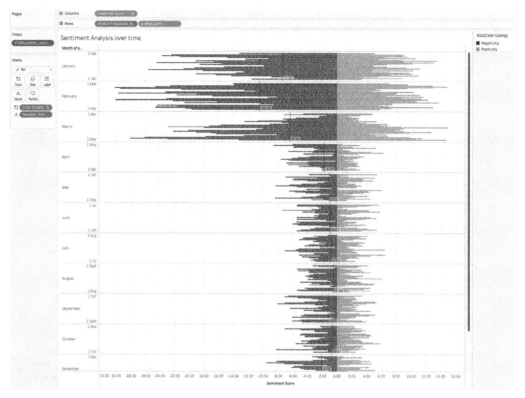

Figure 15.38: Worksheet

So far, we have loaded the dataset and created a Python calculation that uses a pre-trained sentiment analyzer that tells us if a headline is written negative or positive. In the preceding figure, we brought everything together, and you can see that in every month in 2021, the negative news is dominating, with February being the worst (an average score of -10.45) and December being the most positive (an average score of -0.14). We will continue now with a check on what the news is most often reporting about.

To know the topics that were most often discussed in the ABC news, we must count the words used. Perhaps there is a way to do this in Tableau, by splitting the **headline_text** field into one word each, pivoting and counting but it will surely be a tedious process. And there are enough libraries out there to remove things like stop words and reduce words to their core, for example, horse = horses. Therefore, we will deploy another model. Please follow the steps:

1. Create a Start parameter. This one will help us later to define the period we want to search in:

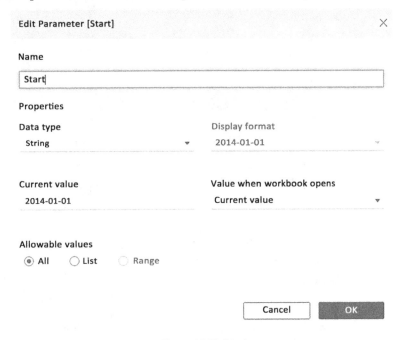

Figure 15.39: Start

2. Also, create an End parameter:

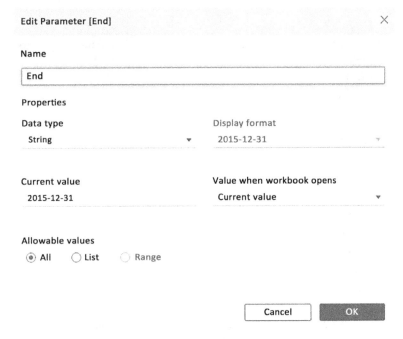

Figure 15.40: End

3. Show both parameters on a new tab in your Tableau workbook called most common words.

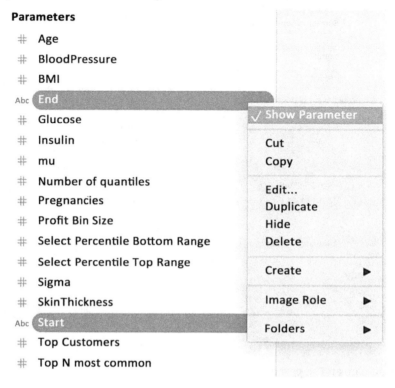

Figure 15.41: Worksheet

4. Next, you will have to write code in your Python IDE of choice (e.g., Jupyter Notebook). For now, copy the following code. The explanation will follow at the end of this section (don't forget to change the location in this line df = pd.read_csv('abcnews-date-text.csv') to exactly where your copy of the file is located:

```
from tabpy.tabpy_tools.client import Client
client = Client('http://localhost:9004/')


def common_words(_arg1, _arg2):

    #load all required libraries
    import pandas as pd
    import nltk
    from nltk.corpus import stopwords
    from nltk.tokenize import word_tokenize
    from nltk.probability import FreqDist
    from nltk.sentiment import SentimentIntensityAnalyzer
```

```
    df = pd.read_csv('abcnews-date-text.csv')
    df['publish_date'] = pd.to_datetime(df['publish_date'],
format='%Y%m%d')

    #convert the Tableau input date to a readable format
    _arg1 = pd.to_datetime(_arg1, format='%Y-%m-%d')[0]
    _arg2 = pd.to_datetime(_arg2, format='%Y-%m-%d')[0]
    df = df.set_index('publish_date')

    #empty lists to be filled
    scores = []
    filtered_sentence = []

    # Select the rows between two dates
    in_range_df = df[df.index.isin(pd.date_range(_arg1, _arg2))]

    #loading english stop words
    stop_words = set(stopwords.words('english'))
    text = in_range_df['headline_text']

    #most used words
    for row in range(0, len(in_range_df)):
        text =  in_range_df['headline_text'][row]
        word_tokens = word_tokenize(text)

        for w in word_tokens:
            if w not in stop_words:
                filtered_sentence.append(w)


    #calculate the frequency of each word
    fdist = FreqDist(filtered_sentence)

    #extract the N most common words
    most_common_words = fdist.most_common(3)
    return str(most_common_words)


client.deploy('common_words', common_words,'Retrieves the most common
words', override = True)
```

Since the indentation is especially important, here is a screenshot of how it should look; you can also see that I specified the location of the abcnews file to be '/Users/marleenmeier/ Downloads/abcnews-date-text.csv' since my file is located there:

```
1  from tabpy.tabpy_tools.client import Client
2  client = Client('http://localhost:9004/')
3
4  def common_words(_arg1, _arg2):
5
6      #load all required libraries
7      import pandas as pd
8      import nltk
9      from nltk.corpus import stopwords
10     from nltk.tokenize import word_tokenize
11     from nltk.probability import FreqDist
12     from nltk.sentiment import SentimentIntensityAnalyzer
13
14     df = pd.read_csv('/Users/marleenmeier/Downloads/abcnews-date-text.csv')
15     df['publish_date'] = pd.to_datetime(df['publish_date'], format='%Y%m%d')
16
17     #convert the Tableau input date to a readable format
18     _arg1 = pd.to_datetime(_arg1, format='%Y-%m-%d')[0]
19     _arg2 = pd.to_datetime(_arg2, format='%Y-%m-%d')[0]
20     df = df.set_index('publish_date')
21
22     #empty lists to be filled
23     scores = []
24     filtered_sentence = []
25
26     # Select the rows between two dates
27     in_range_df = df[df.index.isin(pd.date_range(_arg1, _arg2))]
28
29     #loading english stop words
30     stop_words = set(stopwords.words('english'))
31     text = in_range_df['headline_text']
32
33     #most used words
34     for row in range(0, len(in_range_df)):
35         text =  in_range_df['headline_text'][row]
36         word_tokens = word_tokenize(text)
37
38         for w in word_tokens:
39             if w not in stop_words:
40                 filtered_sentence.append(w)
41
42
43     #calculate the frequency of each word
44     fdist = FreqDist(filtered_sentence)
45
46     #extract the N most common words
47     most_common_words = fdist.most_common(3)
48     return str(most_common_words)
49
50
51 client.deploy('common_words', common_words,'Retrieves the most common words', override = True)
52
53
54
55
```

Figure 15.42: Code

5. Now run the Python script.

6. Go back to the most common words tab in your Tableau dashboard and create the following calculated field common words:

```
MODEL_EXTENSION_STR("common_words", "_arg1, _arg2", [Start], [End])
```

 You can also use the SCRIPT_STR function like we did in the previous exercise, but for deployed TabPy models, Tableau provides this easier syntax of MODEL_EXTENSION functions too.

7. Drag **common words** into the **Rows** and see your first results; between January 2014 and December 2015, the word *new* appeared 4,909 times in the headlines of ABC news, *police* 4,307 times, and *man* 4,171 times. You see the top 3 because it is specified as such in the code, which we will check out in a bit. You can, however, change it to any number!

8. Play with the **Start** and **End** dates and see what happens! Here are two more examples; also notice the word count itself, the top 1 word in 2020 (*coronavirus*, 8,383 times) was used two times more often than the top 1 word between 2014 and 2015 (*new*, 4,909 times):

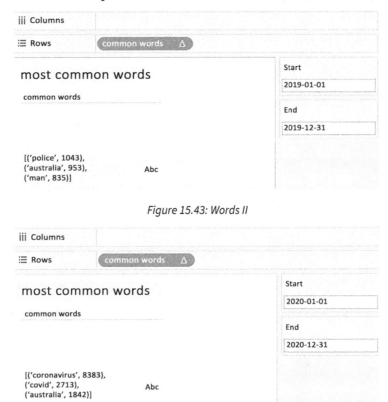

Figure 15.43: Words II

Figure 15.44: Words III

If you want to continue working on this, you could add the top N as a model input parameter, as well as the sentiment score if you wanted to see the top N for a specific sentiment only.

In this exercise, we were able to show that Tableau can analyze text data for its sentiment, something we have not seen before. To do so, we needed to connect Tableau with Python, which is possible by using the external service TabPy. Python can make use of libraries such as nltk.sentiment—which we used in this case. A thorough description of this package can be found here: https://www.nltk.org/api/nltk.sentiment.html. There are many other libraries for sentiment analysis but nltk is used a lot for demonstration purposes and learning. Feel free to try other libraries as well!

Let's demystify some of the new code instances we included in this exercise:

`SCRIPT_REAL`	This Tableau function calls the Python engine and returns a float value.
`from nltk.sentiment import SentimentIntensityAnalyzer`	In this part of the code, we need the Python library `nltk`, and from that library, we need the module `sentiment` from which we will load the function `SentimentIntensityAnalyzer`.

`scores = []`
 	
`text = _arg1`
 	
`sid = SentimentIntensityAnalyzer()`
 	
`ss = sid.polarity_scores(word)`
	This part defines that our `_arg1` will be called `text`, `scores` will be an empty list (and filled later in the code), `sid` will refer to the `SentimentIntensityAnalyzer` function, and lastly, `ss` will be the reference to the scores per word.

`scores.append(ss['compound'])`	In this step, we will fill the empty `scores` table with the polarity scores.
`return scores`	Here, we are returning the now-filled `scores` table as output to Tableau.
`ATTR([Dialog])`	Our `_arg1` is specified as the field `Dialog` from the Tableau workbook.

`from tabpy.tabpy_tools.client import Client`
 	
`client = Client('http://localhost:9004/')`
	In this part of the code, we connect Tableau to the Python instance.

| ```python
import pandas as pd

import nltk

from nltk.corpus import stopwords

from nltk.tokenize import word_tokenize

from nltk.probability import FreqDist

from nltk.sentiment import
SentimentIntensityAnalyzer
``` | Here we load all the required libraries. |
| ```python
df = pd.read_csv('abcnews-date-text.csv')

df['publish_date'] = pd.to_
datetime(df['publish_date'],
format='%Y%m%d')
``` | Next, we read the abcnews file. |
| ```python
_arg1 = pd.to_datetime(_arg1, format='%Y-
%m-%d')[0]

_arg2 = pd.to_datetime(_arg2, format='%Y-
%m-%d')[0]

df = df.set_index('publish_date')
``` | Then, we must convert the input into a readable format for our model. |
| ```python
scores = []

filtered_sentence = []
``` | This part is to create two lists that we will fill in the for loop. |
| ```python
in_range_df = df[df.index.isin(pd.date_
range(_arg1, _arg2))]
``` | Now we will filter the data to be between our start and end date. |
| ```python
stop_words = set(stopwords.
words('english'))

text = in_range_df['headline_text']
``` | Luckily, English stop words are available at our disposal; we are loading them in this step. |
| ```python
for row in range(0, len(in_range_df)):

text =  in_range_df['headline_text'][row]

word_tokens = word_tokenize(text)

for w in word_tokens:

if w not in stop_words: filtered_sentence.
append(w)
``` | In this part of the code, we are converting the remaining headers into a token, which is needed to calculate the frequency, and finally, the non-stop-word words will be stored in the filtered_sentence list. |
| ```python
fdist = FreqDist(filtered_sentence)
``` | By using one of the libraries, we loaded in the beginning, we can now ask to retrieve the frequency for each word. |

`most_common_words = fdist.most_common(3)`
 	
`return str(most_common_words)`
	And since we have the frequency now, we can load the most often-used words.

`client.deploy('common_words', common_words,'Retrieves the most common words', override = True)`	Lastly, we will deploy the model such that we can call it from Tableau Desktop.

We have seen embedded Python code now; you create a calculated field and use fields from your dataset as input. But what if you wanted to use a large model with many lines of code and many different variables, or upfront training of your model? Would this exceed TabPy's capabilities? No! Because next to embedded code, we are also able to write Python scripts outside of Tableau.

Deploying models with TabPy

At times, your script will just be too long to be used in a calculated field, or you'll need upfront training on a different dataset or an extended dataset rather than the one you have in Tableau. In this case, we can use TabPy in a slightly different way. You can write a model outside of Tableau—in Python and deploy it to Tableau such that you can call it from within the desktop.

In the upcoming example, we will build a recommender system that predicts the likelihood of a Pima woman having diabetes when inputting 7 parameters (age, BMI, pregnancies, blood pressure, glucose, insulin, and skin thickness). The dataset is from a 1988 study by *J.W. Smith, J.E. Everhart, W.C. Dickson, W.C. Knowler, and R.S. Johannes*, accessible at the following link: `https://www.ncbi.nlm.nih.gov/pmc/articles/PMC2245318/`.

We will begin with the code in the Jupyter Notebook or your preferred **Integrated Development Environment (IDE)**. Please follow along with the next steps:

1. We start the code by importing the `tabpy` client, which is needed to establish a Python-Tableau connection:

    ```
    from tabpy.tabpy_tools.client import Client
    client = Client('http://localhost:9004/')
    ```

2. Next, we import all the libraries and data needed. Make sure to replace the dataset name with the full path of your file location (for example, `H:/Documents/Diabetes.csv` instead of `Diabetes.csv`):

    ```
    import numpy as np
    import pandas as pd
    from sklearn import ensemble
    from sklearn.model_selection import train_test_split
    df = pd.read_csv("Diabetes.csv", sep = ',')
    df = df[['Pregnancies', 'Glucose', 'BloodPressure', 'SkinThickness',
    'Insulin', 'BMI', 'Age', 'Outcome']]
    ```

3. Now we split the dataset into four; two test datasets that will help us check how accurate our model is, as well as two training datasets to train the model:

```
X_train, X_test, y_train, y_test = train_test_split(df.drop(['Outcome'],
axis = 'columns'),df['Outcome'], test_size = 0.2)
```

4. If you are interested in more detail and the math behind this code, please check https://scikit-learn.org/stable/modules/generated/sklearn.ensemble.GradientBoostingClassifier.html.

5. Next, we will load the `GradientBoosting` model from `sklearn` and fit our data; then; we can immediately visualize the score, which can be interpreted as the percentage of the total that our model predicted the correct value for:

```
gb = ensemble.GradientBoostingClassifier()
gb.fit(X_train, y_train)
gbscore = gb.score(X_test, y_test)
print('gradient boost: ' + str(round(gbscore*100,2)))
```

6. And this is the full code in Jupyter:

```
1  import numpy as np
2  import pandas as pd
3  from sklearn import ensemble
4  from sklearn.model_selection import train_test_split
5  df = pd.read_csv('/Users/marleenmeier/Downloads/Diabetes.csv', sep = ',')
6  df = df[['Pregnancies', 'Glucose', 'BloodPressure', 'SkinThickness', 'Insulin', 'BMI', 'Age', 'Outcome']]
7
8  X_train, X_test, y_train, y_test = train_test_split(df.drop(['Outcome'], axis = 'columns'),df['Outcome'],
9                                                      test_size = 0.2)
10
11 gb = ensemble.GradientBoostingClassifier()
12 gb.fit(X_train, y_train)
13 gbscore = gb.score(X_test, y_test)
14 print('gradient boost: ' + str(round(gbscore*100,2)))

gradient boost: 72.08
```

Figure 15.45: Python script

To conclude this first phase, our model predicted the right outcome in 72.08% of cases, either having diabetes or not having diabetes. This is a fairly good result. To further improve it, we could add more data (in terms of rows), extend our input variables (in terms of columns), or create new features like ratios between variables (hidden information could be emphasized this way). But for now, we can continue working with the model, because eventually, we want to predict the likelihood as a percentage of someone having diabetes. Let's switch over to Tableau:

7. We won't need a dataset for this exercise because all our data lives in the Jupyter Notebook. In Tableau, you can just select one randomly, as we won't use it. In a new Tableau worksheet called Diabetes, create the following seven parameters:

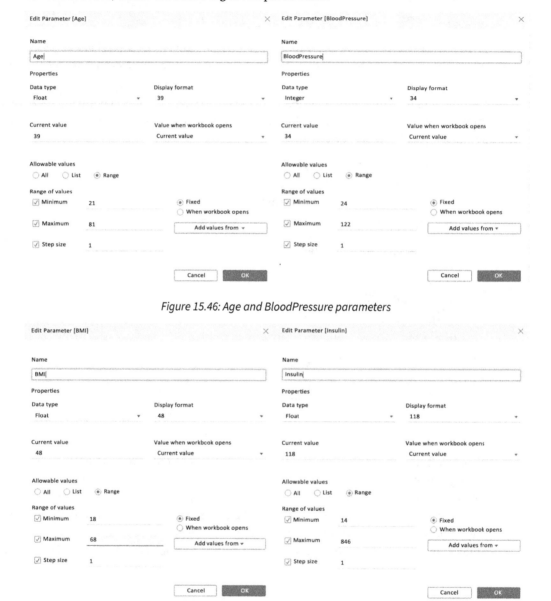

Figure 15.46: Age and BloodPressure parameters

Figure 15.47: BMI and Insulin parameters

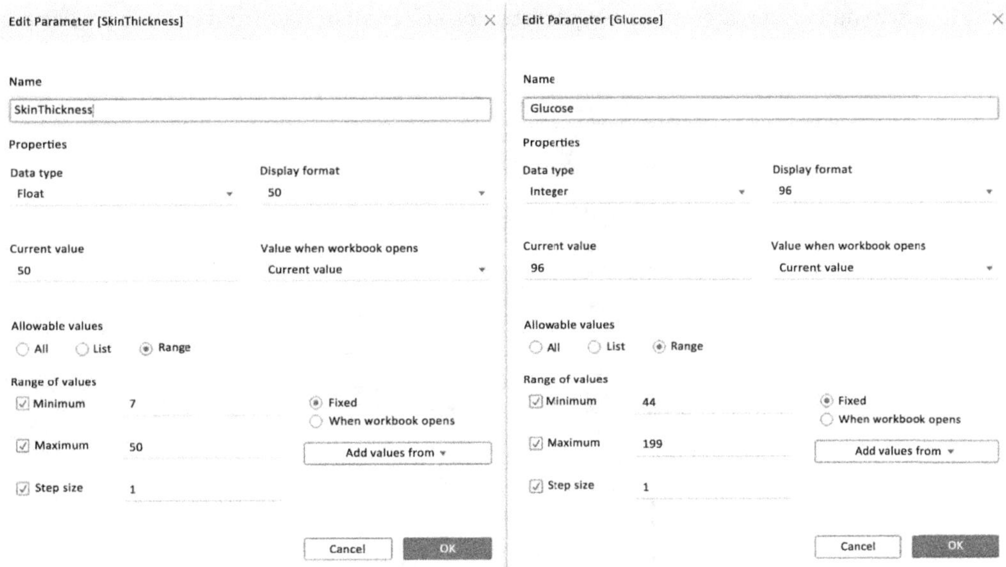

Figure 15.48: SkinThickness and Glucose parameters

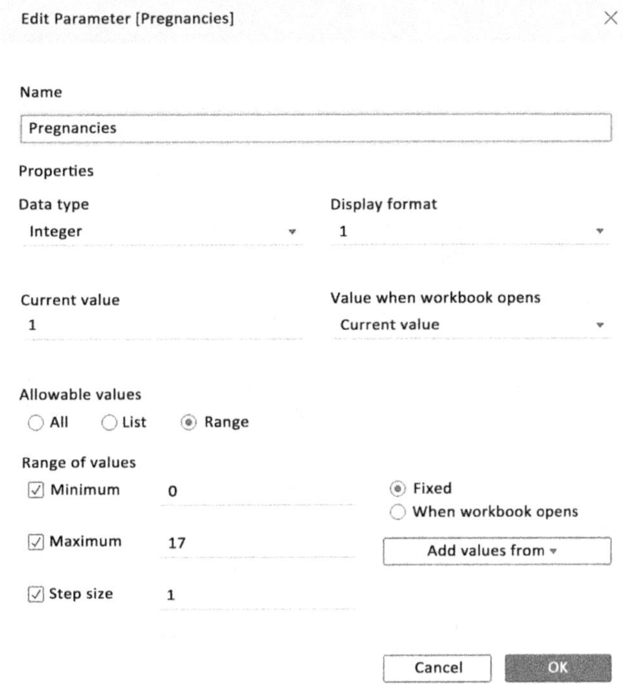

Figure 15.49: The Pregnancies parameter

8. After you have created all seven parameters, select all of them and click **Show Parameter:**

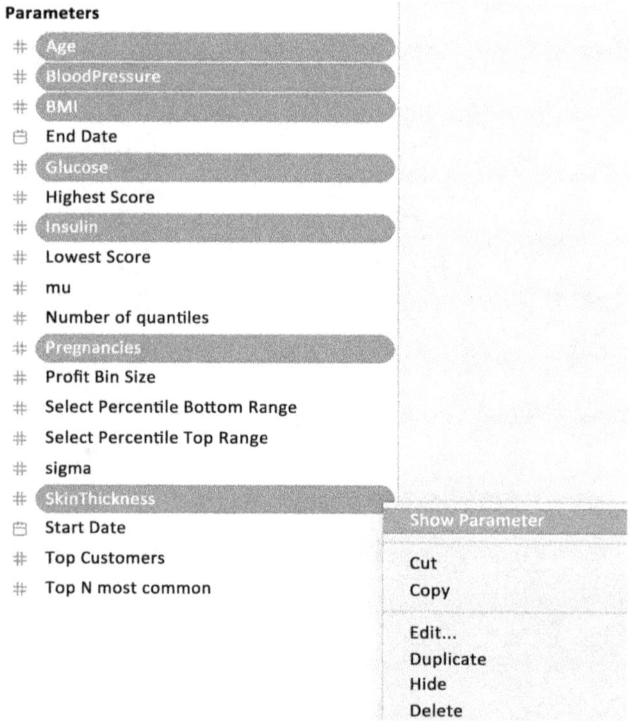

Figure 15.50: Show Parameter

9. Please go back to Jupyter now and execute the two last missing pieces of code that will create a function to call our model:

```
def diabetes_predictor(_arg1, _arg2, _arg3, _arg4, _arg5,_arg6,_arg7):
    import pandas as pd
    row = {'Pregnancies': _arg1, 'Glucose': _arg2, 'BloodPressure':
           _arg3, 'SkinThickness': _arg4, 'Insulin': _arg5, 'BMI':_arg6,
           'Age': _arg7}
    test_data = pd.DataFrame(data = row,index=[0])
    predprob_diabetes = gb.predict_proba(test_data)
    return [probability[1] for probability in predprob_diabetes]
```

10. And lastly, the line that will deploy the function to TabPy:

```
client.deploy('diabetes_predictor', diabetes_predictor,'Predicts the
chances of a Pima female having diabetes', override = True)
```

11. This looks as follows in Jupyter:

```
1  import numpy as np
2  import pandas as pd
3  from sklearn import ensemble
4  from sklearn.model_selection import train_test_split
5  df = pd.read_csv('/Users/marleenmeier/Downloads/Diabetes.csv', sep = ',')
6  df = df[['Pregnancies', 'Glucose', 'BloodPressure', 'SkinThickness', 'Insulin', 'BMI', 'Age', 'Outcome']]
7
8  X_train, X_test, y_train, y_test = train_test_split(df.drop(['Outcome'], axis = 'columns'),df['Outcome'],
9                                                       test_size = 0.2)
10
11  gb = ensemble.GradientBoostingClassifier()
12  gb.fit(X_train, y_train)
13  gbscore = gb.score(X_test, y_test)
14  print('gradient boost: ' + str(round(gbscore*100,2)))
15
16  def diabetes_predictor(_arg1, _arg2, _arg3, _arg4, _arg5,_arg6,_arg7):
17      import pandas as pd
18      row = {'Pregnancies': _arg1, 'Glucose': _arg2, 'BloodPressure':
19          _arg3, 'SkinThickness': _arg4, 'Insulin': _arg5, 'BMI': _arg6, 'Age': _arg7}
20
21      test_data = pd.DataFrame(data = row,index=[0])
22      predprob_diabetes = gb.predict_proba(test_data)
23      return [probability[1] for probability in predprob_diabetes]
24
25
26  client.deploy('diabetes_predictor', diabetes_predictor,'Predicts the chances of a \
27               Pima female having diabetes', override = True)
```

```
gradient boost: 78.57
```

Figure 15.51: Deploying the function

12. To check if your model has been deployed, type `https://localhost:9004/endpoints` in your browser. This will list all the models that have been deployed to TabPy on your machine:

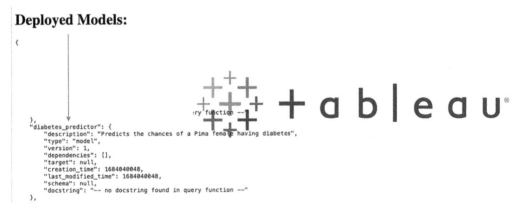

Figure 15.52: Deploying the function

Go back to Tableau and double-check if the connection to TabPy is still active.

13. Create a calculated field called `Diabetes predictor` like so:

```
SCRIPT_REAL("
return tabpy.query('diabetes_predictor',_arg1,_arg2,_arg3,_arg4,_arg5,_
arg6,
_arg7)['response']",
[Pregnancies], [Glucose], [BloodPressure], [SkinThickness], [Insulin],
[BMI],[Age]
)
```

You can see here that since we did all the coding in Python, we only tell Tableau to return a TabPy query called `diabetes_predictor`, then add all the *n* references to variables that are required for the function, and lastly add `['response']` at the end.

Or, since deployed models on TabPy also support the functions `MODEL_EXTENSION_BOOL`, `MODEL_EXTENSION_INT`, `MODEL_EXTENSION_REAL`, and `MODEL_EXTENSION_STR`, you can also use this:

```
MODEL_EXTENSION_REAL("diabetes_predictor", "_arg1, _arg2, _arg3, _arg4,
_arg5, _arg6, _arg7",
[Pregnancies], [Glucose], [BloodPressure], [SkinThickness], [Insulin],
[BMI],[Age]
)
```

The second code is a bit shorter and more intuitive; however, both work!

14. Now place the field **Diabetes predictor** on the **Text** shelf and observe the outcome:

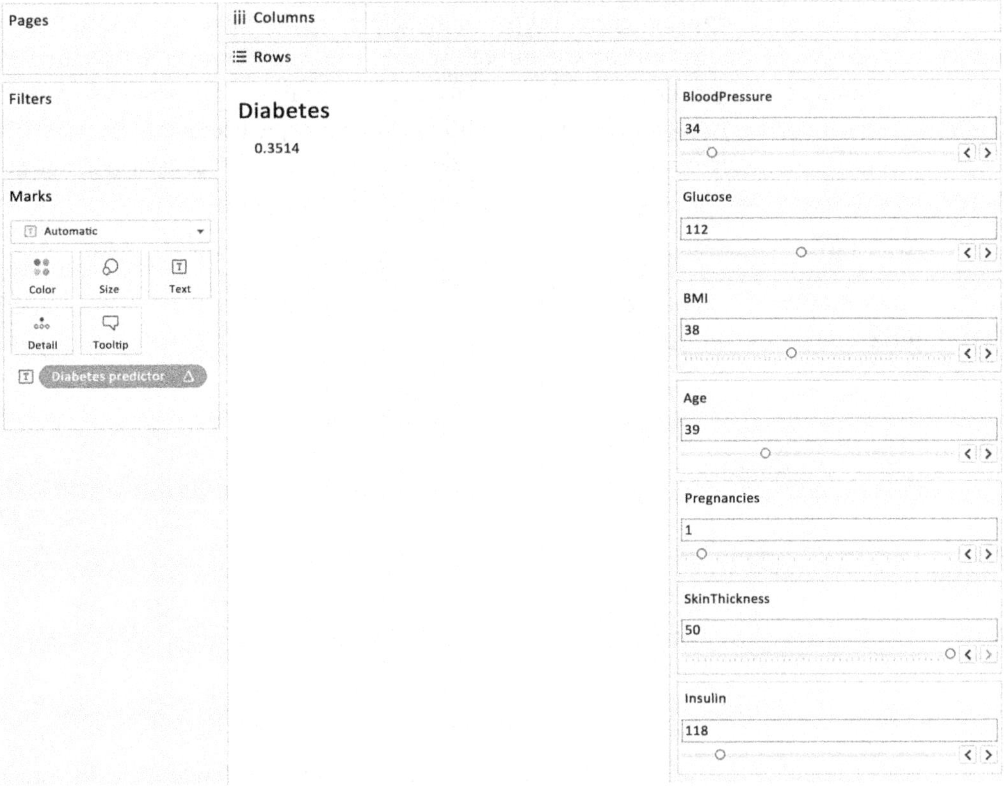

Figure 15.53: Interactive TabPy Diabetes worksheet

By sliding the parameters to the left and right, you will see that the likelihood of diabetes changes. The calculated field sends the data of the parameters via TabPy to Python, where your data will be fitted to the model. And the result will be sent back, and you can see it. Of course, you can build a whole dashboard around it. Examples can be found on the Tableau website: `https://www.tableau.com/about/blog/2017/1/building-advanced-analytics-applications-tabpy-64916`.

If you want to learn more about the Python language itself, a good source of information is, for example, `https://www.w3schools.com/python/default.asp`. The web page will, step by step, guide you through the Python syntax. But Tableau makes it even easier because a set of functions has already been written for you.

Predeployed TabPy functions

Not everyone likes to program outside of Tableau and that's why Tableau has produced a set of widely used, pre-deployed functions you can use out of the box. You will still need to execute one line of code, once! But that is all you need to do in Python itself. The available functions are ANOVA, T-test, sentiment analysis, and PCA but Tableau has mentioned on multiple occasions that more functions might be coming soon. You can find the documentation here: `https://tableau.github.io/TabPy/docs/tabpy-tools.html`.

But let's walk through the steps:

1. In your Jupyter Notebook, execute `tabpy-deploy-models` and see that the four functions are installed:

```
1  !tabpy-deploy-models
```

```
Successfully deployed anova
Successfully deployed ttest
```

```
Successfully deployed Sentiment Analysis
Successfully deployed PCA
```

Figure 15.54: Deploying TabPy default models

2. You can double-check this by typing `http://localhost:9004/endpoints` in your browser, where you should see all deployed models.

   And that's it; calling the function in a calculated field in Tableau is now as easy as the following (using `ttest` as an example function being called):

   ```
   tabpy.query('ttest', _arg1, _arg2)['response']
   ```

3. I challenge you to compare the Sentiment Score from the TabPy default deployed model with the one we created: do they differ? And if so, how?

From Python, you can connect directly to, for example:

- DataRobot (`https://www.tableau.com/solutions/datarobot`)
- Dataiku (`https://www.dataiku.com/partners/tableau/`)
- MATLAB (`https://www.mathworks.com/products/reference-architectures/tableau.html`)

These are all paid third-party tools that help make your data analysis easier. And if you can make a connection from R and Python to another external tool, you can also leverage that capability back to Tableau via Rserve and TabPy, respectively. If you are interested in this type of connection or if you want to refresh the topic of deploying functions, you can check out this video – `https://youtu.be/0BN_Y2CxdYY` – in which Nathan Mannheimer, a former product manager for advanced analytics at Tableau, explains everything we have discussed as well.

What are your personal goals with programming integration? If you have a great idea, feel free to share it with the Tableau community.

Honing your R and Python skills

Some of you might feel overwhelmed by using code and are looking for a simpler way to learn before using R or Python in Tableau. The website www.geeksforgeeks.org introduces you to both and lets you practice on-site programming without any installation.

Einstein Discovery

If you are a Salesforce user and bought the Einstein Discovery license, you can use another out-of-the-box set of models. AI-driven models ship with Einstein Discovery and can be integrated with Tableau workflows. This combination can be leveraged to generate powerful insights for your Salesforce data. You can, for example, forecast sales from data in Salesforce and load it directly into Tableau, then share those insights on your known Tableau Server instance and hence keep all dashboards in one place. Since Salesforce and Tableau are both part of the Salesforce suite, I wanted to mention this; however, it is also yet another kind of software that requires additional licenses, and therefore I decided not to go in-depth on its use (indeed, with what you've learned in this chapter you can replicate much of the functionality with none of the additional cost). If you are interested in learning more, I recommend you check out the following page and subpages on tableau.com: https://www.tableau.com/products/einstein-discovery.

Summary

This chapter just scratched the surface regarding the options of working with R and Python. After finishing this chapter, you should now be able to connect to Python and R from Tableau and recognize and write the basic syntax for both programming languages in Tableau. Most importantly, you are now skilled enough to leverage the power of R and Python functions in Tableau from a simple mean calculation to regressions, all the way to implementing your own machine learning model. Although we covered the installation, integration, and workflow, as well as some of the more popular functions and use cases, there is much more to explore. In fact, the possibilities of Tableau's programming integration remain largely uncharted territory in the BI community.

The intrepid in data visualization are pushing the envelope, but there is much to be done. For those readers looking to enhance their career options, expertise in both packages could offer great advantages. And there is more to come!

During the Tableau Conference 2023, the company sent a clear message, Tableau will continue to develop its advanced analytics and AI capabilities. Newly announced products like Tableau GPT and, with it, Tableau Pulse make me feel impatient for the amazing features to come. Find a summary of what to expect here: https://www.tableau.com/blog/data-innovations-tableau-conference-2023.

While the next chapter is sadly the last chapter of this book, we've still got time to explore another hot topic. Alongside advanced analytics, data governance is an increasingly useful area to explore. Regulations and increasing data security risks force companies to put more emphasis on well-structured guidelines and quality checks. We will introduce you to the other side of Tableau in *Chapter 16, Developing Data Governance Practices*.

Learn more on Discord

To join the Discord community for this book – where you can share feedback, ask questions to the author, and learn about new releases – follow the QR code below:

https://packt.link/tableau

16

Developing Data Governance Practices

This last chapter is slightly different from the others. We will not discuss a feature to be used in a Tableau dashboard or on Tableau Server but rather the data capabilities related to data governance in Tableau – who has access to which data, who viewed which dashboard how often, what the data components of a dashboard are, where the data came from, and more.

We will discuss the following topics:

- What is data governance?
- Data governance principles
- Data governance in Tableau
- Follow-along examples

In recent times, especially in the last 20 years, data governance has gained more importance, which shows the increasing maturity in this field. While in earlier days, data governance was a sole IT task and often limited to data cataloging, today's data governance is a task shared by many. The more data companies store, the more analysts they hire, the more data is used, and the more rules and guidelines are needed. Nowadays, companies get fined for a lack of proper data governance, and massive data security breaches and data leaks make it to the headlines increasingly often. Therefore, many institutions, like the EU, have adopted data protection laws and regulations containing data governance as one of the main pillars. An example is the GDPR for the EU and the CCPA for California.

Even if you are mostly interested in building dashboards and sharing data insights, it is, and will continue to become, more of a joint effort throughout a firm to protect data. Understanding policies and regulations, knowing how to use data governance tools, and acting responsibly are necessary for you too. Therefore, I dedicate this last chapter to data governance and all the built-in functionality Tableau has to offer in this space. Let's start!

What is data governance?

Data governance is all about the generation and implementation of data-related policies following regulations and industry standards. Its primary goal is to guarantee the usefulness, accessibility, and security of information. Enhanced data governance leads to improved data analytics, granting analysts peace of mind by ensuring that the data they rely on originates from reliable sources, has been verified, and has undergone rigorous data quality assessments, among other measures.

On the `www.tableau.com` website, you can find a whitepaper that introduces Tableau users to data management, including data governance: `https://www.tableau.com/learn/whitepapers/tableau-data-management`.

And if you would prefer a video, you will find a walk-through at the following link: `https://www.tableau.com/products/data-management#content-446367`.

Both the whitepaper and the video talk about this setup:

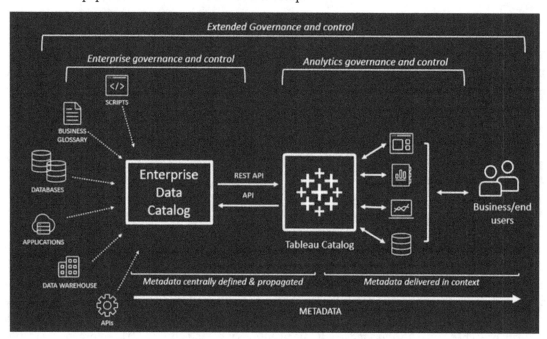

Figure 16.1: Tableau data management

In general, data governance encompasses key aspects such as ensuring data quality, addressing data security and privacy concerns, establishing data policies and standards, assigning data stewards, complying with regulations, and documenting data assets.

So why does data governance matter? Robust data governance leads to improved data quality, lower data management costs, and greater data access. It enhances trustworthiness in data compliance, thus resulting in better decision-making, improved operational efficiency, and reduced risks. Tableau can be a valuable tool for data visualization and analysis within the data governance framework while adhering to proven policies and guidelines.

Data governance principles

If you are planning to work on data governance, you should know that data governance principles are typically the heart and soul of the entire endeavor. To illustrate this, let's examine the seven principles outlined in the GDPR (`https://gdpr-info.eu/`) as an example and explore how Tableau can be employed to enforce them effectively:

- Lawfulness, fairness, and transparency
- Purpose limitation
- Data minimization
- Accuracy
- Storage limitations
- Integrity and confidentiality
- Accountability

Lawfulness, fairness, and transparency

This mandates that personal information collected for providing goods or services must be obtained lawfully and fairly, with individuals informed about the purpose of its use. Furthermore, personal information can only be collected with the explicit consent of the individuals, and a record of this consent must be kept.

Purpose limitation

Personal information should only be collected for a specific and legitimate purpose, and it should not be used for a different or incompatible purpose unless explicit consent is obtained.

Data minimization

The processing of personal information should be restricted to what is necessary to fulfill the intended purpose.

Accuracy

Personal information must be collected accurately and maintained with regular updates to mitigate risks to individuals, and any inaccurate information should be promptly corrected or erased.

Storage limitation

Personal information should be retained only for the duration necessary to fulfill the processing purpose unless it is required for scientific, archival, or public interest purposes, in which case it may be stored for a longer period.

Integrity and confidentiality

Integrity in the GDPR requires maintaining accurate and reliable personal data, while confidentiality mandates protecting personal data from unauthorized access and disclosure, ensuring privacy rights are upheld.

Accountability

For a successful data governance approach, accountability is crucial as it provides direction and effectiveness; establishing a data governance council comprising representatives from all departments, including senior executives, is essential to ensure cross-organization responsibility and the development and enforcement of data processes and policies. Let's see how Tableau can help us stick to these principles in the next section.

Data governance in Tableau

Tableau provides a range of features and capabilities that aid in supporting data governance initiatives within an organization, acting as a complementary tool that aligns with data governance principles.

 Many of the following features are only available when buying the data management add-on for Tableau Server (https://www.tableau.com/products/data-management). Please be aware of this while reading the rest of this chapter.

Data source connectivity

Tableau's data source connectivity allows organizations to set up centralized data governance by connecting to diverse data sources, promoting a trusted and curated approach to data management.

Data source connectivity makes it easier to adhere to the GDPR principle of *integrity and confidentiality* because data is stored securely, and access can be controlled.

Data access controls

Tableau enables administrators to manage user access to data sources and dashboards, implementing user and group permissions to ensure that only authorized individuals can access and interact with specific data assets.

Data access controls make it easier to adhere to the GDPR principle of **integrity and confidentiality** because access can be managed centrally and will thus be limited.

Data security

Tableau offers security features like data encryption, **single sign-on (SSO)** authentication, and integration with identity management systems, enhancing data security by enforcing policies and safeguarding sensitive information.

Data security makes it easier to adhere to the GDPR principle of **integrity and confidentiality** because security breaches and hence unlawful accessing of sensitive data will be limited.

Metadata management

Tableau helps with the creation and management of metadata, offering valuable contextual information such as data definitions, descriptions, and lineage details. This capability supports data governance initiatives by enhancing understanding and control over data assets.

Metadata management makes it easier to adhere to the GDPR principle of **accuracy** because metadata changes can be detected easily.

Data certification

Tableau enables users to certify and promote trusted data sources and dashboards, signifying that the data has undergone quality assurance and can be relied upon for analysis and decision-making. This certification process ensures that users have access to reliable and governed data assets.

Data certification makes it easier to adhere to the GDPR principle of **accuracy** because all users can trust certified data to be monitored on accuracy and timeliness.

Version control

Tableau provides version control capabilities that enable organizations to track changes made to dashboards and data sources, promoting data governance by offering visibility into modifications and facilitating the audit trail process.

Version control makes it easier to adhere to the GDPR principle of **lawfulness, fairness, and transparency** because of its audit trail functionality.

Monitoring and auditing

Tableau's monitoring and auditing features enable administrators to track user activities, access patterns, and data usage, aiding in identifying potential compliance issues and ensuring adherence to data governance policies.

Monitoring and auditing make it easier to adhere to the GDPR principle of **lawfulness, fairness, and transparency** because it helps us to comply with rules and regulations.

Collaboration and documentation

Tableau supports collaboration and documentation by offering features like commenting, annotations, and document attachments, empowering users to document and discuss data assets, definitions, and governance-related information directly within the Tableau environment.

Collaboration and documentation make it easier to adhere to the GDPR principle of **accountability** because comments and annotations are visible and shared between users.

While Tableau offers data governance capabilities, it is crucial for organizations to have a comprehensive data governance strategy and framework that extends beyond the Tableau platform. Tableau's features can enhance, and align with, broader data governance initiatives, but they should be integrated into an overarching governance program to maximize effectiveness.

Follow-along examples

In this last part of the chapter, you can try some of the data governance features yourself; feel free to follow along in your version of Tableau Server.

Certifying data sources

Certifying a data source involves designating it as a trusted and reliable asset through a process that verifies its quality, accuracy, and compliance. This certification instills trust, ensures data quality, supports compliance, promotes consistency, strengthens data governance, enhances decision-making, facilitates data discovery, and is conducted by data governance teams or experts within an organization.

You can certify a data source in Tableau by following these steps:

1. Open Tableau Server.
2. Open a data source.
3. Click on the three dots next to the data source name.
4. Select **Edit Certification…**:

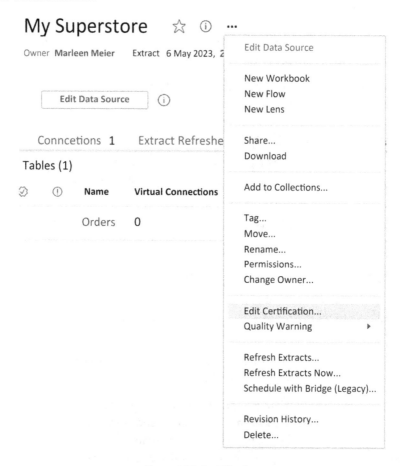

Figure 16.2: Certification

5. You can now type a message visible to data source users holding the reason for the certification or similar. What you type depends on the policies agreed on in your firm. Click **Save**.

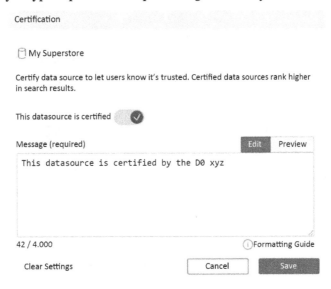

Figure 16.3: Certification message

6. Next to the data source owner and date, you will now see an indication that this data source is certified:

Figure 16.4: Certified

Certified data sources help decision-making, enabling analysts and business users to have heightened confidence in the data they utilize, resulting in more precise insights, well-informed decisions, and enhanced business outcomes.

Data quality warnings

Data quality warnings are notifications that highlight potential issues or anomalies in dataset quality, triggered by incomplete or missing data, inconsistencies, outliers, data integrity problems, validation failures, or outdated information. These warnings signal the need for further investigation and data cleansing to ensure correct analysis and decision-making, emphasizing the importance of addressing data quality issues for reliable insights.

You can set up a data quality warning by following these steps:

1. Open Tableau Server.
2. Open a data source.
3. Click on **the three dots next to** the data source name.
4. Select **Quality Warning** and then choose between **Quality Warning ...** or **Extract Refresh Monitoring ....**

5. The **Data Quality Warning** pop-up will look like this:

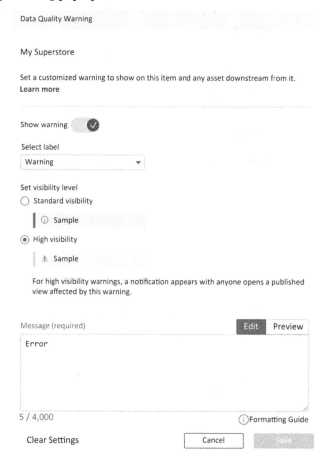

Figure 16.5: Data Quality Warning

6. From here, select one out of five labels from the dropdown **Select label:**

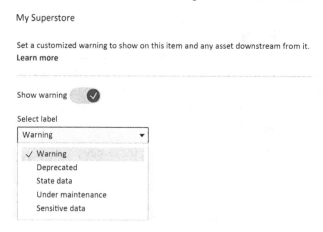

Figure 16.6: Select label

7. The **Extract Refresh Monitoring** pop-up will look very similar, without a dropdown though:

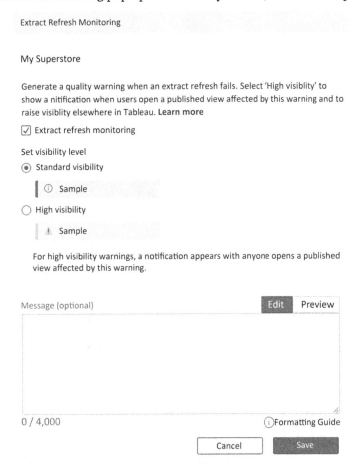

Figure 16.7: Extract Refresh Monitoring

8. In both cases, a **Warning** indicator will appear on the data source overview page:

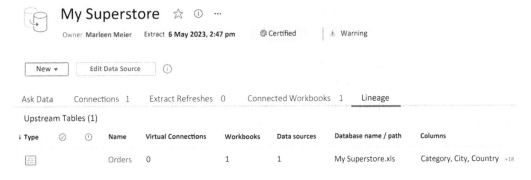

Figure 16.8: Warning

9. If a schedule extraction fails, you can also check the **Schedules** overview page:

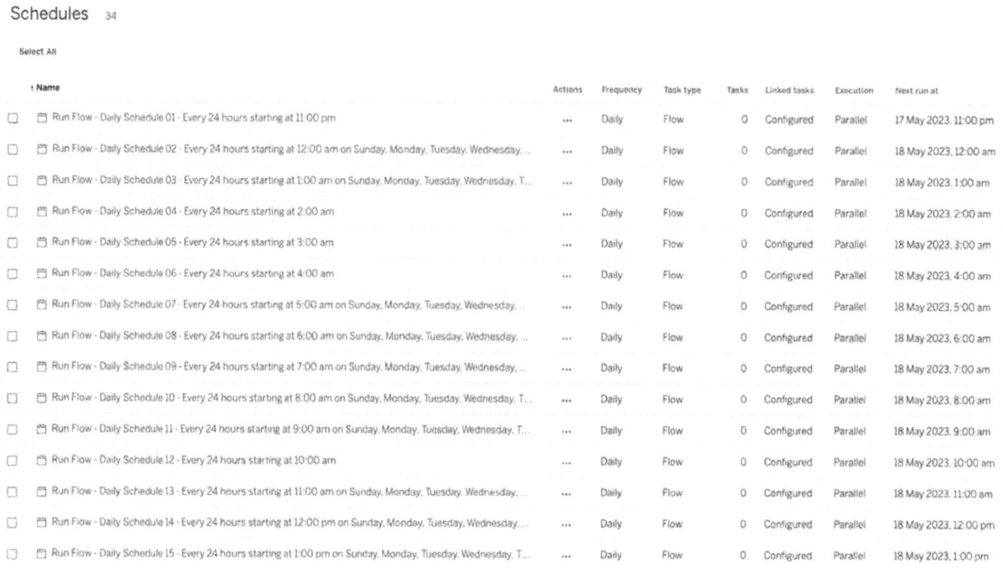

Figure 16.9: Schedules

Data quality warnings serve as indicators that data may require further investigation or cleaning before it can be used for analysis, reporting, or decision-making. They help find potential data issues that could affect the accuracy, reliability, and validity of analytical results. Addressing data quality warnings often involves data cleansing, error correction, and ensuring the data aligns with the required quality standards.

It is important to note that data quality warnings should be acted upon, as they can affect the reliability and validity of insights derived from the data. Resolving data quality issues and keeping high-quality data is crucial to making informed decisions and drawing exact conclusions from data analysis.

Tableau Lineage

Data lineage is important as it establishes trust in data, aids in data quality management and issue resolution, facilitates impact analysis, supports compliance with regulations, strengthens data governance and management practices, assists in troubleshooting and debugging, and enables successful data and system integration. Data lineage provides transparency, understanding, and control over data flows, contributing to improved data governance and decision-making processes.

To see the lineage, you can open any type of overview page, data sources, prep flows, sheets, workbooks, and others on Tableau Server and check the **Lineage** tab:

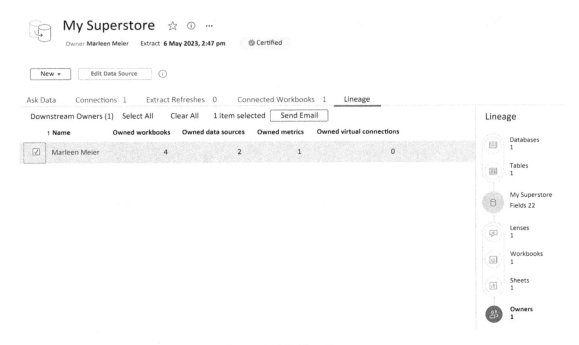

Figure 16.10: Tableau lineage

The right-hand panel provides you with all the details about the respective lineage. From here, you can click on any of the given components and will be redirected there.

Lineage

Databases
1

Tables
1

My Superstore

Fields 22

Lenses
1

Workbooks
1

Sheets
1

Owners
1

Figure 16.11: Detailed lineage

From the table view, you can even check where a column is used; first, go to a table:

Figure 16.12: Upstream tables

Then, click on any of the columns. Observe how the right-hand panel shows that the column **City** is used in the **Databases** and the **Tables** but not anywhere else:

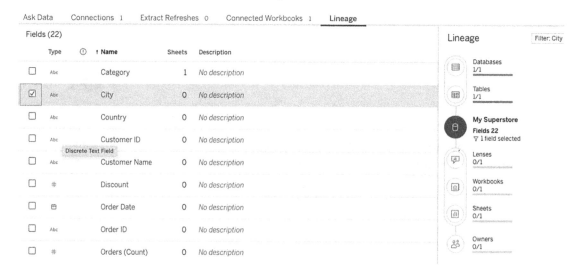

Figure 16.13: Column lineage

Overall, data lineage provides transparency, understanding, and control over data flows. It supports data quality management, compliance efforts, and decision-making processes. By documenting the lineage of data, organizations can improve their data governance practices, enhance data trustworthiness, and mitigate risks associated with data management and analytics.

Data Details

The **Data Details** in Tableau help you and your users understand the data within a published dashboard. To access it, on any given dashboard, click on **Data Details** in the top-left corner and observe the details popping up on the right:

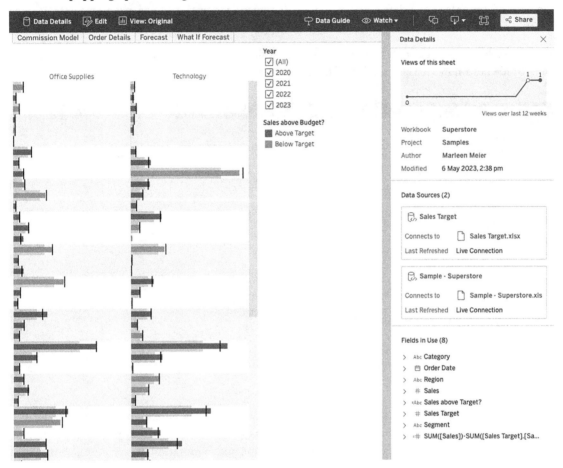

Figure 16.14: Tableau Data Details

In a few seconds, **Data Details** allows you to see the views over time, the data sources, and the fields in use.

Data Guide

A data guide, such as a data dictionary or data reference guide, is a documentation resource that provides detailed information about the structure, content, and meaning of data elements. It is important for data understanding, consistency, integration, quality assessment, governance, collaboration, training, and documentation. A data guide enhances data management practices, promotes data literacy, and supports effective data utilization within organizations.

For the exploration of the data guide, please open a dashboard on Tableau Server and click on the **Data Guide** button in the right section of the blue top bar:

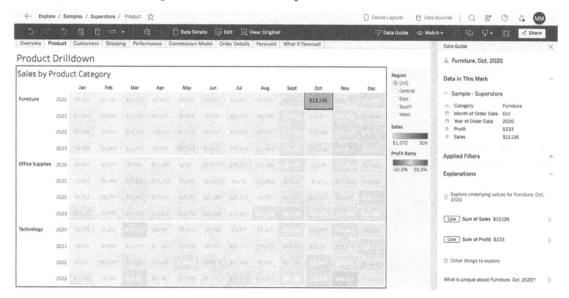

Figure 16.15: Data Guide

By selecting a mark in the view, the data guide automatically populates details about the data point and filters used, and also an explanation. You already know this feature from **Explain Data** in prior chapters of this book, but the data guide makes the explanation and exploration of marks easier than ever.

Here is one more example that clearly shows how Tableau bridges the gap between a single data point and the average of the full dataset:

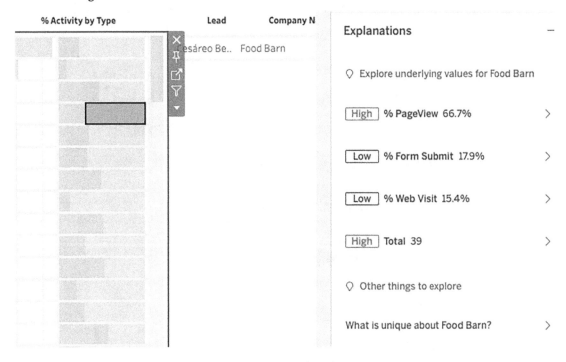

Figure 16.16: Explanations

By clicking on a single arrow, more information comes up:

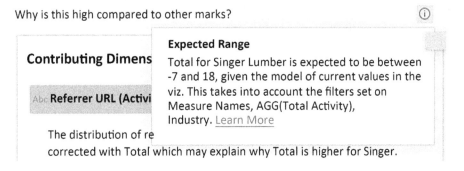

Figure 16.17: Text explanation

And you can even generate graphs that prove the point:

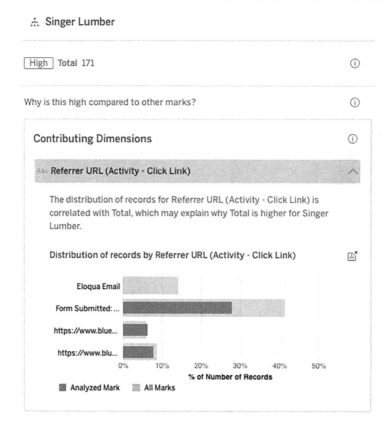

Figure 16.18: Contributing dimensions

The data guide also lets you add descriptions and resources for your users:

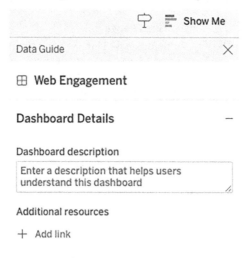

Figure 16.19: Description

And this was the last example in the realm of data governance in Tableau. This is a huge topic and one that extends far beyond the remit of Tableau, so we have only just scratched the surface by looking into the GDPR – one of many data regulations – the data governance functionality in Tableau, and finally some real-life applications. This topic really deserves a book of its own, but I wanted to address it here in short to share the responsibility because even you, as a Tableau developer, have a responsibility and can make a difference in keeping our data safe. Hopefully, this last chapter has given you enough food for thought to start paying more attention to data governance while developing fabulous dashboards.

Now that we've reached the end of the book, consider our journey, which started with loading data into Tableau, creating our first visualizations, and executing our first functions. We moved on by familiarizing ourselves with the level of detail and table calculations, learning about Tableau Prep Builder, Tableau Server, and general visualization best practices before our final round, in which we learned about advanced analytics and leveraging the power of Tableau programming tool integration.

This leaves me with just one question: what will your next Tableau project be? Feel free to share it on Tableau Public and don't forget to add the tag **#MasteringTableau**. I want to congratulate you all for participating and engaging in this learning process! Whether you have more questions, remarks, or feedback, feel free to reach out to me or to the Tableau community. I wish you a lot of success with your personal Tableau career.

Happy Tableau'ing!

Learn more on Discord

To join the Discord community for this book – where you can share feedback, ask questions to the author, and learn about new releases – follow the QR code below:

`https://packt.link/tableau`

packt.com

Subscribe to our online digital library for full access to over 7,000 books and videos, as well as industry leading tools to help you plan your personal development and advance your career. For more information, please visit our website.

Why subscribe?

- Spend less time learning and more time coding with practical eBooks and Videos from over 4,000 industry professionals
- Improve your learning with Skill Plans built especially for you
- Get a free eBook or video every month
- Fully searchable for easy access to vital information
- Copy and paste, print, and bookmark content

At www.packt.com, you can also read a collection of free technical articles, sign up for a range of free newsletters, and receive exclusive discounts and offers on Packt books and eBooks.

Other Books You May Enjoy

If you enjoyed this book, you may be interested in these other books by Packt:

Data Modeling with Tableau

Kirk Munroe

ISBN: 9781803248028

- Showcase Tableau published data sources and embedded connections
- Apply Ask Data in data cataloging and natural language query
- Understand the features of Tableau Prep Builder with the help of hands-on exercises
- Model data with Tableau Desktop using examples
- Formulate a governed data strategy using Tableau Server and Tableau Cloud
- Optimize data models for Ask and Explain Data

Learning Tableau 2022 – Fifth Edition

Joshua N. Milligan

ISBN: 9781801072328

- Develop stunning visualizations to explain complex data with clarity
- Build interactive dashboards to drive actionable user insights
- Explore Data Model capabilities and interlink data from various sources
- Create and use calculations to solve problems and enrich your analytics
- Enable smart decision-making with data clustering, distribution, and forecasting
- Extend Tableau's native functionality with extensions, scripts, and AI through CRM Analytics (formerly Einstein Analytics)
- Leverage Tableau Prep Builder's amazing capabilities for data cleaning and structuring
- Share your data stories to build a culture of trust and action

Packt is searching for authors like you

If you're interested in becoming an author for Packt, please visit authors.packtpub.com and apply today. We have worked with thousands of developers and tech professionals, just like you, to help them share their insight with the global tech community. You can make a general application, apply for a specific hot topic that we are recruiting an author for, or submit your own idea.

Share your thoughts

Now you've finished *Mastering Tableau 2023 - Fourth Edition*, we'd love to hear your thoughts! Scan the QR code below to go straight to the Amazon review page for this book and share your feedback or leave a review on the site that you purchased it from.

https://packt.link/r/1803233761

Your review is important to us and the tech community and will help us make sure we're delivering excellent quality content.

Index

Download a free PDF copy of this book

Thanks for purchasing this book!

Do you like to read on the go but are unable to carry your print books everywhere?

Is your eBook purchase not compatible with the device of your choice?

Don't worry, now with every Packt book you get a DRM-free PDF version of that book at no cost.

Read anywhere, any place, on any device. Search, copy, and paste code from your favorite technical books directly into your application.

The perks don't stop there, you can get exclusive access to discounts, newsletters, and great free content in your inbox daily

Follow these simple steps to get the benefits:

1. Scan the QR code or visit the link below

https://packt.link/free-ebook/9781803233765

2. Submit your proof of purchase
3. That's it! We'll send your free PDF and other benefits to your email directly

Printed in the USA
CPSIA information can be obtained
at www.ICGtesting.com
LVHW071058241223
767331LV00007B/647